T0370519

TALES OF THE HASIDIM

MARTIN BUBER

TALES OF THE
HASIDIM

BOOK ONE: THE EARLY MASTERS

and

BOOK TWO: THE LATER MASTERS

*With a new Foreword
by Chaim Potok*

Schocken Books   New York

Translated by Olga Marx

This work was originally published in two separate volumes,
Tales of the Hasidim: The Early Masters and *Tales of the
Hasidim: The Later Masters (Ten Rungs: Hasidic Sayings)* by
Schocken Books Inc. in 1947.

Frontispiece courtesy of Pictorial Parade

Library of Congress Cataloging in Publication Data
Buber, Martin, 1878–1965.
[Erzählungen der Chassidim. English]
Tales of the Hasidim/by Martin Buber; foreword by Chaim
Potok.
p. cm.
Translation of: Die Erzählungen der Chassidim.
Includes bibliographical references and index.
1. Hasidim—Legends. 2. Parables, Hasidic. I. Title.
BM532.B7613   1991   296.8′332—dc20   90-52921

ISBN 978-0-805-20995-2

Schocken Books Edition 1991

CONTENTS

FOREWORD

by Chaim Potok

Martin Buber, one of the commanding Jewish thinkers of the twentieth century, came to hasidism and its tales in an odd way. The seeds of a lifetime quest are often deeply planted and not easily unearthed. But beginnings can never be entirely buried, and Buber's later interest in hasidism may have originated during his childhood and early adolescence when, because his parents were divorced, he lived in Lemberg with his grandfather, who was an enlightened, renowned scholar and editor of classic rabbinic texts, and at the same time a well-to-do banker, a Jewish communal leader, and a devout Jew, who prayed in a small hasidic synagogue from a prayer book dense with mystical discourse.

Beyond that speculation is the fact that the gathering strength of the sciences at the turn of the century sparked a reaction among some Western European intellectuals: a renewed interest in mysticism. Buber's intellectual idols in the University of Vienna, which he entered in the summer of 1896, were not only the philosophers Schopenhauer and Nietzsche but also the Christian mystics Jakob Böhme, Meister Eckehart, and Nicholas of Cusa. Certain questions haunted Buber from early on. Often we feel ourselves alternately connected to and separated from the world around us. Does the sense of alienation lie at the very root of the human condition? Does it give rise to the mystical yearning for unity with the world and God? Is there a real unity out there somewhere waiting to be discovered by us? Can we realize it, kindle it into existence, by leading authentic, open, honest lives? Can God be realized, made actual, through man?

Buber grew up in an age when Jewry experienced the full power of the secular enlightenment, the subsequent marshaling of Orthodox forces in opposition to secularism, and the birth of modern political Zionism. Newly emancipated Jews, heady with the prospect of participating as partners in Western civilization, attempted to enter fully the mainstream of European life—some by denying their inherited culture, others by taking with them a personal vision of it into the wider world. Those who broke entirely with Judaism and for one reason or another chose later to return, often did so on their own terms. Gone forever was the time when an apostate, like the seventeenth-century Amsterdam Jew, Uriel da Costa, would return unconditionally and at the cost of public contrition and humiliation to the faith established and maintained by repressive communal elders.

The First Zionist Congress, held in Basle in 1897, brought Buber back into the Jewish community. Until then he had lived, as he put it, "in the 'world of confusion,' the mythical dwelling place of the wandering souls . . . in versatile fullness of spirit, but without Judaism, without humanity, and without the presence of the divine." He returned as a Western Jew, who had broken with Jewish observance during adolescence but had retained a deep awareness of the extent to which Western notions of the individual and the community were rooted in the Bible and the Hebraic tradition. In 1901 he joined the staff of the Zionist periodical *Die Welt,* and though he left shortly thereafter, he remained involved in Zionist activity.

He described his odyssey of return in *My Way to Hasidism.* The Hebrew he had learned as a boy and subsequently neglected he now relearned and enriched. He began to grasp the language "in its essence . . . gradually overcoming the strangeness, beholding the essential with growing devotion." And then one day, in his twenty-sixth year, he experienced a remarkable event.

> I opened a little book entitled the *Zevaat Ribesh*—that is the testament of Rabbi Israel Baal-Shem—and the words flashed toward me, "He takes unto himself the quality of fervor. He rises from sleep with fervor, for he is hallowed and become another man and is worthy to create and is become like the Holy One, blessed be He, when he created his world." It was then that, overpowered in an instant, I experienced the Hasidic soul.

Acting on that experience, he withdrew from Zionist activity and for the next six years retired "into the stillness." He began to

viii

gather "not without difficulty, the scattered, partly missing, literature" and immersed himself in it, "discovering mysterious land after mysterious land."

The mysterious land he discovered was the mystical terrain of hasidism.

There had been hasidim, individuals of exceptional piety, in the Talmudic period, and a hasidic community of sorts had existed for a while in medieval Germany. Modern hasidism is the child of Rabbi Israel ben Eliezer of Mezbizh, known as the Baal Shem Tov, Master of the Good Name (1700–1760). He was, it appears, a man both learned and charismatic, a folk healer, one of those who went about curing the sick by invoking the various mystical names of God. Concerning his life, words, and deeds, we have only legends—in shards of writings, tales, pamphlets, books that purport to recount his actual teachings but are clearly infused with excesses of piety and invention.

Hasidism was an explosive act of creation: a response by a single person to the cry of the masses.

By the beginning of the eighteenth century, after a decade of rebellion by Ukrainian peasants against their Polish overlords and a subsequent war with Sweden, in both of which Jews were made to suffer brutally, the once vital Jewish community of Poland was in ruins. In response to this crippling, the world of Polish Jewry turned in upon itself and became so rigorously restrictive and hermetic as to drain it of the possibility of creative spontaneity. The Jewish community lay in a torpor of congealed ritualism; and its most esteemed activity, the learning of Torah, became abstruse, elitist, and far removed from the grim realities and miseries of everyday existence.

Grinding poverty, endless suffering—and learning as the only avenue to God. An ideal mix for revolution. Conjure the bitterness and frustration felt by ordinary unlearned Jews in a culture entirely focused on learning. If learning is the exclusive path to God, how does one come to God when one is a shoemaker, a wagon driver, a water carrier; when one must work day and night and has little time for study?

The answer came from the Baal Shem Tov: Learning is not the

only way to God. One can also approach God through a life of fervor and exaltation experienced for the sake of heaven; through prayer and joy that transcend everyday existence and transform human suffering by imbuing all of life with hope, purpose, sanctity, thereby raising earth to heaven, restoring the unity of creation, and redeeming the world.

"Nowhere in the last centuries," wrote Buber in *Hasidism and Modern Man*, "has the soul-force of Judaism so manifested itself as in Hasidism. . . . Without an iota being altered in the law, in the ritual, in the traditional life-norms, the long-accustomed arose in a fresh light and meaning." He summed up the teachings of hasidism in this way: "God can be beheld in each thing and reached through each pure deed."

Anyone can perform pure deeds; anyone can sing and experience joy. "It is not the man who knows the Torah but the man who lives in it . . . that stands in the highest place," wrote Buber in *The Origin and Meaning of Hasidism*. And anyone can live in Torah.

It was this democratic strain in hasidism that made its appeal to the despairing masses so irresistible. Despite the strong opposition of the rabbis, who initially saw in hasidism and its charismatic leaders, the zaddikim, a threat to their authority, the movement quickly spread. With the advent of the enlightenment, rabbis and zaddikim joined forces against a common enemy: secularism. A tenuous peace was established between the hasidim and their opponents. By the second decade of this century, hasidim constituted about half the population of Eastern European Jewry.

Sixteenth-century Lurianic Kabbalah, endeavoring to fathom the origin and nature of evil in a universe created by a compassionate God, came up with the startling notion of a cosmos gone wrong in the very process of creation. The Creator, while withdrawing His essence from the totality of being in order to make room for the dross of matter, somehow lost control of the process, and elements of God—sacred sparks of His being—spilled from the delicate shells of light that encased them and fell into the created world of matter, where they became trapped, thereby diminishing the being of God and rendering the cosmos awry and prone to instability. The result: exile, persecution, disease, death, war, plague. A vast cosmic error at the very onset of creation set the universe askew and spawned the possibility of evil.

The righting of this terrible wrong—the healing of the world—is the task of the Jewish people. We can repair this broken world by carefully observing the Law, by performing the commandments; each godly act possesses the power to penetrate one of the shells and thereby release the spark within it back to its source in the Creator. Upon the release of all the sparks will come the certain redemption of the world.

The Baal Shem Tov and his disciples reasoned that if there are sparks in the shells, then the shells themselves may contain the possibility of sanctity: the material world may well be a manifestation of the divine. Food, a melody, a sunset—all tell us of the presence of the sacred in the everyday world. "Therefore, one should have mercy on his tools and all he possesses," the Baal Shem Tov is reported to have said; "one should have mercy on the holy sparks."

Buber saw in hasidism powerful affinities with Christian mysticism's quest for unity and admired its passionate vision of the presence of the holy within the ordinary. It is in *this* world that we must find God. If God is absent, it is into this world that we must bring Him. Told once of the enormity of the misery in which humankind finds itself, a hasidic zaddik sat stricken with grief. After a while he roused himself and announced: "Let us draw God into the world and all evil will be stilled."

We make the world a dwelling place for God by hallowing it. A zaddik, aware that both God and man are strangers on this earth, once said to God: "Do not withdraw Yourself from me, but disclose to me Your commandments so that I can become Your friend."

During its first three or four generations of existence, hasidism exemplified the explosive power of myth, and the Baal Shem Tov, in Buber's words, created "the greatest phenomenon we know in the history of the spirit, something which is greater than any solitary genius in art or in the world of thought, a society which lives by its faith." Buber found distasteful the modern inclination to demythologize religion. He saw myth not as "the subsequent clothing of a truth of faith" but as "the unarbitrary testimony of the image-making vision and the image-making memory." Myth is the expression of Jewry's most mercurial and volcanic moments of creative response to the world. It is quickly stilled and repressed by the community, which sees danger in its eruptive nature; reduced and frozen to a cold, small, shriveled point, where, under certain circumstances, it can once again explode, as it did in Eastern Europe when Jewry created hasidism.

"Never yet in Europe has such a community thus established the whole of life as a unity on the basis of the inwardly known," Buber stated in *Hasidism and Modern Man.* "Here is no separation between faith and work, between truth and verification, or, in the language of today, between morality and politics; here all is one kingdom, one spirit, one reality."

Buber saw the early hasidic community as a society that lived by its faith and was entirely open to God, as resonant with that most essential and extraordinary of human abilities: an "I" engaging a "Thou"—a unity achieved through the meeting of man and God in relation, a concept developed in his best-known work, *I and Thou.* Not man swallowed into himself or into the group, but man in full relation to another: a giving by one to another of a living element of one's essential being: compassion, trust, respect, love.

"The fundamental fact of human existence is man with man," wrote Buber in *Between Man and Man.* Hasidism saw the line connecting man to man and man to God as *relation* and not as subject-object; as *sacred betweenness* and not as user to used. That living relation Buber took to be the most unique and vital characteristic of the hasidic community.

Buber has been criticized for his unhistorical and somewhat romanticized view of hasidism, his turning a blind eye to its charlatanism, obscurantism, internecine quarrels, its heavy freight of folk superstition and pietistic excesses, its zaddik worship, its vulgarized and attenuated reading of Lurianic Kabbalah. Most severe has been the charge that Buber has underplayed the importance of the Law in hasidism; that for the hasid the path to relation and dialogue with God lies through the Law.

Buber, however, claimed that the heart of Jewish creativity does not reside in the Law but in the charged visions of the relation between man and God that are found in the Bible and the early decades of hasidism. And though he acknowledged the later decadence of hasidism, he argued that its subsequent decay does not detract from the power and originality found in the early generations of the movement, much of which can still be discerned in its tales.

The hasidic tale, Buber wrote in *The Legend of the Baal Shem,*

> came to life on narrow streets and small, musty rooms, passing from awkward lips to the ears of anxious listeners. A stammer gave birth to it and a stammer bore it onward—from generation to generation. I have received it from folk books, from note-books and pamphlets, at times also from a living mouth, from the mouths of people still living who even in their lifetime heard this stammer. . . . I stand in a chain of narrators, a link between links; I tell once again the old stories, and if they sound new, it is because the new already lay dormant in them when they were told for the first time.

Hasidism and Modern Man contains the account of how Buber dealt with the hasidic tales he came upon at the age of twenty-six. Among the collections of oral teachings and legends of the lives of the zaddikim was one distinctive series of tales that recounted the adventures of Rabbi Nahman of Bratzlav, a great-grandson of the Baal Shem Tov. These tales, told by Rabbi Nahman to his disciples, were written down and published by one of them in clearly distorted form after the zaddik's death. In part imitations of pure Oriental fairy tales and in part symbolic allegories, they were replete with skewing insertions, embellishments, and commentaries.

Buber translated two of the fairy tales, published one of them, and was disappointed with the result. The distortions had become more visible, the original more obscured. "I had to tell the stories that I had taken into myself out of myself, as a true painter takes into himself the lines of the models and achieves the genuine images out of the memory formed of them." Thus he began to experience his "unity with the spirit of Rabbi Nahman." He wrote: "I had found the true faithfulness: more adequately than the direct disciples, I received and completed the task, a later messenger in a foreign realm."

He continued to use this method in his second collection, *The Legend of the Baal Shem*, as he "sought to construct the inner processes in the life of the master out of a selection of traditional legendary motifs." He began by faithfully translating the material at hand. Again the result was heavy disappointment. "The already existing stories were for the most part recorded in crude and clumsy fashion; they did not become more winged in translation. Thus here too I came to my own narrating in growing independence; but the greater the independence became, so much the more deeply I experienced the faithfulness."

Many years later he discovered "another manner of artistic faithfulness to the popular Hasidic narrative." And that new faithfulness we find in the remarkable collection, *Tales of the Hasidism*.

Some have taken Buber to task for the manner in which he reshaped, with the canons of contemporary aesthetics, the tales of Rabbi Nahman and the Baal Shem. Hasidism seems to care little for the artful tale, and by Buber's smoothings and polishings, it is argued, he misrepresented the essential nature of those tales, whose bluntness, distortions, interjections, and general clumsiness should be seen as an expression of the forthrightness and immediacy of hasidic thought.

Buber altered his style in *Tales of the Hasidim* to take into account those features of hasidic storytelling. "I rejected my method of dealing with the transmitted material, on the ground that it was too free," he wrote in the Preface. He tried "to do justice simultaneously to legend and to truth," and described in detail his new approach to the creation of these tales.

> I considered it neither permissible nor desirable to expand the tales or to render them more colorful and diverse, a method the brothers Grimm for instance employed when they wrote down the stories they had by word of mouth from the people. Only in those few cases where the notes at hand were quite fragmentary did I compose a

connected whole by fusing what I had with other fragments, and filling the gaps with related material.

What emerges from these tales is a unique world of the spirit that existed until its destruction by the Germans in World War II. Of the more than one hundred hasidic courts in Eastern Europe, only about forty survived the war, most of them pitiful shades of their former selves. Their current revival and renaissance is one of the more stunning events in contemporary Jewish history—about which tales are now being created for future generations.

The task of the original two volumes, reissued as one in this new edition, may be summed up in the words of the rabbi of Rizhyn, found in its pages:

> This is the service man must perform all of his days: to shape matter into form, to refine the flesh, and to let the light penetrate the darkness until the darkness itself shines and there is no longer any division between the two. . . . (II, p. 59)

Buber considered himself "a man endangered before God, a man wrestling ever anew for God's light, ever anew engulfed in God's abysses. . . ." This collection of tales, which has become a contemporary classic, shows us others "endangered before God." It enables Buber to continue to explore the nature of humankind in its quest for meaning in the face of emptiness, darkness, loneliness. With each tale he makes a fresh attempt at dialogue: He confronts anew a sacred community: a modern man in relation with the premodern world.

Throughout his long life as thinker and activist, Buber retained the integrity of his "I." It was often suggested to him, he wrote in *Hasidism and Modern Man,* that he liberate hasidic thought from its particularist narrowness and offer it as a teaching of all humankind. This he steadfastly refused to do. "Taking such a universal path would have been for me pure arbitrariness. In order to speak to the world what I have heard, I am not bound to step into the street. I may remain standing in the door of my ancestral house. . . ."

He speaks to us through these eternal tales.

PREFACE

One of the most vital aspects of the hasidic movement is that the hasidim tell one another stories about their leaders, their "zaddikim." Great things had happened, the hasidim had been present, they had seen them, and so they felt called upon to relate and bear witness to them. The words used to describe these experiences were more than mere words; they transmitted what had happened to coming generations, and with such actuality that the words in themselves became events. And since they serve to perpetuate holy events, they bear the consecration of holy deeds. It is told that the "Seer" of Lublin once saw a pillar of light rise out of a klaus; when he entered he saw hasidim telling one another about their zaddikim. According to hasidic belief, the primeval light of God poured into the zaddikim; from them it poured into their works, and from these into the words of the hasidim who relate them. The Baal Shem, the founder of hasidism, is supposed to have said that when a hasid spoke in praise of the zaddikim, this was equivalent to dwelling on the mystery of the divine Chariot which Ezekiel once saw. And a zaddik of the fourth generation, Rabbi Mendel of Rymanov, a friend of the "Seer," added in explanation: "For the zaddikim *are* the chariot of God."* But story is more than a mere reflection. The holy essence it testifies to lives on in it. The miracle that is told, acquires new force; power that once was active, is propagated in the living word and continues to be active—even after generations.

A rabbi, whose grandfather had been a disciple of the Baal Shem, was asked to tell a story. "A story," he said, "must be told in such a way that it constitutes help in itself." And he told: "My grandfather was lame. Once they asked him to tell

* Quoted from Midrash Genesis Rabba LXXXII 7; cf. Rashi on Genesis 17:22.

a story about his teacher. And he related how the holy Baal Shem used to hop and dance while he prayed. My grandfather rose as he spoke, and he was so swept away by his story that he himself began to hop and dance to show how the master had done. From that hour on he was cured of his lameness. That's the way to tell a story!"

Side by side with the oral transmission went a written transmission which began far back in the history of the movement, but of the written recollections of the first generations only very few uncorrupted texts have been preserved. In their youth a number of zaddikim wrote down the deeds and utterances of their masters, but apparently for their own use rather than for the public at large. Thus we know from a reliable source that the rabbi of Berditchev, of all rabbis the closest to the people, noted down everything his teacher, Dov Baer of Mezritch, the Great Maggid, said and did, including everyday utterances, and read and re-read the pages, straining his soul to the utmost in the effort to understand the meaning of every word. But his notebook has been lost and very few similar notations have been preserved.

For the most part the legend, this late form of the myth, developed in the literatures of the world in epochs in which the development of the literary narrative either occurs side by side with it or even has already been in the main completed. In the first case, the form of the legend is influenced, in the second it is determined by its sister form. Buddhist legends and tales of India composed as literature, Franciscan legend and the short story of Italy, go hand in hand.

It is quite otherwise with the hasidic legend. The Jews of the Diaspora transmitted legends orally from generation to generation and not until our own era were they couched in literary form. The hasidim could not model the tales they told in praise of their zaddikim on a literary form either extant or in the making, nor could they wholly adapt them to the style of tales current among the people. The inner tempo of the hasidim is frequently too impassioned, too violent for the calm form of such tales, a form which could not contain the abundance of what they had to say. And so the hasidim never shaped their legend into a precious vessel; with few exceptions it never became either the work of an individual artist or a work of folk-art; it remained unformed. But due to the holy element with which it is informed, the life of the zaddikim and the hasidim's rapturous joy therein, it is precious metal, though all too often not pure, but weighted with dross.

Taking the Baal Shem legend as an instance, we can trace the shaping of legendary transmission in hasidism. Even during his lifetime, his family and his disciples circulated tales which were brief indications of his greatness. After his death, these grew into stories which, a quarter of a century later, were set down in book form: the family stories developed into the tales which Rabbi Moshe Hayyim Efraim, the Baal Shem's grandson whom he himself had trained, scattered through his work, "The Camp Flag of Efraim," while the legends perpetuated by his disciples were published at about the same time in the first collection of utterances of the Baal Shem, "The Crown of the Good Name." But twenty-five more years had to pass before the first great legendary biography of the Baal Shem, "In Praise of the Baal Shem Tov," appeared. Every story in this traces back to someone in the immediate circle of the Baal Shem's friends and disciples. Side by side with this are other traditions, such as the oral tradition in the Great Maggid's family, and in the family of Rabbi Meir Margaliot or the written tradition in the school of Koretz. And all of these differ from the published collections and maintain a characteristic life of their own. The second half of the nineteenth century marks the corruption of transmitted motifs. They appear as thin and wordy narratives patched with later inventions and worked into a cheap form of popular literature. But only our own era (since about 1900) heralded the beginnings of critical selection and compiling. These and similar processes are characteristic of the development in hasidic transmission.

After excluding the spurious products in which we frequently cannot find a shred of the original motifs, we still have an enormous mass of largely unformed material: either—and at best!—brief notes with no attempt to shape the event referred to, or—far oftener, unfortunately—crude and confused attempts to give it the form of a tale. In this second category of notes either too much is said or too little, and there is hardly ever a clear thread of narrative to follow. For the most part they constitute neither true art nor true folk-tale but a kind of setting down, the rapturous setting down of stupendous occurrences.

One like myself, whose purpose it is to picture the zaddikim and their lives from extant written (and some oral) material, must above all, to do justice simultaneously to legend and to truth, supply the missing links in the narrative. In the course of this long piece of work I found it most expedient to begin by giving up the available form (or rather formlessness) of the notes with their meagerness or excessive detail, their obscurities and digressions, to reconstruct the events in question with the utmost accuracy (wherever possible, with the aid of variants and other relevant material), and to relate them as coherently as I could in a form suited to the subject matter. Then, however, I went back to the notes and incorporated in my final version whatever felicitous turn or phrase they contained. On the other hand, I considered it neither permissible nor desirable to expand the tales or to render them more colorful and diverse, a method the brothers Grimm for instance employed when they wrote down the stories they had by word of mouth from the people.* Only in those few cases where the notes at hand were quite fragmentary did I compose a connected whole by fusing what I had with other fragments, and filling the gaps with related material.

There are two genera of legend which can be designated in analogy to the two genera of the narrative on which they are modelled: the legendary short story and the legendary anecdote. To exemplify: compare *The Golden Legend* with *The Little*

* See (particularly) Leffz, *Maerchen der Brueder Grimm*, published in their original form from the posthumous papers of Clemens Brentano.

Flower of Saint Francis, or the classical Buddha legend with the tales of the monks of the East-Asiatic Zen sect. Even the formless hasidic material can be grouped in these two categories. For the most part the tales are potential legendary anecdotes. True short stories are rare, but there is a sort of hybrid between story and anecdote. The preponderance of the anecdote is primarily due to the general tendency of the Jewish Diaspora spirit to express the events of history and of the present in a pointed manner: Events are not merely seen and reported so as to signify something, but they are so cleanly hulled from the mass of the irrelevant and so arranged that the report culminates in a significant dictum. In hasidism, life itself favors this mode of interpretation. The zaddik expresses his teachings, deliberately or indeliberately, in actions that are symbolic and frequently go over into utterance which either supplements or helps to interpret them.

By the term short story I mean the recital of a destiny which is represented in a single incident; by anecdote the recital of a single incident which illumines an entire destiny. The legendary anecdote goes one stop beyond: the single incident in question conveys the meaning of life. In the literature of the world, I know of no other group of legendary anecdotes which illustrates this to such a degree, so homogeneously and yet with such variety as the hasidic anecdotes.

The anecdote, as well as the short story, is a species of condensed narrative, that is, of narrative concentrated in one clearly outlined form. Psychology and adornment must be eschewed. The more "naked" it is, the more adequately it fulfills its function.

These considerations determined my attitude toward the material at my disposal.

The zaddik, however, should not be presented merely in actions that tend to go over into dicta, but also in the very act of teaching by word of mouth, for with him speech is an essential part of action. And so this book includes still another species. It includes some pieces which I should like to designate as "Teaching in Answers." The teacher, the zaddik, is asked to interpret a verse in the Scriptures or to expound the meaning of a rite. He replies, and in replying, gives more than the questioner had set out to learn. In the texts I worked on, this species frequently does not employ the form of a conversation; the answer embodies the question. In most instances I have reconstructed the questions and thus restored the dialogue form. And — since a sharp distinction is impossible — this led me to include a number of passages where the speaker puts questions to himself. In addition to these, there are several teachings and sermons which are given because of their profound significance. But not a single passage hails from the extensive theoretical writings of hasidism; all are taken from the popular literature, where they supplement what is told of the lives of the zaddikim. All this has an entirely oral character, not a literary one.

In those selections directly concerned with the teachings, I tried to keep to the actual words of my texts, at least as far as this was compatible with the demands of clarity. But in many cases the texts were so obscure, so fused with alien elements, that it was often necessary to scrape away an entire layer of obvious additions, in order to get down to the true sayings of the master.

This book contains less than a tenth of the material I collected. The first criterion for the inclusion of a tale was, of course, significance *per se*, as well as special significance for the understanding of hasidic life. But many passages which were suitable from this point of view had to be set aside because they did not serve to characterize one of the zaddikim about which this book centers. And this was the deciding factor.

Thus, from the numerous legends transmitted about almost every zaddik, I had to choose those which gave the best account of the character and the way of a certain zaddik, and then to arrange them to give the pattern of his life. Sometimes my material was such that I had only to select among tales and utterances those that furnished together an almost perfect picture of a life; at others there were gaps which I had to fill with my own conjectures, given in my introductions to these two volumes. In a few instances, my data were so meager that I had to resign myself to offering the "static" portrait of a man, instead of the "dynamic" picture of a human life.

Within the individual chapters, I have arranged the tales in biographical, but not in chronological order, since this would have obscured rather than clarified the total effect I had in mind. From the material at hand, it was easier to compose the picture of a man and his way, by projecting the various elements of his character and of his work individually and—if possible—each in the light of its own particular development, until they all fused into a sort of inner biography. Thus, for instance, in the chapter on the Baal Shem, the following sequence was observed: 1) the soul of the Baal Shem; 2) preparation and revelation; 3) ecstasy and fervor; 4) his community; 5) with his disciples; 6) with a variety of people; 7) the strength of vision; 8) holiness and miracles; 9) the Holy Land and redemption; 10) before and after his death. Each passage comes at its appointed place, though occasionally this breaks the chronological order, and the teachings supplement the tales wherever this seems desirable.

At a first quick reading, there will seem to be a number of repetitions in the book, but they are not really repetitions, and wherever a motif recurs, the meaning is altered, or it appears in a different connotation. There is, for example, repeated mention of the "Satan's hasidim," viz., of the false hasidim who join the true and threaten to disrupt the community. But the careful reader will note a different situation and a different form of expression in every single case.

My work of re-telling hasidic legends began more than forty years ago. Its first fruits were the books entitled: "Tales of Rabbi Nahman" (1906), and "The Legend of the Baal Shem" (1907). Subsequently, however, I rejected my method of dealing with the transmitted material, on the grounds that it was too free. I applied my new concept of the task and the means to accomplish it, in the books "The Great Maggid and His Succession" (1921) and "The Hidden Light" (1924). The content of these two books has been reproduced almost entirely in this book, but by far the greater part of it was written since my arrival in Palestine in 1938. Along with much else, I owe the urge to this new and more comprehensive composition to the air of this land. Our sages say that it makes one wise; to me it has granted a different gift: the strength to make a new beginning. I had regarded my work on the hasidic legends as completed. This book is the outcome of a beginning.

Jerusalem, Summer 1946

MARTIN BUBER

TALES OF THE HASIDIM

~~~~~~

BOOK ONE: THE EARLY MASTERS

~~~~~~

INTRODUCTION

1.

The purpose of this book is to introduce the reader to a world of legendary reality. I must call it legendary, for the accounts which have been handed down to us, and which I have here tried to put into fitting form, are not authentic in the sense that a chronicle is authentic. They go back to fervent human beings who set down their recollections of what they saw or thought they had seen, in their fervor, and this means that they included many things which took place, but were apparent only to the gaze of fervor, and others which cannot have happened and could not happen in the way they are told, but which the elated soul perceived as reality and, therefore, related as such. That is why I must call it reality: the reality of the experience of fervent souls, a reality born in all innocence, unalloyed by invention and whimsy. These souls did not give an account of themselves but of what stirred them, and so, whatever we learn from this account is not only a fact in the psychological sense, but a fact of life as well. Something happened to rouse the soul, and it had such and such an effect; by communicating the effect, tradition also reveals its cause; the contact between those who quicken and those who are quickened, the association between the two. That is true legend and that is its reality.

The men who are the subject of these tales, the men who quicken, are the zaddikim, a term which is usually translated by "the righteous," but which actually means "those who stood the test" or "the proven." They are the leaders of the hasidic communities. And the men who do the telling,* whose tales constitute the body of transmitted legends, the men who were

---

* I have prefaced the so-called "miracle tales," i.e., those in which the unreal aspects of reality are especially evident, with the phrase: "It is told."

1

quickened, are the hasidim, "the devout," or, more accurately, those who keep faith with the covenant. They are the members of such communities. This book, then, purports to express and document the association between zaddikim and hasidim, and should be accepted as the expression and documentation of the life of the zaddikim with their hasidim.

2.

The core of hasidic teachings is the concept of a life of fervor, of exalted joy. But this teaching is not a theory which can persist regardless of whether it is translated into reality. It is rather the theoretic supplement to a life which was actually lived by the zaddikim and hasidim, especially in the first six generations of the movement, of which this book treats — three in each volume.

The underlying purpose of all great religions and religious movement is to beget a life of elation, of fervor which cannot be stifled by any experience, which, therefore, must spring from a relationship to the eternal, above and beyond all individual experiences. But since the contacts a man makes with the world and with himself are frequently not calculated to rouse him to fervor, religious concepts refer him to another form of being, to a world of perfection in which his soul may also grow perfect. Compared to this state of perfect being, life on earth seems either only an antechamber, or mere illusion, and the prospect of a higher life has the task of creating fervor in the face of disappointing outer and inner experiences, of creating the fervent conviction that there is such a higher life, and that it is, or can gradually become accessible to the human soul, under certain conditions beyond the bounds of earthly existence. Although faith in a life hereafter is integral to Judaism, there has always been a strong tendency to provide an earthly residence for perfection. The great Messianic concept of coming perfection on earth which everyone can actively help prepare for, could not, in spite of the power it exerted over souls, endow daily life with that constant, undaunted and exalted joy in the Now and Here, which can spring only from fulfilment in the present, not from hope in a future fulfilment.

This was not altered when the Kabbalistic teaching of the transmigration of souls made it possible for everyone to identify his soul with that of a person of the Messianic generation, and thus have the feeling of participating in it. Only in the Messianic movements themselves, which always were based on the belief that perfection was just on the verge of being realized, did the fervor break through and permeate all of life. When the last of these movements, the Sabbatian movement, and its after-effects ended in renegacy and despair, the test for the living strength of religion had come, for here no mere softening of sorrow, but only a life of fervent joy could aid the Jew to survive. The development of hasidism indicates that the test was passed.

The hasidic movement did not weaken the hope in a Messiah, but it kindled both its simple and intellectual followers to joy in the world as it is, in life as it is, in every hour of life in this world, as that hour is. Without dulling the prick of conscience or deadening the sense of chasm between the ideal pattern of the individual limned by his Creator, and what he actually is, hasidism shows men the way to God who dwells with them "in the midst of their uncleannesses," a way which issues forth from every temptation, even from every sin. Without lessening the strong obligation imposed by the Torah, the movement suffused all the traditional commandments with joy-bringing significance, and even set aside the walls separating the sacred and the profane, by teaching that every profane act can be rendered sacred by the manner in which it is performed. It had nothing to do with pantheism which destroys or stunts the greatest of all values: the reciprocal relationship between the human and the divine, the reality of the I and the You which does not cease at the rim of eternity. Hasidism did, however, make manifest the reflection of the divine, the sparks of God that glimmer in all beings and all things, and taught how to approach them, how to deal with them, how to "lift" and redeem them, and re-connect them with their original root. The doctrine of the Shekhinah, contained in the Talmud and expanded in the Kabbalah, of the Shekhinah as the Divine Presence which resides in this world, receives a new and intimate significance and applicability. If you direct the undiminished power of your fervor to God's world-destiny, if you do what you must do at this moment—no matter what it may be!—with your whole strength and with kavvanah, with holy intent, you will bring about the union between God and Shekhinah, eternity and time. You need not be a scholar or a sage to accomplish this. All that is necessary is to have a soul united within itself and indivisibly directed to its divine goal. The world in which you live, just as it is and not otherwise, affords you that association with God, which will redeem you and whatever divine aspect of the world you have been entrusted with. And your own character, the very qualities which make you what you are, constitutes your special approach to God, your special potential use for Him. Do not be vexed at your delight in creatures and things! But do not let it shackle itself to creatures and things; through these, press on to God. Do not rebel against your desires, but seize them and bind them to God. You shall not stifle your surging powers, but let them work at holy work, and rest a holy rest in God. All the contradictions with which the world distresses you are only that you may discover their intrinsic significance, and all the contrary trends tormenting you within yourself, only wait to be exorcised by your word. All innate sorrow wants only to flow into the fervor of your joy.

But this joy must not be the goal toward which you strive. It will be vouchsafed you if you strive to "give joy to God." Your personal joy will rise up when you want nothing but the joy of God—nothing but joy in itself.

3.

But how was man, in particular the "simple man," with whom the hasidic movement is primarily concerned, to arrive at living his life in fervent joy? How, in the fires of temptation, was he to recast the Evil Urge into an urge for what is good? How, in the wonted fulfilling of the commandments was he to develop the rapturous bond with the upper worlds? How, in his meeting with creatures and things, grow aware of the divine sparks hidden within them? How, through holy kavvanah illumine everyday life? We do, indeed, know that all that is necessary is to have a soul united within itself and indivisibly directed to its divine goal. But how, in the chaos of life on our earth, are we to keep the holy goal in sight? How retain unity in the midst of peril and pressure, in the midst of thousands of disappointments and delusions? And once unity is lost, how recover it? Man needs counsel and aid, he must be lifted and redeemed. And he does not need all this only in regard to his soul, for in some way or other, the domains of the soul are intertwined with the big and little cares, the griefs and despairs of life itself, and if these are not dealt with, how shall those loftier concerns be approached? A helper is needed, a helper for both body and soul, for both earthly and heavenly matters. This helper is called the zaddik. He can heal both the ailing body and the ailing soul, for he knows how one is bound up with the other, and this knowledge gives him the power to influence both. It is he who can teach you to conduct your affairs so that your soul remains free, and he can teach you to strengthen your soul, to keep you steadfast beneath the blows of destiny. And over and over he takes you by the hand and guides you until you are able to venture on alone. He does not relieve you of doing what you have grown strong enough to do for yourself. He does not lighten your soul of the struggle it must wage in order to accomplish its particular task in this world. And all this also holds for the communication of the soul with God. The zaddik must make communication with God easier for his hasidim, but he cannot take their place. This is the teaching of the Baal Shem and all the great hasidim followed it; everything else is distortion and the signs of it appear relatively early. The zaddik strengthens his hasid in the hours of doubting, but he does not infiltrate him with truth, he only helps him conquer and reconquer it for himself. He develops the hasid's own power for right prayer, he teaches him how to give the words of prayer the right direction, and he joins his own prayer to that of his disciple and therewith lends him courage, an increase of power—wings. In hours of need, he prays for his disciple and gives all of himself, but he never permits the soul of the hasid to rely so wholly on his own that

5

it relinquishes independent concentration and tension, in other words, that striving-to-God of the soul without which life on this earth is bound to be unfulfilled. Not only in the realm of human passions does the zaddik point over and over to the limits of counsel and help. He does this also in the realm of association with God; again and again he emphasizes the limits of mediation. One man can take the place of another only as far as the threshold of the inner sanctum.

Both in the hasidic teachings and in the tales, we often hear of zaddikim who take upon themselves the sorrow of others, and even atone for others by sacrificing their own lives. But on the very rare occasions (as in the case of Rabbi Nahman of Bratzlav) when we read that the true zaddik can accomplish the act of turning to God for those nearest and dearest to him, the author immediately adds that this act done in place of the other, facilitates the hasid's own turning to God. The zaddik helps everyone, but he does not relieve anyone of what he must do for himself. His helping is a delivery. He even helps the hasid through his death; those near him in the hour of his death receive "a great illumining."

Within these limits the zaddik has the greatest possible influence not only on the faith and mind of the hasid, but on his active everyday life, and even on his sleep, which he renders deep and pure. Through the zaddik, all the senses of the hasid are perfected, not through conscious directing, but through bodily nearness. The fact that the hasid looks at the zaddik perfects his sense of sight, his listening to him, his sense of hearing. Not the teachings of the zaddik but his existence constitute his effectiveness; and not so much the circumstance that he is present on extraordinary occasions as that he is there in the ordinary course of days, unemphatic, undeliberate, unconscious; not that he is there as an intellectual leader but as the complete human being with his whole worldly life in which the completeness of the human being is tested. As a zaddik once said: "I learned the Torah from all the limbs of my teacher." This was the zaddik's influence on his true disciples. But his mere physical presence did not, of course, suffice to exert influence on the many, on the people at large, that influence which made hasidism a popular movement. To achieve this, he had to work with the people until they were ready to receive what he had to give them, to present his teachings in a form the people could accept as their own, he must "participate in the multitude." He had to mix with the people and, in order to raise them to the rung of what perfection they were capable of, he had to descend from his own rung. "If a man falls into the mire," says the Baal Shem, "and his friend wants to fetch him out, he must not hesitate to get himself a little dirty."

One of the great principles of hasidism is that the zaddik and the people are dependent on one another. Again and again, their relationship is compared to that between substance and form in the life of the individual, between body and soul. The soul must not boast that it is more holy than the body, for only in that it has climbed down into the body and works through its limbs can the soul attain to its own perfection. The body, on the other hand, may not brag of supporting the soul, for when the soul leaves, the flesh falls into decay. Thus the zaddikim need the multitude, and the multitude need the zaddikim. The realities of hasidic teaching depend on this inter-relationship. And so the "descending from the rung" is not a true descent. Quite the contrary: "If the zaddik serves God," says Rabbi Nahman of Bratzlav, "but does not take the trouble to teach the multitude, he will descend from his rung."

Rabbi Nahman himself, one of the most spiritual of all the zaddikim, felt a deep and secret sense of union between himself and "simple men." This union is the point of departure for his strange utterances about two months before he died. At first he was in a state of such spiritual exhaustion that he declared he was nothing but a "simple man." But when this state suddenly went over into the loftiest elation of spirit, he said that in such periods of descending, the zaddik was infused with vital strength which poured out from him into all the "simple men" in the world, not only those of Israel, but of all people. And the vital strength which flowed into him, hailed from "the treasure trove of gratuitous gifts" stored up in the land of Canaan from time immemorial, time before Israel, and this treasure trove, he added, consists of that secret substance which is also accorded to the souls of simple men and makes them capable of simple faith.

Here we come to the very foundation of hasidism, on which the life between those who quicken, and those who are quickened, is built up. The quintessence of this life is the relationship between the zaddik and his disciples, which unfolds the interaction between the quickener and the quickened in complete clarity. The teacher helps his disciples find themselves, and in hours of desolation the disciples help their teacher find himself again. The teacher kindles the souls of his disciples and they surround him and light his life with the flame he has kindled. The disciple asks, and by his manner of asking unconsciously evokes a reply, which his teacher's spirit would not have produced without the stimulus of the question.

Two "miracle tales" will serve to demonstrate the lofty function of discipleship.

Once, at the close of the Day of Atonement, the Baal Shem is greatly troubled because the moon cannot pierce the clouds and so he cannot say the Blessing of the New Moon, which in this very hour, an hour when Israel is threatened with grave danger, was to have a particularly salutary effect. In vain he strains his soul to alter the state of the sky. Then his hasidim, who know nothing of all this, begin to dance just as every year at this time, in joyful elation at the service performed by their master, a service like that of the high priest in the Temple of Jerusalem. First they dance in the outer room of the Baal Shem's house, but in their elation they enter his room and dance around him. At last, at the peak of ecstasy, they beg him to join the dance and draw him into the circle. And then the moon breaks through the heavy clouds and shines out, a marvel of flawless light. The joy of the hasidim has brought about what the soul of the zaddik, straining to the utmost of its power, was not able to effect.

Among the disciples of Rabbi Dov Baer the Great Maggid, the greatest disciple of the Baal Shem, Rabbi Elimelekh was the man who kept alive the core of the tradition and preserved the school as such. Once, when his soul rose up to heaven, he learned that with his holiness he was rebuilding the ravaged altar in the sanctuary of heavenly Jerusalem, which corresponds to the sanctuary of Jerusalem on this earth. At the same time, he learned that his disciples were helping him in this task of restoration. In a certain year, two of these were absent from the Festival of Rejoicing in the Law, Rabbi Jacob Yitzhak, later the rabbi of Lublin (the "Seer"), and Rabbi Abraham Joshua Heshel, later the rabbi of Apt. Heaven had told Elimelekh that Jacob Yitzhak would bring the Ark into the sanctuary, and that Abraham Joshua Heshel would bring the tables of the law. Yet now they were both missing! Then the zaddik said to his son: "Eighteen times over I can cry: 'Rise up, O Lord!' (as Israel, in the day of old, called toward the Ark, which was to precede them into battle)—and it will be of no use."

In this second story, the disciples participate in the work of the zaddik as individuals, in the first they take part in it as a "holy community." This form of collective effect is undoubtedly the more significant, though we have many and varied tales concerning the participation of individuals. The community of hasidim who belong to a zaddik, especially the close-knit circle of those who are constantly with him, or—at least—visit him regularly, is felt as a powerful dynamic unit. The zaddik unites with this circle both in prayer and in teaching. They are his point of departure in praying, for he does not pray merely as one speaking for them, but as their focus of strength in which the blaze of the community-soul is gathered, and from which this blaze is borne aloft fused with the flame of his own soul. On the sabbath when, at the third meal, he expounds the Scriptures and reveals what is hidden, his teaching is directed toward them: they are the field of force in which his words make manifest the spirit in expanding circles, like rings widening on the waters. And this meal itself! We can approach an understanding of its tension and bliss only when we realize that all—each giving himself utterly—are united into an elated whole, such as can only form around an elated center, which through its very being, points to the divine center of all being. This is a living connection which sometimes expresses itself strangely and even grotesquely, but the grotesque in itself is so genuine that it bears witness to the genuineness of the impulses. For hasidism must not be interpreted as an esoteric movement but one charged with primitive vitality which—as all primitive vitality—sometimes vents itself rather crudely. It is this very vitality which lends peculiar intensity to the relationship of one hasid toward another. Their common attachment to the zaddik and to the holy life he embodies binds them to one another, not only in the festive hours of common prayer, and of the common meal, but in all the hours of everyday living. In moments of elation, they drink to one another, they sing and dance together, and tell one another abstruse and comforting miracle tales. But they help one another too. They are prepared to risk their lives for a comrade, and this readiness comes from the same deep source as their elation. Everything the true hasid does or does not do mirrors his belief that, in spite of the intolerable suffering men must endure, the heartbeat of life is holy joy, and that always and everywhere, one can force a way through to that joy—provided one devotes one's self entirely to his deed.

There are many distorted aspects of hasidism which are by no means inherent only in the later stages of the movement. Side by side with the fervent love for the zaddik we find a coarsened form of reverence on the part of those who regard him as a great magician, as one who is an intimate of heaven and can right all that is wrong, who relieves his hasidim of straining their own souls and secures them a desirable place in the hereafter. Though the hasidim of a zaddik were often united by a feeling of true brotherliness, they frequently held aloof from and sometimes were even hostile to the followers of other zaddikim. A like contrast obtained between the free life in religion of a hasidic community and their thick-skinned opportunism in regard to the powers of the state. Sometimes, dull superstition settled down side by side with the innocent fantasy of the elated spirit and made shallows of its depths, and sometimes crass fraud made its appearance and abused it. Most of these phenomena are familiar to us through the history of other religious movements that sprang from the vitality of the people, others become understandable when we consider the pathological premises of life in exile. My aim was not to go into all this, but to show what it was that made hasidism one of the most significant phenomena of living and fruitful faith that we know, and—up to this time—the last great flowering of the Jewish will to serve God in this world and to consecrate everyday life to him.

In the very beginnings of the movement, hasidism disintegrated into separate communities whose inner life had small connection, and early in its history individual zaddikim display problematic traits. But every hasidic community still contains a germ of the kingdom of God, a germ—no more than that, but no less, and often this germ lives and grows even in substance which has fallen prey to decay. And even the zaddik who has squandered the spiritual inheritance of his forbears has hours in which his forehead gives forth a glow as though the primordial light had touched it with radiance.

4.

In a crisis of faith, when faith is renewed, the man who initiates and leads the renewal is frequently not a spiritual character in the ordinary sense of the world, but one who draws his strength from an extraordinary union between the spiritual and tellurian powers, between heavenly and earthly fire, but it is the sublime which determines the earth-sustained frame. The life of such a man is a constant receiving of fire and transforming it into light. And this, which is and occurs within himself, is the cause of his twofold effect on the world: he restores to the element of earth those whom preoccupation with thought has removed from it, and those who are burdened with the weight of earth he raises to the heights of heaven.

Israel ben Eliezer of Mezbizh (Miedzyboz), called the Baal Shem Tov (1700-1760), the founder of hasidism, was such a man. He first appears merely as one in a series of Baale Shem, of "Masters of the Name," who knew a Name of God that had magic force, were able to invoke it, and with this art of theirs helped and healed the men who came to them—manifestations of a form of magic which was absorbed by religion. The actual basis for their work was their ability to perceive intrinsic connections between things, connections which lay beyond the bounds of time and space (apparent only to what we usually call intuition) and their peculiar strengthening and consolidating influence on the soul-center of their fellowmen, which enabled this center to regenerate the body and the whole of life— an influence of which the so-called "suggestive powers" are nothing but a distortion. Certain aspects of Israel ben Eliezer's work constitute a continuation of the work of the Baale Shem, but with one marked difference which even expresses itself in the change of the epithet "Baal Shem" to "Baal Shem Tov." This difference and what it signifies is unambiguously stressed in the legendary tradition.

In various versions we are told how either Rabbi Gershon, the Baal Shem's brother-in-law, who first despised him as an ignorant man but later became his faithful disciple, or one of the descendants of the Baal Shem, went to a great rabbi who lived far away—in Palestine or in Germany—and he told him about Rabbi Israel Baal Shem. "Baal Shem?" said the rabbi questioningly. "I don't know any such person." And in the case of the Baal Shem's brother-in-law, the rejection is more pronounced, for when Rabbi Gershon speaks of the Baal Shem as his teacher, he receives the reply: "Baal Shem? No, there is no teacher by that name." But when Rabbi Gershon quickly rights his first words by giving the full name "Baal Shem Tov," the rabbi he is visiting assumes an entirely different attitude. "Oh!" he exclaims. "The Baal Shem Tov! He, to be sure, is a very great teacher. Every morning I see him in the temple of paradise." The sage refuses to have anything to do with common miracle men, but the Baal Shem Tov—that is quite another matter, that is something new. The addition of one word altered the meaning and the character of the epithet. "Shem Tov" is the "Good Name." The Baal Shem Tov, the possessor of the Good Name, is a man who, because he is as he is, gains the confidence of his fellowmen. "Baal Shem Tov" as a general designation, refers to a man in whom the people have confidence, the confident of the people. With this, the term ceases to designate a rather doubtful vocation and comes to apply to a reliable person and, at the same time, transforms what was, after all, a category of magic, into one religious in the truest sense of the word. For the term "Baal Shem Tov" signifies a man who lives with and for his fellowmen on the foundation of his relation to the divine.

There is a story that Rabbi Yitzhak of Drohobycz, one of the ascetic "hasidim" who first rebelled against the Baal Shem, was full of hostility for the innovator because he had heard that he gave people amulets containing slips of paper inscribed with secret names of God. On the occasion of a meeting, he asked the Baal Shem about it. He opened one of the amulets and showed the questioner that on the slip there was nothing but his own name and that of his mother, "Israel ben Sarah." Here the amulet has completely lost its magical attributes. It is nothing but a sign and pledge of the personal bond between the helper and the one who is given help, a bond based on trust. The Baal Shem Tov helps those who trust him. He is able to help them because they trust him. The amulet is the permanent symbol of his direct influence at the given moment. It contains his name and thus represents him. And through this pledge of personal connection, the soul of the recipient is "lifted." The power at work here is the union of the tellurian and spiritual within the Baal Shem and, proceeding from this union, the relationship between him and his hasidim which involves both domains.

This sheds light on his attitude toward the "Men of Spirit" he wishes to win for the hasidic movement, and on the fact that most of them are willing to subject themselves to him. According to one legendary version, for instance, the greatest of his disciples, the actual founder of the hasidic school of teaching: Rabbi Dov Baer, the Maggid (wandering preacher) of Mezritch (Miedzyrzecze), comes to him to be cured of his illness. His physical suffering is only eased, but he is healed of "teaching without soul." This instance clearly demonstrates that Nature, at work in the person of the helper, guides the spirit, which has strayed too far from her, back into her domain, the only milieu in which the soul can thrive through ceaseless contact with her. And the "Great Maggid," whose powers as thinker are far superior to those of the Baal Shem, bows to the infinitely rare and decisive phenomenon: the union of fire and light in a human being. The same holds for another important exponent of hasidic teachings in the second generation, for Rabbi Jacob Joseph of Polnoye (Polonnoje). He was not an independent thinker, such as the Maggid, but well versed in the teachings, and thus enabled to receive and expound the teachings of the Baal Shem who drew him from his ascetic remoteness into a simple life with his fellowmen. There are various versions of how the Baal Shem won him over, but they all have two traits in common: he does not reveal himself directly, but manifests himself through his particular manner of concealment, and he tells him stories (he always likes to tell stories) which stir the hearer just because of their primitive character and apparent lack of intellectual quality, and finally make him see and accept them as a reference to his own secret needs. Here again, in the telling of simple stories and parables which, however, evoke a strong personal application, the connection between spirit and nature becomes manifest, a union which makes it possible for images to serve as symbols, that is as spirit which assumes form in Nature herself. What both of these disciples have to say about the teachings of the Baal Shem, and about their association with him, is characteristic in the same sense: he taught the Maggid (among other things) how to understand the language of birds and trees, and—so the rabbi of Polnoye tells his son-in-law—it was his "holy custom" to converse with animals. The Gaon of Vilna, the great opponent of hasidism, who was responsible for the ban pronounced upon it, the man who wished to proceed against the hasidim "as Elijah proceeded against the prophets of Baal," accused the Baal Shem of "having led astray" the Maggid of Mezritch "through his magic arts." What seemed magic was the union within a person of heavenly light and earthly fire, of spirit and nature. Whenever this union appears incarnate in human form, this person testifies—with the testimony of life—for the divine unity of spirit and nature, reveals this unity anew to the world of man which again and again becomes estranged from it, and evokes ecstatic joy. For true ecstasy hails neither from spirit nor from nature, but from the union of these two.

5.

Not many of the immediate disciples of the Baal Shem stand in the limelight of legendary tradition. It is as though, for the time being, the power of ecstatic vision, which was his to so great a degree, narrowed and concentrated on a few persons beloved by their people, while of the others there are only isolated, though frequently very characteristic tales. Not until the third generation* does the House of Study of the Great Maggid become the focus for a long series of zaddikim, each entirely different from the other, whose memory legend preserved and embroidered with veneration. But aside from this, we are struck by a complete change in tone the moment we turn from the stories which concern the Baal Shem, to those which deal with his disciples and are not immediately connected with his own life. The three men around whom legend has primarily crystallized: the Maggid of Mezritch, Pinhas of Koretz, and Yehiel Mikhal of Zlotchov were, above all, teachers, the first as the head of the hasidic mother-school, the second in a small closed circle which developed hasidic wisdom along its own, independent lines, the third through the powerful influence he exerted in temporary contacts, wide in scope, but not followed up by continuous educational activities. Thus in the case of these three men legend is concerned chiefly with their teachings, while in the stories about the Baal Shem, his teachings only figure as one function, as one part of his life. In the third generation there is a noticeable change: the tales grow more varied, more vivid. They become more like the legends of the Baal Shem. Once more life is expressed in all its abundance — only that the secret of beginnings, the secret of primal magnitude is lacking.

Rabbi Dov Baer, the Maggid of Mezritch (died 1772), was a teaching thinker, or rather, the Baal Shem, who liberated him

---

* In keeping with the contents of this book, this introduction deals only with the first three generations of zaddikim. The introduction to the second volume will treat of the others. This division into generations does not, to be sure, quite correspond to the chronological order: some zaddikim of the third generation chronologically belong to the second volume, some of the fourth to the first.

from his solitude, made a teaching thinker of him. From that time on, the task of teaching determined the deepest core of his thinking. It is significant that his favorite simile is that of the father adjusting himself to his little son who is eager to learn. He regards the world as God's self-adjustment to his little son: Man, whom he rears with tender care to enable him to grow up to his Father. Here then, under the influence of basic pedagogic experience, the Kabbalistic concept of the "contraction" of God to make room for the creation of the world, ceases to be cosmogonic and enters the realm of the anthropological. It is this idea which spurs the Maggid to try to understand the world from the viewpoint of God's educational methods. But the fundamental prerequisite for all education is the strength and tenderness of the relationship between the educator and his pupil. Only one who experienced this like Rabbi Baer could do what he did, could—as Rabbi Shneur Zalman, the most all-inclusive among his disciples, tells us—unite the mercy of God with man's love of God, and the sternness of God with man's fear of God, in other words: set up the reciprocity of this relationship as the fundamental principle. One must understand the tremendous seriousness the Maggid's own experience in receiving teaching had for his soul, to appreciate not only the intensity with which he handles each of his disciples according to his particular character and his inner destiny, but also what is said of his manner of teaching. We are told that his disciples had very divergent interpretations of what he had said, but that the Maggid refused to decide for one or the other of these, because—no matter which of the seventy faces of the Torah one regards with a true spirit—one sees the truth. This sheds light on another aspect of the Maggid's method: When he spoke, he did not supply systematic connections, but threw out a single suggestion, or a single parable without spinning it out and tying together the threads. His disciples had the task—and it was a task which absorbed them completely—of working over what had been said and supplying the missing links. Each did this for himself or they worked together. One of them wrote in a letter: "We were always content with one saying over a long period of time and

kept it alive within us, pure and whole, until we heard another."
The Maggid was concerned with waking the truth inherent in
the spirit of his disciples, with "lighting the candles."

But we cannot grasp all this in its full significance until we
remember that obviously the Maggid had always been a man
given to ecstasy, only that, under the influence of the Baal
Shem, this ecstasy was diverted from ascetic solitude to the
active life of teaching disciples. From that moment on, his
ecstasy assumed the shape of teaching. Many of his disciples
have testified to the ecstatic character of his words. They say
that he had only to open his lips and they all had the impression that he was no longer in this world, that the Divine
Presence was speaking from his throat. And this phenomenon
too cannot be understood until we probe down to the deepest
depths accessible to us: It is apparent that with all the passion
his soul was capable of, the Maggid put himself into the service of the will of God to lift his "little son" up to him. And
to accomplish this service he regarded himself, his thinking
as well as his teaching, only as a vessel for divine truth. To
use his own words, he "changed the something back into the
nothing." From this angle, we can understand that effect on
his disciples which the youngest of them, later the "Seer of
Lublin," described after his very first visit to the Maggid:
"When I came before the master, before the Maggid, I saw
him on his bed: something was lying there, which was nothing
but simple will, the will of the Most High." That was why his
disciples learned even more and greater things from his sheer
being than from his words.

The founder of hasidism, the Baal Shem, had not been a
teacher in the specific sense of the word. Compared to him,
the Maggid represents the quintessence of what makes up the
teacher, and that is the reason for his special influence. The
Baal Shem had lived, wrought, helped, healed, prayed, preached,
and taught. All this was one and the same thing, all was
an organic part of unified, spontaneous life, and so teaching
was only one among other natural manifestations of effective
living. It was different with the Maggid. He was, of course,
not a professional teacher, not a man with one specialized

function. Only in eras when the world of the spirit is on the decline is teaching, even on its highest level, regarded as a profession. In epochs of flowering, disciples live with their master just as apprentices in a trade lived with theirs, and "learn" by being in his presence, learn many things for their work and their life both because he wills it, or without any willing on his part. That is how it was with the disciples of the Maggid. Over and over they say that he himself as a human being was the carrier of teaching, that, in his effect on them, he was a Torah personified. As far as he himself was concerned, however, the will to teach was the mainspring of his existence. He poured into his disciples all the strength of his life, recreated by contact with the Baal Shem. And all the work of his intellect, he put into the service of teaching. He did not write a book; neither had the Baal Shem. But if— unlike the Baal Shem—he permitted others to take down his words, he did this to transmit his teachings to future generations of disciples, as an indestructible prop.

The Great Maggid did not found an institute of learning. His spirit created only disciples, generations of disciples and disciples of disciples. No other religious movement of the modern era has produced so many and so varied independent personalities in so short a space of time.

Concerning the son of the Great Maggid, Rabbi Abraham, "the Angel," who died only a few years after him (1776), Rabbi Pinhas of Koretz said that had he lived longer, all the zaddikim of his generation would have subjected themselves to him. And in the autobiography of one of his contemporaries who, on the ninth day of Av, the commemorative day of the destruction of the Temple, saw him lamenting for a night and a day, we read: "Then I realized that it was not for nothing that all called him an angel, for his was not the strength of one born of woman." But in one most significant respect, he cannot be considered a disciple of Rabbi Baer's, in this one respect he even leaves the teachings of the Baal Shem: he sets out to accomplish the "change of something into nothing" by returning to the way of ascetic solitude. Accordingly, he neither associates with the people at large. like the Baal Shem, nor with disciples, like the

Baal Shem and the Great Maggid. He gave instruction in the Kabbalah to only one person, to Shneur Zalman, a man of his own age. In the preface to his posthumous book, he refers to the fact that the true teachings of the Baal Shem and the Great Maggid "grew dark and material before our eyes," in contrast to the steadfastness of a superior zaddik "who cannot descend to the lowest rung to uplift his generation." Here, as in other instances, the bodily descendants of a leading zaddik cease to transmit the teachings. As early as the second generation the problematic character of hasidic development becomes evident, in its most sublime aspect.

Rabbi Pinhas of Koretz (Korzec, died 1791) was the second among those who belonged to the Baal Shem's circle to become the focus of a tradition. He was not one of his disciples in the strict sense of the word, since he is said to have visited the Baal Shem only twice, the second time during the last days of his life. Apparently his contacts with Rabbi Israel ben Eliezer did not bring about any fundamental change in his views, but only confirmed and strengthened them. Yet he must certainly be included here. Although in his mention of the Baal Shem he does not designate him as his teacher, he and his school give important data about the Baal Shem and cite important utterances of his, for which we have no other source, and which therefore probably go back to oral transmission. One such utterance is the basis of one of the Rabbi Pinhas' major teachings: that we should "love" the evil-doer and hater "more" in order to compensate for the lack of the power of love he himself has caused in his place in the world. And other basic teachings of Rabbi Pinhas also derive from words of the Baal Shem. To gain a better understanding of the relationship, we must remember that the Baal Shem—as we glean from a number of indications—found kindred trends to which his influence afforded increased vitality and, frequently, a deeper rooting. Among these kindred trends, those of Rabbi Pinhas (who was about thirty-two when the Baal Shem died) approximated his own most nearly, and he accepted him more as a companion than as a disciple.

Rabbi Leib, son of Sarah, the zaddik who wandered over the earth for secret purposes of his own, is said to have called Rabbi Pinhas the brain of the world. He was, at any rate, a true and original sage. In the period between the Baal Shem and his great-grandson Nahman of Bratzlav, he has no equal in fresh and direct thinking, in daring and vivid expression. What he says often springs from a profound knowledge of the human soul, and it is always spontaneous and great-hearted. In contrast to the Baal Shem and the Great Maggid, no ecstasies are reported of Rabbi Pinhas. Ecstasy wanes into the background and the mystic teachings are reduced to the precept of constant renewal through immersion in nothingness, a doctrine of dying and arising which, however, sponsors also sturdy living in tune with all the things of this earth, and a give-and-take community with one's fellowmen. Rabbi Pinhas' circle had no great influence on the outside world, but such as it is, it represents a unique and invaluable phenomenon, for its members were distinguished by the simple honesty of their personal faith, the unrhetorical telling of the teaching, a telling even tinged with humor, and by their loyal readiness to satisfy the demands put upon them, at the cost of their very lives.

One cannot consider Rabbi Pinhas apart from his most distinguished disciple, Rafael of Bershad. In the whole history of hasidism, rich in fruitful relationships between master and disciple, there is no other instance of so pure a harmony, of so adequate a continuation of the work. In reading the records, we sometimes hardly know what to ascribe to Pinhas and what to Rafael, and yet we have a number of utterances of the latter which bear the stamp of independent thinking. But more important than his independence is the matter of course devotion with which the disciple embodied his master's teachings in his life and—according to tradition—even in his death, which quietly and solemnly sealed the proclamation of the commandment of truth, for which the master had striven so many years.

Rabbi Yehiel Mikhal, the maggid of Zlotchov (died about 1786) * who first learned from the Baal Shem and, after his

---

* The dates given for his death vary between 1781 and 1792.

death, from the Great Maggid, was also a unique phenomenon, as yet insufficiently understood and difficult to understand. He came from a family of those ascetic mystic hasidim whom the new movement found ready to hand and tried to win for its own, because the earnestness of their faith which colored their whole attitude toward life rendered them particularly valuable for the task of renewal. Mikhal's father was that Rabbi Yitzhak of Drohobycz who had criticized the amulets of the Baal Shem. All manner of uncanny rumors were circulated about him, that he once did a favor to the "prince of the forest," for instance, or that he sent those of his new-born children who displeased him back to the upper world. (It was said that Mikhal remained alive only because his mother refused to let his father see his face, before he had promised to let him live.) Rabbi Yitzhak's mother, who was called "Yente, the prophetess," used to repeat the threefold "holy" of the choir of angels whose song she heard. To understand Mikhal, it is necessary to know his milieu. In spite of the fact that his father was close to the movement, he himself became a follower of the Baal Shem only after some hesitation. From what we are told it is quite evident that his father's suspicion lived on in him and was only gradually overcome. But he never wholly overcame his basic asceticism.

While he was still young, Mikhal became a great preacher, like his father before him, and went preaching from town to town. He fascinated and intimidated his audiences although he emphasized that the reproof in his sermons was directed toward himself as well as them. The Baal Shem chided him for imposing too heavy penances on sinners and apparently induced him to adopt a milder attitude. But even after his death they tell of souls who come to a younger zaddik to complain of Rabbi Mikhal who, as the chief justice of a court in heaven, censures unintentional earthly faults with the utmost severity because he, who remained pure, does not understand the temptations of men. Though he wholly accepted and absorbed the hasidic teachings and followed the trend of the Baal Shem in his doctrine of the Evil Urge as a helper and of the uplifting of sexuality, he never quite rid himself of asceticism whose extreme forms, however, he emphatically rejected. According to a report, which all but crosses the border between the sublime and the ridiculous, he never warmed himself at the stove, for this would have been a concession to sloth, never bent down to his food, for this would have been yielding to greed, and never scratched himself, since this would have verged on voluptuousness. But Rabbi Mikhal's special endowment made for true hasidism in a very significant fashion. The most notable instance of this is that he carried on the tradition of those "first hasidim" of whom the Talmud says that they waited with praying until they had prepared the kavvanah within themselves. But he expanded this motif into something that embraced the whole community: in order to make his prayer representative for the community, he strove to unite with both the mightier and the humbler to form a single, continuous and powerful chain of prayer, and—taking as his point of departure the tradition of his father and a saying of the Baal Shem's—he also wanted to raise up the limp prayers which had not the strength to rise from the ground. This attitude, for which he incurred violent hostility, exerted an effective influence on later generations who accorded him deep veneration. But even a contemporary zaddik said of him that he was "a soul of the soul," and, in his own generation, played the same role as Rabbi Simeon ben Yohai, the founder of the secret teachings, in his.

Like Rabbi Mikhal himself, two of his five sons figure in tales of strange journeys of the soul to heaven. But a third, Rabbi Zev Wolf of Zbarazh (died about 1802),* who was reputed to have been a very wild child, was made of quite other stuff. Like his contemporary Rabbi Moshe Leib of Sasov (who belonged to the fourth generation), he became one of the great friends of man and the earth. In contrast to his father—though we must not forget that Rabbi Mikhal bade his sons pray for their enemies—he obstinately refused to treat the wicked differently from the good. Wolf lavished his love on all human beings who came his way and even on animals. He held that man

* The dates of his death given, vary between 1800 and 1820.

should love all that lives, and that this love must not be determined by the way the object of his love behaves toward him. Among the disciples of Rabbi Mikhal was Rabbi Mordecai of Neskhizh (Niesuchojce, died 1800), whom his teacher took with him to visit the Great Maggid. He figures in a great number of miracle tales, and it is told that even demons recognized his power. The source of such a statement is actual power over the souls of men, and in the case of Rabbi Mordecai such power definitely sprang from the unity in his own soul. This unity, however, did not find adequate expression in power itself, but rather in the unity of his own life. This is what the "Seer" of Lublin must have meant when he said that all his activities were, in reality, one.

6.

According to hasidic tradition, the Great Maggid had three hundred disciples. About forty of these have come down to us as individuals with their personal characteristics, the most of them also through their writings. Ten are represented in this volume, but—as in the case of the Baal Shem's disciples—these ten do not include all of those who were most significant as human beings, because the legends about them, current among the people, do not suffice to give a connected account of their lives. These ten are: Menahem Mendel of Vitebsk (died 1788), whom the Maggid brought to the Baal Shem when he was a boy; Aaron of Karlin (died 1772); Shmelke of Nikolsburg (died 1778); Meshullam Zusya (yiddish Zishe) of Hanipol (Annopol, died 1800); his younger brother, Elimelekh of Lizhensk (Lezajsk, died 1809); Levi Yitzhak of Berditchev (died 1809); Shneur Zalman of Ladi (died 1813); Shelomo of Karlin (died 1792); Israel of Koznitz (Kozienice, died 1814); Jacob Yitzhak of Lublin (died 1815).

What makes Rabbi Menahem Mendel of particular importance in the history of hasidism is that he transplanted the movement to Palestine where, to be sure, other zaddikim had settled before him. From the days of the Baal Shem who, according to legend, had to turn back at the border, the focus of hasidic, as of the pre-hasidic, yearning for redemption, was "the Land." After having taken a leading part in the struggle against those who pronounced the ban, he translated this yearning into action by going to Palestine (1777) with three hundred of his hasidim. There he first settled near Safed, the ancient city of Kabbalists, and later in Tiberias. Thus he gave the movement a site which was not central in location but in spirit, and linked it organically with the past. And he brought the Land an element of new life. Concerning this, a grandson of his friend Shneur Zalman (who had not been able to accompany Mendel to Palestine) said that once, when the Land of Israel was on its highest rung, it had the power to uplift man, but that now that it had sunk so low, and strangely enough kept on sinking, it could no longer uplift man, that now man must uplift the Land, and only a man on so high a rung as Rabbi Mendel had been able to do this. In a letter from Palestine, Rabbi Mendel wrote that he regarded himself as an envoy to the palace of the king, dispatched by the governors of the provinces, that he must not for a moment lose sight of both the physical and spiritual welfare of the provinces. He remained in especially close and constant contact with the hasidim he had left behind in exile, so close that— as one of those who accompanied him writes—everything connected with them, everything taking place in their hearts, was manifest to him when he prayed before falling asleep.

From among all of his disciples, the Maggid chose Aaron of Karlin as his envoy, because he knew how to win souls as none other, even though his courting of them was linked with stern demands upon their whole attitude toward life. He died young, and in his funeral sermon his successor, Rabbi Shelomo of Karlin, said that the Lord had taken him before his time, because his power of converting men to God was so great, that he deprived them of the freedom of choice which is of prime importance. When the Maggid heard of his death, he said: "He was our weapon in war. What shall we do now?" Rabbi Aaron did not wish to go contrary to the folk-character of the movement which not only persisted in the Karlin school but experienced a curious development there. Nevertheless, what he obviously wanted was to create an elite body dedicated to a life of faith. One main device by which he sought to accomplish this was the regulation of one day a week devoted to solitary meditation accompanied by fasting and the ritual bath. But this was to have nothing of the ascetic, for Rabbi Aaron regarded asceticism as a bait thrown out by Satan himself. His demands sprang from his own intrinsic experience. His "testament" expresses his deepest purpose for his own person: to prepare the proper kavvanah for the hour in which the soul departs from the body. His friend Shneur Zalman says of him that he was a veritable fountain of the love of God and that whoever heard him pray was seized by the love for God. But the picture becomes complete only through the words the same zaddik said about Rabbi Aaron's great fear of God after his death.* His love was only the flowering of his fear, for only through great fear—this was Rabbi Aaron's basic feeling—can one attain to great love. He who has not this fear does not love the great and terrible God himself, but only a small convenient idol. One of the sayings of his great-grandson who followed this trend is: "Fear without love is something imperfect; love without fear is nothing at all." And this world in which we live is the site where through fear one can attain to love, and where fear and love can fuse. That is why in another of his sayings we read: "This world is the lowest, and yet the loftiest of all."

Among the disciples of the Great Maggid, Rabbi Shmelke of Nikolsburg was the preacher par excellence; not a preacher who exhorted, as Rabbi Mikhal did in his youth, but a preacher per se. The sermon was his true element because he fervently believed that words inspired by God had the power to transform, and he never gave up this belief, even in the face of disappointments. He regarded the sermon as an action which lifts the prayer of the congregation to the highest level of purity. And so, in his sermons, he repeatedly demanded two things from those who prayed: first, that with the rivers of their love they wash away all separating walls and unite to one true congregation to furnish the site for the union with God; secondly, that they detach their prayers from individual wishes,

* See the story of "The Little Fear and the Great Fear."

and concentrate the full force of their being on the desire that God unite with his Shekhinah. This was the spirit in which he himself prayed and this holy intent of his lifted him to ecstasy, so that in the very midst of prayer, he abandoned the charted track of memory and custom and sang new melodies, never heard before. He left his Polish congregation for Nikolsburg in Moravia, which was utterly remote from the world of hasidism, and where a man such as he was bound to provoke constant annoyance. He exerted a profound influence on many a spirit that was still open and responsive, but the majority of those he stirred up from their usual ways did all they could to make his life in their community intolerable. We have various versions of the tale of how Rabbi Elimelekh, his younger friend in the Maggid's House of Study, visited him and in a coarse and pithy sermon told the burghers that they were not fit patients for so noble a doctor, that first he, Elimelekh, the barber, would have to subject them to drastic treatment. And the next instant, fixing now one, now the other with his gaze, he hurled at them the full description of all their secret vices and faults. Rabbi Shmelke never could have done that, if only because the weaknesses of individuals were not of sufficient importance in his eyes. His basic attitude to all men, including his foes, was love, the vast tide of love which he preached. His House of Study in Nikolsburg became one of the main centers of the movement. He exerted a great influence on his disciples and friends and through them on countless others.

In sharp contrast to Shmelke, Rabbi Meshullam Zusya, known as the Rabbi Reb Zishe, was a true man of the people. Here, in the narrow confines of an eastern ghetto, in a much later century, the "Fool of God" reappears, the singular character, known to us from the legends of Chinese Buddhists, from Sufis, and from the disciples of St. Francis of Assisi. Yet he may also be interpreted as the East European Jewish type of badhan, the jester who figures chiefly at weddings, but now sublimated into something holy. He is a human being who, because of his undamaged direct relationship with God, has quitted the rules and regulations of the social order, though he continues to participate in the life of his fellowmen. He does not sequester himself; he is only detached. His loneliness in the face of the eternal "Thou" is not the loneliness of the recluse, but of one who is composed and true to the world, a loneliness which includes intrinsic oneness with all living creatures. He leads his life among his fellows, detached and yet attached, regarding their faults as his own and rejoicing in them and in all creatures in the freedom of God. But since men are so made that they cannot endure an attitude such as this, which blocks their evasion of the eternal, they are content to jeer at the "fool." They make him suffer. They do not impose sharp and brief martyrdom, but life-long sorrows, and he delights in them. Yet men are also so made that such a destiny kindles them to the most sublime love, and it was with sublime love that Rabbi Zusya was loved by the people.

Rabbi Elimelekh, called the Rabbi Reb Melekh, was Zusya's brother and shared the wanderings of his youth. Year after year, they went on and on without a goal, making their lives an imitation of the journeying of the exiled Presence of God, watching for souls wakened or ready to be wakened. But then they parted ways. Zusya did, to be sure, settle down, but again and again he felt the urge to wander and into his old age he continued to be a boy who whistles a song for God. Elimelekh had the vocation to be a leader of men. He too knew the timeless world of ecstasy, but his clear and unerring reason taught him to protect himself against its dangers and enabled him to combine the life of the spirit with the activities of an organizer. Here again was a man who simultaneously headed the hasidic school and the hasidic congregation, and so Rabbi Elimelekh must be considered the true successor of the Great Maggid. While he did not approach him in originality of teaching, he was almost his equal in his power to build up, and even outstripped him in his intuitive knowledge of the many different types of people, their flaws and their needs, and the means to minister to these. In the legend-shaping memory of the people, he stands out as a doctor of souls, as a man who could exorcise demons, as a wonder-working counselor and guide.

Levi Yitzhak, the rav of Berditchev, the most original of the Maggid's disciples, and the one who came closest to the people, was very different from Elimelekh. He was akin to Zusya, but more of the stuff of this earth, and part and parcel of his nation. His ecstasy penetrated his strong and solid life. The transports of Rabbi Shmelke, whose devoted follower he was, passed over into him, only translated into something more substantial, as it were. In lieu of the strange new songs which broke from Rabbi Shmelke, Rabbi Yitzhak's whole body shook with uncontrollable tremors when he prayed. He liked to converse with crude and ignorant people, but even the worldliest of his words was holy and had for its purpose Yihudim, the uniting of the upper worlds. He was harsh enough when something displeased him about a man, but he was always willing to learn from others and had the greatest reverence for simplicity. Even his communings with God were colored by unvarnished intimacy. He confronted him not only as the passionate intercessor for Israel, he took him to account, made demands on him, and even ventured to hurl threats, a bitter and sublime jest which would have been blasphemy in another, but was irreproachable coming from the lips of this unique character. In his own fashion, however, he also praised God and often interrupted the flow of prescribed prayer by interpolating endearment for him.

Rabbi Shneur Zalman, the rav of Northern White Russia, who was called simply "the rav," or "the Tanya" after the title of his main work, intended to voyage to the Holy Land together with Rabbi Mendel of Vitebsk. But Mendel asked him to turn back—legend makes of it a command received in a dream vision—and the rav later founded the special Lithuanian school of hasidism, the Habad, a term made up of the initial letters of the three upper of the ten Sefirot which, according to the teachings of the Kabbalah, emanated from God: Hokhmah, wisdom; Binah, intelligence; Daat, knowledge. This very name, which detaches the specifically intellectual Sefirot out of the closely linked structure, points to the principle underlying this school: reason and intellect are to be reinstated as a way to find God. The Habad School represents an attempt to reconcile rabbinism with hasidism by incorporating both in a system of thought, a method which of necessity weakened certain fundamental concepts of hasidism. The very separating off of the spheres threatened to deprive hasidism of its strongest base: the teaching that sparks of God are inherent in all things and creatures, in all concepts and urges, sparks which desire us to redeem them and, linked with this teaching, the affirmation of the soul-body entity of man, provided he is able to turn all his stirrings toward God. The average man is no longer asked to transform "alien thoughts"; he is requested to turn away from them and this spells his renunciation of attaining all-embracing unity. The only ones who are not forbidden contact with the powers of temptation are the superior men. (Here, to be sure, the Habad teachings connect up with certain warnings of Rabbi Efraim of Sadylkov, the Baal Shem's grandson.) But in order to give the reason of the individual its due, the zaddik is deprived of the essential office which is his, according to the teachings of the Baal Shem and especially of the Great Maggid, the great office of cosmic helper and mediator. The things misused are discarded together with misuse itself. Yet in spite of everything, the special position of the Habad must not be interpreted as leading to schism. For the rav was exposed to the hostilities of the mitnagdim, the opponents of hasidism, no less, but even more, than the other zaddikim of his time. The anti-hasidic rabbis plotted against him and had him arrested again and again. He was confined in the fortress of Petersburg and subjected to lengthy cross-examination. What he was charged with were distorted teachings of the Baal Shem whose true intent he avowed. A certain zaddik said of the Habad—and he was not altogether wide of the mark—that it resembled a loaded gun in the hand of a man who can aim and who knows the target—only that the fuse was lacking. But even this branch movement with its rationalized mysticism (aided and abetted by the rational tendencies of the Lithuanian Jew) still manifests the old flight of the soul. The life of the zaddik with his hasidim is warmer and stronger than the chilly doctrine, and besides this the rav counted among his disciples distinguished men who again brought the teachings closer to the original tenets of hasidism. Surely the hasidic "flame" burned in the rav himself. We are told of certain traits in his life which give evidence of impassioned personal religiosity, and his clinging to God is documented by his melodies, particularly those known simply as "the rabbi's melodies." Sometimes these are linked with a Kabbalistic song, at others they revolve around "Tatenyu" (little father), a name by which God is addressed. Again and again, at a feast or in solitude, the Habad-hasidim sing them, expressing their fervor and renewing it by its expression.

Rabbi Shelomo of Karlin was instructed by his fellow-pupil Aaron of Karlin and later became his successor. He was a man of prayer in even a stricter sense than Levi Yitzhak, who prayed primarily in behalf of the people while Shelomo prayed only to pray. Rabbi Shelomo as none other accepted as his own the Baal Shem's doctrine that before praying man should prepare to die, because the intention of prayer demands the staking of his entire self. For him prayer was a stupendous venture to which one must give one's self up so completely that thought beyond that point is wholly impossible, that it is impossible to imagine what could take place afterwards. From his youth on, this capacity for self-surrender made his prayer indescribably forceful. Before presenting him to the Great Maggid, Rabbi Aaron told him about this youth who, on the eve of the Day of Atonement, spoke the words of the psalm: "How glorious is Thy name in all the earth," in such a way that not a single one of the fallen sparks remained unlifted. There is a significant story of how some of the hasidim of the "Tanya" came to see him and went into a long ecstasy over the way he recited a psalm before saying grace. The "Tanya" did, indeed, commend him with the words that he was "a hand's-breadth above the world," but it is also told that after Rabbi Mendel of Vitebsk's departure for Palestine, when a number of hasidim thought of joining Rabbi Shelomo, "the Tanya" deterred them with the very same words, saying: "How can you go to him? You know he is a hand's-breath above the world!"—a statement which implied that while Shelomo's ecstasies were commendable, they were not beneficial. This furnishes a clue to what later happened between those two. During a crisis in the hasidic school of Karlin, brought about mostly by the Tanya's growing power of attraction, Rabbi Shelomo conceived the idea of settling in the region of Vitebsk, which had been Rabbi Mendel's main rallying point and which was now included in the Tanya's sphere of influence, and went to him, requesting his consent to this. The rav made three conditions which serve to characterize both men: Rabbi Shelomo was not to look down upon the scholars; he was not to look down upon "natural piety" (that is, piety which lacks ecstasy); and he must no longer declare that the zaddik has to carry the sheep (a phrase by which he designated the zaddik's function to mediate). Shelomo accepted the two first conditions but he rejected the third, and thus relinquished his plan. Later he visited the rav and the two had a lengthy discussion which—so the Habad-hasidim say—"could not be noted down" because of its "shocking" character. In the period of Poland's desperate battles of 1792, in the course of which Shelomo died, he prayed for Poland, while the Tanya (just as twenty years later during Napoleon's campaigns) prayed for Russia. According to tradition, which represents Shelomo of Karlin as a reincarnation of the first, suffering Messiah who re-appears "from generation to generation," he was killed in the midst of prayer by a bullet a Cossack fired, but continued his work of prayer even after his death.

The Great Maggid's youngest disciple, Rabbi Israel, maggid of Koznitz, manifested a gentler, more composed form of Rabbi Shelomo's power of praying. Legend relates that the Baal Shem promised a bookbinder and his wife the birth of a son in their old age, because they had gladdened his heart by their joyful celebration of the sabbath. The son, Rabbi Israel, was sickly all through life and often on the verge of death, but his prayers were so potent that the rows of devotees gazed at that frail form of his as though at a victorious general. When the Great Maggid died, Rabbi Israel attached himself to Rabbi Shmelke, after his death to Rabbi Elimelekh, and after his, to Rabbi Levi Yitzhak. At the very zenith of his life and his work, he still wished to be a disciple. Whenever he cited the words of the talmudic and later masters, he said their names with fear and trembling. On the eve of the Day of Atonement, the entire congregation, men, women, and children, used to come to his threshold and implore atonement with sobs and tears. And he himself came out to them weeping, prostrated himself in the dust, and cried: "I am more sinful than all of you!" Then they wept together and together they went to the House of Prayer to say the Kol Nidre prayer. The power of living prayer—of which he once said that its function was to waken and lift the dead prayers—radiated continually from his sick-bed. People came to him from all over: Jews, peasants, and nobles, to receive his blessing, to implore his mediation, or just to look on his face. No zaddik since the day of the Baal Shem had so many cures of the possessed placed to his credit. And legend even has him play an important role in the history of his time. He is said to have predicted Napoleon's triumph and later his defeat—the outcome of the Russian expedition is traced back to the force of Rabbi Israel's prayers.

Rabbi Jacob Yitzhak of Lublin, a friend of Rabbi Israel and his fellow-pupil in the school of the Great Maggid and later in those of Rabbi Shmelke and Rabbi Elimelekh, also took part in the cosmic struggle. He was called "the Seer" because his intuition was even greater than that of his teacher, Rabbi Elimelekh. One of his disciples said: "If I may take the liberty of saying so, even the Rabbi Reb Melekh did not have the eyes of the Seer of Lublin." He is the only zaddik to whom the people accorded this by-name which is, however, used in quite another sense than in the case of the biblical prophets. The prophet is the mouthpiece of the *will* of God. He does not see or predict a future reality. In fact, the future concerns him only in so far as it cannot yet be grasped and beheld as reality, in so far as it is still latent in the will of God and also in the free relationship of man to this divine will, and hence is, in a certain way, dependent on the inner decision of man. The seer in the hasidic meaning of the word, on the other hand, sees and sees only whatever reality is present in time and space, but his seeing reaches beyond the perception of the senses, beyond the grasp of intelligence on to what is in the process of becoming and back into the past which he recognizes in that and through that which is. Thus the rabbi of Lublin could read not only character and deeds, but the origin of souls (which according to the genealogy of souls, have their own law of propagation) and the migrations of the souls of his visitors. And he read this from their foreheads or even from the notes of request they handed him. Countless men came to him to have their souls illumined and suffused by the light of his eyes. And his disciples felt so secure in the shelter of his radiance that, while they dwelt in its pale, they forgot the exile and thought themselves in the Temple of Jerusalem. But he did not forget the exile. He was filled with ceaseless waiting for the hour of redemption and finally initiated and played the chief part in the secret rites which he and certain other zaddikim—among them Israel of Koznitz, who strove against Napoleon, and Mendel of Rymanov who sided with Napoleon—performed with the purpose of converting the Napoleonic wars into the pre-Messianic final battle of Gog and Magog. The three leaders in this mystic procedure all died in the course of the following year.* They had "forced the end": they died at its coming. The magic, which the Baal Shem had held in check, broke loose and did its work of destruction.

Barukh of Mezbizh (died 1811) grew up under the Great Maggid's care but lived his life remote from the master's other disciples. He was the younger of the two sons of Odel, the Baal Shem's daughter. His elder brother Efraim, whom his grandfather had still been able to educate himself, was a quiet sickly man. We know him almost only through the book in which he cites and interprets the teachings of the Baal Shem and tells the legendary anecdotes about him which—together with similar notes taken down by Rabbi Jacob Joseph of Polnoye—form the nucleus of a legendary biography. Beyond this, the book contains a description of his dreams in which the Baal Shem frequently appeared to him.

Barukh offers us quite another picture, one that is full of contradictions and yet an integrated whole. There has been much and legitimate mention of his interest in wealth and power, his pride and love of splendor, and what we know of these qualities of his would suffice to account for his quarrels with the most

* I have related these happenings in my book *Gog and Magog* (English title: *For the Sake of Heaven*).

prominent zaddikim of his time, even if he had not almost always been the one to start them. And yet it would be a mistake to place him in the category of a later degenerate type of zaddik. Many things we have from his own lips, and others told about him, prove that he led the life of a true and impassioned mystic. But his form of mystic life did not make for harmony with the world of man. It caused him to regard this world as an alien region in which he was an exile, and to consider it his duty to challenge and oppose it. His preference for the Song of Songs, which he recited with such fervor and abandon, helps us to gain insight into his soul, and no less important is the fact that he once designated God and himself as two strangers in an unknown land, two castaways who make friends with each other. But the picture of his soul which takes shape through these characteristics is complicated by the circumstance that Barukh liked to interpret the actions and incidents (even such as seem trivial to us) of his own life as the symbolizing of heavenly events, and wanted others to do likewise. A little deeper probing, however, makes it clear that, in the final analysis, he was concerned with something utterly different from the desire for recognition. Apparently he really meant what he once said: that he would rather be stricken dumb than "coin fine phrases," that is to say, to talk in a manner that would please his hearer rather than unbolt the gates of truth. By and large we must agree with what Rabbi Israel of Rizhyn, the Great Maggid's great-grandson, once said about him: "When a wise man went to the Rabbi Reb Barukh, he could spoon up the fear of God with a ladle, but the fool who visited him, became much more of a fool." And this, of course, does not hold for this one zaddik alone.

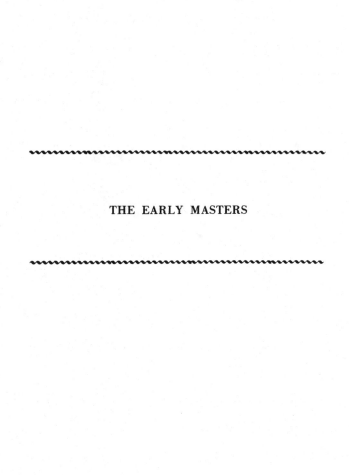

THE EARLY MASTERS

ISRAEL BEN ELIEZER
THE BAAL SHEM TOV

The Tree of Knowledge

They say that once, when all souls were gathered in Adam's soul, at the hour he stood beside the Tree of Knowledge, the soul of the Baal Shem Tov went away, and did not eat of the fruit of the tree.

The Sixty Heroes

It is said that the soul of Rabbi Israel ben Eliezer refused to descend to this world below, for it dreaded the fiery serpents which flicker through every generation, and feared they would weaken its courage and destroy it. So he was given an escort of sixty heroes, like the sixty who stood around King Solomon's bed to guard him against the terrors of night—sixty souls of zaddikim to guard his soul. And these were the disciples of the Baal Shem.

The Test

It is told:

Rabbi Eliezer, the Baal Shem's father, lived in a village. He was so hospitable that he placed guards at the outskirts of the village and had them stop poor wayfarers and bring them to his house for food and shelter. Those in Heaven rejoiced at his doing, and once they decided to try him. Satan offered to do this, but the prophet Elijah begged to be sent in his stead. In the shape of a poor wayfarer, with knapsack and staff, he came to Rabbi Eliezer's house on a sabbath afternoon, and said the greeting. Rabbi Eliezer ignored the desecration of the sabbath, for he did not want to mortify the man. He invited him to the meal and kept him in his house. Nor did he utter a word of reproof the next morning, when his guest took leave of him. Then the prophet revealed himself and promised him a son who would make the eyes of the people of Israel see the light.

His Father's Words

Israel's father died while he was still a child.
When he felt death drawing near, he took the boy in his arms and said: "I see that you will make my light shine out, and it is not given me to rear you to manhood. But, dear son, remember all your days that God is with you, and that because of this, you need fear nothing in all the world."
Israel treasured these words in his heart.

Vain Attempts

After the death of Israel's father, the people looked out for the boy for the sake of Rabbi Eliezer, whose memory was dear to them, and sent his son to a melammed.
Now, Israel studied diligently enough, but always only for a few days running. Then he played truant and they found him somewhere in the woods and alone. They ascribed this behavior to the fact that he was an orphan without proper care and supervision, and returned him to the melammed over and over, and over and over the boy escaped to the woods until the people despaired of ever making an honest and upright man of him.

The First Fight

When the boy grew up, he hired himself out as teacher's assistant. Early in the morning, he called for the children in their homes and brought them to school and the House of Prayer. In a clear and moving voice, he recited to them those words of prayer which are said in chorus, such as "Amen, let His great name be blessed forever and in all eternity." While he walked with them, he sang to them and taught them to sing with him. And when he took them home, he went by way of fields and woods.
The hasidim say that those in heaven rejoiced in these songs every morning, just as they had once rejoiced in the song of the Levites in the Temple of Jerusalem. The hours when the

hosts of Heaven gathered to listen to the voices of mortals, were hours of grace. But Satan was there too. He knew very well that what was in the making down there would threaten his power on earth. So he entered into the body of a sorcerer who could change himself into a werewolf.

Once when Israel was walking through the woods and singing with the little ones in his care, the monster fell on them, and the children screamed and scattered in all directions. Some of them fell ill from the shock and the parents decided to put a stop to the doings of the young school assistant. But he remembered what his father had said as he lay dying, went from house to house, promised the people to protect their children, and succeeded in persuading them to entrust them to him once more. The next time he shepherded them through the wood, he took a sound stick with him and when the werewolf attacked again, he struck him between the eyes, so that he was killed on the instant. The following day they found the sorcerer dead in his bed.

Conjuring

After this, Israel was employed as a servant in the House of Study. Since he had to be there day and night, but felt that Heaven wished him to keep secret his fervor and intentness, he made a habit of sleeping while those in the House of Study were awake, and to pray and study while they slept. But what they thought was that he slept all night and on into the day. The hasidim tell of wonderful happenings that occurred in those days.

Before the time of the Baal Shem Tov—so they say—a wonder-working man by the name of Adam lived, no one knows just where, but it was probably in the imperial city of Vienna. Like the succession of wonder-working men before him, Adam was called Baal Shem, that is the Master of the Name, because he knew the secret, full name of God, and could say it in such a way that—with its help—he was able to effect strange things and especially to heal men in body and soul. When this man knew he was about to die, he did not know to whom to leave the age-old writings from which he had learned his secrets, the writings which had been handed down from Abraham, the patriarch. While his only son was a man both learned and devout, he was not worthy of a heritage such as this. And so Adam, in his dream, asked Heaven what he should do and was told to have the writings given to Rabbi Israel ben Eliezer in the city of Okup, who would then be fourteen years old. On his death-bed, Adam entrusted his son with the errand.

When his son reached Okup, he first found it difficult to believe that the servant in the House of Study, who was generally regarded as a crude and ignorant boy, could be the person he was looking for. He let the boy wait on him in the House of Study, observed him closely and secretly and soon realized that Israel was hiding his true character and preoccupations from the world. Now he told him who he was, gave him the writings and only asked that he might participate in studying them under the boy's direction. Israel consented on condition that their agreement remain secret and that he continue to serve the stranger. Adam's son rented a small house outside the city and apart from others, and the people were only too glad to give him Israel for his servant. They thought, indeed, that this devout and learned man was willing to put up with the boy only because his father had been a person of such merit.

Once Rabbi Adam's son asked the boy to conjure up the Prince of the Torah with the aid of the directions given in the writings, so that they might ask him to solve certain difficulties in the teachings. For a long time, Israel refused to undertake so great a venture, but in the end he let himself be persuaded. They fasted from sabbath to sabbath, immersed themselves in the bath of purification, and—at the close of the sabbath—fulfilled the rites prescribed. But, probably because Adam's son did not fix his soul utterly on the teachings themselves, an error crept in. Instead of the Prince of the Torah, the Prince of Fire appeared and wanted to burn up the entire town. It was only by a great effort that it was saved.

After a long time, Adam's son urged the boy to make another attempt. Israel steadfastly refused to do again what was obviously displeasing to Heaven. But when his companion called on him in the name of his father, who had bequeathed the

38

miraculous writings to the boy, he consented. Again they fasted from one sabbath to the next. Again they immersed themselves in the bath of purification and, at the close of the sabbath, fulfilled the rites prescribed. Suddenly the boy cried out that they were condemned and would die unless they watched through the night with unflagging spiritual intentness. All night they remained standing. But when day was just dawning, Rabbi Adam's son could not fight his drowsiness any longer and fell asleep on his feet. In vain Israel tried to wake him. They buried him with great honors.

His Marriage

In his youth, Israel ben Eliezer was an assistant teacher in a small community not far from the city of Brody. No one knew anything much about him, but the children he taught were so eager and happy to learn, that their fathers also came to like him. Presently it was bruited about that he was wise, and people came to ask his advice. When a quarrel broke out, the young teacher was asked to mediate and this he did so well that a man against whom he decided was no less pleased than his opponent in whose favor he had spoken, and both went their ways serene and happy.

At that time, a great scholar, Rabbi Gershon of Kitov, lived in Brody. His father, Rabbi Efraim, was carrying on a law-suit with a member of the small community whose children the Baal Shem taught. He looked up his opponent and suggested that they both go to Brody to submit their disagreement to the rabbinical court. But the other man kept telling him about the wisdom and sense of justice of the young teacher until Rabbi Efraim agreed to put the matter up to him. When he entered his room and looked at him, he was startled, for shining from Israel's forehead, he saw a curved sign exactly like that he had seen for an instant—and never forgotten!—on the little forehead of his own daughter, when the midwife had shown him the new-born child. He lowered his gaze, his tongue was numb and he could hardly utter his request. When he raised his eyes again, the sign had vanished. Israel listened, put questions, listened again, and then pronounced judgment. Soon after, the hearts of both men were at peace, and it seemed to them that shining justice itself had blazed forth from the mists of their differences.

Later Rabbi Efraim went to the Baal Shem and asked him to take his daughter to wife. Israel consented but insisted on two conditions: that their agreement should remain secret for the time being, and that in the contract about to be drawn up, his scholarship should not even be mentioned; that he should be designated merely by name: Israel ben Eliezer, for—he added —"You want me and not my knowledge, as a husband for your daughter." Everything was done according to his wish.

When Rabbi Efraim returned from his trip, he fell suddenly ill and died after a few hours. His son, Rabbi Gershon Kitover, came to bury him. Among his father's papers he found the marriage contract and read that his sister had been promised to a man who had no learned title and who was not of a famous family. Not even the native town of the stranger was mentioned. He immediately informed his sister of this unheard-of arrangement, but she only replied that since this had been her father's wish, only this and nothing else could be right for her.

Israel waited until he had completed his year of teaching. The fathers of his pupils did not want him to go, but he did not let them hold him back. He put aside his robe and clothed himself in a short sheepskin with a broad leather belt, such as peasants wear, and he adopted their speech and gestures. Thus he came to Brody and to Rabbi Gershon's house. There he stood in the door, on the inner threshold. The scholar, who was just comparing various interpretations of a difficult passage in the Talmud, had them give a coin to the stranger who looked needy to him, but the man said he had something to tell him. They went into the adjoining room together and Israel informed the rabbi that he had come to fetch his wife. In great consternation, Gershon called his sister to see the man her father had chosen for her. All she said was: "If he has commanded this, then it is God's command," and bade them prepare for the wedding. Before they went to the marriage canopy, the Baal Shem talked to his wife and revealed his secret to her. But she had to promise never to breathe a word of it, no matter what might happen. He also told her that great misery and many troubles were in store for them. She only said that all this was as it should be.

After the wedding, Rabbi Gershon spent day after day trying to teach his ignorant brother-in-law the Torah, but it was impossible to get him to remember a single word of the teachings. Finally he said to his sister: "I am ashamed of your husband. It would be a good thing for you to divorce him. If you do not want to do this, I shall buy you horses and a carriage and you can go with him wherever you like." She was well satisfied with the second alternative.

They drove until they came to a little town in the Carpathian Mountains, where the woman found a place to live. Israel went to the nearby hills, built himself a hut, and quarried clay. Two or three times a week, she went to him, helped him load the clay in the wagon, took it into the town and sold it for a small sum. When Israel was hungry, he put water and flour into a little pit, kneaded the dough, and baked it in the sun.

The Helpful Mountain

It is told:

The summits of the mountains on whose gentle slopes Israel ben Eliezer lived are straight and steep. In hours of meditation he liked to climb these peaks and stay at the very top for a time. Once he was so deep in ecstsay, he failed to notice that he was at the edge of an abyss, and calmly lifted his foot to walk on. Instantly a neighboring mountain leaped to the spot, pressed itself close to the other, and the Baal Shem pursued his way.

With Robbers

It is told:

A small band of robbers who lived in the eastern section of the Carpathian Mountains and had witnessed the miraculous happenings which occurred wherever the Baal Shem showed himself, came to him and offered to take him to the Land of Israel by a special route, through caves and holes under the earth, for they had heard—we do not know how—that that was where he wanted to go. The Baal Shem was willing and ready to go with them. The way took them through a gorge filled with mud and slime. Only at the very edge, there was a narrow foothold and there they walked, step by step, holding to blocks of stone which they had rammed into the earth. The robbers went first. But when the Baal Shem wanted to follow them, he saw the flame of the sword wielded in a circle forbidding him to advance, and he turned back.

Obstacles to Blessing

The Baal Shem once asked his disciple Rabbi Meir Margaliot: "Meirly, do you still remember that sabbath, when you were just beginning to study the Pentateuch? The big room in your father's house was full of guests. They had lifted you up on the table and you were reciting what you had learned?"
Rabbi Meir replied: "Certainly I remember. Suddenly my mother rushed up to me and snatched me down from the table in the middle of what I was saying. My father was annoyed, but she pointed to a man standing at the door. He was dressed in a short sheepskin, such as peasants wear, and he was looking straight at me. Then all understood that she feared the Evil Eye. She was still pointing at the door when the man disappeared."
"It was I," said the Baal Shem. "In such hours a glance can flood the soul with great light. But the fear of men builds walls to keep the light away."

The First

When Rabbi Israel ben Eliezer was employed as ritual slaughterer for the village of Koshilovitz, he did not reveal himself and no one could tell the difference between him and an ordinary butcher. Rabbi Zevi Hirsh Margaliot, the rav of the neighboring town of Yaslovitz, had two sons, Yitzhak Dov Baer and Meir. Yitzhak was seventeen at the time, his brother eleven. Suddenly each of the boys was overcome with the burning desire to visit the slaughterer in Koshilovitz. They could see neither rhyme nor reason in it, and even when they had told each other about their longing, they still did not understand it, and both felt that they could not talk about it either to their father nor to anyone else.

One day they stole out of the house and went to the Baal Shem. What was said at this visit, neither he nor they ever told. They stayed with the Baal Shem. At home they were missed. People looked for them all over the town and in the entire region. In Koshilovitz too, they went from house to house until the boys were found and taken home. For the first few days, their father was so happy to have them back that he did not question them. Finally he asked them quietly what was so remarkable about the slaughterer in Koshilovitz. "It is impossible to describe," they replied. "But you can believe us that he is wiser than all the world and more devout than all the world."

Later, when the Baal Shem became known, they attached themselves to him and went to see him every year.

Shaul and Ivan

It is told:

Once when Rabbi Meir Margaliot, the author of the book "Illuminator of the Paths," was visiting the Baal Shem with his seven-year-old son, his host asked him to leave the boy for a time. Little Shaul remained in the house of the Baal Shem Tov. Soon after, the Baal Shem took him and his disciples on a journey. He had the carriage stop in front of a village inn and entered with his companions and the boy. Inside they were playing the fiddle and peasant men and women were dancing. "Your fiddler is no good," the Baal Shem said to the peasants. "Let my boy here sing you a dance song, and then you will be able to dance much better."

The peasants were willing. The boy was stood on the table and in his silvery voice sang a hasidic dance song without words, that went straight to the feet of the villagers. In a reel of wild happiness they danced around the table. Then one of them, a young fellow, stepped forward from among them and asked the boy: "What is your name?" "Shaul," he said. "Go on singing," the peasant cried. The boy started another song and the peasant faced him and danced in time to the tune. But in the midst of his wild leaps and bounds, he repeated over and over in charmed tones: "You Shaul and I Ivan, you Shaul and I Ivan!" After the dance, the peasants treated the Baal Shem and his disciples to vodka, and they drank together.

About thirty years later, Rabbi Shaul, who had become both a wealthy merchant and a Talmud scholar of sorts, was traveling through the country on business. Suddenly robbers attacked him, took his money and wanted to kill him. When he begged them to have pity on him, they took him to their chieftain. He gave Rabbi Shaul a long penetrating look. Finally he asked: "What is your name?" "Shaul," said the other. "You Shaul and I Ivan," said the robber chief. He told his men to return Shaul's money and take him back to his carriage.

The Peasant at the Stream

It is told:

When Rabbi Israel ben Eliezer lived in the village of Koshilovitz, he frequently bathed in the stream. When it was covered with ice, he hacked an opening and dipped down into the water-hole. A peasant whose hut was near the stream once saw him wrenching at his foot which had gotten stuck in the ice, until the skin came off and blood spurted out. After that the peasant watched the weather and put down straw for the Baal Shem to step on. Once he asked the peasant: "What would you like best: to get rich, to die old, or to be mayor?" "Rabbi," said the peasant, "that all sounds pretty good." The Baal Shem had him build a bath-house beside the stream. Soon it became known that the peasant's sick wife had bathed in the water of the stream and recovered from her ailment. The fame of the healing waters spread more and more until the doctors heard of it and made such a to-do about it in government quarters that the bath-house was closed. But in the meantime the peasant who lived near the stream had become rich and the people had chosen him for their mayor. He bathed in the stream every day and grew very old.

Fasting

When Rabbi Elimelekh of Lizhensk once said that fasting was no longer service, they asked him: "Did not the Baal Shem Tov fast very often?"

"When the Baal Shem Tov was young," he replied, "he used to take six loaves of bread and a pitcher of water at the close of the sabbath, when he went into seclusion for the entire week. On a Friday, when he was ready to go home, and about to lift his sack from the ground, he noticed that it was heavy, opened it, and found all the loaves still in it. He was very much surprised. Fasting such as this, is allowed!"

The Tap at the Window

It happened in the days of the Baal Shem's youth, that one Friday he had nothing at all in the house to prepare for the sabbath, not a crumb, not a penny. So early in the morning, he tapped at the window of a well-to-do man, said: "There is some one who has nothing for the sabbath," and walked on. The man, who did not know the Baal Shem, ran after him and asked: "If you need help, why do you run away?" The Baal Shem laughed and replied: "We know from the Gemara that every man is born with his livelihood. Now, of course, the heavier the load of one's sins, the greater effort one must make to get the appointed livelihood to come. But this morning I felt scarcely any weight on my shoulders. Still there was enough to make me do a little something—and that is what I just did."

The Call

When Heaven revealed to the Baal Shem that he was to be the leader of Israel, he went to his wife and said to her: "You must know that I have been appointed to be the leader of Israel." She answered: "What shall we do?" He said: "We must fast." So they fasted for three nights and three days without a break, and one day and one night they lay on the earth with outstretched hands and feet. On the third day, toward evening, the Baal Shem heard a call from above: "My son, rise and lead the people!" He rose and said: "If it is the will of God that I be their leader, I must take this burden upon myself."

The Baal Shem Reveals Himself

It is told:

Israel ben Eliezer had held successively the posts of school assistant, servant in the House of Study, teacher of children, and ritual slaughterer and for a time he acted as driver for his brother-in-law. Finally this man rented a piece of land for him in a village on the Prut River. On the land was an inn which also had rooms for guests. A short distance away, across the ford, a cave had been hewn into the side of a mountain. There the Baal Shem spent the week sunk in meditation. Whenever a guest came to the inn, Israel's wife went to the door and called over to him, and he always responded, and immediately came to wait on the guest. On the sabbath he stayed at home and wore the white sabbath robe.

One day—it was on a Tuesday—a disciple of Rabbi Gershon's, the Baal Shem's brother-in-law, was on the way to his teacher who lived in the town of Brody. He passed through the village on the Prut, stopped, and went into the inn. Then the woman called to her husband and the Baal Shem came and served the guest his meal. When he had finished eating, he said: "Israel, harness the horses; I have to go on."

The Baal Shem harnessed the horses, reported that the carriage was ready, and added: "But how about staying here over the sabbath?" The guest smiled at this foolish suggestion. But hardly had he driven half a mile, when a wheel broke.

He found that it would be some time before it could be fixed, and so he had to go back and spend the night at the inn. The next day, and the next after that, and even on Friday morning, one obstacle after another presented itself, and finally he had no choice but to stay for the sabbath. On Friday morning he went about troubled and sad. To his astonishment he saw that the innkeeper's wife was baking twelve sabbath loaves. He asked her what she needed them for. "Well," she said, "my husband is, to be sure, an ignorant man, but he does the right

46

thing, and I do in my husband's house what I saw done in my brother's."

"Perhaps you also have a bath for the purification?" he asked.

"Certainly," she said. "We have such a bath."

"But what do you need the bath for?" he continued.

"Well," she said, "my husband is, to be sure, an ignorant man, but he does the right thing, and so he immerses himself in the bath every day."

In the afternoon, when the time for prayer was come, he asked the woman where her husband was. "Out in the field with the sheep and cows," she said. So the guest had to say the Afternoon and Evening prayer, and the words to receive the sabbath, alone, and still the innkeeper did not come. For he was praying in his cave. When he finally returned to the house, he again assumed the speech and gestures of a peasant, and greeted his guest in this manner.

"So you see!" he said. "You are spending the sabbath here after all." He stood up against the wall as if to pray, and then —in order not to give himself away by the fervor he knew he could not conceal—he asked his guest to pronounce the benediction over the wine. They sat down and ate together. When they had finished their meal, the Baal Shem asked the guest to say words of teaching. In order not to tax the mental powers of his host too greatly, Rabbi Gershon's disciple merely gave a brief and dry account of the chapter for the week, of the enslavement in Egypt of the children of Israel.

That very night, the last before the day the Baal Shem would complete the thirty-sixth year of his life, Heaven sent him a message that the time for concealment was over.

In the middle of the night, the guest woke up, and from his bed in the main room of the inn, saw a great fire burning in the hearth. He ran there because he thought the logs had caught fire. But then he saw that what he had taken for fire, was a great light. A great white light shone out from the hearth and filled the house. The man started backward and fainted. When the Baal Shem had restored him to consciousness, he said: "A man should not look upon what is not granted to him."

In the morning the Baal Shem went into his cave in his white sabbath robe, came home, head held high, went about in the house, his face shining, and sang: "I shall prepare the meal on the sabbath morning." Then he spoke the "great Kiddush" in his usual manner, with miraculous power of clinging to God. At table, he again asked his guest to say words of the teaching, but he was so confused that all he could utter was a few words interpreting a passage in the Scriptures. "I heard another expounding of that," said the Baal Shem.

Together they said the Afternoon Prayer, and then the Baal Shem spoke words of teaching and revealed secrets of the teachings which no one had ever heard before. Then they said the Evening Prayer together and pronounced the benediction which marks the separation between the sabbath and the workaday week.

When Rabbi Gershon's disciple reached Brody, he went to the community of the "great hasidim" in that town even before visiting his teacher, told what had happened to him and added: "A great light dwells close to you. It would be no more than right that you go and bring it into the city." They went and met the Baal Shem at the edge of the woods which skirts the village. They wove a seat of green withes for him, set him upon it, took it on their shoulders, and he spoke words of teaching to them.

Themselves

The Baal Shem said:

"We say: 'God of Abraham, God of Isaac, and God of Jacob,' and not: 'God of Abraham, Isaac, and Jacob,' for Isaac and Jacob did not base their work on the searching and service of Abraham; they themselves searched for the unity of the Maker and his service."

The Torah Is Perfect

Concerning the verse of the psalm: "The law of the Lord is perfect," the Baal Shem said:

"It is still quite perfect. No one has touched it as yet, not a whit and not a jot of it. Up to this hour, it is still quite perfect."

The hasidim tell:

Rabbi Dov Baer, the maggid of Mezritch, once begged Heaven to show him a man whose every limb and every fibre was holy. Then they showed him the form of the Baal Shem Tov, and it was all of fire. There was no shred of substance in it. It was nothing but flame.

Trembling

1.

On a certain day of the new moon, the Baal Shem joined in the Morning Prayer standing in his own place, for it was his custom to go to the reader's pulpit only when the reading of the psalms began. Suddenly he trembled and the trembling grew greater and greater. They had seen this happen before while he prayed, but it had never been more than a slight quiver running through his body. Now he was violently shaken. When the reader had ended, and the Baal Shem was to go to the desk in his stead, they saw him stand in his place and tremble violently. One of his disciples went up to him and looked him in the face: it was burning like a torch and his eyes were wide open and staring like those of a dying man. Another disciple joined the first, they took him by the hands, and led him to the desk. He stood in front of it and trembled. Trembling he recited the psalms and after he had said the Kaddish, he remained standing and trembled for a good while, and they had to wait with reading the Scriptures until his trembling had left him.

2.

The maggid of Mezritch told:

"Once—it was on a holiday—the Baal Shem was praying in front of the desk with great fervor and in a very loud voice. Because I was ill, it was too much for me, and I had to go into the small room and pray there alone. Before the festival service, the Baal Shem came into the small room to put on his robe. When I looked at him, I saw that he was not in this world. Now, as he was putting on his robe, it wrinkled at the shoulders and I put my hand on it to smooth out the folds. But hardly had I touched it, when I began to tremble. I held fast to the table, but the table began to tremble too. The Baal Shem had already gone into the big hall, but I stood there and begged God to take the trembling from me."

3.

Rabbi Jacob Joseph of Polnoye told:
"Once a large water-trough stood in the room in which the Baal Shem was praying. I saw the water in the trough tremble and sway until he had finished."
Another disciple told:
"Once, on a journey, the Baal Shem was praying at the east wall of a house at whose west wall stood open barrels filled with grain. Then I saw that the grain in the barrels was trembling."

When the Sabbath Drew Near

The disciples of a zaddik who had been a disciple of the Baal Shem Tov, were sitting together at noon, before the sabbath, and telling one another about the miraculous deeds of the Baal Shem. The zaddik, who was seated in his room which adjoined theirs, heard them. He opened the door and said: "What is the sense of telling miracle tales! Tell one another of his fear of God! Every week, on the day before the sabbath, around the hour of noon, his heart began to beat so loudly that all of us who were with him could hear it."

The Fringes

A zaddik told:
The fringes of the prayer robe of the holy Baal Shem Tov had their own life and their own soul. They could move even when his body did not move, for through the holiness of his doing, the holy Baal Shem Tov had drawn into them life and soul.

To His Body

The Baal Shem said to his body: "I am surprised, body, that you have not crumbled to bits for fear of your Maker!"

For You

In the midst of praying, the Baal Shem once said the words in the Song of Songs: " 'New and old, which I have laid up for thee, O my beloved.' " And he added: "Whatever is in me, everything, new and old, for you alone."

They asked him about this, saying: "But the rabbi tells words of teaching to *us* too!" He answered: "As when the barrel overflows."

What the Mouth Will

The Baal Shem said: "When I weld my spirit to God, I let my mouth say what it will, for then all my words are bound to their root in Heaven."

How Ahijah Taught Him

The rav of Polnoye told:

"At first the Baal Shem Tov did not know how to talk to people, so wholly did he cling and cleave to God, and he talked softly to himself. Then his God-sent teacher Ahijah, the prophet, came and taught him which verses of the psalms to say every day, to gain the ability of talking to people without disrupting his clinging to God."

The Money That Stayed in the House

Never did the Baal Shem keep money in his house overnight. When he returned from a journey, he paid all the debts which had accumulated in his absence and distributed whatever he had left, among the needy.

Once he brought a large amount of money back from a journey, paid his debts, and gave the rest away. But in the meantime, his wife had taken a little of the money so that she might not have to buy on credit for a few days. In the evening, the Baal Shem felt something impeding his prayer. He went home and said: "Who took of the money?" His wife confessed it was she who had done so. He took the money from her and had it distributed among the poor that very evening.

Knowledge

The Baal Shem said:

"When I reach a high rung of knowledge, I know that not a single letter of the teachings is within me, and that I have not taken a single step in the service of God."

The Bath of Immersion

The Baal Shem said: "I owe everything to the bath. To immerse oneself is better than to mortify the flesh. Mortifying the flesh weakens the strength you need for devotions and teaching, the bath of immersion heightens this strength."

Against Mortification of the Flesh

Rabbi Barukh, the Baal Shem's grandson, told:

They once asked my grandfather, the Baal Shem Tov: "What is the essence of service? We know that in former times 'men of deeds' lived who fasted from one sabbath to the next. But you have done away with this, for you said that whoever mortifies his flesh will have to render account as a sinner, because he has tormented his soul. So do tell us: what is the essence of service?"

The Baal Shem Tov replied: "I have come into this world to point another way, namely that man should try to attain to three loves: the love of God, the love of Israel, and the love of the Torah—it is not necessary to mortify the flesh."

Without the Coming World

Once the spirit of the Baal Shem was so oppressed that it seemed to him he would have no part in the coming world. Then he said to himself: "If I love God, what need have I of a coming world!"

The Dance of the Hasidim

At the festival of Simhat Torah, the day of rejoicing in the law, the Baal Shem's disciples made merry in his house. They danced and drank and had more and more wine brought up from the cellar. After some hours, the Baal Shem's wife went to his room and said: "If they don't stop drinking, we soon won't have any wine left for the rites of the sabbath, for Kiddush and Havdalah."

He laughed and replied: "You are right. So go and tell them to stop."

When she opened the door to the big room, this is what she saw: The disciples were dancing around in a circle, and around the dancing circle twined a blazing ring of blue fire. Then she herself took a jug in her right hand and a jug in her left and—motioning the servant away—went into the cellar. Soon after she returned with the vessels full to the brim.

The Master Dances Too

One Simhat Torah evening, the Baal Shem himself danced together with his congregation. He took the scroll of the Torah in his hand and danced with it. Then he laid the scroll aside and danced without it. At this moment, one of his disciples who was intimately acquainted with his gestures, said to his companions: "Now our master has laid aside the visible, dimensional teachings, and has taken the spiritual teachings unto himself."

The Deaf Man

Rabbi Moshe Hayyim Efraim, the Baal Shem's grandson told: "I heard this from my grandfather: Once a fiddler played so sweetly that all who heard him began to dance, and whoever came near enough to hear, joined in the dance. Then a deaf man who knew nothing of music, happened along, and to him all he saw seemed the action of madmen—senseless and in bad taste."

The Strength of Community

It is told:

Once, on the evening after the Day of Atonement, the moon was hidden behind the clouds and the Baal Shem could not go out to say the Blessing of the New Moon. This weighed heavily on his spirit, for now, as often before, he felt that destiny too great to be gauged depended on the work of his lips. In vain he concentrated his intrinsic power on the light of the wandering star, to help it throw off the heavy sheath: whenever he sent some one out, he was told that the clouds had grown even more lowering. Finally he gave up hope.

In the meantime, the hasidim who knew nothing of the Baal Shem's grief, had gathered in the front room of the house and begun to dance, for on this evening that was their way of celebrating with festal joy the atonement for the year, brought about by the zaddik's priestly service. When their holy delight mounted higher and higher, they invaded the Baal Shem's chamber, still dancing. Overwhelmed by their own frenzy of happiness they took him by the hands, as he sat there sunk in gloom, and drew him into the round. At this moment, someone called outside. The night had suddenly grown light; in greater radiance than ever before, the moon curved on a flawless sky.

The Bird Nest

Once the Baal Shem stood in the House of Prayer and prayed for a very long time. All his disciples had finished praying, but he continued without paying any attention to them. They waited for him a good while, and then they went home. After several hours when they had attended to their various duties, they returned to the House of Prayer and found him still deep in prayer. Later he said to them: "By going away and leaving me alone, you dealt me a painful separation. I shall tell you a parable.

You know that there are birds of passage who fly to warm countries in the autumn. Well, the people in one of those lands once saw a glorious many-colored bird in the midst of a flock which was journeying through the sky. The eyes of man had never seen a bird so beautiful. He alighted in the top of the tallest tree and nested in the leaves. When the king of the country heard of it, he bade them fetch down the bird with his nest. He ordered a number of men to make a ladder up the tree. One was to stand on the other's shoulders until it was possible to reach up high enough to take the nest. It took a long time to build this living ladder. Those who stood nearest the ground lost patience, shook themselves free, and everything collapsed."

The Address

Every evening after prayer, the Baal Shem went to his room. Two candles were set in front of him and the mysterious Book of Creation put on the table among other books. Then all those who needed his counsel were admitted in a body, and he spoke with them until the eleventh hour.

One evening, when the people left, one of them said to the man beside him how much good the words the Baal Shem had directed to him, had done him. But the other told him not to talk such nonsense, that they had entered the room together and from that moment on the master had spoken to no one except himself. A third, who heard this, joined in the conversation with a smile, saying how curious that both were mistaken, for the rabbi had carried on an intimate conversation with him the entire evening. Then a fourth and a fifth made the same claim, and finally all began to talk at once and tell what they had experienced. But the next instant they all fell silent.

Faith

Rabbi David Leikes, a disciple of the Baal Shem Tov, once asked some hasidim of his son-in-law Rabbi Motel of Tchernobil, who had come to meet him on his way to the town of Tchernobil: "Who are you?"

They said: "We are hasidim of Rabbi Motel of Tchernobil."

But he went on questioning them. "Have you perfect faith in your teacher?" They did not answer, for who would dare to say he had perfect faith! "Then I shall tell you," he said, "what faith is. One sabbath, the third meal—as so often happens—went on into the night. Then we said grace and remained standing and said the Evening Prayer and made Havdalah and at once sat down to the 'escort of the sabbath.' Now we were all poor, and had not a penny of our own, especially on the sabbath. And yet, when the meal was over and the holy Baal Shem Tov said to me: 'David, give something for mead,' I put my hand in my pocket, although I knew I had nothing in it, but I drew out a gulden, and gave it for mead."

The Story Teller

There are many versions of how the Baal Shem gained for his disciple Rabbi Jacob Joseph, later the rav of Polnoye, who subsequently set down the teachings of his master in many a book. These versions include tales of miracles—even the awakening of the dead. I shall here give an account taken from other stories which supplement one another.

When Rabbi Jacob Joseph was still a rav in Szarygrod and bitterly averse to the hasidic way, a man whom no one knew came to his town one summer morning, at the hour when the cattle were taken to pasture, and stopped in the market-place with his wagon. He called to the first man who came along leading his cow, and began to tell him a story, which pleased his listener so well that he could not break away. A second man caught a few words in passing; he wanted to go on and could not, so he stayed and listened. Soon a whole group of people were gathered about the story teller and still their number grew. Right among them stood the servant of the House of Prayer who had been on his way to open the doors, for in summer the rav always prayed there at eight o'clock and the doors had to be opened well ahead of that time, around seven. Now, at eight the rav came to the House of Prayer and found it locked. It is well-known that he was very particular and quick to fly into a temper; now too he angrily set out to look for the servant. But there he was, right in front of him, for the Baal Shem—it was he who was telling the stories—had signed to him to go, and he had run to open the House of Prayer. The rav shouted at him and asked why he had failed in his duty and why the men, who were usually there by that time, had not come. The servant replied that, like himself, all those who had been on the way to the House of Prayer, had been irresistibly captivated by the great story. The angry rav had to say the Morning Prayer alone. But then he told the servant to go to the market-place and fetch the stranger. "I'll have him beaten up!" he cried.

In the meantime, the Baal Shem had finished his story and gone to the inn. There the servant of the House of Prayer found him and delivered his message. The Baal Shem immediately followed him out, smoking his pipe, and in this manner came before the rav. "What do you think you are doing!" shouted the rav. "Keeping people from prayer!"

"Rabbi," said the Baal Shem calmly, "it does not become you to fly into a rage. Rather let me tell you a story."

"What do you think you are doing!" was what the rav wanted to repeat, and then he looked at the man closely for the first time. It is true that he immediately turned his eyes away, nevertheless the words he had been about to say stuck in his throat. The Baal Shem had begun his story, and the rav had to listen like all the others.

"Once I drove cross-country with three horses," said the Baal Shem, "a bay, a piebald, and a white horse. And not one of the three could neigh. Then I met a peasant coming toward me and he called: 'Slacken the reins!' So I slackened the reins, and then all three horses began to neigh." The rav could say nothing for emotion. "Three," the Baal Shem repeated. "Bay, piebald and white did not neigh. The peasant knew what to do; slacken reins—and they neighed." The rav bowed his head in silence. "The peasant gave good advice," said the Baal Shem. "Do you understand?"

"I understand, rabbi," answered the rav and burst into tears. He wept and wept and knew that up to this time he had not known what it was to weep.

"You must be uplifted," said the Baal Shem. The rav looked up to him and saw that he was no longer there.

Every month Rabbi Jacob Joseph fasted one week, from sabbath to sabbath. Since he always took his meals in his room, no one knew this except his niece who brought him his food. In the month which followed his meeting with the Baal Shem, he fasted as always, because it never occurred to him that the uplifting predicted for him could be attained without mortifying the flesh. The Baal Shem was on another one of his journeys, when he suddenly felt: if the rav of Szarygrod continues as he is doing, he will lose his mind. He had the horses urged on so vehemently that one fell and broke a leg. When he entered the rav's room, he said: "My white horse fell because I was in such a hurry to get here. Things cannot go on in this way. Have some food brought for yourself." The rav had food brought and ate. "Your work," said the Baal Shem, "is one of sorrow and gloom. The Divine Presence does not hover over gloom but over joy in the commandments."

The month after this, the rav was sitting over a book in Mezbizh in the "Klaus" of the Baal Shem, when a man entered and immediately began to converse with him. "Where are you from?" he asked. "From Szarygrod," answered the rav. "And what do you do for a living?" the man continued. "I am rav in the city," said Rabbi Jacob Joseph. "And how do you make out?" the other went on to ask. "Do you make a good living or are you strapped for money?" The rav could no longer endure this empty talk. "You are keeping me from my studies," he said impatiently. "If you fly into a temper," said the other, "you curtail God in making his living." "I do not understand what you mean," said the rav. "Well," said the man, "everyone makes his living in the place God has appointed for him. But what is the livelihood of God? It is written: 'And thou, holy one, art enthroned upon the praises of Israel'; that is God's living! If two Jews come together and one asks the other how he makes his living, he answers: 'Praise be to God, I make my living thus and so,' and his praise is the living of God. But you, who do not talk to anyone, you who only want to study, are curtailing God's living." The rav was taken aback. He wanted to reply, but the man had vanished. The rav went back to his book, but he could not study. He shut the book and went into the Baal Shem's room. "Well, rav of Szarygrod," he said smilingly, "Elijah got the best of you, after all, didn't he?"

When the rav had returned to his home, he invited the congregation to the third sabbath meal, as was the custom among the hasidim. Some came, but most of them were annoyed that he had joined that juggler of a hasid! They grew more and more hostile to him until they finally succeeded in driving him out of town. At the last, they would not suffer him to remain in his house for even a day longer and, since it was a Friday, he had to spend the sabbath in a village near by. The Baal Shem was on a journey with some of his intimate friends and on that very Friday he was close to that village. "Let us keep the sabbath together with the rav of Szarygrod and gladden his heart," he said. And that was what they did.

Soon afterward, Rabbi Jacob Joseph became rav in the city of Rashkov. He issued a proclamation far and wide that he would return all fines he had ever received, and there had been many. He did not rest until he had distributed all the money he had. From that time on, he used to say: "Worry and gloom are the roots of all the powers of evil."

The Seventy Languages

Rabbi Leib, son of Sarah, the hidden zaddik, told:

"Once I was with the Baal Shem Tov over the sabbath. Toward evening, his great disciples gathered around the table before the third meal and waited for his coming. And while waiting, they discussed a passage in the Talmud about which they wanted to ask him. It was this: "Gabriel came and taught Joseph seventy languages.' They could not understand this, for does not every language consist of countless words? Then, how could the mind of one man grasp them all in a single night, as the passage implied? The disciples decided that Rabbi Gershon of Kitov, the Baal Shem's brother-in-law, should be the one to ask him.

"When he came and seated himself at the head of the table, Rabbi Gershon put the question. The Baal Shem began to say words of teaching, but what he said seemed to have nothing to do with the subject of the question, and his disciples could not glean an answer from his words. But suddenly something unheard-of and incredible happened. In the middle of the Baal Shem's address, Rabbi Jacob Joseph rapped on the table and called out: 'Turkish!' and after a while: 'Tartar!' and after another interval: 'Greek!' and so on, one language after another. Gradually his companions understood: from the master's speech, which was apparently concerned with quite different things, he had come to know the source and the character of every single language—and he who teaches you the source and character of a language, has taught you the language itself."

The Battle Against Amalek

Once Rabbi Pinhas of Koretz felt confused about his faith in God, and could think of no way to help himself except to travel to the Baal Shem. Then he heard that the master had just arrived in Koretz. Full of happiness he ran to the inn. There he found a number of hasidim gathered about the Baal Shem Tov, and he was expounding to them the verse in the Scriptures in which the hands Moses held up in the hour of the struggle against Amalek, are spoken of as being emunah, that is, trusting and believing. "It sometimes happens," said the Baal Shem, "that a man grows confused about his faith. The remedy for this is to implore God to strengthen his faith. For the real harm Amalek inflicted on Israel was to chill their belief in God through successful attack. That was why Moses taught them to implore God to strengthen their faith, by stretching to Heaven his hands which were, in themselves, like trust and faith, and this is the only thing that matters in the hour of struggle against the power of evil." Rabbi Pinhas heard, and his hearing of it was in itself a prayer, and in the very act of this prayer he felt his faith grow strong.

The Passage of Reproof

When Rabbi Nahum of Tchernobil was young, he once happened to be with the Baal Shem the sabbath on which the great passage of reproof is read from the Scriptures, and which goes by the name of the "Sabbath of Blessings" in order to avoid using the ominous words. On this occasion he was called to the reading of the Torah in the House of Prayer, and it was this very passage of reproof he was to assist with. He was annoyed that just this chapter had fallen to his share. The Baal Shem himself read aloud. Now Rabbi Nahum was sickly and plagued with all manner of aches and pains. But when the Baal Shem began to read, Rabbi Nahum felt pain leave one of his limbs after another with each successive part of the passage of reproof, and when the reading was over, he was rid of all his complaints: sound and well.

Losing the Way

Rabbi Yehiel Mikhal, later the maggid of Zlotchov, did, indeed, seek out the Baal Shem while he was quite young, but was not sure whether or not he should become his disciple. Then the zaddik took him with him on a journey to a certain place. When they had been driving for a while, it became evident that they were not on the right road. "Why, rabbi!" said Mikhal. "Don't you know the way?"

"It will make itself known to me in due time," answered the Baal Shem, and they took another road; but this too did not take them to their destination. "Why, rabbi!" said Mikhal. "Have you lost your way?"

"It is written," the Baal Shem said calmly, "that God 'will fulfill the desire of them that fear him.' And so he has fulfilled your desire to have a chance to laugh at me."

These words pierced young Mikhal to the heart and without further arguing or analyzing, he joined the master with his whole soul.

The Cantor of the Baal Shem Tov

One of the Baal Shem's disciples once asked him: "How shall I make my living in the world?"

"You shall be a cantor," said the master.

"But I can't even sing!" the other objected.

"I shall bind you to the world of music," said the zaddik.

This man became a singer without peer, and far and wide they called him the cantor of the Baal Shem Tov.

After many years he arrived in Lizhensk in the company of his bass singer, who always went with him, and visited Rabbi Elimelekh, the disciple of the disciple of the Baal Shem Tov. For a long time, the rabbi and his son Eleazar could not make up their minds to let these two sing with the chorus in the House of Prayer on the sabbath, for Rabbi Elimelekh feared that the artistry of their singing might disturb his devotions. But Rabbi

Eleazar argued that because of the holiness of the Baal Shem Tov, it would not be right to withhold the honor from the man, and so it was agreed that he should sing at the inauguration of the sabbath. But when he began, Rabbi Elimelekh noticed that the great fervor of his singing flowed into his own, and threatened to drive him out of his mind, and so he had to retract his invitation. But he kept the cantor with him over the sabbath, and paid him many honors.

After the conclusion of the sabbath, the rabbi invited him to his house again and asked him to tell him about the holy Baal Shem Tov, the light of Israel. Then the eyes of the man kindled with new life, and it was clear that there was new life in his throat and in his heart as well. He began to speak and it became manifest that now, since he had not been allowed to sing, all the fervor in his heart, which he usually poured into his song, flowed into his spoken word. He told how, in the great sequence of the songs of praise, the master never recited a verse until he had seen the angel of this verse and heard his special strain. He told of the hours in which the soul of the master rose to Heaven, while his body remained behind as if dead, and that there his soul spoke with whomever it would, with Moses the faithful shepherd, and with the Messiah, and asked and was answered. He told that the master could speak to each creature on earth in its own language, and to every heavenly being in its own language. He told that, the moment the master saw an implement, he at once knew the character of the man who had made it, and what he had thought about, while making it. And then the cantor rose and testified that once he and his companions had received the Torah through the mouth of the master as Israel had once received it at Mount Sinai through the sound of thunder and trumpets, and that the voice of God was not yet silenced on earth, but endured and could still be heard.

Some time after his visit in Lizhensk, the cantor lay down and died. Thirty days after that, and again on a Friday, the bass singer came from the bath of purification and said to his wife: "Summon the Holy Brotherhood quickly to see to my burial, for in paradise they have commissioned my cantor to sing for the inauguration of the sabbath, and he does not want to do that without me." He lay down and died.

The Wrong Answer

It is told:

When Rabbi Wolf Kitzes took leave of his teacher, before setting out for the Holy Land, the Baal Shem stretched out his second finger, touched him on the mouth, and said: "Heed your words, and see to it that you give the right reply!" He refused to say anything more.

The ship on which the Baal Shem's disciple had taken passage was driven from its course by a tempest, and forced to land on an unknown, and apparently desert island. Presently the storm died down, but the vessel had suffered damage and could not put out to sea again immediately. Some of the passengers, Rabbi Wolf among them, went ashore to have a look at the unfamiliar foreign landscape. The others turned back after a while, but he was so deep in meditation that he went on and on and finally came to a big house built in an old-fashioned style, which looked as if no one had ever lived in it. Only then did he remember that the ship would not wait for him, but before he could decide one way or another, a man in a linen garment appeared on the threshold. His features were age-old, his hair was white, but he bore himself erect. "Do not be afraid, Rabbi Wolf," he said. "Spend the sabbath with us. The morning after, you will be able to resume your journey." As in a dream, Rabbi Wolf followed the old man to the bath, prayed in the company of ten tall majestic old men, and ate with them. The sabbath passed as in a dream. The next morning, the age-old man accompanied him down to the shore where his ship was lying at anchor, and blessed him in parting. But just as Rabbi Wolf was hurrying to set foot on the gangplank, his host asked him: "Tell me, Rabbi Wolf: How do the Jews fare in your country?"

"The Lord of the world does not abandon them," Rabbi Wolf replied quickly and walked on. Not until he was on the high seas, did his mind clear. Then he recalled the words of his teacher and was seized with such bitter remorse that he resolved not to continue his voyage to the Holy Land, but to go home at once. He spoke to one of the crew and gathered from his reply that he was already homeward bound.

When Rabbi Wolf came to the Baal Shem, his master looked at him sorrowfully but not angrily and said: "That was the wrong answer you gave our father Abraham! Day after day he asks God: 'How are my children?' And God replies: 'I do not abandon them.' If only you had told him of the sufferings of exile!"

The Axe

Once the Baal Shem had his disciple Rabbi Wolf Kitzes learn the kavvanot of blowing the ram's horn, so that, on New Year's Day, he might announce before him the order of the sounds. Rabbi Wolf learned the kavvanot but, for greater security, noted everything down on a slip of paper which he hid in his bosom. This paper, however, dropped out soon after and he never noticed it. They say that this was the work of the Baal Shem. Now when it was time to blow, Rabbi Wolf looked for his slip in vain. Then he tried to remember the kavvanot, but he had forgotten everything. Tears rose to his eyes, and weeping, he announced the order of sounds quite simply without referring to the kavvanot at all. Later the Baal Shem said to him: "There are many halls in the king's palace, and intricate keys open the doors, but the axe is stronger than all of these, and no bolt can withstand it. What are all kavvanot compared to one really heartfelt grief!"

The Word of the Disciple

On a Friday, at the hour the zaddik examines his soul, the whole world once grew dark for the Baal Shem, and the spark of life almost died within him. That was how one of his great disciples found him. "My master and teacher!" he said. His voice trembled and he could not utter another word. But even so he had caused new strength to flow into the Baal Shem's heart, and the flame of life grew strong within him.

Near and Far

A disciple asked the Baal Shem: "Why is it that one who clings to God and knows he is close to him, sometimes experiences a sense of interruption and remoteness?"

The Baal Shem explained: "When a father sets out to teach his little son to walk, he stands in front of him and holds his two hands on either side of the child, so that he cannot fall, and the boy goes toward his father between his father's hands. But the moment he is close to his father, he moves away a little, and holds his hands farther apart, and he does this over and over, so that the child may learn to walk."

Praying in the Field

A hasid who was traveling to Mezbizh in order to spend the Day of Atonement near the Baal Shem, was forced to interrupt his journey for something or other. When the stars rose, he was still a good way from the town and, to his great grief, had to pray alone in the open field. When he arrived in Mezbizh after the holiday, the Baal Shem received him with particular happiness and cordiality. "Your praying," he said, "lifted up all the prayers which were lying stored in that field."

The Scholars

Moshe Hayyim Efraim, a grandson of the Baal Shem's, dedicated himself to study in his youth and became so great a scholar that this made him deviate somewhat from the hasidic way of life. His grandfather, the Baal Shem, made a point of often going walking with him beyond the town, and Efraim went with him, though with a hint of reluctance, for he begrudged the time he might have spent in studying.

Once they met a man coming from another city. The Baal Shem asked him about one of his fellow-citizens. "He is a great scholar," said the man.

"I envy him his scholarship," said the Baal Shem. "But what am I to do? I have no time to study because I have to serve my Maker." From this hour on, Efraim returned to the hasidic way again with all his strength.

The Limits of Advice

The disciples of the Baal Shem heard that a certain man had a great reputation for learning. Some of them wanted to go to him and find out what he had to teach. The master gave them permission to go, but first they asked him: "And how shall we be able to tell whether he is a true zaddik?"

The Baal Shem replied. "Ask him to advise you what to do to keep unholy thoughts from disturbing you in your prayers and studies. If he gives you advice, then you will know that he belongs to those who are of no account. For this is the service of men in the world to the very hour of their death; to struggle time after time with the extraneous, and time after time to uplift and fit it into the nature of the Divine Name."

Writing Down

A disciple secretly wrote down all the teachings he had heard from the Baal Shem. One day the Baal Shem saw a demon going through the house. In his hand was a book. The Baal Shem asked him: "What book is that you have in your hand?"

"That is the book," the demon replied, "of which you are the author."

Then the Baal Shem knew that some one was secretly setting down in writing what he said. He gathered all his people around him and asked: "Who of you is writing down what I teach you?" The disciple who had been taking notes said it was he, and brought the master what he had written. The Baal Shem studied it for a long time, page for page. Then he said: "In all this, there is not a single word I said. You were not listening for the sake of Heaven, and so the power of evil used you for its sheath, and your ears heard what I did not say."

Beside the Tree of Life

The Baal Shem told:
"Once I went to paradise and many people went with me. The closer I came to the garden, the more of them disappeared, and when I walked through paradise, there were only a very

few left. But when I stood beside the Tree of Life and looked around, I seemed to be alone."

The Sermon

Once they asked the Baal Shem to preach after the prayer of the congregation. He began his sermon, but in the middle of it he was shaken with a fit of trembling, such as sometimes seized him while he was praying. He broke off and said: "O, Lord of the world, you know that I am not speaking to increase my own reputation . . ." Here he stopped again, and then the words rushed from his lips. "Much have I learned, and much have I been able to do, and there is no one to whom I could reveal it." And he said nothing further.

Like Locusts

Rabbi Mikhal of Zlotchov told:
"Once when we were on a journey with our teacher, Rabbi Israel Baal Shem Tov, the Light of the Seven Days, he went into the woods to say the Afternoon Prayer. Suddenly we saw him strike his head against a tree and cry aloud. Later we asked him about it. He said: 'While I plunged into the holy spirit I saw that in the generations which precede the coming of the Messiah, the rabbis of the hasidim will multiply like locusts, and it will be they who delay redemption, for they will bring about the separation of hearts and groundless hatred.' "

Happy Is the People

Concerning the verse in the psalm: "Happy is the people that know the joyful shout; they walk, O Lord, in the light of Thy countenance," the Baal Shem said: "When the people do not depend upon heroes but are themselves versed in the joyful shout of battle, then they will walk in the light of your countenance."

Simplicity

Once the Baal Shem said to his disciples: "Now that I have climbed so many rungs in the service of God, I let go of all of them and hold to the simple faith of making myself a vessel for God. It is, indeed, written: 'The simple believeth every word,' but it is also written: 'The Lord preserveth the simple.' "

The Hose-Maker

Once, in the course of a journey, the Baal Shem stopped in a little town whose name has not come down to us. One morning, before prayer, he smoked his pipe as usual and looked out of the window. He saw a man go by. He carried his prayer shawl and phylacteries in his hand and set his feet as intently and solemnly as though he were going straight to the doors of Heaven. The Baal Shem asked the disciple in whose house he was staying, who the man was. He was told that he was a hose-maker who went to the House of Prayer day after day, both summer and winter, and said his prayer even when the prescribed quorum of ten worshippers was not complete. The Baal Shem wanted to have the man brought to him, but his host said: "That fool would not stop on his way—not if the emperor called him in person."

After prayer, the Baal Shem sent someone to the man with the message that he should bring him four pairs of hose. Soon after, the man stood before him and displayed his wares. They were of good sheep's wool and well-made. "What do you want for a pair?" asked Rabbi Israel.

"One and a half gulden."

"I suppose you will be satisfied with one gulden."

"Then I should have said one gulden," the man replied.

The Baal Shem instantly paid him what he had asked. Then he went on questioning him. "How do you spend your days?"

"I ply my trade," said the man.

"And how do you ply it?"

"I work until I have forty or fifty pairs of hose. Then I put them into a mould with hot water and press them until they are as they should be."

"And how do you sell them?"

"I don't leave my house. The merchants come to me to buy. They also bring me good wool they have bought for me, and I pay them for their pains. This time I left my house only to honor the rabbi."

"And when you get up in the morning, what do you do before you go to pray?"

"I make hose then too."

"And what psalms do you recite?"

"I say those psalms which I know by heart, while I work," said the man.

When the hose-maker had gone home, the Baal Shem said to the disciples who stood around him: "Today you have seen the cornerstone which will uphold the Temple until the Messiah comes."

The Busy Man's Prayer

The Baal Shem said:

"Imagine a man whose business hounds him through many streets and across the market-place the livelong day. He almost forgets that there is a Maker of the world. Only when the time for the Afternoon Prayer comes, does he remember: 'I must pray.' And then, from the bottom of his heart, he heaves a sigh of regret that he has spent his day on vain and idle matters, and he runs into a by-street and stands there, and prays: God holds him dear, very dear and his prayer pierces the firmament."

The Little Whistle

A villager, who year after year prayed in the Baal Shem's House of Prayer in the Days of Awe, had a son who was so dull-witted that he could not even grasp the shapes of the letters, let alone the meaning of the holy words. On the Days of Awe his father did not take him to town with him, because he did not understand anything. But when he was thirteen and of age according to the laws of God, his father took him along on the Day of Atonement, for fear the boy might eat on the fast-day simply because he did not know any better.

Now the boy had a small whistle which he always blew when he sat out in the fields to herd the sheep and the calves. He had taken this with him in the pocket of his smock and his father had not noticed it. Hour after hour, the boy sat in the House of Prayer and had nothing to say. But when the Additional Service commenced, he said: "Father, I have my little whistle with me. I want to sing on it." The father was greatly perturbed and told him to do no such thing, and the boy restrained himself. But when the Afternoon Service was begun, he said again: "Father, do let me blow my little whistle." The father became angry and said: "Where did you put it?" And when the boy told him, he laid his hand on his pocket so that the boy could not take it out. But now the Closing Prayer began. The boy snatched his pocket away from his father's hand, took out the whistle and blew a loud note. All were frightened and confused. But the Baal Shem went on with the prayer, only more quickly and easily than usual. Later he said: "The boy made things easy for me."

The Court Sweeper

Once, just before New Year's, the Baal Shem came to a certain town and asked the people who read the prayers there in the Days of Awe. They replied that this was done by the rav of the town. "And what is his manner of praying?" asked the Baal Shem.

"On the Day of Atonement," they said, "he recites all the confessions of sin in the most cheerful tones."

The Baal Shem sent for the rav and asked him the cause of this strange procedure. The rav answered: "The least among the servants of the king, he, whose task it is to sweep the forecourt free of dirt, sings a merry song as he works, for he does what he is doing to gladden the king."

Said the Baal Shem: "May my lot be with yours."

In the Hour of Doubt

It is told:

In the city of Satanov there was a learned man, whose thinking and brooding took him deeper and deeper into the question why what is, is, and why anything is at all. One Friday he stayed in the House of Study after prayer to go on thinking, for he was snared in his thoughts and tried to untangle them and could not. The holy Baal Shem Tov felt this from afar, got into his carriage and, by dint of his miraculous power which made the road leap to meet him, he reached the House of Study in Satanov in only an instant. There sat the learned man in his predicament. The Baal Shem said to him: "You are brooding on whether God is; I am a fool and believe." The fact that there was a human being who knew of his secret, stirred the doubter's heart and it opened to the Great Secret.

The Famous Miracle

A naturalist came from a great distance to see the Baal Shem and said: "My investigations show that in the course of nature the Red Sea had to divide at the very hour the children of Israel passed through it. Now what about that famous miracle!" The Baal Shem answered: "Don't you know that God created nature? And he created it so, that at the hour the children of Israel passed through the Red Sea, it had to divide. That is the great and famous miracle!"

Truth

The Baal Shem said: "What does it mean, when people say that Truth goes over all the world? It means that Truth is driven out of one place after another, and must wander on and on."

To One Who Admonished

The Baal Shem said this to a zaddik who used to preach admonishing sermons: "What do you know about admonishing! You yourself have remained unacquainted with sin all the days of your life, and you have had nothing to do with the people around you—how should you know what sinning is!"

With the Sinners

The Baal Shem said:
"I let sinners come close to me, if they are not proud. I keep the scholars and the sinless away from me if they are

71

proud. For the sinner who knows that he is a sinner, and therefore considers himself base—God is with him, for He 'dwelleth with them in the midst of their uncleannesses.' But concerning him who prides himself on the fact that he is unburdened
by sin, God says, as we know from the Gemara: 'There is not
enough room in the world for myself and him.' "

Love

The Baal Shem said to one of his disciples:
"The lowest of the low you can think of, is dearer to me than
your only son is to you."

False Hospitality

It is told:
In the days of the Baal Shem, a rich and hospitable man
lived in a nearby city. To every poor wayfarer, he gave food
and drink and money to boot. But he felt the urgent need to
hear words of praise from everyone he received into his house,
and if such words did not come spontaneously, he threw out a
deft phrase as bait, and then a big or little praise-fish was
always sure to bite.

Once the Baal Shem sent one of his disciples, Rabbi Wolf
Kitzes, cross-country, and told him to visit that rich man in
the course of his journey. He was lavishly entertained and
presented with a generous gift, but gave only sparse words of
thanks. Finally his host said: "Don't you think that this is the
proper way to practice hospitality?"

"We shall see," answered Rabbi Wolf. And not another word
could the rich man get out of him. At nightfall, the host
lay down among his guests according to his custom, for before
falling asleep he liked to chat with them and hear something
pleasing to his person. Just as he was dozing off, Rabbi Wolf
touched him on the shoulder with his little finger. In his dream
the man thought he was called to the king and had tea with
him. But suddenly the king fell and was dead and they accused
him of poisoning him and put him in jail. A fire broke out in
the jail and he escaped and fled until he was far away. Then he
became a water-carrier, but that was hard work and got him a

meagre living, so he moved to another region where water was scarce. But there they had a law that you were not paid unless the pail was full to the brim, and to walk with a full pail and never spill a drop was a difficult matter. Once when he was walking carefully, slow step by step, he fell and broke both legs, and there he lay and thought of his former life, and was amazed and wept. Then Rabbi Wolf touched him on the shoulder again with his little finger, and the man woke up and said: "Take me with you to your master."

The Baal Shem received the rich man with a smile. "Would you like to know where all that hospitality of yours has gone to?" he asked. "It has all gone into a dog's mouth."

The man's heart awoke and turned to God, and the Baal Shem instructed him how to lift up his soul.

The Crowded House of Prayer

Once the Baal Shem stopped on the threshold of a House of Prayer and refused to go in. "I cannot go in," he said. "It is crowded with teachings and prayers from wall to wall and from floor to ceiling. How could there be room for me?" And when he saw that those around him were staring at him and did not know what he meant, he added: "The words from the lips of those whose teaching and praying does not come from the hearts lifted to heaven, cannot rise, but fill the house from wall to wall and from floor to ceiling."

The Jug

Once the Baal Shem said to his disciples: "Just as the strength of the root is in the leaf, so the strength of man is in every utensil he makes, and his character and behavior can be gauged from what he has made." Just then his glance fell on a fine beer jug standing in front of him. He pointed to it and continued: "Can't you see from this jug that the man who made it had no feet?"

When the Baal Shem had finished speaking, one of his disciples happened to pick up the jug to set it on the bench. But the moment it stood there it crumbled to bits.

73

In the World of Changes

In the days of the Baal Shem, there lived a man who cruelly mortified his flesh in order to attain a holy spirit. The Baal Shem once said this about him: "In the world of changes, they laugh at him. They bestow on him higher and higher rungs and do it only to make fun of him. If he did not have me to help him, he would be lost."

One Small Hand

Rabbi Nahman of Bratzlav has handed down to us these words of his great-grandfather, the Baal Shem Tov:
"Alas! the world is full of enormous lights and mysteries, and man shuts them from himself with one small hand!"

Across the Dniester

A zaddik told:

When the master was no more than a little boy, the prophet Ahijah, the Shilonite, came to him and taught him the wisdom of the holy names. And because he was still so young, he wanted to find out what he could accomplish. So one day he cast his belt into the Dniester River when the current was very strong, pronounced a name and crossed the river walking on his belt. All his days he did penance for this to erase the flaw from his soul, and he succeeded. For once he had to cross the river at a time the current again ran strong, because a number of Jew-haters were after him with the intent to kill. So again he cast his belt into the waters and crossed on it but without pronouncing a holy name and with the aid of nothing but his great faith in the God of Israel.

The Icicle

A zaddik told:

"On a winter's day, I went to the bath with the master. It was so cold that icicles hung from the roofs. We entered and as soon as he did the Unification, the bath grew warm. He stood in the water for a very long time, until the candle began to drip and gutter. 'Rabbi,' I said, 'the candle is guttering and going out.'

'Fool,' he answered, 'take an icicle from the roof and light it! He who spoke to the oil and it leaped into flame, will speak to this too, and it will kindle.' The icicle burned brightly for a good while, until I went home, and when I got home there was a little water in my hand."

The Creatures

It is told:

Once the Baal Shem was forced to inaugurate the sabbath in an open field. A flock of sheep was at pasture nearby. When he pronounced the hymn to greet the coming Sabbath Bride, the sheep rose on their hind legs and remained in this position, turned toward the master, until he had finished the prayer. For while listening to the Baal Shem's devotions, every creature assumed the original position it had held when it stood at the throne of God.

The Visit

The Baal Shem's disciples could always tell from his face if the Seven Shepherds, or one of them, were with him. Once, at the meal of the New Moon they looked at him and knew that one of the shepherds was present. Later they asked him which of the seven it had been. He said: "When I pronounced the benediction over the bread, I had in mind the secret of eating and plunged into it. Then Moses, our teacher, peace be with him, came to me and said: 'Hail to you, that you have in mind the very secret into which I plunged when I waited at table at the meal of Jethro, my father-in-law.' "

The Debate

It is told:

Once the Baal Shem Tov was seated at his table with his disciples around him. Among them was Rabbi Nahman of Horodenka, whose son married a granddaughter of the Baal Shem and with her begot the other Nahman: Rabbi Nahman of Bratzlav.

The Baal Shem said: "The time has come to reveal to you something of the deeper significance of the bath of immersion."

He paused for a little, and then, with mighty words, built up before them the foundation and structure of meanings. When he had done, he threw back his head, and his face began to shine with that radiance which announced to his disciples that his soul was rising to the worlds above. He was utterly motionless. His disciples rose with trembling hearts and looked at him, for this was one of the times when it was vouchsafed them to see their master as he really was. Rabbi Nahman wanted to rise with the rest, but he could not. Sleep overwhelmed him. He tried to ward it off, but failed.

In his dream he came to a city where tall men were striding through the streets, on toward a great house. He went as far as the gate with them. He could go no further, for the throng of men filled the house. Now, from within, he could catch the voice of a teacher whom he could not see, though he could hear what was said quite clearly. He was speaking about the bath of immersion and revealing all its secret significance. Toward the end of his speech, it became clearer and clearer that he was presenting a teaching different from the traditional doctrine of Ari, the holy "lion" Rabbi Yitzhak Luria, and in conclusion, this was openly stated. And now the throngs moved apart. From the door came Ari himself, pacing toward the pulpit and almost brushing Rabbi Nahman as he went. The movement of the throngs closing behind him swept Rabbi Nahman along. Suddenly he found himself standing in front of the pulpit. He looked up, and recognized the face of his master whose voice he had not recognized. And now the debate took place close before him. The "lion" and the Baal Shem Tov opposed each other by quoting different passages from the holy Book of Splendor and giving different interpretations. Contradictions between one passage and another gaped and closed again, and in the end both flames leaped up in a single blaze which soared to the heart of Heaven. There was no vista through which eyes could see and find a solution. Then those two resolved to ask Heaven to decide. Together they performed the rite that leads to uplifting. What came to pass, happened beyond the confines of time, and instantly Ari said: "The decision has been made in favor of the words of the Baal Shem

Tov." At that Nahman awoke. Before his eyes, the master bowed forward his head which he had flung back, and said to him: "And it was you I chose to accompany me as my witness."

In His Image

Once the Baal Shem summoned Sammael, lord of demons, because of some important matter. The Lord of demons roared at him: "How dare you summon me! Up to now this has happened to me only three times; in the hour at the Tree of Knowledge, the hour of the golden calf, and the hour of the destruction of Jerusalem."

The Baal Shem bade his disciples bare their foreheads, and on every forehead, Sammael saw the sign of the image in which God creates man. He did what was asked of him. But before leaving, he said: "Sons of the living God, permit me to stay here a little longer and look at your foreheads."

The Miraculous Bath

It is told:

Once the Baal Shem bade Rabbi Zevi, the scribe, write the verses for phylacteries and instructed him in the special attitude of the soul which befits this action. Then he said to him: "Now I shall show you the phylacteries of the Lord of the world." He took him to a lonely wood. But another one of his disciples, Rabbi Wolf Kitzes, had discovered where they were going and hid in that same wood. He heard the Baal Shem cry out: "The bath of Israel is the Lord!" And suddenly he saw a bath in a place where there had been none. At the same instant, the Baal Shem said to Rabbi Zevi: "Some man is hiding here." In a moment he discovered Rabbi Wolf and told him to go away. No one has ever found out what happened in the wood after that.

The Effect of the Mixed Multitude

The Baal Shem said:

"The Erev Rav, the mixed multitude, prevented Moses from reaching the rung of an angel."

It is told:

Sabbatai Zevi, the "false Messiah" long dead, came to the Baal Shem and begged him to redeem him. Now it is well known that the work of redemption is accomplished by binding the stuff of life to the stuff of life, by binding mind to mind, and soul to soul. In this way, then, the Baal Shem began to bind himself to that other, but slowly and cautiously, for he feared he might try to harm him. Once, when the Baal Shem lay asleep, Sabbatai Zevi came and tried to tempt him to become as he himself was. Then the Baal Shem hurled him away with such vigor that he fell to the very bottom of the nether world. When the Baal Shem spoke of him, he always said: "A holy spark was within him, but Satan caught him in the snare of pride."

A Halt Is Called

1.

It is told:

In the company of his daughter Odel and Rabbi Zevi, the scribe, the Baal Shem was on his way to the Land of Israel to prepare for the hour of deliverance. But Heaven called a halt to his journey. On the way from Stambul to the Land of Israel, the ship stopped at an unknown island. They went ashore, and when they tried to return to the ship, they lost their way and fell into the hands of robbers. Rabbi Zevi said to the Baal Shem: "Why are you silent? Just do as you usually do and then we shall be free."

But the Baal Shem replied: "I know nothing at all any more. Everything has been taken from me. It is up to you to recall something of all you have learned from me, and stir up my memory."

Rabbi Zevi said: "I too know nothing at all any more! The only thing I still remember is the alphabet."

"Why are you delaying?" cried the Baal Shem. "Recite it to me!" Then the scribe recited the letters of the alphabet, and he said them with the great fervor he always put into his prayers. A bell chimed, an old captain came with a troop of soldiers and freed them without saying a word. He took them aboard his ship and brought them back to Stambul, and neither he nor any of his people said a single word. When they went ashore— it was the seventh day of Passover—the ship and the crew vanished. Then the Baal Shem knew that it was Elijah who had saved them, but he also realized that he was not to travel on, so he set out on his journey home.

2.

But it is also told:
During the festival of Passover, when the Baal Shem and his companions boarded a ship in Stambul, Heaven let him know that he was to go ashore again and start for home. But in his soul he refused to obey, and the ship sailed off with him. Then all the spiritual rungs he had attained were taken from him, and his teaching and his prayer was taken from him too. When he looked into a book, he no longer even understood the symbols. But in his soul he said: "What does it matter! Then I shall enter the Holy Land as a crude and ignorant fellow." But a tempest rose and a huge wave rushed upon the ship and swept Odel, the Baal Shem's daughter, into the sea. At this moment Satan came to him and said what he said. But he cried out: "Hear, o Israel!" He turned his back on Satan and said: "Lord of the world, I am going home." And immediately his teacher, the prophet Ahijah the Shilonite, came through the air, snatched Odel out of the sea, and carried them all back to Stambul through the clouds.

Sound the Great Horn!

A zaddik told:
The holy community had a little house outside the city, and there they met after every sermon of the Baal Shem Tov, to discuss what he had said. I knew where the house was, but I did not dare go there either with them or after them, because I was very young at the time.
The year I was in the house of the Baal Shem Tov, on the first day of the New Year, right after grace, the holy Baal Shem

preached on the words of prayer: "Sound the great horn for our freedom." Immediately after the sermon he went to his room and locked the door. But his disciples went to the house outside the city. I remained behind alone. Then it occurred to me that the Messiah would come this very day, and every moment I grew more and more convinced that now he was walking along the road, soon he would enter the city, and there would be no one there to receive him. And what I imagined seemed to me so overpoweringly true that I could do nothing but run to the disciples to tell them about it. I ran through the town, and the people wanted to stop me and question me. But I ran on until I reached the house where the others were. There I saw them all sitting around a big table, and no one uttered a word, and you could see that not one of them had the strength to utter a word. But later I learned that—in his thoughts—every one of them saw the Messiah coming this very hour. And I did not know what to do except sit down with them. So we sat around the big table until the stars of the second night stood in the sky. Only then the thought broke off in all of us, and we returned to the town.

The Third Failure

It is told:

When the number of renegades who followed Jacob Frank, the false Messiah, grew greater and greater, Heaven revealed to the Baal Shem that their impure strength was stronger than his holy strength, and that, if he hoped to overcome them, he would have to enlist someone to help him, and that this other was to be Rabbi Moshe Pastuch, which means, Rabbi Moshe, the Shepherd. Without a moment's delay, the Baal Shem set out for the city to which he had been directed. When he asked for Rabbi Moshe Pastuch, it evolved that the man who bore that name was a shepherd who pastured his flock in the hills beyond the city. There he found him. The sheep were scattered over the slopes, but the shepherd, whom the Baal Shem approached unobserved, was standing over a ditch and saying to himself: "Dear Lord, how can I serve you? If you had flocks of sheep, I should pasture them for you without pay. But as it is, what can I do?" Suddenly he began to jump back and forth over the ditch. Full of fervor he jumped and jumped and somersaulted and cried: "I am jumping for the love of God! I jump for the love of God!" Then the Baal Shem realized that the service of this shepherd was greater than his own.

When the shepherd paused in his jumping, the Baal Shem went up to him and said: "I must talk with you."

"I am a hired man," said the other, "and may not waste my time."

"But you were just jumping back and forth over the ditch," the Baal Shem reminded him.

"That is true," said the man. "I am permitted to do that because it is for the love of God."

"What I have in mind for you is also for the love of God," said the zaddik. Then the other let him talk and listened, and his soul was just as much aflame as when he had leaped the ditch. He made the Baal Shem tell him everything, beginning with the destruction of the Temple; how twice before, in hours of disaster, when thousands sanctified the great Name with their death, the great work had been undertaken, but that Satan had come between and prevented it, and that now the third hour had come.

"Yes," cried the shepherd. "Let us free the Divine Presence from exile!"

"Is there a place here where we can immerse ourselves?" asked the Baal Shem.

"There is a living spring at the foot of the mountain," said the shepherd, and was already on his way down the slope. The zaddik followed him as best he could. Down below, they both dipped down into the spring, and the Baal Shem prepared to confide to him the secret of the work in hand.

In the meantime, rumor had spread in Heaven that men on earth were about to hasten the hour of salvation. Heavenly powers rose up against the plan, Satan grew strong and went to work. Fire broke out in the city, and soon the alarm rang over to the hills. The shepherd ran to his sheep. "Where are you running and why?" asked the Baal Shem.

The other replied: "The owners of the flocks have most likely heard that the sheep went astray and now they will come and ask what has become of them."

The Baal Shem was unable to hold him back and he realized who it was that had put in his oar.

Before the Coming of the Messiah

The Baal Shem said:

"Before the coming of the Messiah there will be great abundance in the world. The Jews will get rich. They will become accustomed to running their houses in the grand style and moderation will be cast to the winds. Then the lean years will come; want and a meagre livelihood, and the world will be full of poverty. The Jews will not be able to satisfy their needs, grown beyond rhyme or reason. And then the labor which will bring forth the Messiah, will begin."

After the Death of His Wife

A zaddik tells:

The Baal Shem Tov believed that, like Elijah, he would rise up to Heaven in a storm. When his wife died, he said: "I thought that a storm would sweep me up to Heaven like Elijah. But now that I am only half a body, this is no longer possible."

Omission

It is told:

Rabbi Pinhas of Koretz went to the Baal Shem for Passover, and saw that he was very tired.

On the day before the last day of the festival, Rabbi Pinhas debated with his soul whether or not he should go to the bath of immersion. He did not go.

On the last day of Passover he felt in the midst of praying that the Baal Shem was destined to die soon because he had strained himself to the utmost against the throngs of renegades. He concentrated all his strength in prayer, and gave himself wholly up to it, but noticed that he was not accomplishing anything at all. Then he was filled with deep regret that he had not gone to the bath.

After prayer, the Baal Shem asked him: "Did you go to the bath yesterday?" He answered "No." Then the Baal Shem said: "It has already come to pass, and after this there is nothing more."

Of the Baal Shem's Death

After Passover, the Baal Shem fell ill. But he continued to pray before the pulpit in the House of Prayer, as long as his strength permitted.

He did not send word to those of his disciples in other towns who were held to be men whose prayers were effective through their fervor, and sent the disciples who were in Mezbizh, to other places. Rabbi Pinhas of Koretz was the only one who refused to leave.

On the eve of the Feast of Weeks, the congregation met as every year at this time, in order to spend the night in the study of the law. The Baal Shem addressed them on the revelation on Mount Sinai.

When morning came, he sent for his close friends. First he summoned two of them and told them to attend to his corpse and his burial. On his own body he showed them, limb by limb, how the soul wished to depart from it, and instructed them to apply what they had learned in the case of other sick persons, for these two belonged to the Holy Brotherhood who care for the dead and their burial.

Then he bade the quorum of ten worshippers pray with him. He asked for the prayer-book and said: "I want to busy myself with God for a bit more."

After the prayer, Rabbi Nahman of Horodenka went to the House of Study to pray for him. The Baal Shem said: "He is shaking the gates of Heaven in vain! He cannot get in at the door by which he used to enter."

Later, when the servant happened to come into the room, he heard the Baal Shem say: "I give you those two hours," and thought that he was telling the angel of death he need not torment him two hours more, but Rabbi Pinhas knew better what was meant. "He had two hours more to live," he said.

"And he was saying that he would make God a gift of those two hours. This is a true sacrifice of the soul."

Then, just as every year on this day, the people from the city came to him and he spoke words of teaching to them.

Some time later he said to the disciples who stood about him: "I have no worries with regard to myself. For I know quite clearly: I am going out at one door and I shall go in at another." And again he spoke and said: "Now I know for what I was created."

He sat up in bed and spoke brief words of teaching about the "pillar" by means of which the souls, after death, mount from the lower paradise to the upper paradise, to the "Tree of Life," and expounded the verse from the Book of Esther: "And with that the maiden came unto the king." He also said: "I shall surely return, but not as I am now."

After that he had them say the prayer: "And let the graciousness of the Lord our God be upon us," and stretched out in his bed. But several times he sat up again and whispered, as they knew he did when he shaped and directed his soul to fervor. For a while they heard nothing and he lay there quietly. Then he bade them cover him with a sheet. But they still heard him whisper: "My God, Lord of all worlds!" And then the verse of the psalm: "Let not the foot of pride come upon me." Later on, those whom he had bidden attend to his body and his burial, said they had seen the Baal Shem's soul ascend as a blue flame.

The River and the Light

It is told:

A woman who lived in a village not far from Mezbizh often went there and took gifts of fish and poultry, butter and flour, to the house of the Baal Shem. Her way led across a small river. Once the river rose and flooded its banks, and when, notwithstanding, she tried to cross, she was drowned. The Baal Shem grieved for the good woman. In his grief he cursed the river and it dried up. But the prince of the river complained of this in Heaven, and there it was decided that at some time or other for a few hours the bed of the river should fill with water again, that the river should flood its banks, and that one of the descendants of the Baal Shem should try to cross it, and no one should help him but the Baal Shem himself.

Several years after his death, his son lost his way, as he was walking by night, and suddenly found himself close to the river which he did not recognize because of its tiding waters. He tried to cross but was soon seized and swept away by the current. Then, above the shore, he saw a burning light which illumined the banks and the river. He mustered all his strength, fought free of the current, and reached the shore. The burning light was the Baal Shem himself.

The Fiery Mountain

Rabbi Zevi, the Baal Shem's son, told this:
"Some time after my father's death, I saw him in the shape of a fiery mountain, which burst into countless sparks. I asked him: 'Why do you appear in a shape such as this?' He answered: 'In this shape I served God.'"

On the Walls

A zaddik told:
"In a dream I once had the experience of being led to the highest paradise. There I was shown the walls of the Jerusalem of above and they were in ruins. Over these ruins heaped round about, from wall to wall, walked a man incessantly, without stopping. I asked "Who is he?" They replied: "This is Rabbi Israel Baal Shem Tov, who has sworn not to go from here until the Temple has been rebuilt.""

"He Will Be"

Rabbi Nahum of Tchernobil, who in his youth was privileged to see the Baal Shem, said: "It is written: 'The sun also ariseth, and the sun goeth down'—'one generation passeth away and another generation cometh.' As for the Baal Shem Tov, whose merit shall be our protection—no one was before him and no one will be after him until the coming of the Messiah, and when the Messiah comes, he will be." And three times he repeated: "He will be."

If

Rabbi Leib, son of Sarah, the hidden zaddik, once said to some persons who were telling about the Baal Shem: "You ask about the holy Baal Shem Tov? I tell you: if he had lived in the age of the prophets, he would have become a prophet, and if he had lived in the age of the patriarchs, he would have become an outstanding man, so that just as one says: 'God of Abraham, Isaac, and Jacob,' one would say 'God of Israel.'"

BARUKH OF MEZBIZH

The Three Men

An old man once asked the Baal Shem Tov: "Concerning the passage in the Scriptures which relates that Abraham saw three men standing before him, the holy Book of Splendor says that these were Abraham, Isaac, and Jacob. But how could Abraham see Abraham standing before him?"

Barukh, the Baal Shem's grandson, who was three years old at the time, was present and heard the question. He said: "Grandfather, what a silly thing for this old man to ask! Abraham, Isaac, and Jacob—those are of course the attributes which, as everyone knows, became the attributes of the fathers: mercy, rigor, and glory."

The Little Sister

After the death of his grandfather, the Baal Shem Tov, the boy Barukh was taken into the house of Rabbi Pinhas of Koretz. He was very secretive and withdrawn, and even when he was no longer a child, he still would not say a word of teaching.

Once, on the day before the sabbath, Rabbi Pinhas went to the bath with him. When they came home they drank mead together. As soon as the rabbi saw that the youth had grown light of heart, he asked him to say some words of teaching. Barukh said: "In the Song of Songs it is written: 'We have a little sister.' This refers to wisdom, as it is written in Proverbs: 'Say to wisdom: You are my sister.' I have a little wisdom! And further on in the Song of Songs, we read: 'And she hath no breasts.' My little sister wisdom has no breasts from which she can suck, she has no longer a teacher from whom she can receive the teachings. And still further on, it is written: 'What shall we do for our sister in the day when she shall be spoken for?' What shall I do with my little wisdom when I have said all there is to say?"

After his marriage, Rabbi Barukh lived in the house of his father-in-law. The other two sons-in-law, who were learned men, complained that Barukh conducted himself differently from them and from all the rest of the world besides, that when they sat over their books, he slept, and when he was awake, he busied himself with all manner of foolish things. Finally the father-in-law decided to take all three of them to the maggid of Mezritch, and put the matter before him. On the way there they made Barukh sit beside the coachman. When they were about to enter the house, only Barukh was admitted. The others had to wait outside until they were asked to come before the maggid. He said to them: "Barukh is conducting himself very well, and what seems idle play to you is directed to sublime matters and effects sublime things." On the way home they gave Barukh the best seat.

Preparation

When Rabbi Barukh had burned the leaven on the eve of Passover and scattered the ashes, he said the words prescribed for this, and expounded them. " 'Any kind of leaven which remains in my possession'—all that seethes; 'which I have or have not seen'—even though I believe I have looked into myself thoroughly, I have probably not looked thoroughly at all; 'which I have burned or not burned'—the Evil Urge within me tries to convince me that I have burned everything, but not until now do I see that I have not burned it, and so I beg of you, God, 'it shall be null and accounted as the dust of earth.' "

To Himself

When Barukh came to those words in the psalm which read: "I will not give sleep to mine eyes, nor slumber to mine eyelids until I find out a place for the Lord," he stopped and said to himself: "Until I find myself and make myself a place to be ready for the descending of the Divine Presence."

Make Us Holy

Once, when Rabbi Barukh was saying grace and came to these words: "Our Holy One, the Holy One of Jacob," he said to

God in the voice of a child who wants to coax his father: " 'Our Holy One'—make us holy, for you are 'the Holy One of Jacob' —when you wanted to, you made Jacob holy."

The Two Strangers

In the hundred and nineteenth psalm, the psalmist says to God: "I am a sojourner on the earth, hide not thy command-ments from me."

Concerning this verse Rabbi Barukh said: "He whom Life drives into exile and who comes to a land alien to him, has nothing in common with the people there, and not a soul he can talk to. But if a second stranger appears, even though he may come from quite a different place, the two can confide in each other, and live together henceforth, and cherish each other. And had they not both been strangers, they would never have known such close companionship. That is what the psalm-ist means: "You, even as I, are a sojourner on earth and have no abiding place for your glory. So do not withraw from me, but reveal your commandments, that I may become your friend."

Blessed Be He Who Spoke

They asked Rabbi Barukh: "Why do we say: 'Blessed he who spoke and the world existed' and not, 'Blessed he who created the world'?"

He replied: "We praise God because he created our world with the word, and not with the thought, like other worlds. God judges the zaddikim for an evil thought they nurse within them. But how could the rank and file of the people persist if he were to judge them in this way, and not—as he does—only for an evil thought they have expressed and made effective through words."

With Yourself

This is how Rabbi Barukh expounded the words in the Sayings of the Fathers, "and be not wicked by facing yourself only" (that is, do not think that you cannot be redeemed):

"Every man has the vocation of making perfect something in this world. The world has need of every single human being. But there are those who always sit in their rooms behind closed doors and study, and never leave the house to talk with others. For this they are called wicked. If they talked to others, they would bring to perfection something they are destined to make perfect. That is what the words mean: 'Be not wicked by facing yourself only.' Since you face yourself only, and do not go among people, do not become wicked through solitude."

Gifts

When, in saying grace, Rabbi Barukh came to the passage: "Let us not require gifts of flesh and blood and not the loan of them, but only your full, open, and holy hand," he repeated these words three times and with great fervor. When he had ended, his daughter asked him: "Father, why did you pray so fervently that you might be able to do without the gifts of man? Your only means of subsistence is that the people who come to you give you things of their own accord, to show their gratitude."

"My daughter," he replied, "you must know that there are three ways of bringing money to the zaddik. Some say to themselves: 'I'll give him something. I am the kind of man who brings gifts to the zaddik.' The words: 'Let us not require gifts . . .' refers to these. Others think: 'If I give something to this devout man, it will profit me hereafter.' These want heaven to pay them interest. That is the 'loan.' But there are some who know: 'God has put this money in my hand for the zaddik, and I am his messenger.' These serve the 'full and open hand.' "

Sweets

On the eve of the Day of Atonement, at the meal which precedes the fast, Rabbi Barukh distributed sweets among his hasidim at his table, and said: "I love you greatly and whatever good I see in the world, I should like to give you. Keep in mind what is said in the psalm: 'O taste and see that the Lord is good.' Just taste—in the right sense of the word—and you will see:

wherever there is something good, there He is." And he broke into the song: "How good is our God, how fair is our lot."

Right Service

Rabbi Barukh's disciples asked him: "When through Moses God commanded Aaron to make the lamps of the candlestick seven and to light the lamps, the Scriptures simply say: 'And Aaron did so.' Rashi thinks that this is said in praise, because he did not deviate from what he was told. How are we to understand this? Is Aaron, appointed by God, to be considered worthy of praise because he did not deviate from God's command?"

Rabbi Barukh replied: "If the righteous man is to serve God in the right way, he must be a man who, no matter what fires he may feel within him, does not allow the flame to burst from the vessel, but performs every tangible action in the manner proper to it. We are told of a holy servant of God who, when he was to fill the lamps in the House of Prayer, was so flooded with fervor that he spilled the oil. That is why it must be regarded as praise when it is said of Aaron that—although he served his Maker with the whole strength of his soul—he saw to the candlestick in the way prescribed, and lit the lamps."

How We Should Learn

The disciples of Rabbi Barukh asked him: "How can a man ever learn the Talmud adequately? For there we find that Abayyi said this, and Raba said that. It is just as if Abayyi were of one world and Raba of quite another. How is it possible to understand and learn both at the same time?"

The zaddik replied: "He who wants to understand Abayyi's words, must link his soul to the soul of Abayyi; then he will learn the true meaning of the words as Abayyi himself utters them. And after that, if he wants to understand Raba's words, he must link his soul to the soul of Raba. That is what is meant in the Talmud when we read: 'When a word is spoken in the name of its speaker, his lips move in the grave.' And the lips of him who utters the word, move like those of the master who is dead."

Without telling his teacher anything of what he was doing, a disciple of Rabbi Barukh's had inquired into the nature of God, and in his thinking had penetrated further and further until he was tangled in doubts, and what had been certain up to this time, became uncertain. When Rabbi Barukh noticed that the young man no longer came to him as usual, he went to the city where he lived, entered his room unexpectedly, and said to him: "I know what is hidden in your heart. You have passed through the fifty gates of reason. You begin with a question and think, and think up an answer—and the first gate opens, and to a new question! And again you plumb it, find the solution, fling open the second gate—and look into a new question. On and on like this, deeper and deeper, until you have forced open the fiftieth gate. There you stare at a question whose answer no man has ever found, for if there were one who knew it, there would no longer be freedom of choice. But if you dare to probe still further, you plunge into the abyss."

"So I should go back all the way, to the very beginning?" cried the disciple.

"If you turn, you will not be going back," said Rabbi Barukh. "You will be standing beyond the last gate: you will stand in faith."

Thanking in Advance

On a certain eve of the sabbath, Rabbi Barukh went back and forth in his house and, as always, first gave the greeting of peace to the angels of peace, and then said the prayer: "Lord of the worlds, Lord of all souls, Lord of peace," until he came to the words: "I offer thanks to you, O Lord my God, and God of my fathers, for all the grace you have done unto me, and which you will do unto me in the future." Here he stopped and was silent for a time. Then he said: "Why should I give thanks for future grace? Whenever grace is done unto me, that is when I shall offer thanks." But instantly he replied to himself: "Perhaps a time will come when you do a grace unto me, and I shall not be able to offer the thanks which are your due. That is why I must do it now." And he burst into tears.

Rabbi Moshe of Savran, his disciple, had stood in a corner of the room unnoticed and heard his master's words. Now, when he saw him weep, he came forward and said: "Why do you weep? Your question was good and your answer was good!" Rabbi Barukh said: "I wept because suddenly I thought: For what offense shall I be punished by not being able to offer thanks?"

The Great Work

Rabbi Barukh said: "Elijah's great work was not that he performed miracles, but that, when fire fell from Heaven, the people did not speak of miracles, but all cried: 'The Lord is God.'"

Everything Is Wonder

They asked Rabbi Barukh: "In the hymn, God is called 'Creator of remedies, awful in praises, lord of wonders.' Why? Why should remedies stand next to wonders and even precede them?" He answered: "God does not want to be praised as the lord of supernatural miracles. And so here, through the mention of remedies, Nature is introduced and put first. But the truth is that everything is a miracle and wonder."

Medicine

Once Rabbi Barukh went to the city and bought medicine for his sick daughter. The servant set it on the window-sill of his room in the inn. Rabbi Barukh went up and down, looked at the little bottles, and said: "If it is God's will that my daughter Raizel recover, she needs no medicine. But if God made his miraculous power manifest to all eyes, then no one would, any longer, have freedom of choice: everyone would know. But God wanted men to have a choice, so he cloaked his doing in the courses of Nature. That is why he created healing herbs." Then he walked up and down the room again, and asked: "But why does one give poisons to the sick?" And answered: "The 'sparks' that fell from the primeval iniquity of the worlds into the 'shells' and penetrated the stuff of stones, plants, and animals—all ascend back to their source through the sanctification of the devout who work at them, use them, and consume them in holiness. But how shall those sparks that fell into bitter poisons and poisonous herbs, be redeemed? That they might not remain in exile, God appointed them for the sick: to each the carriers of the sparks which belong to the root of his soul. Thus the sick are themselves physicians who heal the poisons."

Apparition

When Rabbi Shelomo of Karlin, whose son was the husband of Rabbi Barukh's daughter, once came to visit the rabbi and was on the very threshold of his room, he started back and closed the door. After a while the same thing recurred. On being questioned, Rabbi Shelomo said: "He is standing at the window and looking out. But beside him stands the holy Baal Shem Tov, and is caressing his hair."

The Argument

Rabbi Moshe of Ludmir, the son of Rabbi Shelomo of Karlin, once called on Rabbi Barukh together with his younger son. When they entered the room, they saw and heard the zaddik arguing with his wife. He paid no attention to his guests. The boy was disturbed because his father was not shown the honor due to him. When Rabbi Moshe observed this, he said: "My son, believe me! What you have just heard was an argument between God and his Presence concerning the lot of the world."

Fine Words

One sabbath, a learned man who was a guest at Rabbi Barukh's table, said to him: "Now let us hear the teachings from you, rabbi. You speak so well!" "Rather than speak so well," said the grandson of the Baal Shem, "I should be stricken dumb."

To a Bridegroom

Rabbi Barukh said this to a bridegroom before he stepped under the wedding canopy: "It is written: 'And as the bridegroom rejoiceth over the bride, so shall thy God rejoice over thee.'

In you, bridegroom, God shall rejoice; the god-like part of
you shall rejoice over the bride."

Sabbath Joy

Once Rabbi Barukh was entertaining a distinguished guest
from the Land of Israel. He was one of those who are forever
mourning for Zion and Jerusalem, and cannot forget their
sorrow for a single second. On the eve of the sabbath, the rabbi
sang: "He who sanctifies the seventh day . . ." in his usual
manner. When he came to the words: "Beloved of the Lord,
you who await the rebuilding of Ariel," he looked up and saw
his guest sitting there as gloomy and sad as always. Then he
interrupted himself and, vehemently and joyfully, shouted in
the very face of the startled man: "Beloved of the Lord, you
who await the rebuilding of Ariel, on this holy day of the
sabbath, be joyful and happy!" After this, he sang the song
on to the end.

Forgetting

A learned man from Lithuania who was proud of his knowledge, was in the habit of interrupting the sermons of Rabbi
Levi Yitzhak of Berditchev with all manner of hair-splitting
objections. Time after time the zaddik invited him to visit him
at his home for discussions of this kind, but the Lithuanian did
not come but continued to appear in the House of Prayer, and
interrupted the rabbi again and again. Rabbi Barukh was told
of this. "If he comes to me," he said, "he will not be able to
say anything at all."
These words were reported to the learned man. "What is the
rabbi specially versed in?" he asked. "In the Book of Splendor," was the answer. So he selected a difficult passage in the
Book of Splendor and went to Mezbizh to ask Rabbi Barukh
about it. When he came into the room, he saw the Book of
Splendor lying on the desk and opened to the very passage he
had in mind. "What an odd coincidence," he thought to himself, and immediately began to cast about for another difficult
passage that might serve to embarrass the rabbi. But the zaddik
anticipated him. "Are you well versed in the Talmud?" he

asked. "Certainly I am well versed in it!" the other replied and laughed. "In the Talmud," said Rabbi Barukh, "it is said that when the child is in the mother's womb a light is kindled above his head and he learns the entire Torah, but that—when his appointed time to issue forth into the air of earth has come —an angel strikes him on the mouth and thereupon he forgets everything. How are we to interpret this? Why should he learn everything only to forget it?" The Lithuanian was silent. Rabbi Barukh continued: "I shall answer the question myself. At first glance, it is not clear why God created forgetfulness. But the meaning of it is this: If there were no forgetting, man would incessantly think of his death. He would build no house, he would launch on no enterprise. That is why God planted forgetting within him. And so one angel is ordered to teach the child in such a way that it will not forget anything, and the second angel is ordered to strike him on the mouth and make him forget. But occasionally he fails to do this, and then I replace him. And now it is your turn. Recite the whole passage to me." The man from Lithuania tried to speak, but he stammered and could not utter a single word. He left the rabbi's house and had forgotten everything. He was an ignorant man! After that he became a servant in the House of Prayer in Berditchev.

Blessing of the Moon

In a certain month of winter, one dark and cloudy night followed upon the other; the moon was hidden and Rabbi Barukh could not say the blessing of the moon. On the last night of those set aside for this, he sent someone out to look at the sky, time after time, but again and again he was told that it was dark as pitch and the snow was falling thick and fast. Finally he said: "If things were with me as they should be, the moon would surely do me a favor! So I ought to do penance. But because I am no longer strong enough to do it, I must at least penitently confess my sins." And this penitent confession broke from his lips with such force that all who were there with him, were shaken. A great shudder pulsed through their hearts, and they turned to God. Then someone came and reported: "It isn't snowing any more. You can see a little light!" The rabbi put on his coat and went out. The clouds had scattered. Among the shining stars shone the moon, and he spoke the blessing.

Hide-and-Seek

Rabbi Barukh's grandson Yehiel was once playing hide-and-seek with another boy. He hid himself well and waited for his playmate to find him. When he had waited for a long time, he came out of his hiding-place, but the other was nowhere to be seen. Now Yehiel realized that he had not looked for him from the very beginning. This made him cry, and crying he ran to his grandfather and complained of his faithless friend. Then tears brimmed in Rabbi Barukh's eyes and he said: "God says the same thing: 'I hide, but no one wants to seek me.'"

The Two Wicks

Rabbi Barukh's other grandchild, young Israel, made a habit of crying aloud while he prayed. Once his grandfather said to him: "My son, do you recall the difference between a wick of cotton and a wick of flax? One burns quietly and the other sputters! Believe me, a single true gesture, even if it be only that of the small toe, is enough."

The Twofold World

Rabbi Barukh once said: "What a good and bright world this is if we do not lose our hearts to it, but what a dark world, if we do!"

DOV BAER OF MEZRITCH
THE GREAT MAGGID

The Family Tree

When Rabbi Baer was five years old, a fire broke out in his father's house. Hearing his mother grieve and cry about this, he asked her: "Mother, do we have to be so unhappy because we have lost a house?"

"I am not grieving for the house," she said, "but for our family tree which burned up. It began with Rabbi Yohanan, the sandal-maker, the master in the Talmud."

"And what does that matter!" exclaimed the boy. "I shall get you a new family tree which begins with me!"

The Curse

When Rabbi Baer was young, he and his wife lived in great poverty. They inhabited a ramshackle house beyond the city limits, because they did not have to pay rent for it, and here the woman brought her son into the world. Up to this time she had not complained. But when the midwife asked for money to buy camomile tea for the child, and she hadn't a penny to give her, she moaned: "This is how his service provides for us!"

The maggid heard these words and said to her: "Now I shall go outside and curse Israel because they leave us to our misery." He went out, stood in front of the door, raised his eyes to Heaven, and cried: "O children of Israel, may abundant blessings come upon you!" Then he went back into the room. When he heard his wife moan a second time, he said to her: "Now I shall really curse them!" Once more he went out, lifted his head, and cried: "Let all happiness come to the children of Israel—but they shall give their money to thorn-bushes and stones!"

Silently his wife held the hungry child. It was too weak to cry. Then—for the first time—the maggid sighed. Instantly the answer came. A voice said to him: "You have lost your share in the coming world."

"Well, then," he said, "the reward has been done away with. Now I can begin to serve in good earnest."

Punishment

When the maggid realized that he had become known to the world, he begged God to tell him what sin of his had brought this guilt upon him.

His Reception

Rabbi Baer was a keen scholar, equally versed in the intricacies of the Gemara and the depths of the Kabbalah. Time and again he had heard about the Baal Shem and finally decided to go to him, in order to see for himself if his wisdom really justified his great reputation.

When he reached the master's house and stood before him, he greeted him and then—without even looking at him properly —waited for teachings to issue from his lips, that he might examine and weigh them. But the Baal Shem only told him that once he had driven through the wilderness for days and lacked bread to feed his coachman. Then a peasant happened along and sold him bread. After this, he dismissed his guest.

The following evening, the maggid again went to the Baal Shem and thought that now surely he would hear something of his teachings. But all Rabbi Israel told him was that once, while he was on the road, he had had no hay for his horses and a farmer had come and fed the animals. The maggid did not know what to make of these stories. He was quite certain that it was useless for him to wait for this man to utter words of wisdom.

When he returned to his inn, he ordered his servant to prepare for the homeward journey; they would start as soon as the moon had scattered the clouds. Around midnight it grew light. Then a man came from the Baal Shem with the message that

Rabbi Baer was to come to him that very hour. He went at once. The Baal Shem received him in his room. "Are you versed in the Kabbalah?" he asked. The maggid said he was. "Take this book, the *Tree of Life*. Open it and read." The maggid read. "Now think!" He thought. "Expound!" He expounded the passage which dealt with the nature of angels. "You have no true knowledge," said the Baal Shem. "Get up!" The maggid rose. The Baal Shem stood in front of him and recited the passage. Then, before the eyes of Rabbi Baer, the room went up in flame, and through the blaze he heard the surging of angels until his senses forsook him. When he awoke, the room was as it had been when he entered it. The Baal Shem stood opposite him and said: "You expounded correctly, but you have no true knowledge, because there is no soul in what you know."

Rabbi Baer went back to the inn, told his servant to go home, and stayed in Mezbizh, the town of the Baal Shem.

The Sign

Once, at parting, the Baal Shem blessed his disciple. Then he bowed his own head to receive the blessing from him. Rabbi Baer drew back, but the Baal Shem took his hand and laid it on his head.

The Succession

Before the Baal Shem died, his disciples asked him who was to be their master in his stead. He said: "Whoever can teach you how pride can be broken, shall be my successor."

After the Baal Shem's death, they first put the question to Rabbi Baer. "How can pride be broken?"

He replied: "Pride belongs to God—as it is written: 'The Lord reigneth; He is clothed in pride.' That is why no counsel can be given on how to break pride. We must struggle with it all the days of our life." Then the disciples knew that it was he who was the Baal Shem's successor.

The Visit

Rabbi Jacob Joseph of Polnoye was the other of the two most distinguished disciples of the Baal Shem who fell heir to his work. It was he who wrote down his master's teachings. After the Baal Shem's death, he lived in Mezritch for a time, and during this period the maggid asked him to be his guest over the sabbath. The rabbi of Polnoye said: "On the sabbath I act like any house-father. I lie down after dining. I do not extend the dinner-hour as you who have many disciples and say Torah at table."

"On the sabbath," answered the maggid, "my disciples and I shall stay in two rooms which lie across the courtyard and leave the house to you, so that you can do just as you would in your own home." So the rabbi of Polnoye and his disciple Rabbi Moshe, who had accompanied him on his trip, remained in the house. On the eve of the sabbath they ate together and then Rabbi Jacob Joseph went to sleep. His disciple wanted very much to sit at the maggid's table, for he knew him for the leader of his generation, but he feared his teacher might wake up and notice his absence.

After the meal on the evening of the sabbath, the holy "third meal," the rabbi of Polnoye said to his disciple: "Let us go to the maggid's table and listen in a little." While they crossed the court, they heard the maggid's voice intoning the teachings, but when they reached his door it ceased. Rabbi Jacob Joseph went back into the court and again he heard the maggid speak. Once more he turned to the door. Once more he stood on the threshold. Once more all was silent within. When this happened a third time, the rabbi of Polnoye walked back and forth in the court, his hands pressed to his heart, and said: "What can we do? On the day our master died, the Divine Presence packed her knapsack and journeyed to Mezritch!" He did not try to go to the maggid's table again. When the sabbath was over, he made his farewells in cordial words and went home with his disciple.

Palm and Cedar

"The righteous [zaddik] shall flourish like the palm-tree; he shall grow like a cedar in Lebanon." Concerning this verse in the psalm, the maggid of Mezritch said: "There are two kinds of zaddikim. Some spend their time on mankind. They teach them and take trouble about them. Others concern themselves only with the teachings themselves. The first bear nourishing fruit, like the date-palm; the second are like the cedar: lofty and unfruitful."

Nearness

A disciple told:

Whenever we rode to our teacher—the moment we were within the limits of the town—all our desires were fulfilled. And if anyone happened to have a wish left, this was satisfied as soon as he entered the house of the maggid. But if there was one among us whose soul was still churned up with wanting—he was at peace when he looked into the face of the maggid.

Effect

A number of disciples once went to the maggid. "We are not going to stay," they said to one another. "We only want to look into his face." They told the coachman to wait in front of the house. The maggid at once told them a story which consisted of twenty-four words. They listened, bade him farewell, and said to the coachman: "Drive on slowly. We'll catch up with you." They walked behind the carriage and talked about the story they had heard. For the rest of that day and the whole of the night, they walked after the carriage. At dawn the coachman stopped, looked back, and said crossly: "Isn't it bad enough that yesterday you forgot the Afternoon and the Evening Prayer! Are you going to skip the Morning Prayer too?" He had to repeat this four times before they even heard him.

In the Maggid's House

Rabbi Shneur Zalman used to say: "What of prophecies! What of miracles! In the house of my teacher, the holy maggid, you drew up holy spirit by the bucketful, and miracles lay around under the benches, only that no one had the time to pick them up!"

102

Teaching

In a certain year, on the eve of Shavuot, the feast of the Revelation, the rabbi of Rizhyn sat at his table and said no word of the teachings to his disciples, as he usually did at this hour. He was silent and wept. It was the same the second evening of the feast. But after grace he said:

"Many a time, when my ancestor, the holy maggid, taught at table, his disciples discussed what their teacher had said, on the way home, and each quoted him differently, and each was positive he had heard it in this, and no other way, and what they said was quite contradictory. There was no possibility of clearing up the matter because when they went to the maggid and asked him, he only repeated the traditional saying: 'Both, these and those are words of the living God.' But when the disciples thought it over, they understood the meaning of the contradiction. For at the source, the Torah is one; in the worlds her face is seventyfold. If, however, a man looks intently at one of these faces, he no longer has need of words or of teachings, for the features of that eternal face speak to him."

In Exile

The maggid of Mezritch said: "Now, in exile, the holy spirit comes upon us more easily than at the time the Temple was still standing.

"A king was driven from his realm and forced to become a wayfarer. When, in the course of his wanderings, he came to the house of poor people, where he was given modest food and shelter, but received as a king, his heart grew light and he chatted with his host as intimately as he had done at court with those who were closest to him.

"Now, that He is in exile, God does the same."

God's Fatherhood

Concerning the verse in the Scriptures: "But from thence ye will seek the Lord thy God, and thou shalt find Him," the maggid of Mezritch said: "You must cry to God and call him father until he becomes your father."

The maggid of Mezritch said:

Nothing in the world can change from one reality into another, unless it first turns into nothing, that is, into the reality of the between-stage. In that stage it is nothing and no one can grasp it, for it has reached the rung of nothingness, just as before creation. And then it is made into a new creature, from the egg to the chick. The moment when the egg is no more and the chick is not yet, is nothingness. And philosophy terms this the primal state which no one can grasp because it is a force which precedes creation; it is called chaos. It is the same with the sprouting seed. It does not begin to sprout until the seed disintegrates in the earth and the quality of seed-dom is destroyed in order that it may attain to nothingness which is the rung before creation. And this rung is called wisdom, that is to say, a thought which cannot be made manifest. Then this thought gives rise to creation, as it is written: "In wisdom hast Thou made them all."

The Last Miracle

The maggid of Mezritch said:

The creation of Heaven and earth is the unfolding of Something out of Nothing, the descent from above to below. But the zaddikim who in their work disengage themselves from what is bodily, and do nothing but think about God, actually see and understand and imagine the universe as it was in the state of nothingness before creation. They change the Something back into the Nothing. This is more miraculous: to begin from the lower state. As it is said in the Talmud: "Greater than the first miracle is the last."

The Strong Thief

The maggid of Mezritch said:

"Every lock has its key which is fitted to it and opens it. But there are strong thieves who know how to open without keys. They break the lock. So every mystery in the world can be unriddled by the particular kind of meditation fitted to it. But God loves the thief who breaks the lock open: I mean the man who breaks his heart for God."

The Ten Principles

Said the maggid to Rabbi Zusya, his disciple: "I cannot teach you the ten principles of service. But a little child and a thief can show you what they are.

"From the child you can learn three things:

He is merry for no particular reason;

Never for a moment is he idle;

When he needs something, he demands it vigorously.

The thief can instruct you in seven things:

He does his service by night;

If he does not finish what he has set out to do, in one night, he devotes the next night to it;

He and those who work with him, love one another;

He risks his life for slight gains;

What he takes has so little value for him, that he gives it up for a very small coin;

He endures blows and hardship, and it matters nothing to him;

He likes his trade and would not exchange it for any other."

The Rabbi and the Angel

The first time—it was on a Friday—that Rabbi Shmelke, the rav of Nikolsburg, and his brother Rabbi Pinhas, the rav of Frankfort-on-the-Main, went to the house of the Great Maggid, they were deeply disappointed. They had expected a long and elaborate welcome, but he dismissed them after a brief greeting and devoted himself to preparing for another, a more distinguished guest: the sabbath. At the three sabbath meals, they were all agog to hear learned and intricate speeches. The maggid said only a few words at each, and without a great show of intellect. At the third, in particular, he did not speak at all like a teacher to his disciples who are avid to learn, but like a good father, united with his sons at a meal only a little more solemn than usual. This was why they took leave of Rabbi Baer the very next day and then went to the House of Study to bid his disciples goodbye. There they saw one whom they had not met: Rabbi Zusya. When they entered, he looked at them for a long time, first at one, then at the other. Finally he fixed his eyes on the floor and said without greeting or any transitional phrase: "Malachi says: 'For the priest's lips should keep knowledge, and they should seek the teaching from his mouth; for he is an angel of the Lord of hosts.' Our sages expounded this as follows: 'If the rabbi resembles an angel, you shall seek the teachings from his lips.' How are we to understand this? Has any one of us ever seen an angel, so that we could compare the rabbi with him? But that is just what is meant! You have never seen an angel, yet, if he stood before you, you would not ask him questions, or examine him, or demand a sign, but believe and know he was an angel. It is the same with the true zaddik. If there is someone who makes you feel such as this—from his lips you shall seek the teachings."

When Rabbi Zusya had ended, the brothers, in their hearts, had already joined the disciples of the maggid.

The Ball

Before the maggid began to teach the two brothers, Shmelke and Pinhas, he told them how to conduct themselves throughout the day, from the moment of waking to falling asleep. His directions took into account all their habits, confirming them or modifying them, as though he knew the whole of their lives. In closing he said: "And before you lie down at night, you add up everything you have done during the day. And when a man calculates his hours and sees that he has not wasted a moment in idleness, when his heart beats high with pride, then—up in Heaven—they take all his good works, crush them into a ball, and hurl it down into the abyss."

Body and Soul

When Rabbi Shmelke returned from his first trip to the Great Maggid, and they asked him what his experience had been, he replied: "Up to that time I had mortified my body so that it might endure the soul. But now I have seen and learned that the soul can endure the body and need not separate from it. This is what we are told in the holy Torah: 'And I will set My abiding presence among you, and My soul shall not abhor you.' For the soul shall not abhor the body."

Its Own Place

Once Rabbi Mikhal of Zlotchov took his young son Yitzhak on a visit to the Great Maggid. The maggid left the room for a short time and while he was absent the boy picked up a snuff box lying on the table, looked at it from every angle, and put it back again. The moment the maggid crossed the threshold he looked at Yitzhak and said to him: "Everything has its own place; every change of place has a meaning. If one does not know, one should not do."

To Say Torah and to Be Torah

Rabbi Leib, son of Sarah, the hidden zaddik who wandered over the earth, following the course of rivers, in order to redeem the souls of the living and the dead, said this: "I did not go to the maggid in order to hear Torah from him, but to see how he unlaces his felt shoes and laces them up again."

How to Say Torah

The maggid once said to his disciples:
"I shall teach you the best way to say Torah. You must cease to be aware of yourselves. You must be nothing but an ear which hears what the universe of the word is constantly saying within you. The moment you start hearing what you yourself are saying, you must stop."

The Stokers' Discussion

The Great Maggid accepted only chosen men as his disciples. Of these he said that they were noble tapers which need only to be lit to burn with a pure flame. Some scholars he rejected because—so he said—his way was not suited to them. But several young men who were not yet considered worthy of being his disciples, remained with him and performed services for him and his disciples. They went by the name of "stokers," because tending the stoves was part of their duties.

One night, as he was about to fall asleep, one of the disciples, Shneur Zalman, the later rav of Northern White Russia, heard three of these young men working at a stove in the adjoining room. They were talking about the sacrifice of Isaac. One of them said: "Why do people make such a great to-do about Abraham? Who would not do as he did, if God himself commanded it! Just think of all those who threw away their lives without such a command, solely to sanctify the Name! What do you think of it?"

The other said: "I see it this way. The children of Israel have within them the heritage of the holy fathers, and so it is no particular virtue for them to give up what they treasure most. But Abraham was the son of a worshipper of idols."

The first of the three stokers answered: "What did that matter at the moment that God, God himself, spoke to him?"

Now the second said: "You must not forget that he rose at early dawn and immediately prepared for the journey without delaying at home with his son even for an hour!"

The first rejected this reason also. "If God spoke to me now," he said, "I should not wait until morning. I should do his bidding right in the middle of the night."

Then the third who had been silent up to this time, said: "In the Scriptures it is written: 'For now I know,' and further on: 'Thou hast not withheld thy son, thine only one, from Me.' You might think that the words 'from Me' were unnecessary. But we learn something just from them: that when the angel held back his hand, Abraham did not rejoice because Isaac was to live, but still—even at this moment—rejoiced more than ever that the will of God was fulfilled by him. That is why it is written, 'for now I know'—*now*, when the angel had already arrested Abraham's hand."

The first of the three stokers did not reply, and the two others were also silent. All Rabbi Shneur Zalman heard was the crackling of the faggots and the hiss of the flames.

How to Become Spiritual

In the days of the Great Maggid, a well-to-do merchant, who refused to have anything to do with hasidic teachings, lived in

Mezritch. His wife took care of the shop. He himself spent only two hours a day in it. The rest of the time he sat over his books in the House of Study. One Friday morning, he saw two young men there whom he did not know. He asked them where they were from and why they had come, and was told they had journeyed a great distance to see and hear the Great Maggid. Then he decided that for once he too would go to his house. He did not want to sacrifice any of his study time for this, so he did not go to his shop on that day.

The maggid's radiant face affected him so strongly that from then on he went to his home more and more frequently and ended up attaching himself to him altogether. From this time on, he had one business failure after another until he was quite poor. He complained to the maggid that this had happened to him since he had become his disciple. The maggid answered: "You know what our sages say: 'He who wants to grow wise, let him go south; he who wants to grow rich, let him go north.' Now what shall one do who wants to grow both rich and wise?" The man did not know what to reply. The maggid continued: ' He who thinks nothing at all of himself, and makes himself nothing, grows spiritual, and spirit does not occupy space. He can be north and south at the same time." These words moved the merchant's heart and he cried out: "Then my fate is sealed!" "No, no," said the maggid. "You have already begun."

The List of Sins

During his stay in Mezritch, the rav of Kolbishov saw an old man come to the Great Maggid and ask him to impose penance on him for his sins. "Go home," said the maggid. "Write all your sins down on a slip of paper and bring it to me." When the man brought him the list, he merely glanced at it. Then he said. "Go home. All is well." But later the rav observed that Rabbi Baer read the list and laughed at every line. This annoyed him. How could anyone laugh at sins!

For years he could not forget the incident, until once he heard someone quote a saying of the Baal Shem: "It is well-known that no one commits a sin unless the spirit of folly possesses him. But what does the sage do if a fool comes to him? He laughs at all this folly, and while he laughs, a breath of gentleness is wafted through the world. What was rigid, thaws, and what was a burden becomes light." The rav reflected. In his soul he said: "Now I understand the laughter of the holy maggid."

From Where?

They tell:

A disciple of the Gaon of Vilna saw his dead father appear to him every night in a dream and ask him to give up his faith and become a Christian. Since Vilna was far away from where he lived, and Mezritch near, he decided to ask the Great Maggid for counsel and aid, in spite of the fact that a serious quarrel had broken out between the two schools. "Open your father's grave," said the maggid. "In it you will find two pieces of wood lying so that they form a cross. Take them out and you will soon have peace again." And everything was just as the maggid had said.

When the man went to Vilna, years later, he told the whole matter to his teacher. The Gaon said: "This is touched on in the Palestinian Talmud. But it is astonishing that the maggid of Mezritch understood the passage."

When, after a time, the man visited Rabbi Baer, he repeated the Gaon's words to him. "Your teacher," said the maggid, "knows it from the Palestinian Talmud, and I know it from where that work knows it."

Failure

Once the maggid concentrated all the force of his being on the coming of redemption. Then a voice asked from Heaven: "Who is trying to hasten the end, and what does he consider himself?"

The maggid replied: "I am the leader of my generation, and it is my duty to use all my strength for that purpose."

Again the voice asked a question. "How can you prove this?"

"My holy congregation," said the maggid, "will rise and testify for me."

110

"Let them rise!" cried the voice.

Then Rabbi Baer went to his disciples and said: "Is it true that I am the leader of my generation?" But all were silent. He repeated his question and still no one said, "It is true." Not until after he had left them, did the numbness leave their minds and tongues, and they were startled at themselves.

Conjuring

During the last years of the maggid's life, the mitnagdim were so hostile to the hasidim that they came to regard them as the builders of the Tower of Babel, reborn, and as such banned them, forbade association with them, marriage, eating of their bread and drinking of their wine. The disciples of the maggid complained of this on each of the three meals of the sabbath. But all three times he was silent as though he had not heard. So, at the close of the sabbath, his disciples, ten in number, formed a congregation of their own and opened the House of Prayer. There, with secret rites, they turned the ban back on those who had banned them. By the third hour after midnight, the thing was done, and they went to the room where they slept. Around the fourth hour, they heard the maggid's crutches drag over the floor. He had been using them for several years because of his weak feet. They rose, washed their hands, and stood before their master. He said: "Children, what have you done?" They replied: "We no longer had the strength to endure it!" He said: "You have done a foolish thing and you have forfeited your head." In that very year the Great Maggid died.

At the Pond

After the maggid's death, his disciples came together and talked about the things he had done. When it was Rabbi Schneur Zalman's turn, he asked them: "Do you know why our master went to the pond every day at dawn and stayed there for a little while before coming home again?" They did not know why. Rabbi Zalman continued: "He was learning the song with which the frogs praise God. It takes a very long time to learn that song."

111

The Left Foot

It is known that the Great Maggid used crutches. Many years after his death, his great disciple, Rabbi Shneur Zalman, once heard his own disciples arguing about who should be called "the zaddik of the generation." "What is there to argue about!" he cried. "The zaddik of the generation is my master, the holy maggid of Mezritch, and none other! 'Let us make man in our image' is written about him, for he was a perfect man. You will object and say: 'How is that possible? His feet were crippled!' But I tell you he *was* perfect, and you know what is said of the perfect man: that with each of his limbs he moves all the worlds, as it is written in the Book of Splendor: 'Mercy—that is the right arm, rigor is the left.' That was why he dragged his left foot. He offered it up, lest he waken rigor within the world!"

From the Look-Out of Heaven

At a time of great anguish for Israel, Rabbi Elimelekh brooded more and more on his griefs. Then his dead master, the maggid of Mezritch, appeared to him. Rabbi Elimelekh cried out: "Why are you silent in such dreadful need?" He answered: "In Heaven we see that all that seems evil to you is a work of mercy."

ABRAHAM, THE ANGEL

The Mothers

They tell:

In the days when the Great Maggid was still poor and unrecognized, it happened on a winter evening that his wife set out for the bath, for her monthly purification. But she was caught in a savage snow-storm, lost her way, and groped about for a long time until finally, at dead of night, she found the bath. When she knocked at the door, the bath-master called to her from within, grumbled that she had waked him from his sleep, and refused to let her in. The woman stood outside in the icy night, but she would not go away. At midnight she heard carriage-bells and the snorting of horses. A fine carriage drove up to the bath-house. Four women got out. They knocked at the door and called. The bath-master came with a light, looked at the women with awe, and admitted them. But before they entered, they took the wife of the maggid between them. They all bathed together. When they had done, they asked her into their carriage and drove her home. She got out and looked around, but the carriage was gone. Softly she entered the room. "So you bathed with the Mothers!" the maggid said. That night she conceived her son Abraham.

Origin

They say that the Great Maggid had purified and unified his body and spirit so utterly that his body was as his spirit, and his spirit was as his body. Therefore in the hour he begot his son, a pure spirit from the world of angels entered his wife's womb, and from there it was born for a brief space into the world of man.

The Face

Sometimes Rabbi Abraham looked so great and awe-inspiring that men could not bear to look at him. One zaddik, who was performing some holy rite, did look at him and forgot whether or not he had said the blessing. On his return home, he refused both food and drink. Another martialled his courage four whole weeks, but when he crossed the threshold, and saw Rabbi Abraham binding on his phylacteries, he trembled and turned away, and did not again venture into his presence.

Barukh and Efraim, the grandsons of the Baal Shem Tov, once said to each other: "Why do you suppose people call the son of the maggid an angel? Let us have a look at him." But when they reached the street in which he lived, and saw Rabbi Abraham's face in the window, they fled in such haste that Efraim dropped his book of psalms.

Marriage

When Rabbi Abraham, the Angel, entered the room on his wedding-night, his face was more awe-inspiring than ever before, and his lips uttered dark sounds of lament. His appearance and his voice terrified the bride to the secret core of her being, and she fell fainting to the ground. Until morning she lay in a fever.

When he entered the room on the following night, his wife's heart filled with heroic strength and she endured his terrible greatness.

Rabbi Abraham begot two sons. After that he lived apart as before.

His Wife's Dream

His wife had a dream. She saw a vast hall and in it thrones, set in a semi-circle. On each throne sat one of the great, and one said: "Let us summon him home." The others nodded in chorus. The woman came forward. She stood before the great on the thrones and pleaded and fought for her husband's life on earth. Her words burned with intensity. The great listened in silence. Finally one said: "Give him to her for twelve earthly years." The others nodded in chorus. The dream melted away. When the maggid said the morning greeting, he laid his hands on the head of his son's wife.

Anniversary

On the eve of the ninth of Av, the day of the burning of the Temple, the men sat on the floor of the dark room of prayer, mourning the destroyed sanctuary, and the reader began: "How doth the city sit solitary, that was full of people!" Rabbi Abraham, the Angel, sitting among the men, cried aloud, "How . . . " and fell silent, his head between his knees. The reader ended the lament. Everyone went home. Rabbi Abraham remained, his head between his knees. They found him in the same position the following day, and he did not rise until he had experienced the destruction to the very end.

Strategic Retreat

Rabbi Abraham said:

"I have learned a new form of service from the wars of Frederick, king of Prussia. It is not necessary to approach the enemy in order to attack him. In fleeing from him, it is possible to circumvent him as he advances, and fall on him from the rear until he is forced to surrender. What is needed is not to strike straight at Evil but to withdraw to the sources of divine power, and from there to circle around Evil, bend it, and transform it into its opposite."

Inheritance

It is told:

After his death, the maggid appeared to his son and—invoking the commandment to honor one's parents—ordered him to give up his life of perfect seclusion, for whoever walks a way such as this, is in danger. Abraham replied: "I do not recognize a father in the flesh. I recognize only one merciful Father of all that lives."

"You accepted your inheritance," said the maggid. "With that you recognized me as your father even after my death."

"I renounce my father's inheritance," cried Rabbi Abraham, the Angel. At that very moment, fire broke out in the house and consumed the few small things the maggid had left his son— but nothing besides.

The White *Pekeshe*

A short time after the fire in which the clothing and utensils the maggid had left his son were burned, Rabbi Abraham's brother-in-law made him a present of a robe of white silk the maggid had worn on high holidays, the famous "white *pekeshe*." On the eve of the Day of Atonement, Abraham put it on to honor his father. The lights in the House of Prayer had already been lit. With a fervent gesture the zaddik leaned over to one of them. The robe caught fire. They snatched it from his body. With a long look of understanding, he watched it crumble to ash.

The Mountain

Once Rabbi Abraham visited his father-in-law in Kremnitz. The most distinguished members of the congregation assembled to welcome the holy man. But he turned his back on them and looked out of the window at the mountain at whose foot the city lay. Among those waiting for him was a man very much aware of his own learning and intent on his own importance. He said impatiently: "Why do you keep staring at the mountain? Have you never seen anything like it before?"

The rabbi answered: "I look and am amazed to see how such a lump of earth made much of itself until it grew into a tall mountain."

Without God

Rabbi Abraham said:

"Lord of the world, if it were possible to imagine a fraction of a second without your influence and providence, of what avail to us were this world, and of what avail to us were that other world? Of what avail to us were the coming of the Messiah, and of what avail to us the resurrection of the dead? What would there be to delight in, in all of this, and what would it be there for?"

The Full Stature

Rabbi Abraham said:

"We say in our prayers: 'Every stature shall bow before thee.' When man reaches the highest rung, when he reaches his full stature, only then does he become truly humble in his own eyes, and knows what it is: to bow before you."

The Other Dream

In the night after the seven days of mourning for Rabbi Abraham, his wife had a dream. She saw a vast hall, and in it thrones, set in a semi-circle. On each throne sat one of the great. A door opened, and one who looked like those others, entered. It was Abraham, her husband. He said: "Friends, my wife bears me a grudge because in my earthly life I lived apart from her. She is right, and therefore I must obtain her forgiveness." His wife cried out: "With all my heart I forgive you," and awoke comforted.

Sanctified

Rabbi Israel of Rizhyn told:
A few years after the death of Rabbi Abraham, the Angel, his widow, my blessed grandmother, received an offer of marriage from the great zaddik Rabbi Nahum of Tchernobil. But the Angel appeared to him in a dream and looked at him threateningly. So he let her be.
My blessed grandmother lived in want. When the Rabbi of Tchernobil had taken her son, my father, into his house, she went to the Land of Israel. She told no one there who she was. She took in washing and supported herself with the money she got for this. She died in the Land of Israel. If only some one could tell me where she lies buried!

PINHAS OF KORETZ AND HIS SCHOOL*

The Black Melammed

In his young years, Rabbi Pinhas earned his livelihood as a melammed, that is, as a teacher of children, in Koretz, where he was generally known as the "Black Melammed." He concealed his true nature from everybody. The only one who knew about him was the rav of Koretz. This rav had a special room in the bath-house and his own bath. Rabbi Pinhas asked his permission to bathe there any time he pleased, day or night, and the rav told the bath-master to admit him at any hour whatsoever.

Once Rabbi Pinhas came after midnight and woke up the bath-master. But he refused to open because, the day before, he had bought some geese and was keeping them in just that room overnight. But the "Black Melammed" would not take no for an answer. He knocked a few shingles out of the roof, climbed through the opening, dipped into the bath, and was going out the same way, when a piece of the wall broke off, and struck him on the head with such force that he lost his footing and fell. He lay on the ground unconscious for several hours. In the morning, people found him and thought he was dead. When the rav heard of it, he said no one must touch him. He himself, however, did not go there, but to the House of Prayer, and prayed: "Lord of the world, keep him alive! Lord of the world, keep this zaddik alive for your own sake!" Then he went to the place where Pinhas was still lying motionless. He shook him and said: "Pinhasel, get up! Go, teach your pupils! Remember, you are a hired man who has his day's work to do!" And Rabbi Pinhas got up and went to his school.

---

* Here I have made an exception to the practice of limiting each chapter to one zaddik. Because the school of Pinhas of Koretz continues and complements his personality and teachings, I am representing it in this chapter in the person of Rabbi Rafael.

Blood-Letting

When Rabbi Pinhas visited the Baal Shem for the first time, his host looked at him for quite a while and then sent for the doctor to let his guest's blood. But before he began, the Baal Shem warned him to be careful to do it right, for, so he said: "That is holy blood, preserved ever since the six days of creation. If you are not quite sure your hand is steady," he added jestingly, "better tap my vein!"

When the Citron Came

When the Baal Shem Tov lay dying, his disciple Rabbi David of Ostrog came to him and said: "Rabbi, how can you leave us behind alone!" The zaddik whispered to him: "The bear is in the woods, and Pinhas is a sage." His disciple knew that these words referred to Rabbi Baer of Mezritch and Rabbi Pinhas of Koretz, although Pinhas did not belong to the group of disciples. But he had come to the Baal Shem twice—the second time just before his death—and the Baal Shem had been to see him twice as well.

After the master's death, Rabbi Baer taught in his place. But Rabbi Pinhas continued to lead an anonymous existence. In the House of Study, he said his prayers behind the stove and no one paid any attention to him.

Now, Rabbi David of Ostrog, who was a well-to-do man, was in the habit of buying two exceptionally fine citrons every year before the Feast of Tabernacles, one for the Baal Shem, the other for himself. The year the master died, he brought three beautiful fruits instead of two before the holiday, one for himself, one for Rabbi Baer, and one for Rabbi Pinhas.

That year citrons were very scarce, and not a single one had gotten to Koretz. On the first day of the feast, the congregation waited with praying to see whether one would perhaps be brought from a neighboring town to which they had sent for it. Finally the heads of the congregation decided that the daily Morning Prayer should be said; that, in the meantime, a messenger might still arrive. But the Morning Prayer was ended, and no one had come. So the reader was asked to begin the liturgy proper to that day. Hesitatingly he went up to the pulpit. He had not yet said the blessing, when the "Black Melammed" came out from behind the stove, walked to the reader, and said to him: "Do not begin yet!" Then he returned to his place behind the stove. The people had not noticed anything, but when they asked the reader why he did not begin, and he referred them to Rabbi Pinhas, they were annoyed and asked for an explanation. "At the right time," he told them, "the citron will be here."

"What do you mean?" they shouted. "What do you mean by 'the right time'?"

"In an hour."

"And if it has not come by then, you'll have to put up with a kick or so, won't you?"

"I have nothing against that," he replied.

Before the hour was up, they reported that a peasant had come on horseback to bring something to Rabbi Pinhas. It was the citron and a letter. Everyone crowded around to read it. The recipient was addressed as the "Head of all the sons of the Diaspora." The writer of the letter was known to many as a holy man. Rabbi Pinhas took the citron, had them bring the palm fronds, and spoke the blessing. They asked him to give them to the reader, so that he might recite the Hallel Psalms. "I shall recite them," he said. He went to the pulpit and prayed before the congregation.

Without a Guest

It is told:

When Rabbi Pinhas had become known, and more and more hasidim came to him with their concerns, he was alarmed to see how much all this diverted him from the service of God and the study of the Torah. The only solution he could think of was that people must stop bringing their problems to him—and his prayer was granted. From that time on, he did not live with his fellow-men—except when he prayed with the congregation—but kept himself apart and devoted himself solely to the service of his Lord.

When the Feast of Tabernacles approached, he had to let a non-Jew make his holiday booth, for the Jews refused to help him. Since he lacked the proper tools, he sent his wife to borrow them from a neighbor, but it was only with the greatest difficulty that she could get what was needed. When he was in the House of Study on the evening of the feast, he asked some wayfarers to dine with him, as he did every year, but he was so thoroughly hated far and wide, that no one would accept his invitation and he had to go home alone. When he had said the words bidding the holy guests, the patriarchs, to enter the booth that evening, he saw our Father Abraham standing outside like someone who has come to a house he is accustomed to visit, and only just sees that it is not the house he thought, and pauses in surprise. "What wrong have I done?" Rabbi Pinhas cried.

"It is not my custom to enter a house where no wayfarers have come as guests," our Father Abraham replied.

From then on, Rabbi Pinhas prayed he might find favor in the eyes of his fellow-men, and again his prayer was granted.

The Breaking of the Vessels

Rabbi Pinhas said: "We all know that very long ago, when God was building worlds and tearing them down, the vessels broke because they could not endure the abundance poured into them. But through this, light penetrated to the lower worlds and they did not remain in darkness. It is the same with the breaking of vessels in the soul of the zaddik."

The Teaching of the Soul

Rabbi Pinhas often cited the words: "'A man's soul will teach him'," and emphasized them by adding: "There is no man who is not incessantly being taught by his soul."

One of his disciples asked: "If this is so, why don't men obey their souls?"

"The soul teaches incessantly," Rabbi Pinhas explained, "but it never repeats."

The Pupil

Rabbi Pinhas said: "Ever since I began giving true service to my Maker, I have not tried to get anything, but only taken what God gave me. It is because the pupil is dark, that it absorbs every ray of light."

Sefirot

Rabbi Pinhas said:

"Every word and every action contains all the ten Sefirot, the ten powers emanating from God, for they fill the entire world. And it is not the way people think: that mercy is a principle in itself and rigor is a principle in itself. For all the ten creative powers are contained in every single thing. Whoever drops his hand, does so in the secret of the efflux of light. Whoever lifts his hand, does so in the secret of the reflux of light. The completed motion of lowering and lifting, houses the secret of mercy and rigor.

"There are no words which, in themselves, are useless. There are no actions which, in themselves, are useless. But one can make useless both actions and words by saying or doing them uselessly."

Hiding

Rabbi Rafael of Bershad, the favorite disciple of Rabbi Pinhas, told:

"On the first day of Hanukkah, I complained to my teacher that in adversity it is very difficult to retain perfect faith in the belief that God provides for every human being. It actually seems as if God were hiding his face from such an unhappy being. What shall he do to strengthen his faith?

"The rabbi replied: 'It ceases to be a hiding, if you know it is hiding.' "

The Doubter

A disciple of Rabbi Pinhas was tormented by doubt, for he could not see how it was possible for God to know all his thoughts, even the vaguest and most fleeting. He went to his teacher in great anguish to beg him to dispel the confusion in his heart. Rabbi Pinhas was standing at the window and saw his visitor arrive. He entered, greeted his master, and was about to tell him his troubles, when the zaddik said: "My friend, I know. And why should God not know?"

On the Throne

Rabbi Pinhas said: "At New Year's, God is in that concealment which is called 'the sitting on the throne,' and everyone can see him, everyone according to his own nature: one in weeping, one in prayer, and one in the song of praise."

Before the Ram's Horn Was Sounded

One New Year's Day, just before the ram's horn was sounded, Rabbi Pinhas said:

"All creatures renew themselves in sleep, even stones and streams. And if man wants to renew his life over and over, then before falling asleep, he must put from him his shape, and commend his naked soul to God. It will ascend and receive new life. But today is the day of the great renewal, and deep sleep falls on all spiritual creatures, on angels, and holy names, and the letters of the Scriptures. This is the meaning of the great judgment in which the spirit is renewed. And so today, man shall be destroyed in deep sleep, and the renewing hand of God will touch him." After these words, he raised the ram's horn to his lips.

On the Day of Destruction

They asked Rabbi Pinhas: "Why should the Messiah be born on the anniversary of the destruction of the Temple—as the tradition has it?"

"The kernel," he replied, "which is sown in earth, must fall to pieces so that the ear of grain may sprout from it. Strength cannot be resurrected until it has dwelt in deep secrecy. To doff a shape, to don a shape—this is done in the instant of pure nothingness. In the husk of forgetting, the power of memory grows. That is the power of redemption. On the day of destruction, power lies at the bottom of the depths, and grows. That is why, on this day, we sit on the ground. That is why, on this day, we visit graves. That is why, on this day, the Messiah is born."

For the Sake of Renewal

Rabbi Pinhas said: "Solomon, the preacher, says: 'Vanity of vanities, all is vanity,' because he wants to destroy the world, so that it may receive new life."

The Miracle of the Light

Rabbi Pinhas said: "Listen, and I shall tell you the meaning of the miracle of the light, at Hanukkah. The light which was hidden since the days of creation was then revealed. And every year, when the lights are lit for Hanukkah, the hidden light is revealed afresh. And it is the light of the Messiah."

A Man on Earth

They asked Rabbi Pinhas: "Why is it written: 'in the day that God created a man on earth,' and not 'in the day that God created Man on earth'?"
He explained: "You should serve your Maker as though there were only one man on earth, only yourself."

The Place of Man

They asked Rabbi Pinhas: "Why is God called 'makom,' that is, place? He certainly is the place of the world, but then he ought to be called that, and not just 'place.' "
He replied: "Man should go into God, so that God may surround him and become his place."

The Easy Death

Once they asked Rabbi Pinhas why, when he prayed, they could hear no sound and see no movement, so that he seemed to lack the fervor which shook the other zaddikim from head to foot.
"Brothers," he answered, "to pray means to cling to God, and to cling to God means to loose oneself from all substance, as if the soul left the body. Our sages say that there is a death which is as hard as drawing a rope through the ring on the mast, and there is a death as easy as drawing a hair out of milk, and this is called the death in the kiss. This is the one which was granted to my prayer."

He Is Your Psalm

Concerning the words in the Scriptures: "He is thy psalm and He is thy God," Rabbi Pinhas said the following:
"He is your psalm and he also is your God. The prayer a man says, the prayer, in itself, is God. It is not as if you were asking something of a friend. He is different and your words are different. It is not so in prayer, for prayer unites the principles. When a man who is praying thinks his prayer is something apart from God, he is like a suppliant to whom the king gives what he has begged from him. But he who knows that prayer in itself is God, is like the king's son who takes whatever he needs from the stores of his father."

The Prayerbook

In the days of Rabbi Pinhas, the prayer-book which is based on the kavvanot of letters, and bears the name of Rabbi Isaak Luria, the great Kabbalist, had just been published. The zaddik's disciples obtained his permission to pray from that book, but after a time they came to him and complained that since they were using it for their prayers, they had lost the sense of intensified life which prayer had always given them. Rabbi Pinhas told them: "You have put all the strength and purposefulness of your thinking into the kavvanot of the holy names, and the combinations of the letters, and have deviated from the essential: to make your hearts whole and dedicate them to God. That is why you have lost the live feeling of holiness."

In Praise of Song

Rabbi Pinhas always spoke in high praise of music and song. Once he said: "Lord of the world, if I could sing, I should not let you remain up above. I should harry you with my song until you came down and stayed here with us."

The One Thing

Once they told Rabbi Pinhas of the great misery among the needy. He listened, sunk in grief. Then he raised his head.

"Let us draw God into the world," he cried, "and all need will be quenched."

Valid Prayer

Rabbi Pinhas said: "A prayer which is not spoken in the name of all Israel, is no prayer at all!"

When Two Sing

Rabbi Pinhas said: "When a man is singing and cannot lift his voice, and another comes and sings with him, another who can lift his voice, then the first will be able to lift his voice too. That is the secret of the bond between spirit and spirit."

The Ear That Is No Ear

Rabbi Pinhas said: "In the book *The Duties of the Heart,* we read that he who conducts his life as he ought, should see with eyes that are no eyes, hear with ears that are no ears. And that is just how it is! For often, when someone comes to ask my advice, I hear him giving himself the answer to his question."

The Quickening

They asked Rabbi Pinhas: "Why is it, that a person who sees his friend after an interval of more than twelve months, says the blessing: 'Who quickenest the dead.'"
He answered: "Every human being has a light in Heaven. When two meet, the lights fuse, and a new light shines out of them. This is called a begetting, and the new light is an angel. But this angel cannot live longer than twelve months, unless those two beings meet on earth again before the time is up. But if they meet after the twelve months have passed, they can quicken the angel again for a time. That is why they say that blessing."

Differences

Rabbi Rafael asked his teacher: "Why is no face like any other?" Rabbi Pinhas replied: "Because Man is created in the image of God. Every human being sucks the living strength of God from another place, and all together they make up Man. That is why their faces all differ from one another."

In Everyone

Rabbi Pinhas said: "In everyone there is something precious, which is in no one else. That is why it is said: 'Despise not any man.'"

And this is how he expounded the saying in the Talmud, that every just man "will burn himself with the baldachin of his neighbor." With the secret core of his neighbor, that is, with the precious thing hidden in the being of his neighbor, and—among all men—only in him.

The Water Carrier

The wife of Rabbi Pinhas once scolded her servant. This annoyed the rabbi and he said to her: "One should never hurt a Jew. A Jew is precious, very precious!" He pointed to a water carrier by the name of Hirsh, who was just taking a pail into the house. The man was very simple-minded, and still unmarried although he was about forty years old. The rabbi said to his wife: "I tremble before Hershele—because he is so precious!"

Country Houses

Rabbi Pinhas said: "God's relationship to the wicked may be compared to that of a prince who, besides his magnificent palaces, owns all manner of little houses hidden away in the woods and in villages, and visits them occasionally to hunt or to rest. The dignity of a palace is no greater than that of such a temporary abode, for the two are not alike, and what the lesser accomplishes, the greater cannot. It is the same with the righteous man. Though his value and service be great, he cannot accomplish what the wicked man accomplishes in the hour he prays, or does something to honor God, and God who is watching the worlds of confusion, rejoices in him. That is why the righteous man should not consider himself better than the wicked."

Concerning Anger

Rabbi Pinhas once said to a hasid: "If a man wishes to guide the people in his house the right way, he must not grow angry at them. For anger does not only make one's soul impure; it transfers impurity to the souls of those with whom one is angry."

Another time he said: "Since I have tamed my anger, I keep it in my pocket. When I need it, I take it out."

Gog

In the intermediate days of the Feast of Tabernacles, Rabbi Pinhas expounded the passage from Ezekiel which is read that week, and which deals with the coming of Gog and Magog. He said: "According to the tradition, the main battle in the wars of Gog falls within the days of the Feast of Tabernacles. People have a way of saying about persons or nations: 'He is as great as Gog; it is as great as Gog.' And why? Because Gog is great in arrogance and brutality. And that is the battle which we must fight at the Feast of Tabernacles: the battle against our own pride."

Endless Struggle

Rabbi Rafael, who was humble all of his days, and avoided being honored, begged his teacher over and over to tell him how he could wholly fend off pride, but received no answer. Again he pressed his master: "O rabbi—pride, pride!"

"What do you want?" said Rabbi Pinhas. "This is a piece of work with which a man must wrestle all his years, and which he can never finish. For pride is the garment of God, as it is written: 'The Lord is king; he is clothed in pride.' But God is boundless, and he who is proud, injures the garment of the unbounded. And so the work of self-conquest is without bounds."

Out of the Net

This was Rabbi Pinhas' comment on the verse in the psalm: "Mine eyes are ever toward the Lord; for he will bring forth my feet out of the net."

128

"As the bird-catcher baits the net, and the bird comes and pecks at it and tangles his foot in the cord, so the Evil Urge confronts men with all the good they have done: learning, charities, and all manner of devout actions, in order to snare them in the net of pride. But if he succeeds in this, man can free himself no more than the captive bird. Then nothing can save him except the help of God."

The Bees

Rabbi Rafael of Bershad said: "They say that the proud are reborn as bees. For, in his heart, the proud man says: 'I am a writer, I am a singer, I am a great one at studying.' And since what is said of such men is true: that they will not turn to God, not even on the threshold of hell, they are reborn after they die. They are born again as bees which hum and buzz: 'I am, I am, I am.' "

A Boon to God

Rabbi Rafael said:
"What a boon that God prohibited pride! If He had bidden us be proud, how could I possibly do God's commandment!"

What You Pursue

Rabbi Pinhas used to say: "What you pursue, you don't get. But what you allow to grow slowly in its own way, comes to you. Cut open a big fish, and in its belly you will find the little fish lying head down."

The Greater Strength

He also used to say: "The strength of him who accepts reproof is greater than his who reproves. For if a man humbles himself to accept reproof and to recognize the truth of it, then God's words apply to him: 'I dwell in the high and holy place, with him also that is of a contrite and humble spirit.' "

More Love

When Rabbi Pinhas and his disciples discussed wicked or hostile persons, they recalled the advice the Baal Shem Tov once gave to the father of a renegade son: that he should love him more. "When you see," they said, "that someone hates you and does you harm, rally your spirit and love him more than before. That is the only way you can make him turn. For the whole of Israel is a vehicle for holiness. If love and unity prevail among them, then the Divine Presence and all holiness is about them. But if—God forbid!—there should be a schism, a rift appears, and through the opening holiness falls down into the 'shells.' And so, if your neighbor grows remote from you in spirit, you must approach him more closely than before—to fill out the rift."

* * *

Rabbi Shemuel told this about Rabbi Rafael of Bershad: "When he was going on his summer trip, he called me and asked me to share his carriage with him. I said: 'I am afraid I should crowd you.' Then he said to me in the manner he always used to express special affection: 'Let us love each other more and we shall have a feeling of spaciousness.' And after we had prayed, he said to me: 'God is a great-hearted friend.' "

* * *

Rabbi Rafael said: "Measured behavior is a dreadful evil. It is a dreadful evil when a man measures his behavior to his fellow-men. It is as if he were always manipulating weights and measures."

* * *

Once Rabbi Rafael was ill, and thought he was going to die. Then he said: "Now all merits must be set aside, lest they separate my heart from the heart of any Jew in the world."

* * *

Rabbi Pinhas said: "We should also pray for the wicked among the peoples in the world; we should love them too. While we do not pray like this, while we do not love like this, the Messiah will not come."

* * *

He used to say: "My Rafael knows how to love the most wicked evil-doers!"

Peace

Concerning the words of the prayer: "He who maketh peace in his high places, may he make peace for us . . ." Rabbi Pinhas said: "We all know that Heaven (shamayim) came into being when God made peace between fire (esh) and water (mayim). And he who could make peace between the utmost extremes, will surely be able to make peace between us."

* * *

Rabbi Rafael of Bershad was very eager to make peace. He often went into the homes of the hasidim and addressed their wives, so that the readiness to keep peace with their husbands might grow in their hearts.

Once, on the ninth day of Av, the anniversary of the destruction of the Temple, he happened to be in a community whose members had for a long time been nursing a quarrel which grew more and more involved and difficult to end. One of the factions approached him with the request to arbitrate. "But the rabbi," so they said, "will probably not want to bother with our affairs in this period of mourning."

"No day is better than this," he replied. "For it was because of an idle quarrel that the city of God was destroyed."

* * *

On the sabbath, when the first chapter in the Scriptures, the story of creation, is read, the hasidim in Bershad sit in a circle all day, and sing over and over: "Sabbath of creation, all in one! sabbath of creation, all in one!"

The Most Important Quality

Rabbi Pinhas used to say: "I am always afraid to be more clever than devout." And then he added: "I should rather be devout than clever, but rather than both devout and clever, I should like to be good."

For Truth

Rabbi Pinhas told his disciples: "I have found nothing more difficult than to overcome lying. It took me fourteen years. I broke every bone I had, and at last I found a way out."

He also said: "For the sake of truth, I served twenty-one

years. Seven years to find out what truth is, seven to drive out falsehood, and seven to absorb truth."

* * *

Once, when Rabbi Pinhas was at the desk, reciting the Evening Prayer, and came to the words: "Who guardest thy people Israel," he screamed aloud from the very bottom of his soul. The countess who owned the region happened to be passing the House of Prayer. She leaned over one of the low window-sills and listened. Then she said to those around her: "How true that scream was! How without any admixture of false-hood!" When they repeated her remark to Rabbi Pinhas, he said with a smile: "Even the peoples of the world know the truth when they hear it."

* * *

On a certain eve of the Day of Atonement, before praying "All Vows," the assembled congregation recited the psalms in noisy confusion. Rabbi Pinhas turned to them and said: "Why do you exert yourselves so much? Probably because you feel that your words are not mounting upward. And why not? Because you have told nothing but lies the entire year. He who lies throughout the year, gets a lying tongue. And how can a lying tongue shape true words which mount to Heaven? I, who am talking to you, know all about it, because I myself had a hard time with this matter. So you can believe me: You must assume the burden of not telling lies. Then you will get a truthful tongue, and the words it shapes will fly to God."

With the Evil Urge

Once, when Rabbi Pinhas entered the House of Study, he saw that his disciples, who had been talking busily. stopped and started at his coming. He asked them: "What were you talking about?"

"Rabbi," they said, "we were saying how afraid we are that the Evil Urge will pursue us."

"Don't worry," he replied. "You have not gotten high enough for it to pursue you. For the time being, you are still pursuing it."

What Is Punishable

A certain zaddik died and soon after appeared in a dream to Rabbi Pinhas, who had been his friend. Rabbi Pinhas asked him: "What is the attitude toward the sins of youth?"

"They are not taken seriously," said the dead man. "Not if a man has atoned. But false piety—that is punished with great severity."

The Pulpit

Once Rabbi Pinhas came into the House of Study and his glance fell on a pulpit. "This pulpit too," he said, "is judged on New Year's Day: whether it is to break or to be preserved."

The Barrier

Rabbi Pinhas said:

"On the sabbath, people come to hear words of teaching. They are full of fervor—and on the very first week-day everything is exactly as it was. For just as the senses, so memory too meets with a barrier. As soon as the holiness of the sabbath is over, all are a thousand miles away from it, and no one remembers it any more. It is as when a madman recovers: he is unable to remember what happened in the days of his madness."

The Pin in the Shirt

Once some women came to Rabbi Pinhas from a nearby town and bothered him with their trivial concerns. When he saw them at his door again on the following morning before prayer, he fled to his son's house and cried: "If only the Messiah came, so that we might get rid of the zaddikim, 'the good Jews.'" After a while, he added: "You think that it is the wicked who delay the coming of the Messiah. Not so—it is 'the good Jews' who are delaying it. A nail somewhere in the wall—what has that to do with me! But a pin sticking in my shirt—that's what pricks!"

Fame

The "Spola grandfather" said:

"To be famous is not a good thing.

"Once I went from town to town with the poor wayfarers. In

our wanderings we came to a town in which Rabbi Pinhas of Koretz was living at that time. There was feasting in his house and a large table was spread with food for the poor. I entered with the rest and sat down. Rabbi Pinhas himself went from one man to the next and gave each a cake. When he came to me, he raised me from the bench until I was level with his face, and kissed me on the forehead.

"When I was beginning to grow famous, I drove to his town to spend the sabbath with him. Dressed in a splendid robe, after the fashion of the famous, I approached and greeted him. He merely glanced at me and asked: 'Where are you from?'

"To be famous is not a good thing."

The Man Who Denies God

Rabbi Pinhas said: "Whoever says that the words of the Torah are one thing and the words of the world another, must be regarded as a man who denies God."

Dreams

Rabbi Pinhas said: "Dreams are a secretion of our thoughts and, through them, our thought is purified. All the wisdom in the world is a secretion of the Torah, and through it the Torah is purified. That is why we read: 'When the Lord brings back those that returned to Zion, we will be like unto them that dream.' For then it will be revealed that wisdom exists only that the Torah may be purified, and exile only that the thought of Israel may be purified, and all will be like a dream."

The Tongue of Tongues

They asked Rabbi Pinhas: "How are we to understand that before the building of the Tower of Babel, all men spoke one tongue in common, but that when God confounded their language, each group of people spoke its own tongue? How was it possible for each people suddenly to speak and understand a language of its own, instead of the tongue which had been common to them all?"

Rabbi Pinhas explained: "Before the building of the tower, all peoples had in common the holy tongue, but each people had its own language besides. That is why it is written: 'And the whole earth was of one language,' that is, the holy language, and 'of one speech' means that besides the holy language they had in common, each people had its own special tongue. This they used to communicate with one another, while the holy tongue was used between different peoples. When God punished them, he took from them the holy tongue."

Originality

Rabbi Pinhas said: "When a man embarks on something great, in the spirit of truth, he need not be afraid that another may imitate him. But if he does not do it in the spirit of truth, but plans to do it in a way no one could imitate, then he drags the great down to the lowest level—and everyone can do the same."

The Eunuchs

Once Rabbi Shmelke and his brother, who subsequently became the rabbi of Frankfort, drove to Rabbi Pinhas of Koretz in order to savor the true taste of the sabbath. They arrived on Friday and found the zaddik in the kitchen where, in honor of the holy hours to come, he was supervising the cooking of the fish. He greeted his guests with the words: "Isaiah says: 'Thus saith the Lord . . . concerning the eunuchs,' that is, those who cannot enjoy holy delight, 'let them keep my sabbaths.' Keep the sabbath and you will savor its full taste."

All Joys

Rabbi Pinhas said: "All joys hail from paradise, and jests too, provided they are uttered in true joy."

The Watchers

A wedding was once celebrated in the house of Rabbi Pinhas. The feasting went on for days, and the number of guests did not lessen, yet during all that time, nothing was damaged, not the smallest flask was broken. When the people expressed surprise at this, the rabbi said: "Why are you astonished? The dead are good watchers!" Now they understood why—while the dance was going on—he had called out: "You dead, you have nothing to do. Watch well that no damage is done!"

The Parting

Rabbi Leib, son of Sarah, the wandering zaddik, used to visit Rabbi Pinhas several times a year. They did not agree concerning worldly matters, because Rabbi Leib did his work all over the world, in a secret manner, while Rabbi Pinhas believed no one could do his work well except in that place which was appointed for him. But at parting he always said to his friend: "We shall never agree, but your work has Heaven for its goal, and my work has Heaven for its goal, and so we are united, and what we do is one and the same thing." Once Rabbi Leib came to Ostrog for the Day of Atonement. At the close of the service, he went to Rabbi Pinhas to exchange wishes for the coming year with him. The two closed the door and talked with each other for a time. When Rabbi Pinhas came out, his cheeks were wet and the tears still streamed from his eyes. As he accompanied Rabbi Leib out, the hasidim heard him say: "What can I do since it is your will to go first?" That year Rabbi Leib died toward the end of the winter, in the month Adar, and Rabbi Pinhas toward the end of summer, in the month Elul.

Mourning

In after years the hasidim related this incident. At the last bend in the road which leads to the west wall of the Temple, the "wailing wall," a zaddik saw a tall woman one evening. She was veiled from head to foot and wept softly to herself. Then his own eyes filled with tears and, for an instant, he could not see. When he looked up, the woman had vanished. "For whom can the Divine Presence be mourning, if not for Rabbi Pinhas!" he exclaimed to his soul, tore his robe, and said the blessing for the dead.

Testimony

Rabbi Rafael of Bershad was known far and wide for his integrity.

Once his testimony was to be the deciding factor in condemning a Jew who had been accused of a crime. Rabbi Rafael knew that the man was guilty. The night before the court was to assemble, he did not go to bed but struggled with himself in prayer until the dawn of day. Then he lay down on the floor, closed his eyes, and died on the instant.

YEHIEL MIKHAL OF ZLOTCHOV

The Want

In early life, Rabbi Yehiel Mikhal lived in great poverty, but not for an hour did happiness desert him.

Someone once asked him: "Rabbi, how can you pray day after day, 'Blessed be thou . . . who has supplied my every want?' For surely you lack everything a man has need of!" He replied: "My want is, most likely, poverty, and that is what I have been supplied with."

On Two Rungs

When Rabbi Mikhal was still poor and taught children in the city of Brusilov, a man who was fond of joking came to him on a Friday, toward evening, and asked him the following question: "How much effort and trouble must a poor man go through before he gets together what he needs for the sabbath! For the well-to-do burgher, on the other hand, it is no trouble at all. But when the sabbath arrives, and the poor man begins to study the tractate for the sabbath, the first thing he reads about are the circumstances under which a poor man who takes, becomes guilty of desecrating the sabbath, while the rich burgher who gives, is considered blameless. Why does it begin with the guilt of the poor man?"

In asking this, the man had nothing in mind but to make a jest, but Rabbi Mikhal took the question seriously. "Come and take the evening meal with me," he said. "I shall think it over until then." After the meal, he repeated the question and gave this answer: "The guilt of the poor man is mentioned in the beginning, because it is he who first stretched out his hand to take."

* * *

Many years later, while Rabbi Mordecai of Neskhizh was visiting his teacher Rabbi Mikhal, the maggid of Zlotchov, a devout and learned man came and asked for a little money. The maggid told Rabbi Mordecai to give him a small sum. A short time after this, a tramp who looked common and coarse also asked for alms. Rabbi Mikhal himself gave him something. When he was asked why he behaved differently in these two instances, he said: "Every act of charity can bring about a sacred union, if the hand of him who gives touches that of him who takes. But when the receiver is a man of slight value, then it is more difficult to accomplish this union."

The Cow

It is told:

During the years when the holy maggid of Zlotchov was still unrecognized, he was so poor that his wife had no shoes and went around in slippers she had made with her own hands. At that time he often fasted from one sabbath to the next, and did not come home from the House of Study the entire week. Each morning, his wife sold the milk of the one cow they owned, and with the proceeds supported herself and her children. One Friday morning the cow gave no milk, lay down, and did not move. After several hours, when all attempts to revive her had failed, the woman gave up in despair and hired a peasant to flay the animal. Before he had started on the job, Rabbi Mikhal came home. When he saw the cow lying in the courtyard he tapped her gently with his stick and said: "Hey there, get up! You have to provide for us!" And the cow got up.

The Baal Shem's Messenger

Before he was recognized, Rabbi Yehiel Mikhal lived in the city of Yampol, not far from Mezbizh, the city of the Baal Shem Tov. At that time the Baal Shem's hasidim included a cattle-dealer who used to come to his master before setting out on a business trip, in order to spend the sabbath near him. Once, when he was taking leave after a visit of this kind, the Baal Shem said to him: "When you get to Yampol, give Rabbi Mekhele my greetings."

But when he got to Yampol, the man asked around in vain

for a rabbi by that name. Finally he went to the House of Study and inquired there. "No," they said, "we have never heard of that rabbi." But someone added: "We do have a Mekhele here, but no one has ever called him 'rabbi.' As a matter of fact, the children call him 'the crazy man,' and no one except the children ever bothers about him. For how can one deal with a man who beats his head against the wall while he prays, until the blood spurts out!"

"I want to talk to him," said the cattle-dealer.

"That will not be so easy," they told him. "When he is at home and sitting over his books, he will not let anyone disturb him. But if you go up to him and whisper: 'I should like something to eat,' he will jump up to get food for his guest, and then you can talk to him."

The dealer asked the way to the "crazy man." He lived in a tumble-down house and ragged children were huddled at his door. Rabbi Mikhal was sitting at the table before an open book of the Kabbalah. He did not look up when his visitor entered. The man went up to him and said in a low tone: "I should like something to eat." Instantly the rabbi rose, looked around, and went through drawers and cupboards, but everything was empty. He picked up a book, ran out with it, took it to the store as a pledge, and brought back bread and herring. While his visitor ate, he said: "The Baal Shem Tov told me to give you his greetings." Rabbi Mikhal bowed his head in silence.

Later the cattle-dealer said: "Rabbi Mekhele, I see that you are a holy man, and since this is so, all you need do is to pray for wealth and you will have it. Why do you live in such want?"

"A king," replied the rabbi, "had made preparations for the wedding of his beloved daughter and invited all the people in the city where he lived into his palace. And inscribed on each invitation was the menu of the wedding-feast. But suddenly the princess fell ill. No doctor could do anything for her, and a few hours later she died. Quietly the people who had gathered for the celebration dispersed. They were full of sorrow for the death of their dear and lovely princess. Only one guest stayed. Holding his invitation in his hand, he asked to be served the entire menu, and they did as he asked. There he sat and smacked his lips over his food in shameless pleasure. Shall I behave as he, now that the Divine Presence, which is the Community of Israel, is in exile?"

Refusal

The people of a certain city begged the Baal Shem Tov to induce his disciple Yehiel Mikhal to accept the position of rabbi, which they had offered him. The Baal Shem Tov urged him to accept, but he persisted in his refusal. "If you do not listen to me," said his master, "you will lose this world and the coming world too."

"Even if I lose both worlds," answered his disciple, "I shall not accept what does not befit me."

"Then, receive my blessing, my son," said the Baal Shem, "that you have withstood temptation."

The Revealed Secret

Rabbi Hayyim, the famous head of the Talmudic Academy in Brody, heard of the powerful effect the exhortations of young Rabbi Mikhal had on his hearers. Since the number of evildoers in Brody was increasing, he asked him to speak in the great House of Prayer on the coming sabbath, and ordered the entire congregation to attend. Rabbi Mikhal ascended the pulpit and put his head down on the desk. For a good while he stood in that position. The congregation became impatient, and the worst of the ne'er-do-wells were most indignant that so young a man had the impudence to make them wait. Some of them went up to him to snatch him from the pulpit, but they did not dare carry out their purpose when they saw the director of the Talmudic Academy leaning against a pillar of the pulpit and clasping it with his hands. At last Rabbi Mikhal raised his head: "It is written," he said: " 'The secret counsel of the Lord is with them that fear Him.' Secret transgressions He reveals to those who fear him, that their warning may strike straight into the hearts of the transgressors." Everyone in the House of Prayer heard these words, although they were uttered in a low voice, and there was not one who could keep back the tears welling in his eyes.

Through the Hat

Once Rabbi Mikhal visited a city where he had never been before. Soon some of the prominent members of the congregation came to call on him. He fixed a long gaze on the forehead of everyone who came, and then told him the flaws in his soul and what he could do to heal them. It got around that there was a zaddik in the city who was versed in reading faces, and could tell the quality of the soul by looking at the forehead. The next visitors pulled their hats down to their noses. "You are mistaken," Rabbi Mikhal said to them. "An eye which can see through the flesh, can certainly see through the hat."

The Time Rabbi Elimelekh Was Frightened

In his later years, Rabbi Elimelekh of Lizhensk, who was on a journey, met a young man with a knapsack on his back. "Where are you bound for?" he asked him.

"I am going to the holy maggid of Zlotchov," was the reply.

"When I was young," said Rabbi Elimelekh, "I heard one day that Rabbi Yehiel Mikhal was visiting a town not far from Lizhensk. I immediately started on my way there. When I arrived, I looked for a place to stay, but all the houses were empty. Finally I found a very old woman busy at her stove. This is what she told me: 'Everyone has gone to the House of Prayer. There's a rabbi there who has made the day into a Day of Atonement. There he stands and is telling everyone his sins, and praying forgiveness for everyone.' When I heard that, I was frightened and went back to Lizhensk."

Heavy Penance

There was once a man who had desecrated the sabbath against his will because his carriage had broken down, and although

142

he walked and almost ran, he did not reach the town before the beginning of the holy hours. For this, young Rabbi Mikhal imposed a very harsh and long penance on him. The man tried to do as he had been told with all his strength, but he soon found that his body could not endure it. He began to feel ill, and even his mind became affected. About this time he learned that the Baal Shem was traveling through this region and had stopped in a place nearby. He went to him, mustered his courage, and begged the master to rid him of the sin he had committed. "Carry a pound of candles to the House of Prayer," said the Baal Shem, "and have them lit for the sabbath. Let that be your penance." The man thought the zaddik had not quite understood what he had told him and repeated his request most urgently. When the Baal Shem insisted on his incredibly mild dictum, the man told him how heavy a penance had been imposed on him. "You just do as I said," the master replied. "And tell Rabbi Mikhal to come to the city of Chvostov where I shall hold the coming sabbath." The man's face had cleared. He took leave of the rabbi. On the way to Chvostov, a wheel broke on Rabbi Mikhal's carriage and he had to continue on foot. Although he hurried all he could, it was dark when he entered the town, and when he crossed the Baal Shem's threshold, he saw he had already risen, his hand on the cup, to say the blessing over the wine to introduce the day of rest. The master paused and said to Rabbi Mikhal who was standing before him numb and speechless: "Good sabbath, my sinless friend! You had never tasted the sorrow of the sinner, your heart had never throbbed with his despair—and so it was easy for your hand to deal out penance."

To Himself

In a sermon which Rabbi Mikhal once gave before a large gathering, he said: "My words shall be heeded." And he added immediately: "I do not say: 'You shall heed my words,' I say: 'My words shall be heeded.' I address myself too! I too must heed my words!"

Humility No Commandment

They asked the maggid of Zlotchov: "All the commandments are written in the Torah. But humility, which is worth all the other virtues put together, is not stated in it as a command-ment. All we read about it is the words in praise of Moses, saying that he was more humble than all other people. What is the significance of this silence concerning humility?"

The rabbi replied: "If anyone were humble in order to keep a commandment, he would never attain to true humility. To think humility is a commandment is the prompting of Satan. He bloats a man's heart telling him he is learned and righteous and devout, a master in all good works, and worthy to think himself better than the general run of people; but that this would be proud and impious since it is a commandment that he must be humble and put himself on a par with others. And a man who interprets this as a commandment and does it, only feeds his pride the more in doing so."

The Help Meet

The maggid of Zlotchov was asked by one of his disciples: "The Talmud says that the child in the womb of his mother looks from one end of the world to the other, and knows all the teachings, but that the instant it comes in contact with the air of earth, an angel strikes it on the mouth, and it forgets everything. I do not understand why this should be: first know everything and then forget it?"

"A trace is left behind in man," the rabbi answered, "by dint of which he can re-acquire knowledge of the world and the teachings, and do his service."

"But why must the angel strike him?" asked the disciple. "If this were not so, there would be no evil."

"Quite true," the rabbi answered. "But if there were no evil, there would be no good, for good is the counterpart of evil. Everlasting delight is no delight. That is how we must interpret what we are taught: that the creation of the world took place for the good of its creatures. And that is why it is written: 'It is not good that the man'—that is to say the primal man

God created—'should be alone,' that is, without the counter-effect and the hindrance of the Evil Urge, as before the creation of the world. For there is no good, unless its counterpart exists. And further on we read: 'I will make him a help meet for him'—the fact that evil confronts good gives man the possibility of victory: of rejecting evil and choosing good, and only then does the good exist truly and perfectly."

Man and the Evil Urge

This is what Rabbi Mikhal said concerning the verse in the Scriptures: "Let us take our journey, and let us go, and I will go before thee."
"That is what the Evil Urge says to man secretly. For this Urge is to become good and wants to become good by driving man to overcome it, and to make it good. And that is his secret request to the man he is trying to seduce: 'Let us leave this disgraceful state and take service with the Creator, so that I too may go and mount with you rung by rung, although I seem to oppose, to disturb, and hinder you.' "

Multiply

A disciple tells:
Once, when my teacher Rabbi Yehiel Mikhal was in his prayer room in Brody, he heard a man reciting the six hundred and thirteen commandments. He said jestingly: "Why are you reciting the commandments? They were given to do, not to recite!" I asked him what he meant by this, whether we are not supposed to teach and learn the commandments too. "In the case of every commandment," he said, "we should try to discover how it can be done. Let us begin with the first of all commandments: 'Be fruitful and multiply.' Why do you think two verbs are used here instead of one?" I was silent because I was ashamed to speak, but when he repeated his question, I said: "Rashi interprets it in this way: If it only said 'be fruitful,' we might think that one man should always beget only one child." "But then," he objected, "it would be enough to say merely: 'multiply.' "

The son of Rabbi Zusya of Hanipol, who was also saying his prayers there, pointed out that in another passage, it is written: "And I will . . . make you fruitful and multiply you," that here also two verbs were used.

"This too is difficult," said Rabbi Mikhal and again put his question to me. I mentioned that Rashi refers the words 'and will multiply you' to the upright posture which distinguishes man from animals.

"But what has it to do with upright posture?" asked the rabbi. I did not know what to say. He said: "This is the way Rabbi Mendel of Primishlan expounded the verse in the Mishnah: 'He who rides the ass shall dismount and pray,' that is, 'he who masters the animal within him, need not suppress it, since—in an eternal prayer—he is devoted and consecrated to God in all that he does, and has become freed of his body.' Thus man can perform bodily acts in this world. He can cohabit, and though—seen from the outside—his movements may be those of an animal, within he is free as an angel, for in what he does, he is devoted and consecrated to God. And this is what is meant by the commandment: 'Be fruitful,' not like animals—but 'multiply,' and that means be *more* than they! Do not walk bent over, but upright, and cling to God as the bough clings to the root, and consecrate your cohabitation to him. This is the will of God; not only to make us fruitful, but to multiply our powers."

Learn from All

They asked Rabbi Mikhal: "In the Sayings of the Fathers we read: 'Who is wise?' He who learns from all men, as it is said, 'From all my teachers I have gotten understanding.' Then why does it not say: 'He who learns from every teacher'?"

Rabbi Mikhal explained: "The master who pronounced these words, is intent on having it clear that we can learn not only from those whose occupation is to teach, but from every man. Even from one who is ignorant, or from one who is wicked, you can gain understanding as to how to conduct your life."

146

The Unity of Qualities

Rabbi Yehiel Mikhal said:

"The words in the Scriptures: 'But ye that cleave unto the Lord your God are alive every one of you this day,' is expounded as follows: 'Cleave to his qualities.' But this must be properly understood. Emanating from God are ten qualities and these come in twos which oppose each other like two colors, one of which is apparently in direct contrast to the other. But seen with the true inner eye, they all form one simple unity. It is the task of man to make them appear a unity to the true outer eye, as well. Perhaps one man finds it difficult to be merciful, because his way is to be rigorous, and another finds it difficult to be rigorous because his way is merciful. But he who binds the rigor within him to its root: to the rigor of God, and the mercy which is in him to its root: to the mercy of God, and so on in all things, such a man will unite the ten qualities within himself, and he himself will become the unity they represent, for he cleaves to the Lord of the world. Such a man has become wax into which both judgment and mercy can set their seal."

Imitation of the Fathers

The maggid of Zlotchov was asked by one of his disciples: "In the book of Elijah we read: 'Everyone in Israel is in duty bound to say: When will my work approach the works of my fathers, Abraham, Isaac and Jacob.' How are we to understand this? How could we ever venture to think that we could do what our fathers could?"

The rabbi expounded: "Just as our fathers invented new ways of serving, each a new service according to his own character: one the service of love, the other that of stern justice, the third that of beauty, so each one of us in his own way shall devise something new in the light of the teachings and of service, and do what has not yet been done."

Not for Wages

They asked the maggid of Zlotchov: "It is written: 'If ye walk in My statutes, and keep My commandments, and do them;

then I will give your rains in their season, and the land shall yield her produce, and the trees of the field shall yield their fruit.' How is it that God promises us wages for serving him? For our sages have told us that we shall not be like servants who serve their master on condition that they receive wages." The zaddik made this reply: "It is true that whoever does a commandment for the sake of gain, even if it be gain in the coming world, gets nothing, for all he wanted to do was serve himself. But he who does a commandment out of the true fear and love of God, his doing shines out into the world and draws an abundance of blessings down upon it. Thus the favor of Heaven and earth is a sign of right doing, not for sake of gain, but for the sake of God himself. That is why it is written: 'I have set before thee life and death, the blessing and the curse; therefore choose life that thou mayst live, thou and thy seed!' Choose the deed of life which brings abundance of life into the world!"

With

This is what Rabbi Mikhal said concerning the verse in the psalm, "Thou hast dealt well with thy servant":
"What you have done, O Lord, can be designated by the word 'with.' When your servant does your commandment, you are acting along with him. But you give him credit for doing it, as though he had acted alone, without your help."

The Nature of the Teachings

No matter what book Rabbi Mikhal was reading, whether a book of the open or the hidden teachings, everything he read seemed to him to point to the service of God. When one of his disciples asked him how this was possible, he replied: "Could there be anything in the teachings which does not point out to us, how to serve God?"

Our Disgrace

Rabbi Mikhal said: "This is our disgrace, that we fear anyone besides God. That is what is said of Jacob in the words: 'Then

148

Jacob was afraid and he was distressed.' We must be distressed because of our fear of Esau."

Keeping the Law

Disciples asked the maggid of Zlotchov: "In the Talmud we read that our Father Abraham kept all the laws. How could this be, since they had not yet been given to him?"

"All that is needful," he said, "is to love God. If you are about to do something and you think it might lessen your love, then you will know it is sin. If you are about to do something and think it will increase your love, you will know that your will is in keeping with the will of God. That is what Abraham did."

Between

Concerning the verse in the Scriptures: "I stood between the Lord and you," Rabbi Mikhal of Zlotchov said: "The 'I' stands between God and us. When a man says 'I' and encroaches upon the word of his Maker, he puts a wall between himself and God. But he who offers his 'I'—there is nothing between him and his Maker. For it is to him that the words refer: 'I am my beloved's and his desire is toward me.' When my 'I' has become my beloved's, then it is toward me that his desire turns."

Sanctification of God

The disciples of the maggid of Zlotchov asked him: "Concerning the words in the Scriptures: 'Ye shall be holy; for I the Lord your God am holy,' the Midrash comments: 'My holiness is beyond your holiness.' But who does not know this? What do we learn through this?"

He expounded: "This is what is meant: My holiness, which is the world, depends upon your holiness. As you sanctify my name below, so is it sanctified in the heights of Heaven. For it is written: 'Give ye strength unto God.' "

The Praying Rabbi

They asked Rabbi Yehiel Mikhal why he was delaying the prayer. He answered: "We are told that the tribe of Dan went last of all the wandering tribes and gathered up everything they had lost. The children of Dan gathered up all the prayers which had been said by the sons of Israel without true fervor, and, therefore, were lying on the ground. That is just what I am doing."

* * *

He expounded the passage in the Talmud which states that the first hasidim waited for a time before they began to pray, in order to concentrate their hearts on God: "During the time they were waiting, they prayed to God to help them concentrate their hearts on him."

* * *

Before beginning to pray, he was in the habit of saying: "I join myself to all of Israel, to those who are more than I, that through them my thought may rise, and to those who are less than I, so that they may rise through my thought."

* * *

Concerning the heading of the psalm, "A prayer of the afflicted when he fainteth," he said: "Join yourself to the prayer of the afflicted and you will cleave to God."

* * *

The Evil Urge once came to him while he was praying. "Go away," he said to it, "and come back when I am eating. While one is praying, there must be no arguments."

* * *

His disciples asked him: "Why is 'every knee shall bow to thee,' mentioned first in the prayer? Why does 'every stature shall prostrate itself before thee alone,' come second? Why is the word 'alone' used only in the one case and not in the other?" He explained: "Knees must be bowed before a king of flesh and blood, so that the gesture of homage can be seen. But only before the King of Kings, only before Him who examines the heart, can what is upright remain upright and yet, in reality, be bowed before Him."

* * *

To Rabbi Wolf of Zbarazh, one of his five sons, Rabbi Mikhal once said: "When I had risen in prayer, and was standing in the hall of truth, I begged God to grant me that my reason might never proceed against his truth."

The Rich Man

Once when Rabbi Mikhal was in the city of Brody on a long visit, he made a habit of praying in the "Klaus" which went by the name of "Hasidim-Study" although many opponents of the hasidic teachings attended the daily service there. Now Rabbi Mikhal did not arrive in the House of Prayer until noon, and even after he had put the prayer shawl over his shoulder, he waited for quite a while before he put it on, bound on the phylacteries, and commenced to pray. His learned enemies were annoyed at this but did not venture to question him themselves. After much reflection and considerable discussion, they sent a rich man, by the name of Zalman Perles, to the rabbi. He went up to the zaddik and asked in respectful tones: "We do not quarrel with the fact that you do not come to the House of Prayer until noon, for, most likely, you are not ready in your heart before then. But what does surprise us is that when you have come, you stand there for such a long time before you finally begin to pray. Why do you do this, and what does it mean?"

Rabbi Mikhal asked in his turn: "Is there no one more learned than you here, to put this question to me?"

"Yes, indeed!" answered Perles. "There are men here, so learned, that I do not reach even to their ankles."

"And why," said the zaddik, "don't they ask me?"

"Well," the other replied, "they are poor, and they have broken hearts—as poor men have. But I am rich and my heart is sound."

"Well, then," said the rabbi, "you yourself admit that the teachings do not ask me why I delay my prayer; only sixty thousand rubles are asking me. But sixty thousand rubles shall not have the pleasure of hearing me reveal why I delay my prayer."

The Great Chorus

Rabbi Mordecai of Kremnitz, the son of Rabbi Mikhal, related: "My father used to intone the verse in the psalm: 'My mouth shall speak the praise of the Lord,' as a question. 'We ask ourselves,' he explained to me, 'how our mouth can speak the praise of God. For do not the seraphim and the hosts of Heaven tremble and grow faint at the greatness of his name? To this the Scriptures reply: And let all flesh bless His holy name. All flesh, all that is living—just because it is flesh, it is called upon to praise Him. We read in the Section of Songs that even the smallest earthworm chants a song to Him. All the more man, who has been granted the power to think up more and more new ways of praising his Maker.' "

Participation

This was Rabbi Mikhal's comment on the words of Hillel, "If I am not for myself, who will be for me? And if I am for myself, what am I?" " 'If I am not for myself,' that is, if I do not work for myself alone, but continually participate in the congregation, 'who will be for me?' In that case, whatever 'who,' that is, whatever any member of the congregation does in my place, counts just as though I had done it myself. But if I am 'for myself'—if I do not participate with others, if I do not join with them, 'what am I?' Then everything in the way of good works which I have wrought alone is less than nothing in the eyes of God, who is the source of all good."

The Naming

They asked the maggid of Zlotchov: "We read in the Scriptures that God brought the animals to Adam that he might name them. And why does it say that whatsoever the man called a creature, according to its living soul, that was to be his name. What is meant by 'living soul'?"
He replied: "You know that every being has the root of its soul, from which it receives its life, in the upper worlds. Now Adam knew the soul-roots of all creatures and gave each its right name, each according to its living soul."

Dubious Faith

A disciple asked the maggid of Zlotchov: "The words in the Scriptures that Noah went into the ark 'because of the waters of the flood' Rashi interprets to the effect that Noah had small faith. He believed, and yet he did not believe, and not until the waters of the flood compelled him, did he go into the ark. Shall we really count Noah, that righteous man, among those who were small of faith?"

The zaddik replied: "There are two sorts of faith: simple faith, which accepts the word and waits to see it fulfilled, and working faith whose power contributes to the fulfillment of that which is to be. With all his heart Noah feared to believe in the coming of the flood, so that his faith might not make that coming more sure. And so he believed and did not believe, until the waters compelled him."

Up the Mountain

Rabbi Yehiel Mikhal said: "It is written: 'Who shall ascend into the mountain of the Lord? And who shall stand in His holy place?' For the sake of comparison, let us take a man who rides up a mountain in his carriage, and when he is half-way up, the horses are tired and he must stop and give them a rest. Now, whoever has no sense at this point, will roll down. But he who has sense will take a stone and put it under the wheel while the carriage is standing. Then he will be able to reach the top. The man who does not fall, when he is forced to interrupt his service, but knows how to pause, will get to the top of the mountain of the Lord."

Temptation

Rabbi Mikhal said: "When the Evil Urge tries to tempt man to sin, it tempts him to become all too righteous."

The Hair Shirt

Rabbi Yudel, a man known for his fear of God and the harsh penances he imposed on himself, once came to visit the maggid of Zlotchov. Rabbi Mikhal said to him: "Yudel, you are wearing a hair shirt against your flesh. If you were not given to sudden anger, you would not need it, and since you are given to sudden anger, it will not help you."

His Sleep

The Rabbi of Apt told, "When my teacher, Rabbi Yehiel Mikhal slept, he looked like one or the other of the angel-beings of the chariot of God: sometimes he had the face of the spiritual animals and sometimes that of the holy wheel-beings; the one when he wanted to mount to the firmament, the other when a call from the firmament reached him."

The Sabbath of Rest

A hasid asked the maggid of Zlotchov: "Rashi, our teacher, says: 'What was lacking in the created world? Nothing but rest. Came the sabbath, and so rest came.' Why does he not just say: 'The world lacked rest until the sabbath came?' For the words 'sabbath' and 'rest' mean exactly the same thing."

"Sabbath," replied the rabbi, "means the homecoming. On that day all the spheres return to their true place. That is what Rashi refers to: during the week, the spheres find no rest because they have been lowered from the place which is theirs. But on the sabbath they find rest because they are allowed to go home."

Satan's Hasidim

In his old age, Rabbi Mikhal fasted on many occasions. Finally one of his disciples ventured to ask him the reason for this self-mortification. The rabbi answered: "I must tell you that Satan has made up his mind to rid the world of hasidim. First he tried to harass us: he instigated persecutions; he had us maligned and denounced. He fanned the flames of enmity in houses and alleys, and thought that in these ways he could make us despair, that we should grow exhausted, and become renegades. But when he realized that his plan had miscarried, and that the ranks he had wanted to weaken, were strengthened, he thought up something new. He decided to make hasidim of his own. Soon after, thousands of Satan's hasidim spread over the land and joined forces with the true hasidim, so that truth was mixed with falsehood. That is why I fasted. I thought I could thwart this plan of his too. But now I shall not fast any more, for I see that I cannot keep Satan from continuing to make his own hasidim. But those who consecrate and truly dedicate themselves to the service of God—those God will separate from the false hasidim. He will light their eyes with the light of His face, so that for them truth will not be mixed with lies."

The Suns and the Earth

Rabbi Mikhal said:

"In every generation there are great zaddikim who shirk the work of salvation by devoting themselves to the Torah. As they fulfil the commandments, each of them ponders on what holy place his soul came from, and is intent on having it go home to that place after its earthly journey is accomplished, to rejoice in the light of heavenly wisdom. That is why to such a man the things of this earth are as nothing. And though he is saddened by the misery among men and the bitter exile of Israel, this is not enough to move his heart to dare in prayer what must be dared. All his great longing is directed solely to his own homecoming, as it is written: 'One generation passeth away, and another generation cometh; and the earth abideth forever. The sun also riseth and the sun goeth down, and hasteth to his place where he ariseth.' Suns rise and go down and let the misery on earth endure."

Banishment and Salvation

A disciple asked the maggid of Zlotchov: "God said to Moses: 'Now shalt thou see what I shall do to Pharaoh; for by a strong hand shall he let them go, and by a strong hand shall he drive them out of his land.' Need the thrall who is freed from heavy servitude be driven into freedom? Will he not hasten from it as the bird from the snare?"

"When Israel is banished," said the maggid, "it is always because it has put the ban on itself, and only when Israel dissolves this self-imposed ban, does it attain to salvation. When it overcomes the power of evil within itself, the demonic power of evil is broken, and instantly the rulers of earth also lose their power to subjugate Israel. Because Israel in Egypt was not willing to return from spiritual exile, Moses said to the Lord: '. . . neither hast thou delivered thy people at all.' This means: 'It is not you who can deliver them.' But God replies: 'Now shalt thou see . . .' And he, who is more powerful than all the powers, keeps the covenant. He casts his great light on the demonic power of Egypt and dazzles it. But the holy sparks which were banned into it, awake; each finds its kin. The sparks behold the primal light and flame toward it, until the demonic power cannot endure them any longer and is forced to drive them out. And the moment this happens above, it also happens below in Israel and in Pharaoh. This is the significance of the plagues."

The Blessing

Rabbi Mikhal once said to his sons: "My life was blessed in that I never needed anything until I had it."

Love for Enemies

Rabbi Mikhal gave this command to his sons: "Pray for your enemies that all may be well with them. And should you think this is not serving God, rest assured that more than all prayers, this is, indeed, the service of God."

Willing

In the last two years before his death, Rabbi Mikhal fell into a trance of ecstasy time after time. On these occasions, he went back and forth in his room, his face aglow with inner light, and one could see that he was clinging to a higher life rather than to earthly existence, and that his soul had only to make one small step to pass into it. That is why his children were always careful to rouse him from his ecstasy at the right moment. Once, after the third sabbath meal, which he always had with his sons, he went to the House of Study as usual, and sang songs of praise. Then he returned to his room and walked up and down. At that time, no one was with him. Suddenly his daughter, who was passing his door, heard him repeat over and over: "Willingly did Moses die. Willingly did Moses die." She was greatly troubled and called one of her brothers. When he entered, he found his father lying on the floor on his back, and heard him whisper the last word of the confession "One," with his last breath.

From World to World

Many years after Rabbi Mikhal's death, young Rabbi Zevi Hirsh of Zhydatchov saw him in a dream. The dead man said to him: "Know, that from the moment I died, I have been wandering from world to world. And the world which yesterday was spread over my head as Heaven, is today the earth under my feet, and the Heaven of today is the earth of tomorrow."

"After He Had Gone in to Bath-sheba"

To Rabbi Aaron Leib of Primishlan, a disciple of the maggid of Zlotchov, came a man on whose face he read signs of having comitted adultery. When he had talked with his caller for a time, he said to him: "It is written: 'A Psalm of David; when Nathan the prophet came unto him, after he had gone in to Bath-sheba.' What can this mean? It means that Nathan chose the right way to move David to turn to God. Had he confronted him publicly and as his judge, he would only have hardened his heart. But he came to censure David in secrecy and love, just as David himself had gone in to Bath-sheba. And then his censure went to the king's heart and melted and recast it, and from it mounted the song of one recast and turned to God." When Rabbi Aaron Leib finished speaking, the man confessed his sin and turned wholly to God.

ZEV WOLF OF ZBARAZH

In the Last Hour

On a certain New Year's night, the maggid of Zlotchov saw a man who had been a reader in his city, and who had died a short time ago. "What are you doing here?" he asked.

"The rabbi knows," said the dead man, "that in this night, souls are incarnated anew. I am such a soul."

"And why were you sent out again?" asked the maggid.

"I led an impeccable life here on earth," the dead man told him.

"And yet you are forced to live once more?" the maggid went on to ask.

"Before my death," said the man, "I thought over everything I had done and found that I had always acted in just the right way. Because of this, my heart swelled with satisfaction and in the midst of this feeling I died. So now they have sent me back into the world to atone for my pride."

At that time a son was born to the maggid. His name was Rabbi Wolf. He was very humble.

His Tears

In his childhood, Rabbi Zev Wolf, the youngest of Rabbi Yehiel Mikhal's five sons, was a wild and self-willed boy. It was in vain that his father tried to curb him. When he was almost thirteen years old and about to become a "son of commandment" who would be responsible for himself and establish his own relation toward the will of God, the zaddik ordered the verses from the Scriptures written for the phylacteries the boy was to wear from this time on. Then he bade the scribe bring him the two empty boxes together with the verses from the Scriptures. The scribe brought them. Rabbi Mikhal took the boxes in his hand and looked at them for a long time. He bowed his head over them and his tears flowed into them. Then he dried the boxes and put into them the verses from the Scriptures. From the hour the boy Wolf put on the phylacteries for the first time, he grew tranquil and was filled with love.

The Servant

Rabbi Wolf's wife had a quarrel with her servant. She accused the girl of having broken a dish and wanted her to pay for the damage. The girl, on the other hand, denied having done what she was accused of, and refused to replace the article. The quarrel became more and more heated. Finally the wife of Rabbi Wolf decided to refer the matter to the court of arbitration of the Torah, and quickly dressed for a visit to the rav of the town. When Rabbi Wolf saw this, he too put on his sabbath clothes. When his wife asked him why, he told her that he intended accompanying her. She objected to this on the grounds that this was not fitting for him, and that besides, she knew very well what to say to the court. "You know it very well," the zaddik replied. "But the poor orphan, your servant, in whose behalf I am coming, does not know it, and who except me is there to defend her cause?"

The Radish Eater

At the third meal on the sabbath, an intimate and holy gathering, the hasidim at Rabbi Wolf's table carried on their conversation in a low voice and with subdued gestures so as not to disturb the zaddik who was deep in thought. Now, it was Rabbi Wolf's wish and the rule in his house that anyone could come in at any time, and seat himself at his table. On this occasion too, a man entered and sat down with the rest, who made room for him although they knew that he was an ill-bred person. After a time, he pulled a large radish out of his pocket, cut it into a number of pieces of convenient size, and began to eat with a great smacking of lips. His neighbors were unable to restrain their annoyance any longer. "You glutton," they said to him. "How dare you offend this festive board with your taproom manners?"

Although they had tried to keep down their voices, the zaddik soon noticed what was going on. "I just feel like eating a really good radish," he said. "I wonder whether anyone here could get me one?" In a sudden flood of happiness which swept away his embarrassment, the radish eater offered Rabbi Wolf a handful of the pieces he had cut.

The Coachman

On a freezing cold day, Rabbi Wolf drove to the celebration of a circumcision. When he had spent a little time in the room, he felt sorry for the coachman waiting outside, went to him, and said: "Come in and get warm."

"I cannot leave my horses alone," the man replied, moved his arms, and stamped his feet.

"I'll take care of them until you get warm and can relieve me again," said Rabbi Wolf. At first the coachman refused to consider such a thing, but after a while he allowed the rabbi to persuade him, and went into the house. There everyone who came, regardless of rank or whether or not he was known to the host, got all the food and drink he wanted. After the tenth glass, the coachman had forgotten who was taking his place with the horses, and stayed hour after hour. In the meantime, people had missed the zaddik but told themselves that he had had something important to attend to, and would return when he was through. A good deal later, some of the guests left. When they came out on the street, where night was already falling, they saw Rabbi Wolf standing beside the carriage, moving his arms and stamping his feet.

The Horses

When Rabbi Wolf drove out in a carriage, he never permitted the whip to be used on the horses. "You do not even have to shout at them," he instructed the coachman. "You just have to know how to talk to them."

The Quarrelers

Rabbi Wolf saw no evil in any man and regarded all human beings as righteous. Once, when two persons were quarreling,

160

and Rabbi Wolf was asked to side against the one who was guilty, he said: "According to me, one is as good as the other —and who would venture to come between two righteous men?"

The Gamblers

A hasid complained to Rabbi Wolf that certain persons were turning night into day, playing cards. "That is good," said the zaddik. "Like all people, they want to serve God and don't know how. But now they are learning to stay awake and persist in doing something. When they have become perfect in this, all they need do is turn to God—and what excellent servants they will make for him then!"

The Thieves

One night, thieves entered Rabbi Wolf's house and took whatever they happened to find. From his room the zaddik watched them but did not do anything to stop them. When they were through, they took some utensils and among them a jug from which a sick man had drunk that very evening. Rabbi Wolf ran after them. "My good people," he said, "whatever you have found here, I beg you to regard as gifts from me. I do not begrudge these things to you at all. But please be careful about that jug! The breath of a sick man is clinging to it, and you might catch his disease!"

From this time on, he said every evening before going to bed: "All my possessions are common property," so that—in case thieves came again—they would not be guilty of theft.

Renegades

A number of zaddikim met in Lwow and discussed the corrupt ways of the new generation. There were many who were giving up the holy customs, wearing shorter robes, cutting their beards and the curls at their temples, and would soon backslide spiritually as well. They thought it imperative to do something to stop the stones from crumbling, or else—on a day none too far off—the entire lofty structure would be bound to collapse. And so those who had met to confer on this matter resolved to set up solid bounds, and to make a beginning by forbidding renegades to appeal to the court of arbitration. But they agreed not to make this decision effective until they had the consent of Rabbi Wolf of Zbarazh. Several zaddikim reported to him the results of the meeting and made their request. "Do you think I love you more than them?" he asked. The decision was never put into effect.

Assistance

While Rabbi Wolf was on a journey, a poor young hasid came up to him and asked for financial assistance. The zaddik looked in his purse, put back a large coin he had happened to find, fetched out a smaller one and gave it to the needy young man. "A young man," he said, "should not have to be ashamed, but neither should he expect Heaven knows what." The hasid went from him with bowed head.

Rabbi Wolf called him back and asked: "Young man, what was that you were just thinking?"

"I have learned a new way to serve God," the other replied. "One should not be ashamed, and one should not expect Heaven knows what."

"That is what I meant," said the zaddik and accorded him help.

MORDECAI OF NESKHIZH

What Does It Matter

Before Rabbi Mordecai of Neskhizh had recognized his vocation, he ran a small business. After every trip he took to sell his wares, he set aside a little money to buy himself a citron for the Feast of Tabernacles. When he had managed to collect a few rubles in this way, he drove to the city and on the way there thought only of whether it would be vouchsafed him to buy the finest of the citrons for sale. Suddenly he saw a water vendor standing in the middle of the road and lamenting his horse which had collapsed. He left his carriage and gave the man all the money he had to buy himself another. "What does it matter?" he said to himself as he turned to go back home. "Everybody will say the blessing over the citron; I shall say mine over this horse!" But when he reached his house, he found a beautiful citron which friends, in the meantime, had brought him as a gift.

With the Prince of the Torah

To those who came to him to share the sabbath meal, Rabbi Mordecai rarely said words of teaching, and then only a very few. When one of his sons once ventured to ask him the reason for this restraint, he replied: "One must unite with the angel-prince of the Torah in order to receive in one's heart the word of teaching. Only then, does what one says enter the heart of one's hearers so that each receives what he requires for his own particular needs."

The Promise

Rabbi Mordecai used to say: "Whoever has eaten of my sabbath meal will not leave the world without having turned to God."

At Dawn

Once Rabbi Mordecai sat with his disciples all night until break of day. When he saw the light of dawn, he said: "We have not transgressed the bounds of day. Rather has day transgressed our bounds and we need not cede to it."

The Standard

Rabbi Mordecai of Neskhizh said to his son, the rabbi of Kovel: "My son, my son! He who does not feel the pains of a woman giving birth within a circuit of fifty miles, who does not suffer with her, and pray that her suffering may be assuaged, is not worthy to be called a zaddik."

His younger son Yitzhak, who later succeeded him in his work, was ten years old at the time. He was present when this was said. When he was old he told the story and added: "I listened well. But it was very long before I understood why he had said it in my presence."

Why People Go to the Zaddik

Rabbi Mordecai said: "People go to the zaddikim for many different reasons. One goes to the zaddik to learn how to pray with fear and love; another to acquire strength to study the Torah for its own sake. Still another goes because he wants to mount to a higher rung of spiritual life, and so on. But none of these things should be the true purpose of going, for each of them can be attained, and then it is no longer necessary to toil for it. The only, the true purpose, should be to seek the reality of God. No bounds are set to this, and it has no end."

The Fish in the Sea

Rabbi Yitzhak of Neskhizh told:

"Once my father said to one of his friends, in the month of Elul: 'Do you know what day this is? It is one of the days when the fish tremble in the ocean.'"

One of the men standing near Rabbi Yitzhak, observed: "People usualy say, 'when the fish tremble in the waters.'"

"The way my father said it," Rabbi Yitzhak replied, "that is the only way it expresses the secret of what occurs between God and the souls."

The Offering

This is how Rabbi Mordecai of Neskhizh expounded the words in the Scriptures: "And in your new moons ye shall present a burnt-offering unto the Lord."

If you want to renew your doing, offer up to God the first thought you have on awaking. God will help him who accomplishes this, to be bonded to Him the whole day, and to bind everything to that first thought.

Seeing and Hearing

A rabbi came to the zaddik of Neskhizh and asked: "Is it true, what people say, that you hear and see all things?"

"Think of the words of our sages," he replied, " 'a seeing eye, and a hearing ear.' Man has been so created that he can see and hear whatever he wants to. It is only a question of his not corrupting his eyes and his ears."

The Skull Cap

It is told:

A woman came to Rabbi Mordecai of Neskhizh and begged him with many tears to find out the whereabouts of her husband who had left her years ago and gone to a foreign country. "What makes you think I could help you?" said the zaddik. "Is he here? Is he perhaps in the water-barrel over there?"

Now, because her faith was great, the woman went to the water-barrel and looked in. "There he is!" she cried. "There he is, sitting in the water!"

"Has he a hat on?" asked the rabbi.

"Only his skull cap."

"Then fetch it."

The woman reached for it and drew it out. At the very same moment her husband, who was carrying on his tailor's trade in a far-away land, was sitting at the window of the house of a lord for whom he happened to be sewing, when a storm-wind rose and blew the cap off his head. The man shook in every limb. The core of his heart trembled and he started on his way home.

Lilith

They tell:

A man of whom Lilith had taken possession traveled to Neskhizh, where he wanted to beg Rabbi Mordecai to free him. The rabbi divined that this man was on the way to him and gave orders throughout the city to have all doors closed at nightfall, and to admit no one. When the man reached the city at dusk, he could not find a lodging, and had to lie down on some hay in a loft. Instantly Lilith appeared and said: "Come down to me."

He asked: "Why do you want to do that? Usually it is you who come to me."

"In the hay, on which you are lying," she replied, "is an herb which prevents me from coming near you."

"Which is it?" he asked. "I shall throw it away and then you will be able to come to me."

He showed her one herb after another, until she said: "That's the one!" Then he bound it to his breast and was free.

The Special Thing

The rabbi of Lublin once asked the rabbi of Apt, who was a guest in his house: "Do you know the old rabbi of Neskhizh?" "I do not know him," he replied. "But tell me: what is there so special about him that you asked me this?"

"The minute you made his acquaintance, you would know," said the rabbi of Lublin. "With him everything: teaching and prayers, eating and sleeping, is all in one piece, and he can elevate his soul to its origin."

Then the rabbi of Apt decided to go to Neskhizh. His carriage was at the door, when he heard that he had been denounced to the authorities and found it necessary to go to the official magistrate of the district. By the time he returned, it was two weeks before Passover and he again postponed his journey. After the holidays, he was told that the rabbi of Neskhizh had died in the week before Passover.

166

FROM THE CIRCLE OF THE BAAL SHEM TOV

Two Candle Holders

For many years Rabbi Moshe Hayyim Efraim, a grandson of the Baal Shem, and his wife lived in great poverty. On the sabbath eve she put the candles into a holder she herself had made out of clay. Later they grew wealthy. One sabbath eve when the rabbi entered the room on his return from the House of Prayer, he saw his wife looking at her wide-branched silver candelabra with joy and pride. "Now it all looks bright to you," he said. "But to me all looked bright in the days gone by."

When the Sabbath Was Over

Rabbi Barukh, a grandson of the Baal Shem told:

"A 'maggid,' a prophetic spirit, used to appear to the rav of Polnoye and teach him. But when the rav attached himself to my grandfather, the Baal Shem Tov, he took that maggid from him and gave him another, one of the Maggidim of Truth.

"Once Rabbi Pinhas of Koretz and I spent the sabbath with the rav of Polnoye. At the close of the sabbath, a messenger arrived to ask Rabbi Pinhas to go home at once, because of some urgent matter. The rav had retired to a room he always went to when he wished to give himself up to meditation. But Rabbi Pinhas could not bear to go away without taking leave of him. So he begged me to tell the rav of the message which had come, but I too hesitated. In the end both of us went to the door and listened. Inadvertently I touched the broken knob and the door flew open. Rabbi Pinhas fled in fright, but I stayed, stood still, and did not turn my eyes away."

So Be It

Rabbi Jacob Joseph the rav of Polnoye, was once invited to a circumcision which was to take place in a nearby village.

When he arrived, one man was still lacking to make up the quorum of ten. The zaddik was very much annoyed that he was forced to wait. Waiting always displeased him. A heavy rain had been falling since early morning, and so they could not get hold of a passerby for quite a while. At last they saw a beggar coming down the street. When they asked him to attend the ceremony as the tenth man, he said: "So be it," and entered. When they offered him warm tea, he said: "So be it." After the circumsicion they invited him to the meal, and he gave the same reply. Finally his host asked him: "Why do you always say the same thing?" The man answered: "For it is written: 'Happy is the people with whom it is so!'" And with that he vanished before the eyes of all.

That night the rav could not sleep. Over and over he heard the beggar say "So be it," until it became manifest to him that it could have been none but Elijah who had come to reprove him for his tendency to grow annoyed. "Happy is the people that is in such a case," he whispered and instantly fell asleep.

The Book

The son of the rabbi of Ostrog told:

When the rav of Polnoye's book "The Genealogies of Jacob Joseph" appeared in print and my father got hold of it, he kept reading and re-reading it. Especially passages which begin: "This I heard from my teacher," he read until he knew them by heart. This went on for a year or even longer. Once, when he was again reading one of these passages, he realized that he did not understand it fully after all. He had the horses harnessed and drove to Polnoye. I was a boy at that time, and he took me with him. He found Rabbi Jacob Joseph ill and wretched. He was lying in his bed which was soon after to be his death-bed. The rav asked my father why he had come. When he was told the reason, he held the book in his arms and spoke in a voice full of strength, and his face was all spirit and flame. Before my very eyes. his bed rose up from the ground.

168

At Market

It is told:

Rabbi Leib, son of Sarah, wandered about all the days of his life and never stayed in one place for any length of time. He often stopped in woods and caves, but he also came to cities and there secretly associated with certain intimate friends of his. He also never failed to appear wherever a large market was held. On such occasions, he rented a booth and stood in it from the beginning to the end of the market. Over and over his disciples begged him to tell them the purpose of this strange habit. Finally he yielded to their importunities.

A man with a heavy load on his shoulders was just passing by. Rabbi Leib called him and whispered in his ear for a while. Then he told his disciples to follow the man and observe him. They saw him go up to one of the merchants, set down his load, and heard him say that he did not want to be a servant any longer. The merchant shouted angrily at him and refused to pay him his due wages, but the man went silently away. Then the disciples who were following him saw that he was wearing a shroud. They ran up to him and adjured him to reveal his secret to them. "Hasty and transitory was my sojourn in the world of chaos," he said to them. "I did not know that I have been dead long since. Now the rabbi told me and has given me redemption."

To Expound Torah and to Be Torah

This is what Rabbi Leib, son of Sarah, used to say about those rabbis who expound the Torah: "What does it amount to—that they expound the Torah! A man should see to it that all his actions are a Torah and that he himself becomes so entirely a Torah that one can learn from his habits and his motions and his motionless clinging to God, that he has become like Heaven itself, of which it is said: 'There is no speech, there are no words, neither is their voice heard. Their line is gone out through all the earth, and their words to the end of the world.'"

The Father and the Little Children

Rabbi Arye of Spola, called the "Spola grandfather," had in his youth known the Baal Shem. One Passover, before the seder, he had his little son recite the mnemotechnical sentence in which the ritual actions are enumerated. When the boy was asked to explain the meaning of the word "kaddesh," "sanctify," he gave the customary response: "When the father returns from the House of Prayer, he should at once say kiddush, that is, say the benediction over the wine," and there he stopped.

The father asked him: "Why do you not add why he should at once say kiddush?"

"My teacher did not tell me anything more," said the boy. So his father taught him to add the words: "so that the little children may not fall asleep but ask the question they are supposed to: 'Why is this night different from all other nights?' "

The next day, when the children's teacher was a guest at the seder, the rabbi asked him why he did not teach the children to follow the word "kaddesh" by giving the reason for saying kaddesh, since this was the traditional sequence. The teacher replied that he had regarded this as superfluous because the rule did not hold only for those fathers who had little children in the house. "That is a grave error on your part," said the rabbi. "You are altering an old custom whose significance you have not plumbed. This is what it signifies: 'When the father returns from the House of Prayer,' that is, when our Father has seen and heard how everyone in Israel, no matter how tired he may be from the preparations for the Passover, said the Evening Prayer full of fervor, and when he now returns to his Heaven, 'he should at once say kiddush,' he should at once renew the holy marriage contracted when he said to Israel: 'And I will betroth thee unto Me for ever,' and redeem us in this very night 'the night of watching,' so that the little children, the people of Israel, may not fall into the deep sleep of despair, but receive a motive for asking their Father in Heaven: 'Why is the night of this exile different from all other nights?'" When the rabbi had said these words, he wept, raised his hands to Heaven, and cried: "Father, father, lead us from our exile, while that which is written still holds for us: 'I sleep, but my earth waketh!' Let us not fall utterly asleep!" All wept with him. But after a while, he roused himself and cried: "Now let us delight our Father and show him that his children can dance, even though they are in darkness." He gave orders to play a merry tune and began to dance.

The "Grandfather's" Dance

When the "Spola grandfather" danced on a sabbath and on feast-days, his feet were as light as those of a four-year-old. And not a single one of those who saw his holy dance failed to turn to God at that very instance, and with his whole soul, for he stirred the hearts of all who beheld him, to both tears and ecstasy.

Once Rabbi Shalom Shakhna, the son of Abraham the Angel, was his guest on a Friday evening. They had just made peace with each other after waging a long dispute. Rabbi Shalom sat there as always on the night of the sabbath, wholly surrendered to his clinging to God. The "grandfather" looked around joyfully as always, and both were silent. But when they had finished eating, Rabbi Arye Leib said: "Son of the Angel, can you dance?"

"I cannot dance," Rabbi Shalom replied.

Rabbi Arye Leib rose. "Then watch the Spola grandfather dance," he said. His heart immediately lifted his feet and he danced around the table. When he had moved once this way and once that, Rabbi Shalom jumped up. "Did you see how the old man can dance!" he called to the hasidim who had accompanied him. He remained standing and kept his eyes fixed on the feet of the dancer. Later he said to his hasidim: "You may believe me: he has made all his limbs so pure and so holy, that with every step he takes, his feet accomplish holy unifications."

Purim Games

At the Purim festival, the "Spola grandfather" was in the habit of organizing a special kind of games. He had a number of hasidim, carefully chosen and directed by him, disguise themselves, one as the "King of Purim," the rest as his princes and counsellors. These sat together in solemn session, in counsel or in judgment, had dicussions, and made resolutions and decisions. Sometimes the "grandfather" himself took part in the masquerade.

The hasidim tell that these games had a powerful effect which traveled through space: that they set at nought doom or the threat of doom decreed for Israel.

Leah and Rachel

In the days when young Nahum, later the Rabbi of Tchernobil, was privileged to live near the Baal Shem, Rabbi Israel ben Eliezer undertook one of his usual journeys. Nahum, who wanted very much to go too, kept walking around the waiting carriage. When the Baal Shem got in, he said to him: "If you can tell me the difference between that sequence of prayer in the Lamentations at Midnight, which bears Leah's name and that which bears Rachel's, you may come with me." Nahum replied without hesitation: "What Leah effects with her tears, Rachel effects with her joy." The Baal Shem at once asked him to get into the carriage.

The Zaddik and His Hasidim

Rabbi Yitzhak of Skvira, a grandson of Rabbi Nahum's, told: "In a small town, not far from Tchernobil, several hasidim of my grandfather's were seated together at the conclusion of the sabbath. They were all honest and devout men and at this meal of 'the escort of the queen,' they were casting the accounts of their souls. They were so humble and so full of the fear of God, that they thought they had sinned very greatly and agreed that there was no hope for them, and that their only consolation was that they were utterly devoted to the great zaddik Rabbi Nahum, and that he would uplift and redeem them. Then they decided that they must immediately go to their teacher. They started out right after the meal and together they went to Tchernobil. But at the end of that same sabbath, my grandfather was sitting in his house and casting the accounts of his soul. Then in his humility and fear of God, it seemed to him that he had sinned very greatly, and that there was no hope for him except one: that those hasidim, so earnest in the service of God, were so deeply devoted to him, and that they would now comfort him. He went to the door and gazed in the direction his disciples lived, and when he had stood there a while, he saw them coming.

At this instant—so Rabbi Yitzhak ended his story—two arcs fused to a ring.

Words of Comfort

Several disciples of Rabbi Nahum of Tchernobil came to him and wept and complained that they had fallen prey to darkness and depression and could not lift up their heads either in the teachings or in prayer. The zaddik saw the state of their hearts and that they sincerely yearned for the nearness of the living God. He said to them: "My dear sons, do not be distressed at this seeming death which has come upon you. For everything that is in the world, is also in man. And just as on New Year's Day life ceases on all the stars and they sink into a deep sleep, in which they are strengthened, and from which they awake with a new power of shining, so those men who truly desire to come close to God, must pass through the state of cessation of spiritual life, and 'the falling is for the sake of the rising.' As it is written that the Lord God caused a deep sleep to fall upon Adam, and he slept and from his sleep he arose, a whole man."

The Quality of God

A Lithuanian once came to Rabbi Nahum of Tchernobil and complained that he had no money to marry off his daughter. The zaddik just happened to have fifty gulden put aside for another purpose. He let the poor man have the money and also gave him his silk robe, so that he might cut a fine figure at the wedding. The man took everything, went straight to an inn and began to drink vodka.

Some hours later, hasidim went to the inn and found him lying on the bench, thoroughly drunk. They took the rest of the money and the silk robe away from him, brought it all back to

Rabbi Nahum, and told him how his confidence had been abused. But the rabbi cried out angrily: "I just caught hold of the tail end of this quality of God's: 'He is good and beneficient to the wicked and to the good,' and you want to snatch it from my hands! Take everything back at once!"

The Rider in the Hen

It is told:
In the course of a journey, Rabbi Nahum was a guest in the house of another zaddik. They had a hen killed in his honor, and served it at the meal. He looked at it for a while and said: "In this fowl, I can see an armed man on horseback." They called the ritual slaughterer and he confessed that at the moment of slaughtering, he had been startled by an armed officer who came riding by, and that from then on he had thought of nothing but that.

Fire Against Fire

It is told:
Once, when the Baal Shem was on a journey, and stopped at the house of one of his disciples, Rabbi David Leikes, a government order was proclaimed to the effect that on a certain day, at noon, the Talmud was to be burned wherever a volume was found. On the morning of that day, Rabbi David hid his Talmud under the wash-tub. At twelve o'clock the bells began to chime. Pale as death he came into the room and saw his teacher calmly walking up and down. "With your fire," said the Baal Shem, "you have put out their fire." The order was rescinded.

The Rope Dancer

Once Rabbi Hayyim of Krosno, a disciple of the Baal Shem's, was watching a rope dancer together with his disciples. He was so absorbed in the spectacle that they asked him what it was that riveted his gaze to this foolish performance. "This man," he said, "is risking his life, and I cannot say why. But I am quite sure that while he is walking the rope, he is not thinking of the fact that he is earning a hundred gulden by what he is doing, for if he did, he would fall."

174

MENAHEM MENDEL OF VITEBSK

His Childhood

From the time he was eleven years old, Menahem studied in the house of the Great Maggid and was dear to him. One sabbath, after the midday meal, the maggid saw him walking up and down the room with a mischievous expression, his cap atilt on his head. He went to the threshold, put his hand on the door-knob, and asked: "How many pages of the Gemara did you learn today?"

"Six," said the boy.

"If," said the maggid, "after six pages, the cap slides to the edge, how many pages do you think are necessary to make it fall off?" Then he closed the door.

Menahem beat against it and said in tears: "Open, rabbi, and tell me what I must do."

The maggid opened the door. "I shall take you to my teacher, the holy Baal Shem," he said.

They arrived in Mezbizh on a Friday. The maggid at once went to the house of Baal Shem Tov. Menahem dressed himself and combed his hair with the greatest care, for this was a habit of his and remained so to his dying day. In the House of Prayer the Baal Shem Tov stood in front of the desk and waited with praying until the boy came. But he did not summon Menahem to him until after the conclusion of the sabbath. The maggid and Rabbi Jacob Joseph of Polnoye, the other great disciple of the Baal Shem, stood in front of their master. He called the boy, looked at him for a long time, and then told him a story about oxen and a plough. His listeners soon realized that it was a parable foretelling the life of Menahem, but the boy understood just so much of it as he had experienced up to this time. The rabbi of Polnoye understood half, and the maggid all.

Later the Baal Shem Tov said to the maggid: "This mischievous boy is full of reverence through and through."

More

On New Year's Day the Great Maggid did not blow the ram's horn himself. This was the office of his disciple Rabbi Menahem Mendel, and the maggid called out what he was to blow. In the last period of his life, when he could no longer walk about on his sore feet, he did this from his room. Once Rabbi Menahem Mendel was absent and Rabbi Levi Yitzhak was to take his place. He put the ram's horn to his lips, but when the maggid called out the first blast, Levi Yitzhak saw a dazzling light and fainted away. "What is the matter with him?" asked the maggid. "Mendel sees much more and still he is not afraid."

Pursued by Honors

The maggid of Mezritch once sent his disciple Rabbi Menahem on a journey to various communities. He was to speak in public and waken desire to study the Torah for its own sake. In one of the towns he visited, a number of learned men came to see Rabbi Mendel at his inn, and showered him with special honors. While talking to them, he brought up the question why it is said that when a man flees from honors, honors pursue him. "If it is good and seemly to be honored," he said, "why is he who flees from honors rewarded for his unseemly fears by having honors pursue him? But if it is wrong to be honored, why should this pursuit punish him for praiseworthy flight? The fact is that the honest man should avoid honors. But—just like everybody else—he is born with a desire for them and must fight against it. Only after a long time, during which he has studied the Torah zealously and for its own sake, will he succeed in overcoming that reprehensible desire and no longer feel satisfaction at being called 'rabbi,' or the like. But the desire for honor which he had in his youth, and which he has conquered, still clings in the very bottom of his soul, and though he knows that now he is free, it pursues him like a tenacious memory, and confuses him. That is the taint of the primeval serpent, and of this too he must cleanse himself."

The Worm

Rabbi Mendel said: "I do not know wherein I could be better than the worm. For see: he does the will of his Maker and destroys nothing."

Vocation

Several hasidim from White Russia came to the Great Maggid and complained that the distance to Mezritch was so great, they could not come as often as they needed to, and in the intervals they were without a teacher and guide. The maggid gave them his belt and his staff and said: "Take this to the man called Mendel, in the city of Vitebsk."

On their arrival in Vitebsk, they inquired for a Rabbi Mendel in every street and alley, but they were told that there was no rabbi by that name. A woman who had been watching them, asked whom they were looking for. "Rabbi Mendel," they replied.

"We haven't a rabbi by that name," she said. "But we certainly have more than enough Mendels. My own son-in-law's name is Mendele."

Then the hasidim knew that this was the man they had been sent to find. They followed the woman to her house and gave her son-in-law the belt and staff. He clasped the belt around him and closed his hand over the knob of the staff. They looked at him and scarcely recognized him. Another man stood before them, a man garbed in the power of God, and the fear of God lifted their hearts.

The Document

The document through which the congregation of Minsk invested Rabbi Mendel with the office of preacher began with the address: "To the holy zaddik, the aloof and holy light," and so forth. It was signed by more than a hundred prominent persons. When Rabbi Mendel had it in hand and read all the encomia and honorary titles, he said: "This would be a fine document to take with one into the World of Truth! But when they question me, I shall have to tell the truth anyway. And the confession of the accused weighs more than the words of a hundred witnesses. So what will all this praise avail me?"

Once Rabbi Menahem fell seriously ill and could not speak. His hasidim surrounded his bed and wept. He rallied his strength and whispered: "Do not be afraid. From the story which the holy Baal Shem once told me, I know that I shall go to the Land of Israel."

Before going on his journey to the Land of Israel, Rabbi Menahem visited the rabbi of Polnoye, who asked him: "Do you remember the story of the oxen and the plough?"

"I remember," he replied.

"And do you know," the rabbi of Polnoye continued, "what point in it you have reached in your life?"

With a little sigh, Rabbi Menahem said: "I've reeled off the greater half of it."

The Heap of Cinders

Before leaving for the Land of Israel, Rabbi Menahem Mendel paid a visit to old Rabbi Jacob Joseph of Polnoye, the great disciple of the Baal Shem Tov. He arrived at the inn in a troika, and this in itself was enough to annoy the hasidim in Polnoye, whose master insisted on a simple life. But when Rabbi Mendel left the inn and went to the zaddik's house hatless and beltless, a long pipe in his mouth, they all thought that Rabbi Jacob Joseph, who was known for his violent temper, would refuse to receive his guest because of this careless and lax behavior. But the old man welcomed him on the threshold with a great show of love, and spent several hours talking to him. When Rabbi Mendel had gone, the disciples asked their master: "What is there to this man who had the impudence to enter your house with only the cap on his head, with silver buckles on his shoes, and a long pipe in his mouth?"

The zaddik said: "A king who went to war hid his treasures in a safe place. But he buried his most precious pearl, which he loved with all his heart, in a heap of cinders because he knew that no one would look for it there. And so that the powers of evil might not touch it, Rabbi Mendel buries his great humility in the cinder-heap of vanity."

A Comparison

Rabbi Israel of Rizhyn said:

"Rabbi Mendel's journey to the Holy Land was like the journey of our Father Abraham. Its purpose was to pave the way for God and Israel."

For Azazel

When someone asked Rabbi Israel of Rizhyn why he did not go to the Land of Israel, he said: "What has a rough fellow like myself to do in the Land of Israel! Now Rabbi Mendel of Vitebsk—he had something to do with the Land of Israel, and the Land of Israel with him." And he went on to tell: "Before Rabbi Mendel set out for the Land of Israel, he invited the officers of the king to dinner in the city of Vitebsk. And they brought their wives with them, as is their custom. Rabbi Mendel had posted several of his young hasidim near the gate, so that they might help the guests, both men and women, from their carriages, a courtesy which officers of the king expect. And he promised the young men that not a shadow of desire should graze their hearts when they lifted those lovely women from the coach. And so it is: If you want to go to the Land of Israel, you must first concentrate your soul on the secret of the goat which is sent into the wilderness for Azazel. That is what Rabbi Mendel meant with that dinner of his. He could do it! But I, who am such a rough fellow—if I came to the Land of Israel, they would ask me: 'Why have you come without your Jews?'"

At the Window

While Rabbi Menahem was living in the Land of Israel, a foolish man climbed the Mount of Olives unobserved. When he got to the top, he blew the ram's horn. The people were startled and soon a rumor sprang up that this was the blowing of the ram's horn which was to precede redemption. When this was reported to Rabbi Menahem, he opened his window, looked out into the world, and said: "This is no renewal!"

Rabbi Menahem used to say: "It is true that the air of the Land of Israel makes a man wise. Before I was in that land, all my thoughts and desires were intent on saying a prayer just once in exactly the right way. But since I am in this land, all I want is just once to say 'Amen' in the right way."

Another thing he said, was: "This is what I attained in the Land of Israel. When I see a bundle of straw lying in the street, it seems to me a sign of the presence of God, that it lies there lengthwise, and not crosswise."

The Signature

When Rabbi Menahem wrote letters from the Land of Israel, he always signed himself: "He, who is truly humble."

The rabbi of Rizhyn once was asked: "If Rabbi Menahem were really humble, how could he call himself so?"

"He was so humble," said the rabbi of Rizhyn, "that just because humility dwelt within him, he no longer regarded it as a virtue."

The Ride to the Leipzig Fair

Among the hasidim who went to the Land of Israel with Rabbi Menahem Mendel was a wise man who had been a great merchant and had become so attached to the zaddik that he gave up his business in order to accompany him to the Holy Land. When after a time it became necessary to send a reliable messenger to the hasidim who had stayed at home, to ask them for financial assistance, this man was entrusted with the errand. But while he was on the ship he suddenly fell ill and died. No one in the Land of Israel knew about it. But after his death, he himself felt as if he were riding in a carriage bound for the fair in Leipzig and talking to an old servant he used to take with him on such trips, and also to the coachman who looked very familiar. And all the while he had a great longing for his teacher. The desire to see him grew stronger and stronger until he decided to turn back and go to him. When he told his two companions of his resolve, they argued vehemently against it: it would be foolish to give up the important business transaction in hand for a mere whim! But he insisted on having his way in the face of all their objections. Finally they told him that he was dead, and that they were evil angels to whom he had been entrusted. Instantly he summoned them before the court of Heaven, and they could not refuse. The verdict was that the angels were to take him to Rabbi Mendel. When he reached the city of Tiberias and entered the zaddik's house, one of the angels went in with him in his true and terrible form. The rabbi was startled at the sight of the angel but bade him wait until he had finished his work. For a whole week he wrought at the soul of the man until it was in the right shape.

This is the story that Rabbi Nahman of Bratzlav told his hasidim.

All the Candles

The hasidim who studied in the "Klaus" of the rabbi of Lubavitch, the son-in-law of Rabbi Shneur Zalman's son, used to light a candle before everyone who sat over his books in the House of Study. But when they had finished their evening work and began to tell one another stories about the zaddikim, they put out all the candles except one, which they left burning. Once, when they were seated around the one burning candle, the rabbi came into the room to fetch a book. He asked them whom they were talking about. "Rabbi Mendel of Vitebsk," they said.

"In his honor," he told them, "you must light all the candles. For when he expounded the teachings, all feeling of self was blotted from his heart, and 'the other side' had no way of getting at him. And so, when you talk about him, you must light all the candles—as if you were studying the holy Torah."

SHMELKE OF NIKOLSBURG

David's Harp

When Rabbi Shmelke and his brother Rabbi Pinhas, later the
rabbi of Frankfort, were in Mezritch, they rented an attic room
so that they might be undisturbed in their studies. Once, after
the conclusion of the sabbath, they were sitting and studying
late at night, when they heard a strange weeping in which they
could clearly detect the voices of both a man and a woman.
They looked out of the window and there, on a bench, in the
alley, they saw the servant and the maid of the house, both in
tears. When they asked them the reason, they said that they had
been employed there for a long time and had been waiting to
get married for years, but the master of the house was against
it, and had managed to prevent it again and again.

At that the brothers declared that all that was necessary was to
set up the marriage canopy; everything else, including the consent of the master of the house, would then come of itself. They
left at once to wake the cantor who immediately fetched ten
men, opened the House of Prayer, and set up the canopy. The
wedding was duly celebrated. Rabbi Shmelke beat time with a
piece of branch, and Rabbi Pinhas clinked two candelabras so
that they gave forth a beautiful sound. Then the maggid came
in. At the "Feast of King David" he had sat there with that remoteness of the soul which sometimes overtook him. Suddenly
he jumped up and ran to the House of Prayer. "Don't you hear
David's harp?" he cried.

New Melodies

Rabbi Moshe Teitelbaum, the disciple of the "Seer" of Lublin,
said: "When Rabbi Shmelke prayed on a sabbath and on feast-
days, but especially on the Day of Atonement when he performed the service of the high priest, the mystery became manifest in the sound of music carrying from word to word, and he
sang new melodies, miracle of miracles, which he had never

heard and which no human ear had ever heard; and he did not even know what he was singing and what melody he was singing, for he clung to the upper world."

* * *

A very old man who had sung in Rabbi Shmelke's choir when he was a boy, used to tell this: "It was the custom to lay out the notes for each text, so that it would not be necessary to fetch them when the praying before the pulpit began. But the rabbi paid no attention to the notes and sang utterly new melodies which no one had ever heard. We singers all fell silent and listened to him. We could not understand from where those melodies came to him."

In Nikolsburg

When Rabbi Shmelke was called to be the rav of Nikolsburg, he prepared an impressive sermon which he intended to preach to the Talmud scholars of Moravia. On the way, he stopped over in the city of Cracow and when the people there begged him to preach to them, he asked his disciple Moshe Leib, later the rabbi of Sasov, who had accompanied him: "Well, Moshe Leib, what shall I preach?"

"The rabbi has prepared a splendid sermon for Nikolsburg. Why should he not preach that here as well?" answered Moshe Leib.

Rabbi Shmelke took his advice. Now a number of men had come from Nikolsburg to Cracow in order to welcome him, and these heard the sermon. So when the zaddik arrived in Nikolsburg, he asked his disciple: "Well, Moshe Leib, now what shall I preach on the sabbath? I cannot dish up the same sermon over again to the men who heard me speak in Cracow."

"We must take some time," said Moshe Leib, "and discuss a problem of the law in preparation for a sermon."

But up to Friday they did not have a moment's time to open a book. Finally Rabbi Shmelke asked: "Well, Moshe, what shall we preach?"

"On Friday evening, they must surely give us a little free time," said Moshe Leib.

They held in readiness a very large candle which was to burn right through the night, and, when the crowd had gone home, they sat down before the book. Then a hen flew in at the window and the whirr of her wings put out the light. Said Rabbi Shmelke: "Well, Moshe Leib, now what are we to preach?"

"Surely," Moshe Leib replied, "there will be no preaching until the afternoon and so in the morning, after prayer, let us go into our room, lock the door, let no one in, and talk over a subject." In the morning they went to prayer. Before the chapter for the week was read, the desk was moved in front of the Ark and the head of the congregation came and asked Rabbi Shmelke to give his sermon. The House of Prayer was filled with the Talmud scholars of Moravia. Rabbi Shmelke had them bring him a volume of the Gemara, opened it at random, posed a problem from the page before him, and asked the scholars to discuss it. Then he too, so he said, would say his say. When they had all spoken, he put the prayer shawl over his head and remained like this for about a quarter of an hour. Then he organized the questions they had raised, one hundred and thirty in number, and gave the replies, seventy-two in number, and there was nothing that was not answered, and solved, and quelled.

Noting Down

When Rabbi Shmelke was called to Nikolsburg in Moravia, a certain custom prevailed in that congregation. Every new rav was asked to note down in the chronicle some new regulation which was to be followed from that time on. He too was asked to do this, but put it off from day to day. He looked at each and every one and postponed noting anything in the book. He looked at them more and more closely and over and over, and put off writing until they gave him to understand that the delay was becoming unduly long. Then he went to where the chronicle lay and wrote down the ten commandments.

The Seven Worldly Wisdoms

When Rabbi Shmelke assumed office in Nikolsburg, he preached on the seven worldly wisdoms on the first seven sabbath-days, one wisdom on each sabbath. From week to week, the congregation grew more surprised at this peculiar choice of subject for a sermon, but no one ventured to question the zaddik about it. On the eighth sabbath he began by saying: "For a long time I did not understand the words of Solomon, the preacher: 'It is better to hear the rebuke of the wise than for a man to hear the song of fools.' Why is it not written: 'than the song of fools'? This is the meaning. It is good to hear the rebuke of a wise man who has heard and understood the song of fools, that is, the seven worldly wisdoms, which—compared to the teachings of God—are a song of fools. To another man the foolish worldly sages could say: 'It is easy for you to scorn our wisdoms, for you have not tasted of their sweetness! If you knew it, you would not want to know anything else!' But he who has studied the seven wisdoms and passed through their inmost core, only to choose the wisdom of the Torah—if such a man cries out: 'Vanity of vanities,' no one can gainsay him."

The Messiah and Those Who Pray

On the first day of the New Year festival, Rabbi Shmelke entered the House of Prayer before the ram's horn was sounded, and prayed, with tears in his eyes: "Alas! Lord of the world! All the people are crying to you, but what of all their clamor! They are thinking of nothing but their own needs, and not of the exile of your glory!" On the second day he again came before the blowing of the ram's horn and wept and said: "It is written in the first book of Samuel: 'Wherefore cometh not the son of Jesse to eat bread, neither yesterday nor today?' Why did the King Messiah not come, not yesterday on the first day of the New Year, and not today, on the second? It is because today, just as yesterday, all their prayers are for nothing but bread, for nothing but the satisfaction of bodily needs!"

The Tears of Esau

Another time he said: "In the Midrash it is written: 'Messiah son of David, will not come before the tears of Esau have ceased to flow.' The children of Israel, who are God's children, pray for mercy day and night, and shall they weep in vain, as long as the children of Esau shed tears? But 'the tears of Esau'—that does not mean the tears which the peoples weep and you do not weep; they are the tears which all human beings weep when they ask something for themselves, and pray for it. And truly: Messiah son of David will not come until such tears have ceased to flow, until you weep because the Divine Presence is exiled, and because you yearn for its return."

A Sermon for Atonement

On the eve of the Day of Atonement, Rabbi Shmelke of Nikolsburg put on his prayer shawl and went to the House of Prayer. On his way from the entrance to the Ark, he called aloud the words of the Scriptures: ". . . for on this day shall atonement be made for you, to cleanse you," and after that he quoted Rabbi Akiba's words from the Mishnah: "Before whom do you atone, and who cleanses you: Your Father in Heaven." All the people burst into tears.

When he stood in front of the Ark, he said: "Brothers of my heart, you must know that the core of turning is the offering up of life itself. For we are of the seed of Abraham who offered his life for the sanctification of the blessed Name and let them cast him into a lime-kiln; we are of the seed of Isaac who offered his life and laid his neck on the stone of the altar—they are surely pleading to our Father in Heaven in our behalf on this holy and awful day of judgment. But let us too walk in their tracks and imitate their works: let us offer up our own lives for the sanctification of the Name of Him who is blessed. Let us unite and sanctify His mighty Name with fervent love and with this as our purpose, let us say together: 'Hear, O Israel!' " And weeping, all the people said: "Hear, O Israel: The Lord our God, the Lord is one."

Then he went on to say: "Dear brothers, now that it was vouchsafed us to unite and sanctify His Name in great love, now that we have offered our lives, and our hearts have become cleansed for the service and fear of the Lord, we must also unite our souls. All souls come from one root, all are carved from the

186

throne of His splendor, and so they are a part of God in Heaven. Let us be united on earth too, so that the branches again may be as the root. Here we stand, cleansed and pure, to unite our souls. And we take upon us the commandment: 'Love thy neighbor as thyself.' " And all the people repeated aloud: "Love thy neighbor as thyself." And he continued: "Now that it has been vouchsafed us to unite His Great Name, and to unite our souls, which are a part of God in Heaven, let the holy Torah plead in our behalf before our Father in Heaven. Once God offered it to all peoples and to all languages, but we alone accepted it and cried: 'All that the Lord hath spoken will we do,' and only then did we say: 'We hear.' And so it is fitting that the Torah ask our Father in heaven for mercy and grace for us on this holy and awful day of judgment." And he opened the doors of the Ark.

Then, in front of the open Ark, he recited the confession of sins, and all the people repeated it after him word for word, and as they did so, they wept. He took out the scroll and, holding it high in his hands, spoke to his congregation about the sins of man. But in the end he said: "You must know that the weeping we do on this day is unblest if it is filled with gloom, for the Divine Presence does not dwell in heaviness of heart, but only in rejoicing in the commandments. And, see, no joy is greater than the joy on this day, when it is granted to us to drive all evil impulses from our hearts, through the power of turning, to come close to our Father in Heaven whose hand is outstretched to receive those who turn to Him. And so, all the tears we shed on this day, should be tears of joy, as it is written: 'Serve the Lord with fear and rejoice with trembling.' "

Sleep

Rabbi Shmelke did not want to interrupt his studies for too long a time, and so he always slept sitting up, his head resting on his arm. In his fingers he held a lit candle which roused him when it guttered and the flame touched his hand. When Rabbi Elimelekh visited him and recognized the power of the holiness which was still locked within him, he prepared a couch for him and with great difficulty persuaded him to lie down for a little while. Then he closed and shuttered the windows. Rabbi Shmelke slept until broad daylight. It did not take him long to notice this, but he was not sorry he had slept, for he was filled with a hitherto unknown sunny clearness. He went to the House of Prayer and prayed before the congregation as usual. But to the congregation it seemed that they had never heard him before. They were entranced and uplifted by the manifest power of his holiness. When he recited the verses about the Red Sea, they gathered up the hems of their kaftans for fear the waves towering to the left and right might wet them with salty foam. Later Shmelke said to Elimelekh: "Not until this day did I know that one can also serve God with sleep."

The Rap

In Apt there was a servant of the House of Prayer whose duty it was to go through the town and, with his hammer, rap at the door of every Jewish house, for the men to come and pray, or learn, or recite psalms. He had only to rap ever so lightly and instantly the sleepers started up, even if it was midnight, and dressed quickly, and hurried to the House of Prayer, and long after he had rapped, the rap of their eager hearts echoed the rap of the hammer. The man had been granted this gift as a boy, when he had served Rabbi Shmelke of Nikolsburg with a heart that was awake and full of devotion.

The Clean Freethinkers

A number of freethinkers in Nikolsburg were carrying on an argument with Rabbi Shmelke. "But you will have to admit," they said in conclusion, "that we, on our part, have virtues which the Poles lack. Our clothing, for instance, is spotlessly clean, and that is more than you can say for that of the Poles, who ignore the bidding of the sages: 'The wise man shall not wear a spotted robe.'"
The rabbi laughed and replied: "You are right. Your clothes are clean, and those of the Poles are not. That is because—according to what the Talmud says of the gradation of virtues—

cleanliness leads to purity, purity to aloofness, and so on higher and higher to the rung of the holy spirit. Now, when the Poles set about beginning with cleanliness, the Evil Urge does all he possibly can to dissuade them from it, for he fears they will rise from rung to rung and attain to the holy spirit. And even when they try to fend off the Evil Urge and assure him that they do not intend to do any such thing, he does not believe them, and will not stop until he has talked them out of cleanliness. But when the Evil Urge takes exception to your cleanliness, you need only assure him that you do not intend to rise, and he instantly takes you at your word, and lets you be just as clean as you like."

The Enemy

A rich and distinguished man in Nikolsburg was hostile to Rabbi Shmelke and tried to think of some way to make him seem ridiculous. On the eve of the Day of Atonement, he came to him and begged him that on this day, when each man forgives his neighbor, they too might become reconciled with each other. He had brought the rabbi a jar of very old and strong wine, and urged him to drink, for he thought that, since the zaddik was unused to drinking, he would become drunk and appear before his congregation in this condition. For the sake of reconciliation, Rabbi Shmelke drank one glass after another and the rich man thought he had accomplished his purpose and went home well-satisfied.

But when evening fell, and the hour of prayer drew near, the shudder of the day of judgment took hold of the rabbi, and in a moment every vestige of the effect of the wine had left him. After the Evening Prayer, Rabbi Shmelke remained in the House of Prayer all night, in the company of other devout people. Just as every year, he sang the psalms and the congregation joined in. When, in the forty-first psalm, he came to the verse: "By this I know that Thou delightest in me: mine enemy will not triumph over me," he repeated it over and over, and translated it, but not in the usual way but freely and boldly: "By this I know that you delight in me: my enemy will suffer no ill because of me." And he added: "Even though there are persons who are hostile to me and try to make me an object of ridicule, forgive them, Lord of the world, and let them not suffer because of me." And he said this in a voice so full of power, that all those who were praying, burst into tears, and each repeated his words from the bottom of his heart. But among them was that rich and distinguished man. In this hour he turned to God and all his malice dropped from him. From this time on, he loved and honored Rabbi Shmelke above all other people.

The Commandment to Love

A disciple asked Rabbi Shmelke: "We are commanded to love our neighbor as ourself. How can I do this, if my neighbor has wronged me?"

The rabbi answered: "You must understand these words aright. Love your neighbor like something which you yourself are. For all souls are one. Each is a spark from the original soul, and this soul is wholly inherent in all souls, just as your soul is in all the members of your body. It may come to pass that your hand makes a mistake and strikes you. But would you then take a stick and chastise your hand, because it lacked understanding, and so increase your pain? It is the same if your neighbor, who is of one soul with you, wrongs you for lack of understanding. If you punish him, you only hurt yourself."

The disciple went on asking: "But if I see a man who is wicked before God, how can I love him?"

"Don't you know," said Rabbi Shmelke, "that the original soul came out of the essence of God, and that every human soul is a part of God? And will you have no mercy on him, when you see that one of his holy sparks has been lost in a maze, and is almost stifled?"

The Ring

A poor man came to Rabbi Shmelke's door. There was no money in the house, so the rabbi gave him a ring. A moment later, his wife heard of it and heaped him with reproaches for throwing to an unknown beggar so valuable a piece of jewelry, with so large and precious a stone. Rabbi Shmelke had the poor man called back and said to him: "I have just learned that the ring I gave you is of great value. Be careful not to sell it for too little money."

The Messengers

A man came to Rabbi Shmelke and complained that he could not make a living, but had to keep on asking kind people to help him. He repeated the words of the prayer: " 'Let us not be in need of the gift of flesh and blood. . .' " Rabbi Shmelke said: "You must not read 'gift' but 'gifts,' for there is one God, but many messengers to do his bidding. And that is what the verse means. Let us not be in need of the gifts we can consider only as the gifts of men. In the hour we take them, let us recognize the givers as your messengers."

Poor Man and Rich Man

Rabbi Shmelke said: "The poor man gives the rich man more than the rich gives the poor. More than the poor man needs the rich man, the rich is in need of the poor."

Be Holy

A man once asked Rabbi Shmelke: "It is written: 'Ye shall be holy, for I the Lord your God am holy. Ye shall fear every man his mother and his father.' How can the lump of clay which is the habitation of evil lusts, strive to acquire a quality which is God's? And what connection is there between this summons to the superhuman, and the commandment to fear father and mother, which is a human law for humans?"
The rabbi replied: "According to the words of our sages, three are concerned with the creation of every child: God, father, and mother. God's part is all holy. The other parts can be sanctified and made as much like it as possible. That is what is meant by the commandment. You are holy and yet you shall become holy. You must, therefore, shun the heritage of your father and mother, which you have within you, and which is opposed to holiness. You must not yield to it, but master it and shape it."

Preparation

A disciple of Rabbi Shmelke's begged his master to teach him how to prepare his soul for the service of God. The zaddik told him to go to Rabbi Abraham Hayyim, who—at that time—was still an innkeeper. The disciple did as he was bidden and lived in the inn for several weeks without observing any vestige of holiness in the innkeeper who from the Morning Prayer till night devoted himself to his business. Finally he asked him what he did all day. "My most important occupation," said Rabbi Abraham, "is to clean the dishes properly, so that not the slightest trace of food is left, and to clean and dry the pots and pans, so that they do not rust." When the disciple returned home and reported to Rabbi Shmelke what he had seen and heard, the rabbi said to him: "Now you know the answer to what you asked me."

The Test

They asked Rabbi Shmelke: "Why is the sacrifice of Isaac considered so glorious? At that time, our Father Abraham had already reached a high rung of holiness, and so it was no wonder that he immediately did as God asked him!"
He answered: "When man is tried, all the rungs and all holiness are taken from him. Stripped of everything he has attained, he stands face to face with Him who is putting him to the test."

Rather Not

Rabbi Shmelke once said: "If I had the choice, I should rather not die. For in the coming world, there are no Days of Awe, and what can the soul of man do without the Days of Judgment?"

Our Generation

Once they asked Rabbi Shmelke: "Some find it difficult to believe that the Messiah could suddenly come in this, our trivial day and age. And how could our generation bring about what the tannaim and amoraim, the 'generations of knowledge,' and the generations after them could not accomplish?"
The zaddik replied: "For many years the host of a king besieged a well-fortified city. All kinds of troops, under the command of expert generals, advanced on the fortress again and again with all the force of which they were capable, until finally

they conquered. Then an army of workers was ordered to clear
away the enormous amount of débris, so that a new beginning
could be made, so that in the city he had vanquished a new
palace could be built for the victorious king. That is our generation."

Thieves' Luck

With regard to Rashi's comment: "He whose ear heard 'Thou
shalt not steal' on Mount Sinai and then went and stole, his ear
shall be pierced," Rabbi Shmelke said:
"Before God gave his commandments down from Mount Sinai,
every one took good care that his property was not stolen from
him. And because the thieves knew this, they did not try to
steal. But after God spoke the words, 'Thou shalt not steal,' and
men felt secure, the trade of thieving began to thrive."

The Brothers

Rabbi Shmelke of Nikolsburg was once entertaining his brother,
Rabbi Pinhas, the rav of Frankfort, as his guest. Now, Rabbi
Shmelke had always eaten in moderation, but in his old age he
ate only a very little food and drank only a little water. When
Rabbi Pinhas, who had not seen him for many years, noticed
this, he said: "Here are two brothers of one father and mother.
The one gobbles and guzzles like a beast, the other is like an
angel of the Lord: he needs neither food nor drink, but savors
the radiance of divine glory." Rabbi Shmelke replied: "Here
are two brothers of one father and of one mother. The one is
like a high priest, the other like a good house-father. The high
priest eats, and his eating is part of the sacrifice which shrives
the house-father."

The Ride on the Danube
It is told:
Dangerous plots against the Jews were brewing in the emperor's
palace. Then Rabbi Shmelke and his disciple Moshe Leib of
Sasov set out for Vienna to put an end to such plans. But it was
freezing weather, and the Danube was full of ice-floes. They
boarded a narrow boat which could not hold more than two

men. They stood up in it and Rabbi Shmelke started singing the song which had been sung beside the Red Sea, and Moshe Leib sang the bass. And the little boat moved safely between the floes. In Vienna the people ran down to the shore and stood there open-mouthed. Soon the news of these strange arrivals reached the court. On the very same day the empress received Rabbi Shmelke and granted his requests.

The Amen to the Blessing

When Rabbi Shmelke felt he was going to die, he said to his hasidim: "I did not want to tell you up to now, but now I must tell it while there is still time. You know that I have always been careful to say grace and blessings before eating and drinking and the like, in a place where there was someone who said 'Amen.' For each blessing begets an angel, and the angel is incomplete unless someone says 'Amen.' But once, on a journey, I had to say a blessing in a lonely place, when—after attending to my bodily needs—I washed my hands at a well, and there was no one anywhere around who could say 'Amen.' Hardly had I begun to feel troubled about this, when two men stood close before me, and before I had time to marvel at their size and grandeur, I was saying the blessing, and they answered 'Amen' with overwhelming sweetness. But when I wanted to look at them more closely, a cloud carried them off."

The Soul of Samuel

On the second day of Iyyar of the year 5538, Rabbi Shmelke summoned his disciples. He was sitting very erect in his big chair, his face was radiant, and his eyes as unclouded as always. He said to them: "Today, you must know, is the day of my death." They began to weep, but he bade them stop, and continued: "You must know that the soul of the prophet Samuel is within me. For this there are three outward signs: my name is Samuel; I am a Levite, as he was; and my life has lasted fifty-two years, just as his. But he was called Samuel, and I Shmelke, and so I remained Shmelke." Soon after this, he told his weeping disciples to leave him, leaned back, and died.

AARON OF KARLIN

The Moment

In his youth, Rabbi Aaron of Karlin was fond of wearing fine clothes, and every day he went driving in a carriage. But a moment came when, as he was leaning back in his carriage, holy insight overwhelmed him and he knew that he must leave this way of his, and enter upon another. He leaned forward; his spirit surged up within him. He set foot on the carriage-step and was flooded with the gift. He set foot on the earth, and all the firmaments were under the sway of his power.

A Whisper

On a Friday evening, after eating in the house of the maggid of Mezritch, Rabbi Aaron returned to his inn and began to recite the Song of Songs in a whisper. Soon after, the maggid's servant came and knocked at his door. He said the maggid could not sleep because the Song of Songs came roaring through his room.

The Long Sleep

Once, when Rabbi Aaron was in the house of the Great Maggid along with other disciples, he was suddenly overcome with weariness. Without realizing what he was doing, he went into his teacher's room and lay down on his bed. Here he slept that whole day and all the following night. His companions wanted to wake him, but the maggid would not let them. He said: "Now he is putting on the phylacteries of Heaven."

Delights

A zaddik told this: The delights of all the worlds wanted to reveal themselves to Rabbi Aaron, but he only shook his head. "Even if they are delights," he said at last, "before I enjoy them, I want to sweat for them."

Rabbi Aaron traveled through all of Russia, from one Jewish city to the next, in search of youths worth bringing his teacher, the Great Maggid, as disciples, so that through them the hasidic teachings might spread through the world. Once he came to the city of Amdur. Now he had heard that, beyond the town, in a lonely wood, lived a devout and learned man, Rabbi Hayke, who kept aloof from the world and from men, and mortified his flesh. In order to bring him to the town, Rabbi Aaron preached in the House of Prayer a number of times, and his words had a powerful effect, but it took a long time for the hermit to hear of it. When the hour for the next sermon drew near, something drove him to the House of Prayer. When Rabbi Aaron heard he had come, he did not preach his sermon, but said only these words: "If a man does not grow better, he grows worse." Like a poison which rouses the very core of life against itself, these words bit into the mind of the ascetic. He ran to the rabbi and begged him to help him out of the maze of error in which he had lost his way. "Only my teacher, the maggid of Mezritch can do that," said Rabbi Aaron.

"Then give me a letter to him," said the man, "so that he may know who I am."

His request was granted, and he started out on his journey confident that before he spoke freely to the maggid, the famous teacher would know that he had before him one of the great men of his generation. The maggid opened the letter and—obviously with deliberate intent—read it aloud. It said that the man who was delivering it did not have a particle of sound goodness in him. Rabbi Hayke burst into tears. "Now, now," said the maggid. "Does what the Lithuanian writes really matter so much to you?"

"Is it true or isn't it?" asked the other.

"Well," said the maggid, "if the Lithuanian says so, it is, very probably, true."

"Then heal me, rabbi!" the ascetic begged him.

For a whole year, the maggid worked over him and healed him. Later, Rabbi Hayke became one of the great men of his generation.

The King

Rabbi Aaron was once reciting the Morning Prayer in the House of Prayer at Mezritch. As he was about to call out God as the "King," tears gushed from his eyes and he could not continue. After prayers, they asked him what had happened. He explained: "At that moment I thought of how Rabbi Yohanan ben Zakkai said to Vespasian: 'Peace be with you, O king. Peace be with you, O king.' And the Roman said to him in anger: 'You deserve the death penalty on two scores. First, I am not the king, yet you called me king. Secondly, supposing I was the king, why did you not come to me before now?' As yet, God is not really king over the world, and I have a part in the blame that this is not so, for why have I still not accomplished the turning; why have I still not come to him?"

The Chandelier

Rabbi Aaron of Tehernobil, son of a daughter of Aaron of Karlin, born long after he died and named after him, was denounced to the authorities and saved only by dint of bribes which the hasidim had given against his will. When he learned of this, he said: "Alas! How weak is my generation! If I stood on the rung of my grandfather, Rabbi Aaron the Great, wrong judgment could have been averted without resorting to bribery." And he went on to tell:

"Once the Haidamaks in the Ukraine and Russia conspired against the Jews and resolved to kill them and seize their property. When word of this reached Mezritch, the heads of the community went to the holy maggid and asked him what to do. Since he saw that Satan had succeeded in gaining the upper hand, he bade all, men, women, and children, hide in the woods around the town, and take with them as much of their possessions as they could carry.

"One group of men hurried to the House of Prayer to save the sacred utensils. From the ceiling hung a large pewter chandelier with thirty-six branches. My grandfather, Rabbi Aaron the Great, had acquired it with the money he had collected, kopek by kopek, among his disciples and the hasidim of the maggid. Every Friday, the holy maggid himself used to light all the branches of this chandelier. It was the only thing left in the House of Prayer. All the other utensils had been removed. My grandfather had been standing at a window, without paying any attention to what was happening around him. Suddenly he noticed them getting at the chandelier. In a moment he was in the middle of the hall. 'Don't touch it!' he cried in a loud voice.

"Messengers went to the maggid to tell him of the incident and find out what he wanted done. The maggid listened to what they had to say and was silent for a time. Then he said: 'All the men, women, and children shall gather in the House of Prayer.' When my grandfather saw the entire community gathering in the House of Prayer, he sent word to the maggid to beg him to come and take pity on him. The maggid gave no reply. Again my grandfather sent to implore him to give him aid of any kind. The maggid did not reply.

"The House of Prayer was filled with the Jews of the community of Mezritch. They were all there: men, women, and children. Only the maggid was missing. Then a man, who had been keeping watch outside, came and reported to my grandfather that the Haidamaks were in the city. My grandfather went out and placed himself in the entrance to the House of Prayer. When the Haidamaks advanced toward him, he hurled the words of the psalm at them in a voice of thunder: 'Why are the nations in an uproar?'

"The leader of the Haidamaks was seized with madness and began to hit out at his own people. They scattered and fled."

On the Earth

This is what Rabbi Aaron of Karlin said concerning the words in the Scriptures: ". . . a ladder set up on the earth, and the top of it reached to Heaven."

"If a man of Israel has himself firmly in hand, and stands solidly on the earth, then his head reaches up to Heaven."

Nothing at All

They asked Rabbi Aaron what he had learned from his teacher, the Great Maggid. "Nothing at all," he said. And when they pressed him to explain what he meant by that, he added: "The nothing-at-all is what I learned. I learned the meaning of nothingness. I learned that I am nothing at all, and that I Am, notwithstanding."

The Little Fear and the Great Fear

Rabbi Shneur Zalman told this about his friend, Rabbi Aaron of Karlin, who died young:

"His fear of God was like the fear of a man who is going to be shot, and stands at the wall and sees the muzzle of the gun pointed at his heart, and looks straight into the muzzle, full of fear and yet undaunted. But this was only his little fear of God, his every-day fear. When the great fear of God came over him —no comparison suffices to describe that!"

Unworthiness and the Hearing of Prayers

They asked Rabbi Aaron: "Concerning Moses' prayer to God to pardon his people, the commentary says: 'that they may not say I was unworthy to plead for mercy in their behalf.' Is not this contrary to the testimony in the Scriptures that Moses was meek above all other men?"

"Just because he was so meek," the zaddik replied, "he said to God: 'Hear my prayer, though I am not worthy of it, so that they may not say that the unworthiness of man became manifest through me, and stop pleading to you with all the strength of their hearts, but rather that they may realize that you hear the prayer of any mouth at all.' "

"I"

A disciple of the Great Maggid had received instruction from him for several years and was now starting on his journey home. On the way, he decided to stop in Karlin to visit Rabbi Aaron, who for a time had been his companion in the maggid's House of Study. It was nearly midnight when he reached the city, but his desire to see his friend was so great that he at once went to his house and knocked at the lit window. He heard the dear, familiar voice ask, "Who is it?" and—certain that his own voice would be recognized—he answered nothing but the word: "I!" But the window remained closed and no other sound came from within, though he knocked again and again. At last he cried out in distress: "Aaron, why don't you open for me?" Then his friend replied, but his voice was so grave and solemn that it sounded almost strange to him: "Who is it that dares call himself 'I' as befits only God himself!" When the disciple heard this, he said to himself: "I have not learned nearly enough," and without delaying he returned to Mezritch.

Conversion

Rabbi Aaron once came to the city where little Mordecai, who later became the rabbi of Lechovitz, was growing up. His father brought the boy to the visiting rabbi and complained that he did not persevere in his studies. "Leave the boy with me for a while," said Rabbi Aaron. When he was alone with little Mordecai, he lay down and took the child to his heart. Silently he held him to his heart until his father returned. "I have given him a good talking-to," he said. "From now on, he will not be lacking in perseverance."

Whenever the rabbi of Lechovitz related this incident, he added: "That was when I learned how to convert men."

The Greeting

A grand-nephew of Rabbi Aaron related: "At the close of the sabbath, when I sat at his table while they said the Elijah-song, I noticed that he and his son Rabbi Asher clasped hands under the table, at the words: "Hail to Him who greeted him, and to him whom He greeted.' And I understand what this meant: Elijah had assumed the shape of the Father, and the Father wanted to accord his son the grace of the greeting."

Permission

It is told:

Passover was coming, and Rabbi Aaron, who was in Mezritch, wanted to go home for the holidays. He asked and received the maggid's permission. But hardly had he left the house, when the maggid called some of his disciples and said to them: "Go

to Aaron's inn at once, and talk him out of going to Karlin."
They went and tried to persuade their friend to celebrate the
festival with them. When they failed to make any impression
on him, they gave away that it was the maggid himself who had
sent them.

Immediately Aaron hurried to him and said: "Rabbi, it is very
necessary for me to go home, and now I am told that you wish
me to spend the holidays with you—is. that so?"

"I shall not keep you," said the rabbi. "If it is necessary for
you to go, go in peace." But when Aaron had left, he again said
to his disciples: "Don't let him go!" This recurred one more
time, but since the maggid did not give him instructions to the
contrary, Rabbi Aaron would not listen to what seemed sheer
foolery, and left for Karlin. When he entered his house, he had
to lie down, and he died three days later. He was thirty-six
years old.

When the maggid heard of his death, he quoted the saying of
our sages: "When Aaron died, the clouds of glory vanished,"
and he added: "He was our weapon. What are we to do in the
world now!"

The disciples reproached their maggid for allowing this radiant
and holy man to go to his death. "Why didn't you tell him?"
they asked.

"What was given a man to administer, he must faithfully administer," he said.

The maggid died the following autumn.

The Foolish Thing

Rabbi Asher, son of Rabbi Aaron, told:

"When I went to see Rabbi Pinhas of Koretz, I did not tell him
who I was, but he said: 'Your father is walking behind you.'
After a while, he added: 'Your father has done a foolish thing.'
I was frightened, for I knew that whatever Rabbi Pinhas said
about a zaddik—and even if he had been in the upper world
these five hundred years—reached the ears of heavenly judgment. 'The foolish thing your father has done,' he went on to
say, 'was not to live longer than he did.' "

Three Generations

When Rabbi Israel of Rizhyn betrothed his son Rabbi Abraham Jacob, later the rabbi of Sadagora, to a daughter of Rabbi Aaron of Karlin, a grandson of the great Rabbi Aaron, and the engagement contract was being written, he said: "It is our custom, at a time such as this, to recite the genealogy of the bride's father. The great Rabbi Aaron was the truth of the world. His son, Rabbi Asher, the grandfather of the bride, has always been close on the track of truth. And the father of the bride—if he knew that a crumb of truth was hidden under a floor-board, he would tear up the floor with his bare hands."

LEVI YITZHAK OF BERDITCHEV

He Who Was Also There

When Levi Yitzhak was young, a rich man chose him for his son-in-law because of his amazing gifts—for such was the custom. As a mark of respect for his prominent father-in-law, they honored him in the first year of his marriage, by asking him to recite the passage, "Unto thee it was shown . . ." before the congregation in the House of Prayer, on the Day of Rejoicing in the Law. He went to the pulpit and, for a while, stood motionless. Then he put out his hand to take his prayer shawl, but laid it down again and stood without moving as before. The heads of the community bade the servant whisper to him not to weary the assemblage, but to begin. "Very well," he said and took the prayer shawl in his hand. But when he had almost covered his shoulders, he laid it back. His father-in-law was ashamed before the congregation, especially since he had often boasted of the excellent young man he had gained for his house. Angrily he sent him a message either to begin the prayer or leave the pulpit. But even before Levi Yitzhak was told these words, his voice suddenly rang through the hall: "If you are versed in the teachings, if you are a hasid," he said, "then speak the prayer!" And with this he returned to his place. His father-in-law said nothing.

But when they were at home and Levi Yitzhak sat opposite him at the festive board, his face bright with the joy befitting the day, he could contain himself no longer and shouted: "Why did you bring this disgrace upon me?"

The rabbi replied: "When I first put out my hand to draw the prayer shawl over my head, the Evil Urge came and whispered in my ear: 'I want to say "Unto thee it was shown . . ." with you!' I asked: 'Who are you that you regard yourself worthy to do this?' And he: 'Who are you that you regard yourself worthy to do this?' 'I am versed in the teachings,' I said. 'I too am versed in the teachings,' he replied. I thought to put an end to this idle talk and said contemptuously: 'Where did you study?' 'Where did you study?' he countered. I told him. 'But I was right there with you,' he murmured laughingly. 'I studied there in your company!' I pondered for a moment. 'I am a hasid,' I informed him triumphantly. And he, unperturbed: 'I too am a hasid.' I: 'To what zaddik did you travel?' And he, again echoing me: 'To whom did you travel?' 'To the holy maggid of Mezritch,' I replied. Whereupon he laughed still more derisively. 'But I tell you that I was there with you and became a hasid just as you did. And that is why I want to say with you, "Unto thee it was shown. . . ." ' Then I had enough of it. I left him. What else could L have done?"

In Tanners' Alley

On one of his journeys, as night was falling, Levi Yitzhak came to a little town where he knew no one at all, nor could he find a lodging until finally a tanner took him home with him. He wanted to say the Evening Prayer, but the smell of the hides was so penetrating that he could not utter a word. So he left and went to the House of Study which was quite empty, and there he prayed. And then, suddenly, he understood how the Divine Presence had descended to exile and now—with bowed head—stood in Tanners' Alley. He burst into tears and wept and wept until he had cried his heart out over the sorrow of the Divine Presence, and he fell in a faint. And then he saw the glory of God in all its splendor, a dazzling light ranged in four-and-twenty rungs of divers colors, and heard the words: "Be strong, my son! Great suffering will come upon you, but have no fear, for I shall be with you."

In Transport

On the morning of the Feast of Tabernacles, when Rabbi Levi Yitzhak was about to reach into the chest where the citron and the sheaf of palm, myrtle and willows of the brook awaited the blessing, he thrust his hand through the glass lid, and did not mark that he had cut himself.

At the Feast of Hanukkah, when he saw the holy lights burning, he was impelled to put his bare hand into the flame, yet felt no hurt.

At the Feast of Purim, before the book of Esther was read, he danced during the benediction, danced on the desk, and almost on the scroll itself.

When he had drawn water for the baking of the unleavened bread, he was so enraptured at fulfilling this holy rite, that he fell into the well.

When at the seder he said the word "matzah," that is, unleavened bread, he was so moved with fervor that he threw himself under the table and tipped it over with the seder-bowl, unleavened bread, and the wine, so that all had to be prepared anew. He donned the fresh clothing they brought him, and—like one savoring an exquisite morsel—said: "Ah! Ah! this matzah!"

The Bath

It is told:

When Rabbi Levi Yitzhak had become rav in Berditchev, those who opposed his teachings beset him with hostilities. Among these was a group, so unfalteringly faithful to the memory of the great Rabbi Liber who had lived and taught in Berditchev, and died fifteen years before, that they did not want to have anything to do with the innovator. Once Rabbi Levi Yitzhak had them come to him and told them that he intended to immerse himself in Rabbi Liber's bath. Now Rabbi Liber had never had a true bath. What they called his bath was nothing but a roof on four posts, and under it a pit full of water. In winter Rabbi Liber used to break the ice with an axe and then immerse himself for his holy ablutions. After his death, the roof had caved in and mud gathered in the pit. And so the zaddik was told that to bathe in it was impossible. But he was firm in his purpose and hired four workingmen who dug for a whole day. So it went for a number of days. His enemies laughed at this curious new rav. It was quite obvious—so they said—that Rabbi Liber did not wish his bath to be used.

Rabbi Levi Yitzhak asked all those of his intimates who had known Rabbi Liber to assemble early the following morning.

He himself went to the bath with them, and once more the workmen began to dig. After two hours one of them cried out: "I see water!" Soon they reported that more water had collected. "There is no need to dig any further," said the rabbi. He took off his clothes and, keeping only his cap on his head, went down into the pit. When he stepped into the water, everyone there saw that it barely lapped his ankles, but in a moment it had risen to his mouth. Then he asked: "Is there anybody here who remembers Rabbi Liber in his youth?" They answered that in the new part of the city lived a beadle who was a hundred and sixteen years old, and had served Rabbi Liber when he was young. The zaddik sent for him and waited in the water which reached to his mouth. At first the old man refused to come. But when he was told what had happened, he went with the man who had come to fetch him.

"Do you still remember the beadle," the rabbi asked him, "who hanged himself from the chandelier in the House of Prayer?" "Surely I remember him," the old man answered in surprise. "But how are you concerned with him? All that was a good seventy years ago, long before you were born!"

"Tell us about it," said the rabbi.

The old man told: "He was a simple man, but he was very devout. And he had his own way of doing things. On Wednesday of every week he began to polish the great chandelier, hanging from the ceiling, for the sabbath, and while he did this he always said: 'I do this for the sake of God.' But one Friday afternoon, when people came to the House of Prayer, they found him hanging from the chandelier in a noose knotted of his belt."

The rabbi said: "That time—on the day before the sabbath—when everything had been cleaned and polished, and there was nothing more to be done, the simple beadle asked himself: 'What more can I do in honor of God? What more can I do in his honor?' His poor, weak mind grew confused, and because of all the great things in the world, to him the chandelier had always been greatest, he hanged himself from it in honor of God. And now that seventy years have passed since that day,

Rabbi Liber appeared to me in a dream and told me to do whatever could be done to release the soul of that simple man. Therefore I had the holy bath restored and immersed myself. Now tell me: Is the hour come for the release of that poor soul?"

"Yes, yes, yes!" they all called as if with a single voice.

"Then I too say: 'Yes, yes, yes!'" said the rabbi. "Go in peace." With that he came out of the water, and the water sank so that it would barely have lapped his ankles.

Rabbi Levi Yitzhak had a bath-house built in that place, and had the old bath restored; for himself he had another dug next to it. Only when he was about to prepare for some difficult work did he use the bath of Rabbi Liber. Even today the house with the two baths still stands in the old part of the city, near the "Klaus," and they still call the one that of Rabbi Liber, and the other that of Rabbi Levi Yitzhak.

Passover Night

Soon after Rabbi Levi Yitzhak had been received as rav by the community of Berditchev, he prayed with great ardor on the first evening of the Feast of Passover, and this lasted for so many hours that the congregation grew tired of waiting, finished their prayers, and went home to prepare the seder meal. Only one man remained, one of those poor wayfarers from another place who, according to the custom, was to take the festive meal at the house of one of the burghers. He had been told that the Jew just reading the prayer was to be his host, and because he was weary with the day's journey he lay down on a bench and was soon fast asleep. Meantime, the rabbi had finished the silent Prayer of Benedictions. When he saw that all the people had gone home, he cried: "O angels, angels on high! Descend on this holy day in praise of the Lord, blessed be He!" At this the stranger half woke from a deep sleep. Still drowsy and dazed, he heard a rushing sound surge through the house and was terrified to the core of his being. But the rabbi recited the hymns in great happiness. Then he caught sight of the stranger and asked him why he alone had remained. The man, who was now fully awake, told him how it had come about, and the rabbi asked him to go to the seder with him. But the stranger was timid and dared not accept. He seemed to fear that—in lieu of food—secret words that work magic would fall to his share. "Calm yourself," said the rabbi. "You will eat at my house just what you would eat at the table of other burghers." Then the man decided to go with him.

The Doubting Innkeeper

The owner of a tavern in Berditchev, where mead was dispensed, was not in favor of the hasidic way of life, but liked to listen when hasidim told each other of the deeds of their leaders. On one such occasion he heard them speak of the praying of Rabbi Levi Yitzhak. In the sabbath service, when—so they told—the rabbi came to the words: "Holy, holy, holy," in the chanting of which denizens of heaven unite with men, the angels came to listen to what his lips were saying.

"Do you really think that this is so?" asked the innkeeper.

"Yes, it is so," they said.

"And where do the angels go after that?" he inquired. "Do they remain floating in air?"

"No," they answered him. "They fly down and stand around the rabbi."

"And where do you go in the meantime?"

"When the rabbi begins to sing mightily, and dances so mightily through all the house, there is no room for us inside."

"Well," said the innkeeper, "I shall see this matter for myself. He won't get me to budge from the spot!"

At the Feast of the New Moon, when the rabbi began to burn with ecstasy, the innkeeper came up close behind him. The rabbi —in his great fervor—turned around, seizing him by the coat-tails, shook him, pushed him, and thus, shaking and pushing him alternately, dragged him from one end of the house to the other, and back again. The innkeeper hardly knew what was happening to him. He was almost out of his mind. There was a roaring in his ears as of a tremendous surge. Rallying the last shreds of his strength, he wrenched himself free from the hands of the zaddik and fled. From that time on, he too believed that other powers were involved than merely those of this earth.

For Israel

Before reciting the Prayer of Benedictions on New Year's Day, the rabbi of Berditchev sang:
"The dwellers above and the dwellers below, they shake and they quake in the fear of your name; the dwellers in chasms, the dwellers in graves, they quiver and shiver for fear of your name. But the just, in the pales of paradise, break into acclaim and sing your name. That is why I, Levi Yitzhak, son of Sarah, am come before you with pleas and with prayers. What have you to do with Israel? To whom do you speak? To the children of Israel! To whom do you give commandments? To the children of Israel! Whom do you bid say the benedictions? The children of Israel! And so I ask you: What have you to do with Israel? Are there not plenty of Chaldeans, and Medes, and Persians? It must be that they are dear to you, the children of Israel—children of God they are called. Blessed art thou, O Lord our God, King of the world!"

The True King

On another New Year's Day he prefaced the liturgy of the sanctification of God in this wise: "*Fonye* [a nickname current among the Jews to designate the Russians—here used to designate the czar], says he is king." And then he proceeded to enumerate the rulers of great countries, calling each by his nickname. In the end he shouted with joy, and cried: "But I say: 'Glorified and sanctified be His great Name!'"

A Deal

In the middle of a prayer Rabbi Levi Yitzhak said:
"Lord of all the world! A time there was when you went around with that Torah of yours and were willing to sell it at a bargain, like apples that have gone bad, yet no one would buy it from you. No one would even look at you! And then we took it!

Because of this I want to propose a deal. We have many sins and misdeeds, and you an abundance of forgiveness and atonement. Let us exchange! But perhaps you will say: 'Like for like!' My answer is: Had we no sins, what would you do with your forgiveness? So you must balance the deal by giving us life, and children, and food besides!"

An Interruption

On the forenoon of the Day of Atonement, when the rabbi of Berditchev came to that place in the recital of the Temple Service where the high priest sprinkles the atoning drops of blood and has to say the words: "And thus did he count: one: one and one: one and two: one and three . . ." he was so overwhelmed with fervor that—when he had said "one" the second time—he fell on the floor and lay as one dead. In vain did those standing near seek to revive him. They lifted him from the floor, carried him to his room, and laid him on his bed. Then the hasidim, who knew very well that this was a state which had to do with the soul, and not a sickness of the body, continued in prayer. Toward evening—they had just begun to say the Closing Prayer —the rabbi rushed in, and up to the pulpit, shouting: ". . . and one!" Then he bethought himself and said the prayers in the correct sequence.

Struggle

Once, on the Day of Atonement, the rabbi of Berditchev was praying in the synagogue of Lwow. In the middle of the Additional Prayer he suddenly stopped, and the people heard him say in Polish, in a threatening voice: "I'll show you . . ."
During the evening meal the son of the rabbi of Lwow said to him of Berditchev: "I shall not take the liberty of criticizing your manner of praying. But may I ask you one thing: How could you interrupt your prayer, and with Polish words at that?"
The rabbi of Berditchev replied: "I managed to down my other enemies, but this was the only way I could get the better of the prince-demon of Poland."

The Wish

Every year on the Day of Atonement a woman came to Berditchev to pray with the congregation of Rabbi Levi Yitzhak. Once she was delayed and when she reached the House of Prayer night had already fallen. The woman was vexed and sorrowful, for she was certain the Evening Service must be over. But the rabbi had not even begun. He had waited for the woman to come —and his astonished congregation with him. When she grew aware that he had not yet recited "All Vows," she was filled with great joy and said to God: "Lord of the world, what shall I wish you in return for the good you have vouchsafed me! I wish you may have as much joy of your children as you have just now granted me!"

Then—even while she was speaking—an hour replete with the grace of God came upon the world.

How to Weigh

Once, when the Day of Atonement was over, Shemuel, the rabbi of Berditchev's favorite disciple, came into his master's room to see how he was after the long fast and the almost superhuman fervor he had put into the day's service. Although the night was well advanced, the zaddik's cup of coffee still stood before him untasted. When he saw his disciple he said: "Good that you have come, Shemuel. Now I can tell it. For you must know that today Satan preferred charges against the judgment of Heaven. 'You, the court of justice,' he said, 'tell me why this is: When a man steals a ruble from his fellow, you weigh the coin in order to measure his sin. But if a man gives his fellow a ruble out of charity, you weigh the recipient and all the persons in his house who have been benefited by the gift. Why do you not merely weigh the coin in this instance too? Or why, in the first instance, do you not put in the scales the man who has been robbed and all those who have suffered because of the robbery?' Then I came forward and explained: 'A benefactor wishes to preserve the lives of people, and so the people must be weighed. But the robber wants only the money. He does not even think of the people he is taking it from, and that is

why—in this instance—the coin alone need be weighed.' That
was how I silenced the plaintiff!"

The Song of "You"

The rabbi of Berditchev used to sing a song, part of which is
as follows.

> Where I wander—you!
> Where I ponder—You!
> Only You, You again, always You!
> You! You! You!
> When I am gladdened—You!
> When I am saddened—You!
> Only You, You again, always You!
> You! You! You!
> Sky is You! Earth is You!
> You above! You below!
> In every trend, at every end,
> Only You, You again, always You!
> You! You! You!

Suffering and Prayer

Whenever Rabbi Levi Yitzhak came to that passage in the Haggadah of Passover which deals with the four sons, and in it
read about the fourth son, about him who "knows not how to
ask," he said: " 'The one who knows not how to ask,' that is myself, Levi Yitzhak of Berditchev. I do not know how to ask you,
Lord of the world, and even if I did know, I could not bear to do
it. How could I venture to ask you why everything happens as it
does, why we are driven from one exile into another, why our
foes are allowed to torment us so. But in the Haggadah, the
father of him 'who knows not how to ask,' is told: 'It is for you
to disclose it to him.' And the Haggadah refers to the Scriptures, in which it is written: 'And thou shalt tell thy son.' And,
Lord of the world, am I not your son? I do not beg you to reveal to me the secret of your ways—I could not bear it! But
show me one thing; show it to me more clearly and more
deeply: show me what this, which is happening at this very

212

moment, means to me, what it demands of me, what you, Lord of the world, are telling me by way of it. Ah, it is not why I suffer, that I wish to know, but only whether I suffer for your sake."

His Wife's Prayer

A prayer has come down to us from Pearl, the rabbi of Berditchev's wife. Whenever she kneaded and baked the loaves for the sabbath, she prayed: "Lord of the world, I beg you to help me that, when my husband Levi Yitzhak says the blessing upon these loaves on the sabbath, he may have in his mind what I have in my mind this very hour that I knead them and bake them."

Two Kinds of Praying

Once, on the eve of the sabbath, Rabbi Levi Yitzhak prayed before the congregation of a town in which he was stopping as a guest. As always, now too he drew out the prayer far beyond its usual length through the many exclamations and gestures not provided for in any liturgy. When he had finished, the rav of that town went up to him, proffered the sabbath greetings, and asked: "Why are you not more careful not to tire the congregation? Do not our sages relate of Rabbi Akiba that, whenever he prayed *with* the congregation, he did so quickly, but that when he prayed alone, he yielded himself to his transports, so that frequently he began in one corner of the room and ended up in another."

The rabbi of Berditchev replied: "How is it possible to assume that Rabbi Akiba with his countless disciples hastened his prayer in order not to tire the congregation! For surely every member of it was more than happy to listen to his master hour after hour! The meaning of this talmudic story is more likely this: When Rabbi Akiba really prayed with the congregation, that is to say, when the congregation felt at heart the same fervor as he, his prayer could well be short, for he had to pray only for himself. But when he prayed alone, that is to say, when he prayed with his congregation, but his was the only heart fervent among them, he had to draw out his prayer to lift their hearts to the level of his."

With Open Eyes

Once Rabbi Levi Yitzhak told the maggid of Koznitz, whose guest he was, that he intended going to Vilna, the center of the opponents of hasidic teachings, in order to debate with them. "I should like to ask you a question," said the maggid. "Why do you go contrary to the custom, in that you recite the Eighteen Benedictions with open eyes?"

"Dear heart," said the rabbi of Berditchev, "do you think that—when I do this—I see anything at all?"

"I know very well," the maggid replied, "that you see nothing whatsoever, but what will you say to those others when they ask you this question?"

The Hoarse Reader

In the congregation of Rabbi Levi Yitzhak there was a reader who had grown hoarse. The rabbi asked him:

"How is it that you are hoarse?"

"Because I prayed before the pulpit," answered the other.

"Quite right," said the rabbi. "If one prays before the pulpit one grows hoarse, but if one prays before the living God, then one does not grow hoarse."

The Absent Ones

Once, after he had recited the Eighteen Benedictions, the rabbi of Berditchev went up to certain persons in the House of Prayer, and greeted them, saying: "Peace be with you," several times over, as though they had just come back from a long journey. When they looked at him in surprise, he said: "Why are you so astonished? You were far away, weren't you? You in a market-place, and you on a ship with a cargo of grain, and when the sound of praying ceased, you returned, and so I greeted you."

Babbling Sounds

Rabbi Levi Yitzhak once came to an inn where many merchants were stopping on the way to market their wares. The place was far from Berditchev and so no one knew the zaddik. In the early morning the guests wanted to pray, but since there was

only a single pair of phylacteries in the whole house, one after
another put them on and rattled off his prayer, and handed
them on to the next. When they had all prayed, the rabbi called
the young men to him, saying that he wanted to ask them something. When they had come close, he looked gravely into their
faces and said: "Ma—ma—ma; va—va—va."

"What do you mean?" cried the young men, but he only repeated the same meaningless syllables. Then they took him for
a fool.

But now he said: "How is it you do not understand this language which you yourselves have just used in speaking to
God?"

For a moment the young men were taken aback and stood silent. Then one of them said: "Have you never seen a child in
the cradle, who does not yet know how to put sounds together
into words? Have you not heard him make babbling sounds,
such as 'ma—ma—ma; va—va—va'? All the sages and scholars
in the world cannot understand him, but the moment his mother
comes, she knows exactly what he means."

When the rabbi heard this answer, he began to dance for joy.
And from that time on, whenever on the Days of Awe he spoke
to God in his own fashion in the midst of prayer, he never
failed to tell this answer to him.

The Foolish Prayer

At the close of the Day of Atonement, the rabbi of Berditchev
said to one of his hasidim: "I know what you prayed for this
day! On the eve, you begged God to give you the thousand
rubles which you need in order to live and usually earn in the
course of a year, all at once, at the beginning of the year, so
that the toil and trouble of business may not distract you from
learning and prayer. But in the morning you thought better of
it and decided that if you had the thousand rubles all at once,
you would probably launch a new and bigger business enterprise which would take up even more of your time. And so you
begged to receive half the amount every half year. And before
the Closing Prayer, this too seemed precarious to you, and you

expressed the wish for quarterly instalments, so you might learn and pray quite undisturbed. But what makes you think that your learning and praying is needed in Heaven? Perhaps what is needed there is that you toil and rack your brains."

The End of Prayers

At the close of the seventy-second psalm are the words: "And let the whole earth be filled with His glory. Amen, and Amen. The prayers of David the son of Jesse are ended."
Concerning this Rabbi Levi Yitzhak said: "All prayers and hymns are a plea to have His glory revealed throughout the world. But if once the whole earth is, indeed, filled with it, there will be no further need to pray."

Worldly Talk

When Rabbi Levi Yitzhak came to Nikolsburg to visit Rabbi Shmelke who had taught him the way of fervor when he was young, and whom he had not seen in a long time, he went into the kitchen, covered with his prayer shawl and with double phylacteries on his forehead, and asked Rabbi Shmelke's wife —on this very first morning—what dishes were being prepared for the noonday meal. His question, though rather surprising, was answered. Then he went on to ask whether the cooks had really mastered their art, and other things of the same sort. Rabbi Shmelke's disciples, who heard of this, took him for a veritable glutton. He, however, now entered the House of Prayer and—while the congregation prayed—began to talk to an utterly insignificant man, despised by all, on quite unimportant worldly subjects, as those standing near could determine. One of the disciples could not bear to observe such behavior any longer and said roughly to the stranger: "Silence! Idle chatter is forbidden here!" But the rabbi of Berditchev paid no attention to him and continued his conversation.
At the midday meal, Rabbi Shmelke greeted him joyfully, bade him sit at his side, and ate from the same bowl as he. His disciples, who had heard of the curious manners of the visitor, marked these signs of favor and friendship with sullen surprise.

When the meal was over, one of them could no longer suppress his annoyance and asked his master why he showered honors on so empty-headed and impudent a man who had behaved in such and such a way. The zaddik replied: "In the Gemara we read: 'Rab (Abba Areka), for all the days of his life never spoke of worldly matters.' Is this praise not strange? Does it indicate that the other masters spent their time in worldly talk? Can nothing worthier be told of Rab? The meaning is this: Whatever worldly affairs he discussed with people in the course of the day, each of his words was, in reality, filled with secret significance and a secret purpose, and made itself felt in the higher world; and his spirit remained steadfast in such service all day long. That is why our sages have accorded him praise of which none other was found worthy. What others could do for only three hours, after which they sank from this level, he could do throughout the day. And the same is true of Rabbi Levi Yitzhak. What I can do for only three hours, he can do the whole day through: concentrate his spirit, so that it makes itself felt in the world of Heaven, even with talk which men consider idle."

He Who Laughed

Rabbi Moshe Leib of Sasov was deeply devoted to the zaddik of Berditchev. His disciple Abraham David, later the rabbi of Buczacz, besieged his master for permission to go to that other, whose manner of teaching he wished very much to observe at close quarters. Rabbi Moshe Leib did not want to grant his request. "In the book of Daniel," he said, "we read that 'they had ability to stand in the king's palace.' Our sages explain these words in this way: that they had learned to restrain themselves from laughing, sleeping, and other things besides. Now Rabbi Levi Yitzhak never ceases to burn with unfailing fire. Into all he does he puts his flame-like soul. And so he who ventures into his presence must be very sure he is able to contain his laughter at observing the curious gestures of the holy man when he prays and when he eats."

The disciple promised he would not give way to laughter, and so the rabbi of Sasov permitted him to go to Berditchev for the sabbath. But when, at table, he saw the convulsive movements of the zaddik, and the faces he made, he could no longer control himself and burst out laughing. Then, he fell into a frenzy; his fits of laughter recurred over and over. Finally he had to be led away from the table and—when the sabbath was over—sent back to Sasov under guard.

When Rabbi Moshe Leib saw him, he wrote to the zaddik: "I sent you a vessel which was whole, and you gave it back to me in pieces."

The sickness of Abraham David lasted thirty days. Then he was suddenly well. From that time on he gave a feast of thanks on the anniversary of that day, and on this occasion told the story of his visit to Berditchev, ending with the words of the psalm: "Give thanks unto the Lord, for He is good, for His mercy endureth forever."

Day After Day

Every evening the rabbi of Berditchev examined in his heart what he had done on that day, and repented every flaw he discovered. He said: "Levi Yitzhak will not do this again." Then he chided himself: "Levi Yitzhak said exactly the same thing yesterday!" And added: "Yesterday Levi Yitzhak did not speak the truth, but he does speak the truth today."

He used to say: "Like a woman who suffers overwhelming pain in child-birth, and swears she will never lie with her husband again, and yet forgets her oath, so on every Day of Atonement we confess our faults and promise to turn, and yet we go on sinning, and You go on forgiving us."

Eternal Beginnings

A student asked the rabbi of Berditchev: "The Talmud teaches that 'Those who are perfect in righteousness cannot stand in that place where those stand who turn to God.' According to this, one who has been stainless from youth comes after one who has transgressed against God many times, and cannot attain to his rung?"

The zaddik replied: "He who sees a new light every day, light he did not see the day before, if he wishes truly to serve, must condemn his imperfect service of yesterday, atone for it, and start afresh. The stainless one who believes he has done perfect service, and persists in it, does not accept the light, and comes after him who ever turns anew."

Envy

Walking in the street, the rabbi of Berditchev once went up to a man who held an important office and was as evil-minded as he was powerful, took hold of the hem of his coat, and said: "Sir, I envy you! When you turn to God, each of your flaws will become a ray of light, and you will shine with a great light. Sir, I envy you your flood of radiance!"

The Seder of the Ignorant Man

Once Rabbi Levi Yitzhak held the seder of the first night of Passover so devoutly, that every word and every rite glowed at the zaddik's table, with all the holiness of its secret significance. In the dawn after the celebration Rabbi Levi Yitzhak sat in his room, joyful and proud that he had performed so successful a service. But, of a sudden, he heard a voice, saying: "More pleasing to me than your seder is that of Hayyim, the water-carrier."

The rabbi summoned the people in his house and his disciples, and inquired about the man whose name he had heard. Nobody knew him. At the zaddik's bidding some of his disciples went in search of him. They had to ask around for a long time before—at the outskirts of the city, where only poor people live— they were shown the house of Hayyim, the water-carrier. They knocked at the door. A woman came out and asked what they wanted. When they told her she was amazed. "Yes," she said, "Hayyim, the water-carrier, is my husband. But he cannot go with you because he drank a lot yesterday and is sleeping it off now. If you wake him you will find that he cannot manage to lift his feet."

All they said in reply was: "It is the rabbi's orders." They went and shook him from his sleep. He only blinked at them, could not understand what they wanted him for, and attempted to turn over and go on sleeping. But they raised him from his bed, took hold of him, and between them brought him to the zaddik, all but carrying him on their shoulders. The rabbi had him put in a chair near him. When he was seated, silent and bewildered, Levi Yitzhak leaned toward him and said: "Rabbi Hayyim, dear heart, what mystic intention was in your mind when you gathered what is leavened?"

The water-carrier looked at him dully, shook his head, and replied: "Master, I just looked into every corner, and gathered it together."

The astonished zaddik continued questioning him: "And what consecration did you think upon in the burning of it?"

The man pondered, looked distressed, and said hesitatingly: "Master, I forgot to burn it. And now I remember—it is all still lying on the shelf."

When Rabbi Levi Yitzhak heard this, he grew more and more uncertain, but he continued asking. "And tell me, Rabbi Hayyim, how did you celebrate the seder?"

Then something seemed to quicken in the eyes and limbs of the man, and he replied in humble tones: "Rabbi, I shall tell you the truth. You see, I always heard that it is forbidden to drink brandy the eight days of the festival, so yesterday morning I drank enough to last me eight days. And so I got tired and fell asleep. Then my wife woke me, and it was evening, and she said to me: 'Why don't you celebrate the seder like all other Jews?' Said I: 'What do you want with me? I am an ignorant man, and my father was an ignorant man, and I don't know what to do and what not to do. But one thing I know: Our fathers and mothers were in captivity in the land of the Gypsies, and we have a God, and he led them out, and into freedom. And see: now we are again in captivity and I know, and I tell you that God will lead us to freedom too.' And then I saw before me a table, and the cloth gleamed like the sun, and on it were platters with matzot and eggs and other dishes, and bottles of red wine. I ate of the matzot and eggs and drank of the wine, and gave my wife to eat and to drink. And then I was overcome with joy, and lifted my cup to God, and said: 'See, God, I drink this cup to you! And do you lean down to us and

220

make us free!' So we sat and drank and rejoiced before God. And then I felt tired, lay down, and fell asleep."

At the Holy Feast of the Seven Shepherds

Rabbi Levi Yitzhak often welcomed at his table an honest and untaught man whom his disciples regarded askance because they thought him incapable of understanding what the rabbi said. And what business has one who boils pitch among those who compound ointments! But because the man was good-natured and simple, he either did not notice the attitude of the rabbi's disciples, or did not let it ruffle him, so that finally they asked the zaddik's wife to show the lout the door. Since she did not want to do this without her husband's permission, she reported to him the misgivings and the request of his disciples. The rabbi replied: "When the Seven Shepherds once sit at the holy feast: Adam, Seth, Methuselah to the right, Abraham, Jacob, Moses to the left, David in the middle, and a poor untutored man, Levi Yitzhak of Berditchev, goes up to them, I believe they will even nod to that lout."

Moses and Mount Sinai

Once the rabbi of Berditchev was asked this question: "How is it that Moses, who in his great humility had implored God not to send him but another to Pharaoh, did not for a single instant hesitate to receive the Torah?"

"He had seen the tall mountains come before God," said the rabbi, "and each beg the privilege of being the one on which the revelation should come to pass. But God chose little Mount Sinai. That is why—when he saw that he too was chosen—Moses did not resist, but followed the call."

His Second Name

Rabbi Levi Yitzhak's second name was *Derbarmdiger*, "Merciful," and by this name which was, however, not his father's, he was known to the authorities and inscribed in their books. And this was how it happened. The king issued a decree that everyone must add to his name a second name, and since the Jews were slow to obey, the sheriff of Berditchev went from house

to house to enforce the new law. When he crossed Rabbi Levi
Yitzhak's threshold and mumbled his question by rote, the zaddik looked at him as one human being looks at another, and—
ignoring the question—said: "Endeavor to imitate the quality
of God. As he is merciful, so you too shall be merciful." But
the sheriff only pulled out his list and noted down: "First name,
Levi Yitzhak, second name Merciful."

The Phylacteries of God

In the middle of a prayer, the rabbi of Berditchev once said to
God: "Lord of the world, you must forgive Israel their sins. If
you do this—good. But if you do not do this, I shall tell all the
world that the phylacteries you wear are invalid. For what is
the verse enclosed in your phylacteries? It is a verse of David's,
of your anointed: 'Who is like thy people Israel, a unique nation on earth!' But if you do not forgive Israel their sins, then
they are no longer a 'unique nation on earth,' the verse contained in your phylacteries is untrue, and they are become invalid."

Another time he said: "Lord of the world, Israel are your
head-phylacteries. When the phylacteries of a simple Jew fall
to the ground, he picks them up carefully, cleans them, and
kisses them. Lord, your phylacteries have fallen to the ground."

The Drayman

Once the rabbi of Berditchev saw a drayman arrayed for the
Morning Service in prayer shawl and phylacteries. He was greas-
ing the wheels of his wagon. "Lord of the world!" he exclaimed
delightedly. "Behold this man! Behold the devoutness of your
people. Even when they grease the wheels of a wagon, they still
are mindful of your name!"

The Woman Who Cried

The rabbi of Berditchev told the following:
"Once, just before New Year's Day, a woman came to me and
cried and cried. I asked her, 'Why are you crying? Why are
you crying?' She said: 'Why shouldn't I cry? My head hurts!

My head hurts!' Said I to her: 'Don't cry. If you cry, your head will only hurt more.' She answered: 'Why shouldn't I cry? Why shouldn't I cry? I have an only son, and now this holy and awful day is coming, and I don't know whether my son will pass when God makes judgment.' Said I to her: 'Don't cry! Don't cry! He will surely pass when God makes judgment, for look, it is written: Is not Ephraim a precious son unto Me? Is he a child of delight? For as often as I speak against him, I do earnestly remember him still. Therefore my heart yearneth for him. I will surely have compassion upon him, saith the Lord.' " This incident the rabbi of Berditchev used to relate in a curious singing tone, and in the same tone the hasidim still tell it today.

On the Ground

A man came to Rabbi Levi Yitzhak and complained: "Rabbi, what shall I do with the lie that keeps sneaking into my heart?" He stopped and then cried aloud: "Oh, and even what I just said was not said truthfully! I shall never find truth!" In despair he threw himself on the ground.

"How fervently this man seeks the truth!" said the rabbi. With a gentle hand he raised him from the ground and said: "It is written: 'The truth will grow out of the ground.' "

The Thick Prayerbook

On one eve of the Day of Atonement, the rabbi of Berditchev waited for a while before going to the pulpit to read the prayers and walked back and forth in the House of Prayer. In a corner he found a man crouched on the floor and weeping. When he questioned him, the man replied: "Up to a short time ago I had all good things, and now I am wretched. Rabbi, I lived in a village and no hungry man went from my door unfed. My wife used to bring home poor wayfarers she met on the road, and see to their needs. And then He comes along"—here the man pointed toward the sky—"takes my wife and my house from one day to the next. There I was with six small children, without a wife, without a house! And I had a thick prayerbook, and all the hymns were in it in just the right order; you didn't have to hunt around, and that burned up along with everything else. Now you tell me, Rabbi, can I forgive Him?"

The zaddik had them look for a prayerbook like the one the man described. When it was brought, the man began to turn the pages to see if everything was in the correct sequence, and the rabbi of Berditchev waited the while. Finally he asked: "Do you forgive Him now?"

"Yes," said the man. Then the rabbi went to the pulpit and intoned the prayer "All Vows."

The Wisdom of Solomon

They asked Rabbi Levi Yitzhak of Berditchev: "With regard to that passage in the Scriptures which states that King Solomon was wiser than all other men, it has been observed: 'Even wiser than fools.' What meaning can there be in these apparently meaningless words?"

The rabbi of Berditchev explained: "One characteristic of a fool is that he considers himself wiser than anyone else, and no one can convince him that he is a fool and that what he does is folly. But Solomon's wisdom was so great that it could assume many different guises, including the guise of the fool. That was why he could hold true converse with fools, and impress their hearts until they recognized and professed the sort of people they were."

Abraham and Lot

In the course of a journey, the rabbi of Berditchev stopped in Lwow and went to the house of a rich and respected man. When he was admitted to the master of the house, he begged for a day's lodging but was silent concerning his name and calling. The rich man answered him gruffly: "I have no use for wayfarers. Why don't you go to an inn?"

"I am not a man to stay at an inn," said the rabbi. "Just give me a little space in one of your rooms and I shall not trouble you for anything else."

"Away with you!" cried the other. "If—as you say—you are not a man to stay at an inn, go to the school-teacher around the corner. He likes to welcome vagrants like yourself with honor, and to give them food and drink."

Rabbi Levi Yitzhak went to the school-teacher, was received with honor, and given food and drink. But on his way there someone had recognized him, and soon the whole town buzzed with the news that the holy rabbi of Berditchev was there and had taken lodgings in the house of the school-teacher. Hardly had he rested a little, when a great throng of people desiring to enter gathered at the door. When it was opened they flooded in to be blessed by the zaddik. Among them was the rich man. He fought his way to the rabbi and said: "May the master forgive me and honor my house with his visit! All the zaddikim who ever came to Lwow were my guests."

Rabbi Levi Yitzhak turned to those standing around him and said: "Do you know the difference between our Father Abraham, peace be with him, and Lot? Why does such a spirit of satisfaction pervade the story of how Abraham set before the angels curd and milk and tender calf? Did not Lot also bake for them and give them to eat? And why is the fact that Abraham received them in his tent regarded as so deserving an action? For Lot also asked them in and gave them shelter. Now this is the truth of the matter: In the case of Lot it is written that angels came to Sodom. But concerning Abraham, the Scriptures say: ' . . . and he lifted up his eyes and looked, and lo, three men stood over against him.' Lot saw angelic shapes, Abraham poor, dusty wayfarers in need of food and rest."

Drudgery

Rabbi Levi Yitzhak discovered that the girls who knead the dough for the unleavened bread drudged from early morning until late at night. Then he cried aloud to the congregation gathered in the House of Prayer: "Those who hate Israel accuse us of baking the unleavened bread with the blood of Christians. But no, we bake them with the blood of Jews!"

Charity

When Levi Yitzhak became rav in Berditchev, he made an agreement with the leaders of the congregation that they were not to ask him to their meetings unless they intended to discuss the introduction of a new usage or a new procedure. One day they asked him to come to a meeting. Immediately after greeting them, he asked: "What is the new procedure you wish to establish?"

They answered: "From now on we do not want the poor to beg at the threshold. We want to put up a box, and all the well-to-do people are to put money into it, each according to his means, and these funds shall be used to provide for the needy."

When the rabbi heard this, he said: "My brothers, did I not beg you not to call me away from my studies and summon me to a meeting for the sake of an old usage or an old procedure?"

The leaders were astonished and protested: "But master, the procedure under discussion today *is* new!"

"You are mistaken," he cried. "It is age-old! It is an old, old procedure that dates back to Sodom and Gomorrah. Do you remember what is told about the girl from Sodom, who gave a beggar a piece of bread? How they took her and stripped her and smeared her naked body with honey, and exposed her for bees to devour, because of the great crime she had committed! Who knows—perhaps they too had a community box into which the well-to-do dropped their alms in order not to be forced to face their poor brothers eye to eye."

In a Hurry

The Rabbi of Berditchev saw a man hurrying along the street, looking neither right nor left. "Why are you rushing so?" he asked him.

"I am after my livelihood," the man replied.

"And how do you know," continued the rabbi, "that your livelihood is running on before you, so that you have to rush after it? Perhaps it is behind you, and all you need do to encounter it is to stand still—but you are running away from it!"

What Are You Doing?

Another time the Rabbi of Berditchev saw a man in the marketplace, a man so intent upon his business that he never looked

226

up. He stopped him and asked: "What are you doing?"

The man answered hurriedly: "I have no time to talk to you now."

But the zaddik refused to be snubbed. He repeated his question: "What are you doing?"

Impatiently the man cried: "Don't delay me. I have to attend to my business."

But the rabbi insisted. "All right," he said. "But you, yourself—what are you doing? Everything you are so worried about is in the hands of God, and all that is in yours is to fear God."

The man looked up—and for the first time he knew what the fear of God was.

The Two Generals

Rabbi Levi Yitzhak said: "Whether a man really loves God—that can be determined by the love he bears his fellow-men. I shall give you a parable.

"Once upon a time a country was suffering from the ravages of war. The general who headed the army which was sent against the foe, was vanquished. The king discharged him and put in his place another man who succeeded in driving out the invader. The first general was suspected of betraying his country. The king wondered whether there was any way to find out whether he really loved or hated him. He realized that there was one unerring sign which would discover the truth to him: if the man, about whom he was in doubt, showed friendship for his rival and expressed unalloyed joy at his success, he might be regarded as trustworthy; but if he plotted against his rival, this would prove his guilt.

"God created man to strive against the evil in his soul. Now there is many a man who does, indeed, love God, but is defeated in that bitter struggle. He can be recognized by his ability to share whole-heartedly and without reservations in the happiness of his victorious fellow-man."

Amalek

This is how Rabbi Levi Yitzhak expounded the verse in the Scriptures: "Remember what Amalek did unto thee."

Because you are a man, you first are permitted to remember what the power of evil has done to you. But when you ascend to the rung of the zaddikim, and your heart has rest from all your enemies round about, then you will "blot out the remembrance of Amalek from under Heaven," and will remember only what the power of evil has done to Heaven: how it set up a wall between God and Israel, and drove into exile the Divine Presence.

The Greatness of Pharaoh

Rabbi Levi Yitzhak said:
"I envy Pharaoh! What glorification of the Name of God did his stubbornness beget!"

Chameleons

Rabbi Levi Yitzhak said:
"It is written: '. . . and shall deal corruptly, and make a graven image, even the form of any thing . . .' This refers to the 'chameleons,' who when they go among hasidim, act like hasidim, and when they are among renegades, adapt themselves to the ways of renegades, and make for themselves the forms of all manner of things."

Perhaps

A very learned man who had heard of the rabbi of Berditchev— one of those who boasted of being enlightened—looked him up in order to debate with him as he was in the habit of doing with others, and refuting his old-fashioned proofs for the truth of his faith. When he entered the zaddik's room, he saw him walking up and down, a book in his hand, immersed in ecstatic thought. The rabbi took no notice of his visitor. After a time, however, he stopped, gave him a brief glance and said: "But perhaps it is true after all!"
In vain did the learned man try to rally his self-confidence. His knees shook, for the zaddik was terrible to behold and his simple words were terrible to hear. But now Rabbi Levi Yitzhak turned to him and calmly addressed him: "My son, the great Torah scholars with whom you debated, wasted their words on you. When you left them you only laughed at what they

had said. They could not set God and his kingdom on the table before you, and I cannot do this either. But, my son, only think! Perhaps it is true. Perhaps it is true after all!" The enlightened man made the utmost effort to reply, but the terrible "perhaps" beat on his ears again and again and broke down his resistance.

The False Messiahs

An unbeliever once expounded to the rabbi of Berditchev that even the great old masters had erred gravely, that Rabbi Akiba, for instance, had taken Bar Kokhba, the rebel, for the Messiah and honored him accordingly.

The rabbi of Berditchev replied: "There was an emperor whose only son fell ill. One physician advised them to spread an acrid salve on a piece of linen and wrap it around the bare body of the patient. Another contradicted him, saying that the boy was too weak to bear the great pain the salve would cause him. A third prescribed a sleeping potion, but the fourth feared it might prove injurious to the patient's heart. Then the fifth suggested that they give the prince a spoonful whenever he woke up and was in pain. And so it was done.

"When God saw that the soul of Israel had sickened, he wrapped it in the acrid linen of the Exile, and that the soul might bear it, he swathed it in numbing sleep. But lest this destroy it, he wakes it from time to time with the hope in a false Messiah, and then lulls it to rest again until the night is past and the true Messiah appears. And for the sake of this, even the eyes of sages are sometimes blinded."

In the Market-Place

The rabbi of Berditchev was once in a big market-place where he saw a welter of men, each possessed with the greed of making profits. He climbed on the roof of a house and called down in a loud voice: "You people, you are forgetting to fear God."

Once and Now

The rabbi of Berditchev said: "What I see before me is a topsy-turvy world. Once the whole truth was in the alleys and market-places of Israel; there everyone told the truth. But when they came to the House of Prayer, they managed to tell lies. Now it is just the other way round. In the streets and in the squares they utter falsehoods, but when they enter the House of Prayer, they confess the truth. For once it was thus in Israel: Truth and faithfulness were the lamps lighting their steps, and when they went to the market-place and into the world of trade, with their souls they proved the words: Your 'yes' be true and your 'no' be true, and all their trading was done in good faith. But when they came to the House of Prayer they beat their breasts and said: 'We have trespassed! We have dealt treacherously! We have robbed!' And all this was a lie because they had kept faith before God and Man. Today the reverse takes place: in trading they lie and cheat; in their prayer they profess the truth."

The Holy of Holies

Rabbi Levi Yitzhak said: "We are forbidden to think evil thoughts, for the mind of man is the Holy of Holies. In it is the Ark with the tablets of the law, and if he permits evil thoughts to arise within him, he is setting an idol up in the Temple. But when, in the midst of praying, the zaddik is seized with great fervor, when he kindles with flame and lifts his hands, it is as once, when—in the Holy of Holies—the cherubim pointed upward their wings."

The Wicked Plot

"We must not mortify our flesh!" That is what the rabbi of Berditchev used to say. "It is nothing but the tempting of the Evil Urge which wants to weaken our spirit, in order to keep us from serving God rightly.

"Once two strong men were wrestling with each other and neither could prevail over his opponent. Then one of them had an idea. 'I must manage to lessen the power of his mind,' he said to himself. 'With that I shall have conquered his body.' That is just what the Evil Urge wants to do when it tempts us to mortify our flesh."

230

True Sorrow and True Joy

When he was asked which was the right way, that of sorrow or that of joy, the rabbi of Berditchev said:
"There are two kinds of sorrow and two kinds of joy. When a man broods over the misfortunes that have come upon him, when he cowers in a corner and despairs of help—that is a bad kind of sorrow, concerning which it is said: 'The Divine Presence does not dwell in a place of dejection.' The other kind is the honest grief of a man who knows what he lacks. The same is true of joy. He who is devoid of inner substance and, in the midst of his empty pleasures, does not feel it, nor tries to fill his lack, is a fool. But he who is truly joyful is like a man whose house has burned down, who feels his need deep in his soul and begins to build anew. Over every stone that is laid, his heart rejoices."

The Dance

When his son had died, Rabbi Levi Yitzhak danced as he followed the bier. Some of his hasidim could not refrain from expressing their astonishment. "A pure soul," said he, "was given to me. A pure soul I render back."

Discipledom

When Rabbi Kalman, the author of the well-known book "Light and Sun," was five years old, he hid under the prayer shawl of the rabbi of Berditchev, as children like to do, and looked up into his veiled face. Then burning strength entered his heart, suffused it, and took possession of him.
After many years Rabbi Elimelekh took some of his noblest disciples to the rabbi of Berditchev. Among them was young Kalman. Rabbi Levi Yitzhak looked at him and recognized him. "That one is mine!" he said.

Knowing

The rabbi of Berditchev and Aaron, his disciple, were on a journey. They stopped in Lizhensk and were the guests of Rabbi Elimelekh. When the rabbi of Berditchev left, his disciple remained behind, settled down in the "Klaus," the House of Study and Prayer of Rabbi Elimelekh, and began to study there without having told him anything about it. In the evening the zaddik went there and noticed him. "Why did you not leave with your rabbi?" he asked.

Aaron replied: "I know my rabbi, and I stayed here because I want to learn to know you too."

Rabbi Elimelekh went close up to him and took him by the coat. "You think you know your rabbi!" he exclaimed. "Why, you don't even know his coat!"

Rabbi Elimelekh's Answer

During the period when, in many places, the enemies of hasidic teachings attacked Rabbi Levi Yitzhak because of his manner of conducting the service, and did him all possible harm, some understanding people wrote to the great Rabbi Elimelekh and asked him how it was that these persons dared to do such things. He answered: "Why does this surprise you? This sort of thing has always gone on in Israel. Alas for our souls! If this were not so, no nation in the whole world could subjugate us!"

The First Page

They asked Rabbi Levi Yitzhak: "Why is the first page number missing in all the tractates of the Babylonian Talmud? Why does each begin with the second?"

He replied: "However much a man may learn, he should always remember that he has not even gotten to the first page."

Hidden Teachings

Rabbi Levi Yitzhak said: "It is written in Isaiah: 'For instruction shall go forth from me.' How shall we interpret this? For we believe with perfect faith that the Torah, which Moses received on Mount Sinai, cannot be changed, and that none other will be given. It is unalterable and we are forbidden to question even one of its letters. But, in reality, not only the black letters but the white gaps in between, are symbols of the teaching, only that we are not able to read those gaps. In time to come God will reveal the white hiddenness of the Torah."

The Last Blowing of the Ram's Horn

On the last New Year's festival in the life of Rabbi Levi Yitzhak, they tried in vain to blow the ram's horn. No one could wring from it a single note. Finally the zaddik himself put it to his lips, but he too did not succeed. It was clear that Satan was involved in this matter. Rabbi Levi Yitzhak put down the horn, laid it aside and cried: "Lord of the world! In your Torah it is written that we Jews are to blow the ram's horn the day on which you created the world. Look down upon us and you will see that all of us have come with our wives and children to do your command. But if we are denied this, if we are no longer your beloved people, well—then let Ivan blow the ram's horn for you!"

All wept and in the depths of their hearts they turned to God. After a time the rabbi put the ram's horn to his lips again, and now it emitted a flawlessly pure sound. After the prayer Rabbi Levi Yitzhak turned to his congregation and said: "I vanquished him, but it will cost me my life. Here I am, a sin-offering for Israel."

He died a few weeks later.

A Period Extended

At the close of the Day of Atonement, as Rabbi Levi Yitzhak came out of the House of Prayer, he said to the people thronging around him: "I tell you that today the time of my life is up and I should be leaving the world this very hour. But I was disturbed and troubled that I would not be able to fulfil the two precious commands, to dwell in the holiday booth and to say the blessing of the citron, that are coming and will be with us in four days. And so I prayed that my time might be extended until after the Feast of Tabernacles, and God heard me." And so it was: on the day after the Rejoicing in the Law the rabbi of Berditchev fell ill, and on the day after that, he died.

The Gates of Prayer

They tell that the hour Rabbi Levi Yitzhak died, a zaddik teaching in a distant city suddenly interrupted his discourse in which he was trying to fuse the power of the doctrine with that of worship, and said to his disciples: "I cannot go on. Everything went dark before my eyes. The gates of prayer are closing. Something must have happened to the great worshipper, to Rabbi Levi Yitzhak."

The Friend

In Rabbi Levi Yitzhak's time, a holy man lived in the city of Berditchev. They called him the rabbi of Morchov because he had grown up in Morchov, in the Ukraine. There was friendship between these two, and in their relation to each other, reproof was open and love hidden. When the zaddik died, the rabbi of Morchov came to walk behind his bier. When they had carried the body out of the house, he went close up to it, leaned down, and whispered something in the ear of the dead. Only the last words were audible: "As it is written: 'Seven weeks you shall count.'" When seven weeks had passed, he himself died.

From That Time On

Rabbi Levi Yitzhak was dead, and from that time on there was no rav in Berditchev. The congregation could find no one to fill the place he had left empty.

ZUSYA OF HANIPOL

The Blessings

Rabbi Zusya used to say: "My mother Mirl, peace be with her, did not pray from the book, because she could not read. All she knew was how to say the blessings. But wherever she said the blessing in the morning, in that place the radiance of the Divine Presence rested the livelong day."

The Parable of the Wood-Cutter

In his youth, Zusya joined the congregation of the Great Maggid, Rabbi Baer of Mezritch. But he did not stay with the other disciples. He roamed through the woods, lay down in hidden places, and sang his praises to God, until the people quoted Solomon's words when they spoke of him: "With her love be thou ravished always." His younger brother Elimelekh, who was still a boy and did not as yet belong to the congregation, sat over his books. He wondered at Zusya and once asked him: "Brother, why do you act so, that everyone in the House of Study says it is strange?" Zusya answered him with a smile: "My brother, I shall tell you a story." And this is the story.

"A poor wood-cutter had a great longing to see the king face to face. So he left his village and walked for many days until he came to the city where the king lived. After trying for a long time, he succeeded in getting employment in the king's palace. He was to tend the stoves. And now he put all the zeal and good sense he was capable of into his work. He went to the forest himself, fetched the best wood, fragrant with resin, split it into even logs, and—at just the right hour—stacked these deftly in the various fire-places. The king enjoyed the good, living warmth. It was better than what he had had, and he asked how this came about. When they told him about the wood-cutter and his work, he sent him a message that he could nave a wish. The poor man begged that he might be allowed to see the king every once in a while. His wish was granted. They made a window in a narrow passage which led to the woodshed and this window faced the king's living-room, so the wood-cutter could look through and satisfy his longing.

"Now once, when the prince was seated at his father's board, he said something which displeased him and was punished by a year's banishment from the king's apartments. For a time he lived in bitter loneliness. Then he began to wander mournfully through the corridors of the palace. When he came to the little window they had made for the wood-cutter, he was seized with still greater longing to see his father again and begged the man to let him look through. They got to talking together.

"My brother," said Zusya to Elimelekh, when he had reached this point in his story, "this is what the wood-cutter told the prince when they were talking to each other. 'You are at home in the rooms of the lord and eat at his table. All you need do is to govern your speech wisely. But I have neither wisdom nor learning, and so I must perform my lowly service that I may sometimes see the lord's face.'"

The Word

This was told by Rabbi Israel of Rizhyn.

"All the pupils of my ancestors, the Great Maggid, transmitted the teachings in his name—all except Rabbi Zusya. And the reason for this was that Rabbi Zusya hardly ever heard his teacher's sermon out to the end. For at the very start, when the maggid recited the verse from the Scriptures which he was going to expound, and began with the words of the Scriptures: 'And God said,' or 'and God spoke,' Rabbi Zusya was overcome with ecstasy, and screamed and gesticulated so wildly that he disturbed the peace of the round table and had to be taken out. And then he stood in the hall or in the woodshed, beat his hands against the walls, and cried aloud: 'And God said!' He did not quiet down until my ancestor had finished expounding the Scriptures. That is why he was not familiar with the sermons of the maggid. But the truth, I tell you—

I tell you, the truth is this: If a man speaks in the spirit of truth and listens in the spirit of truth, one word is enough, for with one word can the world be uplifted, and with one word can the world be redeemed."

Only the Good

Once when young Zusya was in the house of his teacher, Rabbi Baer, a man came before the Great Maggid and begged him to advise and assist him in an enterprise. Zusya saw that this man was full of sin and untouched by any breath of repentance, he grew angry, and spoke to him harshly, saying: "How can a man like yourself, a man who has committed this crime and that, have the boldness to stand before a holy countenance without shame, and without the longing to atone?" The man left in silence, but Zusya regretted what he had said and did not know what to do. Then his teacher pronounced a blessing over him, that from this moment on, he might see only the good in people, even if a person sinned before his very eyes.

But because Zusya's gift of vision could not be taken from him through words spoken by man, it came to pass that from this time on he felt the sins of the people he met, as his own, and blamed himself for them.

Whenever the rabbi of Rizhyn told this about Rabbi Zusya, he was likely to add: "And if all of us were like him, evil would long since have been destroyed, and death overcome, and perfection achieved."

Suffering

When Rabbi Shmelke and his brother visited the maggid of Mezritch, they asked him about the following. "Our sages said certain words which leave us no peace because we do not understand them. They are that men should praise and thank God for suffering just as much as for well-being, and receive it with the same joy. Will you tell us how we are to understand this, rabbi?"

The maggid replied: "Go to the House of Study. There you will find Zusya smoking his pipe. He will give you the explanation." They went to the House of Study and put their question to Rabbi Zusya. He laughed. "You certainly have come to the right man! Better go to someone else rather than to me, for I have never experienced suffering." But the two knew that, from the day he was born to this day, Rabbi Zusya's life had been a web of need and anguish. Then they knew what it was: to accept suffering with love.

The Garments of Mercy

They asked Rabbi Zusya: "We pray, 'And bestow good mercy upon us,' and 'Who bestowest good mercy . . .' Is not every mercy good?"

He explained: "Of course every mercy is good. But the truth of the matter is that all God does is mercy. Only that the world cannot bear the naked fill of his mercy, and so he has sheathed it in garments. That is why we beg him that the garment too may be good."

The Recipient

A man who lived in the same town as Rabbi Zusya saw that he was very poor. So each day he put twenty pennies into the little bag in which Zusya kept his phylacteries, so that he and his family might buy the necessaries of life. From that time on, the man grew richer and richer. The more he had, the more he gave Zusya, and the more he gave Zusya, the more he had.

But once he recalled that Zusya was the disciple of a great maggid, and it occurred to him that if what he gave the disciple was so lavishly rewarded, he might become even more prosperous if he made presents to the master himself. So he traveled to Mezritch and induced Rabbi Baer to accept a substantial gift from him. From this time on, his means shrank until he had lost all the profits he had made during the more fortunate period. He took his trouble to Rabbi Zusya, told him the whole story, and asked him what his present predicament was due to. For had not the rabbi himself told him that his master was immeasurably greater than he?

Zusya replied: "Look! As long as you gave and did not bother to whom, whether to Zusya or another, God gave to you and did not bother to whom. But when you began to seek out especially noble and distinguished recipients, God did exactly the same."

The Offering

They said to Rabbi Zusya: "It is written: 'Speak unto the children of Israel, that they take for Me an offering.' Should it not rather be: 'that they *make* for Me an offering'?"
Rabbi Zusya replied: "It is not enough for him who gives to the needy, to do this in the spirit of holiness. The needy must also take in the spirit of holiness. It is not enough to give in the name of God. What is given, must also be taken in the name of God. That is why it is written: 'that they take for Me an offering.'"

On the Road

For three years Zusya and Elimelekh journeyed through the land, for they wanted to share the lot of the Divine Presence in exile, and convert to it erring mankind. Once they spent the night at an inn where a wedding was being celebrated. The guests were rough and tough fellows to begin with, and had drunk far more than was good for them. They were just trying to think up some new fun for themselves when the poor travelers arrived—in the nick of time for their purpose. They had hardly lain down in a corner, Rabbi Elimelekh against the wall, and Rabbi Zusya beside him, when those fellows came, grabbed Zusya, who was closest to hand, beat him, and tormented him. After a time, they let him slide to the floor and began to dance. Elimelekh was annoyed that they had let him lie on his sack undisturbed. He envied his brother the blows he had received. So he said: "Dear brother, now let me lie in your place, and you sleep in my corner." And they changed places. When the fellows had finished dancing, they wanted to go on with the fun they had had, and laid hands on Rabbi Elimelekh. But one of them cried: "This isn't according to law and order! Let the other one have his share of our gifts of honor!" With that they dragged Zusya out of his corner, gave him a second drubbing, and shouted: "You too shall carry away a souvenir of the wedding!"

Then Zusya laughed and said to Elimelekh: "You see, dear brother. If blows are appointed to a man, they will always find him out, no matter where he puts himself."

The Horses

In the course of their long wanderings, the two brothers, Rabbi Zusya and Rabbi Elimelekh, often came to the city of Ludmir. There they always slept in the house of a poor, devout man. Years later, when their reputation had spread all over the country, they came to Ludmir again, not on foot as before, but in a carriage. The wealthiest man in that little town, who had never wanted to have anything to do with them, came to meet them, the moment he heard they had arrived, and begged them to lodge in his house. But they said: "Nothing has changed in us to make you respect us more than before. What is new is just the horses and the carriage. Take them for your guests, but let us stop with our old host, as usual."

The Fruits of Wandering

When Rabbi Noah of Kobryn, the grandson of Rabbi Moshe of Kobryn, was in Sadagora, he heard someone say, "You will find hasidim up to the point the brothers Rabbi Zusya and Rabbi Elimelekh reached in their long wanderings; beyond that you will not find hasidim."

The Sabbath Feeling

Week after week, from the coming of the Sabbath to the going, and especially when they ate the sabbath meal among the hasidim, and spoke words of teaching, Rabbi Elimelekh and Rabbi Zusya were overcome by a feeling of holiness. Once, when they were together, Rabbi Elimelekh said to Rabbi Zusya: "Brother, I am sometimes afraid that my feeling of holiness on the sabbath may not be a true feeling, and that— in that case—my service may not be the right service."

"Brother," said Zusya, "I too am sometimes afraid of that very thing."

"What shall we do about it?" asked Elimelekh.

Zusya replied: "Let each of us, on a week-day, prepare a meal which is exactly like the sabbath meal. And let us sit with the hasidim and say words of teaching. Then, if we have that feeling of holiness, we shall know that our way is not the true way. But if we do not have it, this will prove that our way is right."

And they did accordingly. They prepared a sabbath meal on a week-day, put on sabbath clothes and the fur caps they wore on the sabbath, ate with the hasidim, and spoke words of teaching. And the feeling of holiness overcame them just as on the sabbath. When they were alone together, Rabbi Elimelekh asked: "Brother, what shall we do?"

"Let us go to the rabbi of Mezritch," said Rabbi Zusya. They went to Mezritch and told their teacher what was weighing upon them.

The maggid said: "If you put on sabbath clothes and sabbath caps, it is quite right that you had a feeling of sabbath holiness. Because sabbath clothes and sabbath caps have the power of drawing the light of sabbath holiness down to earth. So you need have no fears."

Zusya and the Sinner

Once Rabbi Zusya came to an inn, and on the forehead of the innkeeper he saw long years of sin. For a while he neither spoke nor moved. But when he was alone in the room which had been assigned to him, the shudder of vicarious experience overcame him in the midst of singing psalms and he cried aloud: "Zusya, Zusya, you wicked man! What have you done! There is no lie that failed to tempt you, and no crime you have not committed. Zusya, foolish, erring man, what will be the end of this?" Then he enumerated the sins of the innkeeper, giving the time and place of each, as his own, and sobbed. The innkeeper had quietly followed this strange man. He stood at the door and heard him. First he was seized with dull dismay, but then penitence and grace were lit within him, and he woke to God.

Joint Penance

This was told by a reader in the House of Prayer.

When I heard that Rabbi Zusya helped people to turn to God,

241

I decided to go to him. When I arrived in Hanipol, I imme-diately went to his house, put down my stick and knapsack, and asked for him. The rabbi's wife told me to go to the House of Study. I could see the rabbi from the threshold. He was wearing his prayer shawl, had just taken off his phylac-teries, and was reciting the psalm: "Answer me when I call!" While he said these words, he wept more bitterly than I had ever heard or seen anyone weep. And then, on the floor, I saw a man who was moaning quietly to himself. Suddenly he screamed: "I am a great sinner!" It took me quite a while to understand what was going on, and later I learned the whole story.

The man was an assistant in the House of Study of the town he lived in. He had been urged to go to Rabbi Zusya to be told what to do as a penance. But when he stood in front of the rabbi, he refused to do penance. Then—but the rabbi him-self told me what happened then. It was when I discussed my own affairs with him and mentioned what I had seen.

"What did Zusya do then?" he said to me. "I climbed down all the rungs until I was with him, and bound the root of my soul to the root of his. Then he had no choice but to do penance along with me." And it was a very great and very ter-rible penance. But when the man stopped screaming and moaning, I saw the rabbi go up to him. He bent down, took him by the curls at his temples, and gently turned his head around. Finally he lifted him with both hands and set him on his feet. "Thine iniquity is taken away," he said, "and thy sin expiated."

"But I myself"—so the man who told me the story added—"later became the reader in Rabbi Zusya's House of Prayer."

The Bold-faced and the Shame-faced

Our sages say: "The bold-faced go to hell, the shame-faced to paradise." Rabbi Zusya, God's fool, expounded these words as follows. "Whoever is bold in his holiness, may descend to hell in order to raise what is base. He may roam about in alleys and market-places and need not fear evil. But he who

242

is shame-faced, who lacks boldness, must keep to the heights of paradise, to studying and praying. He must beware of coming in contact with evil."

Zaddik and Hasidim

On one of the days of heart-searching, the days between New Year and the Day of Atonement, Rabbi Zusya sat in his chair, and his hasidim stood around him from morning until evening. He had lifted his eyes and his heart to Heaven, and loosed himself from all bodily bonds. While looking at him, one of his hasidim was overcome with the desire to turn to God, and the tears streamed over his face. And just as a burning coal kindles those beside it, so man by man was lit with the flame of turning. Then the zaddik looked around and fixed them with his gaze. Again he lifted his eyes and said to God: "Lord of the world, this is, indeed, the right time for the turning. But you know that I have not the strength to do penance—so accept as penance my love and my shame."

Humility

Rabbi Zusya and his brother Rabbi Elimelekh were once discussing the subject of humility. Elimelekh said: "If a man contemplates the greatness of the Creator, he will arrive at true humility."
But Zusya said: "No! A man must begin by being truly humble. Only then will he recognize the greatness of his Creator."
They asked their teacher, the maggid, who was right. He decided it in this way. "These and those are the words of the living God. But the inner grace is his who begins with himself, and not with the Creator."

Of Adam

Zusya once asked his brother, wise Rabbi Elimelekh: "Dear brother, in the Scriptures we read that the souls of all men were comprised in Adam. So we too must have been present, when he ate the apple. I do not understand how I could have let him eat it! And how could you have let him eat it?"

243

Elimelekh replied: "We had to just as all had to. For had he not eaten, the poison of the snake would have remained within him in all eternity. He would always have thought: 'All I need do is eat of this tree and I shall be as God—all I need do is eat of this tree, and I shall be as God.'"

"Get Thee Out of Thy Country"

Rabbi Zusya taught:

God said to Abraham: "Get thee out of thy country, and from thy kindred, and from thy father's house, unto the land that I will show thee." God says to man: "First, get you out of your country, that means the dimness you have inflicted on yourself. Then out of your birth-place, that means, out of the dimness your mother inflicted on you. After that, out of the house of your father, that means, out of the dimness your father inflicted on you. Only then will you be able to go to the land that I will show you."

"And Israel Saw"

They asked Rabbi Zusya: "It is written: 'And Israel saw Egypt dead upon the sea-shore.' Why are the Egyptians referred to in the singular and not in the plural? And further on it is written: 'And Israel saw the great hand.' Had they not seen it up to then?"

He expounded: "As long as the prince demon of Egypt was alive and ruled, he saw to it that a curtain separated Israel from their Father in Heaven, so that they could not see his splendor. But when the prince demon of Egypt—and this is the reason for the singular—lay dead on the sea-shore, the curtain tore asunder, and with their open eyes they saw His great hand."

Zusya and His Wife

Zusya's wife was a shrew. She kept nagging him to give her a divorce and his heart was weighed down by her words. One night he called her name and said to her: "Look!" And he showed her that his pillow was wet with tears. Then he went on: "In the Gemara it is written that if a man puts his first wife away, the altar itself will shed tears for him. My pillow is wet with these tears. And now—what do you want? Do you still want a letter of divorce?" From this moment on, she grew quiet. And when she was really quiet, she grew happy. And when she was happy, she grew good.

Zusya and the Birds

Once Rabbi Zusya traveled cross-country collecting money to ransom prisoners. He came to an inn at a time when the innkeeper was not at home. He went through the rooms, according to custom, and in one saw a large cage with all kinds of birds. And Zusya saw that the caged creatures wanted to fly through the spaces of the world and be free birds again. He burned with pity for them and said to himself: "Here you are, Zusya, walking your feet off to ransom prisoners. But what greater ransoming of prisoners can there be than to free these birds from their prison?" Then he opened the cage, and the birds flew out into freedom.

When the innkeeper returned and saw the empty cage, he was very angry, and asked the people in the house who had done this to him. They answered: "A man is loitering about here and he looks like a fool. No one but he can have done this thing." The innkeeper shouted at Zusya: "You fool! How could you have the impudence to rob me of my birds and make worthless the good money I paid for them?" Zusya replied: "You have often read and repeated these words in the psalms: 'His tender mercies are over all His works.' " Then the innkeeper beat him until his hand grew tired and finally threw him out of the house. And Zusya went his way serenely.

His Days

Every morning at rising, before he spoke a word to God or to men, it was Rabbi Zusya's custom to call out: "Good morning to all of Israel!"

During the day, he wrote everything he did down on a slip of paper. Before going to bed at night, he fetched it, read it, and wept until the writing was blurred with his tears.

The Blessing

Whenever Zusya met a Jewish boy, he blessed him with the words: "Be healthy and strong as a goy."

The Song

Once, on the eve of the Day of Atonement, Rabbi Zusya heard a cantor in the House of Prayer, chanting the words: "And it is forgiven," in strange and beautiful tones. Then he called to God: "Lord of the world! Had Israel not sinned, how could such a song have been intoned before you?"

He Who Answers Amen

Concerning the words of our sages: "He who answers 'amen' shall not raise his voice above his who says the blessing," Rabbi Zusya said: "The soul says the blessing; the body answers 'amen.' The body shall not dare to speak more fervently than the soul has spoken."

Zusya's Devotions

Zusya was once a guest in the house of the rabbi of Neskhizh. Shortly after midnight, the host heard sounds coming from his guest's room, so he went to the door and listened. Zusya was running back and forth in the room, saying: "Lord of the world, I love you! But what is there for me to do? I can't do anything." And then he started running back and forth again, repeating the same thing, until suddenly he bethought himself and cried: "Why, I know how to whistle, so I shall whistle something for you." But when he began to whistle, the rabbi of Neskhizh grew frightened.

The Fear of God

Once Zusya prayed to God: "Lord, I love you so much, but I do not fear you enough! Lord, I love you so much, but I do not fear you enough! Let me stand in awe of you like your angels, who are penetrated by your awe-inspiring name." And God heard his prayer, and his name penetrated the hidden heart of Zusya as it does those of the angels. But Zusya crawled under the bed like a little dog, and animal fear shook him until he howled: "Lord, let me love you like Zusya again!" And God heard him this time also.

The Creation of Angels

Once Rabbi Zusya was pondering over that passage in the Talmud which deals with hospitality. There it is written: "Those of Israel, holy are they. Many a one wants to, and has not. Many a one has, and does not want to." He could not understand why both, the hospitable man who has not, and the miser, should be called holy. And because he could not understand, he wept. Then the meaning was revealed to him. Everybody knows that an angel springs from each good deed. But angels have a soul and a body, just as we do, only that their body consists of fire and wind. Now, who wants to and has not, can create only the soul of the angel. Who has, and does not want to, and invites a guest only because he is ashamed not to, can create only the body of the angel. But we know that in Israel everyone vouches for everyone else. And so their works fuse as though they were those of a single being. In the same way, the soul and the body of the angel which has been created are fused together. The miser, to be sure, remains just as unholy as he was. But if the created soul finds a body with which it can clothe itself, the fusion of the two creations manifests the holiness of Israel.

The Accuser

This is Rabbi Zusya's comment on the passage in the Sayings of the Fathers: "He who commits one transgression has gotten himself one accuser." "Every sin begets an accusing angel. But I have never seen a complete angel spring from the sin of a devout man of Israel. Sometimes he lacks a head; sometimes his body is crippled. For when a man of Israel believes in God, believes in him even while he is sinning, his heart aches, and what he does, he does not do with all his will, and so the angel never emerges complete."

Above Them

A hasid asked Rabbi Zusya: "Concerning Abraham receiving the three angels, it is written: 'And he took curd and milk and the calf which he had dressed, and set it before them; and he stood above them, under the tree, and they did eat.' It is not strange that here the man stood 'above' the angels?"

Rabbi Zusya expounded: "When a man eats in a state of consecration, he redeems the holy sparks which are imprisoned in food. But the angels are not aware of this service unless the man has told them of it. That is why it is written of Abraham that he 'stood above them.' He let the consecration of the meal descend on them."

The Wheel

Rabbi Israel of Rizhyn had been falsely accused and put in prison. There he said:

"Heaven once revealed to Rabbi Zusya that he was to go to a village not far from Hanipol and guide a tax collector on the true way. He went there immediately and found the man selling vodka to the peasants. He tried to make him stop and say a prayer, but the collector became more and more impatient. When Rabbi Zusya continued to exhort him in spite of his rejection, and even laid an urgent hand on his arm, he took hold of the intruder, shoved him out into the court, and shut the door on him. It was very cold and the rabbi shivered all over. Then he caught sight of an old wagon wheel lying on the ground and put it against his body. And instantly it became a wheel of the Chariot of Heaven and gave out delicious warmth. That was how the tax collector found him. When he saw the blissful smile on Rabbi Zusya's lips, he experienced the truth about life in one small second, and already, with faltering feet and full of amazement at himself, he stood on the true way."

At the Crossroads

On one of his wanderings, Rabbi Zusya came to a crossroads and did not know which of the two roads to take. Then he lifted his eyes and saw the Divine Presence leading the way.

The Poles Have No *Savoir Vivre*

Rabbi Nathan Adler of Frankfort related:

"It is not for nothing that they say the Poles have no *savoir vivre*. No matter when I lift my soul to Heaven, Rabbi Zusya is always there ahead of me. Once I fasted for a long time, in order to reach the gates of Heaven while they are still closed. I stood before the gates, and when they were opened, I was the very first to enter. And whom do you suppose I saw inside? Rabbi Zusya! How he got in, I don't know, but he was certainly there. He had not had the grace to wait until he was admitted. It is not for nothing that they say the Poles have no *savoir vivre*."

Zusya, and Fire and Earth

Zusya once put his hand into the fire. When the flames scorched him and he drew it back, he was surprised and said: "Dear me, how crude is Zusya's body, that it fears fire!"

Another time he said to the earth: "Earth, Earth, you are better than I, and yet I trample on you with my feet. But soon I shall lie under you and be subject to you."

Fire and Cloud

It is told:

On a certain Feast of Tabernacles, before the world had become aware of Zusya, he lived in the booth of the rav of Ostrog. When evening came, the rav lay down on his soft couch heaped high with pillows and blankets, while Zusya slept on the ground in the manner of poor sabbath guests. In the course of the night he said to himself: "Ah, Zishe feels cold; he cannot sleep in the booth." That very instant a fire descended from Heaven and warmed the booth so well that the rav of Ostrog had to throw off feather-beds and blankets. "Now it is warm enough," said Zusya. Immediately the Prince of Fire departed, and the rav of Ostrog had to pull up one cover after another. This recurred a number of times: heat alternated with cold and when morning came the rav of Ostrog no longer addressed his guest as "Zishe," but "Reb Zishe."

When the Feast of Tabernacles was over, Zusya wanted to

continue his journey, but his sore feet would not carry him, and he sighed: "O Lord of the world, Zishe cannot walk!" Then a cloud floated down and said: "Get in."

"Rabbi!" shouted the rav of Ostrog. "I'll rent a carriage for you, but send that cloud away!" From that time on, he no longer called him "Reb Zishe," but "Rebbe Reb Zishe," and ever since then, that was the name he went by in the entire country.

Terror

It is told:

It was after maneuvers, and the victorious army returned via Hanipol. There they made themselves at home in the inn, drank everything in sight, and did not pay a red penny. They wanted to go on drinking, but since there was nothing left, they smashed all the glasses and utensils. Then they demanded more liquor, and because there was none, they beat up the inn-keeper and his helpers. The terrified man finally got a message through to Rabbi Zusya. Zusya came at once, stopped outside the window, looked in at the soldiers, and—three times in succession—said the words of the prayer: "Uvekhen ten pahdekha . . . Lord, our God, lay your terror on all of your creatures." At that, all the soldiers rushed out of the door and the windows in mad haste, left their guns and knapsacks behind, and ran down the street without paying any attention to their commanding officer, who came toward them at the outskirts of the town. Not until he called to them in an angry voice, did they stop. They told him: "An old Jew came and yelled: 'Pahdakh!' Then we were scared to death—we don't know how or why— and even now, we are still afraid." The commander led them back to the inn where they had to pay for the damage they had done and give compensation for the beatings, before he let them march on.

The Shepherd's Song

Rabbi Zusya once passed a meadow where a swine-herd in the midst of his flock was playing a song on a willow-flute. He came close and listened until he had learned it and could take

250

it away with him. In this way the song of David, the shepherd boy, was freed from its long captivity.

Sickness

Rabbi Zusya grew to be very old. He spent the last seven years of his life on a sick-bed, for—so it is written of him—he had taken suffering upon himself in order to shrive Israel.

One day he received as visitors the "Seer" of Lublin and Rabbi Hirsh Leib of Olik. The latter said to the Seer: "Why can you not do what Rabbi Yohanan did for his sick friends: give him your hand so that he may rise?"

The rabbi of Lublin burst into tears. Then the rabbi of Olik asked him: "Why do you weep? Do you think he is sick because such is his destiny? He has taken suffering upon himself of his own free will, and is taking it, and if he wanted to rise, he would not need the hand of a stranger to do so."

The Query of Queries

Before his death, Rabbi Zusya said "In the coming world, they will not ask me: 'Why were you not Moses?' They will ask me: 'Why were you not Zusya?'"

The Tombstone

On Rabbi Zusya's tombstone are the words: "One who served God with love, who rejoiced in suffering, who wrested many from their sins."

The Fire

A certain rav in Hanipol, one of our own day, wrote down the following:

At night, when not a soul was in the graveyard, the lantern above Rabbi Zusya's grave fell to the ground. Rabbi Zusya's "tent" lies between that of the Great Maggid and another zaddik. It was a very old rule that no one should visit these graves without having been in the bath of purification, and without taking off his shoes. Only one watchman was allowed to go there without observing these rules, to tend the everlasting light three times a day. The everlasting light burned in three lamps set into one lantern. It burned over a wooden shrine erected above the graves. The shrine was covered with boards, and in it were hundreds of pleas on slips of paper, each brought by another visitor. On the earth lay twigs, and these too had been laid down on the graves by visitors, for such was the custom. Now, when the lantern fell and fire broke out, all the papers in the shrine were burned, and all the withered sprays on the ground, but the flames did not harm the wood of the shrine itself—though it was very dry.

The Secret of Sleep

Rabbi Zusya's younger son said:
"The zaddikim who, in order to serve, keep going from sanctuary to sanctuary, and from world to world, must cast their life from them, time and again, so that they may receive a new spirit, that over and over, a new revelation may float above them. This is the secret of sleep."

ELIMELEKH OF LIZHENSK

His Watch

When Rabbi Elimelekh said the Prayer of Sanctification on the sabbath, he occasionally took out his watch and looked at it. For in that hour, his soul threatened to dissolve in bliss, and so he looked at his watch in order to steady himself in Time and the world.

When the Sabbath Began

When the sabbath began, Rabbi Elimelekh could not endure the voices proclaiming it. He had to stop up his ears to keep the holy thunder of the sabbath from deafening him.

Good Works

Rabbi Elimelekh once set out for home from a city he had visited and all the hasidim accompanied him for a long stretch of the way. When his carriage drove through the gate, he got out, told the coachman to drive on, and walked behind the carriage in the midst of the throng. The astonished hasidim asked him why he had done this. He answered: "When I saw the great devotion with which you were performing the good work of accompanying me, I could not bear to be excluded from it!"

Answers

Rabbi Elimelekh once said: "I am certain to have a share in the coming world. When I stand in the court of justice above, and they ask me: 'Have you studied all you should?' I shall answer, 'No.' Then they will ask: 'Have you prayed all you should?' And again I shall answer, 'No.' And they will put a third question to me: 'Have you done all the good you should?' And this time too, I shall have to give the same answer. Then they will pronounce the verdict: 'You told the truth. For the sake of truth, you deserve a share in the coming world.'"

The First Light

Rabbi Elimelekh said: "Before the soul enters the air of this world, it is conducted through all worlds. Last of all, it is shown the first light which once—when the world was created—illumined all things, and which God removed when mankind grew corrupt. Why is the soul shown this light? So that, from this hour on, it may yearn to attain it, and approach it rung by rung, in its life on earth. And those who reach it, the zaddikim—into them the light enters, and out of them it shines into the world again. That is the reason why it was hidden."

On Sinai

Rabbi Elimelekh said: "Not only that I remember how all the souls of Israel stood by the burning mountain of Sinai, I even remember what souls stood next to me."

God Sings

The psalm reads: "For singing to our God is good."
Rabbi Elimelekh expounded this: "It is good if man can bring about that God sings within him."

The Servants

A very old woman who, in her youth, had been a servant in Rabbi Elimelekh's house, was often asked to tell some story or other about the zaddik. But whenever they urged her, she said: "I don't know anything. There's only one thing I remember. During the week there were always cross words in the kitchen, for servants are apt to quarrel. But on the eve of the sabbath, something came over us: we embraced, and one said to the other: 'Dear heart, forgive me whatever wrong I have done you during this week!' "

The First Sin

Rabbi Hayyim of Zans told: "My holy master, Rabbi Elimelekh, used to say that, if a man wants to turn to God, he must go back of each sin, back to the one which gave rise to it, and so on to the first sin; and even for this, he has to do penance.

He himself did penance for treading on his mother's breasts with his feet, when he was a babe in arms."

The Penitent

For six years and then for another six years, Rabbi David of Lelov had done great penance: he had fasted from one sabbath to the next, and subjected himself to all manner of rigid discipline. But even when the second six years were up, he felt that he had not reached perfection and did not know how to attain what he still lacked. Since he had heard of Rabbi Elimelekh, the healer of souls, he journeyed to him to ask his help. On the evening of the sabbath, he came before the zaddik with many others. The master shook hands with everyone except Rabbi David, but from him he turned and did not give him a glance. The rabbi of Lelov was appalled and left. But then he thought it over and decided that the master must have taken him for someone else. So he approached him in the evening, after the prayer, and held out his hand. But he was treated just as before. He wept all night and in the morning resolved not to enter the zaddik's House of Prayer again, but to leave for home at the end of the sabbath. And yet—when the hour of the holy third meal had come, the meal at which Rabbi Elimelekh spoke words of teaching, he could not restrain himself and crept up to the window. There he heard the rabbi say:

"Sometimes people come to me who fast and torment themselves, and many a one does penance for six years and then for another six—twelve whole years! And after that, they consider themselves worthy of the holy spirit, and come and ask me to draw it down to them: I am to supply the little they still lack. But the truth of the matter is that all their discipline and all their pains are less than a drop in the sea, and what's more: all that service of theirs does not rise to God, but to the idol of their pride. Such people must turn to God by turning utterly from all they have been doing, and begin to serve from the bottom up and with a truthful heart."

When Rabbi David heard these words, the spirit moved him with such force, that he almost lost consciousness. Trembling and sobbing, he stood at the window. When the Havdalah was concluded, he went to the door with faltering breath, opened it in great fear, and waited on the threshold. Rabbi Elimelekh rose from his chair, ran up to his motionless visitor, embraced him and said: "Blessed be he that comes!" Then he drew him toward the table and seated him at his side. But now Eleazar, the zaddik's son, could no longer restrain his amazement. "Father," he said, "why, that is the man you turned away twice because you could not endure the mere sight of him!"

"No, indeed!" Rabbi Elimelekh answered. "That was an entirely different person! Don't you see that this is our dear Rabbi David!"

The Impure Fire

On his journey to Rabbi Elimelekh whom — after the death of the Great Maggid—he had chosen for his second teacher, young Jacob Yitzak, later the rabbi of Lublin, came to a little town, and in the House of Prayer heard the rav of that place reciting the Morning Prayer with deep fervor. He stayed with him over the sabbath and noticed the same fervor in all he said and did. When he came to know him a little better, he asked him whether he had ever served a zaddik. The answer was "no." This surprised Jacob Yitzhak, for the *way* cannot be learned out of a book, or from hearsay, but can only be communicated from person to person. He asked the devout rav to go to his teacher with him, and he agreed. But when they crossed Rabbi Elimelekh's threshold, he did not come forward to meet his disciple with his customary affectionate greeting, but turned to the window and paid no attention to his visitors. Jacob Yitzhak realized that the rejection was directed to his companion, took the violently excited rav to an inn and returned alone. Rabbi Elimelekh advanced toward him, greeted him fondly, and then said: "What struck you, my friend, to bring with you a man in whose face I can see the tainted image of God?" Jacob Yitzhak listened to these words in dismay, but did not venture to reply or to ask a question. But Rabbi Elimelekh understood what was going on within him and continued: "You know that there is one place lit only by the planet Venus, where good and evil are blended. Sometimes a man begins to serve God and ulterior motives and pride enter into his service. Then, unless he makes a very great effort to change, he comes to live in that dim place and does not even know it. He is even able to exert great fervor, for close by is the place of the impure fire. From there he fetches his blaze and kindles his service with it, and does not know from where he has taken the flame."

Jacob Yitzhak told the stranger the words of Rabbi Elimelekh and the rav recognized the truth in them. In that very hour, he turned to God, ran weeping to the master, who instantly gave him his help, and with this help, he found the way.

Satan's Threat

It is told:

Satan came to Rabbi Elimelekh and said: "I simply won't stand for it any longer that you persecute me with your hasidim! Don't imagine you can get the best of me! I shall make all the world hasidim and then you will no longer have power."

Some time after this, Rabbi Elimelekh went into the House of Study with a cane to drive out some of the hasidim. No one knows why he did not do it. I suppose he did not venture to single out the messengers of Satan.

Elijah

Rabbi Elimelekh told about a man to whom the prophet Elijah had appeared. Someone expressed surprise that this could be, since even Master Ibn Ezra, who had a spirit belonging to a far loftier sphere, had — according to his own words — been denied such a vision. "What you say, is true," said the zaddik. "And yet it is as I have said. You know that after Elijah was transfigured, he became the Angel of the Covenant, and is present at the circumcision of every Jewish boy. But how can this be, since circumcision always takes place in the hour after prayer, and many circumcisions occur in the same hour in all parts of the world? I shall tell you how! Elijah moved all the people of Israel with the spirit of turning, so that they fell on their faces and cried out the name of the true God, and because of this he was given the whole soul of Israel. And so, wherever a boy is brought to the covenant, a part of Elijah's soul is present and enters the boy — a big part or a little part, according to the kind of child and the root of its being. And if the growing boy develops his Elijah-soul to the full, then he has a vision of the Elijah-soul contained within him. Thus the man of whom I was speaking made manifest through his good works the small part of the prophet which was within him. But Ibn Ezra did not have the strength to perfect the great part he had been given."

A Transaction

It is told:

The emperor in Vienna issued an edict which was bound to make thoroughly miserable the already oppressed Jews in Galicia. At that time, an earnest and studious man by the name of Feivel lived in Rabbi Elimelekh's House of Study. One night he rose, entered the zaddik's room, and said to him: "Master, I have a suit against God." And even as he spoke he was horrified at his own words.

But Rabbi Elimelekh answered him: "Very well, but the court is not in session by night."

The next day, two zaddikim came to Lizhensk, Israel of Koznitz and Jacob Yitzhak of Lublin, and stayed in Rabbi Elimelekh's house. After the midday meal, the rabbi had the man who had spoken to him called and said: "Now tell us about your lawsuit."

"I have not the strength to do it now," Feivel said falteringly. "Then I give you the strength," said Rabbi Elimelekh.

And Feivel began to speak. "Why are we held in bondage in this empire? Does not God say in the Torah: 'For unto Me the children of Israel are servants.' And even though he has sent us to alien lands, still, wherever we are, he must leave us full freedom to serve him."

To this Rabbi Elimelekh replied: "We know God's reply, for it also is written in the passage of reproof through Moses and the prophets. But now, both the plaintiff and the defendant shall leave the court-room, as the rule prescribes, so that the judges may not be influenced by them. So go out, Rabbi Feivel. You, Lord of the world, we cannot send out, because your glory fills the earth, and without your presence, not one of us could live for even a moment. But we herewith inform you that we shall not let ourselves be influenced by you either." Then the three sat in judgment, silently and with closed eyes. After an hour, they called in Feivel and gave him the verdict: that he was in the right. In the same hour, the edict in Vienna was cancelled.

Upsetting the Bowl

It is told:

Once Rabbi Elimelekh was eating the sabbath meal with his disciples. The servant set the soup bowl down before him. Rabbi Elimelekh raised it and upset it, so that the soup poured over the table. All at once young Mendel, later the rabbi of Rymanov, cried out: "Rabbi, what are you doing? They will put us all in jail!" The other disciples smiled at these foolish words. They would have laughed out loud, had not the presence of their teacher restrained them. He, however, did not smile. He nodded to young Mendel and said: "Do not be afraid, my son!"

Some time after this, it became known that on that day an edict directed against the Jews of the whole country had been presented to the emperor for his signature. Time after time he took up his pen, but something always happened to interrupt him. Finally he signed the paper. Then he reached for the sand-container but took the inkwell instead and upset it on the document. Hereupon he tore it up and forbade them to put the edict before him again.

The Miraculous Meal

They tell:

On New Year's Day, it was usual for fifteen hasidim to come to Rabbi Elimelekh, and his wife gave them to eat and to drink. But she could not serve them very generous portions, because at that time she did not have much money to spend for the household.

Once—quite late in the day—no less than forty men came

instead of the expected fifteen. "Will you have enough for them to eat?" asked Rabbi Elimelekh.

"You know how we are fixed!" she replied.

Before the Afternoon Prayer he asked her again: "Couldn't we divide what food we have among the forty, for they have—after all—come 'under the shadow of my roof'!"

"We have hardly enough for fifteen," said his wife.

When he said the Evening Prayer, the rabbi prayed fervently to God who provides for all creatures. After the prayer, he announced: "Now let everyone come and eat!" When the forty had eaten all they wanted, the bowls and platters were still full.

The Wine of Life

It is told:

Once, on the second evening of the Feast of Weeks, the hasidim were seated around Rabbi Elimelekh's table and rejoicing in the feast. The rabbi looked around and nodded to each in turn, for he rejoiced in their joy. And he said smilingly: "See, we have everything here to make us joyful. Is there anything still lacking?"

Then a headstrong foolish young man cried out: "All we still lack is to drink of the wine of life, like the devout in paradise." The zaddik said to him: "Take the pole on your shoulders. Fasten two pails to it, and go to the gates of the cemetery. When you get there, set down the pails, turn your back on them, and say: 'Elimelekh has sent me to fetch wine.' Then turn around, lift the full pails, fasten them to the pole, and bring them here to us. But be careful not to talk to anyone—no matter who should speak to you."

The young man shuddered, but did as he was bidden. He fetched the wine at the gate of the cemetery, shuddered, and brought it back with him. All about him the moonless night vibrated with the sound of voices, begging him for a drop: old voices and young voices, and they all sighed and moaned. He hastened on in silence and behind him he heard the dragging of countless ghostly steps. He was almost on Elimelekh's threshhold, when they approached him from the other side. "Now you can't do anything to me!" he shouted. The pole broke in two. The pails fell and cracked, and he felt something strike him on both cheeks. He tottered through the half-open door. Outside all was silent as death. Inside the zaddik spoke: "Fool, sit down at our table."

The Fish Vendor

They say that Rabbi Elimelekh did not celebrate with all due rites the post-sabbath meal, which is called "King David's Feast," and that for this the king was angry with him.

They also tell this:

One Friday afternoon, a man in peasant's dress, who was carrying a basket of fish on his back, came to Rabbi Elimelekh and offered to sell him his wares. He spoke the dialect of that region. The zaddik sent the vendor to his wife, but she told him to go away because she had finished preparing the food for the sabbath several hours ago. The man refused to be denied and again went to the rabbi. He sent word to his wife to buy a little something from him, but she persisted in her rejection. For the third time, the man entered the zaddik's room, fetched his fish out of the basket, threw them on the floor where they wriggled around, and grumbled: "It would be a good idea for you to use them for the King David's Feast." Then Rabbi Elimelekh raised his eyebrows. They were very big and he was in the habit of raising them whenever he wanted to look at anyone closely. He was silent for a while and then said:

"I no longer have the strength to celebrate your meal with all due rites, but I shall command my children to do so."

Gruel

During the last two years of his life, Rabbi Elimelekh ate and drank only very little, and even that little he took only because his family urged him to. Once, when his son Eleazar begged him with tears to eat at least enough to keep him alive, he said with a smile on his lips: "Oh, what coarse food you set before me! Now, if I could only get a plate of gruel, the kind my brother Zusya and I were served in the little red inn on the Dniester, in the days of our wanderings!"

Some time after Rabbi Elimelekh's death, his son set out on a journey to the little red inn on the Dniester. When he arrived there, he asked for a night's lodging and inquired what there was for supper. "We are poor people," said the innkeeper's wife. "We give the peasants vodka in exchange for flour and dried peas and beans. Most of this my husband takes to market and barters for more vodka, and the rest we eat. So I can offer you nothing but gruel for supper."

"Prepare it for me right away," said Rabbi Eleazar. By the time he had said the Evening Prayer, the soup was on the table. He ate one plate of it, and then another, and asked for a third helping. "Tell me what it was you put into the soup to make it so tasty?"

"Believe me, sir," she said. "I put nothing into it at all." But when he pressed her, she finally said: "Well, if it tastes so good to you, paradise itself is responsible for it." And now she told: "It is very long ago, but once two pious men stopped here. You could see that they were true zaddikim. And because I had nothing to serve them except gruel, I prayed to God while I was cooking it: 'Lord of the world, I have nothing else in the house, and you have everything. So have mercy upon your tired and hungry servants and put some herbs from paradise into their soup!' And when the gruel was put on the table, the two of them emptied the whole big bowl, and I refilled it and they emptied it a second time, and one of them said to me: 'Daughter, your soup tastes of paradise.' And just now I prayed again."

The True Wonder

They asked Rabbi Elimelekh: "In the Scriptures we read that Pharaoh said to Moses and Aaron: 'Show a wonder for you.' How are we to understand this? It would have been more logical for him to say: 'Show a wonder to me.'"

Rabbi Elimelekh explained: "Magicians know what they want to accomplish and how to accomplish it. It is not a wonder for them but only for the beholders. But those who work something because God gives them power to do it know of no whence and no how, and the wonder which rises out of their doing, overwhelms them themselves. And this is what Pharaoh meant: 'Do not pretend to me! Get you a wonder from the true world, so that it may thus testify for you.' "

The Hidden Zaddikim

Rabbi Gabriel, a disciple of Rabbi Elimelekh's, once went to visit his master in a carriage he had rented from a man of uncouth bearing who—to his annoyance—insisted on telling him coarse and improper jokes during the entire drive. When they came to the zaddik's house, Elimelekh ran toward the coachman, greeted him with great happiness, and scarcely noticed Rabbi Gabriel. On the way back, the disciple wanted to perform services for the man who had been treated with such respect, but was rejected with a curt phrase.

A few months later, Rabbi Gabriel went to the city and there saw the coachman talking to a mason. He followed the two men to their inn, unobserved, and heard one say to the other: "At Melekh's, you still hear a bit of truth—but nowhere else." And the other repeated: "At Melekh's you hear a bit of truth!" Then they happened to see the rabbi in a corner and shouted at him: "Get out! What are you doing among common folks!" And there was nothing for it; he had to go.

After Rabbi Elimelekh's death, Gabriel was driving through a wood, when the carriage of his friend, Rabbi Uri, came toward him. They dismounted and walked a way together. Then Gabriel told his friend what he had once heard the coachman and the mason say to each other. The two leaned against trees, and wept, and lamented: "A bit of truth was in the world, and now that too has been taken from us!"

The Artery

Rabbi Moshe Efraim, the Baal Shem's grandson, was against the Polish hasidim because he had heard that they mortified their flesh too severely, and destroyed the image of God in themselves instead of making perfect every part of their body, and merging it with the soul into one holy vessel for the service of the Lord. When—after the death of Rabbi Elimelekh—his disciple, Rabbi Mendel of Rymanov, came to Moshe Efraim, to ask him about a successor, as his dying master had bidden him, he was recognized as a Pole and given a rather curt and cool reception. This made him feel so sad that a change came over his face. Rabbi Moshe Efraim watched him attentively: his brow, which had paled, and his wide-open eyes were not those of a base man. He asked him kindly: "Have you studied with a zaddik?"

"I served my teacher, Rabbi Elimelekh," said Mendel.

Then Rabbi Efraim looked at him even more attentively and asked: "And what seemed most wonderful to you about that wonderful man?" But while he was putting this question he thought: "Now this hasid with his luminous face will reveal his true colors and tell me some miracle tale."

Rabbi Mendel replied: "Day by day, when my master was sunk in the contemplation of the awfulness of God, his arteries grew as stiff as hard ropes. And the artery behind the ear, which stirs at nothing in the world, and does not tremble until the hour of death—day after day I saw that artery throb with a strong pulse."

Rabbi Moshe Efraim was silent. Then he said: "I did not know that." Twice he repeated: "I did not know that." And he received Rabbi Mendel like a son.

SHNEUR ZALMAN OF LADI ("THE RAV")

No Returning

In the years immediately after his marriage, Zalman boarded
with his parents-in-law, according to the custom. But his aloofness, his manner of praying, and all the ways in which he
performed his service to God were strange to them and—while
they admired his learning—they thought him a fool. Their
daughter rejected their demands to ask for a letter of divorce
from her husband, and so they had to content themselves with
making life difficult for him. They refused him candles, so
that he had to study at the window by the light of the moon,
and in winter nights, when he often stayed up until dawn,
they let him suffer cold. This went on until—at the age of
twenty—he set out for the Great Maggid in Mezritch.

Later, when the fame of Rabbi Zalman began to spread, his
mother-in-law regretted the hardships which she and her husband—who had died in the meantime—had imposed on the
zaddik, and begged him to live in her house again. She would
see to it, she said, that he lacked nothing, and would also take
care of his hasidim. Rabbi Zalman refused her invitation, and
when the woman did not cease pressing him, he said: "Look!
Who can be better off than the child in his mother's womb?
He need not worry about his food and his drink. A light burns
upon his head, and all day he learns the entire Torah. But
when the child is born, an angel comes and strikes him on the
mouth, and he forgets all he has learned. And yet—even if he
were able to return, he would not want to. Why do you suppose? Because he has reached his full measure."

Permission

Zalman talked it over with his brother, and they decided to
go to study with the holy maggid of Mezritch. Then he asked
his wife to consent to this and she did. But she made him

promise to return after a year and a half. She had saved up thirty rubles. These she gave him and he bought a horse and carriage. His brother, however, had not asked his wife's consent. When they came to the city of Orsha, the horse fell down and died. "That is because you set out without permission," Zalman said to his brother. "And what has happened means that you must not take this course. So you go home, and I shall continue on my way, and whatever I attain, I will share with you." Then they parted, and Zalman proceeded on foot.

The Gaze of the Master

The room of the Great Maggid adjoined that in which his disciples slept. Sometimes he went to them at night, a light in his hand, and looked into their sleeping faces. Once he bent down to the low bench by the stove on which young Zalman lay under a threadbare, three-cornered cover. He looked at him for a long time and then said to himself: "Miracle of miracles that so great a God lives in so frail a dwelling."

Upward

Rabbi Shneur Zalman told: "Before I went to Mezritch, my service was based on reflection, and from this arose my love and my fear of God. In Mezritch I mounted to the rung where awareness is, in itself, love and fear.

"When I first heard the holy maggid say: 'God's attribute of mercy is our love of God; God's attribute of rigor is our fear of God,' I regarded this as an interpretation. But then I saw that it is so: The mercy of God is the love of God; the rigor of God is the fear of God."

The Language of Birds

On his second journey to Mezritch, young Zalman visited Rabbi Pinhas of Koretz. Rabbi Pinhas wanted to teach him the language of birds and the language of plants, but the younger man refused. "There is only *one* thing men need understand," he said.

In his old age, Rabbi Shneur Zalman was once driving through the country with his grandson. Birds were hopping about and twittering everywhere. The rabbi put his head out of the carriage for a while. "How fast they chatter," he said to the child. "They have their own alphabet. All you need do is listen and grasp well, and you will understand their language."

Concerning Ardent Zeal

After the maggid died, Shneur Zalman decided to leave the town of Mezritch for good. When he parted from the maggid's son, from Rabbi Abraham, the Angel, who had instructed him in secret wisdom, his teacher said he would accompany him and got into the carriage. When they were out of the city-gate, Rabbi Abraham called to the coachman: "Urge on your horses and let them run until they forget they are horses." Zalman took the words to heart. "It will take me a while to learn this way of serving, properly," he said, and remained in Mezritch for another year.

At the Lower End

After the death of his teacher, the Great Maggid, Shneur Zalman used to go to Rabbi Menahem of Vitebsk, and was regarded as his disciple, even though his years of studying were actually over. On the sabbath and on feast-days, all the hasidim ate at their rabbi's table. Shneur Zalman always sat at the lower end. On New Year's Eve the rabbi of Vitebsk saw that his place was empty. He went to the House of Study, where he found Zalman standing and praying, listened for a time, unobserved, and went back into the room. "Do not disturb him," he said. "He is delighting in God, and God in him."

To God

Once Zalman interrupted his prayers and said: "I do not want your paradise. I do not want your coming world. I want You, and You only."

Extricated from Time

Rabbi Shneur Zalman told his hasidim:
"I was walking in the street toward evening and happened to see something improper. I was deeply troubled that I had not

guarded my eyes, placed myself with my face to a wall and cried my heart out. When I turned around I saw that it was dark and the time for the Afternoon Prayer had passed. Then I took counsel with myself. I extricated myself from Time and said the Prayer."

Fear

When hasidim began to come to him, and he happened to look out of the window and saw a throng approaching, he was terrified and cried: "What do they want of me? Why do they come to me? What do they see in me?"

Then his wife said to him: "Be calm. They are not coming to you for your sake. They only want you to tell them about the holy maggid, because you have lived in his shadow."

"Then all is well," he said and his heart grew quiet. "I shall tell them, yes, I shall tell them." But when he once began to talk, he could no longer keep back the teachings.

Where Are You?

Rabbi Shneur Zalman, the rav of Northern White Russia, was put in jail in Petersburg, because the mitnagdim had denounced his principles and his way of living to the government. He was awaiting trial when the chief of the gendarmes entered his cell. The majestic and quiet face of the rav, who was so deep in meditation that he did not at first notice his visitor, suggested to the chief, who was a thoughtful person, what manner of man he had before him. He began to converse with his prisoner and brought up a number of questions which had occurred to him in reading the Scriptures. Finally he asked: "How are we to understand that God, the all-knowing, said to Adam: 'Where art thou?'"

"Do you believe," answered the rav, "that the Scriptures are eternal and that every era, every generation, and every man is included in them?"

"I believe this," said the other.

"Well then," said the zaddik, "in every era, God calls to every man: 'Where are you in your world? So many years and days of those allotted to you have passed, and how far

have you gotten in your world?' God says something like this: 'You have lived forty-six years. How far along are you?' "
When the chief of the gendarmes heard his age mentioned, he pulled himself together, laid his hand on the rav's shoulder, and cried: "Bravo!" But his heart trembled.

Question and Answer

The rav asked a disciple who had just entered his room: "Moshe, what do we mean when we say 'God'?" The disciple was silent. The rav asked him a second and third time. Then he said: "Why are you silent?"
"Because I do not know."
"Do you think I know?" said the rav. "But I must say it, for it is so, and therefore I must say it: He is definitely there, and except for him nothing is definitely there—and this is He."

What He Prayed With

The rav once asked his son: "What do you pray with?" The son understood the meaning of the question, namely on what he based his prayer. He answered: "With the verse: 'Every stature shall prostrate itself before thee.' " Then he asked his father: "And with what do you pray?" He said: "With the floor and the bench."

Out of One Bowl

Among the disciples of the maggid of Mezritch was one whose name has been forgotten. No one knows it any more. But once in the maggid's House of Study he was regarded as the foremost among his companions, and all who wanted to have the words of their master repeated and explained, turned to him. Then came the time when the disciples began to talk, and said a worm was gnawing at him. After that he disappeared and rumor had it that he had taken to drinking. He roamed through the countryside with a staff and knapsack and drank silently in some inn until he was drunk; then one wise saying after another came from his lips. Years later he came to the town of Lozhni where Rabbi Shneur Zalman was still living at that time, and entered the House of Study at an hour when the rav was teaching there. No one noticed him in the crowd, and he listened for a while. Then he mumbled to himself: "We all ate out of one bowl, but it is he who has all the food," and left the house. When the rav heard of it, he realized who his visitor was and had them look for him everywhere, for he wanted to persuade him to give up his wandering and stay. But the rover was nowhere to be found.

Reflection

One of the mitnagdim once visited the rav and asked him all sorts of questions. Finally he wished to know why the zaddik had a servant at his door who did not admit visitors to him at all times. The rav put his head in his hands. After a time, he looked up and said: "The head and the trunk form one body, and yet the head must be covered in a different manner and guarded more carefully." The mitnaged was satisfied with this answer and left. But the zaddik's son was not satisfied. "You did not have to put your head in your hands and reflect in order to give the answer you did," he said.

Rabbi Zalman said: "When Korah said to Moses: 'All the congregation are holy, every one of them, and the Lord is among them; wherefore then lift ye up yourselves above the assembly of the Lord,' Moses heard and fell on his face. Only after that, did he answer Korah. But why? He could have said what he had to say, right then and there! But Moses reflected: Perhaps these words are sent from above, and Korah is only a messenger. In that case, how could I reply to him! And so he fell on his face and reflected on whether he really sought to lift himself above the rest. And when he had reflected and come to the conclusion that no vestige of such a desire was within him—and according to God's own words Moses was very humble, more humble than all other men—he knew that Korah had not been sent to him, and he answered his question."

Concerning the Messiah

A man once asked the rav in jest: "Will the Messiah be a hasid or a mitnaged?" He answered: "I think a mitnaged, for if he were a hasid, the mitnagdim would not believe in him; but the hasidim will believe in him, no matter what he is."

The Dark-Tempered and the Light-Tempered

A wealthy man who was devoted to his studies and known for his stinginess, once asked the rav of Ladi: "How are we to interpret the passage in the Talmud, in which we are told that Rabbi Haninah ben Teradion who publicly instructed his disciples in the teachings in an era of rabid persecution, and to the very day he died as a martyr, doubted that he was appointed to life in the coming world? And that, when he expressed his doubt to a friend, he was asked in return, whether he had done a single good work? And that he received a reassuring answer only when he claimed to have distributed his money among the poor. How are we to interpret this?"

"There are two kinds of men," said the rav, "those with black gall and those with light. The dark-tempered sit over the books of the teachings and are of a miserly disposition. The light-tempered love company and are generous. Rabbi Haninah was dark-tempered, devoted to his studies, and withdrawn. His merit did not lie in living for the teachings, but in governing his nature, and giving freely of what he possessed. But once he had done this, and he had learned to live with his fellowmen, his studying was no longer a necessity, but a virtue."

Seeing

On a day shortly before his death, the rav asked his grandson: "Do you see anything?" The boy looked at him in astonishment. Then the rav said: "All I can still see is the divine nothingness which gives life to the world."

The Apparition

One night, the wife of Rabbi Mendel of Lubavitch, the rav's grandson, was awakened by a loud noise coming from her husband's room which was next to hers. She ran to him and saw Rabbi Mendel lying on the floor by his bed. In reply to her questions, he told her that his grandfather had been to see him. She tried to calm him, but he said: "When a soul from the world above and a soul from this world want to be together, the one must put on a garment, and the other must take one off."

Once he said to his close friends: "In the Palestinian Talmud we read that he who says a word in the name of him who originated it, must—in his mind's eye—conjure the author up before him. This is only a fancy, but he who sings a melody another devised—that other is really with him while he sings." And he sang the familiar wordless tune the rav had sung and hummed time and again, the tune: "The Fervor of the Rav."

SHELOMO OF KARLIN

The Meeting

The cities of Pinsk and Karlin lie close to each other, the one on the north, the other on the south bank of a river. When Rabbi Shelomo was a poor young man who taught little children in Karlin, Rabbi Levi Yitzhak, later the rabbi of Berditchev, was the rav of Pinsk. One day he told his servant to go to Karlin, and look for a man by the name of Shelomo, son of Yuta. He was to ask him to come to Pinsk. The servant inquired around for a long time. Finally, at the edge of the town, in a ramshackle little house, he found the melammed Shelomo and gave him his message. "I shall get there in time," said Rabbi Shelomo.

When he crossed Rabbi Levi Yitzhak's threshold a few hours later, the rav rose and said, "Blessed be he that comes," and drew up a chair for his guest himself. For an hour they sat opposite each other, with glowing faces, with intense eyes—in silence. Then they rose and laughed aloud. "What can they be laughing about!" thought the servant who had been listening at the door. And Rabbi Shelomo made his farewells.

But the hasidim said that through the meeting of these two, the exile, which had been threatening the Jews of that region, had been averted, and that this was the cause of their joyful laughter.

He Who Returned

It is told:

Rabbi Aaron of Karlin died young, and Rabbi Shelomo, whose fellow disciple he had been in the house of the Great Maggid and who had followed his elder friend as his teacher, refused to take his place. Then Rabbi Aaron appeared to him in a dream and promised that if he took on himself the yoke of leadership, he would be granted the power of beholding all the wanderings of souls. This promise beguiled him in his dream, and he agreed to assume the succession. The next morning, he was able to see the destinies of the souls of all men. That very day, they brought him a note of request together with a sum of money. The sender was a rich man who lay dying. At the same time, the woman who supervised a home for the poor, came to ask him to pray for a pauper under her care, who had been in labor for days, and still had not borne her child. Rabbi Shelomo saw that the child could not come into the world until the rich man died, for his soul was to pass into the baby. And the news of the death and the birth did, indeed, come, one on the heels of the other. When the rabbi was told a little later that there was not enough fire-wood in the home, and that the young mother and her infant son were freezing, he took some of the money he had received from the rich man, and told them to buy wood with it. For he told himself: this child is really the rich man himself, and so it is his own money. Shortly after, he also gave what remained of the sum for the care of the boy.

Presently the woman left with other beggars and went from town to town. When the boy was six years old, they happened to come to Karlin again and learned that the Bar Mitzvah [confirmation] of the rich man's youngest son was to be celebrated soon. According to the custom, the poor were invited to attend the feast, and mother and son went with the others. But the boy could not be persuaded to sit at the pauper's table. In a loud voice and with arrogant gestures, he demanded a place at the head of the guest-table. Rabbi Shelomo, who noticed this, urged them to give in to the child, so that he might not cause a disturbance. "He is the master of the house, after all," he thought to himself. "And he is asking no more than his due." When the meal was served, the same thing occurred: the boy insisted that he be served with the choicest food, and again the zaddik let him have his way. When the mother was asked whether her son always behaved in this way, she said she had never observed anything of the kind in him. At the end of the feast, when Rabbi Shelomo had already gone home, they distributed money among the poor. When the boy's turn came, he cried: "How dare you offer me coppers! Get gold out of the chest!" Then the sons of the rich man threw him out bodily.

When Rabbi Shelomo discovered how they had treated their returned father, he begged Heaven to take from him his miraculous power.

Refusal

It is told:

Those in Heaven wanted to reveal to Rabbi Shelomo of Karlin the language of birds, the language of trees, and the language of the serving angels. But he refused to learn them, before finding out of what importance each of these languages was for the service of God. Not until after he had been told this, did he consent to learn them, and then he served God with them also.

The Stages

When Rabbi Shelomo of Karlin was traveling through Russia, he kept enumerating the various stages, and said: " 'These are the stages of the children of Israel, by which they went forth out of the land of Egypt.' " When they asked him what he meant by this, he said: "The sacred Book of Splendor interprets God's words, 'Let us make man,' in the following way: that from every world, from the highest to the lowest, God took some part, and from all these parts made man. It was to the worlds, that God said 'Let us.' And that is the meaning of the stages man passes through in his life: he must go from rung to rung until, through him, everything is united in the highest world. And that is why it is written: 'And these are their stages at their goings forth.' The stages of man shall take him to where he has come from."

The Venture of Prayer

Someone asked Rabbi Shelomo of Karlin to promise to visit him the next day. "How can you ask me to make such a promise?" said the zaddik. "This evening I must pray and recite 'Hear, O Israel.' While I say these words, my soul goes out to the utmost rim of life. Then comes the darkness of sleep.

And when it is day, the great Morning Prayer is apacing through all worlds, and finally, when I fall on my face, my soul leans over the rim of life. Perhaps I shall not die this time either, but how can I now promise to do something at a time after the prayer?"

The Piece of Sugar

It is told:

When Rabbi Shelomo drank tea or coffee, it was his custom to take a piece of sugar and hold it in his hand the entire time he was drinking. Once his son asked him: "Father, why do you do that? If you need sugar, put it in your mouth, but if you do not need it, why hold it in your hand!"

When he had emptied his cup, the rabbi gave the piece of sugar he had been holding to his son and said: "Taste it." The son put it in his mouth and was very much astonished, for there was no sweetness at all left in it.

Later, when the son told this story, he said: "A man, in whom everything is unified, can taste with his hand as if with his tongue."

With the Sword at His Throat

Rabbi Shelomo was on a journey in the company of one of his disciples. On the way, they stopped at an inn and sat down at a table. Then the rabbi gave orders to warm mead for him, for he liked his mead warm. In the meantime, soldiers arrived, and when they saw Jews sitting at the table, they told them to get up in loud, angry tones. "Is the mead warm yet?" the rabbi asked the man who served drinks. At that the soldiers struck the table with their fists and shouted: "Off with you, or else . . . !" The rabbi only said: "Isn't it warm yet?" The leader of the soldiers drew his sword from the scabbard and put the blade to the maggid's throat. "Because, you know, it mustn't get really hot!" said Rabbi Shelomo. Then the soldiers left the inn.

Without Ecstasy

Rabbi Shelomo of Karlin said: "When he, who has done all the commandments of the Torah, but has not felt the blaze of holy ecstasy in so doing, comes to that other world, they open the gates of paradise for him. But because he has not felt the blaze of ecstasy in this world, he does not feel the ecstasy of paradise. Now, if he is a fool, and complains, and grumbles: 'And they make so much to-do about paradise!' he is instantly thrown out. But if he is wise, he leaves of his own accord, and goes to the zaddik, and he teaches the poor soul how to feel ecstasy."

A Little Light

"When can one see a little light?" asked Rabbi Shelomo and answered his own question: "If one keeps oneself quite lowly, as it is written: 'If I make my bed in the nether world, behold, Thou art there!'"

Climbing Down

Rabbi Shelomo said: "If you want to raise a man from mud and filth, do not think it is enough to keep standing on top and reaching down to him a helping hand. You must go all the way down yourself, down into mud and filth. Then take hold of him with strong hands and pull him and yourself out into the light."

To Open

Rabbi Shelomo of Karlin said to someone: "I have no key to open you." And the man cried out: "Then pry me open with a nail!" From this time on, the rabbi always said words of warm praise about him.

The Cure

A grandson of Rabbi Shelomo told:
To a zaddik came a man whose soul had become enmeshed in a tangle of oppressive impulses, which defy writing down. "I cannot help you," said the zaddik. "You must go to Rabbi Shelomo of Karlin."
So he came to my grandfather, and arrived just at the hour he was lighting the Hanukkah candles and reciting psalms the

while, for this was his way. The man stopped and listened. My grandfather went on speaking without looking around, but when he came to the words: "And hath delivered us from our oppressors," he turned to his guest, patted him on the shoulder, and asked: "Do you believe that God can wrest us from all oppression?" "I believe," said the man. From that hour on, all his disturbing impulses left him.

The Disciple Speaks

Rabbi Asher of Stolyn said about his teacher, Rabbi Shelomo: "Whenever he prays, the rabbi stands with one foot over here, and the other over there, and it is the foot over there, on which he rests. And everything only in spirit, as it is written: 'And Thy footsteps were not known.' "

Once he entered Rabbi Shelomo's room and said to him: "Rabbi, your footsteps are not known."

"What makes you follow me all the time?" the rabbi retorted. "Come, and I shall tell you when you may, and when you may not."

But the disciple reflected: "Once he has told me, I shall not be able to transgress. So I'd rather not hear it."

Showing and Concealing

Rabbi Asher of Stolyn, a disciple of Rabbi Shelomo's, said concerning the hasidim of his time: "They are peasants of clay and cossacks of straw! When they come to the rabbi, they show him what is good, and what is bad they conceal from him. Now, when I came to my sweet, holy, darling rabbi (and while he said this, he kissed his finger-tips), I concealed the good from him, but I showed him what was bad. For it is written that the priest shall look on the plague."

Into the Inn

Rabbi Shelomo asked his disciple Rabbi Asher: "When did you come to prayer?"

"At just the right time for the inn named, Exult, O ye righteous!" was his reply.

"Well done," said the zaddik. "If you drive, you drive, and if you stop, you look around to see if anything is wrong. For if you stop midway, it is easy to fall behind."

Origin

This is what Rabbi Uri told about his teacher Rabbi Shelomo. "I had been with him a long time, and still he had not asked me my mother's name, as it is the custom to do. Once I mustered my courage and asked him about this. He answered: 'Ox, lion, eagle, man,' and nothing further. I did not dare beg him to expound his words. Only after many years did I come to understand that the great zaddikim, the healers of souls, want to know in which of the four carriers of the throne-chariot of God the soul had its origin, and not in what earthly womb it received its body."

Beyond Music

One day, musicians played for Rabbi Uri of Strelisk, known as "The Seraph." Later he said to his hasidim: "They say that music unites the three principles: life, intellect, and soul. But the musicians of today base their playing only on the principle of life." After a while he continued: "Of all the halls of Heaven, the hall of music is the lowest and the smallest, but he who wants to approach God, has only to enter this hall. My teacher, Rabbi Shelomo of Karlin, had no need of this."

Abel and Cain

Rabbi Uri said: "My teacher, Rabbi Shelomo of Karlin, had the soul of Abel. Now, there are people within whom the good traits of Cain's soul have their habitation, and these are very great."

Leftovers

Rabbi Shelomo and his disciple Rabbi Mordecai of Lechovitz once traveled cross-country. It was toward the end of the period in which the blessing of the New Moon can be spoken, and since the shining sickle had broken from the clouds which had been veiling it, they appeared for the sacred rite. But the coachman anticipated them. The moment he saw the moon, he wiped his hands on the rim of the wheel and mumbled the benediction. Rabbi Mordecai laughed, but his teacher reproved him.

"A king," so he told him, "once gave order to collect all the leftovers of the meal eaten in his army, and store them in a certain place. No one knew the reason for this command. But presently the country was at war, the king's army was surrounded by the enemy and cut off from outside provisions. Then the king fed his army on the leftovers which the enemy laughingly let pass. The army kept up its strength and was victorious."

Out of Travail

Once, at the close of the Day of Atonement, when Rabbi Shelomo was in a gay mood, he said he would tell everyone what he had asked of Heaven on these holy days, and what answer was intended for his request. To the first of his disciples who wanted to be told, he said: "What you asked of God was that he should give you your livelihood at the proper time and without travail, so that you might not be hindered in serving him. And the answer was that what God really wants of you is not study or prayer, but the sighs of your heart, which is breaking because the travail of gaining a livelihood hinders you in the service of God."

What Was Learned

Rabbi Shelomo said to his disciples: "After death, when a man reaches the world of truth, they ask him: 'Who was your teacher?' And when he has told them the name of his teacher, they ask: 'What did you learn from him?' This is what is meant by the words we read in Midrash: 'At some future time, each one will stand and say what he has learned.'"

One of the disciples cried: "I have already prepared what I shall say in your name. It is: 'May God give us a pure heart and pure thinking, and from our thinking, may purity spread

through all of our being, so that in us the word may be ful-
fied: 'Before they call, I will answer.' "

The Dowry

Rabbi Shelomo of Karlin could not bear to have money in his
purse or laid away in the table-drawer. It weighed on his heart
until he had given it to someone who was in need.

On a certain day, he betrothed his son to the daughter of Rabbi
Barukh of Mezbizh, the grandson of the Baal Shem Tov. Rabbi
Barukh was fervent, devout, and wise, but at the same time,
concerned with receiving his due. When the date given in the
engagement-contract for the payment of the dowry had elapsed,
and the money had not been paid, he wrote to Rabbi Shelomo
that he would return the contract and annul the engagement.
The Rabbi of Karlin asked him to set another date, and sent
two of his followers to travel through the country and collect
the amount of the dowry among the hasidim. But when the
sum was in Rabbi Shelomo's hands, and poor people stood in
the court of his house, he could not endure the thought that
out there were the needy, while money was here in his possession. He went into the court and distributed everything he had.
Again Rabbi Barukh sent him a stern letter. The rabbi of
Karlin replied that they should go ahead with preparations
for the wedding, that he himself would bring the dowry. Again
he sent two men to collect the necessary amount, and again they
brought it back with them. But this time they were cautious
and did not give it to the rabbi until he was seated in the
carriage beside his son.

The route took them to a city in which Rabbi Nahum of
Tchernobil was imprisoned as the result of a denunciation, such
as the opponents of hasidim frequently indulged in. The rabbi
of Karlin succeeded in getting the permission of the authorities
to see his friend for a short time. When they stood face to face,
Rabbi Shelomo at once saw that Rabbi Nahum had taken
sorrow upon himself for the sake of Israel, and Rabbi Nahum
at once saw what was going on in him. "How do you know?"
he asked. "For I begged God that neither angel nor seraph
might know."

"An angel or a seraph does not know," said the rabbi of Karlin. "But Shelomo, son of Yuta, knows. But I promise you that when my turn comes, no creature shall know." Now, this was the day just before the rabbi of Tchernobil was to leave the jail. When the rabbi of Karlin had taken leave of him, he went to the official in charge of the prison, gave him the four hundred rubles which constituted the dowry, and thus had his friend released a day sooner. Then he drove on to the wedding with his son.

There are various versions of what happened after this. According to one of them, Rabbi Barukh never mentioned the dowry during the seven days of the celebration. When the rabbi of Karlin was ready to leave for home, his son said to him: "You are going home, and I am staying behind with my father-in-law. What shall I do if he asks me for the dowry?" "Should he ever worry you about it," Rabbi Shelomo replied, "stand somewhere or other, with your face to the wall, and say: 'Father, father, my father-in-law is worrying me about the dowry.' Then he will stop asking you for it."

Some time passed and nothing happened until one Friday evening when Rabbi Barukh recited the Song of Songs and his son-in-law stood opposite him. When Rabbi Barukh came to the words "a bundle of myrrh," he paused and lightly touched his left hand with his right as if he were counting a bundle of bills. Then he continued with the Song of Songs. But his son-in-law could not bear to remain. He rushed into his room, turned his face to the wall, and said: " 'Father, father, my father-in-law is worrying me about the dowry.' " From that moment on, he was left in peace.

The Worst

Rabbi Shelomo asked: "What is the worst thing the Evil Urge can achieve?" And he answered: "To make man forget that he is the son of a king."

How God Loves

Rabbi Shelomo said: "If only I could love the greatest zaddik as much as God loves the greatest ne'er-do-well!"

When Rabbi Shelomo of Karlin was in the little town of Dobromysl, near Lozhny, where his former companion, Rabbi Shneur Zalman, was living at that time, and stopped in the House of Study, Rabbi Zalman said on a Friday, to some hasidim who had come to him: "Now I am not the rabbi. The holy zaddik, our master Rabbi Shelomo, is within my district, so now he is the rabbi. You must go to Dobromysl and stay with him over the sabbath." They did so and ate the three sabbath meals at the table of the rabbi of Karlin. And though he spoke no word of teaching, as their own teacher did on these occasions, their spirit beheld the holy light, and it was incomparably more radiant than ever before. At the third sabbath meal, Rabbi Shelomo preceded the saying of grace by the brief psalm which begins with: "His foundation is in the holy mountains," and ends: "All my springs are in thee," which he translated: "All my springing is in thee." And instantly the springs of their spirit gushed forth. The spirit possessed them so utterly that until long after the sabbath they did not know the difference between day and night. When they returned to Rabbi Zalman and told him what had happened to them, he said: "Yes, who can compare to the holy Rabbi Shelomo! He knows how to translate? We cannot translate. Who can compare to the holy Rabbi Shelomo! For he is a hand's-breadth above the world!"

Armilus

Rabbi Shelomo used to say: "If only the Messiah, the son of David would come! At a pinch, I myself can be the Messiah, son of Joseph, who precedes him and is killed. What is there to fear for me, and whom shall I fear! Shall I fear the crooked cossack?" The people thought he was calling Death a crooked cossack, and were very much surprised at this.

* * * * *

Again and again, the community of Ludmir asked him to come to them, for many of his friends lived there. He always refused. But when envoys from Ludmir came to him once more — it was on Lag ba-Omer, on the thirty-third day of the days of the counting of Omer, between the feasts of Passover and the Revelation — he asked them smilingly: "And what do you do in Ludmir on Lag ba-Omer?"

"Well," said the envoys, "just what is usually done. All the boys, big and the little, go out into the fields with their bows and shoot."

The rabbi laughed and said: "Well, if that's the way it is, if you shoot, that makes all the difference! Then I will come to you."

* * * * *

When the rabbi was already living in Ludmir, the Russians put down a revolt of the Poles in that region, and pursued the defeated rebels right into the town. The Russian commander gave his men permission to loot at will for two hours. It was the day before the Feast of the Revelation which, in that year, fell on a sabbath. The Jews were gathered in the House of Prayer. Rabbi Shelomo was praying, and in such ecstasy that he heard and saw nothing that went on around him. Just then a tall cossack came limping along, went up to the window, looked in, and pointed his gun. In a ringing voice, the rabbi was saying the words, "for thine, O Lord, is the kingdom," when his little grandson, who was standing beside him, timidly tugged at his coat, and he awoke from his ecstasy. But the bullet had already struck him in the side. "Why did you fetch me down?" he asked. When they brought him to his house and laid him down, he had them open the Book of Splendor at a certain passage and prop it up in front of him while they bound up his wound. It stayed there, open before his eyes until the following Wednesday, when he died.

Now, it is said that the name of that limping cossack was Armilus. And that is the name of the fiend who, according to the old tradition, is to kill the Messiah son of Joseph.

The Rope That Gave

A few days before he died of his wound, Rabbi Shelomo wrote to his disciple Mordecai of Lechovitz: "Come, so that I may consecrate you to leadership." Mordecai at once set out on his journey. On the way, he suddenly felt as if a rope which was carrying him safely across an abyss gave, as if he were falling through shoreless space. "I have been severed from my teacher," he screamed, and after that, did not utter another word. His companions took him to the old rabbi of Neskhizh, known as a wonder-worker throughout the land, and asked him to heal Rabbi Mordecai who was quite out of his mind. "Tell him," said the rabbi of Neskhizh, "that his teacher is dead. Then he will recover." They conveyed this news to him very cautiously, for they feared he might do harm to himself. But the moment he grasped their message, his face regained its composure, in a firm voice he pronounced the benediction which is said at the news of death, and cried: "He was my teacher, and he shall remain my teacher."

Out of Mercy

Rabbi Asher of Stolyn told:
My teacher, Rabbi Shelomo, used to say: "I have to prepare what I shall have to do in hell," for he was certain that no better end was in store for him. Now, when his soul ascended after death, and the serving angels received him joyfully, to guide him to the highest paradise, he refused to go with them. "They are making fun of me," he said. "This cannot be the world of truth." At last the Divine Presence herself said to him: "Come, my son! Out of mercy, I shall give you of my treasure." Then he gave in and was content.

"I Am Prayer"

It is told:
A complaint was once lodged in the tribunal of Heaven. It was that most Jews prayed without fixing their souls on prayer. And because this was so, a king was allowed to arise on earth, who wanted to prohibit the Jews in his realm from praying together in a congregation. But some angels objected and would not permit this to happen. Finally they decided to ask the souls of the zaddikim who dwell in the upper world, and they gave their consent to the prohibition. But when they came to Rabbi Shelomo of Karlin, he shook the world with the storm of his prayer, and said: "I am prayer. I take it on myself to pray in lieu of all Israel." And the prohibition did not go through.

ISRAEL OF KOZNITZ

The Story of the Cape

A woman came to Rabbi Israel, the maggid of Koznitz, and told him, with many tears, that she had been married a dozen years and still had not borne a son. "What are you willing to do about it?" he asked her. She did not know what to say.

"My mother," so the maggid told her, "was aging and still had no child. Then she heard that the holy Baal Shem was stopping over in Apt in the course of a journey. She hurried to his inn and begged him to pray she might bear a son. 'What are you willing to do about it?' he asked. 'My husband is a poor book-binder,' she replied, 'but I do have one fine thing that I shall give to the rabbi.' She went home as fast as she could and fetched her good cape, her 'Katinka,' which was carefully stowed away in a chest. But when she returned to the inn with it, she heard that the Baal Shem had already left for Mezbizh. She immediately set out after him and since she had no money to ride, she walked from town to town with her 'Katinka' until she came to Mezbizh. The Baal Shem took the cape and hung it on the wall. 'It is well,' he said. My mother walked all the way back, from town to town, until she reached Apt. A year later, I was born."

"I, too," cried the woman, "will bring you a good cape of mine so that I may get a son."

"That won't work," said the maggid. "You heard the story. My mother had no story to go by."

Studying

When Israel was seven years old, he studied in the Talmud School by day, but in the evening he went to the House of Study and studied on his own. The first night of Hanukkah, his father did not permit him to go to the House of Study, for he suspected him of wanting to play a certain game, popular at this season, with the other boys. But since he had neither a book nor a candle at home, he promised his father to stay in the House of Study only as long at it took a three-penny candle to burn down. Now, either other candles were burning in the room, or the angels, who rejoiced in the studying of the boy, kept the three-penny candle miraculously alight — at any rate, the boy remained in the House of Study long after he was supposed to. When he finally came home, his father beat him until the blood came.

"And did you not tell your father that you were studying all that time?" they asked the maggid when he told the story many years after.

"I might have told him, of course," he answered. "And my father would have believed me, for he knew that I never lied, but is it right to use the greatness of the Torah to save one's own skin?"

Knowledge

They say that, in his youth, Rabbi Israel studied eight hundred books of the Kabbalah. But the first time he saw the maggid of Mezritch face to face, he instantly knew that he knew nothing at all.

His Torah

The maggid of Koznitz said: "Our sages very properly emphasize that in the first psalm, the Torah is called 'the law of the Lord,' and later 'his Torah.' For if a man learns the Torah for its own sake, then it is given to him, and it is his, and he may clothe all his holy thoughts in the holy Torah."

The Sheepskin Coat

It is told:

When he was young, Rabbi Israel was poor and in need. Once he went to visit Rabbi Yitzhak, later the rav of Berditchev, who was then still living in Zelechov, a nearby town. Later the zaddik saw him out. First they stood on the threshold of the house and kept on talking. And they conversed so earnestly, that they walked on and on together. It was bitterly cold, and

Rabbi Levi Yitzhak had not taken his coat. "Lend me your sheepskin for a while," he said to his disciple and friend, and he gladly gave it to him. Freezing in his thin clothing, he walked beside the zaddik and they never stopped talking. This went on for some time. "Now it is enough, Israel," the rabbi finally said. "Now you shall be warm too." From that hour on, Israel's destiny altered.

Sickness and Strength

Rabbi Israel was in poor health from childhood on. He was as lean as a stick and the doctors were surprised that he stayed alive. For the most part, he lay on his bed wrapped in rabbit-skins. When he rose, he put on slippers lined with bear's fur, because he could not stand shoes on his feet. They carried him to the House of Prayer in a litter. But the moment he had said on the threshold: "How full of awe is this place," he was transformed. On Mondays and Thursdays, the days on which the Scriptures are read, he walked in prayer shawl and phylacteries, the scroll of the Torah in his arms, so lightly and quickly through the two rows of waiting people, that the servants who accompanied him carrying the candles could hardly keep up with him. With dancing motion, he leaned toward the holy Ark into which he put the scroll, walked with dancing step to the desk on which the candelabrum stood, and set the candles in it. Then, in his ordinary low voice, he said the first words of the prayer, but from one word to the next his voice gained in power, until he swept upward with it every heart. After prayer, when the servants carried him home in his litter, he was pale as one dying, but his pallor was luminous. That was why they said that his body shone like a thousand souls.

Once, when he had been asked to attend a circumcision, and was about to get into the carriage, some people came forward to help him in. "Fools," he said, "why should I need your strength? It is written: 'But they that wait for the Lord shall change their strength'; I shall change my strength for the strength of God; He has strength to spare." And he jumped into the carriage.

The Coat

Whatever the rabbi of Koznitz said sounded as if he were praying, only weaker and in a lower voice.

He liked to hum to himself proverbs and sayings current among the Polish peasants. After a Purim feast, which he had presided over in great happiness, he said: "How right, what the people say:

> 'Doff your coat, dear soul, and prance
> Merrily at feast and dance.'

But how curious a coat is the body!"

Sometimes he even spoke to God in Polish. When he was alone, they would hear him say: "*Moj kochanku,*" which means: "My darling."

A Prayer

The rabbi of Koznitz said to God: "Lord of the world, I beg of you to redeem Israel. And if you do not want to do that, then redeem the goyim."

Another Prayer

Once the maggid of Koznitz said: "Lord, I stand before you like a messenger boy, and wait for you to tell me where to go."

Testimony

This is what Rabbi Moshe of Koznitz, son of the maggid, writes in his book, the "Well of Moses."

"My father and teacher said to me: 'Believe me, my son, the alien thoughts which seized on me from time to time came only while I was praying, and with the help of God I brought them all home to their source and their root, to where their tent stood in the beginning of time."

Dead and Living Prayers

Once Rabbi Israel heard the "Cursed be . . . " passage in the Scriptures read in the House of Prayer, and cried out at the words: "And thy carcasses shall be food unto all fowls of the air." Later, at the meal, he said: "The prayers which are said without fear and without love, are called the 'carcasses.' But He, who hears the praying of every mouth, has mercy upon His creatures. From above He pours awakening into the heart of man, so that one single time he can pray with his soul as he should, and then his prayer grows great and destroys the prayers which are carcasses, and mounts like a bird to the flood-gates of Heaven."

Music

The maggid of Koznitz said:
" 'Make sweet melody,' is what Isaiah said to Tyre, the 'harlot long forgotten.' Make sweet your way and you shall be given melody."

Every Day

The maggid of Koznitz said:
"Every day, man shall go forth out of Egypt, out of distress."

For His Sick Son

When his beloved little son fell ill, and the doctors had given up hope, the maggid of Koznitz sat up all night and could think of nothing but his great grief. But when the time for the Morning Prayer had come, he said: "It is written: 'And she cast the child under one of the shrubs.' The shrubs, the shrubs, the great shrub of prayer! So that one word of the prayer might be said with rejoicing!"
When Rabbi Levi Yitzhak, who at that time was still living in the neighboring town of Zelechov, heard of it, he went to the bath and dipped under with the holy intent of changing the maggid's trend of thought so that he might pray for the recovery of his son. And he succeeded. While the maggid was praying, the trend of his thoughts was changed, and with great fervor he implored God to let his child recover.
At that time — so the hasidim say — not only little Moshe, the maggid's son, but all the sick children, far and wide, recovered.

Each year, the maggid of Koznitz visited his father's grave in the city of Apt. On one such occasion, the heads of the community came to him to ask him to preach in the great House of Prayer on the sabbath, as he had done the year before. "Is there any reason to believe," he said, "that I accomplished anything with my last year's sermon?" The men left in dismay, and the entire community was stricken with grief. A crowd collected in front of the maggid's inn. All stood silent with bowed heads. But then a man, a craftsman, came forward, went into the maggid's room, and said to him: "You claim that you did not accomplish anything with the sermon you preached last year. You did accomplish something as far as I am concerned. For at that time I heard from your lips the words that every son of Israel must do as it says in the Scriptures: 'I have set the Lord always before me.' Ever since then I see the name of the Lord before me, like black fire on white fire."

"If that is the case," said the maggid, "I shall go and preach a sermon."

Self-Mortification

To the maggid of Koznitz came a man who — in order to mortify himself — wore nothing but a sack on his bare body, and fasted from one sabbath to the next. The maggid said to him: "Do you think the Evil Urge is keeping away from you? It is tricking you into that sack. He who pretends to fast from sabbath to sabbath but secretly eats a little something every day, is spiritually better off than you, for he is only deceiving others, while you are deceiving yourself."

Rejection

A woman came to the maggid of Koznitz and told him, weeping bitterly all the while, that her husband had turned from her, and said she was ugly. "And perhaps you are really ugly?" said Rabbi Israel.

"Rabbi," cried the woman, "did I not seem beautiful and dear to him when we stood under the wedding canopy? Why have I now grown black?"

Then a tremor went through the rabbi, and it was only with difficulty that he could bring himself to comfort the woman, saying he would pray that God might turn her husband's heart back to her. When she had gone, he said to God: "Think of this woman, Lord of the world, and think of Israel. When the people of Israel said at Sinai: 'All that the Lord hath spoken will we do,' and you chose them and wedded them to yourself, were they not beautiful and dear? Why have they now grown black?"

Rich People's Food

A rich man once came to the maggid of Koznitz.

"What are you in the habit of eating?" the maggid asked.

"I am modest in my demands," the rich man replied. "Bread and salt, and a drink of water are all I need."

"What are you thinking of!" the rabbi reproved him. "You must eat roast meat and drink mead, like all rich people." And he did not let the man go until he had promised to do as he said. Later the hasidim asked him the reason for this odd request.

"Not until he eats meat," said the maggid, "will he realize that the poor man needs bread. As long as he himself eats bread, he will think the poor man can live on stones."

In Order

It is told:

A villager and his wife came to the maggid of Koznitz and begged him to pray that they might have a son, for they were childless. "Give me fifty-two gulden," said the maggid, "for this is the numerical value of the word *ben*, son."

"We should be glad to give you ten gulden," said the man, but the maggid refused to accept them. Then the man went to the market-place and staggered back under a sack of copper coins. He spread them out on the table. There were twenty gulden. "Look, what a lot of money!" he cried. But the maggid would not come down with his demand. At that the villager grew angry, gathered up his money, and said to his wife: "Come on, let's go. God will help us without the maggid's prayer."

"You have already been granted his help," said the rabbi. And he was right.

It is told:

When Prince Adam Czartoryski, the friend and counsellor of Czar Alexander, had been married for many years and still had no children, he went to the maggid of Koznitz and asked him to pray for him, and because of his prayer the princess bore a son. At the baptism, the father told of the maggid's intercession with God. His brother who, with his young son, was among the guests, made fun of what he called the prince's superstition. "Let us go to your wonder-worker together," he said, "and I shall show you that he can't tell the difference between left and right."

Together they journeyed to Koznitz, which was close to where they lived. "I beg of you," Adam's brother said to the maggid, "to pray for my sick son."

The maggid bowed his head in silence. "Will you do this for me?" the other urged.

The maggid raised his head. "Go," he said, and Adam saw that he only managed to speak with a great effort. "Go quickly, and perhaps you will still see him alive."

"Well, what did I tell you?" Adam's brother said laughingly as they got into their carriage. Adam was silent during the ride. When they drove into the court of his house, they found the boy dead.

The Pudding

Once a simple man of the people came to the maggid of Koznitz with his wife and said that he wished to divorce her. "Why do you want to do that?" asked the maggid.

"I work very hard all week," said the man, "and on the sabbath I want to have some pleasure. Now at the sabbath meal, my wife first serves the fish, and then the onions and the heavy main dish, and by the time she puts the pudding on the table, I have eaten all I want and have no appetite for it. All week I work for this pudding and when it comes I cannot even taste of it, and all my labor was for nothing! Time after time, I have asked my wife to put the pudding on the table right after the benediction over the wine, but no! She says that the way she does it, is according to the custom."

The maggid turned to the woman. "From now on," he said, "make two puddings. Serve the one right after the benediction over the wine and the other after the main dish, as before." Both husband and wife agreed to this, and went away well pleased.

On the same day, the maggid said to his wife: "From now on, make two puddings on Friday. Serve one right after the benediction over the wine, and the other after the main dish, as you have been doing." From that time on, this was the custom in the maggid's house, and continued to be the custom among his children and his children's children: One pudding was served immediately after the blessing over the wine, and this was called the Peace-at-Home Pudding.

Adam's Share

It is told that once, when the maggid of Koznitz was praying, Adam, the first man, came to him, and said: "You have atoned for your share in my sin — now won't you atone for my share in it too?"

The Cantonist at the Seder

It is told:

In the Russia of those days, it was common to draft Jewish boys into the army, in which they were forced to serve to their sixtieth year. They were known as "cantonists."

On the eve of Passover, a man whose uniform identified him as a cantonist arrived in Koznitz and asked to be admitted to the holy maggid. When he stood in his presence, he begged to be allowed to participate in the Seder, and the maggid gave his permission.

When, in the course of the rites of the Seder, they came to the words: "The Ceremony of the Passover has been celebrated in due order," the guest asked whether he might sing, and his request was granted. After the closing words of the song: ". . . peduyim lezion berina," which means, "Redeemed unto Zion with joy," he cried out in Russian: "Podjom!" that is, "Let's go!" The maggid rose and said in a voice filled with jubilation: "We are ready to go to Zion." But the guest had vanished.

The Man Who Struck the Prophet

A grandson of the maggid of Koznitz told:

"Once a man who was possessed came to the holy maggid — may his memory protect us! — and asked to be redeemed. The maggid called on the spirit to confess his sins. The spirit said: 'When the prophet Zechariah predicted destruction to the people, I was the first to run forward from the throng and strike him in the face. Only then did the others shower blows upon him until they struck him dead. Ever since that time, I am forced to wander from soul to soul and can find no rest.' But when the holy maggid began his work of redemption by rubbing the fringes one against the other, the spirit burst into insolent laughter and cried: 'In my day it was the tailors and the shoemakers who knew how to do this sort of thing.' 'And if you were so clever,' said the maggid, 'why did you strike the prophet dead?' Then the spirit replied: 'It is a law that he who keeps his prophecy to himself incurs the death penalty. On the other hand, it is said that if the prophet does not utter his prophecy, it becomes invalid. So it would have been better if Zechariah had kept his prophecy to himself and thus sacrificed himself for the community. That is why we killed him.' The holy maggid said: 'To tell this — that is the reason why you came here,' and completed the work of redemption."

That is how the grandson of the maggid of Koznitz told the story. But it is also told that when the maggid heard the words of the spirit, he could not complete his work, and that the man who was possessed had to go to Rabbi Issachar Baer of Radoshitz, the wonder-worker, who in his youth had been a disciple of the maggid's, and that he performed the work of redemption.

His Sister's Spirit

It is told:

The maggid of Koznitz had a sister who died young. But in the upper world, they gave her permission to remain in her brother's house.

The maggid always saw to it that clothing was made for poor orphans. When dealers brought him the material for this, he said: "I shall ask my sister whether this stuff is durable and a good buy," and she always gave him correct information.

She watched everything the servants did, and when one or another of them stole a loaf of bread or a piece of meat, she instantly reported the theft to her brother. He detested this tale-bearing, but he could not break her of it. Once his temper grew short and he said to her: "Wouldn't you like to take a little rest?" From that time on, she was gone.

The Soul of the Cymbalist

It is told:

Once, on a midnight, a voice drifted into the room of the maggid of Koznitz and moaned: "Holy man of Israel, have pity on a pour soul which, for ten years, has been wandering from eddy to eddy."

"Who are you?" asked the maggid. "And what did you do while you were on earth?"

"I was a musician," said the voice. "I played the cymbal and I sinned like all wandering musicians."

"And who sent you to me?"

Then the voice groaned: "Why, I played at your wedding, rabbi, and you gave me praise and wanted to hear more, and so I played one piece after another and you were well pleased."

"Do you still remember the tune you played when they conducted me under the wedding-baldachin?" The voice hummed the tune. "Well then, you shall be redeemed on the coming sabbath," said the maggid.

On the Friday evening after that, when the maggid stood in front of the reader's desk, he sang the song: "Come, my friend, to meet the bride," in a tune no one knew, and not even the choir could join in.

The World of Melody

The "Yehudi," the zaddik of Pzhysha, once saw with the eyes of his mind that the maggid of Koznitz, who had fallen ill, was now in danger of dying. Immediately he told two of his faithful men who were excellent singers and players, to go to Koznitz and gladden Rabbi Israel's heart with music. The two set out at once, reached the maggid's house on Friday, and were told to welcome in the sabbath with their singing and playing. When the sounds entered the room where Rabbi Israel lay, he listened intently and his face brightened. Gradually, his breath grew even, his forehead cool, and his hands stopped twitching and lay quietly on the coverlet. When the music ended he looked up as though he had just awakened and said: "The Yehudi saw that I had passed through all the worlds. The only world in which I was not, was the world of melody. So he sent two messengers to lead me back through that world."

The Melody of Angels

Rumor had it that the melody the maggid of Koznitz left behind was one he had heard from the lips of angels who sang it in honor of God. But one of his disciples said this was not so, that the angels had heard it from his lips. In later years, when a son of that disciple told the story, he added: "They were the angels who were born from the deeds of the holy maggid."

With One Look

One sabbath, at the third meal, young Zevi Elimelekh heard his teacher, Rabbi Mendel of Rymanov, say: "He who lives in the era of the maggid of Koznitz, and has not looked upon his face, will not be found worthy to look upon the face of the Messiah, when he comes."

The moment the light was put on the table, Zevi Elimelekh took leave of the rabbi, fetched his stick, slung his knapsack over his shoulder and walked day and night with scarcely any respite, for who knows if the Messiah will not come this very week? When he reached Koznitz, he went straight to the maggid's House of Study, without even stopping to leave his stick and knapsack at an inn, for who knows if the Messiah will not come this very hour? They showed him into a little room where many people were standing around the maggid's bed. Zevi Elimelekh leaned against the wall, rested one hand on his stick, the other on a man in front of him, hoisted himself up, and looked into the maggid's face. "With one look," he said to himself, "one can gain the coming world."

Extension

In his old age, Rabbi Israel said: "There are those zaddikim who—as soon as they have accomplished the task appointed to them for their life on earth—are called to depart. And there are those zaddikim who—the moment they have accomplished the task appointed to them for their life on earth—are given another task, and they live until that too is accomplished. That is the way it was with me."

Pebbles

In the year of Napoleon's Russian campaign, the rabbi of Apt visited the maggid of Koznitz on the Feast of the Revelation. He found him lying on his sick-bed as usual, but saw that his face was quickened with a strange expression of decision. "How are you?" asked the visitor.

"I am a soldier now," said the maggid. "The five pebbles young David picked up for his sling, to fight Goliath the Philistine—those five pebbles I have right here in my bed!"

In the night before the first holiday, two hours after midnight, the maggid went to the desk in the House of Prayer, stood there until morning, said the Morning Prayer, read the Scriptures, recited the liturgy for the feast, and finished his prayer three hours after twelve o'clock noon.

Before the End

When the maggid of Koznitz, who was sick unto death, prayed in front of the Ark, the month before he died, on the eve of the Day of Atonement, he paused before saying the words: "The Lord said: 'I have pardoned,'" and said to God: "Lord of the world, you alone know how great your power is, and you alone know how great is the weakness of my body. And this too you know: that all through this month, day after day, I have prayed in front of the Ark, not for my own sake, but for the sake of this, your people of Israel. And so I ask you: If it grew easy for me to take the yoke of your people upon myself and to perform the service with my wretched body, how can it be difficullt for you, who are all-powerful, to say three words?" Then he bade them sing a song of joy, and called out in a strong voice: "The Lord said: 'I have pardoned'"

JACOB YITZHAK OF LUBLIN ("THE SEER")

His Old Teacher

Rabbi Jacob Yitzhak once journeyed to a distant city in the company of some of his friends and disciples. It was Friday afternoon and they must have been quite close to their destination when they came to a crossroads. The coachman asked which road he was to take. The rabbi did not know and so he said: "Give the horses their head and let them go where they want." After a time they saw the houses of a town. Soon, however, they discovered that it was not the one they were bound for. "Well, after that, better not call me rabbi any more," said the Seer of Lublin.

"But how are we going to get food and shelter for the sabbath," his disciples asked, "if we are not allowed to say who you are?" Now the reason for this question was this: the zaddik never kept overnight even the smallest coins of the gifts of money he had received during the day, but gave everything to the poor.

"Let us go to the House of Prayer," he said. "There some burgher or other will take each of us home with him as his sabbath guest." And that was what happened, only that the rabbi himself took so long over his prayers that the House of Prayer was all but empty when he had done. Looking up, he saw that one man alone, a man of eighty or thereabouts, was still there. This old man asked the stranger: "Where are you going for the consecration of the sabbath?"

"I don't know," said the zaddik.

"Just go to the inn," said the old man, "and when the day of rest is over, I'll take up a collection to settle your bill."

"I cannot keep the sabbath at the inn," said Rabbi Jacob Yitzhak, "because there they do not say the blessing over the lights."

The old man hesitated. Then he said: "In my house I have only a little bread and wine for my wife and myself."

"I am not a big eater," the rabbi of Lublin assured him, and they went off together.

First the old man said the blessing over the wine, and then the rabbi. After the blessing over the bread, the old man asked: "Where do you come from?"

"From Lublin."

"And do you know *him?*"

"I am always in his company."

Then the old man begged his guest in a voice that trembled: "Tell me something about him!"

"Why are you so eager to know?"

"When I was young," said the old man, "I was an assistant at the school and he was one of the children assigned to my care. He did not seem especially gifted. But then I heard that he became a very great man. Since that time I fast one day every week, that I may be found worthy to see him. For I am too poor to ride to Lublin and too weak to walk there."

"Do you remember anything at all about him?" the rabbi inquired.

"Day after day," said the old man, "I had to look for him when the time to study the prayer-book had come, and I never found him. After a fairly long time he came of his own accord, and then I smacked him. Once I watched where he was going and followed. There he sat on an ant-hill in the woods and cried aloud: 'Hear, O Israel, the Lord our God, the Lord is one.' After that I never smacked him any more."

Now Rabbi Jacob Yitzhak knew why his horses had taken him to this town. "I am he," he said. When the old man heard this, he fainted and it took a long time to revive him.

At the end of the sabbath, the zaddik left the city with his disciples, and the old man accompanied him until he grew tired and had to turn back. He reached home, lay down, and died. While this was happening, the rabbi and his companions were having the post-sabbath meal at a village inn. When they had finished eating, he rose, and said: "Now let us return to the city and bury my old teacher."

In the course of his long wanderings, Rabbi Zusya came to the town where the father of the boy Jacob Yitzhak lived. In the House of Study he went back of the stove to pray—for this was his way—and covered his whole head with the prayer shawl. Suddenly he half turned, looked out from it, and without letting his glance rest on anything else, looked the boy Jacob Yitzhak straight in the eyes. Then he turned back to the stove and went on praying. The boy was seized with an irresistible impulse to cry. A well of tears opened up within him and he wept for an hour. Not until his tears ceased to fall, did Zusya go up to him. Then he said: "Your soul has been wakened. Now go to my teacher, the maggid of Mezritch, and study with him, so that your mind may also be roused from its sleep."

In the House of Study

A zaddik told:

"When I lived in Nikolsburg, as a disciple of Rabbi Shmelke, one of my companions was a young man by the name of Jacob Yitzhak. Years later he became the rabbi of Lublin. He and I had both been married for two years. In the House of Study he sat in an inconspicuous place. He never asked questions like the rest. He never looked at any of us, but only at the rabbi. When he was not looking at him, he kept his eyes on the ground. But his face was transfigured with a golden radiance from within, and I saw that the rabbi was very fond of him."

Holy Joy

When Jacob Yitzhak was in Rabbi Shmelke's House of Study, he seemed like an angel remote from all matters of earth, so much so that Rabbi Shmelke, who himself had a tendency to aloofness, found his disciple's attitude excessive. He sent him to Hanipol with a note to Rabbi Zusya which contained only these words: "Make our Itzikel a little lighter of heart!" And Rabbi Zusya, who had once wakened Jacob Yitzhak the boy to holy tears, now succeeded in waking holy joy within him.

At the Brink

Near the city of Lizhensk, where Rabbi Elimelekh taught, there is a hill. It is wooded on all sides except one, but there it is steep and stony, and the rocky peak is called Rabbi Melekh's Table to this very day. Young Jacob Yitzhak was in the habit of going to this place to meditate on how true humility and the annihilation of self can be reached. One day he was in such despair that it seemed to him all he could do was to offer up his own life. He went to the very brink of the rock and wanted to throw himself down. But a comrade of his, young Zalke from Grodzisk, had followed him unobserved. Now he ran toward him, caught him by the belt, and did not stop comforting and encouraging him until he had talked his soul out of its grim purpose.

When Jacob Yitzhak's teacher died, and he was made the rabbi of Lublin, Rabbi Zalke came to visit him. As he entered the room, the zaddik took both his hands in his and said: "Rabbi Zalke, my life, I truly love you. That is because on my soul's first excursion on earth you were my father. But when I recall what you did to me in Lizhensk, I cannot wholly love you."

His Gaze

The hasidim tell:

When the soul of the Seer of Lublin was created, it was endowed with the power of gazing from one end of the world to the other. But when it saw the great mass of evil, it knew that it could not bear this burden and begged to be relieved of its gift. Then its power was limited to seeing everything within a radius of four miles.

In his youth, he kept his eyes closed for seven years, save during the hours of praying and learning, so that he might not see anything unseemly. This made his eyes weak and near-sighted.

When he looked at anyone's forehead, or at his note of request, he saw to the root of his soul and beyond it to the first man. He saw whether that soul came from Abel or from Cain, saw how often, in its wanderings, it had assumed bodily shape, what had been destroyed or bettered in each incarnation, in what sin it had become entangled, and to what vitrue it had ascended.

Once, when he was visiting Rabbi Mordecai of Neskhizh, they spoke of this power. The rabbi of Lublin said: "The fact that I see in each what he has done, lessens my love for Israel. And so I beg you to do something to have this power taken from me."

The rabbi of Neskhizh replied: "The words in the Gemara hold for whatever Heaven decrees: 'Our God gives, but he does not take back.' "

Going Blind

It is told:

In Lublin the Afternoon Prayer was delayed even on the sabbath. Before this prayer, the rabbi sat alone in his room every sabbath, and no one was permitted to enter it. Once a hasid hid there to find out what happened on these occasions. All he saw at first was that the rabbi seated himself at the table and opened a book. But then a vast light began to shine in the narrow room, and when he saw it the hasid became unconscious. He came to himself when the rabbi left the room, and he too went out as soon as he fully regained consciousness. In the entrance, he saw nothing, but he heard them saying the Evening Prayer and realized with horror that the candles must be lit and that he, notwithstanding, was surrounded by utter darkness. He was terrified, implored the rabbi to help him, and was sent to another city, to a man who was known to perform miraculous cures. He asked the hasid about the circumstances of his going blind, and he told him. "There is no cure for you," said the man. "You have seen the original light, the light on the days of creation, which empowered the first people on earth to see from one end of the world to the other, which was hidden after their sinning, and is only revealed to zaddikim in the Torah. Whoever beholds it unlawfully—his eyes will be darkened forever."

Landscape

When Rabbi Jacob Yitzhak was a guest in the house of Rabbi Barukh, the Baal Shem's grandson, that proud and secretive

man who had once said of himself that he would be the super-
visor of all zaddikim, took him with him in his carriage when
he drove to the ritual bath on the day before the sabbath. On
the way, Rabbi Barukh gave himself up to the creative strength
with which he gazed at his surroundings, and the landscape
changed in tune with his thoughts. When they got out of the
carriage, he asked: "What does the Seer see?" Rabbi Yitzhak
replied: "The fields of the Holy Land."

When they crossed the hill between the road and the stream,
Barukh asked: "What does the Seer smell?" He replied: "The
air of the mountain of the Temple."

When they dipped into the stream, the grandson of the Baal
Shem Tov asked: "What does the Seer feel?" And Rabbi Jacob
Yitzhak answered: "The healing stream of paradise."

What Ten Hasidim Can Accomplish

A young man stole away from his wife and parents-in-law to
spend the sabbath in Lublin. But hardly had he greeted the
rabbi, when Jacob Yitzhak—who had looked at him closely—
told him to return to his own town immediately so that he
might reach home before the beginning of the holiday. The
young man begged and begged, but could not induce the rabbi
to change his dictum, and so he went his way deeply disturbed.
He spent the night at an inn and while he lay there, unable to
sleep, a group of hasidim, on the road to the rabbi of Lublin,
entered the room. They heard the man moaning on his bench,
asked him about himself, and discovered what had happened.
Then they got some brandy, kept filling their glasses and his,
drank to one another, and to him, and cried: "To life! To life!"
One after another took him by the hand and then they said to
him: "You are not going home! You are coming to Lublin
with us and shall spend the sabbath there, and don't you worry
about anything!" They drank until morning. Then they all
prayed together, drank to one another and the young man
once more, and went merrily toward Lublin, taking him between them.

The moment they arrived there, they went to the zaddik and
greeted him. The zaddik looked at the young man and was

silent for a time. Finally he asked: "Where have you been? What has happened?" When he had heard everything, the zaddik said: "It was decreed that you should die on this sabbath, and your fate has been averted. The truth of it is that no zaddik can bring about what ten hasidim can accomplish."

The Bed

It was a known fact that frequently the Seer of Lublin could not sleep in a strange bed on occasions when he was a guest in someone's house. And so, when Rabbi Yossel of Ostila heard that the zaddik was coming to his town on his next journey, he immediately gave a devout and able carpenter the order to make a bed of the very best wood and to put into it his most painstaking labor. The carpenter went to the ritual bath, concentrated his mind on his work, and was more successful than ever before. When Jacob Yitzhak had accepted Rabbi Yossel's earnest invitation to stay at his house, his host conducted him to his room, where the bed shone out in all its newness, piled with smooth pillows and soft blankets. But with pained surprise, Rabbi Yossel later heard the zaddik toss about on his bed with many sighs and realized that he could not sleep. For a while he was utterly nonplussed. Finally he offered his guest his own bed. The Seer of Lublin lay down in it, closed his eyes with immediate and evident comfort, and fell asleep. Later Rabbi Yossel mustered his courage and asked what he had found wrong with the bed a God-fearing man had made for him with the most zealous care. The zaddik said: "The man is good and his work is good, but he did it in the nine days before the anniversary of the destruction of the Temple. Since he is devout, he mourned for the Temple unceasingly, and now his sorrow clings to the bed, and exudes from it."

Lighting the Pipe

A zaddik told:
"In my youth I once attended a wedding to which the rabbi of Lublin had also been invited. Among the guests were more than two hundred zaddikim, as for the hasidim—you could

306

not even have counted them! They had rented a house with a great hall for the rabbi of Lublin, but he spent most of the time alone in a little room. Once a great number of hasidim had gathered in the hall and I was with them. Then the rabbi entered, seated himself at a small table and sat there for a time in silence. Then he rose, looked around, and—over the heads of the others pointed at me, standing up against the wall. "That young man over there," he said, "shall light my pipe for me." I made my way through the crowd, took the pipe from his hands, went to the kitchen, fetched a glowing coal, lit the pipe, brought it back into the hall, and handed it to him. At that moment I felt my senses taking leave of me. The next instant the rabbi began to speak and said a few words to me, and at once my senses returned. It was then that I received from him the gift of stripping myself of all that is bodily. Since then, I can do this whenever I want to."

Purification of Souls

Rabbi Naftali of Ropshitz said:

"I testify to this concerning my teacher, Rabbi Itzikel of Lublin: Whenever a new hasid came to him, he instantly took his soul out of him, cleansed it of all stain and rust, and put it back into him, restored to the state it had been in the hour he was born."

The "Casting off of Sins"

Once Rabbi Naftali had missed going to the river with his master, the rabbi of Lublin, for the Casting off of Sins. When the Seer was on the way home with his people, they met Naftali running toward the river. "Why are you running?" one of them asked him. "You see that the rabbi is on the way home, so what difference does it make now, whether you get to the river a little sooner or later?"

Naftali replied: "I am hurrying to gather up some of the sins the rabbi cast into the water, so that I may store them in the treasure-room of my heart."

Lighter

The rabbi of Lublin once said: "How strange! People come to me weighed down with melancholy, and when they leave, their spirit is lighter, although I myself [and here he was going to say: "am melancholy," but he paused and then continued:] am dark and do not shine."

The Little Sanctuary

One of the disciples of the rabbi of Lublin told this: "My master, the rabbi of Lublin, had not only the great disciples whom all the world knows, but also four hundred, who went by the name of 'village people' and had—every one of them!—the gift of the holy spirit."

They asked him: "If such a holy community existed, and the holy Seer was their king, why did they not join in one great attempt to bring about salvation?"

He replied: "Great things were undertaken."

They interposed: "But why didn't the whole community work together?"

He said: "When we were with our holy Seer, we were in a little sanctuary. We lacked nothing, and we did not feel the sadness of exile, nor the darkness that lies over all. Had we felt it, we should have shaken worlds, we should have split the Heavens to bring salvation closer."

The Obstacle

Once Rabbi Jacob Yitzhak confidently expected salvation to come that very year. When the year was over, he said to his disciple the Yehudi: "The rank and file of people either have turned completely to God, or can, at any rate, do so. They present no obstacle. It is the superior people who constitute a hindrance. They cannot attain humility, and therefore they cannot achieve the turning."

Payment

On one Friday evening, before the consecration of the sabbath, the rabbi had retired to his room and locked the door. Suddenly it opened, and he came out. The house was full of his great disciples in the white satin robes the great zaddikim used to wear in those days. The rabbi addressed them: "It is written: 'and repayeth them that hate Him to their face, to destroy them.' This is what it means: He pays his haters for the good works they do in this world in spite of themselves, in order to destroy them in the world which is to come. And so I ask you: given that the wrong-doer is greedy for gold, well then, he will receive his fill of gold; and given the wrong-doer is greedy for honors, well then, he shall have his fill of honors. But now suppose the wrong-doer is not out for honors, and not for gold, but for spiritual rungs, or that he is out to be a rabbi — what then? Well then, he who is out for spiritual rungs, will mount them, and he who is out to be a rabbi, will become one — in order to be destroyed in the coming world."

The Bright Light

A number of hasidim came to Lublin. Before they set out to go to the rabbi, their coachman begged them to take a slip of paper with his name on it, along with other slips of this kind, so that the rabbi might wish him well, and they did as he asked. When the Seer of Lublin read the slip, he cried: "How brightly the name of this man shines out!" The hasidim were astonished and asserted that he was a simple and ignorant man, and that in all the time they had known him, they had not detected any special virtues in him. "At this moment," insisted the rabbi, "his soul is shining out at me like pure light."

When the hasidim went to look for their coachman, they did not find him at the inn, and so they walked from street to street. Presently they met a gay procession coming toward them: first, musicians with cymbals and drums, and behind them a crowd of dancing, skipping, clapping people. In the very middle, gayer and shouting more lustily than all the rest, came the coachman. In answer to their questions, he said: "When you had gone I wanted to amuse myself a bit. So I strolled through the town and suddenly heard music and sounds of merriment from one of the houses. I went in and saw that they were celebrating the wedding of two orphans. So I celebrated along with them, drank, and sang, and had a good time. But after a while there was confusion and quarreling, for it seemed the bride did not have the money to give the groom a prayer shawl according to the custom and what was expected of her. They were just getting ready to tear up the marriage contract! Then my heart beat to bursting. I could not stand seeing the girl humiliated, pulled out my purse, and what do you think? There was just enough in it to pay for the prayer shawl! That is why I am so happy."

The Transition

A rich and powerful man by the name of Shalom, who was generally called Count Shalom, fell dangerously ill. His son at once set out for the rabbi of Lublin, to ask him to pray for mercy. But when, after his long journey, he stood before the zaddik and gave him the slip of paper with his request, Rabbi Jacob Yitzhak said: "Help is no longer possible. He has already passed from the sphere of ruling into that of learning." When the man reached home, he discovered that his father had died that very hour, but that, in the same hour, his wife had borne him a son. He was named Shalom after his grandfather, and grew up to be a master of the teachings.

The Lengthy Lawsuit

The rabbi of Lublin once said to Rabbi Heshel of Komarno, who was a disciple of his: "Why do you never look up the rav of the city? You would do well to go to him from time to time."
Rabbi Heshel was surprised to hear these words, for the rav, who had been nicknamed the "Iron Head," was a declared enemy of the hasidic way. Still, he obeyed his teacher, and began to pray in the rav's house every afternoon. The rav received him most cordially. One day, a lawsuit was presented after prayer. When the parties involved had been sent out of the room, and the discussion was under way, one of the judges took the part of the plaintiff, the other that of the defendant, so that the Iron Head was to tip the scales. Rabbi Heshel was

present and had followed the argument with the closest attention. It was entirely clear to him that the plaintiff was right, but he saw to his distress that the rav inclined to the other side. He did not know what to do, and yet he could not sit in silence and suffer injustice done. Finally he happened to remember a gloss to the passage in the Talmud which presented his own interpretation of the matter as the right one. He fetched the volume of the Gemara, went up to the rav, and asked him to expound the gloss. The Iron Head seemed irritated and refused him on the grounds that this was not the proper time for giving an interpretation. But Heshel repeated his request so insistently that the rav took the book from his hand, and glanced at the page in question. He changed color, told Heshel he would expound the comment to him the next day, and dismissed him.

The following day, when Rabbi Heshel inquired about the result of the session, he was told that the plaintiff had won the case. That same evening, the rabbi of Lublin said to him: "Now you don't have to go to the rav any more." When his disciple looked at him in astonishment, he added: "Those two, the plaintiff and the defendant, had been on earth ninety-nine times, and over and over justice was perverted and both their souls continued to be unredeemed. So I had to send you to help them."

The Rabbi of Lublin and the Iron Head

Rabbi Azriel Hurwitz, rav of the city of Lublin, who was also known by the name of Iron Head, kept plaguing Rabbi Jacob Yitzhak with constant objections and reproaches. Once he said to him: "You, yourself, know and admit that you are no zaddik. Then why do you guide others to your way, and gather a community around you?"

Rabbi Jacob Yitzhak replied: "What can I do about it? They come to me of their own free will, rejoice in my teaching, and desire to hear it."

Then the other said: "Tell all of them, this coming sabbath, that you are not one of the great, and they will turn from you."

The zaddik agreed. On the next sabbath, he begged his as-

sembled listeners not to give him rank and honors that were
not his due. As he spoke, their hearts were set aflame with
humility, and from that moment on, they followed him even
more fervently than before.

When he told the Iron Head of his efforts and their result, the
rav reflected, and then said: "That is the way you hasidim are:
you love the humble and eschew the haughty. Tell them that
you are one of the elect and they will turn from you."

Rabbi Jacob Yitzhak replied: "I am not a zaddik, but neither
am I a liar, and how can I say what is not true!"

On another occasion, Rabbi Azriel Hurwitz asked the Seer:
"How is it that so many flock about you? I am much more
learned than you, yet they do not throng to me."

The zaddik answered: "I too am astonished that so many
should come to one as insignificant as myself, to hear God's
word, instead of looking for it to you whose learning moves
mountains. Perhaps this is the reason: they come to me because I am astonished that they come, and they do not come to
you, because you are astonished that they do not come."

The Rabbi of Lublin and a Preacher

A famous traveling maggid was once preaching in a city, when
word came that the rabbi of Lublin had arrived. And immediately all the maggid's audience left to greet the zaddik.
The preacher found himself quite alone. He waited for a little
while and then he too saw the Seer's table heaped with the
"ransom-money" which petitioners and other visitors had
brought him. The maggid asked: "How is this possible! I
have been preaching here for days and have gotten nothing,
while all this came your way in a single hour!"

Rabbi Yitzhak replied: "It is probably because each wakens
in the hearts of men what he cherishes in his own heart: I, the
hatred of money, and you the love of it."

Truth

A disciple asked the rabbi of Lublin: "Rabbi, you taught us
that if a man knows his own worth and casts honest accounts
with his soul, then this saying of the people can be applied to

him: 'To cast accounts is paying half the bill.' How are we to understand this?"

"When merchandise is shipped across the border," said the rabbi, "the king's seal is put upon it, and thus it is certified. So when a man knows his worth and casts honest accounts with his soul, then truth, the seal of God, is set on him and he is certified."

The Way

Rabbi Baer of Radoshitz once said to his teacher, the rabbi of Lublin: "Show me one general way to the service of God."
The zaddik replied: "It is impossible to tell men what way they should take. For one way to serve God is through the teachings, another through prayer, another through fasting, and still another through eating. Everyone should carefully observe what way his heart draws him to, and then choose this way with all his strength."

In Many Ways

Some time after Rabbi Shalom, the son of Rabbi Abraham, the Angel, had died, two of his disciples came to Lublin to study with the Seer. They found him out in the open, saying the blessing of the New Moon. Now, because he did this a little differently in some details from what their teacher had accustomed them to, they did not promise themselves much from Lublin and decided to leave the town the very next day. When they entered the rabbi's house, shortly after, he spoke words of greetings to them and immediately added: "A God whom one could serve only in one set way — what kind of God would that be!" They bowed before him and became his disciples.

The Reluctant Hand

They asked the rabbi of Lublin: "Why does it say: "And Abraham stretched forth his hand,' and right after that, 'and took the knife . . . ' Is not the first part superfluous?"
He replied: "Abraham had consecrated all his strength and all his limbs, that they might do nothing against the will of God. Now when God commanded him to offer up his son, he

understood this to mean that he was to slay him. But since all his strength and all his limbs were consecrated, that they might do nothing against the will of God, Abraham's hands refused to obey Abraham, and take the knife, since this was not God's true will. Abraham had to overwhelm his hand with the power of his fervor, and send it out like a messenger who must do the errand of his sender. Only then could he take the knife."

True Justice

The words in the Scriptures: "Justice, justice shalt thou follow," were interpreted in the following way by the rabbi of Lublin:

"When a man believes that he is wholly just and need not strive further, then justice does not recognize him. You must follow and follow justice and never stand still, and in your own eyes, you must always be like a new-born child that has not yet achieved anything at all — for that is true justice."

The Second Mother

They asked the Rabbi of Lublin: "Why is it that in the holy Book of Splendor, the turning to God which corresponds to the emanation 'understanding,' is called 'Mother'?"

He explained: "When a man confesses and repents, when his heart accepts Understanding and is converted to it, he becomes like a new-born child, and his own turning to God is his mother."

Dialogue

The rabbi of Lublin was asked by one of his disciples: "Our sages say that God speaks to the community of Israel, as it is written: 'Return unto me, and I will return unto you,' but Israel replies, as it is written: 'Turn thou us unto Thee . . . and we shall be turned.' What does this mean? What God said to them is so, for we know that the awakening from below, brings about that from above."

The rabbi replied: "Our sages say: 'A woman only enters upon a union with him who has made her a vessel, for in the first mating, her husband made of her a vessel, to awaken her

314

womanhood.' And so Israel says to God: 'Make us your vessel once more, that our turning may waken again and again.' And that is why further on in the answer which Israel gave to the Lord, we read: 'Renew our days as of old.' By 'of old' the time before the creation of the world is meant, when nothing existed except the awakening from above."

Sin and Despondency

A hasid complained to the rabbi of Lublin that he was tormented with evil desire and had become despondent over it. The rabbi said to him: "Guard yourself from despondency above all, for it is worse and more harmful than sin. When the Evil Urge wakens desires in man, he is not concerned with plunging him into sin, but with plunging him into despondency by way of his sinning."

The Wicked and the Righteous

The rabbi of Lublin said: "I love the wicked man who knows he is wicked more than the righteous man who knows he is righteous. But concerning the wicked who consider themselves righteous, it is said: 'They do not turn even on the threshold of Hell.' For they think they are being sent to Hell to redeem the souls of others."

The Merry Sinner

In Lublin lived a great sinner. Whenever he wanted to talk to the rabbi, he readily consented and conversed with him as if with a man of integrity and one who was a close friend. Many of the hasidim were annoyed at this, and one said to the other: "Is it possible that our rabbi, who has only to look once into a man's face to know his life from first to last, to know the very origin of his soul, does not see that this fellow is a sinner? And if he does see it, that he considers him worthy to speak to and associate with?" Finally they summoned up courage to go to the rabbi himself with their question. He answered them: "I know all about him as well as you. But you know how I love gayety and hate dejection. And this man is so great a sinner! Others repent the moment they have sinned, are sorry for a moment, and then return to their folly. But he knows no regrets and no doldrums, and lives in his happiness as in a tower. And it is the radiance of his happiness that overwhelms my heart."

Patchwork

A hasid of the rabbi of Lublin once fasted from one sabbath to the next. On Friday afternoon he began to suffer such cruel thirst that he thought he would die. He saw a well, went up to it, and prepared to drink. But instantly he realized that because of the one brief hour he had still to endure, he was about to destroy the work of the entire week. He did not drink and went away from the well. Then he was touched by a feeling of pride for having passed this difficult test. When he became aware of it, he said to himself: "Better I go and drink than let my heart fall prey to pride." He went back to the well, but just as he was going to bend down to draw water, he noticed that his thirst had disappeared. When the sabbath had begun, he entered his teacher's house. "Patchwork!" the rabbi called to him, as he crossed the threshold.

Alien Thoughts

A man came to ask the rabbi of Lublin to help him against alien thoughts which intruded on him while he prayed. The rabbi indicated what he was to do, but the man went on asking him questions and would not stop. Finally the rabbi said: "I don't know why you keep complaining to me of alien thoughts. To him who has holy thoughts, an impure thought comes at times, and such a thought is called 'alien.' But you — you have just your own usual thoughts. To whom do you want to ascribe them?"

Service

Rabbi Jacob Yitzhak was in the habit of taking poor wayfarers into his house and waiting on them himself. Once he had served such a man with food, filled his glass, and stood beside his chair ready to fetch him whatever he needed. After the meal, he took away the empty plates and platters and carried them into the kitchen. Then his guest asked him: "Master, will you tell me something? I know that you, in serving me, have fulfilled the command of God, who wishes the beggar to be honored as his envoy. But why have you taken the trouble to carry out the empty dishes?"

The rabbi replied: "Is not the carrying out of the spoon and the coal-pan from the Holy of Holies part of the service of the high priest, on the Day of Atonement!"

In the Hut

A disciple of the rabbi of Lublin told:
Once I celebrated the Feast of Tabernacles in Lublin. Before the paeans of praise, the rabbi went into the hut to say the blessing over the "Four Plants." For almost an hour I observed his violent movements which seemed impelled by overwhelming fear. All the people who watched thought that this was the essential part of the ceremony; a feeling of great fear passed over into them, and they too moved and trembled. But I sat on a bench and did not take the subsidiary for the essential, but waited until all the restlessness and anxiety was past. Then I rose to see better when the rabbi came to the blessing. And I saw how he — on the highest rung of the spirit — said the blessing motionlessly, and I heard the heavenly blessing. Thus, long ago, Moses did not heed the clap of thunder and the smoking mountain, where the people stood and shuddered, but approached the motionless cloud out of which God spoke to him.

His Clothes

Rabbi Bunam said: "The rabbi of Lublin had better hasidim than I, but I knew him better than all the rest. For once I entered his room when he was not at home, and then I heard a whispering: his clothes were telling one another of his greatness."

The Harpist

In the very act of praying, the rabbi of Lublin would occasionally take a pinch of snuff. A most diligent worshipper noticed

this and said to him: "It is not proper to interrupt the prayer."
"A great king," answered the rabbi of Lublin, "was once walking through his chief city and heard a ragged old street singer
singing a song and playing the harp. The music pleased him.
He took the man into his palace and listened to him day after
day. Now the minstrel had not wanted to part with his old harp
and so he often had to stop and tune it in the middle of playing. Once a courtier snapped at the old man: 'You really
might see to the tuning of your instrument beforehand!' The
harpist answered: 'In his orchestras and choirs, our king has
lots of people better than I. But if they do not satisfy him
and he has picked out me and my harp, it is apparently his
wish to endure its peculiarities and mine.'"

Thanking for Evil

A hasid asked the Seer of Lublin: "To the words in the Mishnah: 'Man should thank God for evil and praise him,' the
Gemara adds: 'with joy and a tranquil heart.' How can that
be?"
The zaddik could hear that the question sprang from a troubled
heart. "You do not understand the Gemara," he said. "And I
do not understand even the Mishnah. For is there really any
evil in the world?"

The Wedding Gift

It was at the wedding of his granddaughter Hinda. At the
very moment the gifts were presented, Rabbi Jacob Yitzhak put
his head in his hands, and seemed to fall asleep. The master
of ceremonies called out again and again: "Wedding gifts from
the family of the bride," and waited for the rabbi, but he did
not move. All fell silent and waited for him to wake up. When
half an hour had passed, his son whispered in his ear: "Father,
they are calling for wedding gifts from the bride's family."
The old man started up from his meditations and replied: "Then
I give myself. After thirteen years, the gift will be brought."
After thirteen years, when Hinda bore a son, he was called
Jacob Yitzhak after his grandfather. When he grew up he
resembled him in every feature, his right eye, for instance, was
a little bigger than his left, just like that of the rabbi of Lublin.

318

NOTES, GLOSSARY,

AND

SELECTED BIBLIOGRAPHY

NOTES

Numerals to the left of each note indicate the page
where the expression to be annotated occurs.

Many zaddikim to whom passing reference is made in these tales are
dealt with in individual chapters, or in the Introduction.

[35] *When all souls were gathered in Adam's soul:* according to the
Kabbalah, the souls of all men were included in the soul of Adam;
from there they set out on their wanderings.

[35] *The sixty:* Cant. 3:8.

[42] *The flame of the sword: see* Gen. 3:24.

[48] *Community of the great hasidim: see* Introduction.

[50] *Rabbi Jacob Joseph of Polnoye: see* "The Story Teller," p. 56, and
"The Visit," p. 100.

[51] *Ahijah the prophet:* according to legend, the biblical prophet Ahijah (I Kings 11-14) came to the Baal Shem and instructed him in the
teachings. *See also* "Across the Dniester," p. 74.

[55] *Rabbi David Leikes: see* "Fire Against Fire," p. 174.

[55] *Rabbi Motel of Tchernobil:* Rabbi Motel (Mordecai) was the son
of Rabbi Nahum of Tchernobil. *See* "From the Circle of the Baal Shem
Tov," pp. 172 ff.; "The Passage of Reproof," p. 60; "He Will Be," p. 85.

[59] *Rabbi Leib, son of Sarah: see* "If," p. 86; "From the Circle of the
Baal Shem Tov," p. 169; "To Say Torah and to Be Torah," p. 107. It is
told that on his wanderings he met with influential lords, among them
the emperor in Vienna, who were unfriendly to Jews. In a miraculous
way he is said to have caused them to change their opinion.

[59] *The hidden zaddik:* there are in each generation thirty-six "hidden"
zaddikim who, secretly, in the disguise of peasants, artisans, or porters,
do their good deeds. These deeds constitute the true foundation of the
created world. Rabbi Leib, son of Sarah, is not numbered among them
since he was known to be a zaddik.

[60] *The Passage of Reproof:* Deut. 28: 15-68.

[64] *Rabbi Wolf Kitzes: see* "False Hospitality," p. 72, and "The Miraculous Bath," p. 77.

[67] *The Light of the Seven Days:* the great zaddik is compared to the
original light of Creation, which he has absorbed.

[74] *Rabbi Nahman of Bratzlav: see* my books *The Tales of Rabbi
Nahman* (in German) , and *A People and Its Land* (in Hebrew) , pp.
91 ff.

[74] *Unification:* sacred ceremonies designed to bring about the unification of the separated divine principles.

[75] *He who spoke to the oil:* this saying is based on a similar story in
the Babylonian Talmud (Taanit 25a) .

[75] *Rabbi Nahman of Horodenka: see* "Of the Baal Shem's Death," p. 83.

[77] *Rabbi Zevi: see* "A Halt Is Called," p. 78.

[77] *The Bath of Israel Is the Lord:* this is Rabbi Akiba's interpretation of Jer. 17:13 (Mishnah Yoma VIII. 9).

[77] *The Erev Rav:* Exod. 12:38; *see also* Neh. 13:3.

[80] *Pastuch:* shepherd (Polish).

[84] *The prince of the river: see* Glossary, *s.v.,* Prince of the Torah.

[94] *And as the bridegroom:* Isa. 62:5.

[103] *The traditional saying:* according to the Babylonian Talmud, a Heavenly Voice spoke this phrase before deciding in favor of the lenient School of Hillel as against the more rigorous School of Shammai (Erubin 13b).

[103] *But from thence:* Deut. 4:29.

[107] *And I will set:* Lev. 26.11.

[119] *The bear is in the woods:* play on the name "Dov Baer" the maggid of Mezritch; "Dov" in the Hebrew language and "Baer" in German and Yiddish mean a bear. The saying seems to imply that the strong "Baer" is to be considered the leader and that "a sage" should stand by his side as an adviser.

[121] *The words:* ascribed to Rabbi Meir, a great teacher during the early talmudic period.

[125] *He is thy psalm:* a possible interpretation of the words "He is thy glory" (Deut. 10:21). The Hebrew term means both "glory" and "psalm."

[127] *Despise not:* Sayings of the Fathers, IV,3.

[128] *The Lord is King:* Ps. 93:1.

[128] *My eyes are ever:* Ps. 25:15.

[129] *God's words:* Isa. 57:15.

[131] *The prayer:* conclusion of the Grace after meals.

[131] *Because of an idle quarrel:* a talmudic tradition (Gittin 55b) holds that a petty quarrel between two Jewish families caused one to denounce the other to the Romans, an event which set off the Roman war against Judaea, and led to the destruction of the Temple.

[141] *The secret counsel:* Ps. 25:14.

[144] *The words in praise of Moses:* Num. 12:3.

[146] *Rabbi Mendel:* a disciple of the Baal Shem Tov, one of the first hasidim to transfer his residence to Palestine.

[146] *From all my teachers:* Ps. 119:99. The correct translation is: "More than all my teachers," but the text also permits this interpretation.

[147] *But ye that cleave:* Deut. 4:4.

[147] *If ye walk in My statutes:* Lev. 26:3.

[149] *I stood:* Deut. 5:5.

[149] *I am my beloved's:* Cant. 7:11.

[149] *Ye shall be holy:* Lev. 19:2.

[151] *My mouth shall speak:* Ps. 145:21.

[153] *Who shall ascend:* Ps. 24:3.

[154] *Means the homecoming: shavat,* to stop, the root of the word *shabbat* (Sabbath), is here combined with the root *shuv,* to return.

[155] *One generation passeth away:* Eccl. 1:4.

[165] *And in your new moons:* Num. 28:11.

[165] *A seeing eye and a hearing ear:* the complete passage (Sayings of the Fathers, II, 1) is as follows: "Know what is above you: a seeing eye, and a hearing ear, and all your deeds are written in a book."

[168] *Happy is the people:* Ps. 144:15.

[168] *Book:* the first comprehensive presentation of the Baal Shem's teachings, written in the form of a commentary on the Bible (1780).

[175] *To make it fall off:* that is, pride leads to faithlessness to the divine law. (An uncovered head is considered a violation of religious respect.)

[180] *It is true:* the following is a quotation from the Babylonian Talmud (Baba Batra 158).

[187] *Serve the Lord:* Ps. 2:11.

[191] *The prayer:* the Grace after meals.

[191] *Three are concerned:* according to the Talmud (Niddah 31), a child's bones, brains, and sinews derive from the father; skin, flesh, and hair from the mother; spirit, soul, senses, and speech from God.

[198] *. . . a ladder set up:* Gen. 28:12.

[199] *Moses' prayer:* Num. 14:19.

[202] *Rabbi Israel of Rizhyn:* grandson of Rabbi Abraham, the Angel.

[203] *Unto thee:* Deut. 4:35.

[210] *Life, and children, and food:* according to the Talmud (Moed Katan 28a), these three are gifts of heaven which are granted independently of man's merit.

[221] *At the Holy Feast:* in the world to come.

[221] *The tall mountains:* a well-known midrashic legend.

[222] *Endeavor to imitate:* a talmudic saying (Shabbat 133).

[223] *Is not Ephraim:* Jer. 31:19.

[223] *The truth will grow:* Ps. 85:12.

[226] *What is told:* a talmudic legend (Sanhedrin 109).

[227] *Remember what Amalek:* Deut. 25:17.

[230] *The words:* in the Babylonian Talmud (Baba Metzia 49).

[230] *We have trespassed . . .:* the confession of sins, recited on the Day of Atonement.

[231] *The Divine Presence:* in the Talmud (Shabbat 30b).

[233] *Here I am, a sin offering:* similar exclamations are reported in the Talmud. The meaning is: May Israel's punishment come upon me.

[235] *With her love:* Prov. 5:12.

[239] *Speak unto:* Exod. 25:2.

[242] *Thine infinity:* see Isa. 6:7.

[251] *Rabbi Hirsh Leib of Olik:* disciple of Rabbi Yehiel Mikhal of Zlotchov; (died 1811).

[254] *For singing:* Ps. 147:1.

[258] *For unto me:* Lev. 25:55.

[277] *If I make:* Ps. 139:8.

[278] *Rabbi Asher of Stolyn:* son of Rabbi Aaron of Karlin; *see* the chapter about him.

[278] *And Thy footsteps:* Ps. 77:20.

[279] *As it is the custom to do:* telling his mother's name, which is a part of his "true" name, is an essential part of the procedure in which a hasid opens his heart to a zaddik.

[288] *How full of awe is this place:* see Gen. 28:17.

[288] *On Mondays and Thursdays:* in addition to being read on the Sabbath, a portion of the Torah is read on these days "so that no three days should go by without Torah."

[288] *But they that wait:* Isa. 40:31.

[290] *Out of distress:* a play on words (*mitzraim*—Egypt, *metzarim*—straits, distress).

[290] *And she cast:* Gen. 21:15.

[290] *The great shrub of prayer:* a play on words (the word *siah* can mean either shrub or speech, word).

[291] *I have set:* Ps. 16:8.

[295] *Fringes:* see Glossary, *s.v.*, Tallit.

[309] *And repayeth them:* Deut. 7:10.

[314] *Justice, justice:* Deut. 16:20.

[314] *Return unto me:* Zech. 1:3.

[314] *Turn Thou us:* Lam. 5:21.

[315] *They do not turn:* in the Babylonian Talmud (Erubin 19).

[318] *He was called:* The custom of naming a boy after his grandfather goes back to a primitive belief, according to which a man is reborn in his grandson.

GLOSSARY

ABAYYI AND RABA: leading talmudic teachers in Babylonia in the first half of the fourth century.

ABRAHAM IBN EZRA of Toledo: outstanding Bible exegete, Hebrew grammarian, religious philosopher, and poet (died 1167).

ADDITIONAL SERVICE: see MUSAF.

ADLER, NATHAN: rabbi of Frankfurt-am-Main, important talmudic scholar and kabbalist (died 1800).

AFTERNOON PRAYER: see MINHAH.

AKIBA: leading Palestinian teacher of the second century C.E.

ALL VOWS: see KOL NIDRE.

AMORA, pl., AMORAIM (speaker, interpreter): masters of the second talmudic epoch (about 200 to 500 C.E.), in which the Gemara originated.

ARI: Abbreviation of Ashkenazi Rabbi Isaak (Luria), the out-outstanding representative of the later Kabbalah (1534-1572). See G. Scholem, *Major Trends in Jewish Mysticism,* Seventh Lecture.

ARIEL: poetic name for Jerusalem (Isa. 29:1). Its probable meaning is "hearth of God," the place from which the sacrifice ascended.

ATTRIBUTES: of God, realized by men in their thoughts and actions. Each one of the three patriarchs symbolically represents one of the divine attributes.

AZAZEL: *see* Leviticus, chap. 16. In biblical times, a mysterious desert creature, to whom, on the Day of Atonement (*see* YOM KIPPUR), a goat was sent "bearing the iniquities" of

325

Israel. In post-biblical times this name was understood as applying to one of the fallen angels.

BADHAN (merry maker) : master of ceremonies at a wedding; at the end of the festive meal he announces the presents, lifting them up one by one and praising, mostly in a humorous manner, the giver and the gift.

BAR KOKHBA ("Son of Stars") : Simeon bar Koziba, the leader of the great rebellion against Emperor Hadrian (132-135 C.E.).

BAR MITZVAH ("son of commandment") : a boy who, upon the completion of his thirteenth year, accepts the responsibility of fulfilling the religious law. Also, the celebration of this event.

BATH: *see* IMMERSION.

BELT AND STAFF: the signs of leadership. By transmitting his staff, the rabbi confers the authority to act in his name.

BLESSED BE HE THAT COMES: greeting given to a guest upon his arrival, who answers: Blessed be the present.

BLESSING OF THE NEW MOON: outdoor benediction service on the appearance of the new moon, which determines the start of the month according to the Hebrew calendar.

BOOK OF CREATION (*Sefer Yetzirah*) : the basic work in the mystical interpretation of the numbers and letters of the alphabet. It is uncertain whether it was composed in talmudic or post-talmudic times.

BOOK OF LAWS: *see* SHULHAN ARUKH.

BOOK OF SPLENDOR: the book *Zohar*, the chief work of the earlier Kabbalah (end of 13th century). *See* G. Scholem, *Major Trends in Jewish Mysticism*, Fifth and Sixth Lectures.

BOOTHS: *see* SUKKOT.

BREAKING OF THE VESSELS: *see* SPARKS.

Burning Of The Leaven: during Passover there must be no leavened food in the house. On the evening preceding the holiday the house is thoroughly cleaned and remnants of leavened food are gathered up and burned in a fire kindled especially for the occasion.

Casting Off Of Sins: *see* **Tashlikh.**

Chariot Of God: the vision of Ezekiel was interpreted to be the mystery of divine revelation, one of the two fundamental principles of Kabbalah. (The other principle was the mystery of creation.)

Citron: *see* **Etrog.**

Court Of Law: the rabbinical court of law, consisting of a head (*av bet din,* father of the court of law), and two judges (*dayanim*).

Day Of Atonement: *see* **Yom Kippur.**

Diaspora (*Gola*) : the dispersion of Israel among the nations.

Divine Nothingness: the Habad school (*see* Introduction), which developed the teachings of the Great Maggid, held that the Divine is without limitation and opposed to all "something," which is limited. The divine is the "nothing" that subsumes all limitation and finiteness.

"Duties Of The Heart" (*Hovot ha-Levavot*) : an important popular work of Jewish religious philosophy and ethics, written in Arabic by Bahya ibn Pakuda in the last quarter of the eleventh century.

Eighteen Benedictions: one of the oldest parts of liturgy, occurring in the regular prayer service. The worshipper, standing, recites it to himself and, according to custom, with his eyes closed. No profane word must interrupt it. After silent recitation by the worshippers it is repeated aloud by the reader.

Elijah: after his ascent to heaven, the prophet Elijah, according to legend, continued to help and instruct the world of man in his function as a messenger of God. Especially, he appears at every feast of circumcision and at every Seder celebration. To behold him and to receive instruction from him are considered an initiation in the mysteries of the Torah.

ELIJAH SONG: in praise of the prophet; in it Elijah is addressed as the good helper.

ELUL: the month preceding the "Days of Awe" and the days of heavenly judgment. It is devoted to inner preparation and self-examination.

ESCORT OF THE SABBATH: the meal taken after the departure of the Sabbath. This meal is understood as bidding farewell to the Queen Sabbath. It "escorts" her away. It is also called "the feast of King David." According to the legend, David was told by God that he would die on a Sabbath; he therefore feasted after every Sabbath in celebration of his continued living.

ETROG: "the fruit of goodly trees" (Lev. 23:40), *citrus medica*, upon which, together with the bouquet of palm branch, myrtle, and willow branch, the Sukkot benediction is spoken.

EVIL URGE: the inclination to evil, which is opposed to "the inclination to good." It is not considered as evil *per se*, but as a power abused by men. It is rather the "passion" in which all human action originates. Man is called upon to serve God "with both inclinations," directing his passion towards the good and holy.

FEAST OF WEEKS: *see* SHAVUOT.

FEAST OF KING DAVID: *see* ESCORT OF THE SABBATH.

FEAST OF REVELATION: *see* SHAVUOT.

FIFTY GATES OF REASON: according to talmudic legend, forty-nine of the fifty gates were disclosed to Moses.

FRANK, JACOB: the last and most dubious of the "false Messiahs"; originator of a radical Sabbatian (*see* SABBATAI

ZEVI) movement in Poland, and later active in Offenbach, Germany. He and his disciples publicly embraced Christianity (died 1791).

FRINGES: *see* TALLIT.

GAON ("excellence") OF VILNA: Rabbi Elijah of Vilna, a renowned rabbinical scholar, leader of a movement against hasidism (died 1797).

GEMARA: "completion" of the teaching; the most extensive portion of the Talmud, an explanation and discussion of the Mishnah, the earlier part of the Talmud. There is a distinction between the Gemara of the Babylonian Talmud and of the Palestinian Talmud.

GOG: *see* WARS OF GOG.

GOOD JEW: a popular designation of the zaddik.

GOY (*pl.*, GOYIM): "nation" (in the physical sense); gentile.

HAGGADAH ("narrative"): the collection of sayings, scriptural interpretations, and hymns pertaining to the exodus from Egypt, as recited in the home service on Passover night (*see* SEDER).

HALLEL ("praise"): a group of psalms recited in the prayer service at certain festivals.

HANINAH BEN TERADION: one of the "ten martyrs" executed by the Romans after the rebellion of Bar Kokhba. They refused to obey the ban on the study of the law.

HANUKKAH ("dedication"): an eight-day holiday beginning on the twenty-fifth day of *Kislev* (November or December) and commemorating the re-dedication of the Sanctuary by the Maccabees (167 B.C.E.) and their victory over the Syrian Greeks who desecrated the Temple. In remembrance of the Maccabean Feast of Lights, candles are lighted in Jewish homes on each of the eight evenings, one candle the first evening, two the second, etc.

HAVDALAH ("separation" of the holy and the profane) : benediction pronounced upon the wine, spices, and light at the
conclusion of the Sabbath and holidays.

HAZAN: cantor, the reader of the prayers in the synagogue.

HEAD OF ALL THE SONS OF THE DIASPORA (exilarch, *resh
galuta*) : the secular head of Babylonian Jewry in talmudic
and post-talmudic times.

HILLEL: a great teacher of the first century B.C.E. His life and
teachings were based on the ideal of universal brotherhood.

HOLY BROTHERHOOD (*hevra kaddisha*, holy society) : its members devote themselves to the burial of the dead.

HOLY NAMES: all the elements of the sacred language are understood as living, super-mundane beings.

HOLY GUEST: the patriarchs are said to visit the devout in the
holiday booths (*see* SUKKOT). The devout recite words of
greeting to them.

HOUSE OF STUDY (*Beth ha-Midrash*) : identical, usually, with
the House of Prayer. It is a place of learning and worship.
Travelers without lodgings are put up in the House of Study.

IBN EZRA: *see* ABRAHAM IBN EZRA.

IMMERSION: the ancient bath which, in the Kabbalah and especially among the hasidim, became an important ceremony
with meanings and mysteries of its own. Immersion in a
river or a stream is higher in value than the ordinary ritual
bath.

JERUSALEM OF ABOVE: the heavenly Jerusalem that corresponds to the earthly Jerusalem. In the same way, a heavenly
sanctuary corresponds to the Temple on Zion.

KADDISH ("holy") : a doxology, especially the one recited as
a memorial of the dead.

KAVVANAH, *pl.*, KAVVANOT ("intention, devotion") : the intention directed towards God while performing a (religious)

deed. In the Kabbalah, kavvanot denote the permutations of the divine name that aim at overcoming the separation of forces in the Upper World.

KIDDUSH ("sanctification") : in addition to its other meanings, this term denotes the benediction pronounced upon the wine at the commencement of the Sabbath and holidays. The marriage ceremony, too, is a Kiddush.

KLAUS: the prayer room of a private (usually hasidic) congregation of worshippers.

KOL NIDRE ("All Vows") : the initial words in the solemn formula of absolution from unfulfilled and unfulfillable vows, pronounced on the eve of the Day of Atonement.

LAG BA-OMER: the thirty-third day of a counting of days that begins with the second day of Passover and ends with the Feast of Weeks.

LAMENTATIONS AT MIDNIGHT: the pious are accustomed to rise at midnight from their beds, sit down on the floor, without shoes, put ashes on their forehead, and read lamentations on the fall of Zion and prayers for redemption.

LETTER OF DIVORCE: the only permissible form of divorce.

LILITH: a female demon that seduces men.

LITHUANIA: the more rationalistically minded Lithuanian Jews, strongly opposed to hasidism.

LURIA, ISAAK: *see* ARI.

MAGGID, *pl.*, MAGGIDIM: a preacher. The maggidim were partly itinerant preachers, partly regularly appointed community preachers; some of the latter at times served as wandering preachers. The term also refers to a spirit that appears to the select and reveals to them secrets of the teachings and the future.

MAKOM ("place") : the designation of God, in whom exists all that exists.

MARRIAGE CONTRACT (*tenaim,* "conditions") : written down and signed at the time of the betrothal; just before the marriage, the *ketubah,* a financial agreement, is added.

MASTER OF CEREMONIES: *see* BADHAN.

MATZAH, *pl.,* MATZOT: unleavened bread, eaten during the week of Passover.

MELAMMED: the teacher of the children.

MENORAH: seven-branched candelabrum, especially the one used in the synagogue.

MERCY-RIGOR: the chief attributes of God.

MESSIAH SON OF JOSEPH: a Messiah who will prepare the way, gathering Israel together and re-establishing the Kingdom, and who will then fall in a war against the Romans led by Armilus. Another tradition holds that he reappears "from generation to generation."

MIDRASH, *pl.,* MIDRASHIM ("exposition, interpretation") : books of the talmudic and post-talmudic times devoted to the homiletic exegesis of the Scriptures. They are rich in legends, parables, similes, and sayings.

MINHAH ("offering") : originally, an afternoon sacrifice (Ezra 9:4), later, as its substitute, the Afternoon Prayer.

MISHNAH ("repetition, teaching") : the earliest and basic part of the Talmud.

MITNAGED, *pl.,* MITNAGDIM ("opponent, antagonist") : the avowed opponents of hasidism.

MUSAF ("addition") : originally, an additional sacrifice on the Sabbath and holidays, later, as its substitute, an additional prayer service recited after the general Morning Prayer.

NEILAH ("closing") : the closing prayer of the Day of Atonement.

NEW YEAR: *see* ROSH HA-SHANAH.

NINTH DAY OF AV: *see* TISHAH BE-AV.

NOTES OF REQUEST (in Yiddish, *Kvittel*) : written on slips of paper containing the name of the supplicant, the name of his mother, and his request.

"ONE": the devout, and especially the martyrs, when they die, avow the Oneness of God.

PASSOVER: *see* PESAH.

PESAH ("passing over," i.e., the sparing of the houses of the children of Israel) : eight-day holiday (in Palestine, seven days) beginning on the fifteenth day of *Nisan* (March or April) and commemorating the exodus from Egypt.

PHYLACTERIES: *see* TEFILLIN.

PRAYER SHAWL: *see* TALLIT.

PRESENCE OF GOD: *see* SHEKHINAH.

PRINCE ADAM CHARTORISKY: on his relations to the maggid of Koznitz, as portrayed in the legendary tradition, *see* M. Buber, *For the Sake of Heaven*, Philadelphia, The Jewish Publication Society, 1945, pp. 195 ff.

PRINCE OF THE TORAH: the angel who represents the Torah in heaven. The elements, the forces of nature, and the nations, which, according to Jewish tradition, are seventy in number, are represented by their respective princes, who are either angels or demons.

PURIM: the feast of "lots" (Esther 9:25) ; the happy holiday commemorating the defeat of the wicked Haman. It is observed by masquerades and games.

RAB (Abba Areka) : a third-century Babylonian master of the Talmud.

RAM'S HORN: *see* SHOFAR.

RANSOM MONEY: the hasid visiting the zaddik hands in, together with a Note of Request, a sum of money. This sum is taken to be a "ransom" for the soul of the applicant.

RASHI: abbreviation for Rabbi Solomon (ben) Isaak (of Troyes), the classical commentator on the Bible and the Babylonian Talmud (died 1105).

RAV ("master, teacher"): the leader of the religious community. He teaches the law and, as the "head of the law court," supervises its fulfillment; whereas *rabbi*, in most cases, denotes the leader of the local hasidic group. In some instances the rabbi was also the rav of his town.

READER: *see* HAZAN.

REJOICING IN THE LAW: *see* SIMHAT TORAH.

ROSH HA-SHANAH ("New Year"): observed on the first and second day of *Tishre* (September or October); the days of judgment.

SABBATAI ZEVI: the central figure of the greatest messianic movement in the history of the Diaspora (died 1676). Soon after Sabbatai Zevi proclaimed himself Messiah, the movement broke down and its founder embraced Islam. *See* G. Scholem, *Major Trends in Jewish Mysticism*, Eighth Lecture.

SACRED UNION: a close and helpful attitude to one's fellow men. It promotes a closeness of the separated heavenly spheres.

SAMMAEL: post-biblical name for Satan, the prince of demons.

SANCTIFICATION OF THE NAME (of God): designates every sacrificial act of man; by it man participates in the establishment of the kingdom of God on earth.

SAYINGS OF THE FATHERS (*Pirke Avot*): a tractate of the Mishnah dealing with ethical teachings and sayings in praise of the study of the law. It begins with a genealogy of tradition.

SECTION OF SONGS (*Perek Shirah*): a compilation of scriptural verses said to be spoken by all kinds of living beings as a praise of God, each one speaking a particular verse.

SEDER ("order") : the festival meal and home service on the first and second (in Palestine, only the first) night of Passover. In this celebration, each succeeding generation identifies itself anew with the generation that fled from Egypt.

SEFIROT: the mystical and organically related hierarchy of the ten creative powers emanating from God, constituting, according to the kabbalistic system, the foundation of the existence of the worlds.

SEVEN SHEPHERDS: mentioned in the Bible (Mic. 5:4), and identified by the Talmud (Sukkah 52 b) as Adam, Seth, Methuselah, Abraham, Jacob, Moses, and David.

SHAVUOT ("weeks") : a two-day holiday (in Palestine, one day), seven weeks after Passover. It is the feast of the first fruits and a season dedicated to the memory of the revelation on Mount Sinai.

SHEKHINAH ("indwelling") : divine hypostasis indwelling in the world and sharing the exile of Israel; Divine Presence among men.

SHOFAR: the ram's horn, sounded in the synagogue, principally on the New Year. A blast on the ram's horn will announce the coming of the Messiah.

SHULHAN ARUKH ("set table") : the book of Jewish law, codified in the sixteenth century.

SIMHAT TORAH ("rejoicing in the law") : feast on the day following Sukkot. The Torah scrolls are taken out of the Ark and are carried through the House of Prayer by an enthusiastic procession.

SON OF COMMANDMENT: *see* **BAR MITZVAH**.

SPARKS: in the primeval creation preceding the creation of our world, the divine light-substance burst and the "sparks" fell into the lower depths, filling the "shells" of the things and creatures of our world.

SUKKAH, *pl.*, SUKKOT ("booths") : tabernacles; an eight-day holiday beginning on the fifth day after the Day of Atonement. It commemorates the wandering in the desert. During this period the houses are abandoned and the people live in booths covered with leaves.

TABERNACLES: *see* SUKKOT.

TALLIT: a rectangular prayer-shawl to whose four corners fringes (*Tzitzit*) are attached.

TANNA, *pl.*, TANNAIM ("repeater, teacher") : the masters of the Mishnah.

TASHLIKH: ceremony of the "casting off" of sins on the New Year. Crumbs of bread symbolizing one's sins are cast into a river.

TEFILLIN (phylacteries) : leather cubicles containing scriptural texts inscribed on parchment. Following the commandment in Deuteronomy 11:18, Tefillin are attached to the left arm and the head during the weekday morning service. They are a sign of the covenant between God and Israel. An error in the written text disqualifies the phylacteries. There is a talmudic conception (Berakhot 5) of the "phylacteries of God." These phylacteries are said to contain the verse II Samuel 7:23.

TEKIAH, *pl.*, TEKIOT: the sounding of the ram's horn (*see* SHOFAR) ; in particular, one of the prescribed sounds. The later Kabbalah enjoined a special Kavvanah on the listener for each of the sounds of the shofar.

THIRD MEAL: the principal meal of the Sabbath, eaten after the Afternoon Prayer, and accompanied by community singing and an address by the zaddik.

TISHAH BE-AV: the "Ninth Day of *Av*" (July or August). A day of fasting and mourning in memory of the destruction of the first Temple by Nebuchadnezzar and the second Temple by Titus. The worshippers sit, like mourners of the dead, without shoes, on the floor of the darkened House of Prayer and recite verses from the Book of Lamentations. According to tradition, the Messiah was born on the Ninth Day of *Av* and will reappear on that day.

TORAH: teaching, law, both the written (biblical) and the oral (traditional) law.

TRAVEL (to the zaddik) : to become a follower of a zaddik, to receive his teaching, and to visit him from time to time.

"TREE OF LIFE" (*Etz Hayyim*) : an exposition of the kabbalistic system of Isaak Luria, written by his most outstanding disciple, Hayyim Vital Calabrese.

TURNING (*Teshuvah*) : man's turning from his aberrations to the "way of God." It is interpreted as the fundamental act by which man contributes to his redemption. (*Teshuvah* is usually translated as "repentance.")

UNLEAVENED BREAD: *see* MATZAH.

WARS OF GOG: the prophecy of Ezekiel (Ezek., chap. 39) is interpreted as a vision of great wars of nations in the time preceding the coming of the Messiah.

WINE OF LIFE: "preserved" from the days of Creation for the pious men in paradise.

YOHANAN THE SANDAL-MAKER: a disciple of Rabbi Akiba.

YOHANAN BEN ZAKKAI: according to a talmudic legend, this leading teacher of the first century C.E. had himself placed in a coffin and carried out of Jerusalem into the presence of Vespasian in order to secure permission to establish a Jewish academy of learning after the fall of Jerusalem.

YOM KIPPUR: the Day of Atonement, the last of the Days of Awe, which commence with the New Year. It is a day of fasting and uninterrupted prayer for atonement.

ZADDIK: the leader of the hasidic community (*see* RAV).

ZECHARIAH: identified by the Targum as "the priest and prophet" who, according to the Bible (Lam. 2:20), "was killed in the sanctuary."

SELECTED BIBLIOGRAPHY
(Only works in English and Hebrew are listed)

Agus, Jacob B., "Hasidism," in *The Evolution of Jewish Thought.* London-New York, 1959, ch. XI.

Baron, Salo W., *A Social and Religious History of the Jews,* vol. II. New York, 1937, ch. X.

Bromberg, Abraham Isaac, *Migedole ha-Hasidut* (a series of monographs). Jerusalem.

Buber, Martin, *Be-Fardes ha-Hasidut.* Jerusalem, 1945.

Buber, Martin, *Or ha-Ganuz.* Jerusalem-Tel Aviv, 1946. (A Hebrew edition of the "Tales of the Hasidim.")

Buber, Martin, *Ten Rungs. Hasidic Sayings.* New York, 1947.

Buber, Martin, *Hasidism.* New York, 1948.

Buber, Martin, *The Way of Man According to the Teachings of the Hasidim.* Chicago, 1951.

Buber, Martin, *For the Sake of Heaven. A Chronicle.* New York, 1953.

Buber, Martin, *The Legend of the Baal-Shem.* New York, 1956.

Buber, Martin, *Darko shel Adam al-pi Torat ha-Hasidut.* Jerusalem, 1957.

Buber, Martin, *Hasidism and Modern Man,* ed. Maurice Friedman. New York, 1958.

Buber, Martin, *The Origin and Meaning of Hasidism,* ed. Maurice Friedman. New York, 1960.

Bunin, H., "Ha-Hasidut ha-Habadit." *Hashiloah* XXVIII, XXIX, XXXI, 1913-15.

Dinaburg, Benzion, "Reshitah shel ha-Hasidut," *Zion* VIII, IX, X, 1934-1945.

Dresner, Samuel H., *The Zaddik.* London-New York, 1960.

Dubnov, Simon, *History of the Jews in Russia and Poland,* vol. I. Philadelphia, 1916, ch. VI and XI.

Dubnov, Simon, *Toledot ha-Hasidut.* Tel Aviv, 1930-32.

Haberman, A. M., "Shaarei Habad." In *Ale Ayin*. Jerusalem, 1953, 293-370.

Halpern, I., *Ha-Aliyot ha-Rishonot shel ha-Hasidim le-Eretz Yisrael*. Jerusalem-Tel Aviv, 1946.

Halpern, I., "Associations for the Study of the Torah and for Good Deeds and the Spread of the Hasidic Movement." *Zion* XXII, 1957, 194-213.

Heschel, A. J., "R. Gershon Kotover." *The Hebrew Union College Annual* XXIII, 1950-51, Part Two, 17-71.

Horodezky, S. A., *Leaders of Hasidism*. London, 1928. *Ha-Hasidut veha-Hasidim*, 3rd ed. Tel Aviv, 1951.

Judaism: A Quarterly Journal, Hasidism Issue, IX, 3 (Summer 1960).

Kahana, Abraham, *Sefer ha-Hasidut*, 2nd ed. Warsaw, 1922.

Kazis, Israel J., "Hasidism Re-examined." *The Reconstructionist*, XXVIII, 8 (May 1957), 7-13.

Kranzler, Gershon, *R. Shneur Zalman of Ladi, Founder of Chabad*. New York.

Marcus, Aaron, *Ha-Hasidut*. Tel Aviv, 1953.

Minkin, Jacob S., *The Romance of Hasidism*. New York, 1935.

Mordecai ben Jeheskel, "Le-Mahut ha-Hasidut." *Hashiloah*, XVII, XX, XXII, XXV, 1909-1912.

Newman, Louis I., and Spitz, Samuel, *A Hasidic Anthology*. New York, 1934.

Newman, Louis I., "The Baal Shem Tov." *Great Jewish Personalities*, ed. Simon Noveck, Washington, D.C., 1959.

Schechter, Solomon, "The Chassidim." *Studies in Judaism* I (1896), 1-45.

Schneersohn, Joseph I., *On the Teachings of Hasidus*. New York.

Schneersohn, Joseph I., *Some Aspects of Hasidus*. New York.

Scholem, G. G., "R. Adam Baal Shem." *Zion* VI, 1941, 89-93.

Scholem, G. G., "The Two First Testimonies on the Relations Between Chassidic Groups and the Baal-Shem-Tov," *Tarbiz* XX (1949), 228-240.

Scholem, G. G., "Dvekuth, the Communion with God in Early Hassidic Doctrine," *Review of Religion* XV, 1950.

Scholem, G. G., *Major Trends in Jewish Mysticism*, 3rd ed., New York, 1954 (Ninth Lecture).

Scholem, G. G., "The Polemic Against Hasidism and its Leaders in the Book Nezed ha-Dema." *Zion* XX, 1955, 73-81.

Scholem, G. G., "New Material on Israel Loebel and his Anti-Hasidic Polemics." *Zion* XX, 1955, 153-162.

Schochat, A., "On Joy in Hasidism." *Zion* XVI, 1951, 30-43.

Spiegel, Shalom, *Hebrew Reborn*. New York, 1930.

Tishby, I., "Beyn Shabtaut le-Hasidut." *Keneset* IX, 1945, 238-268.

Weiss, Joseph, "Beginnings of Hasidism." *Zion* XVI, 1951, 46-105.

Weiss, Joseph, "A Circle of Pneumatics in Pre-Hasidism." *Journal of Jewish Studies* VIII, 1957, 199-213.

Werfel, Yitzhak, *Ha-Hasidut ve-Eretz Yisrael*. Jerusalem, 1940.

Werfel, Yitzhak, *Sefer ha-Hasidut*. Tel Aviv, 1947.

Wilensky, Mordecai L., "The Polemic of R. David of Makow against Hasidism," *Proceedings of the American Academy for Jewish Research*, XXV, 1956.

Zeitlin, Hillel, *Ha-Hasidut*. 1922.

Zweifel, E. Z., *Shalom al Yisrael*, 4 vols. Shitomir, 1868-73.

INDEX TO THE TALES

343

BARUKH OF MEZBIZH

YEHIEL MIKHAL OF ZLOTCHOV

ZEV WOLF OF ZBARAZH

MORDECAI OF NESKHIZH

FROM THE CIRCLE OF THE BAAL SHEM TOV

MENAHEM MENDEL OF VITEBSK

SHMELKE OF NIKOLSBURG

ZUSYA OF HANIPOL

351

ISRAEL OF KOZNITZ

JACOB YITZHAK OF LUBLIN ("THE SEER")

TALES OF THE HASIDIM

~~~~~~

BOOK TWO: THE LATER MASTERS

~~~~~~

INTRODUCTION

The period which followed the first three generations of hasidism is usually treated as one of incipient decline. But that is an over-simplification of what really happened. Confronted by such a development, we must always ask what elements of the movement before us exhibit a deterioration which can, nevertheless, go hand in hand with the enrichment, ramification, and even strengthening of other elements.

There is no doubt that the crude power characteristic of the outset of hasidism lessened during this second epoch, which mainly occupies the first half of the nineteenth century, though certain of the exponents of hasidism lived past that time. The main outlines of the first hasidic tidings and struggles become complicated or blurred, and the sacred passion to bring heaven and earth closer to each other often gives place to the kind of organized religiosity we can trace in every great religious movement which persists past the generations of awakening and revolt. But at the same time comes a variety and abundance of new spiritual life which does not, it is true, deepen the basic ideas of hasidism in any essential respect, but does expand the province in which these ideas can be realized and applies them to the problems of everyday life to a far greater extent than before. The form in which these ideas are expressed has less elemental vigor but often more brilliance. Aphorisms, parables, and symbolic fairy tales which up to that time occurred only as the naive, witty, but unfinished improvisations of genius, achieve literary perfection.

The real problems of the second period are not apparent in the sphere of the spirit and teachings of hasidism, but in that of its inner structure. They emerge in three different sets of relationship: that of the zaddik to the congregation, of the zaddikim and their congregations to one another, and that of the zaddik to his school. In this second period of hasidism all three relationships are occasionally affected by noteworthy and serious changes.

It is common to both periods for the zaddik usually to be "hidden" at first, and only subsequently to "reveal" himself, i.e., let it be known that heaven has called him to its service. In addition to this call there generally is a teacher who appoints him to his office and vouches for him. In other words: The community receives its leader from "on high," directly through the manifest grace of heaven that rests upon him, and indirectly through his election and appointment by his teacher, whose own vocation, in turn, provides the basis for this act. It is only when one of the great teachers dies and the question arises who among his disciples is to succeed him, and then only if there is neither agreement nor schism, that the hasidim themselves make the decision. This is not done according to any prescribed formula, but always in a way suggested and determined by the current situation. If we are to believe legend—and the legendary incidents we are told of correspond to similar known incidents in the history of religion—a decision of this kind is always made and accepted as something mysterious. The congregation is fused to an unprecedented entity, and as such, feeling the will of heaven internally as it were, dares to fulfil that will. In the second period the instances of such decisions multiply. They occur both when a zaddik dies sonless, as well as when he leaves behind a son who is considered a candidate for the succession.

A conversation which has been handed down to us is characteristic of this altered situation. It took place between Rabbi Mendel of Kotzk (a great and tragic figure whom it would be more precise to include in the fourth generation though he really belongs to the fifth) and young Mendel of Vorki, the son of his friend Rabbi Yitzhak of Vorki, nine months after Yitzhak's death. The rabbi of Kotzk is trying to discover who will succeed his friend, for Mendel has rather avoided becoming the successor than striven for that honor. The rabbi of Kotzk asks: "What about the 'world'?" [i.e., the congregation]. His disciple replies: "The world stands" [i.e., the question of the succession has not yet been solved]. Then the rabbi continues: "They say that you will take over the world." And young Mendel answers: "If that were so, I should have a feeling." In conclusion the zaddik says: "They say it is the hasidim who make a rabbi." Thereupon Mendel of Vorki replies: "I was never eager to accept alms." By that he meant that he did not wish to receive the gift of heaven from the hands of the congregation and that he did not recognize their authority, but kept to the great hasidic tradition.

What he is resisting in this way is expressed very clearly in a bitter jest uttered by Rabbi Mendel of Rymanov, a zaddik who lived during the time of the transition from the first period to the second. "If a thousand believing hasidim were to gather around a block of wood," said he, "it too would work miracles." It is obvious that he was using the word "believing" to mean superstitious. These hasidim do not believe that heaven has chosen a zaddik and sent him to them, but that the congregation has the right to have a true zaddik and therefore not merely receives but can even "make" him. The natural consequence of such a point of view is that zaddikim whose aptitude for their vocation is dubious multiply. "One ought not to take the chair until one hears Elijah's call." This saying illustrates the stand of the true zaddikim; the dubious think otherwise.

A second problem rose from the fact that there was a large number of zaddikim but no superior authority, a multiplicity which must be understood as one of the chief bases of the hasidic movement. Historically, hasidism is the reply to the crisis in messianism. The way to hasidism, to the concentrated attempt to preserve the reality of God for the Jew, was paved by the extreme antinomian development of the Sabbatian movement, whose followers thought they could divest the God of Israel of his character of teacher of the right way and still have a Jewish God. Jacob Frank's enterprise, which ran grotesquely amuck and took the final leap into a kind of nihilism draped in mythology, had shown wakeful souls that not only sections of the Jewish people but the whole community was on the edge of the abyss, and this realization had led the most valuable forces to hasidism.

Bitter experience pointed to the necessity of preventing the people from again putting their faith in any single human. Hasidism succeeded in this, on the one hand by setting up the classical picture of biblical eschatology in contrast to the aftermath of the Sabbatian theology, by renewing the concept of the altogether human executor of the divine will to redemption. On the other hand, hasidism repudiated every possible tendency in the direction of endowing a human being with divine attributes, as had happened in those last messianic movements. Not a speck of the idea of incarnation ever attached itself to the Baal Shem, either in regard to his teachings or to the legend which grew around him.

But even more; out of a conscious or unconscious sense of danger (it does not matter which), the structure of the hasidic community was fundamentally characterized by a multiplicity which could not merge into a unity. Every congregation was autonomous and subject to no superior authority. The zaddikim were under no superior leadership. Even the Great Maggid, who headed a hasidic community composed of a number of congregations, did not desire to be anything but a teacher. While in the succeeding generations we find zaddikim competing for higher rank, the rivalry between them being reflected by their congregations, no one laid serious claim to exclusive validity.

Not until the second period did this rivalry degenerate into mutual exclusion. The most striking instance is the quarrel between "Zans" (Rabbi Hayyim of Zans) and "Sadagora" (Rabbi Abraham Yaakov of Sadagora and his brothers) which revived the methods once prevalent in altercation between hasidim and their adversaries (mitnagdim), even to the point of ban and counterban.

What lay behind all this becomes evident in the unmistakable utterances of the rabbi of Zans, who cited the legend of the rivalry between the sun and the moon and the sun's statement that it is not possible for two kings to wear the same crown. Those zaddikim who realized the danger took a firm stand against such deviations from the hasidic way. It is from this point of view that we must interpret the words of Rabbi Hirsh of Zhydatchov, a distinguished disciple of the Seer of Lublin, who said that for hasidim to regard theirs as the only true rabbi is idol worship. But we also find utterances in which plurality is raised to an absolute which verges on the ridiculous, as for example, when the grandson of a distinguished hasidic thinker said that every zaddik should be the Messiah to his hasidim.

The third relationship, that of the zaddik to his school: In the beginnings of hasidism the idea of rivalry between master and disciple never entered the mind of either. On the one hand, the disciple's devotion to his master exerted so powerful a force over his entire life that the thought of acting against the will of his teacher could never occur to him. On the other hand, the teacher, far from seeing his pupils as potential rivals, made those he considered fit for such an office heads of congregations where they served the movement as his representatives, as it were. As an example of this, read how the Great Maggid in truly biblical fashion invests Rabbi Menahem Mendel with belt and staff and appoints him rabbi.

There was a change in the very next generation, toward the end of the first period. Rabbi Elimelekh of Lizhensk, who succeeded to the Great Maggid's teachings, would not suffer his disciples to lead congregations of their own during his lifetime. When one of them, who later became the Seer of Lublin, nevertheless assumed such leadership, a deep and permanent tension resulted. Legend even has it that Rabbi Elimelekh's curse had a fatal effect on those who became the followers of his disciple.

But the same relationship, only in a more acute and complicated form, obtained between the Seer of Lublin and certain of his disciples; it brought gloomy tragedy when the Seer falsely accused the Yehudi, his noblest disciple, of competing with him, and finally—if we may trust the tradition—drove him to his death. There is an oral tradition that the Seer said repeatedly that the Yehudi was above him ("he walks on a higher plane than we"), but that he, the Seer, had been appointed to his place by Rabbi Elimelekh—an utterance which is very strange when viewed in the light of all these occurrences, but undoubtedly reflects the speaker's consciousness.

At this point, though a disciple's leading a congregation was disapproved, still it was endured. In the succeeding generation however, it was generally accepted almost as law that a disciple should not found his own congregation during his teacher's lifetime. Thus a fundamental principle of the hasidic movement, one we might term the inner apostolate, is abandoned. The master no longer sends forth his tried and proven disciples to supplement his work of teaching and construction with their own, each in his autonomous domain; he keeps them chained to himself and his house, and thus prejudices the activities of the movement.

These and similar phenomena are the reason for the sharp criticism which distinguished zaddikim of the second period pronounced upon the zaddikism of their time. After the Yehudi had spoken of the types of leaders who led former generations, and were followed by the zaddikim, he added: "That is why I sigh: I see that the present too will be corrupted. What will Israel do then?"

Another zaddik refuses to expound the hasidic teachings ("say Torah"), because he notes that the instruction of certain zaddikim no longer guards the original complete purity of the hasidic teachings, and that lurking demons might fall upon the teaching and drag them into their realm. It is particularly significant that some descendants of great zaddikim do not want to become rabbis—a son and a grandson of Rabbi Elimelekh's, for instance.

A zaddik of the sixth generation, the grandson of a grandson of the Great Maggid, gives vehement expression to his resentment at a decline which was already apparent. This was Rabbi Dov Baer of Leva, a son of the famous Rabbi Israel of Rizhyn, who went so far as to leave the hasidic camp for a time and fled to the camp of the "enlightened." (This was the incident which set off the quarrel between the followers of Zans and those of Sadagora.)

Rabbi Dov Baer often told a story which ostensibly was about his ancestor, the Great Maggid, but actually referred only to his and not the Maggid's situation. "A tenant farmer," so he told, "once came to the Maggid of Mezritch to ask his help in a matter having to do with his affairs. 'Is it me you are asking?' the Maggid inquired. 'Do you really mean me?' The man replied: 'I ask the rabbi to pray for me in this matter.'— 'Wouldn't it be better,' said the Maggid, 'if you were to ask me to teach you how to pray to God? Then you wouldn't have to come to me any more.'"

In these words which could not by any stretch of the imagination have come from the lips of the Great Maggid, but resemble similar utterances by zaddikim of the second period, despair over the decline of zaddikism has turned into doubt of its very basis. In the early days of hasidism the zaddik also guided his hasidim to a direct relationship with God, but he did not believe that merely teaching people how to pray meant that the man who is an intermediary between heaven and earth could be dispensed with. For, according to the hasidic concept, external help as such is not what matters; it is only the outer husk which makes an inner form of help possible.

This idea emerges most clearly in a story told by Rabbi Shalom Shakhna, the grandson of the Great Maggid and the grandfather of the rabbi of Leva. He tells how a tenant farmer came to him before the beginning of the Sabbath and confided his trouble: that one of his calves was ailing. "And from his words," says the rabbi, "I heard him imploring me: 'You are a lofty soul and I am a lowly soul. Lift me up to yourself!'"

Thus the expedient of external help is not to be abandoned in the least; for teaching how to pray cannot in itself be the true "elevation," and the experience of being uplifted is not a unique event. It is by its very nature a process which is interrupted only by death and, according to a concept we occasionally encounter, not necessarily even then.

Hasidism enters upon its decline when the zaddikim no longer give their hasidim inner help along with and through external help. For here, everything is based on the relationship between zaddikim and hasidim, a living relationship which is all-inclusive and penetrates to the innermost core. When that is lacking, then indeed "the present too will be corrupted."

The series of zaddikim treated in this volume must needs begin with the descendants of the Maggid of Mezritch, with the "Sadagora dynasty." This sequence is essentially different from the succession of the Maggid's disciples, and the disciples of the disciples. Even his son Abraham—as we know from Tales of the Hasidim: The Early Masters—showed his definite opposition to him and his teachings by choosing the way of radical asceticism.

Abraham's son Shalom Shakhna (d. 1802) swerved sharply from his father's path without, however, returning to that of his grandfather. He was educated by Rabbi Nahum of Tchernobil, one of the most faithful disciples of the Baal Shem and the Maggid, and later married his granddaughter.

Shalom expressed his striving toward innovation in his every act. His rich clothing and splendid manner set him apart from his environment, but these outward manifestations apparently symbolized a definite trend and probably because of this people liked to say that his soul was a "spark" of King David's. When his father-in-law reproached him, he replied with the parable of the hen who hatched duck's eggs and then surveyed the swimming ducklings in great dismay. He emphatically rejected Nahum's miracle cures, for while he too wanted to help sufferers, it was to be with the strength of his soul and according to the needs of the moment rather than through the usual magical procedures. To him, all help that came from the outside was only the point of departure and the husk of an inner help.

He surrounded himself with a group of young men who were passionately devoted to him. The conflict between them and their fathers' generation flared up time and again, and that—according to their ideas—was as it should be, for Rabbi Shalom, so we are told, had said: "That which is a result of good cannot take place without opposition." There is even a peculiar story (which I heard in a version still stranger than the one preserved in writing) that Rabbi Shalom made himself appear sinful in public for the purpose of outwitting Satan. For Satan was considered sovereign over Israel in exile, but the secret of redemption was also supposed to have been confided to him, and so Shalom pretended to be sinful in order to gain Satan's confidence and worm the secret out of him. One is tempted to interpret this as an after effect of the Sabbatian tenet of holy sin.

There are several indications that Rabbi Shalom strove to be more than a zaddik. One is the answer he gave Rabbi Barukh, a grandson of the Baal Shem. When Barukh, a proud and imperious man, visited him and suggested: "Let us both lead the world" (world, in this connection, referred to the hasidic community as the center of Israel), he replied: "I can lead the world by myself." But in saying this he was not thinking of reviving the office of exilarch, as has been supposed. His words sprang from the belief in the potential messianic mission of a family in which the potential could become actual in every generation.

Like his father, Rabbi Shalom died young, and before his death had a vision which he told to his son Israel, which allows a deep understanding of this belief. He saw a zaddik sitting in one of the halls of heaven. On the table in front of him lay a magnificent crown shaped out of his teachings and his holiness. But the zaddik was not permitted to place the crown on his head. "I have told you about it," Rabbi Shalom added, "because some day you may need to know it."

His son, Rabbi Israel of Rizhyn (d. 1850), not only adopted his father's manner but carried it further, so that the ceremonial and ritual of his household made it appear like the court of a priest-king. He himself put into words the dynastic character implicit in his mode of life, for he compared Rabbi Abraham Yehoshua Heshel, the old rav of Apt who was generally accepted as "the leader of his generation," to Moses the teacher, but himself to Solomon the king; and the rabbi of Apt himself dubbed him a king in Israel. The throngs which swarmed to his house honored him as such.

It was in this light that his activities were reported to the Czarist regime which arrested him as a leader of the Jews, regarded by them as their king. After two years in prison (for the most part in Kiev) he was liberated and soon afterward fled to Galicia. After much wandering and travail, he settled in Sadagora (Bukovina), which became the goal of mass pilgrimages. But many zaddikim came as well, especially the younger zaddikim, paid homage to him, and delighted in his conversation. Scarcely one among them however became his disciple. He did not wish to bind anyone to himself. He wanted visitors who hung on his words, not disciples who entailed a sustained mutual relationship.

Like the Great Maggid, Rabbi Israel was a distinguished expounder of the Torah, in the hasidic manner, but his homilies are not parts of a unified thinking life. They are sudden lightning conceits—not the work of a fragmentist, like those of the Great Maggid, but of an aphorist, for they flash with the luxuriance of multi-faceted jewels, while the works of the fragmentist show the deep sparkle of plain-cut stones. Modern Western civilization would have called the rabbi of Rizhyn a brilliant improviser, and weighed in the scale of values of that civilization, he was certainly a genius; but he was no longer the vessel and the voice of the religious spirit.

His six sons were gifted epigoni. They too still had something of the spiritual world of the Great Maggid, but it no longer developed into mature personal form. Almost all of them had followers, drew crowds, held court, had congregations and influence; not one of them had disciples. The noblest of his sons, Rabbi David Moshe of Tchortkov (d. 1903), was tender and humane to all creatures. In my youth I spent several summers not far from his home, but I did not make his acquaintance.

Another of his sons, whom I have already mentioned, Rabbi Dov Baer, named for his great-grandfather, was first considered the most notable of the six and attracted the greatest number of people. Later he joined the so-called "enlightened" group and wrote letters in the nature of manifestoes against superstition. This phase, however, lasted only a short while. He returned to Sadagora and remained there from that time on in a sort of half-voluntary confinement. His life merely expressed the situation: the king's highway had come to a dead end.

Since Rabbi Mendel of Vitebsk did not found a school in Palestine, the first place among the disciples of the Maggid must be assigned to Rabbi Shmelke of Nikolsburg, a great preacher, singer of songs, and friend to all humanity. None of his disciples ever equaled him in preaching, but Rabbi Yitzhak Eisik of Kalev fell heir to his gift of song, while Rabbi Moshe Leib of Sasov inherited his love for mankind.

Rabbi Yitzhak Eisik of Kalev (Nagy-Kallo in the north of Hungary; d. 1828) came from a Hungarian village and absorbed its peasant vitality in his childhood. Tradition has it that he tended geese. He not only used the tunes he had learned from the herdsmen for sacral hymns or psalms, such as "By the waters of Babylon," but—without having to make too many changes—converted some of the texts into Jewish mystical verses. The sadness of the pastoral songs is turned into the suffering in exile, their yearning for love into the longing for the Divine Presence. The "unknown melodies" of Rabbi Shmelke played an important part in this transformation, but the rabbi of Kalev's songs were said to have been even more sensuous and enchanting, probably because of the folk elements which entered into them.

His deep attachment to the folk element is illustrated by the curious fact that he always recited the Passover Haggadah in Hungarian. It is told that on the evening of the Seder Rabbi Shmelke could hear all his disciples reciting the Haggadah in their various homes far from Nikolsburg, all except the rabbi of Kalev, because he was speaking Hungarian.

Another instance of his love for the folk element is the story that he had inherited the melody of the hymn "Mighty in dominion . . ." from the Great Maggid, who had learned it from a shepherd. But, so the tale continues, the tune had been in exile with the shepherd, for originally the Levites had sung it in the Temple. This tune, incidentally, returned to the family of the Maggid via the rabbi of Kalev, if the tradition is correct, for Rabbi David Moshe of Tchortkov was fond of singing it.

Many other songs of the rabbi of Kalev spread among his

hasidim. There was Rabbi Hayyim of Zans, for example, who on a Friday evening, when he had paced around the platform in the synagogue seven times, would sing the rabbi of Kalev's song of yearning for the reunion with the "bride," the Divine Presence, until "his bodily strength failed him, because of the vehemence of his ecstasy."

Rabbi Moshe Leib of Sasov (d. 1807) followed his teacher from one Polish village to the next, and from Poland to Nikolsburg. Legend links him with Rabbi Shmelke in miracle tales. We need hardly touch upon him in this introduction, since the stories in themselves suffice to give a clear picture of him. His soul developed the gift of the helpful love which Rabbi Shmelke had roused within him to a level of perfection unusual even in hasidism, a movement so rich in those who knew how to love. A ravishing spontaneity quickened his love and zeal toward both man and beast. In his case, the paradox of the commandment to love one's neighbor as one-self, seems resolved. (Can one love in obedience to command?) And yet even the rabbi of Sasov came up against inner obstacles. He could not love those malicious or self-assured men who disrupt the world. But that was just the sort of thing his teacher used to speak of: that one must love every soul because it is a part of God, or rather that one cannot help loving a soul the moment one grows aware that it is a part of God. And so, since he was very serious in his love for God, the rabbi of Sasov came to love His creatures more and more perfectly. The true meaning of the command to love manifests itself in the inner obstacles to its fulfilment, and in their overcoming.

In order to show the rabbi of Sasov's influence on his immediate circle, the next section of this volume deals with his disciple Rabbi Mendel of Kosov (d. 1825), whose life and work continue the line of love for humanity. He is said to have made especially radical formulations of the belief that the love for one's neighbor is only another side of the love of God. An instance of this is an interpretation he once gave to the words in the Scriptures: "Love thy neighbor as thyself; I am the Lord." He explained: "If a man loves his fellow, the Divine Presence rests with them." And, on another occasion: "The union of loving neighbors effects unity in the upper world." We know that his son Hayyim never ceased in his efforts to have his hasidim live together like good neighbors, to know, help, keep one another company, and love one another.

In Tales of the Hasidim: The Early Masters, I included the Maggid of Koznitz and the Seer of Lublin, both disciples of Rabbi Elimelekh, because they were first disciples of the Great Maggid and may thus be assigned to the third generation. Two others, Rabbi Abraham Yehoshua Heshel of Apt (d. 1825) and Rabbi Menahem Mendel of Rymanov (d. 1815) belong in this volume. It is said that before he died Rabbi Elimelekh left his tongue's judging power to the rabbi of Apt and his spirit's guiding power to the rabbi of Rymanov.

The rabbi of Apt was noted for his judicious character, he discharged the office of judge and arbiter among the hasidim and even the zaddikim of his time. It was through error and effort that he arrived at his profound conception of true justice. He started out with what we usually call justice, i.e., with the wish to be just, but then he learned step by step that human justice as such fails when it attempts to exceed the province of a just social order and encroaches on that of just human relationships.
He learned that God's justice is not in the same category as his love which is the perfection of an attribute we can at least endeavor to imitate, but is something enigmatic which defies comparison with anything men call justice and law. Man should be just within the bounds of his social order, but when he ventures beyond it out on the high seas of human relationships, he is sure to be shipwrecked and then all he can do is to save himself by clinging to love.
The turning point in the life of the rabbi of Apt is, very

probably, the incident related in this book of how he publicly reproved a woman of loose morals, but then, comparing his own attitude with that of God, was overcome and became a changed man. But he did not regard his way to love as that of one individual living on earth; he saw it in connection with the migrations of his soul and realized that he had the task of perfecting that love during their course.

Rabbi Mendel of Rymanov differed from the rabbi of Apt both in his character and his life. He had fallen heir to his teacher's ability to organize, but practiced it within narrower bounds. Of the three circles which surround the zaddik, the disciples, the congregation, and the "transients," he was most concerned with the second. He issued laws to his congregation as if it were a state, and it was more real to him than the state. He did not presume to be just: he simply watched over the just order of those in his charge. When he was forced to reprove, his words penetrated like a natural force to the very heart of the incident which had evoked his censure. And so when it was necessary to preserve custom and maintain order, he who was noted for his sobriety could rise to heights of archaic majesty. This happened when, to rouse and fuse his congregation which was (as congregations always are) in danger of becoming stolid, he spoke to them as God's instituted deputy, liberated them from the compulsion exerted by the Torah and left them free to make their choice anew. To his disciples his power over "the word" made him the model of a man whose every utterance reflects his sense of responsibility.

Rabbi Zevi Hirsh of Rymanov (d. 1846), the disciple who became Rabbi Mendel's successor, was the real "self-made man" among the zaddikim of the second period. He was first apprenticed to a tailor and then became a servant in Rabbi Mendel's house. There he practiced the wisdom and art of serving on so high a plane that the zaddik soon recognized him as a rare human vessel capable of receiving teachings. He accepted young Hirsh as his disciple, but even in that capacity he went on serving the zaddik. He continued his studies for twelve years after his master's death, and then to everyone's surprise assumed the succession.

He was soon recognized by the other zaddikim and occupied a powerful position of a particular kind. Though at times he conducted himself in a haughty manner, he was very humble at heart and often said of his simple and at the same time profound sermons that he only uttered what he had been told to say; sometimes he could not even remember a sermon when he had finished preaching it.

It is also noteworthy that he often asked substantial amounts of money from persons who came to request his intercession. In such cases he named an exact sum, whose numerals were apparently chosen for their mystical significance. On the other hand, he was in the habit of distributing among the needy whatever money he had in the house. It was a sort of redistribution of goods which he practiced among his hasidim, obviously prompted by the feeling that it was his mission to direct superfluous possessions to where they were needed.

Rabbi Shelomo of Karlin, who was known for his great power in prayer, founded a school of ecstatic praying.

His most renowned disciple, who developed his teaching of giving up one's very life in prayer, was Rabbi Uri of Strelisk (d. 1826), called the "Seraph." In this connection ecstatic prayer is not a merely personal transaction; it includes both the zaddik and his hasidim. Almost all of Rabbi Uri's hasidim were poor, but not one of them turned to him in order to attain well-being. All they wanted was to pray together with him, to pray as he prayed, and like him, to give away their life in prayer.

The impression of his marvelous praying was transferred to their whole relationship to him, which became the glorification of a visionary. They really regarded him as a seraph. One hasid tells how he could see that the rabbi had more than one face, another that the rabbi grew taller and taller before his eyes, until he reached up into heaven. The hasidim relate that once when the synagogue had been polluted by the impure prayers of the Sabbatians, his mighty prayers made it burn to the ground the very next evening. But they also tell that the workday week did not begin until he had said the Benediction of Separation (Havdalah) at the close of the Sabbath. Until then the keys to hell were in his hand, and the souls released over the Sabbath could hover in the atmosphere.

Before his death Rabbi Uri ordained Rabbi Yehudah Zevi of Stretyn (d. 1844) to the succession by the laying on of hands recalling the ordination of Joshua by Moses.

Legend has it that he too had possession of the keys to hell over the Sabbath, but the motif is elaborated: all the night after the Sabbath, a hasid saw him standing at an open window, still dressed in his Sabbath clothes, and holding in his hand a great key which he could not bear to lay aside. All the while swarms of evil angels lurked around him, waiting for morning when his strength would fail.

It was his custom to take the ritual bath at night in a river outside the town, and it was said that while he stood in the water he would recite the entire Book of Psalms.

The most outstanding feature of Rabbi Yehudah Zevi's teaching was his emphatic affirmation of the unity of the attributes of God, the unity of God's Rigor and His Mercy.

Rabbi Yehudah's son, Rabbi Abraham of Stretyn (d. 1865), left the world a significant teaching of human unity: that man can bring about such unity between his faculties, that each of his senses can substitute for another and take over its function.

Besides Rabbi Uri of Strelisk, Rabbi Shelomo of Karlin had a second distinguished disciple: Rabbi Mordecai of Lekhovitz (d. 1811), who added new and concrete features to the teaching of giving one's life to prayer. He taught that he who prays should give himself up to his Lord with every word he utters, and he illustrated this by the parable of the legendary bird whose song of praise bursts its own body. Man's entire physical being must enter into every word of his prayer so that it may even "rise from his heel." It is said that Rabbi Mordecai's lung was torn by the fervor of his praying.

But his whole attitude toward life was joyful. Only in joy can the soul be truly raised to God, and "he who wishes to serve God with devotion, and divine light, and joy, and willingness, must have a spirit that is bright, and pure, and clear, and a body that is full of life."

Rabbi Mordecai's son, Rabbi Noah of Lekhovitz (d. 1834), continued along his father's lines though he was more worldly in his outlook. But even among the utterances of Rabbi Noah's grandson, Rabbi Shelomo Hayyim of Kaidanov (d. 1862), we still find sayings informed with the energy of the rabbi of Karlin's teachings on prayer.

Rabbi Shelomo's school reached a late peak in a man who was first Rabbi Mordecai's, and subsequently Rabbi Noah's disciple: Rabbi Moshe of Kobryn (d. 1858). I do not hesitate to count this little-known man among the few late-born great men which the hasidic movement produced in the very midst of its decline. While he did not enrich the teaching, his life and words and the unity between his life and his words lent it a very personal, refreshingly vital expression.

Three sayings suffice to give the gist of his philosophy: "You shall become an altar before God"; "There is nothing in the world which does not contain a commandment"; and "Just as God is limitless, so his service is limitless."

These teachings are integrated with a life which by imaging and exemplifying them, sometimes recalls the early masters of hasidism. For the rest, what is told about him in this book requires no further supplementation or explanation.

Rabbi Hayyim Meir Yehiel of Mogielnica (d. 1849), the grandson of the Maggid of Koznitz, was the most notable among the disciples of that holy man of suffering, who prophesied from the depths of his suffering. Other zaddikim besides his grandfather were his teachers, namely, the rabbi of Apt and the

Seer of Lublin, and he was also close to the Seer's disciple, the Yehudi of Pzhysha, who had so many enemies. Hayyim collected teachings without becoming an eclectic, for though he was not an independent thinker, he had a strong and independent soul which melted all matter received from the outside in the crucible of his own feeling and experience.

Two of his utterances serve to characterize him: "I have no use for spiritual rungs without the garment of the body"; and "I never wanted to win anything without working for it myself." He had insight into himself and liked to tell his hasidim what was happening within his soul. He enjoyed "telling" in any event, and talked readily and freely.

The relationship between him and his hasidim was one of great intimacy; every gesture of his made a lasting impression on them and they served him with love. The disciple for whom his influence was most fruitful was Rabbi Yisakhar of Wolborz (d. 1876).

The rest of this volume gives the story of the school of Lublin and the schools it influenced, including the significant schools of Pzhysha and Kotzk. These developed under the influence of Lublin, especially of the great personality of the Seer, and yet in opposition to both.

Tales of the Hasidim: The Early Masters included ten disciples of Mezritch. Similarly, this volume treats nine of the many disciples of the Seer of Lublin. They are: Rabbi David of Lelov (d. 1813), Rabbi Moshe Teitelbaum of Ohel (Ujhely in Hungary; d. 1841), Rabbi Yisakhar Baer of Radoshitz (d. 1843), Rabbi Shelomo Leib of Lentshno (d. 1843), Rabbi Naftali of Roptchitz (d. 1827), Rabbi Shalom of Belz (d. 1855), Rabbi Zevi Hirsh of Zhydatchov (d. 1831), Rabbi Yaakov Yitzhak of Pzhysha, known as the "Yehudi" (d. 1813), and Rabbi Simha Bunam of Pzhysha (d. 1827). (For the sake of inner relatedness, I have taken them in this non-chronological sequence; and I have not included Rabbi Menahem Mendel of Kotzk, although he was for a time a disciple of the Seer; but have dealt with him in connection with the school of Pzhysha, because he himself never failed to stress that he belonged to Pzhysha rather than to the school of Lublin.)

David of Lelov was one of the most lovable figures in hasidism. He was wise and at the same time childlike, open to all creatures, yet retaining his secret heart, alien to sin and yet protecting the sinner from his persecutors.

He is a notable example of a zaddik who could not become what he was until the truth of hasidism had freed him from his ascetic outlook on the world. He owed this liberation to Rabbi Elimelekh.

The Seer of Lublin was his next teacher, with whom he kept faith throughout his life even though he was, and could not but be, opposed to him in basic issues, while siding wholeheartedly with his friend the Yehudi in the quarrels between Lublin and Pzhysha.

For a long time he refused to be regarded as a zaddik, in spite of the fact that he had numerous reverent followers who compared this unpretentious man to King David, probably with more reason than other zaddikim. For a considerable period of his life he worked in his little shop and frequently sent customers to other shopkeepers who were poorer than he.

He liked to travel through the country, visit unknown village Jews, and warm their hearts with his brotherly words. In the small towns he gathered children about him, took them for drives, and played and made music with them. In the market place he fed and watered animals which had been left untended, as the rabbi of Sasov had done before him. He was particularly fond of horses and went into vehement explanations of how senseless it is to beat them. Because he was more devoted to his own family than to mankind at large, he declared that he was not worthy to be called a zaddik.

He believed that his most important mission was to keep peace among men; that was why—so tradition has it—he had been granted the power of making peace wherever there was enmity by his mere prayer. He taught that one should not reprimand and exhort persons whom one wishes to turn to God, but associate with them like a good friend, quiet the tumult in their hearts and through love lead them to recognize God. This was the method by which he himself led to the right way many who had strayed. (Outstanding among these was a famous physician, Dr. Bernhard, whom the rabbi of Lelov took to the Seer of Lublin, where the doctor developed into a hasid living on a very high rung.)

Rabbi David's own life provided the conclusive example for his teachings. "Everything he did, every day and every hour," said Rabbi Yitzhak of Vorki who studied with him for a time, "was the statute and the word of the Torah."

As Rabbi Elimelekh freed the rabbi of Lelov from the bonds of asceticism, so Rabbi Elimelekh's disciple, the Seer of Lublin, freed Rabbi Moshe Teitelbaum from his preoccupation with scholarliness which isolated him from the world. The Seer recognized in his soul the true flame which only lacked the proper fuel; whoever has that flame is already a hasid at heart, no matter how much he may be opposed to the hasidic way.

Many things had prepared Rabbi Moshe for this way, among others his curious dreams of which we have records, some from the time of his youth. In these dream experiences— including encounters with the masters of the Kabbalah from bygone ages, whom he watched at their secret work—he learned to realize how little good deeds avail if the man who does them is not devoted to God with all his soul, and that both paradise and hell are within the human spirit.

At that point, the Seer became his teacher and taught him the true hasidic joy, but it was not easy for him to reach that state. It was said that Rabbi Moshe was a "spark" from the soul of the prophet Jeremiah. All his life he had sorrowed very deeply for the destruction of the Temple and of Israel. When he learned joy, his hope in the Messiah triumphed over his sorrow, for this hope had an extraordinary sensuous force. No other zaddik is reported to have had such vigorous and concrete faith in the Messiah at every instant of his life.

Rabbi Yisakhar Baer of Radoshitz was known far and wide as a miracle worker and especially famed for his miraculous cures. Chief among these were his cures of "dibbukim," of those who were possessed by demons, and they even gained him the name of "the little Baal Shem." He seems to have had this tendency toward the miraculous from youth on, although for a long time he did not venture to try out his inner powers and was known only as a shy and quiet man. We are told a characteristic incident of his youth: that he accompanied Rabbi Moshe Leib of Sasov on a journey and suggested to Rabbi Moshe Leib his own magical methods of which he himself was not yet aware.

But still stranger than this is the fact that he, who went from one zaddik to another, and after leaving the Seer finally attached himself to the Yehudi, kept his reverence for miracles intact even with this new teacher, the very air around whom was hostile to the miraculous. The tradition affords some explanation for this, for we are told that when the Yehudi's son fell ill, the father himself turned to Rabbi Yisakhar Baer, whose slumbering healing powers he had apparently divined and now decided to actualize. Without any faith in his own gift, in the urgent need of the moment, Rabbi Yisakhar took the child in his arms, laid it in the cradle, rocked it, prayed, and succeeded in healing it.

Many years later, when the school of Pzhysha had produced the last great hasidic school, that of Kotzk, with its atmosphere of tragedy, and the hasidim in both camps, Kotzk and Radoshitz, were opposing one another, Rabbi Yisakhar is said to have uttered a paradox which defined the principle of Kotzk as being the surrender of one's own will, before the will of God, and that of Radoshitz as holding to one's own will, which also springs from the will of God. The saying was: "If you cannot get across it, you must get across it, nevertheless." The followers of the rabbi of Kotzk, however, claimed that in Kotzk they were taught to bring their hearts closer to their Father in Heaven, while in Radoshitz the attempt was made to bring our Father in Heaven closer to the heart of the Jews. By this they meant that instead of striving up to God in all his greatness and austerity, the school of Radoshitz was trying to make him familiar to man—by way of miracles.

This reminds us of what Rabbi Yisakhar himself once said. When one of his most promising disciples asked him why he worked miracles and if it would not be better to purify the soul, he replied that he had been sent "to make the Godhead known to the world."

Rabbi Shelomo of Lentshno was just as unique, though in a different way. He was much praised for his extreme cleanliness because it symbolized his entire mode of life. It is told that he never looked at a coin and never touched one with his fingers; that he never put out his hand to receive anything, not even when any of the zaddikim who were his teachers (viz., Rabbi Mendel of Rymanov, the Seer of Lublin, and the Yehudi) offered him something to eat from his own plate, as the zaddikim often did to their dearest followers; and that he never spoke any idle words or listened to any idle speech.

Even in his youth he made a characteristic comment on the verse in Psalms that God will not despise a broken heart: "But it must, at the same time, be whole." And it is also characteristic that whenever he spoke of the coming of the Messiah, he described the great feeling of shame that would prevail everywhere. Because of his holiness, which though secluded was sympathetic to all creatures, he was regarded as one of the epiphanies of the suffering Messiah. Once he himself said of Messiah the son of Joseph, who according to the tradition was to be killed: "That is no longer the case; he will die of the sufferings of Israel."

He too had enemies among the other zaddikim. The leader of the fight which was waged against him when he remained faithful to the school of Pzhysha was a man who differed from him in all fundamental respects. He was Rabbi Naftali of Roptchitz, who had been taught by Rabbi Elimelekh of Lizhensk and later by his four great disciples: the Rabbi of Apt, the Maggid of Koznitz, Rabbi Mendel of Rymanov, and above all the Seer of Lublin.

We hardly know of another zaddik whose soul harbored such a mass of contradictions as did that of Rabbi Naftali of Roptchitz. But if we consider them all together, they are by no means formless and chaotic, but give the picture of a real human figure. He introduces into the hasidic world a type not uncommon among the distinguished intellectuals of the modern era: a mixture of irony and yearning, skepticism and belief, ambition and humility.

From his youth on, he was given to jests, many of them bitter, and to all manner of pranks including some that were really malicious. In his youth, he reflected on his own endowments with extreme pride, in his age with doubts verging on despair. He once observed that his teacher Rabbi Mendel of Rymanov was holy and knew nothing of cleverness, and added: "So how can he understand what I am like?" On another occasion, when the Seer of Lublin grew impatient with his eternal jesting and reminded him that the verse in the Scripture reads: "Thou shalt be whole-hearted with the Lord thy God," and not "Thou shalt be clever with the Lord thy God," Naftali gave the following bold reply which is utterly out of keeping with the original fundamental point of view of hasidism: "It requires great cleverness to be whole-hearted with the Lord."

But after he himself had become a rabbi, there are more and more quite different reports of him. A number of stories told in this volume, such as "The Watchman," "The Morning Prayer," "Leader and Generation," and above all, "A Wish," the tale of his desire to be reincarnated as a cow, testifies to what had taken place and was still taking place in his soul.

A conversation of his with Rabbi Meir of Stabnitz suggests a conclusion, though rather general, which Rabbi Naftali drew from his life experience. When he met Rabbi Meir, who had been his fellow pupil in Lublin and had in the meantime become to a certain extent the Seer's successor, he told him that from now on the hasidim should stay at home and study rather than go to zaddikim. Rabbi Meir answered: "Do not worry: God will provide! If we are not able to lead the community, other and abler men will appear and be the leaders"—a reply not, however, confirmed by later events.

Together with Rabbi Naftali of Roptchitz we must consider his disciple Rabbi Hayyim of Zans (d. 1876), who, of all the distinguished talmudic scholars among the hasidim, was probably the one that continued the old line of study with the most energy or—to use a curious simile attributed to him—undertook to turn the garment, which had already been turned, back to its original side. But we must not suppose that he attempted the synthesis which the earlier periods of the movement had tried to effect again and again. This synthesis seems to have been renounced, for though Rabbi Hayyim emphasizes that in the final analysis teaching and "service" are the same thing, he admits that as far as he is concerned in learning there is nothing in the world but the Torah, and in praying nothing but service.

He was a master in talmudic debate as well as in ecstasy, and no less distinguished for his generous charities and his deep knowledge of human nature, but he did not approach the great zaddikim in certain all-important qualities, for he lacked the unity of soul, and the unity of a figure shaped by the unity of the soul.

Many great men of the later generations are characterized by the fact that they have everything except the basic unity of everything. Yehezkel of Shenyava, a son of the rabbi of Zans, was a living protest against this trend. It is told of him that he did not want to preach sermons about the Scriptures, but would only read aloud from the Torah. One of his comments on his father was that Rabbi Hayyim had the soul of Abel, but of himself he said that the good element in Cain's soul had entered into his. Another of his sayings which has been handed down to us is that every zaddik comes across men more devout than he among those who follow him, only those men are not aware of it themselves.

The profuse legendary material at my disposal did not yield what I should call a comprehensive picture of Rabbi Shalom of Belz, the famous zaddik and founder of a "dynasty." But certain of his traits are so remarkable that I cannot omit him. Two motifs emerge with peculiar clarity. One is that of confession. Rabbi Shalom had his hasidim tell him all the "alien thoughts" which passed through their minds, that is, all the temptations of fantasy which prevented them from concentrating on prayer. He listened to their confessions with intense activity and this reciprocal relation accomplished the complete liberation of the hasidim.

The other motif has to do with marriage. It is well known that in circles of devout men not merely the presence of women in general, but even that of their own wives, was regarded as a "diverting" factor. This effect was not, however, attributed to the nature of woman as such, but to original sin and that part of it in particular which was due to the female element. In the case of the rabbi of Belz original sin seems to have been conquered. We see him sitting with his wife like Adam and Eve in paradise before the fall, when woman was still man's "help meet" with all her being; the original state of creation is restored.

Rabbi Hirsh of Zhydatchov, who studied not only with the Seer but also with the rabbis of Sasov and Koznitz, presents a new and unique situation. Together with his brothers and nephews he formed a family which was at the same time a school whose leader he was. A story told about one of the five brothers demonstrates the inner connection existing in this circle. It is about one of the brothers who, when the eldest, Rabbi Hirsh, was very sick, offered himself to heaven in his place because "the world needs him more." And his sacrifice was accepted.

Not only in his work, but in his everyday life, Rabbi Hirsh was the true Kabbalist among the disciples of the Seer of Lublin. He never raised a glass of water to his lips without going through a special mystical concentration (kavvanah). Since he had no self-confidence, he feared even after the age of forty that he might be dominated by the planet Venus, in whose sphere good and evil mingle. The fact that so many hasidim came to study with him also filled him with misgivings; could Satan have a hand in it? This doubt assailed him because he took everything very seriously, including the relationship between outer and inner help which he felt he must give to each of his hasidim. But how could he give really personal attention to every individual in such a crowd?

His rejection of any kind of supremacy, of any exclusive claim for himself or any other zaddik, is closely tied to this general attitude. He believed that a hasid who thought that his was the only true rabbi was an idolater, and that all that mattered was for everyone to find the rabbi fitted to his character and to his particular needs, the proper rabbi to give him individual help.

Rabbi Yehudah Zevi of Rozdol (d. 1847), a nephew of Rabbi Hirsh, developed the problem of the zaddik which his uncle had newly posed, in connection with his own self-doubting. He felt that he lacked the power the great zaddikim of earlier times possessed, the power to change the world. The determining principle of his own soul was, he discovered, a kind of yielding of his own, so to speak, space, a space making. He called this element nothingness and believed that it too was necessary for the existence of the world.

Rabbi Yitzhak Eisik of Zhydatchov (d. 1873), another nephew of Rabbi Hirsh, did not make any greater claims for the zaddik, but stressed the positive factor in his relationship to the hasidim, in two ways: first, by his view that all human relationships, hence those of zaddik and hasidim as well, are based on a mutual give and take, and secondly by interpreting the frequently misunderstood moral influence of the zaddik on the hasid as an action which is not independent but conditioned by and included in the religious operation. On the whole, we may say that the school of Zhydatchov substantially contributed the critical evaluation of the entire sphere of relationship existing between zaddik and hasidim, and to their new and more precise delimitation.

The school of Pzhysha, which originated in that of Lublin, and the school of Kotzk, the offspring of that of Pzhysha, present a large, independent, communal structure. But we cannot properly understand the salient feature of these two schools without knowing that of their founder, the Yehudi.*

Like his master, the Yehudi was called Yaakov Yitzhak, but since it was not fitting to use his teacher's name in his teacher's entourage, he is said to have been known as "the Yehudi," i. e., the Jew. This became so popular that later on other zaddikim addressed the rabbi of Pzhysha simply as "holy Jew." But the name is symbolic as well and points to the special character of the man. Even as a boy Yehudi refused to pray at stated intervals and in the company of others. Neither rebukes nor blows were of any avail. But then his father noticed that after the House of Prayer had been closed the boy climbed over the roof and in through a window to say his prayer, and did this day after day. As a youth he liked to pray in a granary where no one could see him.

In those days he already had the reputation of being a great talmudic scholar but one who knew nothing of the service of the heart. It was generally supposed that he did not take the bath of immersion for he was never seen in any of the groups of ten or more who descended the ninety steps to the ice-cold pool. They went together in order to relieve the weirdness of the long slippery stair, and also to light a fire and warm the water a little. But the Yehudi went alone at midnight, immersed himself without making a fire, returned as secretly as he had come, and studied the Kabbalah. At dawn his young wife sometimes found him lying unconscious over his book.

His wife's parents lived in the city of Apt. At that time, Rabbi Moshe Leib of Sasov resided in the same city. He took an interest in the youth, became fond of him, and had a profound influence on his sensitive and reticent soul. Presently Rabbi Abraham Yehoshua Heshel of Apt also discovered the greatness of Yehudi's soul. For many years he taught children in various villages. Then he was filled with

---

*See my book *For the Sake of Heaven* (Philadelphia, 1945) which tells of the ambivalent relationship between the Seer and the Yehudi.

a yearning for death which he regarded as the perfection of being. He did not know whether this yearning was divine truth or self-delusion. He sought support and leadership and it is said that Rabbi David of Lelov took him to the Seer of Lublin.

There, so we are told, he was received like one who has been expected, and a feeling of deep calm came over him. When we remember the restlessness of his youth, we can understand what he meant by saying that in Lublin he learned to fall asleep. But the Seer was not like his teacher the Maggid of Mezritch. He did not have the same great clarity which evoked the confidence of those he educated. The Maggid of Mezritch helped the disciples under his care to build up the substance of their life, each out of his own particular elements. The Seer lived in the world of his own spiritual urges, the greatest of which was his "seeing." His humility—though passionate like all his other qualities—impelled him time and again to strike a compromise between his personal world and the world at large, yet he could not really understand a human being like the Yehudi or the premises of his nature, for he lacked the one essential to such a man: the confidence of one soul in another. The Yehudi, in turn, could never realize this failing in the Seer's personality. That was why the relationship between the two was one of both intimacy and remoteness.

Finally the Yehudi founded a congregation of his own, a step which though taken at his teacher's suggestion provided fuel for the Seer's suspicions. With the help of Rabbi Bunam, who had been a fellow student of the Yehudi's and had then become his disciple, this congregation grew into the school of Pzhysha. But the focal point in the Yehudi's life continued to be his disturbed and bitter relations with the rabbi of Lublin, and time and again he felt a compulsion to bridge the unbridgeable gap.

He started out on his own way in the shadow of this conflict, and after years of struggle, the people flocked to him. "Turn!" he cried to them. "Turn quickly, for the day is near, there is not time for new migrations of souls; redemption is close at hand!" What he meant by this was that redemption was so imminent that people had no more time to strive toward perfection in new incarnations, that they had to take the decisive step now, with one stupendous effort, in the great turning. The Yehudi kept on the other side of the realm of magic which the Seer and his friends entered at that time in an attempt to reach the messianic sphere by affecting current events; he did not wish to hasten the end, but to prepare man for the end.

Rabbi Uri of Strelisk, the "Seraph," said of him that "he wanted to bring a new way down to men: to fuse teaching and prayer into one service." He went on to say that that had never happened before, but I think that it had happened in the beginnings of the hasidic innovation, but had by that time disappeared. And Rabbi Uri continued: "But he died in the midst of his work and did not complete it."

The gravest accusation the Yehudi's enemies proffered against him was that he did not pray at the prescribed hours, but waited until he was filled with the desire to pray. This was however nothing but the first necessary consequence of his will to concentrate. He did not have the opportunity to draw the further consequences, for he died in the fulness of his strength, before he was fifty, some two years before his teacher. According to one legend, the Seer had bidden him die, so that through the Yehudi the Seer might learn from the upper world what next step to take in the great messianic enterprise.

According to another legend, the upper world gave him the choice of either dying himself or having his teacher die—and he chose. There is still another version which suggests that the secret of his youth which had expressed itself in a yearning for death was at that time renewed on a higher plane, and that the highest "unification" is bound up with bodily death when it is performed by those who are uprooted—and this late bloom of hasidism no longer had any true roots. The story of his death is enveloped in more mystery than that of any other zaddik.

He himself once formulated the teaching which took shape in his life in a few terse words which are a commentary on the verse in the Scriptures: "Justice, justice shalt thou follow." They were: "We ought to follow justice with justice and not with unrighteousness." In this volume the passages about the Yehudi are supplemented by stories selected from a mass of kindred material about his sons and grandsons intended to show that here a peculiarity of character is preserved through several generations.

Rabbi Simha Bunam of Pzhysha was the greatest of the Yehudi's disciples and assumed the succession. He had traveled about as a copyist, lumber merchant, and pharmacist, went to Hungary to study the Talmud, and also made repeated business trips to Danzig. Wherever he went he kept his eyes open and experienced life sympathetically and freely. "I know all about sinners," he once said. "And so I also know how to straighten a young tree that is growing warped."

When Bunam first grew aware of the hasidic truth, he studied with the Maggid of Koznitz whom he frequently visited. Later he journeyed to Lublin where the Seer immediately became fond of this "worldly" man. Finally he made the acquaintance of the Yehudi and was soon his most trusted disciple.

After the Yehudi's death, the great majority of the hasidim of Pzhysha chose Bunam for their rabbi, but he was very reluctant to follow the call and let many who came to see him wait for days because he found it so difficult to practice his new vocation. He had no contact with the masses, not even that which the Yehudi had with his followers during the last period of his life: that of accepting their enthusiasm. But once he began seriously to teach, his teaching became his most vital function and one he discharged with a strong sense of responsibility. He shook and revolutionized the entire lives of the young men who came from everywhere and begged permission to remain near him. Since these youths were leaving their homes and business for his sake, families from far and wide expressed more enmity to him than to any other zaddik.

Many zaddikim of his time were hostile to him for objective reasons. Rabbi Naftali of Roptchitz, who had fought most vehemently against the Yehudi, once told a young man who had come to ask his blessing on his marriage to a girl from the neighborhood of Pzhysha: "I am not saying anything against the rabbi, for he is a zaddik: but his way is dangerous to the disciples who follow him. We serve so many years to arrive at the power and fervor they acquire in so short a time. With those methods 'the other side' may slip in—God forbid!—with the help of the demoniacal planet Venus." Finally, at the great zaddikim wedding at Ostila there was something very like a court session, in which the rabbi of Apt presided and dismissed the case, which was however more legitimate than the accusation guessed.

Bunam tried to continue to lead his hasidim along the way the Yehudi had taken, but he could not maintain it, for he did not share his teacher's belief that man must be prepared for redemption here and now and that redemption was really so close at hand. The Yehudi had tried to strike roots in the *goal*. But Bunam could no longer conceive this goal as the direct aim of his own personal actions, and so the heritage of his master was left hanging in air. The prospect of a new fusion of teaching and prayer, which had brightened the horizon for a brief moment, now vanished. It passed because the old rootedness was no more and it had proved impossible to strike new roots. Wisdom could still prosper in the atmosphere of "individualism," of abandonment which now became the abandonment of the goal, but holiness could not ripen in it. Wise Bunam was known as "the man versed in the mystery" but he was no longer close to the mystery itself, as the Yehudi like the early zaddikim had been. His profound table talk and crystalline parables bear powerful witness to the religious truth, but he cannot be regarded as the body and voice of the religious spirit. Prayer, which the Yehudi had "delayed," i.e., subjectivized, was made subsidiary to teaching—a natural result of the supremacy of the school over the congregation. And under the influence of rootlessness, teaching itself ceased to be the transmission of the unutterable and again became mere preoccupation with the study of contents.

The sinister quality of this later period of disintegration, which was only glossed over by Rabbi Bunam's clear wisdom, plainly comes out in the legend about his son, Rabbi Abraham Moshe, who died before his thirtieth year, soon after his father. He was all awareness of death and longing for death. His father said of his son that he had the soul of King Jeroboam I who separated Israel from Judah; that now his way could lead either to utter evil or to perfect goodness and an early death—and it led to the second.

What the young rabbi says concerning the sacrifice of Isaac has a dark personal ring: Abraham's love for his son was expressed in his very readiness to sacrifice him, for Isaac dwelt in Abraham's house "only as a son," while in reality he was the sacrificial lamb of God.

There is a strange story that before his wedding—he married one of the Yehudi's granddaughters—Rabbi Bunam sent him to the graveyard to invite one of the dead, and Moshe made a mistake and invited the wrong one. He did not remain at home after he was married, but took to the woods with a group of youths "attached to him" and with them "learned the hasidic way." (We know of a youth group of this kind around Rabbi Shalom Shakhna, and shall find the same situation in the case of Rabbi Mendel of Vorki.) It was the same wood through which the Seer of Lublin had once driven, where he had said that "the entire manifest and hidden teachings together with the Divine Presence" would once be present there. His father came to fetch him home to his young wife. As if waking from sleep, he said: "I forgot."

The story entitled "The Secrets of Dying" tells how he was involved in the death of his father, who "all his life had learned to die." He hesitated to become his father's successor, for he knew that by so doing he would cut short his own life. Yet in the end he decided for it. Only two years later, however, he "craved" death, and died. He was as beautiful in death as he had been in life. A zaddik who approached as he was being carried to the grave cried: "Alas for the beauty which must rot in the earth," and then lapsed into a silence which he did not break the whole of that day.

It is said that Rabbi Abraham Moshe was a great musician. As far as we know, he was Rabbi Bunam's only son.

If we follow Rabbi Hanokh in regarding Rabbi Bunam's disciples as commentaries on his teachings, then we must consider Rabbi Menahem Mendel of Kotzk (d. 1859) as that commentary which was itself in need of a commentary; but he never found one, for his disciples were not such a commentary.

From childhood on Rabbi Mendel was a rebel who zealously guarded his own independent way. It is told that when the Seer of Lublin sent for the youth and according to his custom asked him questions which revealed his own gift of "seeing," Mendel answered only under protest, and later when the Seer rebuked him for his way because it led to melancholy, Mendel left Lublin and went to Pzhysha. There he did indeed submit to the Yehudi's guidance, but soon after his master's death his irrepressible soul again revolted, not only in anger at the swarms of idle visitors: it was mutiny of the spirit.

When he himself became a rabbi, it grew quite clear that he was fanatically intent on a fundamental renovation of the movement. Hasidism was to remember the purpose of man's creation: "To lift up the heavens." He declared: "Holy revelation has deteriorated into habit," and every ounce of strength had to be concentrated to press on to revelation, to that point from which the heavens can be "lifted up."

This could no longer be the task of the congregation; it was the task of the disciples. The bond between congregation and school seems to be definitely severed. The congregation still had prayer, and prayer had as superior a significance at Kotzk as anywhere else. The rabbi himself was praised for having prayed without effort or ostentation "like one conversing with his friend." But in order to deceive the world—and at Kotzk they were always intent on dissembling in the sight of the world—prayers were "quickly gotten over with." Indeed, there was no longer any real feeling for congregational prayer as such. Prayer and teaching had finally become two worlds which were related only through knowledge of the goal, but not through the warmth of the heart and enthusiasm of practice. The "temple of love," where the great love between the hasidim once lived, was closed because of the abuse of the holy fire, and could not be opened again. Everything depended on the discipleship as an elite which was to press forward to revelation.

Toward the end of his life Rabbi Mendel hinted at what he had originally had in mind, saying that he had intended going "into the woods" with four hundred hasidim and giving them "manna" so that they might know the kingly power of God. This is the vision of a new wandering through the desert to receive the new revelation. Rabbi Mendel interpreted the words in the Talmud that "the Torah was given only to those who eat manna" as referring only to those who had no care for the morrow (Exod. 16:19 ff.) In this connection it is significant that even as a child he insisted that he remembered standing at Sinai, and as a rabbi, he enjoined everyone to imagine the stand at Sinai in his heart.

Certain of his utterances which have been transmitted indicate his hope that every member of his selected group would be able to "see straight into heaven" and become like the Baal Shem. This was quite consistent, for he regarded himself as the Sabbath on which the work of the great week, begun with the Baal Shem, reached its culmination. But these visions soon faded. The overwhelming disappointments he had suffered in his early years led him to concentrate on learning with fanatic intensity. His disciples (most of whom, incidentally, had to gain their livelihood by manual labor) thought themselves far above the rest of the world, and this led to undesirable developments.

After his first bold hopes had been wrecked, his only concern was to maintain, internally and externally, what he considered the truth, which was not a content, but a personal quality, something "which cannot be imitated." He expounded the words in the psalm that God is close to all who call on him in truth, by interpreting it to mean: Who call on him by the quality of truth dwelling in their soul, and he refused to make peace even with the school of a friend, if it had to be on terms that violated this quality.

He was even more uncompromising in his defense of inner truth. God's commandment, he taught, must not be made an idol to hide the truth, and when we say "God" we must mean the true God and not a "molten image" of our fantasy. It is quite understandable that only a few of his disciples— disciples and former companions, such as the rabbi of Ger, who saw in Mendel a "spark of the true fire" and "lay down under it"—incorporated the stern teaching of personal truth in their lives and made it live. (One disciple later defined this teaching to mean: "There is no truth until one's entire person is internally one and unified in His service, until one's entire person is one truth from the first to the last of the letters of the Scriptures.")

Most of them probably enjoyed listening to Rabbi Mendel's utterances, such as his praise of Pharaoh because he "was a man" and had remained steadfast in the face of the plagues, but they did not realize the implications of his utterances. His disappointment in his hasidim certainly did much to make him somber and aloof for the last twenty years of his life.

But it would be taking this tragic figure of hasidic agony too lightly if we were to explain the events of his life in terms of his personal experiences, without analyzing the change in faith itself. It seems to me that the decline of a great movement, above all of a great religious movement, is the most severe test to which the faith of a really believing man can be put, a far more difficult test than any personal fate. And Rabbi Mendel was a really believing man. He once said to himself: "I have faith; faith is clearer than vision."

To me the most important of all questionings of fate is how such closeness to God could change into such remoteness from God. In the history of hasidism, this question appears in the school of Pzhysha. The Yehudi's words: "This too will be corrupted," are evidence that he had already sensed it; he tried to combat it by powerfully calling for a turning. This question also threw its shadow over Rabbi Bunam—as we know, among other things, from his radical elaboration of the theme of "Satan's hasidim"—and he answered it by teaching that the shepherd is there even when the sheep do not see him. In Rabbi Mendel's time the decline had advanced so far and he was so sensitive to it, that the question felled him with cruel force, and he succumbed to its blows.

The crisis came on a Friday evening on which the rabbi did not pronounce the Benediction of Sanctification (Kiddush) until midnight and did not leave his room to come to the Sabbath table until that time. The oral reports, almost all of which have been preserved, differ considerably on what happened then, but all agree on a certain more or less outspoken antinomian note, on the transference of Rabbi Mendel's inner rebelliousness to his relation to the Torah. This holds even though we do not know whether he really said the words attributed to him by the so-called "enlightened" group; that man with all his urges and lusts is part of God; and whether he finally cried out: "There is no judgment and there is no judge!" —or whether he only touched the candlestick and thus ostentatiously sinned against the law of the Sabbath.

At all events something profoundly shocking must have occurred, for otherwise we could not explain one incident on which all the reports are fairly agreed. It is that Rabbi Mordecai Joseph, once Rabbi Mendel's fellow student at Rabbi Bunam's, later his disciple, and always his secret rival, called to the hasidim: "The tablets and the broken tablets were both preserved in the Ark of the Covenant, but when God's name is desecrated, there is no place for consideration of a rabbi's honor—tie him up!" Rabbi Mendel's brother-in-law, the faithful rabbi of Ger, opposed Rabbi Joseph and succeeded in quieting a large number of hasidim.

The rest left Kotzk after the Sabbath, Rabbi Mordecai Joseph at their head. He settled in the town of Izbica and later declared that "Heaven had commanded" him to leave his former teacher.

From that time on, throughout the remaining twenty years of his life, Rabbi Mendel kept to his room behind two doors which were almost always closed. Two holes were bored through one door, through which he heard the service in the adjoining House of Prayer, sometimes probably watching. The other door he occasionally opened himself, when hasidim were gathered outside. On such occasions he stood on the threshold without his kaftan. His face was awful to behold. He cursed them in choppy words that burst from his lips with such force that they were seized with terror and fled from the house through doors and windows. But sometimes, on a Friday evening, he issued from his room dressed in his white pekeshe and greeted his visitors, whom he otherwise gave only the tips of his fingers through the hole in the door. But he never sat down at the Sabbath table and almost never ate more than a plate of soup in the evening. When called to read the Torah on a Sabbath, he would go to the pulpit, his prayer shawl drawn over his face, and would go back again as soon as he had read the scriptural portion. Mice came and went in his room as they pleased, and when the hasidim heard them scuttling about, they whispered to the newcomers that these were souls who had come to the rabbi for redemption. And if you were to ask a hasid of Kotzk what the rabbi did about the bath of immersion, you would be told to this day that the legendary well of Miriam, which, locked in stone, once accompanied the Jews on their journey through the desert, had opened up in the rabbi's room.

I have told the story of the rabbi of Kotzk in such detail because it is so striking an illustration of the end of a process; it gives the impression of being the final act in a drama. But to regard it as an end from the purely chronological point of view would be a mistake. On the contrary: Kotzk became a focus for hasidic life and work which went on as though this were not the close of a phase, but the middle.
Three zaddikim who were close friends of Rabbi Mendel are a good example of this. They were: Yitzhak of Vorki, who died a decade before Mendel (1848), and must be considered together with his son whose name was also Mendel (d. 1868); and Yitzhak Meir of Ger (d. 1866), and Hanokh of Alexander

(d. 1870), who both survived Rabbi Mendel of Kotzk by almost ten years. But if we listen intently, we can hear midnight striking in the lives of these disciples too—though much more slowly.

I shall take Rabbi Hanokh—the last of the three—first, because of them all he was a disciple of the rabbi of Kotzk in the truest sense of the word. Rabbi Mendel and these three had all studied together at Rabbi Bunam's. When their teacher died, the rabbi of Ger, who was then twenty-eight and had already attained to his own spiritual position and his own sphere of work, deliberately subordinated himself to the rabbi of Kotzk after talking with him in the woods all through one night—so tradition has it—because he saw "the light shining from Tomashow" (Rabbi Mendel's first home).

The rabbi of Vorki, who was twenty years older than the other two, visited the Seer of Lublin when he was a mere boy and later studied with David of Lelov and Bunam. When Rabbi Bunam died, he attached himself to Abraham Moshe for the brief period of his rabbinate and then headed a congregation of his own, for a time even in Pzhysha. All through his life, however, he was a true friend to Rabbi Mendel. But Rabbi Hanokh was the disciple par excellence of the rabbi of Kotzk who had once been his fellow student in Rabbi Bunam's House of Study. Rabbi Hanokh always said that prior to the rabbi of Kotzk no one had taught him that a hasid was a human being who asked for the meaning. Even in Kotzk he continued to hide his deep and burning nature under all sorts of foolery. He actually developed in the teachings of Rabbi Mendel only the old, the original hasidic element. His main contribution was that he gave a more concrete and perfect form to the concept of "lifting up the heavens." He taught that the so-called two worlds, heaven and earth, are in reality one single world which has split apart but will grow whole again if man makes the earth entrusted to him like heaven. (Here he seems to demand the opposite of "lifting up the heavens," and yet it is the same thing, for a heaven which is no longer separate from earth, no longer deprived of earth, a heaven which has no gaps, must certainly have been "lifted.") All men, moreover, have the possibility of making the earth like heaven, for at the bottom of every heart there is a residue of the substance and the power of heaven, which can operate from its human habitation. Israel is in exile; man is in exile, but it is the exile of his own baseness, to which he lends the control of his heavenly heart. This must be taken as the point of departure for man's sharing in the redemption. Here we have the classical hasidic teachings in a new form approaching the views even of the era in which we are living. The parable of the Maggid's disciple, Rabbi Aaron of Karlin, about the negation of the ego reappears in a new practical form when we hear that Rabbi Hanokh never referred to himself as "I" because that pronoun belongs to God alone. But melancholy, though not despairing utterances, such as his words concerning the aging of melodies, testify to his deep insight into the decline of hasidism and its need for regeneration.

In contrast, the brilliant sayings of Rabbi Yitzhak Meir of Ger cannot be worked into a unified and relatively independent doctrine like those of Rabbi Hanokh. The rabbi of Ger was an aphorist somewhat like Rabbi Israel of Rizhyn, whom he resembled in other respects as well. He too was a representative zaddik of far-reaching influence, but he concerned himself with and represented the social and cultural affairs of Polish Jewry to a far greater extent than the rabbi of Rizhyn, and he spoke of himself with a humble self-criticism quite foreign to Rabbi Israel.

His critical and yet not hopeless attitude toward the movement, whose decline he recognized, is expressed very clearly in a certain description—surely not without reference to his own experience—which he drew in his old age of a congregation which had everything: a leader and members and a House of Study and all the appurtenances. Suddenly Satan bore out the innermost point. "But everything else remained just as it was, and the wheel kept on turning, only that the innermost point was lacking." He was speaking intimately to his grandson, but suddenly the description wrested a cry from him: "God help us! We must not let it happen!"

Rabbi Yitzhak of Vorki, the third of the three disciples of Kotzk, was also given to self-criticism, but he did not have such clear-cut resolution in the face of the declining movement. This noble man, who among all the disciples came closest to the mature wisdom of Rabbi Bunam, seems not to have realized the problems of that late hour. But I think that what he said about the seemingly hopeless and yet not hopeless turning of the great sinner goes beyond the sphere of personal experience.

His son Mendel of Vorki, on the other hand, gave direct and forceful expression to the crisis, not so much in one or the other of his sayings, as through his silence. The variations handed down to us on the theme of his "silence" form a curious picture. With him silence is not a rite, as with the Quakers, nor is it ascetic practice, as with some Hindu sects. The rabbi of Kotzk called it an "art." Silence was his way. It was not based on a negative principle; nor was it merely the absence of speech. It was positive and had a positive effect. Mendel's silence was a shell filled with invisible essence, and those who were with him breathed it. There is a story of how he met another zaddik for the first time, how they sat opposite each other for an hour in complete silence, somewhat like Aegidius, St. Francis' disciple, and St. Louis of France, and both derived benefit from this experience. He spent a night of silence with his hasidim, and they felt themselves uplifted toward the One.

There is no doubt that silence was his special kind of fervor, of hasidism. But it was not only that. When he himself spoke of silence—though not of his own, which he never touched on directly—he did not interpret it as soundless prayer but as soundless weeping or as "a soundless scream." The soundless scream is the reaction to a great sorrow. It is in general the Jew's reaction to his own great sorrow; it "befits us." By reading between the lines we discover that it is particularly his, Mendel of Vorki's reaction to the hour in which "the present too is corrupted." The time for words is past. It has become late.

THE LATER MASTERS

SHALOM SHAKHNA OF PROBISHTCH

The Hen and the Ducklings

Rabbi Shalom Shakhna, the son of Abraham the Angel, lost both his parents when he was very young, and grew up in the house of Rabbi Nahum of Tchernobil, who gave him his granddaughter to wife. However, some of his ways were different from Rabbi Nahum's and unpleasing to him. He seemed to be very fond of show, nor was he constant in his devotion to the teachings. The hasidim kept urging Rabbi Nahum to force Rabbi Shalom to live more austerely.

One year during the month of Elul, a time when everyone contemplates the turning to God and prepares for the Day of Judgment, Rabbi Shalom, instead of going to the House of Study with the others, would betake himself to the woods every morning and not come home until evening. Finally Rabbi Nahum sent for him and admonished him to learn a chapter of the Kabbalah every day, and to recite the psalms, as did the other young people at this season. Instead, he was idling and loafing in a way particularly ill becoming to one of his descent.

Rabbi Shalom listened silently and attentively. Then he said: "It once happened that a duck's eggs were put into a hen's nest and she hatched them. The first time she went to the brook with the ducklings they plunged into the water and swam merrily out. The hen ran along the bank in great distress, clucking to the audacious youngsters to come back immediately lest they drown. 'Don't worry about us, mother,' called the ducklings. 'We needn't be afraid of the water. We know how to swim.'"

The Powerful Prayer

Once on the eve of the New Year in the House of Prayer, while Rabbi Nahum of Tchernobil was reciting the Afternoon Prayer with great fervor, his grandson-in-law Rabbi Shalom,

49

who used to recite this prayer at the reader's desk, suddenly felt a sinking of the spirit. All around him were praying with great concentration, but it needed all the strength he had just to utter one word after the other, and to grasp the simple meaning of each word. Afterward Rabbi Nahum said to him: "My son, how your prayer took Heaven by storm today! It lifted up thousands of banished souls."

In Peace

Once when Rabbi Shalom Shakhna happened to be staying in a small town of the district of Kiev, the old zaddik Rabbi Zev of Zhytomir arrived to spend the sabbath there. On Thursday evening Rabbi Shalom prepared to leave and went to bid Rabbi Zev farewell. The zaddik inquired when Rabbi Shalom expected to reach his destination. "Tomorrow, around three in the afternoon," was the reply.

"Why do you plan to be on the road after the noon hour on the day before the sabbath?" Rabbi Zev asked in surprise.

"At twelve o'clock I usually put on my sabbath clothes and start singing the Song of Songs, which is Solomon's, king of peace. By that time the sabbath peace has already begun for me."

"And what am I to do," replied Rabbi Shalom, "if a tenant farmer comes to me toward evening and tells me his troubles, tells me that his calf has fallen sick, and from his words I gather that he is saying to me: 'You are a lofty soul, and I am a lowly soul; lift me up to you!' What am I to do then?"

From off the table the old man took the two candlesticks with the lighted candles, and grasping them in his two hands, he accompanied his young guest through the long corridor to the outer door. "Go in peace," he said. "Go in peace."

The Streets of Nehardea

Rabbi Shalom said:

"The Talmud tells of a wise man versed in the lore of the stars and relates that the paths of the firmament were as bright and clear to him as the streets in the town of Nehardea where he lived. Now if only we could say about ourselves that the streets of our city are as clear and bright to us as the paths of the firmament! For to let the hidden life of God shine out in this lowest world, the world of bodiliness, that is the greater feat of the two!"

With the Same Passion

It is written: "A Psalm of David," and following: ". . . after he had gone in to Bathsheba." This is how Rabbi Shalom expounded the verse: "David returned to God and said his psalm to him with the same passion with which he had gone to Bathsheba. That was why God forgave him on the instant."

On the Highest Rung

A hasid of Rabbi Shalom living in a certain town happened to be present when the "Rav," Rabbi Shneur Zalman, on a visit to the town in the course of a journey on the Sabbath, said Torah with great fervor. But suddenly it seemed to the hasid that the "Rav" grew less fervent, that what he said now appeared to lack the admirable passion of what had gone before. The next time the hasid was with his teacher Rabbi Shalom, he told of the incident, and openly stated his surprise. "How can you venture to judge such matters!" said the zaddik. "You don't know enough to do that. But I shall tell you: There is a very high and holy rung, and he who reaches it is freed of all the stuff of earth and can no longer kindle to flame."

ISRAEL OF RIZHYN

The New Heaven

When the rabbi of Rizhyn was a child, he was once walking up and down in the yard on a Friday toward evening time, when the hasidim had already gone off to pray. A hasid went up to him and said: "Why don't you go in? The sabbath has already begun."

"The sabbath hasn't begun yet," he replied.

"How do you know that?" asked the hasid.

"On the sabbath," he answered, "there always appears a new Heaven, and I can't see any sign of it yet."

On Earth

Rabbi Israel of Rizhyn, the son of Rabbi Shalom Shakhna, and Rabbi Moshe of Savran had quarreled. The rabbi of Savran, prompted by the wish to make peace, paid his adversary a visit. Rabbi Israel asked him: "Do you believe there is a zaddik who clings to God unceasingly?" The other answered as one who wants to hide a doubt: "There might well be." To which the rabbi of Rizhyn replied: "My grandfather was like that; my grandfather Rabbi Abraham, whom they called the Angel." Then the other said: "He did not, come to think of it, spend many days on this earth." And the rabbi of Rizhyn: "And my father Rabbi Shalom was like that." And again the rabbi of Savran remarked: "He too, come to think of it, did not spend many days on this earth."

Then the rabbi of Rizhyn replied: "Why speak of years and days! Do you think they were on earth in order to dry up here? They came, accomplished their service, and returned."

The Tale about Smoke

Once Rabbi Moshe of Kobryn came to visit the rabbi of Rizhyn on the eve of the sabbath. He found his host standing in the middle of the room, his pipe in his hand and clouds of smoke wreathing round him. The rabbi of Rizhyn immediately began to tell a story:

"There was once a man who lost his way in the woods at twilight on the eve of the sabbath. Suddenly he saw a house in the distance. He walked toward it. When he entered he found himself face to face with a robber, a fierce-looking robber, and on the table in front of him lay a gun. The robber jumped up, but before he could get hold of the gun the man had seized it, and quick as lightning he thought: "If I hit him, it will be well, if I miss, the room will at least be full of smoke and I can escape.'"

When the rabbi of Rizhyn reached this point in his story he put down his pipe and said: "Sabbath!"

Two Kinds of Zaddikim

The rabbi of Rizhyn told how the people of Jassy sneered at the rabbi of Apt after his sermons. He added: "In every generation there are people who grumble about the zaddik and look askance at Moses. For the rabbi of Apt is the Moses of his generation." He paused, and after a while he continued: "There are two kinds of service and two kinds of zaddikim. One sort serves God with learning and prayer, the other with eating and drinking and earthly delights, raising all this to holiness. This is the kind the grumbling is about. But God has made them as they are because he does not want man to be caged in his lusts, but to be free in them. That is the calling of these zaddikim: to make men free. Those others are the lords of the manifest, these are the lords of the hidden world. It is to them that secrets are revealed and the meaning of dreams unfolded, as it was to Joseph, who curled his beautiful hair and served God with the delights of this world."

On another occasion he spoke about the verse: "The heavens are the heavens of the Lord; but the earth hath He given to the children of men," saying: "There are two kinds of zaddikim. Those of the one sort learn and pray the livelong day and hold themselves far from lowly matters in order to attain to holiness. While the others do not think of themselves, but only of delivering the holy sparks which are buried in all things back to God, and they make all lowly things their concern. The former, who are always busy preparing for Heaven, the verse calls 'the heavens,' and they have set themselves apart for the Lord. But the others are the earth given to the children of men."

Zaddikim and Hasidim

The rabbi of Rizhyn said:

"Just as the holy letters of the alphabet are voiceless without the vowel signs, and the vowel signs cannot stand without the letters, so zaddikim and hasidim are bound up with one another. The zaddikim are the letters and the hasidim who journey to them are the vowel signs. The hasidim need the zaddik, but he has just as much need of them. Through them he can be uplifted. Because of them he can sink—God forbid! They carry his voice, they sow his work in the world. Suppose that one of the hasidim who come to me is on the road and meets a carriage full of so-called enlightened passengers. He persuades the coachman to let him ride beside him, and when the time comes to say the Afternoon Prayer he gets down from his seat, and makes ready, and prays while the carriage waits. And the passengers are annoyed and revile the coachman and shout at him. In the midst of all this, perhaps through all this, they experience a change of soul."

The Roof

Jacob Ornstein, the rav of Lwow, opposed the hasidic way. And so once when the rabbi of Rizhyn was calling on him, he thought his visitor would launch into subtle interpretations of the Scriptures in order to impress him with the scholarship of the hasidim. But the zaddik only asked: "What are the roofs of the houses in Lwow made of?"

"Out of sheet iron," said the rav.

"And why out of sheet iron?"

"To be protected against fire."

"Then they might just as well be made of brick," said Rabbi Israel and took his leave. When he was gone, the rav laughed and exclaimed: "And that is the man people flock to!"

A few days later Rabbi Meir of Primishlan came to Lwow to see the rabbi of Rizhyn, who was his friend, but found he had already left. They told him what he had said. His face lit up and he said: "Truly, the roof, the heart of the man who watches over the congregation, should be of brick: so shaken with all their sorrows that it threatens to break every moment, and yet endures; but instead it is of sheet iron!"

The Other Way

Once when the Jews were passing through a period of great stress, the rabbi of Apt who was then the eldest of his generation issued a command for a universal fast, in order to call down God's mercy. But Rabbi Israel summoned his musicians, whom he carefully selected from a number of different towns, and night after night he had them play their most beautiful melodies on the balcony of his house. Whenever the sound of the clarinet and the delicate tinkle of the little bells floated down from above, the hasidim began to gather in the garden, until there was a whole crowd of them. The music would soon triumph over their dejection and they would dance, stamping their feet and clapping their hands. People who were indignant at these doings reported to the rabbi of Apt that the day of fasting he had ordered had been turned into a day of rejoicing. He answered:

"It is not up to me to call him to account who has kept the memory of the command in the Scriptures green in his heart: 'And when ye go to war in your land against the adversary that oppresseth you, then ye shall sound an alarm with the trumpets; and ye shall be remembered before the Lord your God.' "

The Counterruse

Several mitnagdim of Sanok came to the rabbi of Rizhyn when he was passing through their city, and complained to him: "In our congregation we pray at dawn, and after that we sit wrapped in our prayer shawls, with our phylacteries on head and arm, and learn a chapter of the Mishnah. Not so the hasidim! They pray after the hour set for prayer has passed, and when they have finished praying they sit down together and drink schnapps. And yet they are called the 'devout' and we the 'adversaries.' "

Leib, the rabbi of Rizhyn's servant, was seized with an irresistible desire to laugh as he listened to this complaint, and not troubling to conceal the reason for his laughter, he said: "The service and prayer of the mitnagdim are ice-cold and have no warmth at all, just like a corpse, and when you watch by the side of a body you study the chapter from the Mishnah prescribed for this occasion. But when the hasidim have done their bit of service, their heart glows and is warm like one who is alive, and whoever is alive must drink schnapps."

The rabbi said: "We'll let the jest pass. But the truth of the matter is this: You know that ever since the day our Temple was destroyed, we pray instead of making sacrifice. And just as the sacrifice was disqualified if the thought was impure, so it is with prayer. That is why the Evil Urge devises ruse upon ruse to confuse him who prays with thoughts alien to prayer. Now for this the hasidim have invented a counter-ruse. After praying they sit down together and drink to one another. 'To life!' Each tells what is burdening his heart and then they say to one another: 'May God grant your desire!' And since—so our sages say—prayers can be said in any language whatsoever, this speaking and answering of theirs while drinking is also regarded as prayer. But all the Evil Urge sees is that they are eating and drinking and using everyday speech, and so he stops bothering his head about them."

"Thee"

The hasidim were once sitting together and drinking, when the rabbi entered the room. It seemed to them that he did not eye them with favor. "Are you displeased to find us drinking, rabbi?" they asked. "Yet it is said that when hasidim sit together over their cups, it is just as though they were studying the Torah!"

"There is many a word in the Torah," said the rabbi of Rizhyn, "which is holy in one passage and unholy in another. So for instance, it is written: 'And the Lord said to Moses: Hew thee two tables of stone,' but also: 'Thou shalt not

56

make unto thee a hewn image.' Why is it that the same word is holy in the first passage and unholy in the second? It is because there the word 'thee' comes after, and here it precedes. So it is with all we do. Whenever the 'thee' comes after, all is holy, when it precedes, all is unholy."

The Judgment of the Messiah

Many heads of families of Berditchev complained to the rabbi of Rizhyn that their sons-in-law had left wives and children in order to become his disciples, and when they asked him to persuade the youths to return home, he told them about a young man who had lived in the days of the Great Maggid. He had quitted his father-in-law's house to go to the maggid. They had fetched him back and he had pledged on a hand-clasp that he would stay at home. Yet shortly thereafter he was gone. Now his father-in-law got the rav of the town to declare that this broken promise was cause for divorce. The young man was thus deprived of all means of subsistence. Soon he fell ill and died.

When the zaddik had finished his story, he added: "And now, my good men, when the Messiah comes, the young man will hale his father-in-law before his court of justice. The father-in-law will quote the rav of the town, and the rav will quote a passage from the commentary on the Shulhan Arukh. Then the Messiah will ask the young man why after giving his hand on it that he would remain at home he broke his promise just the same, and the young man will say, 'I just had to go to the rabbi!' In the end the Messiah will pronounce judgment. To the father-in-law he will say: 'You took the rav's word as your authority and so you are justified.' And to the rav he will say: 'You took the law as your authority and so you are justified.'

"And then he will add: 'But I have come for those who are not justified.' "

The Zaddik and the People

The rabbi of Rizhyn said:

"As when someone prepares to split a tree with an ax, and

takes a great swing at it but misses, and the ax goes into the earth, so it is when the zaddik talks to people in order to rouse their hearts to the service of God, but they do not heed him, and admire only the cleverness and artfulness of his sermon."

The Hidden Teachings

Concerning the verse: "For instruction shall go forth from Me," the rabbi of Rizhyn said:

"The teachings will never be altered. The first book of Moses will forever be the book of beginnings, which tells what happened to our fathers from the day God created the world. But there is something which is hidden from us: what God wrought before he created the world. And that is what is meant by the words: 'Now will it be said to Jacob and of Israel, what God hath wrought.' And the same is meant by the words: 'For instruction shall go forth from Me'—telling what I wrought before I created the world."

Ezekiel and Aristotle

Once when many wise men were gathered about his board, the rabbi of Rizhyn asked: "Why are the people so set against our master Moses ben Maimon?" A rabbi answered: "Because in a certain passage he asserts that Aristotle knew more about the spheres of Heaven than Ezekiel. So why should we not be set against him?"

The rabbi of Rizhyn said: "It is just as our master Moses ben Maimon says. Two people entered the palace of a king. One took a long time over each room, examined the gorgeous stuffs and treasures with the eyes of an expert and could not see enough. The other walked through the halls and knew nothing but this: 'This is the king's house, this is the king's robe. A few steps more and I shall behold my Lord, the King.'"

The Road Makers

When the rabbi of Ger visited the rabbi of Rizhyn in Sadagora, his host asked: "Are there good roads in Poland?"

"Yes," he replied.

"And who," the rabbi of Rizhyn continued, "is responsible for the work and directs it, Jews or non-Jews?"

"Jews," answered the rabbi of Ger.

"Who else," exclaimed the rabbi of Rizhyn, "could be versed in the work of making roads!"

Who May Be Called Man?

Concerning the words in the Scriptures: "When any man of you bringeth an offering to the Lord . . ." the rabbi of Rizhyn said: "Only he who brings himself to the Lord as an offering may be called man."

The Right Kind of Altar

It is written: "An altar of earth thou shalt make unto Me . . . and if thou make Me an altar of stone, thou shalt not build it of hewn stones, for if thou lift up thy tool upon it, thou hast profaned it."

The rabbi of Rizhyn expounded this as follows: "The altar of earth is the altar of silence which is most pleasing to God. But if you do make an altar of words, do not hew and chisel them, for such artifice would profane it."

The Nature of Service

The rabbi of Rizhyn said:

"This is the service man must perform all of his days: to shape matter into form, to refine the flesh, and to let the light penetrate the darkness until the darkness itself shines and there is no longer any division between the two. As it is written: 'And there was evening and there was morning—one day.'"

And another time he said:

"One should not make a great to-do about serving God. Does the hand boast when it carries out the will of the heart?"

Walking the Tight Rope

Once the hasidim were seated together in all brotherliness, when Rabbi Israel joined them, his pipe in his hand. Because he was so friendly, they asked him: "Tell us, dear rabbi, how should we serve God?" He was surprised at the question and replied: "How should I know!" But then he went right on talking and told them this story:

There were two friends, and both were accused before the king of a crime. Since he loved them he wanted to show them mercy. He could not acquit them because even the king's word cannot prevail over a law. So he gave this verdict: A rope was to be stretched across a deep chasm and the two accused were to walk it, one after the other; whoever reached the other side was to be granted his life. It was done as the king ordered, and the first of the friends got safely across. The other, still standing in the same spot, cried to him: "Tell me, my friend, how did you manage to cross that terrible chasm?" The first called back: "I don't know anything but this: whenever I felt myself toppling over to one side, I leaned to the other."

Breaking Impulses

A young man gave a note of request to the rabbi of Rizhyn. He had written to ask God's help in breaking his evil impulse. The rabbi's eyes laughed as he looked at him: "You want to break impulses? You will break your back and your hip, yet you will not break an impulse. But if you pray and learn and work in all seriousness, the evil in your impulses will vanish of itself."

Suffering

A man who was afflicted with a terrible disease complained to Rabbi Israel that his suffering interfered with his learning and praying. The rabbi put his hand on his shoulder and said: "How do you know, friend, what is more pleasing to God, your studying or your suffering?"

God the Forgiver

The time the rabbi of Rizhyn followed the advice of his physicians and went to Odessa to bathe in the sea, a grandson of the famous Rabbi Jacob Emden was living there. His name was Meir and he had strayed from the path of his fathers. When Rabbi Israel heard about him, he sent for him and invited him to come to Rizhyn. He promised that all his expenses would be taken care of. Meir agreed.

He had sat at the rabbi's table in Rizhyn only a short time when he made complete penance. One day, however, the zaddik noticed that he was looking depressed, and asked: "Meir, my son, what is troubling you? If it is your sins, remember that the turning makes up for everything."

Meir answered: "Why should I not be troubled? After doing penance I keep returning to sin over and over again as a dog returns to his vomit—and how can I know whether my penance is still accepted?"

The rabbi of Rizhyn touched his arm and said: "Have you never wondered why we read in the prayer: '. . . For thou art a forgiver of Israel and a pardoner of the tribes of Jeshurun.' Would it not be enough to write: 'You forgive and pardon'? But just as it is man's way and compulsion to sin and sin again and again, so it is God's way and his divine compulsion to forgive and pardon again and again."

Penance

A confirmed sinner who allowed no evil desire to pass him by came to Rabbi Motel of Tchernobil, handed him a slip on which he had listed the sins he had committed in his life, and asked to have a penance imposed on him. When Rabbi Motel had read the slip of paper, he said: "I am too old to assume the burden of someone who requires such heavy penance. Go to the rabbi of Rizhyn. He is young, he will take it upon himself." So the man went to the rabbi of Rizhyn and gave him the list. And now the rabbi of Rizhyn read the whole long column, the big items and the small, and the sinner waited.

Finally the zaddik said: "This shall be your penance. No matter what word of prayer you utter, from now until you die, you shall not utter a single word of prayer with empty lips; but you shall preserve the fulness of every word."

61

God and Gladness

Concerning the words in the Scriptures: "And it shall be, if thou shalt forget the Lord thy God . . ." the rabbi of Rizhyn said: "It is well known that by every 'and it shall be' in the Scriptures, gladness is meant. Here too this is what is meant. Here we are told: 'If you forget gladness and fall into a depression, you are forgetting the Lord your God.' For it is written: 'Strength and gladness are in His place.'"

The Child Thinks of His Father

The rabbi of Rizhyn said:

"In certain prayer books we do not read: 'Cause us, O Lord our God, to lie down,' but 'Cause us, our Father, to lie down.' For when man thinks of God as God, whose glory fills the world and there is no thing in which God is not, then he is ashamed to lie down on a bed in his sight. But if he thinks of God as his father, then he feels like a fond child whose father sees after him when he goes to bed, and tucks him in, and watches over his sleep. As we pray: 'Spread over us the covering of thy peace.'"

Afar Off

This question was put to the rabbi of Rizhyn: "Of the children of Israel standing at the foot of Mount Sinai, it is written: 'And the people saw it and stirred and stood afar off . . .' How shall we interpret this? Is not the entire earth filled with the glory of God? How can one stand 'afar off' from him?"

He expounded: "Miracles are for those who have little faith. When Israel saw that God was performing miracles, they knew that they had still to stand afar off; their hearts stirred, and—in spirit—they stood afar off at a place which was still befitting to them, but at the same time they yearned for perfect faith with all the strength of their stirring hearts."

To Walk with One's Own Light

A young rabbi complained to the rabbi of Rizhyn: "During the hours when I devote myself to my studies I feel life and light, but the moment I stop studying it is all gone. What shall I do?"

The rabbi of Rizhyn replied: "That is just as when a man walks through the woods on a dark night, and for a time another joins him, lantern in hand, but at the crossroads they part and the first must grope his way on alone. But if a man carries his own light with him he need not be afraid of any darkness."

Holy Spirit

The rabbi of Rizhyn was asked: "What does it mean when they say of some person or other that he has a holy spirit?"
He answered: "If a man really has spirit and he does not allow it to grow impure, that is called holy spirit."

Controversy for the Sake of Heaven

The rabbi of Rizhyn said:
"When the hasidim see one rabbi carrying on a controversy with another, they too begin to argue with one another. But in reality only the zaddikim are permitted to carry on a controversy, for it is a controversy for the sake of Heaven. That is why it says in the Talmud: 'Which controversy was for the sake of Heaven? That of Hillel and Shammai.' It does not say 'of the school of Shammai and the school of Hillel,' for a controversy for the sake of Heaven can be waged only by the teachers, not by their disciples."

The Time for Prayer

Once when Rabbi Israel was visiting the rabbi of Apt, he waited a long time before saying the Morning Prayer—something he did quite frequently. When they asked him when he was going to pray, he said he did not know just yet, and told this story:
A king had set an hour at which every one of his subjects was to have a free hearing. One day a beggar came to the palace at another hour and asked to be taken to the king. The guards snapped at him, and demanded whether he was not acquainted with the ruling. The beggar said: "I know all about it, but it only holds for those who want to talk to the king about the things they have need of; but I want

to talk to the king about what the realm has need of." The beggar was instantly admitted.

"And so," the rabbi of Rizhyn ended his story, "how am I to know when I shall pray?"

A Dish of Beans

A number of young men came to Rizhyn from a distant town in order to spend the Days of Awe near Rabbi Israel. When they noticed that he did not keep the prescribed hours for prayer but waited until he was seized with fervor, they wanted to imitate him and also waited, though they did not quite know what for. After the Feast of the Rejoicing in the Law, they went to the rabbi to take leave of him. He gave them his blessing and said: "See to it that you do not delay your prayers, but say each at its proper time. I shall tell you the story of the man whose wife served him a dish of beans for dinner year in, year out, day after day. Once she was delayed and the meal was put on the table an hour late. When her husband saw the beans, he grew angry and cried: 'I thought that today you were going to serve me an especially fine dish, and that the cooking of it had taken up so much time because it required many ingredients and particular care. But I am not in the mood to wait for the beans I eat every day!'" With that the zaddik ended his tale.

The young men bowed, and started on their homeward journey. In an inn, where they stopped on the way, they met an old man whose face was unfamiliar to them, but with whom they immediately entered into conversation. When they told him what the rabbi had said to them in parting, he smiled and said: "The cause of the man's anger was that there was as yet no perfect love between him and his wife. If there is such love, the man is well pleased if his wife lets him wait a long time, and then serves him a dish he eats every day, and there is nothing his heart does not regard as new and good."

These words struck the young men deeply. When they went to Rizhyn again on the Days of Awe, they told the rabbi of the incident. He was silent for a time, and then said: "What the old man said to you he also said to me, and he also said it to God."

In the Attic

This story is told:
Every night the rabbi of Rizhyn was in the habit of climbing to the attic and staying there for two hours. During that time his servant Shmulik who accompanied him waited sitting on the stairs. Once the zaddik's daughter wanted to fetch something from a cupboard which was in the attic, and found Shmulik sitting there and weeping. She asked him what was the matter. "Someone," he said, "slipped me a lot of money so that I should let him go in to the rabbi, and now he is inside." He opened his hand and showed her the money. Just then the rabbi came out at the door. There was no one in the room. In Shmulik's palm lay a few shards of clay.

Of a Hidden Zaddik

This story is told:
A hasid of the rabbi of Rizhyn had a daughter who was afflicted with serious eye trouble which no doctor knew how to cure. Time and again he begged the rabbi to help him, but no help was granted him. Finally, when the girl was stricken blind, the zaddik said to him unasked: "Take your daughter to Lwow, and when you get there, wait for the vendors who go about the streets and call out their wares, each with his own singsong cry, for instance: 'Fine pretzels, fresh pretzels!' He whose cry you like best is the one who can heal your daughter."
The hasid did as he was told and soon discovered the man who sang out his wares most to his liking. He bought a pretzel from him and asked him to bring some to the inn the next day. When the vendor entered his room, the hasid locked the door, and repeated the words of the rabbi of Rizhyn. The vendor's eyes snapped and he shouted: "You let me out of here, or I'll make a heap of bones of you along with your rabbi." The hasid opened the door in terror. The man disappeared, but the girl was cured.

Return, O Israel

This is what Rabbi Israel of Rizhyn said on the "Sabbath of the Turning":

"Hosea says: 'Return, O Israel, unto the Lord thy God.' That was said to the whole world and to all the creatures of Heaven and earth. For everything that has been created, below and above, all the servants of the Most High, the angels, the seraphim, the heavenly creatures, the holy wheels, all up to the throne of God himself, must accomplish the turning. And that is what the words 'unto the Lord thy God' mean: all creatures of all rungs to the very highest, up to the throne of God, must accomplish the turning."

But when he had said this, Rabbi Israel addressed himself: "O Israel, return Israel, unto the Lord thy God."

Turning and Redemption

The rabbi of Rizhyn said:

"They say that the zaddik of Spola, the Grandfather, once called out: 'Messiah, why don't you come? What are you waiting for? I swear to you by my beard that the Jews will not atone.' And I shall not contradict the Grandfather of Spola. But this I promise you, Lord of the world, I promise you that they will atone just as soon as Messiah, the king, appears. And they have some justification. For before ever we sinned, You in your covenant with Abraham between the section of the sacrifice sentenced us to four exiles; therefore you must redeem us before we do penance."

On another occasion the rabbi of Rizhyn laid the fingers of his right hand on the table after the morning meal, and said: "God says to Israel: 'Return unto me . . . and I will return unto you.'" Then he turned his right hand palm up and said: "But we children of Israel reply: 'Turn Thou us unto Thee, O Lord, and we shall be turned; renew our days as of old.' For our exile is heavy on us and we have not the strength to return to you of ourselves." And then he turned his hand palm down again and said: "But the Holy One, blessed be he, says: 'First you must return unto me.'" Four times the rabbi of Rizhyn turned his hand, palm up and palm down. But in the end he said: "The children of Israel are right, though, because it is true that the waves of anguish close over them, and they cannot govern their hearts and turn to God."

The Time to Come

It was on a sabbath and the rabbi of Rizhyn sat at his table surrounded by his hasidim. Then he said to them: "The days are near when all will be well with the common man both in body and in soul, but all will not be well with the extraordinary man, not in body and not in soul, and he will not even be able to recite one psalm."

And he concluded: "Why do I tell you this? So that your hearts shall not grieve: it ought to be so, it must be so."

Another time he said: "In the last three hours before redemption it will be as difficult to cling to Jewishness as to climb a smooth wall of ice. That is why in the Hoshanot prayer we say: 'Three hours—pray help!' Those are the last hours."

Labor Pains

The rabbi of Rizhyn said:

"If a pregnant woman goes into labor in the eighth month when her time is not yet come, they try to stop her labor. But not so in the ninth month. If the woman goes into labor then, they try to hasten it, so that she may soon give birth. That is why formerly when people called to Heaven begging God to free the earth of some misery, their prayer was granted, for the time was not yet come. But now that redemption is near, no prayer which ascends in behalf of the sorrowful world is of avail, but sorrow is heaped upon sorrow so that the birth may soon be accomplished."

Blowing the Ram's Horn on the Sabbath

On a New Year's Day which fell on a sabbath the rabbi of Rizhyn said:

"On a New Year's Day which falls on the sabbath, the ram's horn which summons the world to the new year must not be blown. On that day God himself blows the ram's horn. And

he certainly knows how to blow! That is why on this day our
hope is so wide-awake; the source of mercy itself has wakened
it."

The Two Caps

Rabbi David Moshe, the son of the rabbi of Rizhyn, once said
to a hasid:

"You knew my father when he lived in Sadagora and was
already wearing the black cap and going his way in dejection;
but you did not see him when he lived in Rizhyn and was still
wearing his golden cap." The hasid was astonished. "How is
it possible that the holy man from Rizhyn ever went his way
in dejection! Did not I myself hear him say that dejection is
the lowest condition!"

"And after he had reached the summit," Rabbi David replied,
"he had to descend to that condition time and again in order
to redeem the souls which had sunk down to it."

The Sound of the Ram's Horn

Rabbi David Moshe told this story:

The year he died my father could no longer go to the House
of Prayer on New Year's Day. I prayed with him in his room.
His service was more wonderful than ever before. When he
had ended, he said to me: "Today I heard the Messiah blow
the ram's horn."

The Meal at the Close of the Sabbath

In his old age the rabbi of Rizhyn spent his summers in the
little town of Potok. Once Rabbi Moshe of Kobryn visited him
over the sabbath. That day, the rabbi of Rizhyn did not eat
the meal at the close of the sabbath, but sat in his garden in
the evening, and the rabbi of Kobryn kept him company. For
a long time the rabbi of Rizhyn was silent. Then he said: "We
could eat the fruits of this tree in place of the meal, couldn't
we?" Then he touched the rabbi of Kobryn's belt and said:
"Let's take a little walk." And as they walked, he repeated
what he had said before: "Dear Rabbi Moshe, you are a
learned man. Is it not true that we are permitted to replace
the meal at the close of the sabbath with fruits?" Then the

rabbi of Kobryn understood that the rabbi of Rizhyn was speaking of his own end and of his sons, and cried out: "Our holy rabbi, the world still has need of you!" But a month and a half after this sabbath, Rabbi Israel died.

ABRAHAM YAAKOV OF SADAGORA

Creatures

On the fifteenth day of the month Shevat, the "New Year of
the Trees," when they were placing fruit on the table, as is
the custom on this day, Rabbi Abraham Yaakov, the eldest
son of the rabbi of Rizhyn, said:

"It is written: 'When any man of you bringeth an offering
unto the Lord, ye shall bring your offering of the cattle, even
of the herd or of the flock.' All creatures and plants and
animals bring and offer themselves to man, but through man
they are all brought and offered to God. When man purifies
and sanctifies himself in all his members as an offering to
God, he purifies and sanctifies all the creatures."

Of Modern Inventions

"You can learn something from everything," the rabbi of
Sadagora once said to his hasidim. "Everything can teach
us something, and not only everything God has created. What
man has made has also something to teach us."

"What can we learn from a train?" one hasid asked dubiously.

"That because of one second one can miss everything."

"And from the telegraph?"

"That every word is counted and charged."

"And the telephone?"

"That what we say here is heard there."

Bird Song

On the Sabbath of Song when the song from the Torah is
read, which Moses and Israel sang at the Red Sea, the rabbi
of Sadagora was asked: "Why is it customary to scatter buck-
wheat grits for the birds on this day?"

"A king," he replied, "had a little pavilion where he could
be quite alone. It was built well away from all his palaces.
Nobody was allowed to enter it but himself, nor could any of

his servants set foot in it. Only a songbird shared the room with him, and the king listened to his song which was dearer to him than all the music of his singers.

"In the hour when the waters of the Red Sea were divided, all the angels and seraphim sang praise to the Lord. But he was listening to the song of his little bird Israel.

"That is why we feed the birds on this day."

On the Sabbath of Song

On the Sabbath of Song when the song sung beside the Red Sea was read, the rabbi of Sadagora said:

"It is not written that they sang the song immediately after they crossed the sea. First they had to reach the rung of perfect faith, as it is written: . . . 'and they believed in the Lord, and in his servant Moses.' Only after that come the words: 'Then sang Moses and the children of Israel . . .' Only he who believes can sing the song."

All the Melodies

Rabbi Abraham Yaakov said:

"Every people has its own melody, and none sings that of another. But Israel sings all of them, in order to bring them to God. Thus in the Section of Songs all the creatures that live on the earth and all the birds utter each his own song, but Israel makes a song out of all of their songs in order to bring them to God."

Testimony

One Friday evening a group of so-called enlightened men entered the house of the rabbi of Sadagora uninvited, to hear him say the Kiddush and then to make fun of it. When the zaddik noticed this, he said: "The words from Genesis which we say to inaugurate the sabbath: 'And the heaven and the earth were finished,' are spoken here, as we all know, in testimony of the work of creation of the one and only God, and where could testimony be more in place than where there is denial? So let us testify in the face of these who deny that God created the world and that he guides it." He rose and said the Kiddush.

Everyone Has His Place

Rabbi Abraham was asked:

"Our sages say: 'And there is not a thing that has not its place.' And so man too has his own place. Then why do people sometimes feel so crowded?" He replied: "Because each wants to occupy the place of the other."

Sufferings and Pangs

Once the rabbi of Sadagora sat at his midday meal, and sighed, and did not eat. His sister asked him what was troubling him and repeated her question several times. At last he answered her with a question of his own: "Have you heard the reports about the sad condition of our brothers in Russia?"

"It seems to me," she answered, "that these sufferings might be the birth pangs that herald the coming of the Messiah."

The zaddik considered this. "Perhaps, perhaps," he finally said, "but when suffering is about to reach its peak, Israel cries out to God, saying it can bear it no longer, and God is merciful and hears them: he relieves the suffering and postpones redemption."

The Wandering Light

A friend once asked the rabbi of Sadagora: "How can this be? A number of holy men who lived before our time alluded to a date on which redemption was to come. The era they indicated has come and gone, but redemption has not come to pass."

The zaddik replied: "My father, may his memory be a blessing unto us, said this: 'In the Talmud we read that all the calculated dates of redemption have passed. But just as the Divine Presence left the sanctuary and went into exile in the course of ten journeys, so she cannot return all at once, and the light of redemption loiters between Heaven and earth. At every date it descended one rung. The light of redemption is now dwelling in the lowest Heaven, which is called the "curtain."' That is what my father said. But I say: the light of redemption is spread about us at the level of our heads. We do not notice it because our heads are bowed beneath the burden of exile. Oh, that God might lift up our heads!"

NAHUM OF STEPINESHT

Playing Checkers

On one of the days of Hanukkah, Rabbi Nahum, the son of the rabbi of Rizhyn, entered the House of Study at a time when he was not expected, and found his disciples playing checkers, as was the custom on those days. When they saw the zaddik they were embarrassed and stopped playing. But he gave them a kindly nod and asked: "Do you know the rules of the game of checkers?" And when they did not reply for shyness he himself gave the answer: "I shall tell you the rules of the game of checkers. The first is that one must not make two moves at once. The second is that one may only move forward and not backward. And the third is that when one has reached the last row, one may move to where he likes."

The Choice

Rabbi Nahum once said to the hasidim gathered about him: "If we could hang all our sorrows on pegs and were allowed to choose those we liked best, every one of us would take back his own, for all the rest would seem even more difficult to bear."

The Pious Man

In a certain city lived a man whose piety was so much talked of that the people had given him the byname of "the Pious One." He fell ill, and when his family heard that several people in the town were going to Rabbi Nahum to beg his blessing, they asked them to mention "the Pious One" when they got to the zaddik. The people agreed. Along with the slips of paper on which they had written their names they also gave Rabbi Nahum a slip bearing the name of the sick man, and told him this was a man who was famed far and wide for the austere life he led, and went by the name of "the Pious One." The rabbi commented: "I do not know what a pious man is, and I never learned anything about it from my father either. But I fancy it must have to do with a kind of cloak: the material is made of arrogance, the lining of grudges, and it is sewed with the threads of dejection."

DAVID MOSHE OF TCHORTKOV

Who Makes the Bands of Sleep to Fall

The hasidim tell this story:

When Rabbi David Moshe, a son of the rabbi of Rizhyn, was seven years old, a fire broke out in his father's house one night. The children were assembled, and David Moshe was found to be missing. His father sent a servant to fetch him. The servant found the boy lying in bed fully awake and asked whether he had not noticed that there was a fire. David Moshe said nothing but gave the servant to understand through signs that he had of course noticed it, but that since he had already said the nightly prayer beginning: ". . . who makes the bands of sleep to fall upon mine eyes," he did not want to interrupt his falling asleep and was certain he would be saved. While the servant was reporting this to the father, the fire died down.

The Faithful Servant

Rabbi Nahum of Stepinesht once said this of his brother, Rabbi David Moshe of Tchortkov:

"When my brother David Moshe opens the Book of Psalms and begins to recite the praises, God calls down to him: 'David Moshe my son, I am putting the whole world into your hands. Now do with it just as you like.' Oh, if he only gave me the world, I should know very well what to do with it! But David Moshe is so faithful a servant that when he gives the world back it is exactly as it was when he received it."

The Birth of a Melody

The rabbi of Tchortkov once said:

"Sometimes it happens that war breaks out between two kingdoms, and the war drags on for thirty years. Then out of the groans of those who fell in battle and the cries of the victors a melody is born so that it may be sung before the zaddik."

In a Thick Cloud

Rabbi David Moshe said:

"God says to Moses: 'Lo, I come unto thee in a thick cloud that the people may hear when I speak with thee.' There is always danger that the spirit of the zaddik may mount too high and lose touch with his generation. That is why God masses the dark cloud of sorrow over the zaddik and sets limits to his soul, and then the word which he received can get to the people again. But when sorrow descends upon the zaddik, he finds God even in the sorrow, as it is written: '. . . but Moses drew near unto the thick darkness where God was.' "

The Meekness of Moses

Once Rabbi David Moshe said with tears in his eyes:

"It is written that Moses was meek above all men. How are we to interpret this? He with whom God spoke face to face and whose work was so mighty—how could he think himself less than all others? The reason is this: In those forty days which Moses spent on the heights his body had become pure and luminous like that of the ministering angels. After that time he said to himself: 'Of what importance is it, if I, whose body was purified, give service to God? But if one of Israel who is still clad in his turbid flesh serves God—how much greater is he than I!' "

The Scroll of the Torah

Once a new Torah Scroll was being dedicated in the House of Prayer. Rabbi David Moshe held it in his hands and rejoiced in it. But since it was large and obviously very heavy, one of his hasidim went up to him and wanted to relieve him of it. "Once you hold it," said the rabbi, "it isn't heavy any more."

The Natural Way

Rabbi David Moshe once asked after one of his hasidim who was in great straits and in need of the help of God. The rabbi wanted to know whether that help had been accorded him. He was told that that was not the case, and that the nature of his trouble was such it was hardly possible to imagine that help could come in a natural way.

"Most likely the man has not perfect faith," said the zaddik. When he saw that the hasidim did not understand him, he continued: "At first glance it seems as though there were no reason to separate the natural way from the supernatural. This event was sent by God and that other too was sent by God—so why make a distinction? But the distinction is real nevertheless. You know, when the world was created, the flood of light was so unbounded that the world could not bear it, and the vessels broke. And so the light was limited in order that it might be received and contained. And that is the meaning of the natural way: the limiting of the abundance into the bounded measure of the vessels. Now such a vessel is the readiness of man, and the readiness of man is faith. But just as all men have not the same faith, and no man has the same faith at all times, so the bounds of the natural way differ. He whose faith is stronger, whose vessel is more spacious, is accorded a greater measure of the natural way, for that way reaches to the bounds of faith. Yesterday when your faith was small, you had to seek the help you had need of beyond nature, but today your faith has grown great and so all the help you are accorded is possible by the natural way. This is the meaning of what is told of Nahshon, the son of Amminadab: When Israel stood by the Red Sea he leaped into the waters before they were divided, and when they reached his throat, he said: 'Save me, O God, for the waters are come in even unto the soul.' He did not cry aloud, he spoke in a gentle voice, for his faith was great, and so everything that took place was natural."

Praise of This Generation

Once on the eighth day of the Feast of Booths there was great rejoicing at the table of the rabbi of Tchortkov. He laughed and asked: "Why are you people so exceedingly happy? Have you had a drop to drink?"

"There hasn't been time to drink," they replied. "We stayed in the House of Prayer for a long time, and then we came straight to the rabbi's table. We are just happy because of the festival and because we are with our rabbi."

"It is true," said he, "that the moment the people of Israel feel the least bit of revelation, they are filled with an overwhelming joy." And after a while he went on: "I say that this generation of ours from whom God hides in great secrecy is better than the wilderness generation. They were vouchsafed that great revelation, of which a serving-maid, so it is told, saw more than the prophet Ezekiel saw later on, and they had tremendous spiritual powers, and their master was Moses. But now God is hidden, and our strength is slight, and yet the moment we sense the least bit of revelation we are uplifted and full of joy. That is why I say: This generation is better than the wilderness generation."

FROM THE SCHOOL OF

RABBI SHMELKE OF NIKOLSBURG

MOSHE LEIB OF SASOV

By Night

In his youth Moshe Leib sometimes secretly changed his dress of an evening, left the house unobserved, and shared in the amusements of some young men of his own age, singing and dancing with them. They all loved him, and his most casual word was their law; yet he never commanded them. When he went to Nikolsburg to study with Rabbi Shmelke, they gave up their revelry because without him they took no pleasure in it. After many years, one of them who had been traveling in foreign lands stopped in Sasov on his way home. In the inn and on the street everyone he talked to told him about a wonderful man, the great zaddik Moshe Leib. When he heard the name, which was quite a common one, it did not occur to him that this could be his companion in the delights of days gone by, but his curiosity got the better of him. He went to the rabbi and instantly recognized him. And the thought crossed his mind: "My, my, he is certainly an adept at deceiving the world!" But as he looked into Rabbi Moshe Leib's face, a face he knew so well and that yet commanded his reverence, he realized the implication of his memories and suddenly understood that in those nights he and his friends had been guided without knowing it, and that time and again their celebrations had been uplifted under the influence of a law they could not grasp.

He bowed before the zaddik, who was regarding him with kindness, and said: "Master, I thank you."

The Rod

Moshe Leib's father was bitterly opposed to the hasidic way. When he learned that Moshe Leib had left the house without his knowledge and gone to Rabbi Shmelke's House of Study in Nikolsburg, he flew into a rage. He cut a vicious rod and kept it in his room against his son's return. Whenever he saw a more suitable twig on a tree, he cut a new rod which he thought would be more effective, and threw the old one away. Time passed and many rods were exchanged. In the course of a thorough house-cleaning a servant once took the rod up to the attic.

Soon afterward Moshe Leib asked his teacher's leave to absent himself for a short while and went home. When he saw his father jump at sight of him and start on a furious search, he went straight up to the attic, fetched the rod, and laid it down in front of the old man. The latter gazed into the grave and loving face of his son and was won over.

The Khalat

Moshe Leib spent seven years in the House of Study of the holy Rabbi Shmelke of Nikolsburg. When the seven years were up, the rabbi summoned him and said nothing but: "Now you may go home." Then he gave him three things to take with him: a ducat, a loaf of bread, and the kind of long white robe that is called khalat, and he added: "May the love of Israel enter your heart."

Moshe Leib walked all day and grew very tired. In the evening, as he approached a village where he intended to eat his bread and pass the night, he heard the sound of groaning and found that it came from behind a barred cellar window. He went up to it, spoke to the person inside, and soon learned that it was a Jewish innkeeper who had been imprisoned because he had not been able to pay his three hundred gulden rent to the lord of the estate. The first thing Moshe Leib did was to throw his loaf of bread through the bars.

Then without asking the way, just as though he were at home in that region, he made straight for the manor house, asked to be taken to the lord, and requested him to release the Jew. He offered his ducat as ransom. The manor lord merely looked over this impudent fellow who was attempting to settle a debt of three hundred gulden with a ducat, and sent him packing. But the instant Moshe Leib was outside, he was so overcome with the suffering of the imprisoned Jew that he burst in at the door again and cried: "But you must let him go! Take my ducat and let the man go free!"

Now in those days every lord in the state of Poland was a king on his own estate and had the power of life and death. So the lord ordered his servants to seize Moshe Leib and throw him into the kennel. And because Moshe Leib saw death in the eyes of the dogs who rushed at him, he quickly put on his white khalat, so as to die in a festive robe. But at sight of the khalat the dogs backed toward the wall and howled. When the lord entered the kennel, Moshe Leib was still leaning close to the door, and the dogs stood around in a wide circle, howling and shivering. He was told to get out and be off, but Moshe Leib insisted: "Not until you take my ducat and let the man go free!" Then the lord took the ducat and himself went to the house where the Jew was imprisoned, opened the cellar door, and bade the man go home in peace. And Moshe Leib continued his journey.

The rabbi of Tchortkov loved to tell this story, and when he had finished he always added: "Oh, where can that kind of khalat be found!"

A Jew Lives Here!

When Moshe Leib visited Rabbi Elimelekh for the first time, his host honored him at the sabbath meal by asking him to say Torah. Now on this particular sabbath the passage of the Scriptures to be read dealt with God's smiting the Egyptians and passing over the houses of the Israelites. Moshe Leib said: "This cannot possibly mean that God passed over a certain place, because there is no place where he is not. But when he passed through the Egyptians' houses, and saw the corruption of their souls, and then came to a house full of piety and goodness, he was overjoyed and cried: 'A Jew lives here!' "

When Rabbi Elimelekh heard this explanation, he jumped on the table, danced upon it, and sang over and over: "A Jew lives here! A Jew lives here!"

When Moshe Leib was young, he and his wife and children lived in great poverty. One of his neighbors who wished him well offered him a sum of money so that he might ride to market, buy goods, and sell them in his home town. Rabbi Moshe Leib rode to market with the other dealers. When they arrived at their destination they all attended to their business, but he went to the House of Study. When he left it and went to the market place, without realizing how many hours had passed, they were just getting ready to start for home, and when he said he wanted to buy some goods, they laughed at him. So he went home with the rest.

His children were waiting for him in front of his house and called: "What did you bring us?" At these words he fainted.

Just as Moshe Leib regained consciousness, the well-to-do neighbor arrived to inquire how he had made out. He saw how wretched Moshe Leib looked and asked: "What's the matter, Rabbi? Have you lost the money? But don't let that worry you: I'll give you more." Rabbi Moshe Leib only said: "Oh, what shall I do if in the future I come home, and they ask, 'What have you brought us?'"

"Well, if that's the way it is," said the neighbor, "you had better carry on your business at home."

After this, he made known to the world that Rabbi Moshe Leib was a zaddik.

How Long?

Long after Rabbi Moshe Leib's death, his son, Rabbi Shmelke of Sasov, was asked to tell about his father. He said: "He died when I was still a boy and at that time I did not have the understanding to grasp his actions. But there is something I can tell you anyway. I must have been about five years old. It was New Year's and my father was praying at the reader's desk. I had crept under his prayer shawl and heard how in the middle of his low-voiced Prayer of Benedictions he complained to God in the half-coaxing, half-affectionate tone of a child and the language used by the common people. He said something like this: 'Dear God, please send us the Messiah sometime! How long are you going to let us suffer in the dark exile? We can't stand it any more!' "

How a Thief Instructed the Rabbi of Sasov

The rabbi of Sasov once traveled about trying to collect money to ransom persons in the debtors' prison, but he did not succeed in getting together the sum he needed. Then he regretted having wasted time he might have spent studying and praying, and resolved that henceforth he would stay home. On the same day he heard that a Jew who had stolen an article of clothing had been soundly beaten and put in jail. Rabbi Moshe Leib interceded with the judge and gained the thief's release.

When the zaddik went to fetch the thief from jail, he warned him: "Remember the beating they gave you and don't ever do anything like that again!"

"Why not?" said the thief. "If you don't succeed the first time, you may succeed the next."

"If that's the case," said the rabbi to himself, "then I must keep trying at my job, too."

Interruption

One midnight when Rabbi Moshe Leib was absorbed in the mystic teachings, he heard a knock at his window. A drunken peasant stood outside and asked to be let in and given a bed for the night. For a moment the zaddik's heart was full of anger and he said to himself: "How can a drunk have the insolence to ask to be let in, and what business has he in this house!" But then he said silently in his heart: "And what business has he in God's world? But if God gets along with him, can I reject him?" He opened the door at once, and prepared a bed.

Imitatio Dei

The rabbi of Sasov once gave the last money he had in his pocket to a man of ill repute. His disciples threw it up to him. He answered them: "Shall I be more finicky than God, who gave it to me?"

How the Rabbi of Sasov Learned How to Love

Rabbi Moshe Leib told this story:

"How to love men is something I learned from a peasant. He was sitting in an inn along with other peasants, drinking. For a long time he was as silent as all the rest, but when he was moved by the wine, he asked one of the men seated beside him: 'Tell me, do you love me or don't you love me?' The other replied: 'I love you very much.' But the first peasant replied: 'You say that you love me, but you do not know what I need. If you really loved me, you would know.' The other had not a word to say to this, and the peasant who had put the question fell silent again.

"But I understood. To know the needs of men and to bear the burden of their sorrow—that is the true love of men."

His Own Suffering

Whenever the rabbi of Sasov saw anyone's suffering either of spirit or of body, he shared it so earnestly that the other's suffering became his own. Once someone expressed his astonishment at this capacity to share in another's troubles.

"What do you mean 'share'?" said the rabbi. "It is my own sorrow; how can I help but suffer it?"

At the Fair

Rabbi Moshe Leib used to go to the fair and keep a sharp lookout for anyone who might need his help. On one such occasion the traders had left the stalls to watch the performance of a troop of jugglers or some other spectacle, and their cattle remained in the market place, untended. The calves were thirsty and hung their heads. When the rabbi noticed this he took a bucket and watered the animals as if that had been his job all his life. Just then one of the traders returned, and when he saw a man tending the cattle of the others he asked him to see to his cattle, too. They were standing in one of the side streets, he said, and he wouldn't argue over the cattle tender's fee. The rabbi obeyed and stayed on his job until he had finished.

The Love of Man

The rabbi of Sasov used to visit all the sick boys in the town, sit at their bedside, and nurse and take care of them. Once he said: "He who is not willing to suck the pus from the sore of a child sick with the plague has not climbed even halfway up the mountain to the love of his fellow men."

The Delay

On the eve of the Day of Atonement, when the time had come to say Kol Nidre, all the hasidim were gathered together in the House of Prayer waiting for the rabbi. But time passed and he did not come. Then one of the women of the congregation said to herself: "I guess it will be quite a while before they begin, and I was in such a hurry and my child is alone in the house. I'll just run home and look after it to make sure it hasn't awakened. I can be back in a few minutes."

She ran home and listened at the door. Everything was quiet. Softly she turned the knob and put her head into the room— and there stood the rabbi holding her child in his arms. He had heard the child crying on his way to the House of Prayer, and had played with it and sung to it until it fell asleep.

Lamentations at Midnight

Rabbi Moshe Leib was unusually tall and broad but a protracted disease was sapping his strength. However, even when he had retired exhausted with pain, he rose from his bed every midnight, left his room wide-awake and with a firm step, and recited the lamentation over Jerusalem. That was why his hasidim said that the words in the Song of Songs: "Hark! my beloved knocketh," applied to him. For it was clear that the voice of the mournful Divine Presence was knocking at his heart and waking him.

Rabbi Hirsh of Zhydatchov had heard of the rabbi of Sasov's strange doings at midnight. Once when he was a guest in his house he hid so that he might watch him. At midnight he saw the rabbi of Sasov put on peasant's dress, go into the snow-covered yard, fetch a load of wood out of the cellar, lash the logs together, and hoist them on his back. Then he walked away and Rabbi Hirsh followed him in the crackling cold of the winter night to the end of the town. There Rabbi Moshe stopped in front of a miserable hut and unloaded the wood. His disciple crept up to a back window and looked into a bare room. The stove was out. On the bed lay a woman pressing a newborn child to her breast with a gesture of utter despair.

But at that moment the rabbi of Sasov entered the room. Rabbi Hirsh saw him go up to the woman and heard him address her in Ruthenian: "I have a load of wood for sale and don't want to carry it any further. Will you buy it at a bargain price?" The woman answered: "I haven't a penny in the house." But the rabbi refused to be put off. "I'll come back for the money some other time," he said. "If you'll just take the wood!" The woman objected: "What shall I do with the wood! I can't chop it up myself and there isn't an ax anyway." The rabbi of Sasov replied, "You just let me take care of that," left the room, took his ax, and chopped the wood into small pieces.

And while he was chopping, Rabbi Hirsh heard him reciting that part of the Lamentations at Midnight associated with the name of our Mother Rachel. He caught the words: "Shake thyself from the dust; arise, and sit down, O Jerusalem!" Then the rabbi took the wood, stooped in order to enter through the low door, and made a fire in the stove. While he put in the wood, he softly recited the other part of the lamentations associated with the name of our Mother Leah, and ended with: "Thou wilt arise, and have compassion upon Zion; build Thou Jerusalem." Then he left the room and went home, walking very quickly.

Below and Above

The rabbi of Sasov was entertaining two singers at his house. Their singing was excellent, but—as is so often the case with singers—they were mischievous fellows. Once his wife put some coffee on the table for him, but while he was getting ready the two of them drank it up and filled the pot with water. His wife did not have another warm drink to serve him, for things were none too plentiful in that house. She grew very angry at the ne'er-do-wells and cried: "What do you need singers for! All they give you is trouble!" He said: "Their beautiful songs waken my heart so that I can hear the angels sing."

God and Man

A woman who lived next door to Rabbi Moshe Leib lost one child after another before they were a year old. Once when she was in the zaddik's house, she cried aloud: "A God who gives you children just to take them away again is not good: he is a cruel God!" Rabbi Leib's wife scolded her: "That's no way to talk! What you should say is: 'We cannot fathom God's mercy, and what he does is well done.' "

"Oh, no!" said the rabbi, who heard them talking from where he sat in his room and came out to join them. "You must not be resigned. Take courage, woman, and take strength. A year from now you will have a son, and in time to come I shall lead him under the bridal canopy." And so it was.

When It Is Good to Deny the Existence of God

Rabbi Moshe Leib said:

"There is no quality and there is no power of man that was created to no purpose. And even base and corrupt qualities can be uplifted to serve God. When, for example, haughty self-assurance is uplifted it changes into a high assurance in the ways of God. But to what end can the denial of God have been created? This too can be uplifted through deeds of charity. For if someone comes to you and asks your help, you shall not turn him off with pious words, saying: 'Have faith and take your troubles to God!' You shall act as if there were no God, as if there were only one person in all the world who could help this man—only yourself."

Pouring the Mead

Rabbi Hayyim of Zans told this story:

"When I was a little under three, a great fire broke out in Brody, the town where I was born, and my nurse took me and fled to Sasov. She stayed there with me over the last days of the Feast of Booths. Now on the Day of Rejoicing in the Law, Rabbi Moshe Leib of Sasov was in the habit of going to the market place together with his entire congregation. This time, too, tables and benches had been set up, and they all sat around the tables while the rabbi—blessed be his memory!— took a pitcher of mead, walked from one to the other, and poured. The women came to the market place to watch, and on this occasion my nurse joined them, carrying me in her arms. The rabbi said, 'The women shall stand to one side,' and they did so, my nurse along with them. At that I craned my head across my nurse's shoulder and watched. I watched carefully and I still know everything I saw."

A zaddik who was among his listeners asked: "Does the rabbi really remember how he craned his head across his nurse's shoulder?" Rabbi Hayyim replied: "It was imposed on me to remember, for I had got a beautiful little soul and if I had not spoiled it later on, it would have amounted to something. So I was given this memory to keep on my way."

The Dance of Healing

News was brought to Rabbi Moshe Leib that his friend the rabbi of Berditchev had fallen ill. On the sabbath he said his name over and over and prayed for his recovery. Then he put on new shoes made of morocco leather, laced them up tight and danced.

A zaddik who was present said: "Power flowed forth from his dancing. Every step was a powerful mystery. An unfamiliar light suffused the house, and everyone watching saw the heavenly hosts join in his dance."

The Bridal Dance

A hasid related:

"I was at the wedding of Rabbi Moshe Leib's grandson and there were many guests. When they formed the ring for the bridal dance, a man in a short peasant's smock with a short peasant's pipe in his mouth suddenly leaped into the ring and danced alone in the very middle. I was just about to take him by the sleeve, for I thought he must be out of his

90

mind to break into a circle of zaddikim; but when I saw them all watching him in silence, I let him be. After the dance, I found out that it was the rabbi."

This Is the Time to Dance

A zaddik who was near death got up and danced. And when those around him tried to get him to stop, he said: "This is the time to dance." Then he related: "When Rabbi Uri of Strelisk was traveling around to collect money for some charitable purpose, he called on the rabbi of Sasov. 'I have no money,' said the rabbi, 'but I'll dance a bit for you.' He danced the whole night through and Rabbi Uri did not take his eyes off him, for in every step was a holy meaning. When morning dawned Rabbi Moshe Leib said: 'Now I'll go and collect some money in the market places and streets.'

"He left and did not return until after two days. When they asked him where he had been, he said: 'When I was young, I once needed money to ransom prisoners and started out to collect it with a boy who was to show me where the rich people lived. The boy did his job so cleverly and well that I soon had the required sum. Because of this I promised him that I should once dance at his wedding. Now when I arrived in Zlotchov I heard the sound of gay music, followed it, and learned that the boy I had traveled with was celebrating his wedding. And so I danced and made merry with the merry until now.'

"And that is why I say," the zaddik who was telling the story added, "when they come to you with a demand, it is time to dance."

How the Rabbi of Sasov Helped a Woman Bear Her Child

The story is told:
In a certain village a woman had been lying in labor for days, and the hour of her delivery would not come. They sent a messenger to the rabbi of Sasov to ask him to beg God to have mercy on her. At dead of night the man arrived in the city where he knew no one, not even the zaddik, and could not find his way in the dark. Only one house was still

lit. The messenger knocked. An old man opened the door, poured him a glass of brandy to refresh him, and asked why he had come. When he heard the cause of the journey, he said: "It is too late to go there now. You just sleep here and in the morning I'll take you to the rabbi." He gave him something to eat and prepared a bed for him.

The man woke up early in the morning and was sorry that he had given in to his own weariness and the words of the old man, and postponed his pressing errand. Just then his host came up to him and said: "Be of good cheer! I have just learned that the woman has given birth to a healthy boy. Go to the nearby villages and tell her relatives." When the man was outside the house, he discovered from the questions people asked him that he had been a guest of the rabbi; but he did not venture to go back in.

The Way of Life

Rabbi Moshe Leib said:

"The way in this world is like the edge of a blade. On this side is the netherworld, and on that side is the netherworld, and the way of life lies in between."

An Hour

Rabbi Moshe Leib said:

"A human being who has not a single hour for his own every day is no human being."

Depending on God

Rabbi Moshe Leib said:

"How easy it is for a poor man to depend on God! What else has he to depend on? And how hard it is for a rich man to depend on God! All his possessions call out to him: 'Depend on us!'"

Generations

The rabbi of Rizhyn related:

"Once when the holy Baal Shem Tov wanted to save the life of a sick boy he was very much attached to, he ordered a candle made of pure wax, carried it to the woods, fastened it to a tree, and lit it. Then he pronounced a long prayer. The candle burned all night. When morning came, the boy was well.

"When my grandfather, the Great Maggid, who was the holy Baal Shem's disciple, wanted to work a like cure, he no longer knew the secret meaning of the words on which he had to concentrate. He did as his master had done and called on his name. And his efforts met with success.

"When Rabbi Moshe Leib, the disciple of the disciple of the Great Maggid, wanted to work a cure of this kind, he said: 'We have no longer the power even to do what was done. But I shall relate the story of how it was done, and God will help.' And his efforts met with success."

The Love of Israel

Rabbi Moshe Leib wanted most earnestly to acquire only one of all the virtues of his teacher Rabbi Shmelke of Nikolsburg: his love of Israel. And he did acquire it and in abundance. For when he fell very ill and lay on his bed for two and a half years, racked with pain, he grew more and more certain that he was suffering for the sake of Israel, and his pain did not grow less, but it was transfigured.

The Wedding Tune

Once Rabbi Moshe Leib married off two orphans and saw to it that they did not feel deserted on their wedding day. When the two young people stood under the bridal canopy, the rabbi's face was transfigured with radiance, for at that moment he felt himself a father twice over. He listened to the tune the musicians were playing. Then he said to the people standing around him: "I wish it were vouchsafed me to go to my eternal home on the day destined to the sound of this tune."

After many years, when this hour and these words were long forgotten, a number of musicians were traveling to play at a wedding in Brody, on a snowy winter's day. Suddenly the horses began to pull harder and broke into a rapid trot. The driver could not slow them up. They went faster and faster, jolted the sleigh worse and worse, and ran unerringly toward some goal. They finally stopped at a cemetery. The musicians saw many people gathered there, and asked where they were, and who was being buried. When they heard the name of Rabbi Moshe Leib, they remembered how years ago when they were young they had played before him at the wedding of the two orphans. And now the people too recalled the incident and they all cried: "Play the wedding tune!"

After Death

It is told:

When Rabbi Moshe Leib had died he said to himself: "Now I am free from fulfilling the commandments. What can I do now that will be in obedience to the will of God?" He thought for a while. "It must surely be God's will that I be punished for my countless sins!" And immediately he began to run with all his might and jumped straight into hell. Heaven was very much perturbed at this, and soon the prince of hell was told not to stoke his fires while the rabbi of Sasov was down there. Thereupon the prince begged the zaddik to take himself off to paradise, for this was clearly not the place for him. It just would not do to call a holiday in hell for his sake.

"If that is the case," said Moshe Leib, "I won't stir from here until all the souls are allowed to go with me. On earth I made it my business to ransom prisoners, and so I certainly will not let this big crowd suffer in this prison." And they say that he had his way.

The Dancing Bear

Some guests who had attended the wedding of the daughter of Rabbi Shmelke of Sasov, who was Rabbi Moshe Leib's son, paid a visit to Rabbi Meir of Primishlan on their way home. He questioned them eagerly as to what special thing they had seen at the celebration, refused to be satisfied with what they told him, and kept on asking: "And what else happened?" Finally they said: "While the traditional dances with the bride and groom were going on, an enormous man completely disguised as a bear leaped into the circle and did a most magnificent bear's dance. Everybody marveled at his really wonderful bounds, and there was a great clapping of hands. And then just as suddenly as he had come, he was gone. No one knew him."

"I'll tell you," said Rabbi Meir. "That was none other than our holy teacher Rabbi Moshe Leib of Sasov—may his memory help us—who came down from the uppermost paradise to rejoice with his family."

His Heart

Once Rabbi Bunam was asked: "Have you ever known a zaddik whose heart was broken and crushed and yet sound and whole?" Rabbi Bunam replied: "Yes, I did know such a zaddik. It was Rabbi Moshe Leib of Sasov."

He Who Lives Forever

The hour before he died Rabbi Shmelke of Sasov saw his father Rabbi Moshe Leib and his great teacher Rabbi Mikhal, the maggid of Zlotchov, standing beside him. Then he began to sing the hymn: "Glory and faithfulness are His who lives forever." When he came to the verse, "Cognition and expression are His who lives forever," he stopped singing and said: "When a man approaches his end, when the power of expression and the power of cognition are being taken from him, he shall give these two, cognition and expression, to Him who lives forever."

MENAHEM MENDEL OF KOSOV AND HAYYIM
OF KOSOV

"Wherefore?"

Once when they asked Rabbi Mendel of Kosov with great insistence, "Why doesn't the Messiah come?" he replied: "It is written: 'Wherefore did the son of Jesse not come neither yesterday nor today?' Why does he not come? Because today we are no different from what we were yesterday."

Destroying a Man

A deputation came to Rabbi Mendel of Kosov to complain of a certain slaughterer in their town. After they had enumerated a long list of misdeeds the people asked the zaddik to relieve this objectionable person of his office. But one who had come along with the rest disputed their testimony, saying that it was slander and sprang from hatred. Rabbi Mendel decided in favor of the slaughterer. The others reproached him bitterly because he had believed the words of one single man and ignored the majority.

"The Scriptures relate," he said, "that God bade Abraham offer his son as a burnt-offering, and Abraham prepared to obey. But an angel stopped him and instantly he heeded the angel's voice even though God had not himself revoked his command. What the Torah teaches us thereby is this: None but God can command us to destroy a man, and if the very smallest angel comes after the command has been given and cautions us: 'Lay not thy hand upon . . . ' we must obey him."

The Right Kind of Help

Among Rabbi Mendel's hasidim was a man by the name of Rabbi Moshe, who was both well-to-do and fond of doing good deeds. And then the wheel of fortune turned—to use a popular phrase—and he lost all his money and fell into debt. He went to the zaddik and told him about his predicament. "Go to my brother-in-law, the Seraph of Strelisk," said Rabbi Mendel, "and pour your heart out to him." The man did so. When Rabbi Uri of Strelisk had heard his story he said: "I shall take the bath of immersion for you and the merit of this bath will accrue to your benefit." The man returned to his master and reported what had happened. "Go back to my brother-in-law," said the rabbi of Kosov, "and say to him: 'The bath of immersion will not serve to pay my creditors.' "

The man rode to Strelisk a second time and said what he had been told to. "Very well, my son," the Seraph replied. "In that case I shall also dedicate to your welfare the merit of the phylacteries which I shall put on today." When the man repeated this in Kosov, Rabbi Mendel said: "Give my brother-in-law this message from me: 'The phylacteries can't get rid of tormentors, either.' "

The man did as he was bidden. The Seraph reflected. "Well," said he, "if that is the case, I shall do my utmost for you. I shall dedicate to you the merit of all the prayers I say today, and thus from this hour on the three merits will unite in giving you help." Rabbi Moshe returned to Kosov and gave his report.

"Go," said the zaddik, and he spoke as softly as always, only more slowly, and when he spoke slowly the effect on those who were listening was greater than if he had raised his voice, "go, speak to my brother-in-law in my name and say: 'All this will not settle a single debt.' "

When the Seraph received this message, he immediately put on his fur coat and set out for Kosov. The moment he arrived at his brother-in-law's he asked: "What do you want of me?" "What I want," said Rabbi Mendel, "is for both of us to travel around for a number of weeks, and collect money from our people. For it is written: 'Thou shalt uphold him.' " And that is what they did.

The Snuffbox

Once when Rabbi David of Zablotov, the son of Rabbi Mendel of Kosov, was visiting Rabbi Zevi Hirsh in Zhydatchov, he happened to pull his snuffbox out of his pocket to take a pinch. Hardly had Rabbi Hirsh laid eyes on the box when he asked: "Where did you get that?"

"From my father," said Rabbi David.

"This box," said the rabbi of Zhydatchov, "conjures up for me the Tent of Meeting, and it conjures up all the secret holy meanings which Bezalel the builder had in mind when he put up the Tent of Meeting."

Rabbi David replied: "They told me this about my father: When he had this box made he gave the silversmith a piece of solid silver and told him exactly what to do. He even told him how many times he was to strike with his hammer— just so many and no more. And he stood by the entire time and saw to it that everything was done just as he said."

"Now everything is perfectly clear," said the rabbi of Zhydatchov.

The Gift to His Adversary

A Jew from Kosov who was known to be opposed to the hasidic way once came to Rabbi Mendel and complained that he was about to marry off his daughter and did not have the money for her dowry. He begged the rabbi for advice on how to earn the sum he needed. "How much do you need?" asked the rabbi. It came to a few hundred gulden. Rabbi Mendel opened a drawer in his desk, emptied it, and gave the money to the man.

Soon after, the zaddik's brother learned what had occurred. He came and took the zaddik to task, saying that whenever something was needed in his own house he said he had no money to spare, yet now he had given such a large sum to an adversary. "Someone was here before you," said Rabbi Mendel, "and said exactly the same thing, except that he expressed himself much better than you."

"Who was it?" asked his brother.

Rabbi Mendel replied: "It was Satan."

Dancing and Pain

On every sabbath eve Rabbi Hayyim of Kosov, the son of Rabbi Mendel, danced before his assembled disciples. His face was aflame and they all knew that every step was informed with sublime meanings and effected sublime things.

Once while he was in the midst of dancing, a heavy bench fell on his foot and he had to pause because of the pain. Later they asked him about it. "It seems to me," he said, "that the pain made itself felt because I interrupted the dance."

In Every Generation

One evening several of Rabbi Hayyim of Kosov's hasidim sat together in his House of Study and told one another stories about zaddikim, above all about the Baal Shem Tov. And because both the telling and the listening were very sweet to them, they were at it even after midnight. Then one of them told still another story about the Baal Shem Tov. When he had ended, another sighed from the bottom of his heart. "Alas!" said he, half to himself. "Where could we find such a man today?"

At that instant, they heard steps coming down the wooden stair which led from the zaddik's room. The door opened and Rabbi Hayyim appeared on the threshold, in the short jacket he usually wore in the evening. "Fools," he said softly, "he is present in every generation, he, the Baal Shem Tov, only that in those days he was manifest while now he is hidden." He closed the door and went back up the stair. The hasidim sat together in silence.

YITZHAK EISIK OF KALEV

The Song of the Gooseboy

Rabbi Leib, the son of Sarah, the roving zaddik who never stayed in one place for any length of time, was always on the search for souls, the souls of the dead which longed for redemption, and living souls which needed to be discovered and uplifted.

The story goes that once when he was in the north of Russia, he heard of a holy soul in the south of Hungary which was hiding rather than becoming manifest in the body of a boy. He immediately set out on one of his wonderfully swift journeys. When he arrived in the little town he had been told of, he prayed in the House of Prayer and then went into the adjoining wood and walked until he came to a clearing which was threaded by a stream. There he found a boy of about eight walking slowly along the bank with eyes and ears only for his flock, which obeyed his every whistle and gesture. Rabbi Leib followed unobserved, and soon the boy began to hum a little song, repeating the few words over and over:

> "Shekhinah, Shekhinah, how far, how far!
> Galut, Galut, how endless you are!
> But if the Galut were taken away,
> We could be together, together to stay."

After listening for a while, Rabbi Leib approached the boy and asked him where he had learned his song. "Why, all the herdsmen here sing it," answered the boy. "Do they really sing those words?" the zaddik insisted. "Well," said the boy, "they say 'beloved' instead of 'Shekhinah,' and 'wood' instead of 'Galut,' but that's just stupid. For who could our beloved be if not the Shekhinah and every child knows that the wood which separates us from her is the Galut, so why not say so in the first place?"

Then Rabbi Leib went with the boy and his flock of geese to the poor widow who was his mother and offered to take her son with him and see to it that he grew up to be a rabbi. He brought him to Rabbi Shmelke of Nikolsburg and the boy grew up in his House of Study. Rabbi Shmelke's melodies formed his soul, but to the end of his days he sang to himself the songs of the Hungarian herdsmen, changing only a word here and there.

Miriam's Well

This story was told by a grandson of Jacob Fisch, a man both rich and devout, whom the Baal Shem had blessed with both hands and wished a very long life, and who actually lived to the age of one hundred and thirteen years, his face remaining youthful to the day of his death.

"My grandfather's estate was close to the town of Kalev. Once in the late afternoon before the Day of Atonement, when everybody was already assembled in the House of Prayer, wearing shrouds and reciting the Prayer of Purity with much weeping, the rabbi of Kalev called my grandfather and said to him: 'Rabbi Jacob, have your horses harnessed; let us go for a drive.' My grandfather was very much surprised, but since he was well acquainted with the zaddik's ways he said nothing, but sent word home to have the carriage brought around. They got in and drove across my grandfather's fields. In one place there was a narrow body of water. Quickly the rabbi took off his clothes and immersed himself again and again. My grandfather stood beside him and did not know what to do. But the zaddik was already putting on his clothes. They drove straight to the House of Prayer, and the zaddik went up to the reader's desk.

"My grandfather could not get over his amazement, for never before had he seen any water in that place in his fields. When the Day of Atonement was over, he went back there and looked around, but nowhere could he find a trace of the stream. Then he went to the zaddik and said: 'Rabbi, you know that I never ask you about your own concerns, but now I beg you to explain to me what happened.'

" 'Rabbi Jacob,' answered the zaddik, 'if Miriam's Well, which accompanied Israel in the wilderness, comes through our part of the country unexpectedly, why in the world do you just

stand there instead of immersing yourself in it along with
me?' "

Immersion without Water

Once on the afternoon before the Day of Atonement, when
the time for the ritual bath had come, the rabbi of Kalev
went to the stream near which the town is situated. But instead
of immersing himself in it he lay down on the grassy bank
and said: "Oh, what a good place to sleep!" When it was
almost evening, and the hasidim who had accompanied him
had all dipped down in the stream, he awoke and stretched.
Then without immersing himself, but looking and moving
as though he were quickened with new life, as he always
appeared after the bath, he returned to the town with the rest.

Enduring Pain

From youth until old age Rabbi Yitzhak Eisik suffered from
an ailment which was known to involve very great pain. His
physician once asked him how he managed to endure such
pain without complaining or groaning. He replied: "You
would understand that readily enough if you thought of the
pain as scrubbing and soaking the soul in a strong solution.
Since this is so, one cannot do otherwise than accept such
pain with love and not grumble. After a time, one gains the
strength to endure the present pain. It is always only the question of a moment, for the pain which has passed is no longer
present, and who would be so foolish as to concern himself
with future pain!"

Like Lye

One sabbath, after Rabbi Yitzhak Eisik had sung the song,
"When I the sabbath keep," which contains the words: "That
is why I wash my heart like lye," he paused and said: "One
does not wash lye; one washes with lye!" Then he replied
to his own objection: "But the holiness of the holy sabbath
can make a heart so pure that it becomes strong enough to
purify other hearts, as lye purifies objects."
The disciple who related this incident, later—when he had
become a zaddik—told his own hasidim: "Do you know how
I became a Jew? My teacher, the holy rabbi of Kalev, took

the soul out of my body and soaped and beat it and rinsed it and dried it and rolled it, like women washing clothes at a brook, and then he put this cleansed soul back into me."

"And the Fire Abated"

The tale is told:

The rabbi of Kalev once spent the sabbath in a nearby village as the guest of one of the hasidim. When the hour to receive the sabbath had come, someone suddenly screamed, and a servant rushed in and cried that the barn in which the grain was stored was on fire. The owner wanted to run out, but the rabbi took him by the hand. "Stay!" he said. "I am going to tell you a story." The hasid stayed.

"When our master Rabbi Zusya was young," said the zaddik, "he stoked the stoves in the house of the Great Maggid, for this duty was always assigned to the youngest disciples. Once when he was saying the psalms with great fervor just before the coming of the sabbath, he was startled by screams from within the house. Sparks had fallen from the stove which he had filled with wood, and since no one was in the living room, a fire had started.

" 'Zusya!' he was reproached. 'There's a fire!'

" 'No matter,' he replied. 'Is it not written: And the fire abated!' At that very same moment the fire abated."

The rabbi of Kalev fell silent. The hasid, whom he still held by the hand, did not dare move. A moment passed and some-one called in at the window that the fire in the barn had gone out.

The Visit on the Seder Evening

They tell this story:

Reizel, the daughter of Rabbi Zevi Hirsh of Zhydatchov, who had married a son of the rabbi of Kalev, lived with him in her father's house. Once they received an invitation to spend the Passover in Kalev. She was against it since she did not want to be absent from her father's Seder, but her husband kept urging her to accept, until finally she consented.

The customs in her father-in-law's house were different from those she was familiar with. But what vexed her more than anything else was that the rabbi did not sit down at the table early on the Seder evening as her father did, but walked back and forth in the room for a long time without saying a word. Suddenly he threw open the window. A carriage drawn by two great white horses stopped in front of the house. In it were three men and four women of princely appearance. The rabbi went out to them. They embraced and kissed him, exchanged a few words: then the coachman cracked his whip and the carriage was gone. The rabbi re-entered the room, closed the window and sat down at the table. Reizel did not dare to question him.

When the festival was over and she was back home, she told her father all that had happened. "You must know," he instructed her, "that those were the patriarchs and the matriarchs. The holy rabbi did not want to sit down to the Seder before the advent of salvation, and he besieged the upper worlds with his prayers. And so the fathers and the mothers had to appear and tell him that the time was not yet come."

FROM THE SCHOOL OF

RABBI ELIMELEKH OF LIZHENSK

ABRAHAM YEHOSHUA HESHEL OF APT

Knowing the Future

When young Heshel walked across the field, he heard the future in the rustle of growing things; and when he walked through the street, he heard the future in men's footsteps. But when he fled from the world and withdrew to the silence of his room, his own limbs told him the future. Then he began to fear, being uncertain whether he could keep to the true way now that he knew where his feet were taking him. So he gathered courage and prayed that this knowledge be taken from him. And God in his mercy granted his prayer.

The Bribe

In his youth Rabbi Abraham Yehoshua was head of the law court in Kolbishov, and there were five cities in his district. Once he was to decide a lawsuit together with two judges who had been bribed. Since he obstinately opposed all their suggestions, they finally advised the person who had bribed them, who knew as well as they that the rabbi was incorruptible, to slip a considerable sum of money into the pocket of the special coat which Rabbi Abraham Yehoshua wore only on the day of the New Moon. The man took their advice and managed it unobserved. At the next court session the rabbi felt himself inclining to the opinion of his fellow judges. For a while he was silent. Then he postponed decision for a day, went to his room and cried his heart out to God. On the day of the New Moon he put on his special coat and found the money. He summoned the man and forced him to confess what he had done.

Whenever the rabbi of Apt related this incident, he would cite a verse from the fifth book of Moses: "For a gift doth blind the eyes of the wise, and pervert the words of the righteous."

Rabbi Shmelke of Sasov, the son of Rabbi Moshe Leib of Sasov, was still a child at the time of his father's death. Once when he was a young man, he visited the rabbi of Apt. In honor of his guest the rabbi had the candles lit in the House of Study and received him with such kindness that the youth was embarrassed. The moment he had rather reluctantly seated himself in the armchair drawn up for him, the rabbi of Apt turned to him and told him the following:

"I owe it to your father that I began to serve God in the right way. At that time I was rav in the little town of Kolbishov and thought the finest thing in the world was to learn for the sake of learning. One afternoon when I was sitting over my books I heard a carriage drive past. I left the room and found two men just getting off, the older short and frail, the younger a veritable giant. They walked up to me, but since I resented being disturbed in my studies I did not ask who they were. I only offered them some pastries and a sweet liqueur and went back to my books. They sat and talked to each other without paying any attention to me.

"I took myself firmly in hand and tried to go on studying without being distracted, yet I could not help hearing some of their words, especially as there was something majestic and solemn in their voices and the expression of their faces. They were indeed speaking of solemn matters, apparently continuing a discussion they had begun on their journey. But in my soul I rejected the idea of having anything to do with it, for I said to myself: 'That is not my way—so why should I concern myself with it?' Later I accompanied them to the House of Prayer. After the prayer, they asked me whether I could put them up for the night. At that time there was not much room in my house, but it was impossible to turn away men such as these—that was perfectly clear to me. So I said yes, served them coffee, and went on studying. And the same thing happened as before: they continued their discussion and my mind was torn between trying to concentrate on my reading and fighting against listening. Then I prepared a place for them to sleep and I too lay down. Around midnight

I rose as always and began to study. In the next room I heard them talking about sublime matters.

"Early in the morning they came to bid me farewell and asked me in a way that seemed quite casual what passage in the Talmud I was studying at the moment. When I told them, they began to discuss that passage. The older man made a remark about it, the younger raised an objection, and when half an hour was up, between them they had completely illuminated the passage and I realized that I had not understood it properly until then. Then to cite an example for something he had said the older man told a story about the Baal Shem Tov and in the same way the younger told one too.

"When they had finished their stories they took leave of me, and even then I did not ask them anything, for I was glad to continue my studies undisturbed. But as, in my usual custom, I was walking up and down the balcony a little before going to the House of Prayer, I suddenly thought: 'Why didn't I ask those men who they were and why they came?' And then, bit by bit, the words I had caught while I was studying came back to me and formed a connected whole. Only then did I know with certainty that what they had said had been sublime. From that time on I could do nothing but think of them. I repeated their words to myself and saw that they were intended to be properly learned. But then I noticed that from day to day my prayer was becoming purer and stronger. The words I had heard surrounded the prayer and purified and strengthened it. I grew sadder and sadder at the thought that I had let the men go without becoming acquainted with them, and my longing to see them again increased.

"Another early morning, two weeks afterward, I was walking up and down the balcony with just a skullcap on (for I was in the habit of putting on my fur cap only before going to the House of Prayer), when I saw a carriage passing the house. Evidently it was not going to stop. The two men were in it. I rushed out with only my cap on my head and called a word of greeting. The carriage stopped, they returned my greeting indifferently, and the older man added: 'We are in a hurry. We want to pray in the next village.'

" 'Can't I get you something to eat?' I asked.

" 'Well, all right,' said the younger, a little more cordially.

" 'Get us a few pretzels, but quickly.'

"It took a few moments to fetch them, and when I came out of the house the carriage was making off at full speed. I swiftly snatched up prayer shawl and phylacteries and holding them in one hand and the pretzels in the other, I ran after the carriage in my skullcap and shouted to them to stop. But they did not seem to hear me, and not until I had mustered all my strength to catch up with them did the carriage stop. I got in and we began to talk. I found out that the older man was the rav of Berditchev and the younger Rabbi Moshe Leib of Sasov, your father. After we had prayed in the next village, I offered them the pretzels and they said the blessing and ate, and I with them. Then they wanted to send me home but I begged to be allowed to accompany them a short way. So we drove off together and they spoke to me, and then I asked questions and they answered. The talk continued and the carriage rolled along and I was not aware that the hours were passing. When the carriage stopped, I discovered that we were in Lizhensk, in front of Rabbi Elimelekh's house. 'Here you are,' said your father. 'This is where your light lives.'

"And so I stayed on in Lizhensk."

Temptations

Joseph Landau, the rabbi of Jassy in Rumania, had rejected a bribe offered him by a prominent member of his congregation whom he had opposed because the man had violated a religious law. Shortly after this he visited the rabbi of Apt, and with a self-satisfied air told him how he had resisted temptation. When the zaddik bade him farewell he blessed him and expressed the hope that he would become an honest and God-fearing man. "I am delighted with the blessing of my teacher and master," said Rabbi Joseph Landau, "and what more could I ask! But why did you wish me this just at this time?"

The rabbi of Apt replied: "It is written: 'Also unto Thee, O Lord, belongeth mercy; for Thou renderest to every man

110

according to his work.' Those who expounded these verses asked themselves time and again why paying a hired man his proper wages should be called 'mercy.' But the truth of the matter is that God has mercy when he leads every man into the temptation befitting his inner level: the common man into petty, the superior man into grave, temptation. The fact that you were exposed to so slight a temptation is a sign that you have not yet reached one of the upper rungs to perfection. That is why I blessed you asking God to let you ascend to them and be found worthy of a greater test."

In Hell

The rabbi of Apt said to God:
"Lord of the world, I know that I have no virtue and no merit for which, after my death, you could set me in paradise among the righteous. But if you are thinking of putting me in hell among the evil-doers, please remember that I cannot get along with them. So I beg of you to take all the wicked out of hell, so you can put me in."

The Turning Point

A respected woman once came to ask the advice of the rabbi of Apt. The instant he set eyes on her he shouted: "Adulteress! You sinned only a short while ago, and yet now you have the insolence to step into this pure house!" Then from the depths of her heart the woman replied: "The Lord of the world has patience with the wicked. He is in no hurry to make them pay their debts and he does not disclose their secret to any creature, lest they be ashamed to turn to him. Nor does he hide his face from them. But the rabbi of Apt sits there in his chair and cannot resist revealing at once what the Creator has covered." From that time on the rabbi of Apt used to say: "No one ever got the better of me except once—and then it was a woman."

The Proud and the Humble

Once the rabbi of Apt came to a city in which two men competed for the privilege of giving him lodgings. Both houses were equally roomy and comfortable and in both households all the rules were observed with pious exactness. But one of the men was in ill repute for his many love affairs and other sinful doings and he knew quite well that he was weak and thought little of himself. The other man, however, no one in the whole community could accuse of the slightest breach of conduct. With proud and stately steps he walked abroad, thoroughly aware of his spotless purity.

The rabbi selected the house of the man with the bad reputation. When he was asked the reason for his choice, he answered: "Concerning the proud, God says: 'I and he cannot live together in this world.' And if God himself, blessed be he, cannot share a room with the proud, then how could I! We read in the Torah, on the other hand: '. . . who dwelleth with them in the midst of their uncleannesses.' And if God takes lodgings there, why shouldn't I?"

The Golden Scale

Rabbi Naftali, a disciple of the rabbi of Apt, who later became the rabbi of Roptchitz, asked a fellow pupil to find out what their teacher thought of him. For half a year his friend made every effort to get the rabbi to say something, but he said nothing about Naftali, nothing good and nothing bad. So his fellow disciple told Naftali, saying: "You see, the master has a golden scale in his mouth. He never passes judgment on anyone, for fear he might wrong him. Has he not forbidden us to judge even those who are supposed wicked through and through? For if anyone were to wrong them, he would be wronging God himself."

Tall Stories

The rabbi of Apt liked to tell tall stories. You might have taken them for meaningless exaggerations, and yet not only his disciples but others too saw meaning in them and found enlightenment.

Once when he was visiting Rabbi Barukh of Mezbizh, a grandson of the Baal Shem, and was just about to begin a story, Rabbi Barukh asked him to accompany him to the well which was called "the spring of the Baal Shem." The moment they reached the well the rabbi of Apt started talking and Rabbi Barukh stood by, leaning on his cane and listening. Among other things, the rabbi of Apt told about his son's wedding: "The batter for the noodle dish was spread on leaves over the fences and even hung down from the roof-tops!"

The Mezbizh hasidim who surrounded the two watched the wise lips of their rabbi and prepared to burst out laughing as soon as he did, but they saw that he was listening attentively and his lips were not twitching. Later, when the rabbi of Apt had left, Rabbi Barukh said: "Never have I heard such a golden tongue!"

On another occasion, when the rabbi of Apt went to Berditchev to call on Rabbi Levi Yitzhak, the people came in droves to see and greet him. Scarcely had he tasted the sweet liqueur and the cakes that had been set before him, when he began to walk up and down the room telling a story. He told how when he was a rav in the town of Jassy they had wanted to build a big bridge in front of his house, and what huge quantities of wood they had carted to the spot. A merchant who often went to Jassy to trade was among the listeners, and nodded eagerly: "Yes, Rabbi, that's just the way it was!" The rabbi of Apt turned to him in surprise. "And how do you know about it?" he asked.

Denunciation

Two young men who had been friends from childhood on lived in the same city. After they married they decided to be partners in a business, and their business throve. But the wife of the one, who was clever and smooth in her dealings with customers, was displeased that her husband's friend who had a good but somewhat stupid wife should have half the profits. Her husband did indeed tell her that it is not our shrewdness or strength that matters, but only that which pleases God. She however would not accept his instruction and pressed him more and more until finally he said to his friend: "We must separate, dear friend, for I cannot stand this any longer." They divided up the business, but from that time on the man with the dull wife had all the luck, while the clever wife made nothing but blunders in her buying and selling. She grew more and more malicious and finally hit on the idea of having two bribed witnesses take a false oath that the other woman had committed adultery.

The matter came before the religious court. When Rabbi Abraham Yehoshua had examined the witnesses, he sent for his son and said to him: "Have this posted all over the district: 'Whoever from this time on gives the rabbi of Apt a ruble is a sinner in Israel.' For it says in the Torah: 'At the mouth of two witnesses . . . shall he that is to die be put to death.' But I can see that this woman is without guilt. Thus what I see is contrary to the holy Torah, and whoever pays me taxes sins."

When the rabbi of Apt had uttered these words with all solemnity, the witnesses were seized with terror. They nudged each other with their elbows and then confessed the truth.

The World of Illusion

Once the rabbi of Apt spoke of the world of illusion in which the souls of all those who die deluded by their own vanity stray. And he told this story:

"A few years ago during a very cold winter a poor man went to buy wood in the market place of our town. He wanted to warm the room for his wife who had just borne a child. There were only a few fagots left and he was just about to purchase them when the head of the community appeared and outbid him. The poor man who could not pay a higher price begged him in vain to have pity on his wife and child. That night the woman and baby fell sick, and they died a few days later. The man survived them for only a short while; but on the very day he died the head of the community died too.

"Then the souls of both men appeared to me in a dream. For the poor man had summoned his opponent to my court. I pronounced the judgment. Many times in the course of his life the head of the community had been brought before worldly judges on the complaints of those he had oppressed and tormented, but since he was well versed in all the intricacies of the law, he had always had the suits referred to one higher court after another until he managed to get himself acquitted. Even now, in the world of illusion, he seemed just as sure of himself as he had been on earth and appealed to a higher judge. He came without delay, but contrary to expectations he not only agreed with my judgment but pronounced an even harsher sentence.

" 'I'll teach the judge!' shouted the accused and again appealed to a still higher court. But when the court convened, his sentence was again raised.

" 'If I have to go to the emperor himself, I'll see this thing through!' shouted the head of the community.

"By now he has gotten as far as the governor."

Those Who Are to Hear, Hear

Once a great throng of people collected about the rabbi of Apt to hear his teachings.

"That won't help you," he cried to them. "Those who are to hear, will hear even at a distance; those who are not to hear, will not hear no matter how near they come."

Ways

A disciple asked the rabbi of Apt: "It is written: 'For the Lord regardeth the way of the righteous; but the way of the wicked shall perish.' The two parts of this sentence do not seem to belong together."

The rabbi explained: "The righteous have many and devious ways, and the wicked have also many and devious ways. But the Lord knows the ways of the righteous by the fact that they are all one way and that is the Way. But the ways of the wicked are numerous and manifold, for they are nothing but many ways of losing the one way. In the end they themselves realize that each is losing his own way and all the ways.

"It is as though someone were walking through a wood and keeping to a certain path not knowing why he has taken this particular path rather than another. He keeps walking day and night until he comes to a tall beech standing at the end of the path and at that point the way is lost. The man cannot

go forward and he does not dare to go back, for he has
lost the way."

Freedom of Choice

Rabbi Heshel said:

It is God's will that there be freedom of choice. That is why
he has waited until this day. For in the days of the Temple
they had the death penalty and whipping, and so there was
no freedom. After that Israel had penal codes, so there was
still no freedom. But now everyone can sin openly and without shame, and prosper. And so whoever leads a good life
today is worthy in the eyes of God, and redemption depends
on him.

A Great Nation

The rabbi of Apt was asked: "The Midrash points out that
God said 'Go' twice to Abraham, once when he bade him leave
his father's house, and once when he commanded him to
sacrifice his son. The explanation in the Midrash is that the
first bidding as well as the second was a test. How are we
to understand that?"

He replied: "When God bade Abraham leave his father's
house, he promised to make of him 'a great nation.' The
Evil Urge observed with what eagerness he prepared himself
for the journey and whispered to him: 'You are doing the
right thing. A great nation—that means power, that means
possessions!'

"But Abraham only laughed at him. 'I understand better
than you,' he said. 'A great nation—means a people that
sanctifies the name of God.' "

Every Day

The rabbi of Apt said:

"Every one of Israel is told to consider himself to be standing
at Mount Sinai to receive the Torah. For man there are past
and future events, but not for God; day in, day out, he gives
the Torah."

Two Kinds of Love

This question was put to the rabbi of Apt: "It is written:
'And Jacob served seven years for Rachel; and they seemed

116

unto him but a few days, for the love he had to her.' How shall we interpret this? One would think that the time seemed overlong for the lover and that a day seemed as long as a year!"

The rabbi of Apt explained: "There are two kinds of love. The first attaches itself to the loved object and returns to the lover, and so every hour is long and hangs heavy on his hands because the lover longs to go to his beloved. But the second, the love for one's true mate, does not return to the lover. So it does not matter whether he lives one or a thousand miles away from his beloved. That is why we read: 'And Jacob served seven years for Rachel; and they seemed unto him but a few days, for the love he had to her.' It was her he loved; his love clung to her and did not return to him. He was not concerned with himself and his desire. His was the true love."

Like a Vessel

Rabbi Heshel said:

"A man should be like a vessel that willingly receives what its owner pours into it, whether it be wine or vinegar."

We Shape a Human Likeness for God

Our sages said: "Know what is above you." This is how the rabbi of Apt expounded those words:

"'Know what is above, is from you.' And what is it that is above you? This is what Ezekiel says: 'And upon the likeness of the throne was a likeness as the appearance of a man upon it above.' How can this be said with reference to God? For is it not written: 'To whom then will ye liken Me, that I should resemble him?' But the truth of the matter is that it is we who make 'a likeness as the appearance of a man.' It is the likeness we shape when we serve with devout hearts. With such a heart we shape a human likeness for our Creator, for him, blessed be he and blessed be his name, who can be likened to none. When a man is merciful and renders loving help he assists in shaping God's right hand. And when a man fights the battle of God and crushes Evil, he assists in shaping

God's left hand. He who is above the throne—it is you who have made him."

The Widow

A disciple of the rabbi of Apt related this story:
"Once I was present at a conversation my teacher carried on with a widow. He spoke to her of her widowhood in good, comforting words, and she allowed her soul to be comforted and found new strength. But I saw that he wept and I too began to weep; for suddenly I knew that he was speaking to the Divine Presence, that is forsaken."

The Soul

On the Day of Atonement, when Rabbi Abraham Yehoshua would recite the Avodah, the prayer that repeats the service of the high priest in the Temple of Jerusalem, and would come to the passage: "And thus he spoke," he would never say those words, but would say: "And thus I spoke." For he had not forgotten the time his soul was in the body of a high priest of Jerusalem, and he had no need to learn from the outside how they had served in the Temple.

Once he himself related: "Ten times have I been in this world. I was a high priest, I was a prince, I was a king, I was an exilarch. I was ten different kinds of dignitary. But I never learned to love mankind perfectly. And so I was sent forth again and again in order to perfect my love. If I succeed this time, I shall never return again."

Tears and Laughter

A man once confessed a sin to the rabbi of Apt and told him with tears how he had atoned for it. The zaddik laughed. The man went on to tell what more he intended doing to atone for his sin; the rabbi went on laughing. The man wanted to speak on, but the laughter robbed him of his speech. He stared at the zaddik in horror. And then his very soul held its breath and he heard that which is spoken deep within. He realized how trivial all his fuss about atoning had been and turned to God.

Later the rabbi of Apt told his hasidim: "Two thousand years ago, before I became a high priest in the Temple of Jerusalem, I had to learn the service step by step. First I was accepted into the company of young priests. At that time this man who has just gone was one of those who lived remote from the rest. He was stern with himself, pure and proven in the practice of all the virtues. But unexpectedly he was snared in a serious sin. In accordance with the law he prepared to bring a sin-offering.

"This was the custom in those days: When a man came to the keeper in charge to choose an animal for the sacrifice, the official asked him what sin he was about to atone for. When the man would begin to speak, the sorrow of his secret would spill over, and he would pour his heart out like water. Then he would take the animal and walk through the streets of Jerusalem to the hall of the Temple where the animal was to be slaughtered. There the young priests would come to meet him and they too would inquire what his sin had been, and again his heart would melt like wax in fire. By the time such a man would reach the high priest and confess his innermost secret, he would be wholly transformed.

"Now when this man entered the Temple hall with his sacrificial animal, I took pity on his ravaged and tear-stained face. I comforted him, wept with him, and eased his heart, until he began to regain his composure and his sin weighed on him less and less. When he came to the high priest he did not experience the turning to God, and his offering was not graciously accepted. So, in the course of time, he had to come down to earth once more and appear before me again. But this time I loved him more."

The Servant of the Lord

The rabbi of Apt was asked:
"In the last chapter of the fifth book of Moses we read: 'So Moses, the servant of the Lord, died there . . .' And we read again in the first chapter of Joshua: ' . . . After the death of Moses, the servant of the Lord.' Why should Moses be desig-

nated a servant of the Lord in the hour of his death and after it, just as if this were something new? For chapter after chapter before this we read how he served his Lord with all his heart and substance."

The rabbi of Apt expounded: "Before Moses died, the Lord showed him the land from the top of Mount Nebo and said to him: 'This is the land which I swore unto Abraham, unto Isaac, and unto Jacob.' Rashi comments on this: 'God sent Moses forth and said: Go and tell the patriarchs that I shall now fulfil the oath which I swore unto them.' So even in his death Moses was the messenger and faithful servant of God, and he died in order to serve in all eternity."

The Table

On the day of the New Moon in the month he was to die, the rabbi of Apt discussed at his table the death of the righteous man. When he had said grace he rose and began to walk back and forth in the room. His face glowed. Then he stopped by the table and said: "Table, pure table, you will testify in my behalf that I have properly eaten and properly taught at your board."

Later he bade that his coffin be made out of the table.

The Inscription

Before he died the rabbi of Apt ordered his sons to have no other words of praise carved on his tombstone than: "He who loved Israel." That is the inscription on the stone.

In Dying

When he lay dying the rabbi of Apt cried out: "Why does the son of Jesse delay?"

He wept and said: "Before his death the rabbi of Berditchev promised that he would disturb the peace of all the holy men, and that he would not stop until the Messiah came. But then they showered him with such delights in hall after hall that he forgot. But I shall not forget. I do not want to enter paradise before the coming of the Messiah."

Beyond Our Vision

After the rabbi of Apt's death, two zaddikim met, Rabbi Yitzhak of Radzivil, the son of the maggid of Zlotchov, and Rabbi Israel of Rizhyn, the rabbi of Mezritch's great-grandson. Rabbi Israel asked: "What did he mean by saying that he did not want to enter paradise before the coming of the Messiah?" Rabbi Yitzhak replied: "In the psalm we read: 'We have thought on Thy lovingkindness, Elohim, in the midst of Thy temple.' My reading of this verse is this: 'We thought of Elohim. Your lovingkindness is in the midst of your temple.' The name Elohim refers to the divine attribute of rigor. So, when we 'think,' we think of our troubles *here*, seeing in them only the divine attribute of rigor, or Elohim. But *there*, 'in the midst of Thy temple,' everyone who comes, if only to the threshold, knows that everything there is the 'lovingkindness' of God."

The Vision of the Vegetable Vendor

Rabbi Yitzhak of Neskhizh, the son of Rabbi Mordecai of Neskhizh, told this story:

"On the day before the rabbi of Apt suddenly fell ill and died, an old woman who sold vegetables in the market place said to her neighbor: 'This morning at dawn—I don't know whether I was awake or dreaming—I saw my husband, may he rest in peace, who has been dead these many years. I saw him rush past without looking at me. Then I burst into tears and cried to him: "First you go and leave me to a miserable life with my orphaned children and now you don't even look at me!" But he kept on running and didn't turn to give me a glance. As I sat there crying, I saw him coming back. He stopped and said: "I couldn't take any time off before. We had to fumigate the road and cleanse the air because the zaddikim from the Land of Israel cannot stand the air here, and they will soon be coming to receive the rabbi of Apt and escort him to the other side."'

"Isn't that a fine story?"

The Grave in Tiberias

This tale is told:

Once the rabbi of Apt sat deep in thought. He looked bewildered and a little sad. When his hasidim asked whether anything was troubling him, he said: "Up to now, during my soul's every sojourn on earth I occupied some post of honor in Israel: but this time I have none." At that very moment a messenger from the Land of Israel arrived and handed the rabbi an official letter. In it was stated that the Palestinian community made up of emigrants from Volhynia whose seat was in Tiberias, nominated him their head. The rabbi of Apt had a feast prepared to celebrate his happiness. Then he gave the messenger a sum of money for the purpose of acquiring a plot of ground for him beside the grave of the prophet Hosea, and of the same size.

The night Rabbi Abraham Yehoshua died, a knocking was heard at the window of the Volhynia meeting house in Tiberias: "Go out and escort the rabbi of Apt to his eternal rest," it said. When the caretaker opened the door he saw a bier being borne through the air. Thousands of souls were swarming around it. He followed it to the cemetery and watched them lower the body into the grave.

MENAHEM MENDEL OF RYMANOV

The Song of Praise

The only way young Mendel could manage to travel from his home to the city where Rabbi Elimelekh lived was to hire himself out as servant to a coachman. His duties included watching the carriage and the horses during the stops on the journey. It was a bitterly cold day. The driver and his passengers were warming themselves in the inn, eating and drinking. Rabbi Mendel in his thin coat and his shoes full of holes walked back and forth beside the carriage and rubbed his hands. "Praise be to the Creator," he sang to himself, "that I am cold. Praise be to the Creator that I am hungry." He hopped from one foot to the other, and sang his song of praise as though it were a dance tune.

A guest coming toward him from the inn saw and heard him, and was amazed. "Young man," said he, "what are you mumbling to yourself?"

Mendel answered: "I am thanking God that I am in good health and can be so enormously hungry."

"But why don't you eat until you are full?" asked the man.

Mendel thought this over. "You have to have money for that," he said.

The man called a servant to watch the carriage, took Mendel into the inn, and had food and a warm drink brought to him. Then he saw to it that he got sturdy shoes and a short sheepskin coat of the sort the village Jews wear.

When Mendel reached Lizhensk he immediately went to Rabbi Elimelekh's house and, so quickly that the servants did not notice him, walked into the room of the zaddik, who was sitting over a book, absorbed in the profundities of the teachings. His son Eleazar motioned to the unmannerly stranger to go and wait outside until his presence would not disturb the zaddik in his studies. But Rabbi Elimelekh had already looked up. He took his son by the arm and said almost singing, as though he were chanting a song of praise: "Lazar, Lazar, what do you want of that little Jew? Why, sparks of fire are flying all around his head."

Barter

Rabbi Mendel's wife's parents kept urging their daughter to get a divorce from a husband who turned away from this-world things and whose inefficiency in business only equaled his dislike for it. When she refused, they put out the couple, who up to this time had been living with them, as was customary. Then the two were in bitter need. Occasionally with the cook's connivance the woman managed to steal a few provisions from her father's kitchen, or a few fagots from her father's cellar. But once when her parents were away on a trip and the tradesmen refused to give her anything more on credit, she could not bring Rabbi Mendel, who was sitting over his books in the House of Study, a thing to eat for three days. On the third day she ventured to cross the baker's threshold one more time. He turned her away. Silently she left the shop. But he followed her and offered her bread and other food, as much as she could carry, if she on her part would promise him her share in the world to come. She hesitated only an instant. Then she accepted his offer.

When she entered the House of Study she saw her husband sitting in his seat. He was almost unconscious, but the book was gripped firmly in both his hands. She spread the cloth, served him, and watched him while he ate. He looked up, for never before had she remained. They looked at each other. When their eyes met, she saw he knew what she had done. And then she saw that at that moment she had received a new share in the coming world.

The Hungry Child

Once when there was not a piece of bread in Rabbi Mendel's house, his son ran to him crying and complained his hunger was so great he could bear it no longer.

"Your hunger is not so great as all that," said his father. "For otherwise I should have something to quiet it."

The boy slunk off without a word. But before he reached the door, the rabbi saw a small coin lying on the table.

"I wronged you," he called out. "You are really very hungry indeed."

The Spoon

Rabbi Elimelekh's servant once forgot a spoon for Rabbi Mendel who was a guest at Rabbi Elimelekh's table. Everyone ate except Rabbi Mendel. The zaddik observed this and asked: "Why aren't you eating?"

"I have no spoon," said his guest.

"Look," said Rabbi Elimelekh, "one must know enough to ask for a spoon, and a plate too, if need be!"

Rabbi Mendel took the word of his teacher to heart. From that day on his fortunes were on the mend.

In Youth

Rabbi Mendel once boasted to his teacher Rabbi Elimelekh that evenings he saw the angel who rolls away the light before the darkness, and mornings the angel who rolls away the darkness before the light. "Yes," said Rabbi Elimelekh, "in my youth I saw that too. Later on you don't see those things any more."

The Call

A man came to Rabbi Mendel and begged him to confirm him in the feeling that he had the call to be a rabbi. He said he felt that he had reached that rung and was capable of pouring blessings upon Israel. For a time the zaddik looked at him in silence. Then he said:

"When I was young the voice of a man used to wake me every night at midnight. It would call to me: 'Mendel, rise for the Lamentations at Midnight!'

"I had grown accustomed to the voice. But one night I heard another voice call. 'Rabbi Mendel,' said the voice, 'rise for the Lamentations at Midnight.' I was terrified. I trembled until dawn and all day I was seized by terror. 'Perhaps I heard wrong,' I said to calm my heart. But the next night the voice again said: 'Rabbi Mendel!'

"For forty days afterward I mortified my flesh and prayed without ceasing that the voice be taken from me. But the gates of Heaven remained closed to me, and the voice kept calling. So I resigned myself."

The Testament

Before he died Rabbi Elimelekh laid his hands on the heads of his four favorite disciples and divided what he owned among them. To the Seer of Lublin he gave his eyes' power to see; to Abraham Yehoshua, his lips' power to pronounce judgment; to Israel of Koznitz, his heart's power to pray; but to Mendel he gave his spirit's power to guide.

Nothing to Offer

After Rabbi Elimelekh's death a number of his younger disciples agreed to go to Rabbi Mendel, who at that time was still living in Prystyk. They arrived at his house on a Friday afternoon. On the table were two sabbath loaves made of rye flour and two small candles in crude clay holders. They asked his wife where he was and were told that he had not yet returned from the ritual bath. Naftali, later the rabbi of Roptchitz, at once went to the city and bought all the necessary things: a white tablecloth, real white sabbath loaves both large and small, and tall candles in handsome holders. The table was set properly and they all sat down to it.

When Rabbi Mendel entered the room, they all rose to show him that they accepted him as their father. He fixed one after the other with a long, searching gaze.

Then he said: "If you bring the right things with you, you may come even to me, who have nothing to offer."

Refusal

On the eve of the New Year Rabbi Mendel entered the House of Prayer. He surveyed the many people who had come together from near and far. "A fine crowd!" he called out to them. "But I want you to know that I cannot carry you all on my shoulders. Every one of you must work for himself."

Women's Wear

The first ruling Rabbi Mendel had made in Rymanov was that the daughters of Israel should not parade up and down the streets in gay-colored, lavishly trimmed dresses. From then on the Jewish girls and women of Rymanov faithfully followed the zaddik's orders. But the daughter-in-law of the wealthiest man in town, the wife he had just fetched for his son from the capital of the district, refused to let her finery turn yellow in her chest with none to admire it.

When Rabbi Mendel saw her strutting up and down the main street, dressed in her best, he sent for the most mischievous guttersnipes and gave them permission to call after the woman whatever went through their heads. The rich man, who was one of the pillars of the community, came to the rabbi in a rage and tried to make clear to him that his ruling was contrary to the Torah, for Ezra the Scribe had included in his ordinances permission for traders to travel from place to place so that the daughters of Israel might adorn themselves.

"Do you think," asked Rabbi Mendel, "that Ezra meant them to parade up and down the streets? Do you think he did not know that a woman can receive the honors due her nowhere save in her home?"

Weights and Measures

On the last day of every month Rabbi Mendel had the weights and measures in every Jewish shop examined. Once in the place of business of a rich man his agents discovered a liquid measure which had been declared invalid. The proprietor asserted that he no longer used it for measuring. "Even if you only use it for a spittoon, the law forbids you to have it on your premises," said one of the investigators, Rabbi Hirsh, the faithful "Servant" of Rabbi Mendel, whom the zaddik had secretly chosen for his successor. He hurled the measure to the ground and smashed it with his foot.

"Is Saul also among the prophets?" sneered the merchant. "Are you already competent to lay down the law?"

When Hirsh returned to the zaddik he reported that everything was in good order, but the others told Rabbi Mendel what had happened. He immediately sent out a crier to hammer on the doors of all the people and summon them to a sermon in the House of Prayer. But he forbade the man to knock at the rich merchant's door.

The congregation assembled. Rabbi Mendel preached on the subject of just weights and measures. Only then did the rich man, who had come along with the others, realize why he had not been summoned. The fact that the rabbi was speaking about him to everyone but him, wounded him to the heart. After the sermon he went up to Rabbi Mendel and begged to be given a penance and pardoned.

Concerning Hospitality

A man came and complained to Rabbi Mendel that he could not fulfil the commandment to be hospitable because his wife did not like to have guests, and whenever he brought people to the house it gave rise to quarrels which threatened his domestic peace.

The rabbi said, "Our sages say: 'Welcoming guests is a greater virtue than welcoming the Divine Presence.' This may sound exaggerated to us. But we must understand it properly. It is said that when there is peace between husband and wife the Divine Presence rests in their minds. That is why welcoming guests is described as being more important than welcoming the Divine Presence. Even if hospitality destroys the peace that exists between a man and his wife, the commandment to be hospitable is still the more important."

Guest Loaves

During a period when the cost of living was very high, Rabbi Mendel noticed that the many needy people whom he entertained as guests in his house received smaller loaves than usual. He gave orders to make the loaves larger than before, since loaves were intended to adjust to hunger and not to the price.

The Leaky Roof

Government officials came to Rymanov to requisition a house in which to store provisions for the army. The only house suitable for their purpose proved to be the House of Prayer of the Jewish congregation. When the heads of the community heard of this, they did not know what to do and consulted Rabbi Mendel in great dismay. But one of them recalled a circumstance which might lead to a change in the decision: the roof of the House of Prayer had been leaking for quite a while and if a heavy rain were to fall, the provisions would certainly have to be stored elsewhere.

"Then the decision to make a storehouse of the House of Prayer is just," said the rabbi. "For it is a judgment upon your idleness and neglect. Have the roof mended at once!"

The roof was mended the same day. From that time on nothing further was heard concerning the decision of the officials. Only after some weeks did the people of Rymanov hear that on that very day the officials had decided in favor of another town.

At Court

When the rabbis of Apt and Rymanov were staying with the Seer of Lublin in the city of Lantzut where he lived before going to Lublin, his enemies denounced his guests to the authorities, who had them jailed. They decided that since Rabbi Mendel could speak the best German and German was the language used in the court, he was to do the talking for all when they were examined.

The judge asked: "What is your business?"

The rabbi of Rymanov replied: "Serving the king."

"What king?"

"The King over all kings."

"And why did you two strangers come to Lantzut?"

"To learn greater zeal in serving, from this man here."

"And why do you wear white robes?"

"It is the color of our office."

The judge said: "We have no quarrel with this sort of people." And he dismissed them.

The Two Lights

Rabbi Mendel of Rymanov was asked: "Why cannot two zaddikim have their seats in the same city?"

He replied: "Zaddikim are like the lights up in Heaven. When God created the two great lights of Heaven he placed both in the firmament, each to do its own special service. Ever since, they have been friends. The great light does not boast of being great and the small light is content with being small. And so it was in the days of our sages: there was a whole skyful of stars, large stars and small stars, and they lived together in all brotherliness. Not so the zaddikim of our day! Now no one wants to be a small light and bow to a greater. So it is better for each to have his own firmament all for himself."

The Acceptance of the Torah

One morning on the first day of the Feast of Weeks, before the reading from the Torah, Rabbi Mendel left the prayer room to go into his own room. After a time he returned to the prayer room and said: "When Mount Sinai was raised to hang above you like a huge hollow bell, you were compelled to accept the Law. Today I release you from this compulsion and from this responsibility. You are once more free to choose."

Then all cried aloud: "Now too we accept the Torah!"

A disciple of the rabbi of Lublin, who happened to be there because he had been unable to go as usual to his teacher over the holidays, added the following whenever he told this story: "And all their impurities melted away as they had that time, at Mount Sinai."

At a Time of Good Will

Rabbi Mendel was asked: "On the sabbath, when we say the Afternoon Prayer, why do we speak the words of the psalm: 'And as for me, may my prayer unto thee, O Lord, be at a time of good will.' "

He replied: "Because the will of the Most High to create the world for the good of his creatures already existed on the afternoon of the sabbath before the first day of creation. Every sabbath at this same time, it is as if that original will again wakes, and so we pray that this time before the sabbath draws to a close, the will to do good to His creatures may manifest itself once more."

A Day's Portion

Rabbi Kalman of Cracow asked Rabbi Hirsh the Servant, Rabbi Mendel's successor: "What is your way in the service of prayer?"

He replied: "My way was shown to me by my holy teacher, may he merit life in the world to come. Concerning manna, it is written: 'And the people shall go out and gather a day's portion every day.' Every day has its own portion of prayer, and one must concentrate on the particular meaning of each portion every day."

Belief and Trust

Rabbi Mendel of Rymanov was asked how to interpret the words God added when he told Moses that the people were to gather a day's portion of manna every day: " . . . that I may prove them whether they will walk in my law or not."

He explained: "If you ask even a very simple man whether he believes that God is the only God in the world, he will give the emphatic answer: 'How can you ask! Do not all creatures know that He is the only one in the world!' But should you ask him if he trusts that the Creator will see to it that he has all that he needs, he will be taken aback and after a while he will say: 'Well, I guess I haven't reached that rung yet.'

"But in reality belief and trust are linked, and one cannot exist without the other. He who firmly believes, trusts completely. But if anyone—God forbid—has not perfect confidence in God, his belief will be faint as well. That is why God says: 'I will cause to rain bread from heaven for you'; that means 'I *can* cause bread to rain from heaven for you.' But he who goes in the path of my teachings, and that means he who has belief in me, and that means, he who has trust in me, gathers a day's portion every day and does not worry about the morrow."

The Lord of the Manor and the Peasant

At the Seder, on the night of Passover, Rabbi Mendel of Rymanov liked to tell the following story after the song about "one only kid":

A peasant stood in the market place and offered a calf for sale. Along came the lord of the manor and asked: "What do you want for that dog?" Said the peasant: "That's a calf and not a dog." Each insisted that he was right and so they wrangled for a while, until the lord gave the peasant a box on the ear, saying: "Here's something to help you remember that when the lord say it's a dog, it *is* a dog." The peasant replied: "I shall remember."

Some time later, a friend of the peasant came running into the village which adjoined the manor. He was all out of breath and shouted for the firemen. It seemed that where he lived, quite a distance away, the community threshing barn and the house of the mayor, who was popular for miles around, had caught fire. The entire squad of firemen set out and took all their equipment with them. In the meantime the peasant set fire to the four corners of the manor and it burned down.

A few weeks later, when he heard that the lord was going to rebuild his house, he disguised himself, pretended to be an architect and told the lord he would draw up a plan. This he at once proceeded to do, for he was a clever peasant. They sat over the plan, calculated the amount of wood necessary for the building, and decided to go into the forest which belonged to the lord to measure the circumference of the trees which were suitable for lumber.

When they reached the forest, the peasant was contemptuous of the trees standing at the edge. There were better trees farther along, said the lord; they walked on, keeping a sharp lookout, until they were right in the middle of the forest. There the architect stopped and pointed enthusiastically to a giant of a tree, saying it was so and so many ells around and would make splendid planks.

"That's a lot more ells than you think," said the lord. The architect went up to the tree and put his arm about the trunk. "Just as I figured!" he cried.

Then the lord went up to the tree and did just as the other before him. The peasant pulled out his measuring cord, tied the lord to the trunk by his arms and legs, gave him a sound drubbing and said: "This is the first reminder, so that you'll know when the peasant says it's a calf, it *is* a calf and not a dog." Then he went his way, but the lord howled for hours until someone happened along and cut his bonds.

When the lord got home he felt ill and went to bed. He grew worse from day to day and had doctor after doctor called, but none of them could give him any relief. At that time a rumor spread through the neighboring town that a great miracle-healer would stop there for a day in the course of his travels and would heal all the sick who came to consult him.

Soon after, the peasant disguised as a doctor arrived in the town, and gave out very good advice—for he was a clever peasant. The lord, who had heard of him, had him summoned to his bedside and promised to pay him whatever he asked if he would cure him.

The doctor came, took one look at the patient, and said peremptorily to the persons around him: "You must leave me alone with him and not disturb me in my rather severe but infallible cure—not even if he should scream." As soon as they were gone, he bolted the door and gave the lord another first-rate drubbing.

Those who stood outside heard the pitiful shrieks and said: "There's a real fellow for you! He is doing a thorough job." But the peasant was saying to the lord: "This is a second reminder, so you'll be sure to know once and for all: when a peasant says it's a calf, it *is* a calf and not a dog." Then he went off with such ease and self-confidence that no one even thought of stopping him.

When the lord recovered from his illness and his bruises, he set out to find the peasant, but did not succeed, for the latter had not only dyed his skin and changed the cut of his hair but had also assumed manners and gestures that were so different that he was quite unrecognizable. Early in the morning on the next market day, he saw the lord sitting in his coach close to the market place which was still almost empty, peering in all directions. The peasant turned to an acquaintance of his who had come with his horse and had the reputation of being a good rider, and said: "Do you want to do me a favor, friend?" "Surely," said the other, "if it isn't anything too difficult." "All you have to do," answered the peasant, "is to ride up to that gentleman in the coach, bend down and whisper to him: 'If the peasant says it's a calf, it *is* a calf.' Then ride off as fast as you can, and don't stop until you have left those who will pursue you far behind. After that, meet me at the inn—you know which—and I'll have them serve you the best old plum brandy ever."

His friend did as he had been told. When the lord heard his words, he started up, for he was sure the man he had been looking for was there in front of him. He shouted to his coachman and servant to unhitch the horses and make after the fellow. They mounted the horses and galloped off.

When the peasant saw the lord alone in his coach, he went up to him, boxed his ears soundly and said: "This is the third reminder, and now I guess you have learned that when the peasant says it's a calf, it *is* a calf and not a dog." Then he went off to the inn.

And the calf—so Rabbi Mendel ended his tale at every Seder—the calf remained a calf and never became a dog.

And when the children asked: "And what was the name of the clever peasant?" Rabbi Mendel answered, "Michael."

When they asked: "What was the name of the bad lord?" he said: "Sammael."

And when they asked: "What was the name of the calf that never became a dog?" he replied: "That is the well-known calf, Israel."

Roads

Rabbi Mendel often complained:

"As long as there were no roads, you had to interrupt a journey at nightfall. Then you had all the leisure in the world to recite psalms at the inn, to open a book, and to have a good talk with one another. But nowadays you can ride on these roads day and night and there is no peace any more."

134

Fulfilling the Law

A disciple asked Rabbi Mendel of Rymanov:
"The Talmud says that Abraham fulfilled all the commandments. How is that possible, since they had not yet been given?"
"You know," said the rabbi, "that the commandments of the
Torah correspond to the bones, and the prohibitions to the
sinews of man. Thus the entire Law includes the entire body
of man. But Abraham had made every part of his body so
pure and holy that each of itself fulfilled the command
intended for it."

The Heart

Rabbi Mendel of Rymanov used to say that during the time he
was silently reciting the Eighteen Benedictions, all the people
who had ever asked him to pray to God in their behalf would
pass through his mind.
Someone once asked how that was possible, since there was
surely not enough time. Rabbi Mendel replied: "The need
of every single one leaves a trace in my heart. In the hour
of prayer I open my heart and say: 'Lord of the world, read
what is written here!' "

The Pause

Rabbi Hirsh the Servant related:
"When my holy teacher recited the Penitential Prayers at the
Reader's desk on the day before the New Year, he would always
pause after saying the prayer with the phrase: "When everyone has truly turned to you with all his heart and soul," and
would stand a moment in silence before he resumed. Many
thought that during this time he busied himself with the permutations of the names of God, but his intimates knew he
only waited until he saw that everyone in the congregation was
determined to turn with all his heart and soul.

The Sounds of Work

This question was put to Rabbi Mendel: "The Scriptures say
that when Moses was told that the people were bringing far
too many offerings for the building of the sanctuary in the

wilderness, he issued the command that no one henceforth was to work at the sanctuary. How does that follow? All Moses had to do was to command that no further offerings be brought."

Rabbi Mendel expounded: "It is well known that those who worked at the sanctuary were most holy men, and that their work had a holy effect. When one of them struck the anvil with his hammer, and another split wood with his ax, the sounds echoed in the hearts of all those who heard, and the people were driven by a holy desire to bring more than was needful. That is why Moses bade the workers stop their work."

The Disciples Band Together

Rabbi Mendel's disciples formed an association. They wrote a charter which began with these words: "We wish to found an association of comrades who seek the truth and strive to be righteous and humble; who strive to turn to God with a whole heart, with a heart rendered pure, so that we may no longer be barred by a wall from his holiness."

Whenever they made a new resolution as to how they should conduct themselves, they inscribed it on the roll which began with the above charter. One of their resolutions read: "To beware of untoward words, concerning which our holy rabbi has said that their utterance is a violation of the commandment: Thou shalt not murder."

Rabbi Mendel's utterance which is here cited was: "Every word has a perfect shape of its own, and he who casts the sound of the word to the demons is sinning against it, like one who rises against his neighbor and slays him."

The Ark of the Covenant and Its Carriers

Rabbi Mendel said:

"When a man wants to serve God in the right way and does not succeed, walls rise up before him. His prayer lacks tone, his learning light. Then his heart rises up against him, and he comes to the zaddik as one whom his own heart has cast out, and stands trembling, waiting for the zaddik to help him— then his own humility makes the zaddik humble as well. For he who is to give help sees the bowed and fervent soul of him who has come for help, and thinks: 'He is better than I!' And at that instant, the zaddik is lifted to the very heights by his service and has the power to loosen that which is bound. To this we may apply the phrase: 'The Ark of the Covenant carried its carriers.'"

They Blessed Each Other

Rabbi Feivish of Zbarazh once came to Rabbi Mendel in order to spend the sabbath near him. On Sunday when he took his farewell he wept and said: "I am seventy-four years old and I still have not truly turned to God."
Weeping, Rabbi Mendel replied: "That troubles me too."
Then they decided to bless one another with the blessing that they might be able to accomplish the true turning.

The Ultimate Joy

Soon after the death of Rabbi Mendel's wife, his daughter also died. People whispered to one another not to tell him of it just yet, but when his son-in-law entered the House of Prayer weeping, while the rabbi was saying the Morning Prayer, he at once realized what had happened. He finished the Prayer of Benedictions, and said: "Lord of the world, you took my wife from me. But I still had my daughter and could rejoice in her. Now you have taken her from me too. Now I have no one left to rejoice in, except you alone. So I shall rejoice in you." And he said the Additional Prayer in a transport of joy.

ZEVI HIRSH OF RYMANOV

Genealogy

When the rabbi of Rizhyn betrothed his grandson to the daughter of Rabbi Hirsh of Rymanov, before the writing of the marriage contract he said: "It is the custom in my family to recite our genealogy at the time of betrothal. And that is what I shall now do. My grandfather's father was Rabbi Baer, my grandfather was Rabbi Abraham the Angel, and my father Rabbi Shalom Shahkna." He had given merely the names of the Great Maggid, his son, and his grandson, without adding the usual honorary titles. Then he said to Rabbi Hirsh: "Now it is your turn to tell us from whom you are descended."

Rabbi Hirsh replied: "My father and mother left this earth when I was ten years old, and so I did not know them well enough to be able to speak of them, but I have been told that they were upright and honest folk. When they died, my relatives apprenticed me to a tailor. I stayed with him for five years, and even though I was very young I worked well. I was careful not to ruin what was new, and to repair what was old."

"The marriage is agreeable to both sides," cried the rabbi of Rizhyn.

Bed-Making

One of the duties of Rabbi Menahem Mendel of Rymanov's servant was making his bed, and he never let anyone else do this in his stead. Now when young Zevi Hirsh quitted the tailor's trade and was taken into the zaddik's house as a stoker, he begged the servant to let him make the zaddik's bed, but the man refused, saying that the rabbi would certainly notice that another's hand had performed this service. Once, however, the servant was called away before evening, and since he had to go at once, he transferred his duties to the young stoker and gave him minute directions on how to

138

make the bed. Hirsh promised to do exactly as he had been told.

When Rabbi Mendel rose the following morning he called his servant and asked who had made the bed. Trembling, the man answered, and begged forgiveness.

"I never knew," said the zaddik, "that one could sleep so sweetly. From now on the stoker is to make my bed."

The Power to Cleanse

Rabbi Nathan Yehudah, the son of Rabbi Mendel of Rymanov, told this story.

"The morning after Rabbi Hirsh the Servant had celebrated his wedding, I entered the House of Study and found the bridegroom cleaning out the place with the same devotion to his task as ever. I was annoyed, went to my father, and said: 'Father, it isn't right for your Servant to ignore his marriage and do such lowly work on the Seven Days of the Feast!'

"My father replied: 'You have made me happy, my son. I was much troubled as to how I should be able to pray today if Zevi Hirsh the Servant did not clean the House of Study himself. For when he does the cleaning he drives out all the demons, and the air grows pure, and then that house is a good place to pray in.'

"On that very day my father accepted Rabbi Hirsh as his disciple."

The Loftiest Prayer

Rabbi Hirsh once complained to his teacher that whenever he prayed he saw fiery letters and words flash before his eyes.

"These," said Rabbi Mendel, "are the mystical concentrations of our sacred master Rabbi Isaac Luria. So what cause have you to complain?"

"But I want to pray concentrating only on the meaning of the words," answered Rabbi Hirsh.

"What you have in mind," said Rabbi Mendel, "is a very high rung which only one man in a whole generation can reach: that of having learned all secret wisdom and then praying like a little child."

There are many reports on how Rabbi Hirsh became the successor of his teacher and master. One of them says that Rabbi Mendel dreamed that the angel Metatron, "the prince of the innermost chamber," led Hirsh the Servant to the zaddik's chair. Afterward the zaddik observed that Hirsh saw the souls of the dead who came to him for redemption as clearly as the zaddik himself. This lessened his uneasiness, yet from that time on he no longer permitted the Servant to live in his house and perform personal services for him. The only thing he allowed him to do was to help him put on his phylacteries— for Hirsh had begged this of him as a very great favor.

According to another account, Rabbi Mendel's two sons drove to Rabbi Naftali of Roptchitz after their father's death to ask him to decide which of them should become his father's successor. They took Rabbi Hirsh with them as their servant, and were already agreed that whichever of them became the rabbi would take the Servant into his house. On the way they were accosted by a villager who had been among their father's hasidim. When he heard of his master's death, he wanted to hand the note of request he had with him to them because they were Rabbi Mendel's sons, but they did not wish to take it, since neither of them had yet been ordained rabbi. So the younger son gently told the man to give the note to Rabbi Hirsh and the man did so in the simplicity of his heart. They were amazed and somewhat confounded to see Rabbi Hirsh take the note with a matter of fact air. When they came to Rabbi Naftali, he greeted Rabbi Hirsh with the title of rabbi and gave him the place of honor.

They say that a group of hasidim wanted to elect as their rabbi Nathan Yehudah, Rabbi Mendel's eldest son, but he not only refused, but went away to foreign parts for a considerable period of time.

The Renewed Soul

Rabbi Hirsh once said to his hasidim:

"When a man rises in the morning and sees that God has returned his soul to him and that he has become a new creature, he should turn singer and sing to God. My holy master

Rabbi Menahem Mendel had a hasid who whenever he came to the words in the Morning Prayer: 'My God, the soul you have placed in me is pure,' danced and broke into a song of praise."

The Perfection of the Torah

A woman once came to Rabbi Hirsh, her eyes streaming with tears, and complained that she had been the victim of a miscarriage of justice in the rabbinical court. The zaddik summoned the judges and said: "Show me the source from which you derived your verdict, for it seems to me that there has been some error." Together they looked up the passage in the book Breastplate of Judgment on which the verdict had been based, and discovered that there had indeed been a misinterpretation.

One of the judges asked the rabbi how he had known beforehand that there had been an error. He answered: "It is written: 'The law of the Lord is perfect, restoring the soul.' Had the verdict been in accordance with the true law, the woman could never have wept as she did."

The Quintessence of the Torah

Before his death Rabbi Hirsh of Rymanov repeated over and over the words in the song of Moses: "A God of faithfulness and without iniquity." Then he said: "The quintessence of the holy Torah is to know that He is a God of faithfulness and that therefore there can be no iniquity. You may ask: 'If this is so, then why the whole Torah? It would have been enough for God to say that one verse at Sinai!' The answer is: No one can grasp this one truth until he has learned and fulfilled the whole Torah."

FROM THE SCHOOL OF

RABBI SHELOMO OF KARLIN

URI OF STRELISK

With a Quorum of Ten Pulpits

When, after visiting with his teacher Rabbi Shelomo of Karlin, Rabbi Uri returned to Lwow, he did not have a quorum of ten needed for community prayer, but prayed alone during an entire year. One day while he was studying the Book of Splendor, he came to a passage in praise of those who listen to the reading of the Torah and decided from then on to go to the House of Prayer every sabbath to hear the Torah read. But the first sabbath he listened he noticed that they were not reading what was really written in the Torah! So he did not go the following week. But soon after this he again found a passage in the Book of Splendor in praise of those who pray together with the community. He assembled ten men to pray with him and said to himself: "Even if God commanded me to pray with a quorum of ten pulpits, I would pray with them."

Acceptable Offering

Rabbi Uri said:
"It is written: 'And Abel brought, also he . . . ' He brought his own 'he,' his own self. Only when a man offers himself as well, is his offering acceptable."

Before Going to Pray

Every morning before going to pray Rabbi Uri saw to his house, and said his last goodbye to his wife and children.

The Secret Prayer

This is how Rabbi Uri expounded the words of the prayer: "May He who knows that which is hidden accept our call for help and listen to our cry."
"We know very well how we ought to pray; and still we cry for help in the need of the moment. The soul wishes us to cry out in spiritual need, but we are not able to express what the

soul means. And so we pray that God may accept our call for
help, but also that he, who knows that which is hidden, may
hear the silent cry of the soul."

To Walk Hidden with God

Rabbi Uri said:

"It is written: 'And to walk hidden with thy God.' Know that
angels stand. Ceaselessly they stand, each on his own rung,
but we move, we move from rung to rung. For angels are not
garmented in flesh; they cannot remain hidden while they perform their service, and no matter on what rung they stand, they
are always manifest. But man on this earth is clothed in flesh
and can hide within this body of his. And so hidden from sight,
he can move from rung to rung."

There and Here

Rabbi Uri taught:

"We read in the psalm: 'If I ascend up into heaven, Thou art
there; if I make my bed in the nether world, here Thou art.'
When I consider myself great and think I can touch the sky,
I discover that God is the faraway There, and the higher I
reach, the farther away he is. But if I make my bed in the
depths, if I bow my soul down to the nether world, he is here
with me."

Open Thou Mine Eyes

Once at table Rabbi Uri said the words of the psalm with
great fervor: "Open Thou mine eyes, that I may behold
wondrous things out of Thy law," and expounded them in
this way:

"We know that God created a great light, that man might be
able to look from one end of the world to the other and no
curtain might separate the sight of the eyes from that which
is seen. But then God hid this light. That is why David pleads:
'Open Thou mine eyes.' For it is really not the eye, with its
white and its pupil, that produces sight; the eye has sight
because the power of God lends sight to the eye. But a curtain
prevents the eye from seeing that which is distant in the same
way as it sees that which is near. David pleaded that this
curtain be removed, that he might behold the wonder of all

146

that is. For, he says, 'out of Thy law,' that is, according to Thy law I see that no separation is intended."

Where?

Rabbi Uri once said to the hasidim who had come together in Strelisk: "You journey to me, and where do I journey? I journey and journey continually to that place where I can cling to God."

The Wish

A zaddik who was visiting Rabbi Uri asked him: "Why is it that none of your hasidim is rich?"

"I shall show you why," answered the rabbi of Strelisk. "Call in any one of the people who are in the anteroom." His visitor did so.

"This is a season of grace," said Rabbi Uri to the hasid who had entered. "Whatever wish you utter now shall be granted to you."

"If I may make a wish," said the man in a voice both shy and burning, "I wish that every morning I may be able to say the prayer 'Blessed be He who spake and the world came into being' just like our rabbi says it."

Generation after Generation

Rabbi Uri said:

"One does not help only one's own generation. Generation after generation David pours enthusiasm into somber souls; generation after generation Samson arms weak souls with the strength of heroes."

Each His Own

Rabbi Uri said:

"David could compose the psalms, and what can I do? I can recite the psalms."

Letters and Souls

Rabbi Uri said:

"The myriads of letters in the Torah correspond to the myriads of souls in Israel. If one single letter is left out of the Torah, it becomes unfit for use; if one single soul is left out of the union of Israel, the Divine Presence will not rest upon it.

Like the letters, so the souls must unite and form a union. But why is it forbidden for one letter in the Torah to touch its neighbor? Because every soul in Israel must have hours when it is alone with its Maker."

The Growing Tree

Rabbi Uri taught:

"Man is like a tree. If you stand in front of a tree and watch it incessantly to see how it grows and to see how much it has grown, you will see nothing at all. But tend to it at all times, prune the runners, and keep the vermin from it, and— all in good time—it will come into its growth. It is the same with man: all that is necessary is for him to overcome his obstacles, and he will thrive and grow. But it is not right to examine him every hour to see how much has been added to his growth."

Into Freedom

Tradition has it that until Rabbi Uri recited the Benediction of Separation at the close of the sabbath, and separated the sabbath from the weekday, the keys of hell were in his hand, and souls who had been freed from torment for the duration of the holy day of rest could fly about in the world unhindered.

The Sign

For a number of hours Rabbi Uri lay unconscious in the agony of death. His favorite disciple, Rabbi Yehudah Zevi, opened the door from time to time, looked at the dying man, and closed the door again. At last he entered the room and went up to the bed. The next moment the hasidim who had followed him in saw their master stretch out one last time, and die. Later, when they asked Rabbi Yehudah how he had known that death was imminent, he replied: "It is written: 'For man shall not see Me and live.' I saw that he saw."

Testimony of the Disciple

The rabbi of Kalev once asked Rabbi Yehudah Zevi to tell him words of the teachings which he had heard from his teacher, Rabbi Uri. "The teachings of my teacher," said Rabbi

Yehudah Zevi, "are like manna that enters the body but does not leave it." But when the rabbi of Kalev would not stop pressing him, Rabbi Yehudah Zevi tore open the coat over his breast and cried: "Look into my heart! There you will learn what my teacher is."

YEHUDAH ZEVI OF STRETYN AND HIS
SON ABRAHAM OF STRETYN

Men Can Meet

In the course of a journey, Rabbi Yehudah Zevi of Stretyn learned that Rabbi Shimon of Yaroslav was traveling the same road from the opposite direction. He got out of his carriage and went to meet him. Now Rabbi Shimon had heard of Rabbi Yehudah Zevi's coming, got out of his carriage, and went toward him. They greeted each other like brothers.

Then Rabbi Yehudah Zevi said: "Now I understand the meaning of the popular saying: 'Men can meet, but mountains never.' When one man considers himself just a human being, pure and simple, and the other does so too, they can meet. But if the one considers himself a lofty mountain, and the other thinks the same, then they cannot meet."

A Pregnancy

Rabbi Yehudah Zevi said:

"When a man grows aware of a new way in which to serve God, he should carry it around with him secretly and without uttering it for nine months, as though he were pregnant with it, and let others know of it only at the end of that time, as though it were a birth."

The Lord Is God

Rabbi Yehudah Zevi said:

"It is written: 'Unto thee it was shown that thou mightest know that the Lord, He is God; there is none else beside Him.' He who is learned knows that there is really no distinction between the name YHVH (which is translated as 'the Lord'), that is, the attribute of mercy, and the name Elohim (which is translated as 'God'), that is, the attribute of rigor. He knows that in reality everything is good. That is the secret meaning of the people's cry after Elijah had overcome the prophets of Baal: 'YHVH is Elohim!' "

Messiah the Son of Joseph

A hasid told this story:

"Once Rabbi Yehudah Zevi said to us at table: 'Today Messiah the son of Joseph will be born in Hungary, and he will become one of the hidden zaddikim. And if God lets me live long enough, I shall go there and see him.'

"Eighteen years later the rabbi traveled to the city of Pest and took me with him along with other hasidim. We stayed in Pest for several weeks and not one of us disciples knew why we had come.

"One day a youth appeared at the inn. He wore a short coat and his face was as beautiful as an angel's. Without asking permission he went straight into the rabbi's room and closed the door behind him. I remembered those words I had heard long ago, kept near the door, and waited to greet him as he came out and ask his blessing. But when hours later he did come out, the rabbi accompanied him to the gate, and when I ran out into the little street, he had vanished. Even now after so many years, my heart still beats with the living impulse I received from him as he went by."

The Suffering He Took Over

During the last three years of his life Rabbi Yehudah Zevi was afflicted with a terrible disease which caused painful ulcers to break out all over his body. The doctors said that from what they knew of human fortitude it was impossible for a man to bear such pain. When one of the rabbi's close friends asked him about this, he said: "When I was young and one who was sick came to me, I could pray with all the force of my soul that his suffering might be taken from him. Later the strength of my prayer flagged and all I could do was to take the suffering upon myself. And so now I bear it."

Drugs

A learned but ungenerous man said to Rabbi Abraham of Stretyn: "They say that you give people mysterious drugs and that your drugs are effective. Give me one that I may attain to the fear of God."

151

"I don't know any drug for the fear of God," said Rabbi Abraham. "But if you like I can give you one for the love of God."

"That's even better!" cried the other. "Just you give it to me."

"It is the love of one's fellow men," answered the zaddik.

The Unity of Senses

Rabbi Hayyim of Zans was surprised when Rabbi Abraham of Stretyn, who was visiting him, failed to put sugar in his coffee. When he questioned him about it, Rabbi Abraham said: "It is said: 'There is no unity in my bones because of my sin.' Why is there a division between the powers of the limbs of man that are all wrought out of the same matter? Why can eyes only see and ears only hear? Because of the sin of the first man they are not in harmony. But whoever sets himself right to the very root of his soul, to Adam's sin, will bring unity to his body. And such a man can taste sweetness even with his eyes."

MORDECAI OF LEKHOVITZ
AND HIS DESCENDANTS

The Chain

Rabbi Mordecai of Lekhovitz said to his disciples:
"The zaddik cannot say any words of the teachings unless he
first links his soul to the soul of his dead teacher or to that
of his teacher's teacher. Only then is link joined to link, and
the teachings flow from Moses to Joshua, from Joshua to the
elders, and so on to the zaddik's own teacher, and from his
teacher to him."

The Nature of Prayer

Rabbi Moshe of Kobryn related:
"My teacher, Rabbi Mordecai of Lekhovitz, taught me how to
pray. He instructed me as follows: 'He who utters the word
"Lord" and in doing so prepares to say "of the world," is not
speaking as he should. At the moment he is saying "Lord,"
he must only think of offering himself up to the Lord, so that
even if his soul should leave him with the "Lord," and he were
not able to add the word "world," it would be enough for him
that he had been able to say "Lord." '
"This is the essence of prayer."

In Your Kingdom

An emissary from the Land of Israel, a devout and honest man,
feared that great honors would be conferred upon him (for
at that time such was the custom with regard to emissaries)
and that he might feel satisfaction thereat. So he prayed to
God if that happened, to send him stomach cramps, for the
bodily pain would make him forget all about the honors. His
prayer was granted. When he arrived in Lekhovitz—it was
on a Friday—Rabbi Mordecai received him with great honors.
Soon after, the emissary was in such pain that he had to lie
down and was unable to sit at the zaddik's table. But from

his bed he could hear the hasidim in the next room singing, "They shall rejoice in Your kingdom," the zaddik leading the chorus.

The emissary jumped up. His pains had left him. Just as he was, without his coat and shoes, wearing only the skullcap on his head, he ran into the room and danced around the table. "Praised be the Lord," he cried, keeping time with the singing, "who has brought me to the right place. I heard it: 'They shall rejoice in Your kingdom.' Not in a wife and children, not in sheep and cattle, but in Your kingdom! Praise be the Lord that I have come to the right place. But in Your kingdom! But in Your kingdom!"

The Hole in the Lung

Rabbi Mordecai of Lekhovitz once said to himself:

"We have heard of a bird that sings his praise of God with such fervor that his body bursts. But I pray and yet I remain whole and sound. So what good are my prayers?" After a time the great fervor of his praying tore a hole in his lung. The doctors in the town of Lwow gave him up, but he said to God: "I did not mean to say only one prayer in that way; I want to go on praying." Then God helped him and he recovered. When he happened to be in Lwow again, and a crowd of hasidim surrounded his house, a doctor passed by and asked who had arrived. "The rabbi of Lekhovitz," they answered. "Is he still alive?" cried the doctor. "Then he certainly must be living without a lung."

Miracles

The rabbi of Kobryn said: "We paid no attention to the miracles our teachers worked, and when sometimes a miracle did not come to pass, he gained in our eyes."

Against Worrying

Rabbi Mordecai of Lekhovitz said:

"We must not worry. Only one worry is permissible: a man should worry about nothing but worry."

154

Why the Rejoicing?

This is what Rabbi Mordecai once said in connection with the verse in the psalm: "Rejoice the soul of Thy servant."

"Why the rejoicing?" said he. " 'For unto Thee, O Lord, do I lift my soul'—it is by rejoicing that I can lift my soul to You."

A Blessing

Once when Rabbi Mordecai attended the circumcision of the son of his friend Rabbi Asher of Stolyn, and they brought him the boy afterward that he might bless him, he said: "May you not fool God, may you not fool yourself, and may you not fool people."

A Sign for Cain

This is how Rabbi Mordecai expounded the verse: "And the Lord set a sign for Cain, lest any finding him should smite him." "God gave Cain, the penitent, a sign of strength and holiness, so that no accident he met with should beat his spirit down and disturb him in his work of repentance."

Wholesome Insolence

A learned old man who was hostile to the hasidic way once asked Rabbi Mordecai of Lekhovitz: "Tell me why it is that so long as a young man learns in the House of Study and has nothing to do with the oddities of hasidim, he is well behaved and has good manners, but as soon as he joins the hasidim he grows insolent."

The zaddik replied: "Haven't you heard about that learned old fellow who has been taking a great deal of time and trouble with mankind from time immemorial? King Solomon called him an old king, and the fact that he learns along with all those who learn proves his learning. Now when this learned old fellow comes to a timid young man who has nothing but good manners with which to meet people, and tries to tempt him to follow him in his ways, the youth does not dare turn him out. But the hasid, the insolent hasid, seizes the old fellow in both his arms, presses him close to himself till his ribs crack, and kicks him out of the door."

The Verse Within

Once when Rabbi Mordecai was in the great town of Minsk expounding the Torah to a number of men hostile to his way, they laughed at him. "What you say does not explain the verse in the least!" they cried.

"Do you really think," he replied, "that I was trying to explain the verse in the book? That doesn't need explanation! I want to explain the verse that is within me."

For the Joy of Others

The mitnagdim were making fun of the rabbi of Lekhovitz on another occasion. But when they laughed he did nothing but smile and say: "God has not created a single creature that does not give joy to others. So I too have been created for the joy of others, for those who are near to my heart because my nearness is pleasing to them, and for you because you mock me." The mitnagdim listened and grew silent and gloomy.

Hasid and Mitnagid

A hasid of the zaddik of Lekhovitz had a business partner who was a mitnagid. The hasid kept urging him to go to the rabbi with him, but the mitnagid was obstinate in his refusal. Finally, however, when they happened to be in Lekhovitz on business, he let himself be persuaded and agreed to go to the zaddik's for the sabbath meal.

In the course of the meal the hasid saw his friend's face light up with joy. Later he asked him about it. "When the zaddik ate, he looked as holy as the high priest making the offering!" was the reply. After a while the hasid went to the rabbi, much troubled in spirit, and wanted to know why the other had seen something on his very first visit which he, the rabbi's close friend, had not.

"The mitnagid must see, the hasid must believe," answered Rabbi Mordecai.

Fraud

Rabbi Mordecai of Lekhovitz busied himself collecting money for the Land of Israel, and he himself gave large amounts for this cause. At all times—when he rose from his bed in the morning, before Morning Prayer, after Morning Prayer, before studying, after studying, before dining and after dining, and so on until evening he put aside gifts for the Land of Israel. When a sum of money had accumulated he sent it to Rabbi Abraham Kalisker who at that time was the collector for the Land of Israel, and he appended a slip of paper which bore the names of the donors. But since Rabbi Mordecai himself had contributed considerable sums and did not wish anyone to know how large a share of the money was due to him, he added something of what he had given under the name of every other donor listed on the slip.

When the list came to Rabbi Abraham's hand, he looked at it, smiled, shook his head, and pointed to one item after another, saying: "The rabbi of Lekhovitz has something of his own in this! And here there's something more of the rabbi of Lekhovitz!"

Before Thee

Once when Rabbi Mordecai was saying the verse from the psalm: "But I was brutish and ignorant; I was as a beast before Thee," he interrupted himself and cried: "Lord of the world, I want to be ignorant, I want to be brutish, if only I can be before Thee."

In His Father's Footsteps

When Rabbi Noah, Rabbi Mordecai's son, assumed the succession after his father's death, his disciples noticed that there were a number of ways in which he conducted himself differently from his father, and asked him about this.

"I do just as my father did," he replied. "He did not imitate, and I do not imitate."

Against Hypocrisy

Rabbi Noah of Lekhovitz said:

"He who works in the service of God deceitfully—what good does it do him? God cannot be fooled, and if you succeed in fooling the people, it will turn out wrong in the end. Whoever tries to fool others only fools himself, and keeps on being a fool."

"I Believe"

Once when Rabbi Noah was in his room, he heard how one of his disciples began to recite the Principles of Faith in the House of Study next door, but stopping immediately after the words "I believe with perfect faith" whispered to himself: "I don't understand that!" and then once more: "I don't understand that." The zaddik left his room and went to the House of Study.

"What is it you do not understand?" he asked.

"I don't understand what it's all about," said the man. "I say 'I believe.' If I really do believe, then how can I possibly sin? But if I do not really believe, why am I telling lies?"

"It means," answered the rabbi, "that the words 'I believe' are a prayer, meaning 'oh, that I may believe!'" Then the hasid was suffused with a glow from within. "That is right!" he cried. "That is right! Oh, that I may believe, Lord of the world, oh, that I may believe!"

Light

"And God said: 'Let there be light.'"

Rabbi Shelomo Hayyim of Kaidanov, a grandson of Rabbi Mordecai of Lekhovitz, read this verse thus: "And he said: 'God, let there be light!'" When a man prays with true fervor, "God, let there be light," then he shall see the light.

A Jew

Before he died Rabbi Shelomo Hayyim said to his sons: "You are not to think that your father was a zaddik, a 'rebbe,' a 'good Jew.' But all the same I haven't been a hypocrite. I did try to be a Jew."

MOSHE OF KOBRYN

The Fish in the Water

Rabbi Moshe of Kobryn told this story:

"When I was a boy I was once playing with other children on the first day of the month of Elul. Then my elder sister said: 'How can you play today at the beginning of the month of preparation for the great judgment, when even the fish in the water tremble?'

"When I heard this I began to tremble and could not stop for hours. And even now as it comes back to me, I feel as if I were a fish in water on the first day of the month of Elul, and like the fish I tremble before the judgment of the world."

Charity

Rabbi Moshe of Kobryn was the son of villagers who labored hard to earn a meager livelihood. When he was a boy there was a famine in Lithuania. Poor men left the cities with their wives and children and swarmed all over the countryside in search of food. Every day throngs of hungry people passed through the village in which Moshe's parents lived. His mother ground grain with a hand mill and each morning she baked bread and distributed it among them.

One day, more people came than usual and there was not enough bread to go around. But the oven was still hot and the bowls were full of dough. So she quickly took some of the dough, kneaded it and formed loaves, and slipped them into the oven. Meanwhile the hungry people complained because they had to wait, and a few insolent fellows among them even railed and cursed. At that, Rabbi Moshe's mother burst into tears. "Do not cry, mother," said the boy. "Let them curse. Just do your work, and fulfil the commandment of God. If they praised you and showered blessings on you, it would not perhaps be fulfilled so well."

To Be a Soldier

The rabbi of Kobryn told this story:

"When I was young I once spent Purim with my teacher Rabbi Mordecai of Lekhovitz. In the middle of the meal he cried: 'Today is the day of gifts, the hour for giving has come. Whoever reaches out his hand, will get from me whatever strength in the service of God he desires for himself.' His disciples asked for a variety of spiritual gifts. Each got what he wanted and kept it.

"Finally the rabbi inquired: 'Well, Moshe, and what do you want?'

"I fought down my shyness and replied: 'I don't want any gratuitous gift. I want to be a common soldier and serve until I deserve what I get.' "

One Thing after Another

The rabbi of Kobryn told this story:

"When my teacher instructed me in one way to serve, I did not want to hear anything more from him until I had done what he had taught me. Not until then did I open up my ears again."

The Faithful Follower

Rabbi Mordecai of Lekhovitz was a disciple of Rabbi Shelomo of Karlin. When this rabbi died, his disciples Rabbi Mordecai and Rabbi Asher of Stolyn divided the communities of his hasidim between them. But they could not come to an agreement about Kobryn, which each wanted to include in his own area. Rabbi Mordecai suggested a solution. "I have a hasid in Kobryn," he said, "Rabbi Moshe. I give you a year to get him to visit you. If he does, you shall have Kobryn. During this year you may do anything you like to attract him to you and I shall do everything I can to drive him from me."

And so it came to pass. The next time Rabbi Moshe went to Lekhovitz, his teacher did not greet him. But Moshe neither questioned nor doubted; he was just as devoted to Rabbi Mordecai as before. And even though Rabbi Asher called on him, put himself out to be agreeable, and promised him all kinds of

160

good things in this and the coming world, Moshe remained faithful. And so Kobryn fell to his teacher's share.

Angels and Humans

The rabbi of Kobryn once looked at the Heavens and cried: "Angel, little angel! It is no great trick to be an angel up there in the sky! You don't have to eat and drink, beget children and earn money. Just you come down to earth and worry about eating and drinking, about raising children and earning money, and we shall see if you keep on being an angel. If you succeed, you may boast—but not now!"

An Answer

The rabbi of Kobryn liked to tell the story of the answer General Gowin gave to Czar Nicholas. The general was very old and had served fifty years. At maneuvers which the Czar attended the general headed one of the armies.

Nicholas rode down the first row and addressed the general: "Well, Gowin, I see you are up and doing. Is your blood still hot?"

Said Gowin: "Not my blood, your majesty. The service is still hot in me."

Books

Once he said:

"If it were within my power, I should hide everything written by the zaddikim. For when a man has too much knowledge, his wisdom is apt to be greater than his deeds."

The End of the Matter

The rabbi of Kobryn taught:

"At the close of Ecclesiastes we read: 'The end of the matter, all having been heard: fear God!' Now whatever matter you come to the end of, you will always hear this one maxim, 'Fear God!' and this one is the whole. There is not a single thing in all the world that does not show you a way to fear God and to serve him. All is commandment."

Up and Down

Rabbi Moshe of Kobryn taught:

"When you walk over a freshly ploughed field, furrows alternate with ridges. The way in the service of God is like that. Now you go up, now you go down, now the Evil Urge gets a hold on you, now you get a hold on him. Just you see to it that it is you who deal the last blow!"

For the King

"And if one of you should suddenly fall from the heights he has reached," said the rabbi of Kobryn to his hasidim, "and plunge into the abyss, let him not give way to despair! Let him take the yoke of the Kingdom of Heaven upon him anew, and begin the fight all over again.

"When the Saxons in our region were fighting the Russians, a Russian soldier got one of them in his power. 'Cry for mercy,' he shouted, 'and I'll let you go!'

"'Nothing doing,' the Saxon panted in his face. 'It would be a disgrace to my king.'

"The Russian bellowed back: 'Cry mercy or I'll knock off your head.' But as the steel cut the artery in his throat, the Saxon repeated: 'It would be a disgrace to my king.'"

Simply to Act

Before drawing water for the baking of the unleavened bread, the rabbi of Kobryn said to those standing around him: "The king teaches his men all manner of military thrusts and feints, but when they are in the thick of the fight, they throw all they have learned overboard and simply shoot. In respect to the drawing of water there are also many mysteries to be learned, but when it comes to the action itself all I know is what I am bidden to do."

The Dress That Did Not Fit

The wife of a high-ranking officer had told a tailor to make her an expensive dress. But it turned out too tight and he was thrown out of the house in disgrace. The tailor went to the rabbi of Kobryn and begged him to tell him what to do so as not to lose all his customers among the gentry.

"Go back," said the zaddik, "and offer to make the dress over. Then rip it up and sew the pieces together again just as they are."

The man did as he was told. Timidly and humbly he made over the dress he had botched in his proud assurance, and it turned out perfect.

This is a story Rabbi Moshe was fond of telling himself.

The Soul and the Evil Urge

The rabbi of Kobryn taught:

The soul says to the Evil Urge what Abraham said to Lot: " . . . If thou wilt take the left hand, then I will go to the right; or if thou take the right hand, then I will go to the left." The soul says: "When you try to lead me left, I will not heed you and go the right. But should you by any chance advise me to go right in your company, I'd prefer to go left."

Bitter, Not Bad

The rabbi of Kobryn taught:

"When a man suffers, he ought not to say: 'That's bad! That's bad!' Nothing that God imposes on man is bad. But it is all right to say: 'That's bitter!' For among medicines there are some that are made with bitter herbs."

Not By Bread Only

In the course of the sabbath meal Rabbi Moshe once took a piece of bread in his hand and said to his hasidim:

"It is written: 'Man doth not live by bread only, but by every thing that proceedeth out of the mouth of the Lord doth man live.' The life of man is not sustained by the stuff of bread but by the sparks of divine life that are within it. He is here. All exists because of his life-giving life, and when he withdraws from anything, it crumbles away to nothing."

By Whose Word

One of the rabbi of Kobryn's hasidim was employed in public
works. One morning while he was attending to his business,
he was overcome by a worry. He did not know what to do.
Finally he let everything go, returned to town and without
stopping at his own house went straight to the zaddik, who
was just about to have breakfast. A dish of barley had been
set before the zaddik and he was saying the blessing over it,
ending: "by whose word all things exist."
The zaddik did not look at his hasid who had just crossed the
threshold, and he did not offer to shake hands with him. So
the man stood to one side and waited for an opportunity to
present his problem. Finally the rabbi said to him: "Zalman,
I thought you were like your father, but now I see you are not
like him. Your father once came to me with a whole load
of troubles. As he entered, I was saying the blessing, ending
'by whose word all things exist,' just like today. When I had
ended I saw that your father was preparing to leave. 'Abramele,'
I asked, 'didn't you have something on your mind?'
" 'No,' said he, and took leave of me.
"Do you understand? When a Jew hears that everything exists
because of the word of God—what is there left to ask? For
this is the answer to all his questions and worries."
And Rabbi Moshe gave the hasid his hand in greeting. For
a while the hasid was silent, then he bade his master farewell
and went back to his work comforted.

Where Is Man?

The time for the sabbath meal had come and many young men
were standing around the table of the rabbi of Kobryn. He fixed
his eyes on one of them who had often been at his house and
asked the servant: "Who is that?" The servant was surprised,
but gave the visitor's name. "I do not know him," said Rabbi
Moshe. The servant gave the names of the young man's father
and father-in-law, and when this too failed to jog the rabbi's
memory, the servant told him when the young man had come
to Kobryn and how he had heard the rabbi's teachings.
At this the zaddik seemed to remember, and he addressed

the subject of his inquiries who was standing before him in great distress: "Now I know why I did not recognize you. Where a man sends his thoughts, there he is himself, and since your thoughts were very far away, all I saw was a lump of flesh."

Do Not Crowd

Once on a Hanukkah evening the people crowded around to see the rabbi of Kobryn light the candles. But he said: "It is written: 'The people saw, they tottered, they stood afar off.' When you jostle and crowd, you are very far off."

The Flame Goes Out

A hasid complained to the rabbi of Kobryn that every time he set out to see him, his heart was aflame with fervor and he thought he would fly straight to Heaven the moment he stood before his teacher; yet every time he saw him face to face, the flame went out, and then his heart felt more shriveled and cold than at home.

The rabbi said: "Remember what David says in the psalm: 'My soul thirsteth for God,' and further on, 'So have I looked for Thee in the sanctuary.' David implores God to let him feel the same fervor in the holy sanctuary that he felt when he was 'in a dry and weary land where no water was.' For first the all-merciful God wakens a man to holiness, but once he is kindled to act the flame is taken from him, so that he may act for himself and of himself attain to the state of perfect awakening."

Satan's Ruse

"In olden times," so said the rabbi of Kobryn, "when Satan wanted to prevent a hasid from going to the zaddik, he assumed the shape of his father, or his mother, or his wife, and tried his utmost to persuade him to give up his plan. But when he saw that resistance only strengthened the hasid in his faithfulness, he changed his tactics. He made his peace with the man he was dealing with, grew very friendly, and said, all gentleness and docility: 'You have converted me. Just you go to your rabbi, but permit me to join you; just you pray in your own

way, and let me pray along with you; just you learn whatever you can, and I shall help you learn.'

"And so the time comes when Satan says: 'Just you sit down
in the zaddik's seat, and I shall sit beside you. We two shall
stay together!' "

Accepting the World

One of Rabbi Moshe's hasidim was very poor. He complained
to the zaddik that his wretched circumstances were an obstacle
to learning and praying.

"In this day and age," said Rabbi Moshe, "the greatest devotion, greater than learning and praying, consists in accepting
the world exactly as it happens to be."

The Original Meaning

This is what Rabbi Moshe said to an author who put questions
to him concerning the Kabbalah, the secret teachings, and the
kavvanot, the mystical concentrations, which are directed
toward superhuman effects. "You must keep in mind that the
word Kabbalah is derived from *kabbel:* to accept; and the
word kavvanah from *kavven:* to direct. For the ultimate significance of all the wisdom of the Kabbalah is to accept the yoke
of the Kingdom of God, and the ultimate significance of all the
art of the kavvanot is to direct one's heart to God. When a man
says: 'The Lord is my God,' meaning: 'He is mine and I am
His,' must not his soul go forth from his body?" The moment
the rabbi said this, he fell into a deep faint.

A Free Gift

After Rabbi Yitzhak of Vorki's death one of his hasidim went
to Rabbi Moshe of Kobryn. "What do you hope to get from
me, here in Lithuania," asked the rabbi, "that you could not
get just as much of, or even more, from any zaddik in Poland?"

"My teacher," the man replied, "often said that is was a sacred
duty to learn to know the rabbi of Kobryn because he spoke
the truth that is in his heart. And so I decided to go to you
and hoped you might teach me how to attain to truth."

"Truth," said the rabbi of Kobryn, "is not something that can be attained. God looks at a man who has devoted his entire life to attaining the truth—and suddenly he gives him a free gift of it. That is why it is written: 'You will give truth to Jacob.' "

He took a pinch of snuff between two fingers and scattered it on the floor. "Look, even less than this!" Again he took some snuff—only a few shreds of tobacco. "And it can be even less, if only it is the truth!"

True Fear of God

"Had I the true fear of God," said the rabbi of Kobryn, "I should run through the streets and shout: 'You are sinning against the Torah in which is written: Ye shall be holy.' "

The Peg and the Crown

The rabbi of Kobryn said:

"He who is a leader in Israel must not think that the Lord of the world chose him because he is a great man. If the king chose to hang his crown on a wooden peg in the wall, would the peg boast that its beauty drew the king's gaze to it?"

For the Sake of the Others

On the eve of New Year's Day, before the Afternoon Prayer, the rabbi of Kobryn once laid his head on all the notes of request which were spread out before him, and said:

"Lord of the world, 'Thou knowest my folly, and my trespasses are not hid from Thee.' But what shall I do about all these people? They think I really am something! And so I beg of you: 'Let not them that wait for Thee be ashamed through me!' "

Self-Conquest

Once on the eve of the New Year, when Rabbi Moshe went up to the reader's desk to pray, he began to tremble in every limb. He clung to the pulpit, but the pulpit too swayed back and forth. The zaddik could keep his balance only by bending way back. He looked as though he were driving his trembling inward. Only then did he stand firmly in his place and begin to pray.

The Reader

Before praying on New Year's Day, Rabbi Moshe of Kobryn said:

"Once a king was angered at his rebellious people and sat in judgment upon them. No one dared come before him and plead for mercy. But among the throng was the man who had led the revolt. He knew that his head was forfeit, and came forward and pleaded with the king. So, during the Days of Awe, the reader stands before the Ark and prays for the congregation."

He Called to Them

On New Year's Day before the blowing of the ram's horn, the rabbi of Kobryn used to call out:

"Little brothers, do not depend upon me! Every one had better take his own part!"

The Offering

Once on a sabbath Rabbi Moshe of Kobryn was standing before the Ark and praying the Additional Prayer, which is a substitute for the offerings of sabbaths and feast days. When he said the words: "Lead us into our land and there we shall prepare unto thee the offerings that are obligatory for us," he fell to the floor in a faint. They had great difficulty in reviving him, and he finished the prayer.

That evening, Rabbi Moshe spoke again at his own table: "There in our land we shall bring the special offering for this sabbath, for here we have no sanctuary and no service by sacrifices." And he kindled at the words and cried aloud: "Lord of the world, we, we, we ourselves shall bring ourselves to you in place of the offering!"

Then all understood why in the House of Prayer he had fallen to the floor as if all life had left him.

The Fool

The rabbi of Kobryn was asked: "Why is it that a cantor is always called a fool?"

"You know," he replied, "that the world of music verges on that of the turning to God. When the cantor sings he is in the world of music and quite close to that other. How can he manage to keep from leaping over into it and giving himself up to the true turning? Is there any foolishness as foolish as that?"

Exchange of Strength

Rabbi Moshe taught:

When a Jew is about to say: "Blessed art thou, O Lord our God, king of the world," and prepares to utter the first word, the word "blessed," he shall do so with all his strength, so that he will have no strength left to say "art thou." And this is the meaning of the verse in the Scriptures: "But they that wait for the Lord shall exchange their strength." What we are really saying is: "Our Father in Heaven, I am giving you all the strength that is within me in that very first word; now will you, in exchange, give me an abundance of new strength, so that I can go on with my prayer."

Into the Word

Rabbi Moshe of Kobryn said:

"When you utter a word before God, then enter into that word with every one of your limbs."

One of his listeners asked: "How can a big human being possibly enter into a little word?"

"Anyone who thinks himself bigger than the word," said the zaddik, "is not the kind of person we are talking about."

The One Who Knows Not How to Ask

When the rabbi of Kobryn came to that part in the Passover Haggadah which tells of the four sons whose father instructs them in the meaning of the Seder, and what is said about the youngest: "And with the one who knows not how to ask— you must open," he always paused, sighed, and said to God: "And the one, alas! who does not know how to pray—open his heart so that he may be able to pray."

One, Who Knows One?

This is what Rabbi Moshe of Kobryn said concerning the first question in the game of riddles which is sung at the close of the Passover Haggadah: "One, who knows One? One, I know One."

" 'One, who knows One?' Who can know the One who is sheer oneness? For do not even the seraphim ask: 'Where is the place of His glory?' One, and I know it in spite of everything! For, as the sage says: 'God, where can I find you? And where can I not find you!' And the seraphim too reply: 'The whole earth is full of His glory.' I know the One who is sheer oneness by his works within me."

The Ladder

Rabbi Moshe taught:

It is written: "And he dreamed, and behold a ladder set up on the earth." That "he" is every man. Every man must know: I am clay, I am one of countless shards of clay, but "the top of it reached to heaven"—my soul reaches to Heaven; "and behold the angels of God ascending and descending on it"— even the ascent and descent of the angels depend upon my deeds.

Everywhere

The rabbi of Kobryn taught:

God says to man, as he said to Moses: "Put off thy shoes from thy feet"—put off the habitual which encloses your foot, and you will know that the place on which you are now standing is holy ground. For there is no rung of human life on which we cannot find the holiness of God everywhere and at all times.

He Cometh!

The rabbi of Kobryn taught:

In the Midrash we read that when Moses proclaimed to the people that God would deliver them from servitude, they said to him: "How can we be delivered, for the whole land of Egypt is full of our idol worship!" But he answered them: "Because God wants to deliver you, he does not heed your idol worship. As it is written: 'Hark! my beloved! Behold he cometh, leaping upon the mountains, skipping upon the hills!' " And that is the way it is now. When a man bethinks himself and yearns to be delivered from his evil ways, the Evil Urge whispers to him: "How can you hope for deliverance! Have you not wasted all your days on trivial matters!" But the zaddikim say: "Because God wants to deliver you he will not heed what has been, he will leap across all and everything and deliver you."

For the Sake of God

The rabbi of Kobryn taught:

It is written: "And Moses reported the words of the people unto the Lord." In obedience to God's command Moses had brought Israel the message that they were to be a "kingdom of priests and a holy nation," and the people had replied: "All that the Lord has spoken, we will do." This means: It is not to attain a high rung that we desire to serve God, but only because he has spoken to us. Their answer pleased Moses, and he reported it to God in their name and his own.

Not to Fear Death

When the hasidim sat around the rabbi of Kobryn's table at the Feast of Weeks, he said to them: "It is written that at Mount Sinai the people said to Moses: 'Speak thou with us and we will hear; but let no God speak with us, lest we die.' How is it possible that in their greatest hour Israel refused to hear the voice of God for fear of death that is nothing but a wresting of the soul from its husk to cling to the light of life!"

Over and over again and more and more earnestly the zaddik repeated his question. The third time he uttered it, he fainted away and lay motionless a while. It took them a long time to revive him, but then he straightened up in his chair and concluded his teaching: "'. . . lest we die.' For it was very hard for them to give up serving God on earth."

The Most Humble

The rabbi of Kobryn was asked: "How is it possible that Dathan and Abiram reproached Moses with wanting to make himself a prince over them? For does not the Torah testify that he was the most humble of all men?"

The rabbi expounded: "When Moses sat in the zaddik's chair,

he pronounced judgment with great force. That is why they thought he wanted to make himself a prince over them. But deep in his heart he was the most humble of men. How different are the people who go their way, head bowed to the earth, and term themselves humble. That is a worthless sort of humility. True humility is hidden in the heart."

Words Not Taken to Heart

Once after the rabbi of Kobryn had "said Torah" at the sabbath meal, he said to the hasidim seated around his table: "I see that all the words I have spoken have not found a single man who took them into his heart. And if you ask me how I know this, since I am neither a prophet myself nor the son of a prophet, let me tell you. Words that come from the heart go to the heart in all their truth. But if they find no heart that will receive them, then God shows mercy to the man who spoke them: He does not let them err about in space, but they all return to the heart from which they were spoken. That is what has happened to me. I felt something like a thrust—and they all thronged back into my heart."

* * *

Some time after Rabbi Moshe's death, a friend said: "If there had been someone to whom he could have talked, he would still be alive."

Rest

Once when he was old, he was seated at the sabbath meal and anyone could see that he was very weak. His trusted servant urged him to go and take a rest. "Fool," cried the rabbi, "the only rest I know is when I sit together with Israel. I have no other rest."

"If I Knew"

Rabbi Moshe once said:
"If I knew for sure that I had helped a single one of my hasidim to serve God, I should have nothing to worry me."
Another time he said:
"If I knew I had said 'Amen' just once in the way it ought to be said, I should have nothing to worry me."

And on still another occasion he said:

"If I knew that after my death it would be said in Heaven that a Jew was coming, I should have nothing to worry me at all."

The End

On the Great Sabbath not many days before he died, Rabbi Moshe of Kobryn repeated the words of the psalm over and over again: "Praise the Lord, O my soul!" Then he added softly: "Soul of mine, you will praise the Lord in every world, no matter in what world you are. But this is what I beg of God: 'I will praise the Lord while I live'—as long as I still live here, I want to be able to praise him."

On the last day of Passover he talked at table a long time before grace was said. Then he concluded: "Now I have nothing more to say. Let us say grace."

On the following night he lay down on his deathbed, and he died a week later.

Most Important

Soon after the death of Rabbi Moshe, Rabbi Mendel of Kotzk asked one of his disciples:

"What was most important to your teacher?"

The disciple thought and then replied:

"Whatever he happened to be doing at the moment."

FROM THE HOUSE OF

THE MAGGID OF KOZNITZ

MOSHE AND ELEAZAR OF KOZNITZ

For the Light

Rabbi Moshe, the son of the maggid of Koznitz, said:
"It is written: 'Pure olive oil beaten for the light.' We are to
be beaten and bruised, but in order to glow with light."

The Window and the Curtain

When young Rabbi Eleazar of Koznitz, Rabbi Moshe's son,
was a guest in the house of Rabbi Naftali of Roptchitz, he
once cast a surprised glance at the window, where the curtains
had been drawn. When his host asked him the cause of his
surprise, he said: "If you want people to look in, then why
the curtains? And if you do not want them to, why the
window?"

"And what explanation have you found for this?" asked
Rabbi Naftali.

"When you want someone you love to look in," said the young
rabbi, "you draw aside the curtain."

HAYYIM MEIR YEHIEL OF MOGIELNICA AND
YISAKHAR OF WOLBORZ

Rabbi Hayyim Meir Yehiel told this story:

"My mother, peace be with her, lost one child after another in early infancy. Finally she gave birth to a child they named Moshe, and he looked as though he might survive. The first time he sat at the table of his grandfather the holy maggid, for the third sabbath meal, was when he was seven years old. On that day the passage in the Scriptures had been read which deals with how God commanded Moses to speak to the rock 'that it give forth its water' and Moses smote the rock and 'water came forth abundantly.' While they were at the meal, the boy Moshe suddenly leaped on the table and cried: 'The Torah speaks of the sin of Moses—but was it sin for him to smite the rock? Did not God himself say to him: "Take the rod!"'

"And he spoke on and on and gave a logical justification for Moses our teacher. Then he got down from the table and said to his mother: 'Mother, my head aches.' He went to his room, lay down on his bed, and died. Later, the zaddikim of that generation said that the soul of our teacher Moses had been in the boy and that he had been born only to justify Moses, our teacher.

"When he died, my mother implored her father, the holy maggid, to help her so that she might rear a son to manhood. He answered her: 'My daughter, when you lie with your husband your soul soars high in ecstasy and that is why the children you conceive do not get enough of the stuff of earth. You must bring your soul down to earth and then you will conceive a son who will live.' My mother absorbed this counsel with all her heart and soon afterward she conceived me.

"The night before I was born she dreamed that she was led into a great hall, where old men wearing crowns and white robes were seated at a long table listening to a boy, to her son Moshe, who sat at the head of the board. She wanted to run up to him and embrace him, but he called to her: 'Do not touch me!' Then he blessed her for the hour of birth."

Not without the Garment of Flesh

Rabbi Hayyim Meir Yehiel told this story:

"When I was five years old I said to my grandfather, the holy maggid: 'Grandfather, you go to a rabbi, and my father goes to a rabbi. I am the only one who doesn't go to a rabbi; I want to go to a rabbi too.' I began to cry.

"Said my grandfather to me: 'But I too am a rabbi.'

"Said I to him: 'Then why do you go to a rabbi?'

"Said he: 'What makes you think I go to a rabbi?'

"Said I: 'Because at night I see an old man with you, and you are seated before him as a servant before his master—so he must be your rabbi.'

" 'My child,' said he, 'that is the Baal Shem Tov, may his merits shield us. When you are older you will also be able to study with him.'

"Said I: 'No, I don't want a dead rabbi.'

"And I think the same to this very day. For I do not want the rungs of the spirit without the garment of the flesh. When learning from a rabbi, the disciple must resemble his teacher at least in one thing—in having a garment of flesh. That is the mystery of the Divine Presence in exile."

Only on My Own

Rabbi Hayyim Meir Yehiel, the grandson of the maggid of Koznitz, told this incident.

"When I was a boy of eleven, my grandfather summoned me and said: 'Come to me at dawn and I shall teach you the Kabbalah.' I did not do as he said, but from that time on I studied alone at dawn and did my service, for I did not want anything I could not get on my own.

"After a time my grandfather again summoned me and said: 'First I thought you did not like getting up early. But now I have found out that you are up early, and nevertheless you do not come to me.' But he had grasped the fact that I wanted to study on my own, for he went on to say: 'Well, just make a point of being there every morning when I pray, and I shall see to it that you receive holy insight.'

"But I did not even want to get this without working for it myself, and so I was present only at the beginning and end of the prayer. Time passed, and then one night I had a vision. My teacher, the rabbi of Apt, blessed be his memory, appeared to me and brought me phylacteries from paradise. When I had bound one of the phylacteries to my forehead I sensed a holy insight."

The Choice of a Soul

Rabbi Hayyim Meir Yehiel once said to his hasidim:

"I know a man who as a boy was removed to the upper worlds on the night he became Bar Mitzvah, and there they allowed him to choose a soul to his own liking. And so he selected a great soul. But it did not reach any high rung after all, and he remained a little man."

The hasidim realized that he had been speaking of himself.

The Secret of the Counting

The rabbi of Mogielnica once said to his hasidim: "I shall explain to you the secret of the counting of the fifty days between Passover and the Feast of Weeks. First it is dark, then it grows very light, but after that it grows dark again, and then, from day to day, from step to step, more and more light appears until it is all light again, and the receiving of the Torah, for which we have prepared ourselves, comes to pass."

Against Pious Thoughts

On a certain Purim when the rabbi of Mogielnica was reading the scroll of Esther, a young man stood near by and said to him when the reading was over: "I fear I did not listen closely enough and perhaps skipped over one word or another while I was silently reciting the scroll with you."

Later the rabbi said to his friends: "There's your superpious man! All he cares about is doing exactly what is prescribed. But he whose soul is directed toward doing the will of God within the commandment, and clings wholly to God's will, may very possibly fail to do something of what is prescribed, but it does not trouble him. For it is written: 'In thy love for her wilt thou err constantly.'"

No Contradictions

The rabbi of Mogielnica said:
"It is well known that the sayings of our sages which seem to contradict one another are all 'words of the living God.' Each of them decided according to the depth of his root in Heaven, and up there all their words are truth, for in the upper worlds there are no contradictions. There all opposites, such as prohibition and permission, guilt and guiltlessness, are one unified whole. The distinction between prohibition and permission appears only in their actions on earth."

There Is a Difference

Rabbi Hayyim of Mogielnica was about to go on a journey, but because he was so old and weak he could not manage to get into the carriage. Some of the hasidim who were present went in search of a stool. But when Rabbi Yisakhar saw his teacher standing and waiting he lay down on the ground. The zaddik set foot on his back and got into the carriage.
Later, the disciples discussed the incident. One of them said: "What is there so remarkable about it? I am ready to lie under the rabbi's feet for two hours!"
On Friday evening before the zaddik came to the meal, the youth lay down under the table. His master noticed it at once. "Now, now," he said, "come out from under that table!"

Marriage

Rabbi Yisakhar of Wolborz recounted:
"After my wedding a friend and I were studying the marital laws in the House of Study, when our teacher, Rabbi Hayyim of Mogielnica, came in and gave us a document which, he said, would explain itself. He left immediately. The document was a marriage contract in which we did not notice anything that required explanation. We asked the rabbi's son about it.

181

" 'Don't you see,' said he, 'that there is a drawing of two clasping hands on the sheet? That's what he was referring to.'
"Later his father confirmed him and interpreted the symbol. 'You can see by the sleeves,' he explained, 'that the hands are those of the groom and the bride. The groom gives his hand to the bride and says: "I betroth thee unto Me for ever"—one hand shall nevermore be withdrawn from the other—"in righteousness and in justice"—now a pat and now a slap— "in lovingkindness and in compassion"—now a tidbit and now a good drink—but we shall remain together "for ever"; we dare not lose our tempers. That is how a Jew should be with the Lord of the world—he mustn't lose his temper!' "

In the World of Confusion

They tell this story:
To Rabbi Yisakhar of Wolborz there came a dead man whom he had once known when he was alive and prominent in his community, and begged the rabbi's help, saying that his wife had died some time ago and now he needed money to arrange for his marriage with another.
"Don't you know," the zaddik asked him, "that you are no longer among the living, that you are in the world of confusion?"
When the man refused to believe him, he lifted the tails of the dead man's coat and showed him that he was dressed in his shroud.
Later Rabbi Yisakhar's son asked: "Well, if that is so—perhaps I too am in the world of confusion?"
"Once you know that there is such a thing as that world," answered his father, "you are not in it."

FROM THE SCHOOL OF

THE RABBI OF LUBLIN

DAVID OF LELOV

The New Suit

Little David's father was a poor man. During the first months of an exceptionally severe winter he could not buy his son a warm suit of clothes. At long last he managed to scrape together the money. When David arrived at the school in his new suit, he saw a younger boy shivering in rags, and immediately changed clothes with him.

As soon as David reached home he went to his mother and told her what had happened. "Put on your old suit," she said, "and go back to school. If your father comes home and finds out what you have done he will be angry and beat you."

"But mother," answered the boy, "it is better for him to beat me and work off his anger."

The Name of God

Rabbi David of Lelov once heard a simple man who was praying say the name of God after every verse. The reason he did this was that there are two dots one above the other at the close of each verse. The man took each to be the tiny letter Yud or Yod, and since the name of God is sometimes abbreviated in the form of two Yuds, he thought that what he saw at the end of every verse was the name of God.

The zaddik instructed him: "Wherever you find two Jews [Yuds] side by side and on a par, there is the name of God. But whenever it looks to you as if one Jew [Yud] were standing above the other, then they are not Jews [Yuds] and it is not the name of God."

Concerning Those Who Ply a Trade

Rabbi Yitzhak of Vorki told this story:

"Once when I was traveling with Rabbi David Lelov, of blessed memory, we arrived in the little town of Elkish about an hour past midnight. Rabbi David did not want to wake

anyone, so we went to Rabbi Berish, the baker. He was standing at his oven and doing his work. When we entered I saw
his face cloud over because we had found him working.
" 'Oh,' said Rabbi David, 'if only God let me earn my bread
by the work of my hands! The truth of the matter is that everyone in Israel has an inner urge he himself does not know of.
What he wants is to work for his fellow men. Everyone who
plies a trade, the cobbler, the tailor, or the baker, takes money
in return for his work only that he may live and continue
to work for his fellow men.' While Rabbi David was speaking,
I saw the baker's face clear and grow brighter and brighter."

The Mistake

Rabbi Yitzhak of Vorki told this story:
"Once when I was on the road with my holy teacher Rabbi
David of Lelov, and we stopped over in a town far from our
home, a woman suddenly fell upon him in the street and
began to beat him. She thought he was her husband who had
abandoned her many years ago. After a few moments, she
saw her error and burst into a flood of tears.
" 'Stop crying,' Rabbi David said to her. 'You were not striking
me, but your husband.' And he added in a low tone: 'How
often we strike someone because we take him for another!' "

Peace-Making

Rabbi David and his disciple Yitzhak, later the rabbi of Vorki,
were once on their way to a place Rabbi David had been
asked to come to in order to make peace between two men
who had a long-standing quarrel. On the sabbath he acted
as the reader of the prayers. The two adversaries were present.
After the close of the sabbath he ordered the horses harnessed
for the journey home.
"But the rabbi has not carried out what he came for," said
his disciple.
"You are mistaken," said Rabbi David. "When in the course
of my prayer I said: 'He who maketh peace in his high places,
may he make peace for us,' the peace was made." And it was
really so.

With the Children

Whenever Rabbi David of Lelov came to a Jewish town he gathered all the children around him and gave each a little whistle. Then he packed them into the big wagon he used for traveling, and drove them all over town. The children whistled with might and main the entire time, and the entire time Rabbi David's face was wreathed in smiles.

With Animals

Once Rabbi David went to Lublin with his disciple Rabbi Yitzhak, in order to spend the New Year with his teacher, the Seer, as he did year after year. On New Year's Day, before the blowing of the ram's horn, the Seer looked around and noticed that Rabbi David was not there. Yitzhak immediately ran to the inn to look for him. He found Rabbi David standing in front of the gate to the house, holding out his cap full of barley to the horses, which their driver in his hurry to get to the House of Prayer had left behind unfed.

When Rabbi David, having finished feeding the horses, came to the House of Prayer, the Seer said: "That was fine blowing of the ram's horn Rabbi David treated us to!"

*　　*　　*

One Friday afternoon Rabbi David was on a journey, when suddenly the horse stopped and refused to go on. The driver beat the horse, but the zaddik objected.

"Rabbi," cried the driver, "the sun will soon be setting and the sabbath is almost here."

"You are quite right," answered Rabbi David, "but what you have to do is to make the animal understand you. Otherwise, it will some day summon you to court in Heaven, and that will not be to your honor."

Concerning Joseph's Brothers

The rabbi of Lelov said to his hasidim:

"A man cannot be redeemed until he recognizes the flaws in his soul and tries to mend them. A nation cannot be redeemed until it recognizes the flaws in its soul and tries to mend them. Whoever permits no recognition of his flaws, be it man or nation, permits no redemption. We can be redeemed to the extent to which we recognize ourselves.

"When Jacob's sons said to Joseph: 'We are upright men,' he answered: 'That is it that I spoke unto you saying: Ye are spies.' But later, when they confessed the truth with their lips and with their hearts and said to one another: 'We are verily guilty concerning our brother,' the first gleam of their redemption dawned. Overcome with compassion, Joseph turned aside and wept."

MOSHE TEITELBAUM

The Enemy

In his youth Rabbi Moshe Teitelbaum had been an enemy of the hasidic teachings, for he regarded them as rank heresy. Once he was staying with his friend Rabbi Joseph Asher, who was also opposed to these innovators. At just about this time, the prayer-book of the holy Rabbi Isaac Luria had appeared in print. When the volume was brought to the two friends, Rabbi Moshe snatched the heavy tome from the messenger, and threw it on the floor. But Rabbi Joseph Asher picked it up and said: "After all, it is a prayer-book, and we must not treat it disrespectfully."

When the rabbi of Lublin was told of the incident, he said: "Rabbi Moshe will become a hasid; Rabbi Joseph Asher will remain an opponent of the hasidic way. For he who can burn with enmity can also burn with love for God, but he who is coldly hostile will always find the way closed." And so it was.

Fear

In the notes Rabbi Moshe Teitelbaum made on the dreams he had in his youth we find the following.

"I was looking ou of the window on the eve of the New Year and there were the people running to the House of Prayer, and I saw that they were driven by the fear of the Day of Judgment. And I said to myself: 'God be thanked, I have been doing the right thing all through the year! I have studied right and prayed right, so I do not have to be afraid.' And then my dreams showed me all my good works. I looked and looked: They were torn, ragged, ruined! And at that instant I woke up. Overcome with fear I ran to the House of Prayer along with the rest."

Paradise

In Rabbi Moshe Teitelbaum's notes on his dreams there is an entry which reads: "I have been in the paradise of the Tannaim." He had also kept a sheet with the words: "The angels will immerse you, and you shall suffer no harm." In his dream he stood near a mountain and wanted to get into the paradise of the Tannaim. But he was told that first he had to immerse himself in Miriam's Well. And at that very instant he looked into the deep water and shuddered. But angels laid hold of him and immersed him and carried him up from the depths. Then he entered the paradise of the Tannaim. There he saw one of the masters sitting with a fur cap on his head and studying the tractate called "The First Gate." There the path stopped. Rabbi Moshe was surprised. "That can't be paradise!" he cried. "Listen, child," said the angels, "you seem to think that the Tannaim are in paradise, but that's not so: paradise is in the Tannaim."

Mourning and Joy

When Rabbi Moshe Teitelbaum became a disciple of the Seer of Lublin, he studied the hasidic way of life for a time and liked it well. But once a question rose in his heart. He noticed that they were always joyful, that they performed every labor with joy, walked and rested with joy and prayed with sublime joy. Then he remembered the words in the Path of Life: "Every God-fearing man must mourn and lament the destruction of the Temple." The next time he was on the way to the rabbi of Lublin he was filled with doubts but he curbed them and said to God: "Lord, you know all my thoughts, and know that it is my purpose not to permit my eyes to regard the ways of good men as wrong. So be with me, and help me when I come to my master, to propound my question. For our sages say: 'If a man comes to be cleansed, they will assist him.' The word 'they' is used, not 'he.' For the 'they' refers to human beings." In this way he prayed and communed with God all the way to Lublin.

The moment he crossed the Seer's threshold, the master said to him: "Why is your face clouded today? It does, indeed, say in the Path of Life that every God-fearing man should mourn and lament the destruction of the Temple. But believe me, we too break into lamentation for Jerusalem at midnight, and we moan and weep, and yet it is all done in a spirit of joy. Do you know the story of the king who was sent into exile? He wandered about for a long time until he found refuge with a friend. This faithful friend shed tears whenever he remembered that the king had been driven out of his realm. But at the same time he rejoiced that the king was lodging in his house. Now, you see, dear friend, that the exiled Divine Presence is lodging with us. I really should not reveal this thing, for we are bidden to keep silence on matters concerning God, but our sages have said: 'If a man comes to be cleansed, they will assist him.' The word 'they' is used, not 'he.' For the 'they' refers to human beings."

Waiting

Rabbi Moshe Teitelbaum was always waiting for the coming of the Messiah.

Whenever he heard a noise in the street, he asked in trembling tones: "Has the messenger come?"

Before going to sleep he would lay out his sabbath clothes near the bed and lean his pilgrim's staff against them. A watchman had orders to wake the rabbi at the very first sign he saw.

Once someone wanted to sell Rabbi Moshe a fine house right next to the House of Prayer. "What would I do with it?" he cried. "Soon the Messiah will come and I shall go to Jerusalem."

The great zaddikim of his era said that a spark from the soul of Jeremiah had been reborn in him. When anyone wondered at the greatness of his sorrow on the day commemorating the destruction of the Temple, he said: "Why should you be astonished? 'I am the man that hath seen affliction,' but God will let me see the restoration as well."

Even when he was very old, it never occurred to him that he could possibly die before the coming of the Messiah.

* * *

Once while he was walking in the procession around the pulpit on the seventh day of the Feast of Booths, the day of the Great Prayer for Salvation, he prayed: "Lord of the world, grant us the coming of the end. And do not think that I am concerned about my own welfare! I agree that I shall not be liberated and redeemed; I am ready to be as the stone hurled from the sling, and to suffer every anguish—for the one and only purpose that your Divine Presence may suffer no more."

* * *

When he was eighty-two, he prayed on the eve of the Day of Atonement before "All Vows": "Lord of the world, you know that I am a wicked sinner, but you also know that I intend to speak the truth. I do not lie and so I shall say only what is so. Had I, Moshe, the son of Hannah, known that my hair would turn gray before the Messiah came, I would very probably not have stood it. But you, Lord of the world, have made a fool of me day after day, until I turned gray. By my life, it is indeed a great trick for the Almighty to make a fool of an old fool! I implore you, Lord of the world, let it come now! Not for our sake, but for your own, that your Name may be sanctified amongst the many!"

* * *

Before his death he said: "I am thinking about my holy teachers, whose soul is in the uppermost paradise. Why do they keep silence? Why do they not shake all the worlds to bring the Messiah down to earth?" And after a little he continued: "In the realm of delight they have most likely been so deluged with joy that they have forgotten the earth, and to them it seems as if the Messiah had already come." And presently he added: "Even if they try to do the same to me—I shall not abandon my people."

NAFTALI OF ROPTCHITZ

The Watchman

In Roptchitz, the town where Rabbi Naftali lived, it was the custom for the rich people whose houses stood isolated or at the far end of the town to hire men to watch over their property by night. Late one evening when Rabbi Naftali was skirting the woods which circled the city, he met such a watchman walking up and down. "For whom are you working?" he asked. The man told him and then inquired in his turn: "And whom are you working for, Rabbi?"

The words struck the zaddik like a shaft. "I am not working for anybody just yet," he barely managed to say. Then he walked up and down beside the man for a long time. "Will you be my servant?" he finally asked. "I should like to," the man replied, "but what would be my duties?"

"To remind me," said Rabbi Naftali.

The Morning Prayer

"There are zaddikim," said Rabbi Naftali, "who pray that those in need of help may come to them and find help through their prayers. But the rabbi of Roptchitz gets up early in the morning and prays that all those in need of help may find it in their own homes, not have to go to Roptchitz, and not be deluded into thinking that the rabbi has helped them."

A Wish

Once, after the Additional Prayer on the Day of Atonement, the rabbi of Roptchitz said: "I wish that I could be reborn as a cow, that a Jew might come to me in the morning to take some of my milk to refresh himself before beginning the service of God."

Leader and Generation

Rabbi Naftali was once talking about the story of the Midrash which tells that God showed Moses all the generations to come, generation after generation with its preachers, generation after generation with its judges.

"Why," asked one of his disciples, "is the generation mentioned first and the leader afterward? Should he not take precedence?"

"You know," said the rabbi, "that the radiance of Moses' face was like that of the sun, of Joshua's like that of the moon, and so the faces of the successive leaders grew paler and paler. If God had inadvertently shown to Moses, Naftali, the school assistant [for so he liked to call himself], as a rabbi, Moses would have cried out: 'Is that supposed to be a rabbi!' and fainted with the shock. That is why God first showed him the generation and then the leader befitting it."

The Foolish Request

The rabbi of Roptchitz told the following incident:

"During the siege of Sebastopol Czar Nicholas was once riding along one of the walls when an enemy archer took aim at him. A Russian soldier who observed this from afar screamed and startled the emperor's horse so that it swerved to the side and the arrow missed its target. The Czar told the man to ask any favor he pleased. 'Our sergeant is so brutal,' the soldier faltered. 'He is always beating me. If only I could serve under another sergeant!'

" 'Fool,' cried Nicholas, 'be a sergeant yourself!'

"We are like that: we pray for the petty needs of the hour and do not know how to pray for our redemption."

The Twin Loaves

Two youths who were deeply devoted to each other used to go to Rabbi Naftali together to sit at his table. When he distributed the bread, for such was his custom, he always gave the two friends twin loaves clinging each to each. Once they were vexed with each other. They did not know how this feeling had entered their hearts and could not overcome it. Soon after when they again went to Roptchitz and were seated at the rabbi's table on the eve of the sabbath, he took the twin loaves, cut them apart, and gave one to each of the youths. On their way home from the meal they were overcome with

194

emotion and both cried out in the same breath: "We are at fault, we are at fault!" They went to an inn, ordered schnapps and drank a toast to each other. The next day at the midday meal of the sabbath Rabbi Naftali again put twin loaves into the hands of the friends.

Conflagration

Young Rabbi Feyvish, a disciple of the rabbi of Roptchitz, recited the Lamentations every midnight as if Jerusalem the city of God had been destroyed that very day. Time after time he was overwhelmed with an infinite sorrow.

Late one evening the rabbi of Roptchitz asked the hasidim who were with him to follow him into the House of Study. "I shall show you," he said, "the meaning of the prophet's words: 'Arise, cry out in the night!'" In the semidarkness of the House of Study they found young Feyvish lying on a bench in a deep sleep. For a while they stood in front of him and wondered why the zaddik had taken them here. Suddenly the youth slipped to the floor, tore open his shirt collar, and cried: "Mother, I am burning up!" Just then the clock struck twelve.

Later on Feyvish left the rabbi of Roptchitz and became the disciple of the rabbi of Apt. His first teacher was much grieved about this. "With all my strength," he said, "I tried to keep down the fire. With the rabbi of Apt he will be a burnt-offering in the conflagration of his heart." Soon after this Rabbi Feyvish died in the House of Prayer during the saying of the prayer: "The breath of all that lives shall bless your name."

The Teacher

Rabbi Naftali of Roptchitz received a man who came with a long list of sins in his hand. He said that he had already been to another zaddik, but that he had imposed so heavy a penance upon him that he was physically unable to endure it. The rabbi cut him short. "And what wrong did our Father do to you," he cried in a terrible voice, "that you have betrayed him?" These words struck the man down. He lost consciousness and fell.

Several hasidim from Hungary who were standing by began

to laugh. Rabbi Naftali turned on them angrily. "I have all but slain a human soul," he cried, "and you laugh!"

"Forgive us," they said. "When our teacher Rabbi Eisik of Kalev lay on his deathbed, he gave us a sign: 'If you find a man who can take the insides out of a sinner, cleanse them, and put them back again that he may live, that is the man you shall take for your rabbi.' That was why we laughed. We have found a new master and we shall keep him until the coming of the Messiah; then we shall return to our old teacher." Then the zaddik laughed with them. He raised the penitent sinner from the floor. " 'Thine iniquity is taken away, and thy sin expiated.' " he said. "Go in peace; keep to the way of God, and he will help you."

The Penitent Who Felt Ashamed

A sinner who wanted to atone came to the rabbi of Roptchitz to learn what penance he should do. He was ashamed to confess all his sins to the zaddik and yet he had to disclose each and every one, for otherwise the rabbi could not have told him the proper form of atonement. So he said that one of his friends had done such and such a thing, but had been too ashamed to come in person and had commissioned him to go in his stead and find out for him the purification for every one of his sins.

Rabbi Naftali looked smilingly into the man's sly and tense face. "Your friend," said he, "is a fool. He could easily have come to me himself and pretended to represent someone who was ashamed to come in his own person."

The Arrogant Ascetic

When Rabbi Naftali was young, there was a man in his native city who fasted and kept vigils until he considered himself quite close to perfection, and his heart swelled. Rabbi Naftali, who knew very well what was going on within that man, once happened to be in the House of Study when a boy grazed the man with his elbow while he was sunk in meditation. The rabbi rebuked the boy: "How dare you disturb this man! Don't you know that he has been fasting for four and twenty hours?"

"Rather say from one sabbath to the next," the ascetic corrected his statement. And with that, what was hidden became manifest.

The Other Half

Once on the Great Sabbath the rabbi of Roptchitz came home from the House of Prayer with weary steps. "What made you so tired?" asked his wife. "It was the sermon," he replied. "I had to speak of the poor and their many needs for the coming Passover, for unleavened bread and wine and everything else is terribly high this year."

"And what did you accomplish with your sermon?" his wife went on to ask.

"Half of what is necessary," he answered. "You see, the poor are now ready to take. As for the other half, whether the rich are ready to give—I don't know about that yet."

Do Not Stop!

On the Day of Rejoicing in the Law, the rabbi of Ulanov, who was a dear friend of the rabbi of Roptchitz, lay dying. In Roptchitz the hasidim had just begun the great round dance in the court of the zaddik's house. He was standing at the window and looking down at them with a smile, when suddenly he raised his hand. Instantly they stopped and gazed up at him with faltering breath. For a while he kept silent and seemed as someone who has been overcome by bad news. Then he signed to the hasidim with his hand and cried: "When one of the generals falls in battle, do the companies scatter and take to flight? The fight goes on! Rejoice and dance!" Later it became known that the rabbi of Ulanov had died that very hour.

SHELOMO LEIB OF LENTSHNO

Refractory Eyes

"When I was a boy," said Rabbi Shelomo Leib of Lentshno, "I adjured all the parts of my body to do nothing save what was the will of God. And they all consented; all except my eyes. So I said I would not open my eyes, and kept lying down. When my mother asked me why I did not get up, I refused to tell, so she beat me with a stick. Then I asked my eyes whether they were now ready to take the oath. But they still held out. Finally my mother beat me so hard that they took pity on me and said 'yes.' So then I could get up."

Fearless

Rabbi Zevi Elimelekh of Dynov was asked how it was that he had always remained true to his friend Rabbi Shemolo Leib of Lentshno, even though he belonged to another school. He answered: "How could I be against him! When the two of us were studying with Rabbi Mendel in Rymanov, everyone there was so overcome with fear that not even the greatest dared raise his eyebrows. But he, Shelomo Leib, took off his shoes and danced on the table in his stocking feet, right in front of the rabbi, who sat there, and watched, and never uttered a word."

In the Image of God

The Yehudi once told his friend Rabbi Kalman of Cracow that among his disciples there was one in whose face one could still see the full image of God. Kalman took a candle and went to the House of Study where the disciples slept. He studied every face intently, but did not find what he was seeking.

"I guess you didn't look behind the stove," said the Yehudi when his friend told him of his vain search; and he accompanied him back. Behind the stove they found young Shelomo

Leib. Rabbi Kalman looked at him for a very long time by the light of his candle. "It is true," he said then. "It is true."

A Wanderer and Fugitive

After studying in Lublin and Rymanov for a time, Rabbi Shelomo Leib attached himself to the Yehudi, who said to him: "The most effective penance is to become a wanderer and fugitive." So Rabbi Shelomo decided in his soul to become a fugitive and wanderer.

Many years later a hasid who lived in Lentshno visited Rabbi Mendel of Kotzk. The rabbi asked him: "Did you see the rabbi of Lentshno?"

"I took leave of him before coming here," answered the hasid. "And was he cheerful?" asked the rabbi of Kotzk. "Yes," replied the hasid. "That's the way it is," the rabbi of Kotzk said sorrowfully. "He who is first a wanderer and fugitive becomes cheerful afterward."

The Four Hundred

Rabbi Yitzhak of Vorki once asked Rabbi Shelomo Leib of Lentshno: "Why do your hasidim look so broken in spirit and depressed?"

He replied: "Don't you know that my men are part of the four hundred who went into exile with David, and of whom it is written: 'And everyone that was in distress, and everyone that was in debt, and everyone that was discontented. . . . '"

The Perfect Swimmer

When the rabbi of Lentshno's son was a boy he once saw Rabbi Yitzhak of Vorki praying. Full of amazement he came running to his father and asked how it was possible for such a zaddik to pray quietly and simply, without giving any sign of ecstasy.

"A poor swimmer," answered his father, "has to thrash around in order to stay up in the water. The perfect swimmer rests on the tide and it carries him."

YISAKHAR BAER OF RADOSHITZ

Two Ways

A grandson of the rabbi of Radoshitz told this:
"In his youth Rabbi Yisakhar Baer had been a disciple of
Rabbi Moshe Leib of Sasov. The rabbi of Sasov used to take
him along on his trips to ransom prisoners. Once they were
on the Vistula, when a storm broke out and almost capsized
the boat. The rabbi of Sasov rose and cried: 'We are going
to our Father!' and clamped his hands as wedding guests do
during the bridal dance. They were saved.

"Some time after this they went to Warsaw to see the governor.
When they arrived at his palace they saw that it was surrounded by armed guards who refused to admit anyone without a written permit. Rabbi Moshe Leib asked my grandfather:
'What shall I tell them?' He replied: 'Say to them in their
own language: Puszczaj!' That means 'Let pass' and also
'Let go!'

"Rabbi Moshe Leib, who was almost a giant in stature, went
up to one of the guards and roared the word 'Puszczaj' at
him. The man retreated in alarm and let the two proceed.
We do not know just what happened after that, but the rabbi
of Sasov must have roared 'Puszczaj' to the governor as well,
because all the prisoners on whose behalf they had come
were released."

In the Bowl

Rabbi Yisakhar Baer was very poor in his youth. One year
he had to fast after as well as before the Day of Atonement,
and when the Feast of Booths drew near he did not have
the wherewithal to celebrate it. So he stayed in the House of
Study after prayer, for he knew that there was no food in his
house. But his wife had sold a piece of jewelry she still had,
without telling him about it, and had bought holiday loaves
and potatoes and candles for the sum she received.
Toward evening when the rabbi came home and entered the

booth, he found a festive table awaiting him, and was filled with joy. He washed his hands, seated himself, and began to eat the potatoes with great gusto, for he had gone hungry for days.

But when Rabbi Yisakhar Baer grew aware of how preoccupied he was with eating, he stopped. "Berel," he said to himself, "you are not sitting in the festive booth; why, you are sitting right in the bowl!" And he did not take another bite.

The Terror of the Ritual Bath

This story is told:

Once young Yishakhar was so very poor that he had eaten nothing for a number of days, for it went against his grain to confide his trouble to others. So one evening when he felt that he could not keep alive much longer, he said to himself that he had better take one more ritual bath before he grew too weak. In those days the bath in Radoshitz lay sixty or seventy steps below the level of the ground. He undressed down to his shirt and started on his way. As he descended the stairs he heard a noise as though someone were striking his hand on water, but he went on. The noise grew louder and louder and it was clear that there were many hands beating on water. Yishakhar Baer paused a moment and then resumed his way. A gust of wind extinguished his lantern. In the darkness he heard a hideous clamor down below. He noticed creatures rising out of the depths to block his path. Quickly he threw off his shirt and jumped into the water. It grew very quiet. All he heard was one more sound as though someone were saying: "Lost," and snapping his fingers. Yisakhar Baer immersed himself again and again. Then he climbed up the stairs, dressed and went home. In front of his house stood a wagon loaded with sacks of flour and other food. "Are you Rabbi Yisakhar Baer?" asked the driver. "I was told to deliver these goods to you."

Now a few hours earlier on that very day, a farm wagon had driven up to the house of a liquor merchant, a hasid who lived near the town. In the wagon was a tall, very old man. As the merchant came to the door to greet him, he looked at him piercingly with his rather nearsighted eyes, and asked: "Where is the rabbi of this place?"

"We have no rabbi here," answered the distiller.

"Don't you know any extraordinary man in the town of Radoshitz?" the old man went on to ask. "Any 'fine Jew'?"

"There is no 'fine man' here," the hasid assured him. "We have nothing extraordinary of any description, unless you would consider the man who teaches our children something extraordinary. He certainly is a singular fellow, what you might call a 'pious' man. What we call him is just Berel, the idler."

At that the old man straightened up in the wagon so that he looked even taller than he was, and fairly snorted: "What's that? You call him an idler? He's no idler, he's a great man! He shakes the world the way an ordinary person might shake a tree in the woods." Then he called to his driver: "Back to Lublin!" and on the instant the wagon with the two men vanished.

Suddenly the hasid realized that the tall man he had seen was the rabbi of Lublin, for someone had once given him a description of the Seer of Lublin. But the next moment he thought: "Why, the rabbi of Lublin died two years ago!" Then he loaded a wagon with sacks of flour and other food and sent it to Radoshitz.

His First Healing

Once when young Yisakhar Baer was on his way to Pzhysha to see his teacher the Yehudi, and was about to cross a hill which lies before the town, he heard screams and sobs from the valley below. There could be no doubt that the sounds came from his master's house. He ran down in great bewilderment. The moment the Yehudi caught sight of Yisakhar Baer, he told him with tears streaming down his cheeks that his son was ill and on the verge of death. "We don't know what to do next," he said. "But here you are, just in the nick of time. Take the child, and I know you will make him well."

Yisakhar Baer listened in great dismay. He had never had anything to do with such matters, nor ever felt any extraordinary powers within himself. But he took up the child, put him down in his cradle again, and rocked him, and rocking, he poured his pleading soul out before God. In an hour the boy was out of danger.

Peasant Wisdom

Rabbi Yisakhar Baer once met an old peasant from the village of Oleshnye who had known him when he was young, but was not aware of his rise in the world. "Berel," the peasant called to him, "what's new with you?"

"And what's new with you?" asked the rabbi.

"Well, Berel, what shall I tell you," answered the other. "What you don't get by your own work you don't have."

From that time on whenever Rabbi Baer spoke of the proper way to conduct one's life, he added: "And the old man of Oleshnye said: 'What you don't get by your own work you don't have.' "

The Confession

Once when Rabbi Yisakhar Baer was very ill, he said to himself: "It is usual for a sick man to confess his sins. Now what shall I confess? Shall I say: 'I have sinned'? But a man in the condition I am in now cannot lie, and I have not sinned. Or shall I say: 'I have done too little in the service of God'? But I did whatever I possibly could. There is one thing though that I can confess: My feeling toward God was not clear and not pure enough, not wholly turned to him and him alone. I can take on myself the task of making it clearer and purer. For in this there are no bounds to improvement, since our feeling is based on our grasp of the magnitude of God, of boundless God. And so that is the task I shall take on myself. If God helps me recover, I shall try to make my feeling for him clearer, purer and more wholly turned to him."

He recovered and lived for another twenty years.

The Imitator

The rabbi of Radoshitz had a disciple who could imitate his teacher's way of pronouncing the sabbath eve Benediction of Sanctification so perfectly that whoever heard him from a distance thought it was the rabbi himself. Once when he happened to be in Radoshitz, the zaddik summoned him. "I am told," said he, "that you can utter the Benediction of Sanctification in exact imitation of my voice and gestures. Do it for me!"

"If the rabbi will promise not to be annoyed," said his disciple, "I shall be glad to do it."

"You need have no fears," said the zaddik.

The disciple pronounced the blessing over the wine just like the rabbi, and made exactly the same gestures. But when he came to a certain passage, he paused, grew motionless, and then finished the Benediction as best he could.

When his disciple had ended, the zaddik asked him: "Why didn't you go on?"

"Rabbi," answered his disciple, "when you come to that passage, you offer yourself up, and I am under no obligation to do that."

Strange Assistance

Rabbi Moshe of Lelov's daughter, a granddaughter of Rabbi David of Lelov who had been the Yehudi's friend and protector, was childless. Time after time she beset her father with requests to pray for her. Finally he told her that only the rabbi of Radoshitz could assist her in this matter. She immediately made preparation for the journey and traveled to Radoshitz in the company of her mother-in-law, who was also the daughter of a distinguished zaddik. When she had told Rabbi Yisakhar Baer her trouble, he turned on her and berated her as one scolds a spoiled child: "What's all this about wanting children, you impudent baggage! Out with you!"

The young woman, who had been delicately reared and never heard a rough word, fled, dissolved in tears. "Now I shall cry and cry till I die," she said to herself. But her mother-in-law went to the rabbi and asked him why he had shamed the poor woman as he did, whether she had by any chance committed some sin.

"Wish her good luck," answered the rabbi. "Everything is right with her now. There was no other way than to stir her to the very depths." The woman returned to him and he gave her his blessing. Soon after she came home she conceived a son.

I and You

The rabbi of Radoshitz was asked: "How are we to interpret the passage in the Talmud where Rabbi Simeon ben Yohai says to his son: 'My son, you and I are enough for the world'?" He replied: "In the Tosefta we read: 'The meaning which underlies the creation of the world is that the creature says: You are our God, and the Holy One, blessed be he, says: I am the Lord your God.' This 'you' and this 'I' are enough for the world."

God's Prayer

This question was put to the rabbi of Radoshitz: "There is one sentence in the Talmud which we do not understand. We read: 'Whence do you deduce that God himself prays? It says: And I shall bring them to my holy mountain, and make them joyful in the house of prayer. It does not say "their prayer" but "my prayer." And it follows from this that God himself prays.'

"How shall we interpret this? Is the 'but' supposed to exclude the prayers of man?"

He answered: "Not at all. God takes pleasure in the prayer of righteous men. And more than that: It is he who wakens those prayers within them and gives them the strength to pray. And so man's prayer is God's prayer."

The Light behind the Window

On a certain Passover before the Seder celebration, Rabbi Yisakhar Baer called his guest the rabbi of Mogielnica, a grandson of the maggid of Koznitz, to the window, and pointed to something outside. "Do you see, Rav of Mogielnica?" he said. "Do you see?"

After the feast was over the rabbi of Mogielnica danced around the table and sang in a low voice: "The holy old man, our brother, has shown me a light. Great is the light he has shown me. But who knows, who knows how many years must pass, how long we still must sleep before it comes to us, before it comes to us."

SHALOM OF BELZ

Transformation

Rabbi Shalom's elder brother once asked him: "How did you happen to attain to such perfection? When we were quite young I learned more quickly than you."

"This is how it happened, brother," the rabbi of Belz replied. "When I became Bar Mitzvah, my grandfather Rabbi Eleazar of Amsterdam, of blessed memory, came to me one night in a vision and gave me another soul in exchange for mine. Ever since that time I have been a different person."

The Light of the Teachings

Young Shalom's first teacher was the rabbi of Lutzk in Sokal. Then he heard about the Seer of Lublin, and the more he heard about him the more his heart burned with longing to hear his Torah. But when he asked his teacher's permission to go to the Seer, it was refused. "If you go to Lublin," he said, "I shall take from you all you have accomplished here."

Shalom did not let this stop him, however, and went to Lublin notwithstanding. When he returned and passed his teacher's house, the rabbi happened to be standing at the window. He called his wife. "Just look," said he, "how the light of the Torah shines out from the face of my disciple!"

The Confession

A hasid relates:

"Once I went to Rabbi Shalom of Belz and told him my trouble: that while I prayed alien thoughts came and confused me, not thoughts about the business of the day but evil and frightening visions; and I begged him to heal my soul. When I had finished he said to me: 'Feel no shame before me, my son. Tell me everything that is disturbing and perplexing you.' I started right in, and told him about every terror and every lust which had attacked me. While I was speaking he kept his eyes closed, but I looked at him and saw how his holy thoughts were laboring to draw those aliens thoughts up from the depths of my soul. When I had ended he said: 'God will help you to keep them away from now on.' And ever since they have never come into my mind."

Tomorrow

It was before the Passover and while the hasidim were drawing water for the baking of the unleavened bread, they called to one another: "Next year in Jerusalem!" Then Rabbi Shalom said: "Why not before next year? With this water which we are now drawing we may be baking unleavened bread in Jerusalem tomorrow on the day before the feast, and may eat it—if the Messiah comes to redeem us."

Adam and Eve

On one of his frequent visits to the rabbi of Belz, Rabbi Hayyim of Zans took his young son Barukh with him. They found Rabbi Shalom and his wife sitting at table in a room with plain board walls. They stayed for a while, and on their way home Rabbi Hayyim asked his son: "What impression did those two make on you—the holy rabbi and his wife?"

"As we entered the room," said the boy, "they seemed to me like Adam and Eve before they sinned."

"That is just how they seemed to me," said his father. "And how did the room in which they were seated look to you?"

"Like paradise," said Barukh.

"That is just how it looked to me," said Rabbi Hayyim.

Why?

When his wife died, Rabbi Shalom said:

"Lord of the world! If I had the strength to wake her, should I not have done so by now? I am simply not able to do it. But you, Lord of the world, you have the strength, and you can do it—why don't you waken Israel?"

HAYYIM OF ZANS AND YEHEZKEL OF SHENYAVA

The Fire

When the town of Brody burned and little Hayyim was taken to Rabbi Moshe Leib's house in Sasov, the zaddik said to him: "Hayyim, tell me what you saw during the fire."
The boy replied: "On the one side I saw Jews putting out the fire, and on the other I saw 'Germans' [the name given to those who had rejected Jewish dress and customs] setting fires. So I asked myself: 'Why are the Jews taking so much trouble putting out the flames? It would be simpler just to drive away the Germans, and there would soon be an end to the fire.'"

Nothing But...

When Rabbi Hayyim was a boy, someone once heard him running back and forth in his room and whispering to himself without stopping: "I mean nothing but You, nothing but You alone."

His Bad Foot

In his youth Rabbi Hayyim Zans was a disciple of the zaddik of Roptchitz. His fervor in praying was so great that he stamped on the floor with both feet. But one foot was lame. Once when the zaddik's wife had watched Hayyim pray, she went to her husband and said: "What a heartless person you are! Why do you let him pound the floor with his bad foot? Tell him to use only his good foot."
"I could do that right enough," answered the zaddik, "if, in praying, he knew every time whether he was using his good or his bad foot."

For the Smallest Spark

A zaddik who bore Rabbi Hayyim of Zans a grudge once said to him: "You climb around in the upper worlds and I accomplish just as much as you when I recite ten psalms."
"It is true that I climb around in those worlds," the rabbi

of Zans replied, "but for the smallest spark of the fear of God
I give up everything else."

Teaching and Service

A certain rav, very anxious to discuss sublime subjects with
the rabbi of Zans with no one to listen in on their conversation, finally managed to have the zaddik invite him on the
drive he always took before the Afternoon Prayer. When the
town lay behind them, Rabbi Hayyim asked him what he had
on his mind. "The question I should like to put to you," said
the rav, "is this: What is the difference between the way of
teaching and the way of service?"

The rabbi lit his pipe and blew thick clouds of smoke into
the clear air. In between he uttered long low growls like a
restless lion. The rav felt very ill at ease and wished he had
never put his question.

When they had driven about a mile, the zaddik roused himself and said: "You want to know the difference between the
way of teaching and the way of service. I shall tell you: The
way of teaching is when a man is always ready to give his
soul for the glory of God, and the way of service is when
a man is always prepared to fulfil the verse: 'My soul failed
me when he spoke.'" He knocked at the window, and this
indicated to the coachman that he was to start back home.

To the People

A rather officious man once insisted on presenting a request
to Rabbi Hayyim after the Afternoon Prayer. When he refused
to take "no" for an answer, the zaddik spoke roughly to him.
A friend who was present asked him why he was so angry,
and he answered that whoever uttered the Afternoon Prayer
was face to face with the World of Emanation; why should he
not be angry, coming from that world, to be annoyed with
the petty troubles of a petty man.

His friend replied: "Following the passage in the Scriptures
which tells of God's first revelation to Moses on Sinai, we
read: 'And Moses went down from the mount unto the people.'
Rashi's comment on this is: 'This informs us that when Moses

left the mount he did not return to his own affairs, but to the people.' How are we to interpret that? What affairs in the desert did our teacher Moses, peace be upon him, renounce in order to go to the people? We must interpret it as follows: When Moses descended from the mountain he was still clinging to the upper worlds, and in them was accomplishing his sublime work of permeating the divine attribute of rigor with that of mercy. Those were the affairs Moses had to attend to. And yet he paused in his great work, disengaged himself from the upper worlds, and turned to the people. He listened to all their petty troubles, stored the heaviness of heart of all Israel within himself, and then bore it upward in prayer."

When Rabbi Hayyim heard this, his anger melted away. He asked someone to call back the man he had shouted at, and gave ear to his request. Almost all that night he listened to the troubles and wishes of the hasidim gathered about him.

His Reason

The rabbi of Zans once said: "I love the poor. And do you know why? It is because God loves them."

What You Get Out of Life

The rabbi of Zans told the following story and accompanied his words with gestures that conjured up a picture.

"People come to me who ride to market every day in the week. One such man approached me and cried: 'My dear rabbi! I haven't gotten anything out of life. All week I get out of one wagon and into another. But when a man stops to think that he is permitted to pray to God himself, he lacks nothing at all in the world.' "

The Apples

A poor woman, an apple vendor whose stand was near Rabbi Hayyim's house, once came to him complaining: "Rabbi, I have no money to buy what I need for the sabbath."

"And what about your apple stand?" asked the zaddik.

"People say my apples are bad," she answered, "and they won't buy."

Rabbi Hayyim immediately ran out on the street and called: "Who wants to buy good apples?" A crowd collected around him in no time at all; they handed out coins without looking at them or counting them, and soon all the apples were sold for two and three times what they were worth.

"Now you see," he said to the woman as he turned to go, "your apples were good; all that was the matter was that people just didn't know about it."

The Turkey

Rabbi Hayyim had singled out certain poor people in his town, and gave them money every month. Not merely alms; he gave each what he required to support himself and his family.

On a certain market day a poultry dealer brought an unusually fine turkey to Zans. He took it straight to the rabbi's house and tried to sell it to his wife for the sabbath. But she thought it too dear, and so the man went off with his high-priced bird. A little later the woman found out that one of the men who received his sustenance from her husband had bought the turkey. "Now look at your poor!" she complained to the rabbi. "I wasn't able to buy the bird because the price was too high, but that man went and bought it!" "That shows," said the zaddik, "that he wants a good turkey as well for the sabbath. I didn't know that, but now that I do know it, I must raise the amount I give him every month."

Putting to Shame

A poor schoolteacher once came to visit Rabbi Hayyim of Zans. "I suppose you are preparing for your daughter's wedding,"-said the zaddik. "I don't know," said the other. Rabbi Hayyim looked at him inquiringly. "I still haven't the money to buy the bridegroom a prayer shawl and a fur cap, as custom demands," said the schoolteacher sadly.

Rabbi Yehezkel, the rabbi's son, who was listening to the conversation, interrupted at this point. "Father," he cried,

"just a few days ago I saw this man buying both these things!"
The teacher reddened and left the room in silence.

"What have you done!" said Rabbi Hayyim. "Perhaps he was not able to pay for what he bought, or perhaps he needs money to have a dress made for his wife to wear at the wedding, but does not want to say so. And now you have put a man to shame."

Rabbi Yehezkel ran into the street, caught up with the schoolteacher, and begged his forgiveness. But the man refused to forgive him and insisted that the zaddik should judge the matter. Soon they both stood before him.

"Don't forgive him," the old man said to the schoolteacher. "Don't forgive him until he has paid the entire cost of the wedding down to the last shoe lace." And so it was done.

True Wisdom

One day the rabbi of Zans was standing at the window and looking out into the street. Seeing a passer-by, he knocked on the pane and signed to the man to come into the house. When the stranger entered the room Rabbi Hayyim asked him: "Tell me, if you found a purse full of ducats, would you return it to its owner?"

"Rabbi," said the man, "if I knew the owner I should return the purse without a moment's delay."

"You are a fool," said the rabbi of Zans. Then he resumed his position at the window, called another passer-by, and put the same question to him. "I'm not so foolish as all that," said this man. "I am not such a fool as to give up a purse full of money that comes my way!"

"You're a bad lot," said the rabbi of Zans, and called in a third man. He replied: "Rabbi, how can I know on what rung I shall be when I find the purse, or whether I shall succeed in fending off the Evil Urge? Perhaps it will get the better of me, and I shall appropriate what belongs to another. But perhaps God, blessed be he, will help me fight it, and in that case I shall return what I have found to its rightful owner."

"Those are good words!" cried the zaddik. "You are a true sage!"

The Story of the General

Once when Rabbi Hayyim was on a journey, great honors were showered upon him. Later he said to his son who had accompanied him: "I shall tell you a story about a general. It is customary for the guards to accord greater honor to a general than to a colonel. Now it once happened that a general was court-martialed because of some wrong he had done and demoted to colonel. When he left the house in which the military court had sat and passed the guards, they did not notice that he no longer wore a general's insignia and saluted him just as always. Only then was he pierced to the heart."

Looking for the Way

In the month of Elul when men prepare their souls for the days of judgment, Rabbi Hayyim was in the habit of telling stories to a tune that moved all his listeners to turn to God. Once he told this story: "A man lost his way in a great forest. After a while another lost his way and chanced on the first. Without knowing what had happened to him, he asked the way out of the woods. 'I don't know,' said the first. 'But I can point out the ways that lead further into the thicket, and after that let us try to find the way together.'

"So, my congregation," the rabbi concluded his story, "let us look for the way together."

In the King's Uniform

The servant of the rabbi of Zans told this story:

"One morning before prayers the rabbi lay down again for a short while because he was suddenly tired. Just then—and later we discovered that it was by mistake, because all practical affairs were usually referred to the zaddik's son, the rabbi of the district—a soldier came to collect taxes. The zaddik was startled when he laid eyes on him. When the soldier had gone he said to me: 'This soldier is a simple peasant, but when he appears in the king's uniform, we fear him. Let us put on the King's uniform, the prayer shawl and the phylacteries, and all the nations will fear the King.'"

The rabbi of Zans used to say: "All zaddikim serve, each in his own way, each according to his rung, and whoever says: 'Only my rabbi is righteous,' loses both worlds."

A Piece of Advice

Rabbi Hayyim had married his son to the daughter of Rabbi Eliezer of Dzikov, who was a son of Rabbi Naftali of Roptchitz. The day after the wedding he visited the father of the bride and said: "Now that we are related, I feel close to you and can tell you what is eating at my heart. Look! My hair and beard have turned white, and I have not yet atoned!"

"O my friend," replied Rabbi Eliezer, "you are thinking only of yourself. How about forgetting yourself and thinking of the world?"

Resignation

The rabbi of Zans used to tell this story about himself:

"In my youth when I was fired with the love of God, I thought I would convert the whole world to God. But soon I discovered that it would be quite enough to convert the people who lived in my town, and I tried for a long time, but did not succeed. Then I realized that my program was still much too ambitious, and I concentrated on the persons in my own household. But I could not convert them either. Finally it dawned on me: I must work upon myself, so that I may give true service to God. But I did not accomplish even this."

The Missing Number

Shortly before his death Rabbi Hayyim said to a man who had come to visit him: "If I had nine true friends whose hearts were one with mine, we should each put a loaf in his knapsack and go out into the field together and walk in the field and pray and pray, until our prayers were granted and redemption came."

In the Pulpit

When Rabbi Yehezkel, the son of the rabbi of Zans, was stopping in the town of Ujhely in Hungary, he had the crier announce that he would preach in the House of Prayer. The entire congregation gathered at the appointed time. The rabbi ascended the pulpit and said: "My friends! Once I preached in this place, and my heart was not wholly directed toward Heaven. But to pray with a divided heart is a great sin. And so I decided to do penance. Now according to the word of our sages, wrong must be expiated where it was done, and so I have again come to this pulpit. And I pray to the Holy One, blessed be he, to forgive me."

Thereupon the whole congregation recognized the power of the word of God; the fear of God entered their hearts, and all accomplished the turning.

His Discourse

When Rabbi Yehezkel was elected rav of the town he was still a young man. The entire congregation expected him to preach a sermon on the first sabbath after his arrival, for such was the custom, but he denied them their wish. At the third sabbath meal the most distinguished men of the town, who were guests at his table, begged him to expound the Torah to them. He called for a Bible, opened to the weekly portion, and read it through from beginning to end. Then he said: "This is the Torah of God. It is holy, and it is not my office to talk about it." He kissed the book and had it put back in its place.

ZEVI HIRSH OF ZHYDATCHOV, YEHUDAH ZEVI OF ROZDOL AND YITZHAK EISIK OF ZHYDATCHOV

From the Depths

Rabbi Hirsh of Zhydatchov told this story:

"On the day before the sabbath they drove me out of the town of Brody and I was in great disgrace. I walked on and on without stopping and when I got home toward evening, just before the beginning of the sabbath, I went to the House of Prayer in my workaday clothes and could only just manage to say the words of the prayer. But in the morning before I prayed I spoke to God, saying: 'Lord of the world, you see the humiliation of those who have been humiliated, and you see my crushed heart. Give me light so that I can pray to you.' Then suddenly my heart caught fire. My prayer was a flowing flame. Never before had that happened to me, and it will never happen again."

The Double Answer

Rabbi Hirsh once said to his hasidim:

"When a man comes to me and asks me to pray for help in some need of his in this world—one on behalf of a lease, another on behalf of a shop—his soul besieges me at that instant and asks for redemption in the upper world. And it is my duty to reply to both of his entreaties—with a single answer."

It Is Not the Multitude That Does It

Once when Rabbi Hirsh of Zhydatchov entered the House of Prayer, he said to the hasidim who were gathered there: "My sons, it is written: 'A king is not saved by the multitude of a host.' It is of no help to God when a zaddik has a multitude of hasidim."

His Suspicion

The rabbi of Komarno, who was a nephew of Rabbi Hirsh, related this incident.

"It was the Feast of Weeks. Dawn was just breaking when I

entered the room of my teacher and uncle, but he did not notice me. He was walking back and forth and I heard him crying out his heart to God. Now at that time four or five hundred people had come to him over the holidays. He said: 'Perhaps Sammael has sent me this multitude to tempt me away from you? Have pity on my poor soul that I may not be exiled from your presence!' "

Every Rabbi Is Good

One sabbath Rabbi Zevi Hirsh interrupted his teachings at the third meal and said:

"There are hasidim who travel to their rabbi and say that save for him there is no rabbi in all the world. That is idol worship. What then should they say? They should say: 'Every rabbi is good for his people, but our rabbi is best for what concerns us.' "

Illuminated

When Rabbi Moshe of Sambor, Rabbi Zevi Hirsh's younger brother, was a youth, he went about in the villages and traded with the peasants. But when he came home and said the Afternoon Prayer he felt as if his whole body were lit by a great light.

He himself tells this story: "I once asked my brother and teacher: 'Why is it: Sometimes when I have been traveling on business and come home and begin to pray, I feel illuminated, almost as though the Divine Presence had come to me?'

"And my brother answered me in his usual clear, direct way: 'Why should you be surprised at that? When a traveler walks in the way of God, then whether he knows it or not all the holy sparks which cling to the herbs of the field and the trees of the forest rush forth and attach themselves to such a man, and this illuminates him with a great light.' "

Not Yet!

When Rabbi Hirsh was on his way to Munkacs, he visited old Rabbi Moshe in Ujhely, and Rabbi Moshe complained to him as he had done so often before that the Messiah had not yet come. "You know," said Rabbi Hirsh, "I stake my whole self for everyone, even the most unfaithful, and probe down to the root of his apostasy where wickedness can be recognized as need and lust. And if I get that far, I can pull him out all right! What do you say: shall we give all those souls up as lost? For wouldn't they be lost if the Messiah came today?"

The Change in the Work

When Rabbi Hirsh returned from his wife's funeral and went up the stairs to his room, he was heard saying to himself: "Up to now I have accomplished holy unification by marriage here below, now I shall try to accomplish unification by marriage up above."

Two weeks later he died.

The Everlasting Foundation

The wife of Rabbi Yehudah Zevi of Rozdol, whose uncle was Rabbi Hirsh, once asked him: "Why don't you say something to your enemies who are out to hurt you, and why do you even do them favors when you could be bringing God's punishment down upon them by prayer?"

He said: "Did you never stop to think why so many people go to the zaddik and bring him gifts, hundreds and thousands of gifts just to one man? It is because every building must have a foundation, and without it the structure cannot stand. Now the structure of the world stands because of the zaddik, as it is written: 'The righteous is the foundation of the world.' And so it is only right that all support him who supports them all. But why should people come to me as well, and bring gifts to me even though I am not a zaddik? I have thought about this and weighed the question. Then it occurred to me that the world requires still another foundation. For it is written: 'He hangeth the world over nothingness,' and the Talmud comments on this: 'The world rests upon him who, in the hour of conflict, reduces himself to nothing, and does not say anything against those who hate him.' So you see, it is because people need nothingness in addition to the zaddik that they support me."

The Greatest Lust

A learned man once said to the rabbi of Rozdol: "It seems to me that the condition of being a zaddik is the greatest of all lusts."

"That's how it is," the rabbi replied, "but to attain to it, you first have to get the better of all the lesser lusts."

Remembering and Forgetting

On New Year's Day Rabbi Yehudah Zevi of Rozdol said:
"Today we have prayed: 'For thou art he who remembereth from eternity all forgotten things.' What is the meaning of this? That God remembers only what man forgets. When someone does a good deed and it slips his mind and he does not remember having done anything good at all, then God remembers his service. But when a man's heart swells with pride and he says to himself: 'How well I spoke! How well I learned!' then nothing of all of this persists in the eyes of God. When a man falls into sin and later dwells upon it and repents, God will forget that sin. But he remembers sins which are lightly thrust aside."

The Cord of Grace

Rabbi Yitzhak Eisik of Zhydatchov, Rabbi Hirsh's nephew, was an only son. Once when he was little more than a boy, his father asked him: "How do you interpret the words of our sages: 'Whoever occupies himself with the Torah by night, around him God strings a cord of grace by day.' Do we not always rise at midnight to occupy ourselves with the Torah, and are we not in need and trouble by day notwithstanding? So where does the cord of grace come in?"

The boy answered: "Father, the fact that we rise midnight after midnight, and occupy ourselves with the Torah, without heeding our troubles—that in itself is the cord of grace."

Three Signs

On one of his visits to Rabbi Zevi Hirsh, Rabbi Shalom of Kaminka took his son, young Yehoshua, to Zhydatchov with him. At the midday meal the boy saw a youth with heavy black curls enter the room. In one hand he carried a pitcher of water, in the other a bowl, and a towel was slung over his shoulder. He went from one person to the next all around the table with a joy that shone from his face and animated his whole body, and waited on them until they had all washed their hands. "Father," asked Yehoshua, "who is that dark youth?" "Take a good look at him," answered Rabbi Shalom. "He will be a prince in Israel."

Many years later, when Rabbi Hirsh had died and his younger brother Yitzhak Eisik, that same "dark youth," had become rabbi of Zhydatchov, and hasidim were streaming to him from all over, his fame reached Rabbi Yehoshua, who had become his father's successor in Kaminka. "I'll go to him," he decided, "and watch him to find out whether his way is right, and whether I should become his disciple. And I shall think up three signs I must have for this: first he must come to greet me when I arrive, second he must invite me to eat with him, third he must guess one of my thoughts."

Rabbi Yehoshua set out for Zhydatchov, but as he approached the town he suddenly felt feverish and when he arrived he had to be carried from his carriage and put to bed. When Rabbi Yitzhak heard of this he visited Rabbi Yehoshua and said he would surely be well that very day, and so he should have supper with him. Later, when Rabbi Yehoshua, who really had gotten over his fever, was seated at Rabbi Yitzhak's table, his host said to him smilingly: "Well, rav of Kaminka, and if a man is not able to guess another's thoughts, does that mean he isn't a rabbi?"

Rabbi Yehoshua became one of Rabbi Yitzhak's favorite disciples.

Give and Take

Rabbi Yitzhak Eisik said:
"The motto of life is 'Give and take.' Everyone must be both a giver and a receiver. He who is not both is as a barren tree."

Through the Darkness

Rabbi Yitzhak Eisik never exhibited any violent emotion in praying. He prayed in a gentle and holy voice, but his words trembled through every heart in the House of Prayer.

220

Once on the Feast of Weeks when he spoke the song of praise which precedes the reading of the Torah, one of his disciples who had known the Seer of Lublin was so deeply stirred that he lost the use of his eyes. He did not regain his sight until the zaddik stopped speaking. After prayers he told his teacher what had happened, and Rabbi Yitzhak Eisik explained it to him, saying: "That was because your soul which was caught up in the word went through the 'darkness, cloud, and thick darkness' of Mount Sinai."

A Breath

A disciple of Rabbi Yitzhak Eisik told this story:
"In the beginning when I came to hear our master speak but was not yet able to understand him, I opened my mouth wide, so that at least his holy breath might enter into me."

Moralizing

Rabbi Yitzhak Eisik of Zhydatchov was once host to Rabbi Zalman Leib of Sziget in Hungary, who brought with him a number of his hasidim, among them several farm and vineyard owners, who were beginning to behave somewhat like the so-called "enlightened" group. Rabbi Zalman begged his host to admonish them. "Admonishing is not the custom here," replied the zaddik. "When I face my congregation on the sabbath and say the prayer: 'All shall thank thee and all shall praise thee,' those are our words of admonition. If they fail to rouse a man to the turning, moralizing will not do any good."
On the following day while Rabbi Yitzhak, standing in front of the Ark, was saying, All shall thank thee," the rabbi from Hungary happened to look at those of his people who were worrying him, and he saw that they were weeping.

The Exile Festival

Rabbi Yitzhak Eisik wanted to go to the Holy Land and settle there. His sons and his friends tried to shake his resolve and did not succeed. But then something very strange happened.
On the evening before the second day of Passover, the zaddik entered the House of Prayer in the prayer shawl he wore on

weekdays. After the Prayer of Benedictions, he stood silent instead of beginning on the festival psalms, and his congregation waited in astonishment, for the like had never happened before. After a time he began to recite the psalms and he spoke with the same sublime animation as always.

Later, in the course of the meal, he said: "Today during the Evening Prayer I was wholly deprived of the power to think, and not only that: I felt I was wearing my everyday prayer shawl. I did not know what God had done to me, but finally it was revealed to me: Because I wanted to go to the Land of Israel, I no longer had any connection with the holiness of the second day of the festival which is observed only in the countries outside Palestine, and I remained in the weekday. When I realized this I thought over everything very thoroughly and decided not to give up this holiness, but rather to renounce settling in the Holy Land. Not until then was the power of thought restored to me."

But even though Rabbi Yitzhak had renounced his intention of going to the Land of Israel, he was there at all times with his eyes and his heart. He had a House of Prayer built in the holy city of Safed, and it was named for him. From then on he used to say that it was through it that his prayers rose to Heaven. He also said that every day after the Morning Prayer he made an excursion to the Holy Land. And when some passage in the Book of Splendor would not reveal itself to his understanding, he would lean his head on the box into which one puts donations for the Holy Land in the name of Rabbi Meir, the worker of miracles (a box he always kept on his table), and would repeat the saying of our sages: "The air of the Land of Israel makes wise," and instantly the gates of light swung open to him.

They Traveled Together

A hasid wished to go to the Land of Israel and went to Rabbi Yitzhak to ask his advice in the matter. The zaddik said: "Wait a while. You and I will go to the Land of Israel together." The hasid thought that Rabbi Yitzhak intended traveling there and waited to hear from him. But the message he received was news of the zaddik's death. When he heard this he said: "Then I must prepare for the journey." He immersed himself in the ritual bath, bade them call the Holy Brotherhood, and confessed his sins. Then he wrote his last will and testament and lay down. A few days later he died.

Free

During the last year of his life Rabbi Eisik of Zhydatchov often lifted his hands toward the window that gave on the street and said to himself: "Take a look at it—take a look at the coarse world!"

On the morning of the day of his death—he died toward evening—he put on his prayer shawl and phylacteries as always. But when he had uttered the first benediction of the Morning Prayer, he ordered his prayer shawl and phylacteries taken off, and said: "Today I am free of prayer shawl and phylacteries and commandments, and I shall soon be free of the world."

YAAKOV YITZHAK OF PZHYSHA (THE YEHUDI)*
AND HIS DESCENDANTS

The Peacemaker

Yaakov Yitzhak's father sometimes received visits from his
brother, who lived off the main road in a little town where
he worked for small pay as a servant in the House of Prayer.
In reality, he was one of the thirty-six hidden zaddikim who,
according to tradition, uphold the world. Whenever he came
to see his brother, the two went walking in the fields beyond
the town and spoke of the mysteries of the Torah. Once they
took the boy with them and he walked behind his elders. They
came to a meadow in which sheep were grazing. Suddenly
they noticed that the animals had started a fight about their
share in the pasture. The bellwethers were making for each
other with lowered horns and neither shepherd nor dog was
in sight. Instantly the boy sprang forward, assumed control of
the meadow, and ordered his realm. He separated the opponents
and made peace between them. In a trice every sheep and every
lamb had been allotted what it required. But now a number
of the creatures seemed in no hurry to eat, but pressed close
to the boy, who scratched their coats and talked to them.
"Brother," said the servant in the House of Prayer, "that
boy will some day be a shepherd of the flock."

The Road to Perfection

Once the Yehudi was asked to examine thirteen-year-old
Hanokh, later the rabbi of Alexander, in the Talmud. It took
the boy an hour to think over the passage which had been
assigned to him before he could expound it. When he had
done, the zaddik cupped his hand around Hanokh's cheek and
said: "When I was thirteen I plumbed passages more difficult
than this in no time at all, and when I was eighteen, I had

*"Yehudi" means a Jew; see "Anger Placates a Foe," "The Festival
of the Exile" and "Elijah" in this chapter.

the reputation of being a great scholar in the Torah. But one day it dawned on me that man cannot attain to perfection by learning alone. I understood what is told of our father Abraham; that he explored the sun, the moon, and the stars, and did not find God, and how in this very not-finding the presence of God was revealed to him. For three months I mulled over this realization. Then I explored until I too reached the truth of not-finding."

The Smith

When Rabbi Yaakov Yitzhak was young and had board and lodging in the house of his father-in-law, his next-door neighbor was a smith. The smith got up very early in the morning and struck hammer on anvil until the sound roared like thunder in the ears of the sleeping youth. Yaakov Yitzhak woke up and thought: "If this man tears himself away from sleep so early for worldly work and worldly profit, shall I not be able to do the same for the service of the eternal God?"
The following morning he rose before the smith, who, as he entered his smithy, heard the young man reading in a low tone. This irritated him: "There he is at work already, and he doesn't need to! I certainly won't let a fellow like that get ahead of me!" On the following night he got up before the Yehudi. But the young rabbi took up the challenge and won the race. In later years he used to say: "Whatever I have attained I owe first and foremost to a smith."

What He Learned in Lublin

When the rav of Leipnik, who was opposed to the hasidic way, became acquainted with young Yitzhak and his learning, he asked him: "What do you want of the rabbi of Lublin? What can you learn from him? What have you learned from him?"
The Yehudi replied: "Even if there were nothing else, I certainly learned one thing from my teacher, the holy rabbi of Lublin: when I get into bed, I fall asleep on the instant."

The Angel's Lot

The Yehudi told this story:
"A hasid died and was faced with the judgment of Heaven.

He had powerful advocates and it seemed that the verdict would be favorable, when a great angel appeared and accused him of a wrongdoing. 'Why did you do this?' he was asked, and all he could think of as an excuse was: 'My wife talked me into it.' Then the angel laughed aloud and said: 'That is indeed a peculiar kind of vindication! He could not resist the voice of a woman!' Sentence was passed: the man was punished for the wrong he had done, the angel was to be tested by entering an earthly body and becoming some woman's husband."

When the hasidim heard the end of this story, they decided that the rabbi had been talking about himself.

Answering Back

The Yehudi's wife often subjected him to long quarrelsome speeches. He always listened to what she had to say, but remained silent and accepted it cheerfully. Once however when her nagging was a good deal worse than usual, he answered her back. Later his disciple Rabbi Bunam asked him: "In what way is this day different from others?" The Yehudi answered him: "I saw that her soul was about to leave her body for rage because I did not let her scolding annoy me. And so I said a trifling word, that she might feel that her words troubled me and draw strength from this feeling."

Anger Placates a Foe

There were people who never tired of slandering the Yehudi to his teacher, the rabbi of Lublin. They asserted he was trying to usurp the rabbi's place. Among them was the rabbi of Lublin's wife. When she died quite suddenly, her husband sent for the Yehudi and said to him: "That's your work!"

"God forbid!"

"Well, what did you do when you heard that she was maligning you?"

"I recited the psalms."

"And you call that doing nothing?"

"What should I have done?"

"Got angry," said the rabbi of Lublin.

"Rabbi," said the Yehudi, "look into my eyes, and through

my eyes into my heart, and examine it to see if it is possible for me to become angry."

The Seer looked into the eyes of his disciple. "It is true," he said. " 'The Jew' doesn't know how to be angry."

Making Up

Once when the Yehudi was seated at the table of the maggid of Koznitz on the second day of the Feast of Weeks, his host said to him: "It troubles me that on this second day of the festival, which is observed only in the countries outside Palestine, I have a greater sense of holiness and light than on the first, which is the only one kept in the Land of Israel. Can you, holy Jew, tell me, why it is that the day celebrated in exile seems holier to my heart than the single great day celebrated in our homeland?"

The Yehudi replied: "When a man has quarreled with his wife and they make up, their love is greater than before."

"You have given me new life," said the maggid, and kissed him on the forehead.

Elijah

This story is told:

The Yehudi used to put on a peasant's smock and a cap with a visor such as peasants wear, and ride to market with his servant, who had also donned this kind of dress, to look for Elijah wandering through the world in the guise of a peasant.

On one such occasion he met a villager leading a mare by the rein. The Yehudi took his servant by the arm and cried: "There he is!" The stranger flashed his anger full in the Yehudi's face. "Jew!" he cried. "If you know, why let your tongue wag!" And he vanished on the instant.

Some say that it was from this time on that people called the rabbi of Pzhysha just Yehudi, the "Jew," and nothing else.

A Temptation

Once the Yehudi was walking up and down the street. For hours he talked about apparently idle and worldly matters with the plain people, but in reality he was accomplishing marvelous unifications in the upper worlds. Then the Evil Urge came and

227

whispered to him: "See how great and splendid is the power of your soul!" But he replied: "What do you want to make me conceited about? I am sure that everybody does what I do, only that I notice it as little in them as they do in me."

Can and Want To

Once when the Yehudi was walking cross-country, he happened on a hay wagon which had turned over. "Help me raise it up!" said the driver. The rabbi tried but he could not budge it. "I can't," he finally said. The peasant looked at him sternly. "You can all right," said he, "but you don't want to."
On the evening of that day the Yehudi went to his disciples: "I was told today: We can raise up the Name of God, but we don't want to."

Silence and Speech

A man had taken upon himself the discipline of silence and for three years had spoken no words save those of the Torah and of prayer. Finally the Yehudi sent for him. "Young man," he said, "how is it that I do not see a single word of yours in the world of truth?"
"Rabbi," said the other to justify himself, "why should I indulge in the vanity of speech? Is it not better just to learn and to pray?"
"If you do that," said the Yehudi, "not a word of your own reaches the world of truth. He who only learns and prays is murdering the word of his own soul. What do you mean by 'vanity of speech'? Whatever you have to say can be vanity or it can be truth. And now I am going to have a pipe and some tobacco brought for you to smoke tonight. Come to me after the Evening Prayer and I shall teach you how to talk."
They sat together the whole night. When morning came, the young man's apprenticeship was over.

Speech

The Yehudi and Peretz his disciple were crossing a meadow. Cattle put out to pasture there were lowing, and where it was watered by a stream a flock of geese rose from the water with a great cackling and beating of wings. "If only one could understand what all of them are saying!" cried Peretz.

"When you get to the point of understanding the very core of what you yourself are saying," said the rabbi, "you will understand the language of all creatures."

Not What Goes in at the Mouth...

The Yehudi once told his disciple Rabbi Bunam to go on a journey. Bunam did not ask any questions but left the town with a number of other hasidim and just followed the highway. Toward noon they came to a village and stopped at an inn. The innkeeper was so pleased with his pious guests that he invited them to have dinner with him. Rabbi Bunam sat down in the main room, while the others went in and out and asked all sorts of questions concerning the meat which was to be served them: whether the animal was unblemished, what the butcher was like, and just how carefully the meat had been salted. At that a man dressed in rags spoke up. He had been sitting behind the stove and still had his staff in his hand. "O you hasidim," he said, "you make a big to-do about what you put into your mouths being clean, but you don't worry half as much about the purity of what comes out of your mouths!"

Rabbi Bunam was about to reply, but the wayfarer had already disappeared—for this is Elijah's habit. Then the rabbi understood why his teacher had sent him on this journey.

Honoring One's Parents

The Yehudi was studying the Talmud with his disciples. A certain passage puzzled him and he fell silent and became absorbed in thinking about it. Among his disciples was a boy whose father had died soon after he was born. Since he knew that such interruptions on the part of his teacher were apt to last quite a while, he hurried home because he was very hungry. Just as he started on his way back to the House of Study, his mother called to him and asked him to carry a heavy bundle of hay down from the loft for her. But he did not turn back to the house because he feared to be late. Then suddenly he thought better of it. "The purpose of learning is doing," he told himself, ran back, and obeyed his mother. Then he went on to the House of Study.

The instant the boy crossed the threshold, the Yehudi roused himself from his meditations, rose to his full height, and said joyfully to him: "I am sure you must have honored your mother this hour. We know that Abayyi was the only one of the masters of the Talmud who knew neither his father nor his mother, and that because of this his soul from time to time slips into the body of those who keep the commandment of honoring their parents, which it was not vouchsafed him to do. Well, Abayyi just appeared to me and expounded that difficult passage."

Holy Despair

This is what the Yehudi said concerning the verse in the psalm: "How long shall I take counsel in my soul, having sorrow in my heart by day?"

"So long as I take counsel in my soul, there must needs be sorrow in my heart by day. It is only when I realize that no counsel can help me, and no longer take counsel and know of no help save that which comes from God—it is only then that help is accorded me." And then he added: "This is the mystic meaning of the ritual bath."

Expounding the Scriptures

Rabbi Bunam once came into his teacher the Yehudi's room. He looked up from his book like one who is interrupting, but not loath to interrupt, his work, and said almost playfully: "Say a verse from the Torah and I will expound it to you." Bunam said the first verse that occurred to him: "And Moses spoke in the ears of all the assembly of Israel the words of this song until they were consummated."

"Until they were consummated," the Yehudi repeated and turned back to his book. The interview was at an end.

Rabbi Bunam left the room full of great happiness. Fifteen-year-old Hanokh, who had been in the room with him, asked him how he could be so happy since he had not received the promised interpretation.

"Just think a bit!" said Bunam. Then the other understood too: again and again Moses had spoken his song to the children of Israel, until he had made them consummated and perfect.

Abraham and His Guests

This is what the Yehudi said concerning the verse in the Scriptures that tells about Abraham being visited by angels: "And he stood over them and they did eat."

"Why is this said in the Scriptures? It is not customary for the host who does not eat with his guests to stand over them while they eat. Now this is what is meant by these words in the Scriptures: The angels have their virtues and flaws, and men have their virtues and flaws. The virtue of angels is that they cannot deteriorate, and their flaw is that they cannot improve. Man's flaw is that he can deteriorate, and his virtue that he can improve. But a man who practices hospitality in the true sense of the word, acquires the virtues of his guests. Thus Abraham acquired the virtue of angels, that of not being able to deteriorate. And so he was over and above them."

The Right Child

After a sabbath meal at which many fathers of families were present, the Yehudi said: "You people! If any one of you is asked why he toils so on earth, he replies: 'To bring up my son to study and serve God.' And after the son is grown up, he forgets why his father toiled on earth, and toils in his turn, and if you ask him why, he will say: 'I must bring up my son to be studious and do good works.' And so it goes on, you people, from generation to generation. But when shall we get to see the right child?"

Unmixed

The Yehudi used to say:
"The main thing is not to mix the good with the bad. A hair of goodness is enough if only it has not the slightest trace of admixture."

The Stork

The Yehudi was asked: "In the Talmud it says that the stork is called *hasidah* in Hebrew, that is, the devout or the loving one, because he gives so much love to his mate and his young. Then why is he classed in the Scriptures with the unclean birds?"

He answered: "Because he gives love only to his own."

Our Test

The Yehudi said:

"Everything can be tested in some particular way to discover whether it is any good. And what is the test for the man of Israel? It is the love of Israel. When he sees the love of Israel growing in his soul day after day, he knows that he is ascending in the service of God."

The Most Valuable

The Yehudi used to say:

"I should be glad to give up my share in this and the coming world for a single ounce of Jewishness."

The Most Difficult

The Yehudi once said:

"It's no great trick to be a worker of miracles, a man who has reached a certain spiritual rung can shift Heaven and earth— but to be a Jew, that's difficult!"

Deterioration

One night the Yehudi and his disciple Rabbi Bunam shared a room. Contrary to his habit, the Yehudi did not fall asleep, but kept thinking and sighing.

Rabbi Bunam asked: "Why are you sighing?"

The Yehudi replied: "I can't stop thinking about how the judges came after Moses, the prophets after the judges, then the Men of the Great Assembly, then the Tannaim and Amoraim, and so on to the moralists, and when they too deteriorated and false moralists multiplied, the zaddikim appeared. I am sighing because I see that they too will deteriorate. What will Israel do then?"

He Who Went Before

When young Peretz lay dying, the Yehudi sat by his disciple's bed and said to him: "Peretz, your time is not come."

The other answered: "Rabbi, I know that, but have I permission to say something?"

"Speak," said the Yehudi.

"I saw," said Peretz, "that the rabbi will soon have to leave this earth, and I do not want to stay here without you."

The Yehudi died a few weeks after him.

Ultimate Insight

Sometimes the Yehudi said that every New Year's Day gave him fresh insight into the service of God, and then everything he had done in the past year seemed insignificant compared to the new, and thus he went from one crossing to the next, on an endless way. But once toward the end of a year when he was reading the Book of the Angel Raziel, it was revealed to him that he would die soon after New Year's Day. He went to his teacher, the Seer of Lublin, and told him this. "Stay with us over New Year's," said the Seer, "and you will be spared." But the Yehudi bade him farewell and returned to his own house.

The day the Yehudi died, Rabbi Kalman was walking with Rabbi Shemuel in a distant part of the country. Rabbi Kalman said: "There is a certain unification which can be accomplished on this day, but only in the Land of Israel. Whoever accomplishes it in any other place must die on the selfsame day. That was what happened to Moses, our master, peace be with him."

The Watch He Took Apart

Rabbi Yerahmiel, the Yehudi's eldest son, who was a watchmaker before he became a rabbi, once told this story to the congregation assembled in the House of Study:

"When I had learned the watchmaker's trade, I lived with my father-in-law, and he too knew quite a bit about watches. Once I wanted to go to a great zaddik and had no money for the journey. Then I told my father-in-law that if he gave me ten gulden, I would repair his watch which had been out of order for a long time, and which he had not been able to repair himself. He agreed. So I took the whole watch apart to see what was wrong with it. And then I saw that there was nothing wrong with it at all, except that one hair spring was the least bit bent. I straightened it out, and the watch was as good and true as when it left the hand of its maker."

When Rabbi Yerahmiel had ended his story, the entire congregation wept.

Playing with a Watch

A hasid of Rabbi Pinhas of Kinsk, a grandson of Rabbi Yerahmiel, once came into the master's room and found him lying down and playing with his watch. He was surprised because it was almost noon and the rabbi had not yet prayed. Just then Rabbi Yerahmiel said to the hasid: "You are surprised at what I am doing? But do you really know what I am doing? I am learning how to leave the world."

After the Close of the Sabbath

One Friday on his return from the ritual bath, Rabbi Yehoshua Asher, the Yehudi's second son, asked his sons not to come to his house for the sabbath meal as they usually did, but to go to bed early, so that they might be able to stay with him a long time the night after the close of the sabbath. They did not however do as he said, and appeared at his table that evening as always. After the meal he said to them: "Do not visit me tomorrow during the day as you usually do, and see to it that you rest after midday meal." But again they failed to heed his words and appeared at their father's table as always. At the third sabbath meal the rabbi bade his eldest son cut the bread in his place, and when he was reluctant to do this, his father said: "You must learn to cut bread for Israel and to accord them abundance of blessings."

After they had eaten, said the Evening Prayer, and recited the Benediction of Separation, the rabbi ate the meal of escort of the sabbath with all those dear to him, and again he bade his eldest son cut the bread. After the meal he said to his sons: "I beg you not to go away but to do me the favor of staying with me." A little later he ordered clean underwear brought to his room. His wife was surprised that he wished this at so unusual an hour, but she gave the servant the garments, and the rabbi put them on. Then he told the servant to light candles in the House of Study and in all the rooms. At first his wife objected, but when she heard that the rabbi really wished it, she fetched the candles. Shortly after this, the rabbi had the doors thrown open and sent for his sons and his close friends who were waiting in the House of Study and in the entrance to the house.

The rabbi was in his bed. He then asked to have his pipe handed to him. He puffed at it slowly and calmly for a little and put it down on the chair. Then he drew the covers up over his face. All they could hear, just barely hear, was a sigh, and he had passed away.

Not to Seek the Righteous

A man who had done something wrong and was suffering from the consequences of his action asked the maggid of Trisk to advise him in this matter. But he sternly refused to have anything to do with it. "It is proper to ask advice *before* acting, not afterward," said he.

Then the man turned to Rabbi Yaakov Zevi of Parysov, a son of Rabbi Yehoshua Asher. "You must be helped," Rabbi Yaakov Zevi said. "We must not be set on seeking the righteous, but on imploring mercy for sinners. Abraham sought the righteous, and so he did not succeed in what he undertook. But Moses prayed: 'Pardon, I pray Thee, the iniquity of this people,' and God answered him: 'I have pardoned according to Thy word.'"

Where to Find God

A merchant once came to Rabbi Meir Shalom, a son of Rabbi Yehoshua Asher, and complained of another merchant who had opened his shop right next door to him. "You seem to think," said the zaddik, "that it is your shop that supports you, and are setting your heart upon it instead of on God who is your support. But perhaps you do not know where God lives? It is written: 'Love thy neighbor as thyself: I am the Lord.' This means: 'You shall want for your neighbor what he needs, just as you do for yourself—and therein you will find the Lord.'"

The Wayfarer's Greeting

A grandson of Rabbi Nehemiah, the Yehudi's third son, told this story:

"When my grandfather was returning from Sadagora where he had been visiting with the rabbi of Rizhyn, he began to doze in the carriage which he was driving with one of his hasidim. A man with a great sack on his back passed them on the road. When he was about a hundred ells away he turned and called to my grandfather who was wakened by the sound: 'Nehemiah, is that you?' My grandfather leaned out of the carriage. 'Little Nehemiah,' the man continued, 'you're bound for Poland? Then give my greetings to the holy rabbi of Radoshitz, give my greetings to the holy rabbi of Mogielnica and give my greetings to your holy brother, Rabbi Yerahmiel!' Then he walked on. But all the persons to whom he had sent his greetings were dead. Soon after he reached home my grandfather died."

PZHYSHA AND ITS DAUGHTER SCHOOLS

SIMHA BUNAM OF PZHYSHA

Verses for Chess

When Rabbi Bunam was young and a trader in lumber, he liked to play chess with persons of rather dubious reputation. Whenever he made a move he did it with inner fervor as serene as if he were intent on some holy rite, and from time to time he accompanied his actions by a jesting verse which he half spoke, half sang. For instance: "Be careful when you move at chess, or you'll end up with one pawn less." The verses always suited the stage of the game, but the tone in which they were said was such that his audience felt impelled to listen. They realized more and more that the verses had to do with their very lives. They did not want to admit it, they resisted, they yielded. Their hearts were possessed with the great turning.

The Wrong Move

Once Rabbi Bunam was playing chess with a man he was particularly anxious to turn from his evil way. He made a wrong move, and now it was the move of his opponent, who put him in a difficult position. Rabbi Bunam begged to be allowed to take back his move and the man consented. But when the same thing happened again, the other refused to give in to him a second time. "I let it pass once," he said, "but this time it must count."

"Woe to the man," the zaddik cried, "who has crept so deep into evil that prayer can no longer help him turn!" His fellow player stared at him silent and motionless, his soul on fire.

Worldly Talk

Rabbi Bunam took his lumber down the Vistula to Danzig where he intended to sell it. But in between he studied with the holy Yehudi.

Once he came to the Yehudi straight from Danzig. "Did you

hear any news there?" the holy Yehudi asked him. Bunam at once began to tell him all manner of things. Yerahmiel, the son of the Yehudi, was annoyed to see them wasting his father's time with idle worldly talk. But later when the guest had left, Rabbi the Yehudi said to his son "Do you know that what he told me reached from under the great abyss up to the throne of glory?"

The Walls

On a business trip to Leipzig, Rabbi Bunam, together with a number of merchants who had accompanied him, stopped at the house of a Jew in order to say the Afternoon Prayer. But the moment he entered he realized that he had come to an ill-smelling house; never had he prayed in such a room. He gave the others a sign and they left. The rabbi turned to go to the next house. But after a few steps he stopped. "We must go back!" he cried. "The walls are summoning me to judgment because I scorned and put them to shame."

Do They Deny God?

When Rabbi Bunam was in Danzig he sat down at table every Saturday with the "Germans"—that was how those Jews who had given up the Torah and Jewish ways were called—and spoke about the Torah. But the "Germans" only made fun of his strange talk. Indignantly his son Rabbi Abraham Moshe begged him to stop talking about the Torah to unbelievers who only mocked it.

"What can I do?" said Rabbi Bunam. "When the time comes and the word wakens within me—how can I restrain it? All the same though—next sabbath when I am getting ready to talk, step on my foot under the table to remind me to keep quiet." And so his son did on the following sabbath when they were again seated at table.

But Rabbi Bunam reproved him: "No! These people here are not unbelievers! I just heard one of them who has a bad headache cry out: 'Hear, O Israel!' Now Pharaoh really was an unbeliever, for when he was suffering under the blows of God he declared that he did not know Him."

In the days when Rabbi Bunam still traded in lumber, a number of merchants in Danzig asked him why he who was so well versed in the sacred writings went to visit zaddikim; what could they tell him that he could not learn from his books just as well? He answered them, but they did not understand him. In the evening they invited him to go to the play with them, but he refused. When they returned from the theater they told him they had seen many wonderful things. "I know all about those wonderful things," said he. "I have read the program."

"But from that," they said, "you cannot possibly know what we have seen with our own eyes."

"That's just how it is," he said, "with the books and the zaddikim."

In a Brothel

A lumber merchant once asked Rabbi Bunam to take his son, who was to attend to some business for him, to Danzig, and begged him to keep an eye on the youth.

One evening Rabbi Bunam could not find him at the inn. He left immediately and walked along the street until he came to a house where he heard someone playing the piano and singing. He went in. When he entered, the song had just come to an end, and he saw the lumber merchant's son leave the room. "Sing your best selection," he said to the girl who had been singing, and gave her a gulden. She sang, the door of the room opened, and the youth returned.

Rabbi Bunam went up to him and said in a casual tone, "Oh, so there you are. They have been asking for you. How about coming right back with me?" When they reached the inn, Rabbi Bunam played cards with the youth for a while and then they went to bed. The next evening he went to the theater with him. But when they returned Rabbi Bunam began to recite psalms and spoke with great force until he had extricated the youth completely from the power of materiality, and brought him to the point of perfect turning.

Years later the zaddik once told his friends: "That time in the

brothel I learned that the Divine Presence can descend anywhere and if, in a certain place, there is only a single being
who receives it, that being receives all of its blessing."

In the Public Park

One evening when Rabbi Bunam was in Danzig he went to the
public gardens. They were lit with many lights, and young men
and girls were strolling about in bright-colored dress. "These
lights are the candles of the Day of Atonement," he said to
himself. "And these garments are the shrouds of those who
pray."

Charity

When Rabbi Bunam still traded in lumber and went to Danzig
every year to the market, he stopped on the way in a little
town where he intended to spend the sabbath and there heard
of a devout and learned man who lived in great poverty. Rabbi
Bunam invited himself to the man's house as his sabbath guest,
had furnishings, dishes, and food taken to the empty house and
even managed to persuade him to accept suitable clothing.
When the sabbath was over, Rabbi Bunam, in parting, presented his host with a considerable sum of money. But the
latter refused to accept it, saying that he had already received
more than enough.

"The rest," said Rabbi Bunam, "I did not give you, but myself,
in order to heal the wound of pity which your wretchedness
dealt me; only now can I fulfil the commandment of charity.
That is why it is written: 'Thou shalt surely give him, and
thy heart shall not be grieved when thou givest unto him.'
He who cannot endure the sight of poverty must allay it until
the grievance of his heart is overcome; only then can he really
give to his fellow man."

The Pharmacist

Later, Rabbi Bunam became a pharmacist in Pzhysha. But at
night he studied with Rabbi Yaakov Yitzhak, the holy Yehudi.
When the rabbi had difficulty in healing a soul in the course
of his work with his hasidim, he used to say: "Call the pharmacist; he will help me."

242

The Guitar

Rabbi Yehezkel of Koznitz told a disciple of Rabbi Bunam: "When your teacher was a pharmacist in Pzhysha we saw a great deal of each other. One time I would go to him, the next he would come to me. One evening when I entered his pharmacy I saw an instrument lying on a bench, the kind whose strings you pluck with your fingers. Just then a peasant woman came to have a prescription filled. With one hand Rabbi Bunam made up the medicine, with the other he fingered the strings. When the woman had left I said to him: "Rabbi Bunam, that is unholy conduct!" Said he: "Rabbi Yehezkel, you are no real hasid!"

I went home and in my heart I bore him a grudge. But that night my grandfather appeared to me, boxed my ears, and shouted: "Don't spy on that man, he shines into all the halls of Heaven."

The Decision

When his teacher the holy Yehudi died, Rabbi Bunam remained in the town of Pzhysha. Once when his wife was sitting at the window, she saw a carriage full of people stop in front of their house. She ran to her husband and cried: "Bunam, a whole carriage-load of hasidim has come to you!"

"What are you thinking of," he said. "You know that that's not my business." But an hour later, when they had all left, he said to her: "There's no helping it. I cannot hold out against it any longer. The moment they came in, I knew the needs and wishes of every one of them."

The Shepherd

After the death of Yehudi, for a time his disciples did not know whom to choose for their master. They asked Rabbi Bunam to advise them.

He said: "A shepherd was pasturing his sheep near the edge of a meadow. He grew very tired, lay down on the ground, and fell asleep. Such a thing had never happened to him before. At midnight he awoke. There was a full moon high in the Heavens, and the night was cool and clear. The shepherd drank some water from the brook and felt better. But at the same time he remembered his sheep and his heart skipped a beat. He looked around and saw his beasts lying a few steps off, one crowded up against the next, as if they were in the fold. He counted them and not one was missing. He cried: 'Dear God, how can I repay you! Entrust your sheep to me and I shall guard them like the apple of my eye.' Find such a shepherd and make him your rabbi."

Rabbi Abele Neustaedter, who long before had instructed the Yehudi in the Kabbalah, and whom many among those present regarded as his former disciple's successor, rose from his chair and seated Rabbi Bunam in his place.

The Expensive Doctor

When Rabbi Bunam became the successor of his teacher the Yehudi, many young men came to him and forgot their homes and callings. This caused their fathers great annoyance and Rabbi Bunam was more harshly persecuted than any of the zaddikim of his generation. Once a young man's father-in-law came after him, had his carriage wait at the rabbi's door, rushed into the house, and shouted from the threshold: "You corrupt our best sons until they throw up everything and waste years here with you. And then you say that you are teaching them the fear of God! Teaching the fear of God! We don't need you for that. We have plenty of books for that purpose and they can find more in them than they can get from you."

Rabbi Bunam waited until the man ran out of words. Then he said: "You know that I used to be a pharmacist. In those days I observed that a doctor who visited all the sick without being called and without asking money for his services met with less confidence and respect for his orders than another who charged big fees. The pain and the trouble they suffer from their fathers and fathers-in-law is the fee these sick souls must pay who come to me, and they believe in the doctor who proves such a fearful expense to them."

The Cloak

A disciple of Rabbi Bunam was asked: "What is so wonderful about your teacher that you make such a great to-do over him?"

He replied: "Elijah found Elisha when he was ploughing the field with his oxen. You must not think of Elisha as a prophet, but as a real farmer who calls to his team: 'Giddap! Giddap!' Then the master came and cast his cloak over him and instantly Elisha's soul burned bright as a flame. He slaughtered his beasts, he broke his plough.

" 'What have I done to you?' asked Elijah.

" 'Oh,' Elisha cried, 'What you have done to me!'

"He left his father and mother and ran after his teacher, and no one could tear him away from Elijah. That is how it is when Rabbi Bunam takes one of his disciples by the hand. No matter how simple a man he is, life begins to stir within him so strongly that he yearns to offer himself up on the altar to God."

The Treasure

Rabbi Bunam used to tell young men who came to him for the first time the story of Rabbi Eisik, son of Rabbi Yekel in Cracow. After many years of great poverty which had never shaken his faith in God, he dreamed someone bade him look for a treasure in Prague, under the bridge which leads to the king's palace. When the dream recurred a third time, Rabbi Eisik prepared for the journey and set out for Prague. But the bridge was guarded day and night and he did not dare to start digging. Nevertheless he went to the bridge every morning and kept walking around it until evening.

Finally the captain of the guards, who had been watching him, asked in a kindly way whether he was looking for something or waiting for somebody. Rabbi Eisik told him of the dream which had brought him here from a faraway country. The captain laughed: "And so to please the dream, you poor fellow wore out your shoes to come here! As for having faith in dreams, if I had had it, I should have had to get going when a dream once told me to go to Cracow and dig for treasure under the stove in the room of a Jew—Eisik, son of Yekel, that was the name! Eisik, son of Yekel! I can just imagine what it would be like, how I should have to try every house over there, where one half of the Jews are named Eisik,

and the other Yekel!" And he laughed again. Rabbi Eisik
bowed, traveled home, dug up the treasure from under the
stove, and built the House of Prayer which is called "Reb
Eisik's Shul."

"Take this story to heart," Rabbi Bunam used to add, "and
make what it says your own: There is something you cannot
find anywhere in the world, not even at the zaddik's, and there
is, nevertheless, a place where you can find it."

The Watchman Who Brooded

Rabbi Bunam once said: "It sometimes happens that a man
becomes sinful and he himself does not know how it came
about, for there was not a single moment when all his thoughts
were not on guard." And he told this parable:

A great nobleman once had a race horse in his stable. He
valued it more than anything he possessed and had it well
guarded. The door of the stable was bolted and a watchman
was always posted in front of it. One night the owner felt
restless. He went to the stable. There sat the watchman and was
obviously brooding over something with great effort.

"What are you brooding about?" asked the master.

"I am wondering," said the man, "where the clay goes to
when you drive a nail into the wall."

"Just you go on thinking about it," said the master. He returned
to the house and went to bed. But he was unable to sleep and
after a while he could not stand it, and went back to the stable.
Again he found the watchman brooding in front of the door.
"What are you thinking about now?" asked his master.

"I am wondering," he said, "where the batter goes to when
you bake a doughnut."

"Just you go on thinking about that," said his master approv-
ingly. Again he retired and again he could not stay in bed and
went to the stable a third time. The watchman was sitting
in his place and brooding. "What is going through your head
now?" asked the master.

"I am just wondering," said the watchman. "There is the door and it is bolted. Here am I, sitting in front of it and watching: and yet the horse has been stolen. How is that possible?"

The Three Prisoners

After the death of Rabbi Uri of Strelisk, who was called the Seraph, one of his hasidim came to Rabbi Bunam and wanted to become his disciple. Rabbi Bunam asked: "What was your teacher's way of instructing you to serve?"

"His way," said the hasid, "was to plant humility in our hearts. That was why everyone who came to him, whether he was a nobleman or a scholar, had first to fill two large buckets at the well in the market place, or to do some other hard and menial labor in the street."

Rabbi Bunam said: "I shall tell you a story. Three men, two of them wise and one foolish, were once put in a dungeon black as night, and every day food and eating utensils were lowered down to them. The darkness and the misery of imprisonment had deprived the fool of his last bit of sense, so that he no longer knew how to use the utensils he could not see. One of his companions showed him, but the next day he had forgotten again, and so his wise companion had to teach him continually.

"But the third prisoner sat in silence and did not bother about the fool. Once the second prisoner asked him why he never offered his help.

" 'Look!' said the other. 'You take infinite trouble and yet you never reach the goal, because every day destroys your work. But I sit here and try to think out how I can manage to bore a hole in the wall so that light and sun can enter, and all three of us can see everything.' "

Saved

Rabbi Bunam told this story:

"Rabbi Eleazar of Amsterdam was at sea on a journey to the Holy Land, when, on the eve of New Year's Day, a storm almost sank the ship. Before dawn Rabbi Eleazar told all his people to go on deck and blow the ram's horn at the first ray of light. When they had done this, the storm died down."

"But do not think," Rabbi Bunam added, "that Rabbi Eleazar intended to save the ship. On the contrary, he was quite certain it would go down, but before dying with his people he wanted to fulfil a holy commandment, that of blowing the ram's horn. Had he been out to save the ship through a miracle, he would not have succeeded."

The Story He Told

Rabbi Bunam said:

"Once when I was on the road near Warsaw, I felt that I had to tell a certain story. But this story was of a worldly nature and I knew that it would only rouse laughter among the many people who had gathered about me. The Evil Urge tried very hard to dissuade me, saying that I should lose all those people because once they heard this story they would no longer consider me a rabbi. But I said to my heart: 'Why should you be concerned about the secret ways of God?' And I remembered the words of Rabbi Pinhas of Koretz: 'All joys hail from paradise, and jests too, provided they are uttered in true joy.' And so in my heart of hearts I renounced my rabbi's office and told the story. The gathering burst out laughing. And those who up to this point had been distant from me attached themselves to me."

All and Each

Rabbi Bunam once said:

"On a sabbath, when my room is full of people, it is difficult for me to 'say Torah.' For each person requires his own Torah, and each wishes to find his own perfection. And so what I give to all I withhold from each."

Ears and Mouth

Once when Rabbi Bunam was "saying Torah" at his table, everyone crowded so close up to him that the servant shouted at them to stop.

"Let them be," the zaddik said to him. "Believe me, just as

they bend their ears toward me to hear what I am saying, I too bend down my ears to hear what my mouth is saying."

A Bit of Sand

Rabbi Bunam was once walking outside the city with some of his disciples. He bent, picked up a speck of sand, looked at it, and put it back exactly where he had found it. "He who does not believe," he said, "that God wants this bit of sand to lie in this particular place, does not believe at all."

The Beginning of Teaching

Rabbi Bunam began his teaching with the words:
"We thank you, who are blessed and are the source of blessing, and are manifest and hidden." Then he said: "The man of feeling must feel His divinity as he feels the place on which he stands. And just as he cannot imagine himself without such a place, so in all simplicity he ought to become aware of Him who is the Place of the world, the manifest locus comprising the world; but at the same time, he must know that it is He who is the hidden life which fills the world."

The Taste of Bread

Rabbi Bunam once said at the third sabbath meal:
"It is written: 'Taste and see that the Lord is good.' What you taste in bread is not its true taste. Only the zaddikim who have purified all their limbs taste the true taste of the bread, as God created it. They taste and see that the Lord is good."

All Bones

When Rabbi Bunam's enemies asked him why he delayed praying every morning, he replied: "Man has bones which sleep on even after he is awake. But it is written: 'All my bones shall say: Lord, who is like unto Thee?' That is why man must wait to pray until all his bones are awake."

Two Pockets

Rabbi Bunam said to his disciples:
"Everyone must have two pockets, so that he can reach into

the one or the other, according to his needs. In his right pocket are to be the words: 'For my sake was the world created,' and in his left: 'I am earth and ashes.' "

Two Doors

Rabbi Bunam said:
"Man is always passing through two doors: out of this world and into the next, and out and in again."

The Wedding Ring

Rabbi Bunam taught:
"Like one who has made all the preparations for the wedding and forgotten to buy the wedding ring, so is he who has toiled a whole life long and forgotten to hallow himself—in the end he wrings his hands and devours himself in remorse."

The Scarf

Rabbi Bunam's favorite disciple had lost his scarf and looked all over for it with great zeal. His companions laughed at him. "He is right," said the zaddik, "to treasure a thing which has served him. Just so after death the soul visits the body that has sunk and leans above it."

Gifts

Rabbi Bunam said to his hasidim:
"He among you who is concerned with nothing but love is a philanderer; he among you who is nothing but devout is a thief; he among you who is nothing but clever is an unbeliever. Only he who has all these three gifts together can serve God as he should."

The Mead

Rabbi Bunam was informed that his disciples gathered at feasts of friendship. So he told his disciples this story:
"A man desired a good livelihood and so he asked around to find out what he should do. He was advised to learn how to make mead, since people like to drink mead. So he went to another city and had an experienced mead brewer teach him the principles of this trade. Then he returned home. And first of all—for such was the custom—he arranged a mead feast

and invited a great many people who, he thought, would spread the fame of his mead. But when the mead was brought to the table and the guests tasted it, they made wry faces, for it was bitter and undrinkable.

"The man returned to his instructor and angrily demanded the return of the money he had paid. The brewer asked him whether he had used the right amount of all the ingredients, and the man answered yes to every question in a furious voice. Finally the brewer said: 'And of course you put the honey in all right?'

" 'Honey!' said the man. 'No, I never thought of that!'

" 'You fool,' cried the master brewer, 'do you have to be told that too?'

"And that's the way it is with you," Rabbi Bunam concluded his story. "A feast is all very well, but along with it there must be a full measure of hasidic honey."

Master and Disciple

Rabbi Hanokh told this story:

"For a whole year I felt a longing to go to my master Rabbi Bunam and talk with him. But every time I entered the house, I felt I wasn't man enough. Once though, when I was walking across a field and weeping, I knew that I must run to the rabbi without delay. He asked: 'Why are you weeping?'

"I answered: 'I am after all alive in this world, a being created with all the senses and all the limbs, but I do not know what it is I was created for and what I am good for in this world.'

" 'Little fool,' he replied, 'that's the same question I have carried around with me all my life. You will come and eat the evening meal with me today.' "

Self-Confidence

Rabbi Hanokh told this story:

"In the house of my teacher Rabbi Bunam, it was customary for all his hasidim to assemble on the eve of the Day of Atonement, and to recall themselves to him. Once when I had settled the accounts of my soul, I was ashamed to have him see me. But I decided to go with the others, to remind him of me, and then leave hurriedly. And that is what I did. The moment he saw me getting ready to go, however, he called me to him. It flattered my vanity that the rabbi wanted to look upon me. But the very moment I felt flattered at heart, he said to me: 'Now there is no longer any need for it.'"

A Saying of the Fathers

A disciple told this story:

"My master Rabbi Simha Bunam once drew my head toward him with his holy hand until his lips touched the inside of my ear. Three times he whispered to me the words from the Sayings of the Fathers: 'Be not like servants who minister to their master on condition that they receive a reward.' My brain seemed to split with the holy and awesome breath of his mouth."

Blow!

Once when Rabbi Bunam honored a man in his House of Prayer by asking him to blow the ram's horn, and the fellow began to make lengthy preparations to concentrate on the meaning of the sounds, the zaddik cried out: "Fool, go ahead and blow!"

To Clutch at Life

Rabbi Bunam said:

"On New Year's the world begins anew, and before it begins anew, it comes to a close. Just as before dying, all the powers of the body clutch hard at life, so man at the turn of the year ought to clutch at life with all his might and main."

In Exile

On New Year's Day, when he had returned from the service, Rabbi Bunam told this story to the hasidim who had gathered in his house:

A king's son rebelled against his father and was banished from the sight of his face. After a time, the king was moved to pity his son's fate and bade him be sought out. It was long before one of the messengers found him, far from home. He was at a village inn, dancing barefoot and in a torn shirt in the midst of drunken peasants.

The courtier bowed and said: "Your father has sent me to

ask you what you desire. Whatever it may be, he is prepared to grant your wish."

The prince began to weep. "Oh," said he, "if only I had some warm clothing and a pair of stout shoes!"

"See," added Rabbi Bunam, "that is how we whine for the small needs of the hour and forget that the Divine Presence is in exile!"

I Am Prayer

This is what Rabbi Bunam said concerning the verse in the psalm: "And I am prayer."

"It is as if a poor man, who has not eaten in three days and whose clothes are in rags, should appear before the king. Is there any need for him to say what he wants? That is how David faced God—he was the prayer."

The Butcher on the Sabbath

Rabbi Bunam once said:

"How I envy the butcher who weighs out meat for the sabbath all day Friday, and before evening goes from house to house to collect his money. And then he hears the call that the sabbath is being welcomed in the House of Prayer and he runs there as fast as his legs will carry him, so that he too can welcome the sabbath, and hurries home to pronounce the blessing, and sighs and says: 'Praise be to God who has given us the sabbath as a day of rest.'

"Oh, if I could only savor the sabbath as he does!"

The Sign of Pardon

"In this day and age, when there are no prophets," Rabbi Bunam once said to his disciples, "how can we tell when a sin we have committed has been pardoned?"

His disciples gave various answers, but none of them pleased the rabbi. "We can tell," he said, "by the fact that we no longer commit that sin."

The Exception

Rabbi Bunam once said:

"Yes, I know how to bring all sinners to the point of turning—all except the liars!"

Result of Mortification of the Flesh

A man once told Rabbi Bunam: "Time and again I have mortified my flesh and done all I should, and yet Elijah has not appeared to me."

In reply the zaddik told him this story: "The holy Baal Shem
Tov once went on a long journey. He hired a team, seated
himself in the carriage, and uttered one of the holy Names.
Immediately the road leaped to meet the straining horses and
hardly had they begun to trot when they had reached the
first inn, not knowing what had happened to them. At this
stop they were usually fed, but they had scarcely calmed
down when the second inn rushed past them. Finally it occurred
to the beasts that they must have become men and so would
not receive food until evening, in the town where they were
to spend the night. But when evening came and the carriage
failed to stop, but raced on from town to town, the horses
agreed that the only possible explanation was that they must
have been transformed into angels and no longer required
either food or drink. At that moment the carriage reached its
destination. They were stabled, given their measure of oats,
and they thrust their heads into their feed bags as starved
horses do."

"As long as you are in a like situation," said Rabbi Bunam,
"you would do well to be content."

The Obliging Dream

A man who pursued honors came to Rabbi Bunam and told
him his father had appeared to him in a dream and said: "I
herewith announce to you that you are destined to be a leader."
The zaddik accepted the story in silence. Soon afterward, the
man returned and said that he had the same dream over
again.

"I see," said Rabbi Bunam, "that you are prepared to become
a leader of men. If your father comes to you once more, answer
him that you are ready to lead, but that now he should also
appear to the people whom you are supposed to lead."

Reluctant Honor

Someone said to Rabbi Bunam: "My case certainly proves the falseness of the saying that honor will run after him who flees from her and will flee from him who runs after her. For I ran diligently away from her, but she did not take a single step to catch up with me."

"Evidently she noticed that you were looking back at her," answered the rabbi, "and was no longer attracted by the game."

Sacrificing to Idols

Rabbi Bunam was asked: "What is meant by the expression 'sacrificing to idols'? It is unthinkable that a man should really bring a sacrifice to idols!"

He said: "I shall give you an example. When a devout and righteous man sits at table with others and would like to eat a little more but refrains because of what the people might think of him—that is sacrificing to idols."

The Maze

Rabbi Bunam was told about zaddikim who wore themselves out in the ecstasies of solitary service.

He replied: "A king had a broad maze with many intricate windings built around his palace. Whoever wanted to look upon him had to go through this maze where every step might lead into unending confusion. Those who dared enter because of their great love for the king were of two kinds. The one thought only of fighting their way forward bit by bit, the others left signs at the most puzzling twists and turns to encourage later comers to proceed on their way, without however making the way any easier. The first submitted to the intention in the *orders* of the king; the second trusted in the purpose of his mercy."

I See

One day, after he had gone blind, Rabbi Bunam visited Rabbi Fishel, the fame of whose miracle-cures had spread through the land. "Entrust yourself to my care," said his host. "I shall restore your light."

"That is not necessary," answered Bunam. "I see what I need to see."

Do Not Change Places

Rabbi Bunam once said:

"I should not like to change places with our father Abraham! What good would it do God if Abraham became like blind Bunam, and blind Bunam became like Abraham? Rather than have this happen, I think I shall try to grow a little over and beyond myself."

The Fool and the Sage

Rabbi Bunam once said:

"If I were to set out to give learned and subtle interpretations of the Scriptures, I could say a great many things. But a fool says what he knows, while a sage knows what he says."

The Solitary Tree

Rabbi Bunam once said:

"When I look at the world, it sometimes seems to me that every man is a tree in a wilderness, and that God has no one in his world but him, and that he has no one to turn to, save only God."

The Unredeemed Place

Once Rabbi Bunam was praying at an inn. People jostled and pushed him, but he did not go into his room. Later he said to his disciples: "Sometimes it seems impossible to pray in a certain place and one seeks out another place. But that is not the right thing to do. For the place we have quitted cries out mournfully: 'Why did you refuse to make your devotions here with me? If you met with obstacles, it was a sign that it was up to you to redeem me.'"

The Forbidden Way

The story is told:

Rabbi Bunam once drove out into the country with his disciples. While they were on the way they all fell asleep. Suddenly the disciples woke up. The carriage had come to a standstill in the tangled depths of a wood. Not a path as far as eye could see and no one could understand how they ever got there. They roused the zaddik. He looked around and cried: "Watchman!"

"Who goes?" the answer came from the thicket.

"The pharmacist of Pzhysha."

Threateningly the voice replied: "This time, but never again!"

A road opened up, the carriage drove on, the disciples recognized the region, but never had they seen a wood in those parts. They did not dare to look back.

The Great Crime

Rabbi Bunam said to his hasidim:

"The sins which man commits—those are not his great crime. Temptation is powerful and his strength is slight! The great crime of man is that he can turn at every moment, and does not do so."

David and We

Rabbi Bunam was asked: "We confess our sins so many times on the Day of Atonement. Why do we not receive a message of forgiveness? Now David had hardly finished saying: 'I have sinned,' when he was told: 'The Lord has put away thy sin.'"

He replied: "What David said was, 'I have sinned against the Lord,' and what he meant was: 'Do with me according to your will and I shall accept it with love, for you, O Lord, are just.' But when we say 'we have sinned,' we think that it is fitting for God to forgive us, and when immediately after that we add: 'We have betrayed you,' we think that now, after God has forgiven us, it is fitting that he favor us with all manner of good things."

Young Trees

Rabbi Meir of Stabnitz was always opposing Rabbi Bunam and his way. Once he compelled two of his hasidim to swear they would do whatever he asked them to. When they had taken this oath, he charged them to journey to Pzhysha and give the following message to Rabbi Bunam: "How is it possible that you are a rabbi? Can one acquire what one needs to be a rabbi by selling lumber in Danzig?"

The men arrived in Pzhysha with heavy hearts. They begged

Rabbi Bunam to forgive them for the insult they were forced to inflict on him, and repeated the message.

"Tell your teacher," the zaddik answered, "that had I known what was ahead of me when I was young, I should have lived as he did. But it is better that I did not know."

Later he said to his disciples: "Meir has been a man of God from his youth on and does not know how to sin. Then how can he know what is wrong with the people who seek him out? I was in Danzig and in the theaters, and I know what sinning is like—and ever since then I have known how to straighten out a young tree that is growing crooked."

At the Big Wedding

In Ostila, at the wedding of a grandson of the great rabbi of Apt where more than two hundred zaddikim in white robes had assembled, Rabbi Bunam's opponents preferred all manner of false charges against him and his hasidim, and tried to have all of them excommunicated. Several disciples of Rabbi Bunam defended their cause with great strength and passion, and one of them even leaped upon the table, tore open his shirt so that his breast was bared, and called to the rabbi of Apt: "Look into my heart, and you will see what my master is!"

Finally the rabbi of Apt, who was the chairman, said: "The son of my friend the holy Yehudi, of blessed memory, is here; let us ask him to tell us the truth about this matter."

Rabbi Yerahmiel, the son of the holy Yehudi, rose. Since, after his father's death, there had been a number of unpleasant incidents between his followers and those of Rabbi Bunam, everyone expected him to express doubts as to the new way. But he said: "My father used to say: 'Bunam is the very tip of my heart.' And once when I thought he was wasting my father's time with worldly talk, my father said to me afterward: 'Do you know that what he told me reaches from under the great abyss up to the throne of glory?'"

Everyone fell silent. Only Rabbi Simeon Deutsch, who had in days gone by maligned the holy Yehudi to his teacher the Seer of Lublin, launched forth into fresh accusations and compared Rabbi Bunam to Sabbatai Zevi, the false Messiah.

Then the old rabbi of Apt rose and thundered at him with his great voice: "Rabbi Simeon, you are a wrangler! If you were in an empty wood, you would pick a quarrel with the very leaves on the trees. We have not forgotten what you did at Lublin! We shall not lend you an ear." After these words, nothing more was said of this matter throughout the wedding.

Eternal Creation

Rabbi Bunam taught:

"This is how we must interpret the first words in the Scriptures: 'In the beginning of God's creation of the heaven and the earth.' For even now, the world is still in a state of creation. When a craftsman makes a tool and it is finished, it does not require him any longer. Not so with the world! Day after day, instant after instant, the world requires the renewal of the powers of the primordial word through which it was created, and if the power of these powers were withdrawn from it for a single moment, it would lapse into tohu bohu."

Curse and Blessing

Someone asked Rabbi Bunam: "Why did God put such a strange curse upon the serpent? Why did he say that it was to eat dust? When God endowed the serpent with the ability to feed on dust, I think it was a blessing rather than a curse, for it can find whatever it needs for life everywhere."

Rabbi Bunam replied: "God told man that he must eat his bread in the sweat of his face, and if he has no bread he can pray to God for help. To woman God said she was to bear her children in pain, and if the hour of birth is very difficult, she can pray to God to ease her pain. Thus both are still bound to God and can find a way to him. But to the serpent which was the source of evil, God gave everything it requires, so that it might never have to ask him for anything at all. Thus at all times, God supplies the wicked with an abundance of riches."

For the Sake of Redemption

Rabbi Bunam expounded:

"It is written: 'And now, lest he put forth his hand, and take also of the tree of life, and eat and live forever.' When human beings committed their first sin, God in the fulness of his mercy permitted them to live in the world of death, so that they might achieve perfect redemption. That is why he decided to prevent them from taking also of the tree of life, for then their spirit would never have fought free of matter and prepared for redemption. So he drove them out of paradise."

The Sacrifice of Isaac

Rabbi Bunam was asked: "Why in the story of the sacrifice of Isaac is it especially stated and related that they went 'both of them together'? For is it not self-evident?"

He replied: "The temptation which Isaac resisted was greater than that of Abraham. Abraham heard the command from the lips of God. When Isaac heard his father say that God himself would provide the lamb for the burnt-offering, he understood—though he heard the command from the lips of man. But Abraham brooded: 'Whence has my son this great strength? It must be the strength of his youth!' Then he fetched forth from within himself the strength of his own youth. Only then did both of them really go together."

Two Kinds of Service

On a sabbath, at table, Rabbi Bunam was explaining the Scriptures.

"It is written: 'And the children of Israel sighed by reason of their service, and they cried, and their cry came up unto God out of their service.' Why is the word 'service' used twice? The first time it refers to the bondage in Egypt, but the second time it refers to the service of God. 'Away from the service of flesh and blood!' That was what they meant when they cried to God for help. 'Through the service of God, up to God.'"

Burdens

Rabbi Bunam expounded:

"It is written: 'I will bring you out from under the burdens of the Egyptians.' Why is the word 'burdens' used here rather than bondage? Because Israel had grown accustomed to bondage. When God saw that they no longer felt what was happening to them, he said: 'I will bring you out from under the burdens of Egypt. Suffering these burdens is not doing you any good; I shall have to redeem you.' "

No More than This

Rabbi Bunam was asked: "It is written: 'And ye shall be unto me a kingdom of priests, and a holy nation. These are the words which thou shalt speak unto the children of Israel.' Our teacher Rashi comments: 'These are the words, no more and no less.' What does he mean by that?"

Rabbi Bunam explained: "Moses was good. He wanted to reveal more to the people, but he was not allowed. For it was God's will that the people make an effort of their own. Moses was to say just these words to them, no more, and no less, so that they might feel: something is hidden here, and we must strive to discover it for ourselves. That is why, further on, we read: 'And he set before them all these words.' No more and no less."

It Is I

Rabbi Bunam was asked: "It is written: 'I am the Lord thy God, who brought thee out of the land of Egypt.' Why does it not read: 'I am the Lord thy God, who created heaven and earth'?"

Rabbi Bunam expounded: " 'Heaven and earth!' Then man might have said: 'Heaven—that is too much for me.' So God said to man: 'I am the one who fished you out of the mud. Now you come here and listen to me!' "

We Want Water

Rabbi Bunam expounded:

"It is written that Israel said at Sinai: 'We will do and obey.' Ought it not read: 'I will do and obey,' since every individual was speaking for himself? But it was as if a great throng of people were in prison dying of thirst on a scorching day, and as if suddenly someone came and asked whether they wanted water, and everyone were to answer: 'Yes, we want water!' For every one of them would know how thirsty they all were.

So at Sinai they were all thirsting for a drink of the Torah, and each one of them felt the thirst of all, and when the word came to them, each one cried: 'We.' "

Moses and Korah

Rabbi Bunam taught:

"In every generation the soul of Moses and the soul of Korah return. But if once, in days to come, the soul of Korah is willing to subject itself to the soul of Moses, Korah will be redeemed."

True and False Turning

Rabbi Bunam was asked: "Why was the sin of worshipping the golden calf forgiven, though we do not find it said in the Scriptures that the people turned and did penance, and why was the sin of the spies not forgiven, although we read that the people mourned greatly because of it? Do we not know that there is nothing which can resist the turning?"

He replied: "This is the nature of turning: When a man knows he has nothing to hope for and feels like a shard of clay because he has upset the order of life, and how can that which was upset be righted again? Nevertheless, though he has no hope, he prepares to serve God from that time on and does so. That is true turning, and nothing can resist it. That is how it was with the sin of worshipping the golden calf. It was the first sin and the people knew nothing of the power of turning, and so they turned with all their heart. But it was different with the sin of the spies. The people already knew what turning can accomplish, and they thought that if they did penance they would return to their former state; so they did not turn with all their hearts, and their turning accomplished nothing."

The Shepherd Is There

Rabbi Bunam once commented on the verse in the Scriptures: "I saw all Israel scattered upon the mountains, as sheep that have no shepherd."

He said: "This does not mean that the shepherd is not there. The shepherd is always there. But sometimes he hides, and then he is indeed not there for the sheep, because they do not see him."

262

Against Dejection

Rabbi Bunam expounded:

"In the psalm we read: 'Who healeth the broken in heart . . . '
Why are we told that? For it is a good thing to have a broken
heart, and pleasing to God, as it is written: 'The sacrifices of
God are a broken spirit . . . ' But further on in the psalm we
read: 'And bindeth up their wounds.' God does not entirely
heal those who have broken hearts. He only eases their suffering, lest it torment and deject them. For dejection is not good
and not pleasing to God. A broken heart prepares man for
the service of God, but dejection corrodes service. We must
distinguish as carefully between the two, as between joy and
wantonness; they are so easily confused, and yet are as far
removed from one another as the ends of the earth."

In Water

Rabbi Bunam said:

"It is written in Proverbs: 'As in water face answereth to face,
so the heart of man to man.' Why does the verse read 'in
water' and not 'in a mirror'? Man can see his reflection in
water only when he bends close to it, and the heart of man too
must lean down to the heart of his fellow; then it will see
itself within his heart."

The Gate

This is what Rabbi Bunam said about the words in the psalm:
"Open to me the gates of righteousness": "It is the way of
honest service, that a man will always feel himself to be on
the outside and beg God to open to him the gates of true
service. This is what David meant when he said: 'This is the
gate of the Lord; the righteous shall enter into it.' There is no
gate to the Lord, save prayer such as this."

The Covenant with the Philistines

Rabbi Bunam once had the horses harnessed and drove to
Warsaw with several of his hasidim. When they arrived there
he told the coachman to stop at an inn. They entered and sat
down at a table. At a corner table near theirs sat two porters
who were drinking schnapps and talking about all sorts of

things. After a while the first asked: "Have you already studied the weekly portion of the Torah?"

"Yes," answered the second.

"I too have learned it," said the first, "and I found one thing very hard to understand. It is the passage about our father Abraham and Abimelech, the king of the Philistines, where it says: '. . . and they two made a covenant.' I asked myself: Why say 'they two'? That seems utterly superfluous."

"A good question!" cried the second. "But I wonder what answer you will find to it."

"What I think," said the first, "is that they made a covenant, but still they did not become one; they remained two."

Rabbi Bunam rose, left the inn with his hasidim, and got into the carriage. "Now that we heard what these hidden zaddikim had to tell us," he said, "we can go back home."

World-Peace and Soul-Peace

Rabbi Bunam taught:

"Our sages say: 'Seek peace in your own place.' You cannot find peace anywhere save in your own self. In the psalm we read: 'There is no peace in my bones because of my sin.' When a man has made peace within himself, he will be able to make peace in the whole world."

Concealment

Rabbi Bunam said:

"Before the coming of the Messiah, concealment will be so great that even the zaddikim who walk in white robes will not know their way about, and even they will be confused and flinch in their faith in the Messiah."

* * *

Another time he said:

"Before the coming of the Messiah, there will be summers without heat, and winters without cold, scholars will be without Torah, and hasidim without the hasidic way."

The Test

"The Baal Shem Tov," said Rabbi Bunam, "was wiser than Aher, the great heretic. When Aher heard a voice from Heaven crying: 'Return, O backsliding children—all except Aher,' he gave up everything and left the community. But the Baal Shem —once when he noticed that all his great gifts were suddenly leaving him, he said: 'Well then, I shall serve God as a simple man does. I am a fool, but I have faith,' and he began to pray like a little child. Instantly he was lifted higher than before, for it had only been a test."

The Book of Adam

Rabbi Bunam once said:
"I thought of writing a book. I was going to entitle it 'Adam' and the whole of man was to be in it. But then I thought it over and decided it would be better not to write such a book."

A "Good Jew"

Rabbi Bunam once asked: "Why do they call a zaddik 'a good Jew'?" Jestingly he answered his own question: "If they meant by that that he prays well, they would have to call him 'a good prayer'; if they meant that he learns well, they would have to say 'a good learner.' Now 'a good Jew' thinks well, and drinks well, and everything about him is good."

But to a disciple who had been in Pzhysha only a short time, he said: "You must know why you have come to me. If you think to become 'a good Jew,' you have come in vain. But if you are here in order to become simply a good Jew, you did right."

Abraham and Isaac

Rabbi Bunam explained the tradition that Abraham represented the attribute of mercy, and Isaac that of rigor.

"Abraham's house was wide open on all four sides. He was hospitable to everyone and gave of all the good things he had. Through this he revealed the great Name of God to the world. But when Isaac became rabbi in his stead, he went to a shop, bought iron bolts and locked all the doors. He himself went in to the innermost chamber, isolated himself from men, and devoted himself to the Torah night and day. Fear and trembling seized all his hasidim and all those who came to ask his counsel. In this way he revealed to the world that there is 'rigor.' When, from time to time, a door was opened and people were admitted, everyone who looked on his face instantly accomplished the perfect turning."

Satan's Hasidim

Rabbi Bunam told this story:

"When the Baal Shem Tov made the first hasidim, the Evil Urge was in great straits, for, as he said to his followers, 'now the hasidim of the Baal Shem Tov will set the world ablaze with their holiness.' But then he thought of a way out.

"He disguised himself, pretended to be someone else, and went to two hasidim who lived together in a certain town. 'Your work is praiseworthy,' he said to them. 'But there ought to be at. least ten of you, so that you can pray in a quorum.' He fetched eight of his people and joined them to those two hasidim. And since they had no money to purchase a scroll and other things they needed, he brought them a rich man—also one of his adherents—who provided them with whatever was necessary. He did the same everywhere. When he had finished he said to his hosts: 'Now we no longer need be afraid of anything, for we have the majority, and that is what counts.' "

Repetition

Rabbi Bunam once said to Rabbi Mendel, his disciple: "What do I need so many hasidim like these for? A few who really are hasidim would be enough for me."

"Why did the former zaddikim not do the same?" answered Rabbi Mendel. Long afterward, when his master had been dead for many years and he himself was the rabbi of Kotzk, Rabbi Mendel once said to his disciple Rabbi Hirsh of Tomashov: "What do I need so many hasidim like these for? A few who really are hasidim would be enough for me."

"Why did the former zaddikim not do the same?" answered Rabbi Hirsh.

By Night

Two hours every night, as he lay in bed, Rabbi Bunam would listen to his disciple Mendel, later the rabbi of Kotzk, while he read to him out of the Book of Splendor. Sometimes Rabbi

Bunam fell asleep for a little while, and the reading was interrupted. When he awoke he himself resumed it.

But once when he woke he said to his disciple: "Mendel, I have been thinking it over: Why should I go on living as I do? People keep coming to me and prevent me from serving God. I want to give up my service as a rabbi; I want to devote myself to the service of God." He repeated this again and again. His disciple listened and said nothing.

Finally Rabbi Bunam dozed again. After a few breaths, he sat up and said: "Mendel, no rabbi has been permitted to do so, I am not permitted to do it either."

The Order That Was Rescinded

The Russian government gave orders that the hasidim were no longer to be allowed to visit the zaddikim. Temeril, a noble lady who had provided for Rabbi Bunam in his youth and in whose service he used to sail down the Vistula to take lumber to Danzig, spoke to the governor of Warsaw and succeeded in having the order rescinded.

When Rabbi Bunam was told about it, he said: "Her intentions were good. But it would have been better had she induced the government to build a wall about every zaddik's house, and surround it with Cossacks to allow no one to enter. Then they would let us live on bread and water and do our job."

The Good Enemy

The quarrel that broke out between Rabbi Bunam and Rabbi Meir of Stabnitz lasted for many years. When Rabbi Meir died, a hasid of Rabbi Bunam's came and brought him the good news.

The zaddik jumped up and struck his hands together. "That is meant for me," he cried, "for he was my support." Rabbi Bunam died that same summer.

The Keys

The rabbi of Ger told this story:

"Rabbi Bunam had the keys to all the firmaments. And why not? The man who does not think of himself is the man who is given all the keys. He could have quickened the dead, but he was an honest man and did not take what was not his due."

The Meaning

When Rabbi Bunam lay dying his wife burst into tears.
He said: "What are you crying for? My whole life was only that I might learn how to die."

The Secrets of Dying

Rabbi Yudel, who had given faithful service to Rabbi Abraham Moshe, the son of Rabbi Bunam, told this story:

"On the eve of the last sabbath before Rabbi Bunam's death, Rabbi Abraham Moshe told me that he wanted to go to his father. So we went there together and Rabbi Abraham Moshe seated himself at the head of the bed. Then he heard his father saying the Evening Prayer, but immediately afterward he heard him say the Morning Prayer.

"He said: 'Father, now is the time for the Evening Prayer.' But just then his father began to say the Afternoon Prayer.

"When Rabbi Abraham Moshe heard that, he fainted and hit the floor with the back of his head. I ran to him from the opposite corner of the room where I had been standing, and managed to bring him to consciousness. The moment he was conscious he said to me: 'Let us go home,' and we went home.

"When we were back home he told me to say the Benediction of Sanctification in his stead, because he had to go to sleep immediately. He also ordered me not to admit anyone, no matter what happened. He stayed in bed until Tuesday. From time to time I brought him a small glass of wine. That was all he took.

"On Tuesday people came running and reported that Rabbi Bunam was failing rapidly, but I turned them away. Then Rabbi Abraham Moshe's mother, Rabbi Bunam's wife, peace be with her, came to the door and said: 'My son, I beg you to go to your sick father. Do you want people to say that in the hour of his death you did not wish to be with him?'

" 'Mother,' he replied, 'believe me, if I could go, I would go, but I cannot.'

"Later I heard that his mother then went to Rabbi Yitzhak of

Vorki, Rabbi Bunam's disciple, and begged him to persuade his friend Rabbi Abraham Moshe to come to his father's deathbed.

"Rabbi Yitzhak answered her: 'If Your Reverence were to order me to climb up on the roof and jump down, I should obey. But in this matter I cannot obey Your Reverence. For Rabbi Abraham and his holy father are concerned with something in which neither angels nor seraphim may interfere, and I cannot meddle in it.'

"But soon after that, at the very moment Rabbi Bunam, may his merit protect us, died, Rabbi Abraham Moshe opened his eyes and said to me: 'Yudel, now there is darkness all over the world.'

"When they carried the bier into the House of Life they went by Rabbi Abraham Moshe's door. He came out and remained standing until they had passed; then he went back in.

"Many years later I was with Rabbi Menahem Mendel of Vorki for the Passover, on the last day of which his father Rabbi Yitzhak of Vorki died. And Rabbi Menahem Mendel ordered me not to let anyone come to him, no matter what happened."

From Now On

After Rabbi Bunam's death, his disciple Yitzhak of Vorki came to his master's son, Abraham Moshe, to speak words of comfort to him. The son lamented: "And who will teach me now?"

"Take courage," said the disciple. "Up to now he has taught you in his coat; from now on, he will teach you without his coat on."

The Craving

On Hanukkah, when Rabbi Abraham Moshe was in the city of Biala with his mother, he said to her: "Mother, I have a craving to die." She answered: "I heard from your father that one has to learn to die." He answered: "I have learned it." Again she said: "I heard from your father that one has to learn for a very long time, to learn it properly." He answered: "I have learned long enough," and lay down. He died on the seventh day of the feast. Later his mother found out that before going on his journey he had visited his favorite disciples and taken leave of them.

MENAHEM MENDEL OF KOTZK

Two Kinds of Teaching

When Mendel was already the far-famed and much-hated rabbi of Kotzk, he once returned to the little town in which he was born. There he visited the teacher who had taught him his alphabet when he was a child and read the five books of Moses with him. But he did not go to see the teacher who had given him further instruction, and at a chance meeting the man asked his former pupil whether he had any cause to be ashamed of his teacher. Mendel replied: "You taught me things that can be refuted, for according to one interpretation they can mean this, according to another, that. But my first teacher taught me true teachings which cannot be refuted, and they have remained with me as such. That is why I owe him special reverence."

How He Became a Hasid

Rabbi Mendel said:

"I became a hasid because in the town where I lived there was an old man who told stories about zaddikim. He told what he knew, and I heard what I needed."

This Is My God

When Mendel was fifteen he rode to the Seer of Lublin without asking permission of his parents. Soon after, his father came to Lublin to fetch him back. "Why have you left the ways of your fathers," he cried, "and attached yourself to the hasidim!" "In the song sung by the Red Sea," said Mendel, "what we read first is: 'This is my God and I will glorify him,' and only then, 'My father's God and I will exalt him.'"

From Lublin to Pzhysha

When Mendel, together with one of his friends, left Lublin in disappointment and drove to Pzhysha to study with the holy Yehudi, the Seer's disciple, he fell sick on the way. His friend ran to the Yehudi and begged him to remember Mendel in his prayers. "Did you leave Lublin without asking the rabbi's permission?" asked the Yehudi. When he was told that was so, he went to the inn. "As soon as you are well," he said to Mendel, "you must take it upon yourself to return to Lublin and ask the rabbi's permission to leave." Mendel shook his head. "I have never regretted the truth," he said. The Yehudi looked at him long and searchingly. Finally he said: "If you are so sure of your own judgment, you will get well in any case." And so it was.

But when Mendel had recovered and came to him, the Yehudi said: "It is written: 'It is good for a man to bear a yoke in his youth.'" At that the young man felt a readiness to serve truly enter into every limb.

Later on the Seer once asked the Yehudi if he had worthwhile young men about him. "Mendel," he replied, "wants to be worthwhile." Many years later, when Rabbi Mendel of Kotzk was old, he quoted this question and this answer. "At that time," he added, "I did not yet want to be worthwhile. But from the moment the holy Yehudi said it, I did, and I do."

After the Yehudi's Death

Rabbi Mendel told this story to Rabbi Hanokh, his disciple: "When the holy Yehudi lay in bed ill, all the people recited psalms, but I stood by the stove and did not want to recite psalms. Then Rabbi Bunam came up to me and asked: 'Why do you press Heaven so hard?' But I did not understand what he wanted of me. After the Yehudi's death he said to me: 'It is over; the rabbi is no more, but he has left us the fear of God, and where the rabbi's word is, there he himself is.' I said nothing. After that I looked elsewhere for the rabbi's word, but it was not there. And so I went to Rabbi Bunam."

The Offer

The story is also told that when his master had died and Rabbi Mendel was greatly troubled as to who would now be his teacher, the Yehudi appeared to him in a dream and tried to comfort him, saying that he was willing to continue to teach

him. "I do not want a teacher from the other world," answered
Mendel.

Disgust

Temeril, a lady who lived in Warsaw and was known for her
charitable works, visited Rabbi Bunam in Pzhysha and gave
him a sum of money to be distributed among worthy poor young
men in his House of Study. The zaddik entrusted one of his
pupils with this task. When he had just finished allotting the
money, Rabbi Mendel arrived in a torn coat with the cotton
showing through the ragged lining. "What a pity!" cried the
youth who had distributed the funds. "I forgot about you and
now I have no more money!"

"Money!" said Rabbi Mendel and spat. For weeks afterward,
the youth could not see a coin without feeling his gorge rise
within him.

A Conversation

Rabbi Bunam once said to Rabbi Mendel, his disciple: "If I
am sentenced to hell—what shall I do?"

Mendel was silent.

After a while Rabbi Bunam said: "This is what I'll do. Our
sages say: 'If a disciple is banished, his teachers are banished
together with him.' Well then, I shall say: 'Bring me my teachers, the Seer of Lublin and the holy Yehudi!'"

Then Mendel answered: "This cannot of course come up as far
as you are concerned," he said, "but knowing it can be of great
use to me."

The Secret Burial

Rabbi Mendel was not present when his master Rabbi Bunam
died, for just at that time his son was to be married. On his
deathbed Rabbi Bunam had bidden Mendel leave him and go
to the wedding, and had refused to listen to his objections.

After the wedding Rabbi Mendel learned that his teacher had
died and the burial had already taken place. He traveled to
Pzhysha, asked for the keys to the room in which his master
died, and locked himself in it. After a long time he came out
and said to his assembled friends: "Only I and no one else
was present at the rabbi's burial."

Why the Castle Was Built

Once when Rabbi Mendel was in the neighborhood of Pilev—
that is, Pulavy—he visited the castle of Prince Czartoryski. He
went from room to room and finally to the garden, where he
stayed for a long time. Just at that time Rabbi Israel, the son
of the Seer of Lublin, happened to be taking a trip and was
stopping over in Pilev. When he heard that Rabbi Mendel was
at the castle of the Czartoryskis, he told this story:

"I passed by here with my father, of blessed memory, when the
castle was just being built. My father looked at it and said:
'For whom are they building this castle? For the zaddik who
will some day stay there.' Since that zaddik is now in the castle,
it is only right that I go there so that I may see him."

The Sabbath

Rabbi Mendel of Kotzk once said to one of his hasidim: "Do
you know who I am? There was Rabbi Baer, and there was
Rabbi Shmelke; there was Rabbi Elimelekh, there was the rabbi
of Lublin, there was the holy Yehudi, and there was Rabbi
Bunam. I am the seventh. I am the quintessence of all of them;
I am the sabbath."

Concerning His Soul

Rabbi Mendel of Kotzk once said to his son-in-law: "My soul
is one of those that hail from the time before the destruction of
the Temple. I do not belong among the people of today. And
the reason I have come into this world is to draw the distinction
between what is holy and what is profane."

The Firmaments

A zaddik who was opposed to the rabbi of Kotzk sent him a
message: "I am so great that I reach into the seventh firmament." The rabbi of Kotzk sent back his answer: "I am so small
that all the seven firmaments rest upon me."

A Trustworthy Man

A disciple told this story:

"Once when I was standing in the room of my master and
teacher, the rabbi of Kotzk, I understood the meaning of what

is written in Proverbs: 'But a trustworthy man who can find?' This does not mean that you can find only one in a thousand. It means that a trustworthy man, that is to say a man who can really be trusted, cannot be found at all, for he is well hidden —you may stand right in front of him and yet you will not find him."

Sight and Faith

The rabbi of Kotzk made this comment on certain zaddikim of his time: "They claim that, during the Feast of Booths, they saw the Seven Shepherds in their booth as guests. I rely on my faith. Faith is clearer than sight."

In a Fur Coat

The rabbi of Kotzk once said of a famous rabbi: "That's a zaddik in a fur coat." His disciples asked him what he meant by this. "Well," he explained, "one man buys himself a fur coat in winter, another buys kindling. What is the difference between them? The first wants to keep only himself warm, the second wants to give warmth to others too."

Korah's Error

A disciple asked the rabbi of Kotzk what it was that caused Korah to rebel against Moses and Aaron.

"He had observed," answered the rabbi, "that whenever he stood up above, among the singing Levites, great gifts of the spirit descended upon him. And so he thought that if he stood within the tabernacle with his censer, still greater gifts would accrue to him. He did not know that the power he had felt came upon him because Aaron stood in his place and he in his."

In Pacing

A hasid told his son:

"Once when I was in Kotzk on the Day of Rejoicing in the Law, the rabbi paced around the pulpit with the scroll of the Torah in his hand, came to where I was standing, and said the verse: 'And in His temple all say: Glory.' Then I felt as though I were up in the temple of Heaven and heard all the angels cry: 'Glory,' I grew faint and I became a different man."

From the Outside

The rabbi of Kotzk was asked how he knew what advice to give the hasidim who came to him in regard to their business affairs, since he certainly was above and beyond all such matters. He replied: "From where can you get the best all-round view of everything?"

It Is Written

When Rabbi Yitzhak Meir, later the rabbi of Ger, was in Kotzk for the first time, he soon noticed that the zaddik's house was neither well-run nor supervised, for something or other was always being stolen. Once he heard Feyvel the servant reproach the rabbi's wife: "Why shouldn't there be stealing, if things aren't locked up but just lie around for the taking!" At that the zaddik's voice rang out from his room: "Feyvel, it is written: 'Thou shalt not steal'!" When Rabbi Yitzhak Meir heard this, he was instantly overwhelmed with the feeling that it was altogether impossible for anyone to steal anything.

After Waking

One morning after prayer the rabbi of Kotzk said: "When I woke up today, it seemed to me that I was not alive. I opened my eyes, looked at my hands, and saw that I could use them. So I washed them. Then I looked at my feet and saw that I could walk with them. So I took a few steps. Now I said the blessing: 'Blessed art thou who quickenest the dead,' and knew that I was alive."

The Lord of the Castle

Rabbi Mendel once spoke to his hasidim about a certain parable in Midrash: How a man passed by a castle and, seeing it on fire and no one trying to put out the blaze, thought that this must be a castle without an owner, until the lord of the castle looked down on him and said: "I am the lord of the castle." When Rabbi Mendel said the words: "I am the lord of the castle," all those around him were struck with great reverence, for they all felt: "The castle is burning, but it has a lord."

God's Back

Concerning the verse in the Scriptures: "And thou shalt see My back; but My face shall not be seen," the rabbi of Kotzk said: "Everything puzzling and confused people see, is called God's back. But no man can see his face, where everything is in harmony."

All Together

The rabbi of Kotzk said:

"It is written: 'The ordinances of the Lord are true, they are righteous altogether.' In this world you see one ordinance decreed for one man, and an apparently contradictory ordinance for another, and you are astonished and cannot understand how both can be righteous. But in the coming world you will see them all together and you will find them altogether righteous."

To What Purpose Was Man Created?

Rabbi Mendel of Kotzk once asked his disciple Rabbi Yaakov of Radzimin: "Yaakov, to what purpose was man created?" He answered: "So that he might perfect his soul."

"Yaakov," said the zaddik, "is that what we learned from our teacher, Rabbi Bunam? No, indeed! Man was created so that he might lift up the Heavens."

The Ladder

Rabbi Mendel of Kotzk said to his disciples: "The souls descended from the realms of Heaven to earth on a ladder. Then it was taken away. Now up there they are calling the souls home. Some do not budge from the spot, for how can one get to Heaven without a ladder? Others leap and fall, and leap again and give up. But there are those who know very well that they cannot make it, but try and try over and over again until God catches hold of them and pulls them up."

Man's Advantage

This is what Rabbi Mendel said about the words in the Scriptures: "This is the law of the burnt-offering":

"Why does God demand sacrifice of man and not of the angels? That of the angels would be purer than that of man could ever be. But what God desires is not the deed but the preparation. The holy angels cannot prepare themselves; they can only do the deed. Preparation is the task of man who is caught in the thicket of tremendous obstacles and must free himself. This is the advantage of the works of man."

Immersion

This is what the rabbi of Kotzk said concerning Rabbi Akiba's saying that "God is the waters of immersion of Israel": "The waters of immersion only purify the soul if one is wholly immersed, so that not a hair is showing. That is how we should be immersed in God."

God's Dwelling

"Where is the dwelling of God?"
This was the question with which the rabbi of Kotzk surprised a number of learned men who happened to be visiting him.
They laughed at him: "What a thing to ask! Is not the whole world full of his glory!"
Then he answered his own question:
"God dwells wherever man lets him in."

Fathers and Sons

A man came to the rabbi of Kotzk and complained of his sons who refused to support him, though he was old and no longer able to earn his own livelihood. "I was always ready to do anything at all for them," he said, "and now they won't have anything to do with me." Silently the rabbi raised his eyes to Heaven. "That's how it is," he said softly. "The father shares in the sorrow of his sons, but the sons do not share in the sorrow of their father."

The Vessel

A disciple of Rabbi Mendel told this story in his old age, shortly before he died:
"I shall tell you the first saying I heard from the rabbi. I heard many after that, but with this first he kindled my heart forever. It was on a sabbath eve after the Benediction of Sanctification. The rabbi sat in his big chair, and his face was transformed as though his soul had left his body and was floating about him. He stretched out his arms with a gesture of great decision,

poured water over our hands, spoke the benediction over the bread, and broke the bread. Then he said:

" 'In the world there are sages, students, and thinkers. They all think of and study the mystery of God. But what can they find out about it? No more than they can grasp from their rung of reason. But the holy children of Israel have a vessel: it is to do God's will and with this vessel they can hold more than is accorded their rung, they can grasp what is accorded on the rung of the ministering angels. That is what is meant by the words spoken at Sinai: "We do, we hear." It is with our doing that we grasp.' "

Giving and Receiving

The rabbi of Kotzk was asked: "Why is the Feast of Weeks designated as 'the time the Torah was given' us, rather than the time we received the Torah?"

He answered: "The giving took place on the day commemorated by this feast, but the receiving takes place at all times. It was given to all equally, but they did not all receive in equal measure."

Upon Thy Heart

Rabbi Mendel of Kotzk said:

" 'And these words which I command thee this day, shall be *upon* thy heart.' The verse does not say: '*in* thy heart.' For there are times when the heart is shut. But the words lie upon the heart, and when the heart opens in holy hours, they sink deep down into it."

No Strange God

They asked the rabbi of Kotzk: "What is new about King David's saying, 'There shall no strange God be in thee'? For was it not specifically stated in the decalogue: 'Thou shalt have no other gods before Me.' "

He replied: "The meaning is this: God ought not to be a stranger to you."

Molten Gods

The rabbi of Kotzk said:

"It is written: 'Thou shalt make thee no molten gods.' When you think God, you should really think of him, and not of a molten god whom you have made in your own image."

278

No Graven Image

The disciples of the rabbi of Kotzk were once discussing why it is written: "Take heed unto yourselves, lest ye forget the covenant of the Lord your God, which He made with you, and make you a graven image, even in the likeness of any thing which the Lord thy God hath bidden thee," and not—as the meaning really demands—"which the Lord thy God hath forbidden thee." The zaddik who had been listening joined in the discussion. "The Torah warns us," said he, "not to make a graven image of any thing the Lord our God has bidden us."

The Hunter

Rabbi Mendel of Kotzk told the story of the hunter whom the prophet Elijah met in the wilderness and asked why he was living there without the Torah and without the commandments. The hunter tried to defend himself. "I never could find the gate that leads to the presence of God," he said.

"You were certainly not born a hunter," said Elijah. "So from whom did you learn to follow this calling?"

"My need taught me," answered the hunter.

Then the prophet said: "And had your need been equally great because you had lost your way far from God, do you think it would have failed to show you the way to Him?"

Fear

The rabbi of Kotzk asked one of his hasidim:

"Have you ever seen a wolf?"

"Yes," he replied.

"And were you afraid of him?"

"Yes."

"But were you aware of the fact that you were afraid?"

"No," answered the hasid. "I was simply afraid."

"That is how it should be with us when we fear God," said the rabbi.

Two Kinds of Fear

The rabbi of Kotzk was asked: "When they stood at Mount Sinai, the people said to Moses: 'Speak thou with us, and we will hear; but let not God speak with us, lest we die.' And

Moses answered: 'Fear not.' He went on to say that God had come 'that His fear may be before you, that ye sin not.' Is not that a contradiction?"

Rabbi Mendel said: " 'Fear not'—that means: This fear of yours, the fear of death, is not the fear God wants of you. He wants you to fear him, he wants you to fear his remoteness, and not to fall into sin which removes you from him."

What Does It Matter to You?

A hasid came to the rabbi of Kotzk. "Rabbi," he complained, "I keep brooding and brooding, and don't seem to be able to stop."

"What do you brood about?" asked the rabbi.

"I keep brooding about whether there really is a judgment and a judge."

"What does it matter to you!"

"Rabbi! If there is no judgment and no judge, then what does all creation mean!"

"What does that matter to you!"

"Rabbi! If there is no judgment and no judge, then what do the words of the Torah mean!"

"What does that matter to you?"

"Rabbi! 'What does it matter to me?' What does the rabbi think? What else could matter to me?"

"Well, if it matters to you as much as all that," said the rabbi of Kotzk, "then you are a good Jew after all—and it is quite all right for a good Jew to brood: nothing can go wrong with him."

Worry

A hasid told the rabbi of Kotzk about his poverty and troubles. "Don't worry," advised the rabbi. "Pray to God with all your heart, and the merciful Lord will have mercy upon you."

"But I don't know how to pray," said the other.

Pity surged up in the rabbi of Kotzk as he looked at him. "Then," he said, "you have indeed a great deal to worry about."

Holiness

It is written: "And ye shall be holy men unto Me."
The rabbi of Kotzk explained: "Ye shall be holy unto me, but as men, ye shall be humanly holy unto me."

Infirmity

A man came to the rabbi of Kotzk and told him his trouble. "People call me a bigot," he said. "What kind of an infirmity are they ascribing to me? Why a bigot? Why not a pious man?"
"A bigot," the rabbi answered him, "converts the main issue in piety into a side issue, and a side issue into the main issue."

Afar Off

This is how Rabbi Mendel expounded the verse from the Scriptures: "Am I a God near at hand . . . and not a God afar off?"
" 'Afar off' refers to the wicked. 'Near at hand' refers to the righteous. God says: 'Do I want him who is already close to me, do I want the righteous? Why, I also want him who is afar off, I want him who is wicked!"

The "Way" of the Wicked

The rabbi of Kotzk commented on the verse in the Scriptures: "Let the wicked forsake his way."
"Does the wicked man have a way? What he has is a mire, not a way. Now what is meant is this: Let the wicked man leave his 'way,' that is, his illusion of having a way."

The Setting

Rabbi Mendel said:
"The larger and more luminous the jewel, the larger the setting. The greater and more luminous the soul, the greater the 'shell' which surrounds it."

Great Guilt

Rabbi Mendel said:
"He who learns the Torah and is not troubled by it, who sins

and forgives himself, who prays because he prayed yesterday—a very scoundrel is better than he!"

The Week and the Sabbath

Once the rabbi of Kotzk said to Rabbi Yitzhak Meir of Ger: "I don't know what they want of me! All week everyone does as he pleases, but come sabbath he puts on his black gown and girds himself with his black belt, and sets the black fur hat on his head, and there he is: hand-in-glove with the Bride of the Sabbath! What I say is: As a man does the week, so let him do on the sabbath."

Earnestness

The rabbi of Kotzk called to some of his hasidim: "What is all this talk of praying 'earnestly'! What is the meaning of to pray 'earnestly'?"
They did not understand what he had in mind.
"Is there anything at all," he said, "that one ought not to do earnestly?"

No Break

Rabbi Mendel saw to it that his hasidim wore nothing around the neck while praying, for, he said, there must be no break between the heart and the brain.

Praying and Eating

Rabbi Mendel was asked: "It is written: 'Ye shall serve the Lord your God, and he will bless thy bread.' Why is 'ye' written first, and later 'thy'?"
He explained: "To serve—that means to pray. When a man prays, and even if he does so alone in his room, he ought first to unite with all of Israel; thus, in every true prayer, it is the community that is praying. But when one eats, and even if it is at a table full of people, each man eats for himself."

Three Principles

Rabbi Mendel of Kotzk once said to his congregation:
"What do I ask of you? Only three things: Not to look fur-

tively outside yourselves, not to look furtively into others, and not to have yourselves in mind."

Comparing One to Another

Someone once told Rabbi Mendel that a certain person was greater than another whom he also mentioned by name. Rabbi Mendel replied: "If I am I because I am I, and you are you because you are you, then I am I, and you are you. But if I am I because you are you, and you are you because I am I, then I am not I, and you are not you."

Idol Worship

The rabbi of Kotzk said:
"When a man makes a reverent face before a face that is no face—that is idol worship!"

The False Peace

Rabbi Mendel of Kotzk and Rabbi Yitzhak of Vorki, who had both been taught by wise Rabbi Bunam, were friends, and their brotherly good will toward each other had never been troubled. But their hasidim had many arguments concerning the teachings and could not reconcile their opinions. Once both zaddikim happened to be in the same city. When they had greeted each other, Rabbi Yitzhak said: "I have news for you. Our disciples have made peace with one another." But at that the rabbi of Kotzk grew angry. His eyes flashed and he cried: "So the power of deception has gained in strength and Satan is about to blot out the truth from the world!"
"What's that you say!" Rabbi Yitzhak stammered.
The rabbi of Kotzk continued: "Remember what the Midrash tells about the hour when God prepared to create man: how the angels formed two factions. Love said: 'Let him be created, for he will do works of love.' Truth said: 'Let him not be created, for he will practice deception.' Justice said: 'Let him be created, for he will do justice.' Peace said: 'Let him not be created, for he will be all controversy.' What did God do? He seized truth and hurled it to earth. Have you ever thought this story over? Is it not strange? Truth, to be sure, lay on the

ground and no longer hindered the creation of man. But what did God do with peace, and what answer did he give peace?" The rabbi of Vorki was silent.

"Look!" said the rabbi of Kotzk. "Our sages taught us that controversies in the name of Heaven spring from the root of truth. After truth had fallen to earth, peace understood that a peace without truth is a false peace."

What Cannot Be Imitated

The rabbi of Kotzk said:
"Everything in the world can be imitated except truth. For truth that is imitated is no longer truth."

To Increase Knowledge

This is what the rabbi of Kotzk said about the words of Solomon: "He that increaseth knowledge, increaseth sorrow."
"A man should increase his knowledge, even though by so doing he will inevitably increase his sorrow."

The Sons

A man came to the rabbi of Kotzk and asked how he could make his sons devote themselves to the Torah. The rabbi answered: "If you really want them to do this, then you yourself must spend time over the Torah, and they will do as you do. Otherwise, they will not devote themselves to the Torah but will tell their sons to do it, and so it will go on. For it is written: 'Only take heed to thyself . . . lest thou forget the things which thine eyes saw . . .! Make them known unto thy children and thy children's children.' If you yourself forget the Torah, your sons will also forget it, only urging their sons to know it, and they too will forget the Torah and tell their sons that they should know it, and no one will ever know the Torah."

High Prices

Once when prices in the region of Kotzk were very high, the hasidim who had come for over the sabbath wanted to start home on the following day, but the rabbi kept putting off their departure. His wife was at the stove when he came up to her, his pipe in his mouth. "Mendel," she said, "why detain the hasidim? Prices are high at the inn and they will have to pay so much for their food!"

"Why is food so dear?" he countered. "Because people want to eat all the time. If everyone wanted to learn all the time, learning would be dear and food would be cheap."

Miracles

The rabbi of Kotzk was told of a wonder-worker who was versed in the secret art of making a robot. "That is unimportant," he said. "But does he know the secret art of making a hasid?"

Like a Cooper

Rabbi Mendel of Vorki, the son of Rabbi Yitzhak of Vorki, once came out of the rabbi of Kotzk's room exhausted and covered with sweat. He sat down against the wall of the entrance to rest a little, and said to the hasidim who clustered around him: "Let me tell you: that holy old man examined me limb by limb, from head to toe, the way a cooper examines a cask."

First Prize

Rabbi Yehiel Meir, later the rabbi of Gostynin, who was a poor man, went in to his teacher, the rabbi of Kotzk, with a beaming face and told him he had won the first prize in a lottery. "That wasn't through any fault of mine," said the zaddik. Rabbi Yehiel went home and distributed the money among needy friends.

Different Customs

A hasid of the rabbi of Kotzk and a hasid of the rabbi of Tchernobil were discussing their ways of doing things.

The disciple of the rabbi of Tchernobil said: "We stay awake all night between Thursday and Friday, on Friday we give alms in proportion to what we have, and on the sabbath we recite the entire Book of Psalms."

"And we," said the man from Kotzk, "stay awake every night as long as we can; we give alms whenever we run across a poor man and happen to have money in our pockets, and we do not say the psalms it took David seventy years of hard work to make, all in a row, but according to the needs of the hour."

Thou Shalt Not Steal

Rabbi Yehiel Meir of Gostynin had gone to his teacher in Kotzk for the Feast of Weeks. When he came home, his father-in-law asked him: "Well, did your people over there receive the Torah differently than anywhere else?"

"Certainly!" said his son-in-law.

"What do you mean?" asked the other.

"Well, to give you an instance," said Rabbi Yehiel. "How do you here interpret 'thou shalt not steal'?"

"That we shall not steal from our fellow men," answered his father-in-law. "That's perfectly clear."

"We don't need to be told that any more," said Rabbi Yehiel. "In Kotzk this is interpreted to mean: You shall not steal from yourself."

The Difference

While the quarrel between the hasidim of Kotzk and those of Radoshitz was in full swing, Rabbi Yisakhar Baer of Radoshitz once said to a hasid from Kotzk: "What your teacher believes in is: 'If you can't get over it, you must get under it,' but what I believe in is: 'If you can't get over it, you must get over it anyway.'"

Rabbi Yitzhak Meir of Ger, the disciple and friend of the rabbi of Kotzk, formulated the difference in another way when a hasid of the rabbi of Radoshitz visited him after his master's death. "The world thinks," said he, "that there was hatred and quarreling between Kotzk and Radoshitz. That is a grave mistake. There was only one difference of opinion: in Kotzk they aimed to bring the heart of the Jews closer to their Father in Heaven; in Radoshitz they aimed to bring our Father in Heaven closer to the heart of the Jews."

Between Kotzk and Izbica

Some time after Rabbi Mordecai Joseph of Izbica had broken away from Kotzk and founded a congregation of his own, a hasid who had followed him to Izbica visited Kotzk and went to the rabbi. Rabbi Mendel looked up, gazed at him fixedly, and said loudly: "Who is this?" as though he had never seen him before. When the hasid asked him in great distress: "Rabbi, don't you know me?"—he said: "That can't possibly be you! For the sages say: 'And let the fear of thy master be like the fear of Heaven.' Can there be two Heavens?"

Speak unto the Children of Israel

When a disciple of the rabbi of Lentshno visited the rabbi of Kotzk, his host said to him: "Give my greetings to your teacher. I love him very much. But why does he cry to God to send the Messiah? Why does he not rather cry to Israel to turn to God? It is written: 'Wherefore criest thou unto Me? Speak unto the children of Israel.' "

The Three Pillars

Rabbi Mendel said:

"Three pillars support the world: Torah, service, and good deeds, and as the world approaches its end the two first will shrink, and only good deeds will grow. And then what is written will become truth: 'Zion shall be redeemed with justice.' "

The Hour

The rabbi of Kotzk said:

"Generation after generation has toiled to bring the Messiah, each generation in its own way, and they have not succeeded. One cannot bring the Messiah. Some day when the Jews are all busy with caring for their daily bread, and bewildered in spirit —he will come."

Those Who Cannot Pray

On the eve of the Day of Atonement the rabbi of Kotzk said to one of his hasidim: "Hersh, you shall pray for the Jews who cannot pray, for the Jews in fields and woods, for those who are here and for those who are not here, and not only for the living, but also for the dead. For I tell you the walls are swarming with souls!"

The Sanctuary of Love

The rabbi of Kotzk was asked: "Once there was so much love among the hasidim. Why is this not so in our time?"

He replied: "In Heaven there is a sanctuary of love. The rabbi of Berditchev opened it for mankind, and that is how the hasidim came to love one another so much. But the wicked managed to get in too, and took out love for their trivial loves. Then the zaddik locked up the sanctuary again."

The Corner

It is written: "He setteth an end to darkness."
Whenever he read these words, the rabbi of Kotzk said: "One little corner—God left one little corner in darkness so that we may hide in it!"

Why Write a Book?

Rabbi Mendel's hasidim asked him why he did not write a book. For a while he was silent, then he answered:
"Well, let's say I have written a book. Now who is going to buy it? Our own people will buy it. But when do our people get to read a book, since all through the week they are absorbed in earning their livelihood? They will get to read it on a sabbath. And when will they get to it on a sabbath? First they have to take the ritual bath, then they must learn and pray, and then comes the sabbath meal. But after the sabbath meal is over, they have time to read. Well, suppose one of them stretches out on the sofa, takes the book, and opens it. But he is full and he feels drowsy, so he falls asleep and the book slips to the floor. Now tell me, why should I write a book?"

The Sacred Goat

Rabbi Yitzhak of Vorki was one of the very few who were admitted to Rabbi Mendel during the period when he kept away from the world. Once he visited Kotzk after a long absence, knocked, entered Rabbi Mendel's room and said in greeting: "Peace be with you, Rabbi."
"Why do you say rabbi to me," grumbled the rabbi of Kotzk. "I am no rabbi! Don't you recognize me! I'm the goat! I'm the sacred goat. Don't you remember the story?
"An old Jew once lost his snuffbox made of horn, on his way to the House of Study. He wailed: 'Just as if the dreadful exile weren't enough, this must happen to me! Oh me, oh my, I've

lost my snuffbox made of horn!' And then he came upon the sacred goat. The sacred goat was pacing the earth, and the tips of his black horns touched the stars. When he heard the old Jew lamenting, he leaned down to him, and said: 'Cut a piece from my horns, whatever you need to make a new snuffbox.' The old Jew did this, made a new snuffbox, and filled it with tobacco. Then he went to the House of Study and offered everyone a pinch. They snuffed and snuffed, and everyone who snuffed it cried: 'Oh, what wonderful tobacco! It must be because of the box. Oh, what a wonderful box! Wherever did you get it?' So the old man told them about the good sacred goat. And then one after the other they went out on the street and looked for the sacred goat. The sacred goat was pacing the earth and the tips of his black horns touched the stars. One after another they went up to him and begged permission to cut off a bit of his horns. Time after time the sacred goat leaned down to grant the request. Box after box was made and filled with tobacco. The fame of the boxes spread far and wide. At every step he took the sacred goat met someone who asked for a piece of his horns.

"Now the sacred goat still paces the earth—but he has no horns."

No Glasses

As he grew older, the rabbi of Kotzk suffered pain in his eyes. He was advised to wear glasses for reading, but he refused: "I do not want to get a wall between my eyes and the holy Torah."

Into the Woods

Toward the close of his life the rabbi of Kotzk said: "I always thought I should have only four hundred hasidim, and that I should go into the woods with them and give them manna, and that they would recognize the kingly power of God."

YITZHAK OF VORKI

The Servant Who Neglected His Work

Rabbi Yitzhak of Vorki once rebuked one of his sons because
he was neglecting the study of the Torah. When the son, who
was already the head of a family, excused himself on the score
of his many domestic worries, the rabbi told him this story:
"When I was still working for the charitable lady Temeril
as a copyist, I once saw her superintendent beat a servant for
neglecting his work. And oddly enough the man swung his
scythe even while he was being beaten, and cut the grain with
tremendous zeal. Later on I asked him why he had done this.
'You stupid Jew,' said he, 'I was dealt all those blows because
I had neglected my work. So what wonder I went at it with
might and main!' It is the same with you, my son. All your
troubles arise from your neglect of the Torah."

Himself

Once when Rabbi Yitzhak was playing host to certain prominent men of Israel, they discussed the value to a household of
an honest and efficient servant. They said that a good servant
made for good management and cited Joseph at whose hands
everything prospered. Rabbi Yitzhak objected. "I once thought
that too," he said. "But then my teacher showed me that everything depends on the master of the house. You see, in my youth
my wife gave me a great deal of trouble, and though I myself
put up with her as best I could, I was sorry for the servants.
So I went to my teacher, Rabbi David of Lelov, and asked him
whether I should oppose my wife. All he said was: 'Why do
you speak to me? Speak to yourself!' I thought over these
words for quite a while before I understood them. But I did
understand them when I recalled a certain saying of the Baal
Shem Tov: 'There is thought, speech, and action. Thought corresponds to one's wife, speech to one's children, and action
to one's servants. Whoever straightens himself out in regard to

all three of these will find that everything prospers at his hands.' Then I understood what my teacher had meant: that everything depended on myself."

Dying and Living

As a comment to the words in the psalm: "I shall not die but live," Rabbi Yitzhak said: "In order really to live, a man must give himself to death. But when he has done so, he discovers that he is not to die—but to live."

Adam's Sin

Rabbi Yitzhak was asked: "What do you think was Adam's real sin?"

"Adam's real sin," said he, "was that he worried about the morrow. The serpent set out to reason with him: 'There is no service you can perform, for you cannot distinguish between good and evil and are unable to make a choice. Eat of this fruit and you will be able to distinguish; you will choose the good and receive the reward.' That he gave ear to this—that is where Adam was at fault. He worried that he would not be able to serve, yet at that very hour he had his service: to obey God and to resist the serpent."

The Slanderer

A certain man tried to make Rabbi Yitzhak of Vorki's hasidim rebel against their master by slandering him in every possible way. An uproar ensued. The zaddik was told of the matter. He summoned the man and received him without witnesses. "Fool," he said to him, "why do you tell untruths and lay yourself open to being called a liar? Let me tell you everything bad about myself. Then when you leave here and proclaim that to the world, no argument advanced against you will hold water."

The Offering

On the sabbath on which the weekly portion from the Torah dealing with the Offering is read, Rabbi Yitzhak happened to be visiting the rabbi of Kotzk, who at that time had just begun to live in great seclusion and received only close friends, like the rabbi of Vorki.

"Why," asked Rabbi Yitzhak, "have you gone to such extremes in withdrawing from men?"

Rabbi Mendel replied: "The answer is in the weekly portion we read today: 'That they take for Me an offering'; and that is explained as meaning, 'For Me, that is, for My Name.' When a Jew wishes to take the right way, God's way, then he has no alternative but to make an 'offering.' He must offer up all companionship, not only that of evil men, but also that of good men; for a little further on we read: 'Of every man whose heart maketh him willing.'"

"The answer to what you just said," replied the rabbi of Vorki, "is in today's weekly portion, in the very same verse: 'That they take for Me an offering.' When a Jew wishes to take the right way, God's way, he must take what every man has to offer him. He should accept the companionship of every man and by associating with every man receive from him whatever that man can give him for the way of God. But there is one qualification. From the man whose heart is locked he will receive nothing at all. Only the man 'whose heart maketh him willing' can give."

His Merit

Someone came to Rabbi Yitzhak with a question. "I cannot understand the story the Talmud tells about Rabbi Zera," he said. "It says that when his disciples asked him how he had lived so long, he answered that he had never rejoiced over anyone's misfortune. How can that be a merit?"

The rabbi said: "This is what it means: I could not rejoice in the good fortune life offered me when I heard of someone else's misfortune."

The Alphabet

Rabbi Yitzhak was asked: "Why on the Day of Atonement is the confession of sins arranged in alphabetical order?"

He replied: "If it were otherwise we should not know when to stop beating our breasts. For there is no end to sin, and no end to the awareness of sin, but there *is* an end to the alphabet."

The Heavenly Voice

They asked Rabbi Yitzhak how the following saying of our sages should be interpreted: "You shall do all your host tells you, all save going away." For it seems we certainly ought to obey our host when he bids us go!

The rabbi replied: "Those who believe that the word 'host' here refers to God are right. We should obey him in all things, save when he bids us to go from him. For we know that 'he that is banished is not banished from him.' The truth of the matter is that he who has done much evil must travel a most stormy road in order to turn to God. Heaven announces that his turning is no longer desired and would not be accepted. But if he does not allow this to discourage him, if just then his will breaks through and nevertheless turns to God, then he will be healed. They say that the arch-heretic Elisha ben Abuyah, who was called 'Aher' or 'the Other,' heard a voice calling down from Heaven: 'Return O backsliding children— all except Aher!' Then he broke the last bonds which held him to the Torah and the congregation, and renounced the truth. Should he have refused to believe the voice which addressed itself to him and therefore wanted something of him? That would have been of no avail. Yet grace hangs on a hair: if he had turned, his turning would have been accepted."

The Lost Woman

A widow complained to Rabbi Yitzhak that certain merchants who had employed her husband as copyist refused to pay her a sum of money they still owed him, and had no pity on her in her wretchedness. The zaddik had the merchants brought before him. When they caught sight of the woman they cried out as with one voice: "Are you listening to that lost woman! Her husband has been dead these three years, and half a year ago she bore a bastard!"

"So, she was so poor," said the rabbi, "that she had to lose her self!"

After Thirty Years

A certain man had lived in seclusion for thirty years and devoted himself to the Torah. When he returned to the company of men, he heard about Rabbi Yitzhak of Vorki and decided to go to him. On the way there he pictured to himself the joy and honor with which the zaddik would receive so learned a man who had devoted all his efforts to the Torah for so long a time. When he stood in Rabbi Yitzhak's presence, the rabbi said to him: "You are so learned a man and have devoted all your efforts to the Torah for so long a time—surely you know what God says?" The man grew embarrassed and uncertain. Finally he said hesitantly: "God says we should pray and study." The zaddik laughed. "You do not understand my question," he said. The man left in an unhappy frame of mind.

But he went to the zaddik again and again, and each time Rabbi Yitzhak received him with the same words. Then came the day when he made his farewell.

"What are you taking home with you," asked the zaddik, "since you don't know what God says!" Tears rose in the man's eyes as he said: "Rabbi, that is just why I came to you—to learn something!"

"It is written in Jeremiah," said the zaddik, " 'Can any hide himself in secret places'—that means, anyone who locks himself into his room for thirty years and studies the Torah; 'that I shall not see him?'—that means, I may not want to see such a man; 'saith the Lord'—that is what God says."

Moved to the depths of his being, the man stood there, and for a time he could not speak, he could not even think. Then the spirit moved him. "Rabbi," he sighed, "I should like to ask you a question."

"Speak," said the zaddik. "What is the prescribed thing to do," asked the man, "when scraps of a holy book which has been torn fall to the ground?"

"They should be picked up," said the zaddik, "lest they be destroyed."

The man threw himself on the floor. "Rabbi, rabbi," he cried, "a vessel filled with scraps of the Holy Scriptures lies before you. Do not let them be destroyed!" With both hands the zaddik raised him and seated him at his side. Then he talked to him and helped him with his words.

When Rabbi Yitzhak lived in the town of Kinzk, a very well-to-do man invited him to a banquet. When the zaddik came to the house he saw that the forecourt was lit with large lanterns and the steps covered with rugs. Then he refused to proceed unless his host had the lanterns put out and the rugs removed, or promised to receive even the most unimportant guest with like magnificence from that time on.

"We are bidden to be hospitable," the zaddik said. "And just as we must not differentiate between one ram's horn and another when it comes to blowing the ram's horn, so in his capacity of guest one man is just like another." His host begged him to retract the demand, but in vain. In the end he had to yield, and since he was unable to give the required promise he had the house restored to its everyday appearance.

Commandment and Money

Rabbi Yitzhak once praised an innkeeper who was eager to satisfy every wish of his guests. "How anxious this man is to fulfil the commandment to be hospitable!" he said. "But he takes pay for it," someone remarked. "He accepts money," answered the zaddik, "so that it may be possible for him to fulfil the commandment."

The Zaddikim That Build

Rabbi Yitzhak was asked: "How are we to understand the saying: 'Every zaddik in whose days the Temple is not built is no zaddik at all.' That would mean that all the zaddikim who have lived since the destruction of the Temple were not zaddikim." He explained: "The zaddikim are always building at the upper sanctuary. The zaddik who does not do his share in the building is no zaddik at all."

The Faithful Servant

It is told in the Midrash:
The ministering angels once said to God: "You have permitted Moses to write whatever he wants to, so there is nothing to prevent him from saying to Israel: I have given you the Torah."

God replied: "This he would not do, but if he did, he would still be keeping faith with me."

Rabbi Yitzhak of Vorki's disciples once asked him to interpret this. He answered by telling them a parable:

A merchant wanted to go on a journey. He took on an assistant and let him work in his shop. He himself spent most of his time in the adjoining room from where he could hear what was going on next door. During the first year he sometimes heard his assistant tell a customer: "The master cannot let this go for so low a price." The merchant did not go on his journey. In the course of the second year he occasionally heard the voice next door say: "We cannot let it go for so low a price." He postponed his journey. But in the third year he heard his ·assistant say: "I can't let this go for so low a price." It was then that he started on his journey.

The Dwelling

Rabbi Yitzhak's disciples said to him: "Concerning the account in the Scriptures that 'the stuff' the people had brought for the building of the sanctuary was 'sufficient and too much,' so that there was something left over when the work was completed, the Midrash tells that Moses asked God what to do with it, and God replied: 'Make of it a dwelling for the tabernacle of the testimony,' and Moses did so. How are we to interpret this? Is it not the Ark which holds the tablets that is called the tabernacle of the testimony, and had it not already been completed?"

"You know," answered the rabbi, "that the sanctuary was holy because the Divine Presence had entered it. But over and over again people have asked how the splendor of Him about whom it is written: 'the heavens and the heaven of heavens cannot contain Thee,' could possibly be confined in the space between the staves of the Ark. But listen to the words in the Song of Songs: 'King Solomon made himself a palanquin of the wood of Lebanon. He made the pillars thereof of silver, the top thereof of gold, the seat thereof of purple.' And if you doubt that it was possible to rest on such a bed, here is the answer: 'The inside thereof being inlaid with love.' It was the love of the people who contributed to the building of the sanctuary that drew the Divine Presence down between the staves of the Ark. But because there was too much of their will to love, more than was needed for the work, Moses asked: 'What's to be done with all this will?' and God replied: 'Make of it,' and this means: make of the overflow of the innermost heart of Israel 'a dwelling for the tabernacle of the testimony' —the testimony that your love has drawn me into the world shall dwell within it."

On the Highest Rung

Rabbi Yitzhak was asked: "It is written: 'And this is the blessing, wherewith Moses the man of God blessed the children of Israel before his death.' Of the words 'before his death' Rashi says, 'just before his death,' and, in support of his interpretation, adds: 'If not now, when?'

"In what way does this mean more than what anyone can glean from the Scriptures?"

"Note," answered the rabbi, "that this is the only passage in which Moses is called 'a man of God.' Now this is how it was: Because of his great love for Israel, Moses wanted to bless them, time and again. But each time he felt he would reach a higher rung, and that his blessing would then have greater strength, and that was why he delayed giving it. But when he had reached the rung of 'a man of God,' and that is the rung of the angels who do not move from rung to rung like men, but remain fixed, he knew that he must be very close to death, and then he blessed Israel—for, 'If not now, when?' "

Faith

A hasid of Rabbi Yitzhak had no children. Time after time he begged his teacher to pray for him and time after time Rabbi Yitzhak referred him to Rabbi Baer of Radoshitz, the famous miracle-worker. But the hasid did not follow his suggestion. The other hasidim asked him why he did not go to Radoshitz. "If I go," he said, "and go without faith, I will not be helped. But if I scrape up some faith in the rabbi of Radoshitz, it means that I shall forfeit just that much of the faith I have in my rabbi. And if, God forbid, my faith in my rabbi became imperfect, then what would I want children for?"

MENAHEM MENDEL OF VORKI

The Test

Rabbi Yitzhak of Vorki once took his sons to see his teacher Rabbi Bunam, who gave each of them a glass of bock beer and asked them what it was. The elder boy said: "I don't know." Menahem Mendel, the younger, who was three years old at the time, said: "Bitter and good."

"This one will become the leader of a great congregation," said Rabbi Bunam.

The Driver

When Rabbi Yitzhak of Vorki and Mendel, his young son, were visiting Rabbi Israel of Rizhyn, their host invited his friend to go driving with him. Mendel begged to be allowed to accompany them. "One who does not yet know the mystery of the Divine Chariot may not come," said the rabbi of Rizhyn. "But I know how to drive," said Mendel. The rabbi of Rizhyn gave him a long look. "Then do it," he said. Mendel mounted the coachman's box and took the reins in his hands.

In the course of their drive the rabbi of Rizhyn asked: "Rav of Vorki, how did you deserve such a son?" Rabbi Yitzhak replied: "He is an undeserved gift."

The Gang in the Wine Cellar

The group of contemporaries with whom young Mendel gadded about consisted of youths on a high rung, but like himself all of them were well versed in hiding their true character.

Rabbi Berish, later the rabbi of Biala, who was at the time a disciple of the rabbi of Vorki and known as a learned man, could not get over his surprise at not seeing them engage in study. Once on the first night of the Feast of Weeks, when everyone had left the table and day was already breaking, he noticed the group with Mendel in the van going down into the cellar. He stole after them, hid, and saw them put on their prayer shawls, rattle off the Morning Prayer, and then sit down together and drink. This displeased Rabbi Berish mightily. But then he noticed that the moment all of them had finished the second glass Mendel spoke to them in a low tone—he could not catch the words from his hiding place—and instantly they all bowed their heads over the table and wept. It looked to Rabbi Berish as though all the small glasses filled up with their tears. Later he asked them to accept him as a member of their group, but a period of waiting was imposed on him.

One Thing Is Needful

At Rabbi Mendel's wedding the *badhan* in the midst of his half-jesting, half-serious harangues uttered this singsong: "Pray and learn and serve your God." Rabbi Mendel took up the very same tune: "Don't pray and don't learn and don't anger your God."

Swift Obedience

When Rabbi Yitzhak of Vorki was in Warsaw on an errand concerning his congregation, he became ill, and his elder son Rabbi David of Omshinov implored him to go home. After holding out for a considerable time his father at last consented. Rabbi David summoned the coachman and told him to harness the horses. In the meantime Rabbi Mendel, the younger son, who had not been present during the discussion, arrived and heard from the coachman that his father was preparing to drive back to Vorki. "You can go home," said Mendel, "the rabbi is not leaving." When Rabbi David learned of the incident he complained to his father.

"What do you want of him?" said the rabbi of Vorki. "He obeys even before I give him an order."

You Have Done Too Little

When Rabbi Yitzhak of Vorki was seriously ill, his elder son fasted and recited psalms, but Rabbi Mendel, the younger, went about with a group of hasidim of his own age who had been devoted to him from boyhood on and called themselves his bodyguard. They toasted each other's health in schnapps. But there were times when he walked in the woods unaccompanied. When Rabbi Yitzhak recovered, a banquet was prepared to celebrate the event. Mendel said to his brother: "You have done too little to rejoice in good earnest—you did nothing but fast and pray."

The Voice

After Rabbi Yitzhak's death many hasidim came to Vorki for the Feast of Weeks. Among them was Rabbi Benjamin of Lublin, who had been a disciple of the Seer but had gone over to the much-maligned Yehudi, the Seer's disciple, while his first teacher was still alive. Since Rabbi Benjamin was very old and sickly, he had to lie down soon after his arrival. After prayers Rabbi Yitzhak's two sons went to see him. "Children," he said to them, "I wish you'd tell me how we are to interpret the words in the Scriptures: 'And all the people saw the voice.' " Rabbi Yaakov David, the elder son, gave a most perspicacious interpretation, but Rabbi Menahem Mendel, the younger, was silent as usual. "And what have you to say?" asked Rabbi Benjamin.

"I say," answered Menahem Mendel, "that we must take it to mean: they saw and realized that one must take the voice into oneself and make it one's own."

No Speech and No Words

Some time after Rabbi Yitzhak's death, when each of his sons already had his own congregation, they once met in a town far from the home of either and a banquet was held in their honor. Rabbi David delivered a lengthy sermon but Rabbi Mendel said nothing. "Why don't you also 'say Torah'?" asked his brother.

"Concerning the Heavens we read in the psalms," Mendel replied, " 'There is no speech, there are no words, neither is their voice heard. Their line is gone out through all the earth.' "

* * *

But on another occasion, when a great zaddik asked him why he did not "say Torah," he replied: "The Talmud says that Simeon of Emmaus interpreted all the passages in the Scriptures in which the word *et* [which indicates the accusative] is used. But when he came to the verse where this word introduces the command: 'Thou shalt fear the Lord thy God,' he refrained from interpretation."

A Night of Silence

Once Rabbi Menahem Mendel spent an entire night in the company of his hasidim. No one spoke, but all were filled with great reverence and experienced great elation. Finally the rabbi said: "Well for the Jew who knows that the meaning of 'One' is one!"

Speech in Silence

Rabbi Mendel's hasidim once sat at his table in silence. The silence was so profound that one could hear the fly on the wall. After grace the rabbi of Biala said to his neighbor: "What a table we had today! I was probed so deeply that I thought my veins would burst, but I managed to hold out and answer every question I was asked."

The Way of Silence

The first time Rabbi Mendel, the son of the zaddik of Vorki, met Rabbi Eleazar, the grandson of the maggid of Koznitz, the two retired to a room. They seated themselves opposite each other and sat in silence for a whole hour. Then they admitted the others. "Now we are ready," said Rabbi Mendel.

* * *

When Mendel was in Kotzk, the rabbi of that town asked him: "Where did you learn the art of silence?" He was on the verge of answering the question, but then he changed his mind, and practiced his art.

Soundless Cry and Soundless Weeping

Rabbi Mendel once commented on the verse in the Scriptures: "For God hath heard the voice of the lad." He explained it in this way: "Nothing in the preceding verses indicates that Ishmael cried out. No, it was a soundless cry, and God heard it."

* * *

On another occasion he discussed the verse in the Scriptures which tells about Pharaoh's daughter in these words: "And she opened it, and *saw* . . . a boy that wept."

"What we should expect to be told," said he, "is that she *heard* the child Moses weeping. But the child was weeping inside himself. That is why later on we find the words: 'and (she) said: This is one of the Hebrews' children.' It was the Jewish kind of weeping."

Basic Attitudes

Rabbi Menahem Mendel of Vorki was asked what constitutes a true Jew. He said: "Three things are fitting for us: upright kneeling, silent screaming, motionless dance."

The Honest Sleep

It was the day before the New Year and people from all over had come to Vorki and gathered in the House of Study. Some were seated at the tables studying, others who had not been able to find a place for the night were lying on the floor with their heads on their knapsacks, for many of them had come on foot. Just then Rabbi Mendel entered, but the noise those at the tables made was so great that no one noticed him. First he looked at those who were studying, and then at those lying on the floor. "The way these folk sleep," he said, "pleases me more than the way those others are studying."

A Beautiful Death

Soon after the death of a zaddik who was a friend of the rabbi of Vorki, one of his hasidim, who had been present at the death, came to Rabbi Mendel and told him about it.

"How was it?" asked Rabbi Mendel.

"Very beautiful," said the hasid. "It was as though he went from one room into the next."

"From one room into the next?" said Rabbi Mendel. "No, from one corner of the room into another corner."

YITZHAK MEIR OF GER

Where Does God Live?

When Rabbi Yitzhak Meir was a little boy his mother once took him to see the maggid of Koznitz. There someone said to him: "Yitzhak Meir, I'll give you a gulden if you tell me where God lives!" He replied: "And I'll give you two gulden if you tell me where he doesn't!"

In Praise of Grammar

The rabbi of Ger told this story:

"As a child I did not want to study grammar, for I thought it was just a subject like many others. But later I devoted myself to it because I realized that the secrets of the Torah depend upon it."

The Malcontent

When Rabbi Yitzhak Meir was quite young he became a disciple of Rabbi Moshe of Koznitz, the son of the maggid of Koznitz. One day his teacher kissed him on the forehead because he had helped him solve a difficult problem with astonishing acumen. "What I need," said Yitzhak Meir to himself, "is a rabbi who rends the flesh from my bones—not one who kisses me."

Soon after he left Koznitz.

A Quick Sleep

Rabbi Yitzhak Meir's wife once asked him why he slept so little, and she worried that this might be bad for his health. He laughed and answered: "Why did your father choose me as a husband for you? Because I was a gifted student. And what does it mean to be a gifted student? It means that one person learns in two hours what it takes another a whole day to learn. Well, I sleep as much in two hours as another sleeps a whole night."

Like the Ox

A hasid complained to the rabbi of Ger: "I have worked and toiled and yet I have not the satisfaction of a master-craftsman who, after twenty years of effort, finds some result of his labors in his work: either it is better than it was at first, or he can do it more quickly. I see nothing at all. Just as I prayed twenty years ago, so I pray today."

The zaddik answered: "It is taught in Elijah's name: 'Man should take the Torah upon himself, as the ox takes the yoke and the ass his burden.' You see, the ox leaves his stall in the morning, goes to the field, plows, and is led home, and this happens day after day, and nothing changes with regard to the ox, but the ploughed field bears the harvest."

Coming Tests

The rabbi of Ger said:

"There will be many and grave temptations and he who has not prepared himself for them will be lost. For it is too late to prepare when temptation is actually at hand. Temptation is only a test; it shows what within you is dross and what is true metal."

Danger

The rabbi of Ger was on a journey with one of his favorite hasidim. The way led down a steep hill, and the startled horses ran for all they were worth and could not be reined in. The hasid looked out of the carriage and shuddered; but when he glanced at the zaddik, he saw that his face had lost nothing of its usual composure. "How is it that you are not afraid of the danger we are in?" he asked.

"Whoever is aware of the real danger at every instant," the zaddik replied, "is not terrified by any danger of the moment."

The Fortress

When the large House of Study the rabbi of Ger was having built was completed, the rav of Warsaw came to inspect it, and said: "Most likely you have a very good reason for moving away from us and building your house outside the town." The rabbi of Ger said nothing, so the rav continued: "I understand your reason. You wanted to put up a fortress for the protection of Warsaw, and such a fortress must of course be outside the town. And sometimes one must even use it as a point of vantage from which to fire into the town." Still the rabbi of Ger did not utter a word, but he laughed like one who agrees with the speaker.

About Eating

The rabbi of Ger once asked a hasid what he had learned from the lips of the rabbi of Kotzk. "I heard him say," said the hasid, "that he was surprised that merely saying grace is not enough to make man God-fearing and good."

"I think differently," said the rabbi of Ger. "I am surprised that merely eating is not enough to make man God-fearing and good. For it is written: 'The ox knoweth his owner and the ass his master's crib.' "

* * *

When the rabbi of Ger was asked the difference between ordinary fathers of families and hasidim, he laughed and replied: "Ordinary fathers of families pray and then study, but the hasidim pray and then eat. For when the hasid discovers that neither in his solitary reflection before prayer nor in prayer itself has he experienced the greatness of God, he goes to his meal and thinks: 'Though I am not yet like the ox who knows his owner, I can at least emulate the ass and stand at my master's crib.' "

"Throw Up the World"

The rabbi of Ger said: "I often hear men say: 'I want to throw up the world.' But I ask you: Is the world yours to throw up?"

The Sins of the People

Some time after the Feast of Weeks the rabbi of Radzimin came to visit the rabbi of Ger, who thought that his friend's face looked thin and tired. "What's the matter with you?" the rabbi of Ger asked. "Is it only the great heat we are having or is something troubling you?"

"I am like this every year," said the other, "in the summer months, when those chapters in the Scriptures which deal with Israel's wanderings through the wilderness are read. For there we hear of sin after sin; terrible sins, like those of the spies and those when 'Israel joined himself unto the Baal of Peor.' That such sins are reported as having been committed by a generation of knowledge—that is what keeps tormenting me!" The rabbi of Ger replied: "When they committed what is called their sin they must have had a great purpose in mind, for it is out of their sins that the Torah was made. Do you think that a Torah could have been made out of our good deeds?"

A Sermon

Before the Day of Atonement the rabbi of Ger said to the hasidim gathered around his table:

"Hillel, our teacher, says: 'If I am not for myself, who will be for me?' If I do not perform my service, who will perform it for me? Everyone must perform his own service. And further along, he says: 'And if not now, when?' When will this Now be? The Now that is now, this instant in which we are speaking, did not exist at any time since the world was created, and it will never exist again. Formerly there was another Now, and later there will be another Now, and every Now has its own service; as we read in the Book of Splendor: 'The garments of morning are not the garments of evening.'

"Strive for the Torah with all your strength and you will be linked to the Torah—but the sixty myriad letters in the Torah correspond to the sixty myriad souls in Israel, of whom the Torah is speaking: in this way you will become related to the whole. And if you proffer yourself to the whole, you receive from the whole; you receive even more than you put into it. And so to your own Now you can add something of your neighbor's Now, of the good he accomplishes in that Now. Furthermore Hillel, our teacher, says: 'And if I am only for myself, what am I?' If—God forbid—I should be separated from the community, when could I catch up on my Now? No other Now can make up for this Now, for every moment is concentrated in its particular light.

"He who has done ill and talks about it and thinks about it all the time does not cast the base thing he did out of his thoughts, and whatever one thinks, therein one is; one's soul is wholly and utterly in what one thinks, and so much a man dwells in baseness. He will certainly not be able to turn, for his spirit will grow coarse and his heart stubborn, and in addition to this he may be overcome by gloom. What would you? Rake the muck this way, rack the muck that way—it will always be muck. Have I sinned, or have I not sinned—what does Heaven get out of it? In the time I am brooding over it I could be stringing pearls for the delight of Heaven. That is why it is written: 'Depart from evil and do good'—turn wholly away from evil, do not dwell upon it, and do good. You have done wrong? Then counteract it by doing right.

"And so on this day before the Day of Atonement let us feel a withdrawal from sin and a strengthening of the spirit, feel it in our innermost heart and not through forced ecstasy, receive it in our hearts for all future time, and be merry. Let us recite the list of our sins as quickly as possible, and not dwell upon it, but rather dwell upon the words of the prayer: 'And thou, O Lord, shalt reign, thou alone . . .'"

Shame

While the rabbi of Ger was in the midst of "saying Torah," he heaved a deep sigh and said:

"Something our sages said touches me to the marrow, and devours at my vitals. They said: 'He who has no shame, his fathers did not stand at Mount Sinai.' Well then, and where is shame?"

Emphasis

The rabbi of Ger taught his disciples:

"Merely by emphasizing a word ever so slightly a man can cool his neighbor's fervor in the service of God. So for instance the serpent said to Eve: 'And though God did say'—as if someone said to you: Well, and suppose God did say that—what of it? A slight emphasis and Eve's faith was cooled and she ate of the forbidden fruit."

The Motive

The rabbi of Ger was asked: "What is the meaning of God's asking Cain why his countenance had fallen? How could his face not 'fall' since God had not accepted his gift?"

He replied: "God asked Cain: 'Why is thy countenance fallen?' Because I did not accept your gift, or because I accepted that of your brother?"

The Three Questions

When in expounding the Torah the rabbi of Ger came to the words Jacob says to his servant: "When Esau my brother meeteth thee, and asketh thee, saying: Whose art thou, and whither goest thou? and whose are these before thee?"—he said to his disciples: "Note how much Esau's questions resemble the saying of our sages: 'Reflect upon three things: know whence you have come, where you are going, and to whom you will some time have to give account and reckoning.' Note it well, for whoever reflects on these three things needs much self-examination, lest Esau ask within him. For Esau too can ask about these, and bring heaviness into the heart of man."

The Darkness of the Soul

Concerning the passage in the Scriptures which deals with the thick darkness in the land of Egypt, where "they saw not every man his brother, neither rose any from his place," the rabbi of Ger said: "He who does not want to look at his brother soon gets to the point where he cleaves to his place and is not able to move from it."

Seeing and Believing

The rabbi of Ger was asked:

"It is written: 'And Israel saw the great hand,' and further on it is written: 'And they believed in the Lord and in his servant Moses.' Why is this said? The question as to whether or not one believes can only be put while one does not as yet see."

He answered: "You are mistaken. It is only then that the true question can be put. Seeing the great hand does not mean that faith can be dispensed with. It is only after seeing that we feel how much we are in need of it. Seeing the great hand is the beginning of belief in that which we cannot see."

The Real Exodus

The rabbi of Ger was asked: "Why is it that the Feast of Weeks, which was instituted to commemorate revelation, is referred to with the words 'a commemoration of the departure from Egypt'?"

He expounded: "Did not God speak to Moses out of the midst of the burning bush, saying: 'And this shall be the token unto thee, that I have sent thee: when thou hast brought forth the people out of Egypt, ye shall serve God upon this mountain.' Their receiving the Torah at Sinai was the sign that they were now out of Egypt. Up to that time they were still caught in the bondage of Egypt."

The Eternal Voice

The rabbi of Ger said:

"Concerning the voice over Sinai, the Scriptures say that 'it went on no more,' and the Targumim take this to mean that it went on uninterruptedly. And the voice does indeed speak today as it did long ago. But now as then it requires preparation to hear it. As it is written: 'Now therefore, if ye will hearken unto My voice.' Whenever we hear it, that 'Now' has arrived."

The Wheel and the Innermost Point

On an evening in late summer, Rabbi Yitzhak Meir was walking back and forth in the court of the House of Study in the company of his grandson. It was the first day of the month of Elul and the new moon was in the sky. The zaddik asked whether they had blown the ram's horn, for this should be done a month before the New Year. Then he said: "When a man becomes a leader, all the necessary things must be at hand: a House of Study and tables and chairs, and one man is made the manager, one the servant, and so on. And then Satan comes and wrests out the innermost point, but everything remains just as it was and the wheel keeps on turning, only that the innermost point is missing." The rabbi raised his voice: "But, so help us God, we must not let it happen!"

Forgive Me

When Rabbi Yitzhak Meir's mother died he followed the bier weeping and begged her to forgive him. And before they closed the grave, he cried: "In this world I am a man who is much honored and many call me rabbi. But now you will enter the world of truth and see that it is not as they think. So forgive me and do not bear me a grudge. What can I do, if people are mistaken in me!"

Who Is to Come?

On a certain Passover many people were gathered in the house of the rabbi of Ger. Suddenly he raised his voice and said to them: "You should know that I'm not just like any rabbi. I do not crave money and I am not out for honors. All I care about is turning the hearts of Jews to Heaven in the few years still allotted to me. And I beg anyone who has no longing in that direction to stop coming to me. Those who seek me out because they want to gain a livelihood or have children or be cured would do better to go to someone else. But he who feels that something is lacking in the service he gives God, and is troubled because sickness or worry about his livelihood or the desire for children are obstacles in the way of his service—I can help a man such as this both on the one score and the other."

Two Points of View

The rabbi of Ger once asked one of his disciples who was a guest in his house what thoughts he had had on the way to him. The man replied: "Hasidim come to the rabbi with all manner of requests, some because they have business troubles, other because they are sick or the like. 'What has all this to do with the rabbi?' I asked myself."

"And what did you answer yourself?" asked the zaddik.

"I told myself," said the disciple, "that the rabbi helps those who come to him to make the turning and thus raises them to a higher rung, from which their prayers will more readily be heard."

"I see it differently," said the zaddik. "The rabbi reflects: 'What am I and what is my life that these people should come to me and ask me to pray for them! Why I am nothing but a drop in the bucket!' And in this way he makes the turning and is uplifted and since he has linked his being to those who sought him out, salvation flows from him into them."

This was the last journey this disciple made to his teacher, for soon after this the rabbi died.

In the Dust

Someone asked the rabbi of Ger: "Why do people always weep when they say the words in the prayer: 'Man, his origin is of the dust and his end is in the dust'? If man sprang from gold and turned to dust, it would be proper to weep, but not if he returns whence he has come."

The zaddik replied: "The origin of the world is dust, and man has been placed in it that he may raise the dust to spirit. But man always fails in the end and everything crumbles into dust."

The Heart Remains

In his old age the rabbi of Ger told this story:

"When I was still a student, Rabbi Shelomo Leib came up to me in the House of Study and said: 'Young man, you are known as the gifted Jew from Poland, so tell me why our sages commented on the verse in the Scripture: "Thou shalt love the Lord thy God with all thy heart and with all thy soul," with the words: "Even if He takes your soul"; but failed to comment: "Even if He takes your heart," concerning the other part of the verse which says we should love Him with all our heart.'

"I did not know what to say, for I did not consider his question a question at all. For to take one's soul simply means to take one's life. But what was the matter with me that I did not even wish to know what he meant? The older I get, the larger his question looms before me. If God so desires, let him take our life, but he must leave us that with which we love him—he must leave us our heart."

The Fear of Death

The rabbi of Ger once said:

"Why is man afraid of dying? For does he not then go to his Father! What man fears is the moment he will survey from the other world everything he has experienced on this earth."

HANOKH OF ALEXANDER

Before God

In his youth when Rabbi Hanokh of Alexander was living in Pzhysha as Rabbi Bunam's disciple, it was his duty to act as congregational reader of the Morning Prayer in a house adjoining that of his teacher. Now he was in the habit of praying with vehement gestures and loud cries, quite differently from Rabbi Bunam, who spoke with his characteristic composure even when he conducted the services for the congregation. Once young Hanokh was praying when the rabbi entered the room, and he immediately lowered his voice and stopped gesturing. But hardly had he done this, when he reflected and said in his soul: "I am after all not concerned with the rabbi; I am standing before God!" And instantly he resumed his stormy manner of praying.

After the service Rabbi Bunam had him summoned. "Hanokh," he said to him, "today I took great pleasure in your praying."

Revelation

In his youth, Rabbi Yehiel Meir of Gostynin once attended a wedding in Pzhysha. At the inn they put him up in the same room with young Rabbi Hanokh of Alexander, whom he had never met, and he was forced to share the bed with him. On the eve of the wedding Rabbi Hanokh played the wag both in his actions and words, and this did not exactly serve to give his roommate a better opinion of him. But that night he noticed Hanokh leave the bed very softly and—thinking himself unobserved—go into the anteroom. Yehiel Meir listened intently. He heard a whispering that touched him to his very marrow. Whispered verses of psalms came to his ears and moved him as though he had never heard them before. When Hanokh returned, Yehiel Meir pretended to be asleep. During one of the evenings when the "Seven Benedictions" were recited, Rabbi Hanokh again clowned for all he was worth. He told of the merry pranks of a woman known as Hannele the thief, and his account was so vivid that the wedding guests were convulsed with laughter. Yehiel Meir stared at him in bewilderment. Was this the same man on whose fervent words he had eavesdropped that other night? Then suddenly in the midst of his wildest jest Hanokh turned his head and looked straight into his eyes. And now Yehiel Meir saw before him what he had heard that night, and it was addressed to him. He trembled from head to foot.

Secret

Rabbi Bunam used to say: "A secret is something you say in such a way that everyone can hear it, and yet no one who is not supposed to know can know it."

But Rabbi Hanokh, his disciple, added: "The secrets of the Torah are so well hidden that they cannot be communicated at all. As it is written: 'The secret counsel of the Lord is with them that fear him.' They can be grasped only through the fear of God, and save through the fear of God they cannot be grasped at all."

Look into the Book

A hasid came to Rabbi Hanokh and wept and complained about some misfortune which had overtaken him.

"When I was in the elementary school," the rabbi replied, "and a certain boy began to cry in class, the teacher said to him: 'He who looks into his book stops crying.'"

The Threat

A prominent man threatened to thrust Rabbi Hanokh down from all the spiritual rungs he had attained at a single blow. He replied: "You could not thrust me down to a lowlier place than the one I am already in."

The Butcher's Sigh

Shortly after he had become a rabbi, Rabbi Hanokh said: "A butcher was plying his chopping knife for all he was worth and chopped right on into the sabbath. Suddenly it dawned on him that the sabbath had come. He ran off to the House of Prayer, and just as he rushed in he heard them singing the hymn: 'Come, my friends, to meet the bride.' Then he heaved a deep sigh, and it was not the butcher who was sighing, it was the Jew who sighed out of him. For it is written: 'The children of Israel sighed out of their bondage.' It was Israel, it was the Jew that sighed out of them."

The House of Weddings

Rabbi Hanokh told this parable:

A man from a small town moved to Warsaw. From a house near the one in which he had rented a room he heard the sound of music and dancing. "They must be celebrating a wedding there," he thought to himself. But the next day he again heard festive music, and the same thing happened on the day after that. "I wonder who the owner of that house can be," he said to friends he had in the city. "He seems to have a lot of sons he is marrying off!" They laughed at him. "That house," they said, "is rented out every day for the purpose of celebrating weddings. Then the musicians play and the guests dance. Because of this we call it the house of weddings."

And then Rabbi Hanokh added: "That is why our sages compare this world to a house of weddings."

A Vain Search

Rabbi Hanokh told this story:

There was once a man who was very stupid. When he got up in the morning it was so hard for him to find his clothes that at night he almost hesitated to go to bed for thinking of the trouble he would have on waking. One evening he finally made a great effort, took paper and pencil and as he undressed noted down exactly where he put everything he had on. The next morning, very well pleased with himself, he took the slip of paper in hand and read: 'cap'—there it was, he set it on his head; 'pants'—there they lay, he got into them; and so it went until he was fully dressed.

"That's all very well, but now where am I myself?" he asked in great consternation. "Where in the world am I?" He looked and looked, but it was a vain search; he could not find himself. "And that is how it is with us," said the rabbi.

"Scaring Off"

Rabbi Hanokh told this story:

A servant girl from Poland hired herself out to work in Germany. In that country they use the term "to scare off" in their cookery. By this they mean pouring cold water into a pot in which meat is boiling, to make it easier to take off the scum. Once when the lady of the house in which the girl was working had to go off to market while the dinner was cooking, she said to her: "Watch the soup and don't forget 'to scare off.'" The girl did not understand the term, but she was ashamed to admit it. When she saw the scum rise to overflowing, she took a broom and threatened the pot on all sides, until it upset and the soup spilled all over the stove.

"Now if you try to scare off the Evil Urge when it rises up within you," the rabbi added, "you will upset everything. You must learn to skim off the scum."

The Real Exile

Rabbi Hanokh said:

"The real exile of Israel in Egypt was that they had learned to endure it."

Baseness

Rabbi Hanokh was asked: "It is written: 'The children of Israel lifted up their eyes and, behold, the Egyptians were marching after them; and they were much afraid; and the children of Israel cried out unto the Lord.' Why were they so afraid, since they knew that God himself was aiding them?"

Rabbi Hanokh answered: "When they were in Egypt, when they were in baseness up to their ears, they did not see it. But now they lifted their eyes and saw baseness coming after them. They had thought that since God had led them out of Egypt, all that was over and done with. Now suddenly they realized that baseness was still with them—and they cried out to God. 'And Moses said unto the people: Fear ye not, stand still, and see the salvation of the Lord, which He will work for you today; for whereas you have seen Egypt today, ye shall see them again no more for ever.' That means that now you see the baseness which is with you—that in itself is aid and succor. 'The

Lord will fight for you.' Now that you yourselves see that you are base, the Lord will help you out of your baseness. 'And ye shall hold your peace.' Hold your peace, for help has already been granted you."

Beyond the Pale of Nature

Rabbi Hanokh was asked: "Why does one speak of the 'rending asunder' of the Red Sea and not of its 'splitting asunder,' since it is written: 'He split the sea and caused them to pass through.'"

Rabbi Hanokh gave this explanation: " 'Split' indicates only a slight crack, but 'rend asunder' points to a great opening. In the Midrash we are told that when Moses bade the sea split, it replied that it did not intend to obey flesh and blood and go beyond the pale of nature; not until it saw Joseph's coffin did it do as it was bidden. That is why the verse in the psalm reads: 'The sea saw it and fled.' It saw and it realized that Joseph, whose bones the people were taking with them to the Promised Land, had once gone beyond the pale of nature in that he resisted temptation. Then the sea too went beyond the pale of nature and rent itself asunder. That is why we say 'rending asunder of the Red Sea.'"

Seeing and Hearing

Rabbi Hanokh was asked: "It is written: 'Lo, I come unto thee in a thick cloud, that the people may hear when I speak with thee.' Why should hearing be helped by the fact that He comes in a thick cloud?"

Rabbi Hanokh interpreted the words in this way: "The sense of seeing takes precedence over the sense of hearing. But the thick cloud makes it impossible to utilize the sense of seeing, and so hearing is everything."

Unto the Heart of Heaven

This is how Rabbi Hanokh interpreted the words in the Scriptures: ". . . and the mountain burned with fire unto the heart of heaven": The fire of Sinai burned into the core of men until it made them a heavenly heart.

Their Desire

Rabbi Hanokh was asked: "In the Book of Psalms, it is written: 'He will do the desire of them that fear Him.' How can one claim that God will do everything that those who fear Him desire? Do not the God-fearing, above all, have to suffer much that they do not desire, and do without much they do desire?" He said: "You must take it to mean that it is He who makes the desire of those who fear him. God created the desire itself. All that is necessary for man is to desire this desire."

To the Children of Men

When Rabbi Hanokh had said the verse in the psalms: "The heavens are the heavens of the Lord, but the earth hath He given to the children of men," he paused and then went on to say: " 'The heavens are the heavens of the Lord'—you see they are already of a heavenly character. 'But the earth hath He given to the children of men'—so that they might make of it something heavenly."

Two Worlds

Rabbi Hanokh said: "The other nations too believe that there are two worlds. They too say: 'In the other world.' The difference is this: They think that the two are separate and severed, but Israel professes that the two worlds are essentially one and shall, indeed, become one."

The Fight

Rabbi Hanokh was asked why the hasidim did not begin to pray at the set time.

"While soldiers are going through their training," he replied, "there is a certain set time for everything they have to do, and they must follow their schedule. But when they are in the thick of battle they forget what was prescribed and fight as the hour demands.

"The hasidim," the rabbi concluded, "are fighters."

At the Meal

Once when Rabbi Hanokh was eating the meal with his hasidim on one of the nine days which precede the Ninth Day of Av, the day of lamenting the destruction of the Temple, he said to them:

"Formerly when these days came around, everyone was shaken with anguish because the Temple was burned, and we have no sanctuary in which to make our offerings. But now the hasidim eat their meal as if they were making an offering, and say: 'The Lord was, is, and will be; the sanctuary was, is, and will be.'"

Once he said: "When the Messiah comes, we shall see what the tables at which we eat have effected."

On Growing Old

A fiddler once played Rabbi Hanokh a tune. He said: "Even melodies that grow old lose their savor. When we heard this one at Rabbi Bunam's long ago, it made our hearts leap. Now it has lost its savor. And that is how it really is. We must be very well prepared and ready for old age. We pray: 'Cast me not off in the time of old age!' For then we lose our savor. But sometimes this is a good thing. For when I see that after all I have done I am nothing at all, I must start my work over again. And it is said of God: 'Who reneweth the creation every day continually.'"

NOTES, GLOSSARY,

AND

GENEALOGY OF THE HASIDIC MASTERS

NOTES

Numerals to the left of each note indicate the page
on which the expression occurs.

[19] *Love thy neighbor:* Lev. 19:18.
[28] *God will not despise:* Ps. 51:19.
[29] *Thou shalt be whole-hearted:* Deut. 18:13.
[36] *Justice:* Deut. 16:20.
[40] *The Torah was given:* Mekhilta on Exod. 16:4.
[40] *God is close:* Ps. 145:18.
[42] *There is no judgment:* Leviticus Rabbah XXVIII.1.
[42] *The tablets:* Berakhot 8b.
[50] *A wise man:* Samuel: Babylonia, 3rd cent.; Talmud Berakhot 58b.
[51] *A Psalm of David:* Ps. 51:1.
[53] *The heavens are the heavens of the Lord:* Ps. 115:16.
[55] *And when ye go to war:* Num. 10:9.
[56] *Hew thee:* Exod. 34:1.
[56] *Thou shalt not make:* Exod. 20:4.
[58] *For instruction:* Isa. 51:4.
[58] *What hath God wrought:* Num. 23:23.
[59] *When any man of you:* Lev. 1:2.
[59] *An altar of earth:* Exod. 20:21.
[59] *And there was evening:* Gen. 1:5.
[62] *And it shall be:* Deut. 8:19.
[62] *Strength and gladness:* I Chron. 16:27.
[62] *And the people saw it:* Exod. 20:18.
[63] *Which controversy:* Sayings of the Fathers, V,19.
[66] *Return, O Israel:* Hos. 14:2.
[66] *Between the sections of the sacrifice:* see Gen. 14:17.
[66] *Return unto me:* Zech. 1:3; Mal. 3:7.
[66] *Turn Thou us unto Thee:* Lam. 5:21.
[70] *When any man of you:* Lev. 1:2.
[71] *And they believed:* Exod. 14:31.
[71] *And the heaven and the earth:* Gen. 2:1.
[72] *There is not a thing:* Sayings of the Fathers, IV, 3.
[72] *Birth-pangs that herald:* a talmudic tradition (Sanhedrin 98b).
[72] *All the calculated dates:* Sanhedrin 97a.
[76] *Lo, I come unto thee:* Exod. 19:9.
[76] *Moses drew near:* Exod. 20:18.

[76] *Meek above all men:* Num. 12:3.

[77] *Nahshon:* a talmudic legend (Sotah 37a).

[77] *Even unto the soul:* Ps. 69:2.

[78] *A serving-maid saw more:* a midrashic teaching (Mekhilta on 15:12).

[87] *My beloved knocketh:* Cant. 5:2.

[88] *Awake and rise:* Isa. 52:2.

[88] *You will have pity on Zion:* Pss. 102:14; 51:20.

[96] *Wherefore did the son of Jesse:* I Sam. 20:27.

[96] *Lay not thy hand:* Gen. 22:12.

[97] *Uphold him:* Lev. 25:35.

[103] *And the fire abated:* Num. 11:2

[107] *For a gift doth blind:* Deut. 16:20.

[110] *Also unto Thee:* Ps. 62:13.

[112] *I and he cannot:* Talmud (Sotah 5a).

[112] *That dwelleth with them:* Lev. 16:16.

[114] *At the mouth of two witnesses:* Deut. 17:6.

[115] *For the Lord regardeth:* Ps. 1:6.

[116] *Go:* Gen. 12:1; 22:2.

[116] *And Jacob served:* Gen. 29:20.

[117] *Know what is above you:* Sayings of the Fathers, II,1.

[117] *And upon the likeness:* Ezek. 1:26.

[117] *To whom then:* Isa. 40:25.

[119] *So Moses:* Deut. 34:5.

[119] *After the death:* Josh. 1:1.

[120] *This is the land:* Deut. 34:4.

[121] *We have thought:* Ps. 48:10.

[128] *Welcoming guests:* Talmud (Shabbat 127a).

[128] *Divine Presence rests:* Talmud (Sotah 17a)

[130] *When the mount:* a talmudic tradition (Shabbat 88a).

[130] *And as for me:* Ps. 69:14.

[131] *And the people shall go out:* Exod. 16:4.

[131] *That I may prove them:* Exod. 16:4.

[131] *I will cause to rain bread:* Exod. 16:4.

[135] *Abraham fulfilled:* Yoma 28b.

[135] *Moses was told:* Exod. 36:5-6.

[137] *The Ark . . . carried its carriers:* a talmudic tradition (Sotah 35a) referring to the story of the crossing of the Jordan (Josh. 3).

[141] *The law of the Lord:* Ps. 19:8.

[141] *A God of faithfulness:* Deut. 32:4.

[145] *He also brought:* Gen. 4:4.

[146] *And to walk hidden:* Mic. 6:8.

[146] *If I ascend:* Ps. 139:8.

[146] *Open Thou mine eyes:* Ps. 119:18.

[146] *A great light:* this refers to the talmudic tradition (Hagigah 12a)

about the light created on the first day of creation which preceded the creation of the sun and the stars.

[148] *For man shall not see me:* Exod. 33:20.
[149] *Manna that enters . . . :* a talmudic legend (Yoma 75b).
[150] *Unto thee it was shown:* Deut. 4:35.
[150] *YHVH is Elohim:* I Kings 18:39.
[152] *There is no unity:* Ps. 38:4.
[153] *From Moses to Joshua:* Sayings of the Fathers, I,1.
[155] *Rejoice the soul:* Ps. 86:4.
[155] *And the Lord set:* Gen. 4:15.
[155] *Called him an old king:* Eccles. 4:13.
[157] *But I was brutish:* Ps. 73:22.
[158] *Let there be light:* Gen. 1:13.
[161] *The end of the matter:* Eccles. 12:13.
[163] *If thou wilt take the left hand:* Gen. 13:9.
[163] *Man doth not live:* Deut. 8:3.
[165] *The people saw:* Exod. 20:15.
[165] *My soul thirsteth:* Pss. 42:3; 63:3.
[167] *You will give truth:* Mic. 7:20.
[167] *Ye shall be holy:* Lev. 19:2.
[167] *Thou knowest:* Ps. 69:6.
[169] *Blessed art thou, O Lord our God:* introductory words in a benediction.
[169] *But they that wait:* Isa. 40:31.
[170] *The sage:* Judah ha-Levi, medieval Hebrew liturgical poet.
[170] *The whole earth:* Isa. 6:3.
[170] *And he dreamed:* Gen. 28:12.
[170] *Put off thy shoes:* Exod. 3:5.
[170] *How can we be delivered:* see Yalkut Shimeoni on Exodus, No. 190.
[170] *Hark! my beloved:* Cant. 2:8.
[171] *And Moses reported the words:* Exod. 19:6.
[171] *Speak thou with us:* Exod. 20:19.
[171] *Dathan and Abiram:* Num. 16:13.
[173] *Praise the Lord:* Ps. 146:1.
[173] *I will praise the Lord:* Ps. 146:2.
[177] *Pure olive oil:* Exod. 27:20.
[178] *Give forth its water:* see Num. 20:8.
[181] *In thy love:* Prov. 5:19.
[181] *Words of the living God:* talmudic tradition (Erubin 13b).
[182] *I will betroth thee:* Hos. 2:21.
[188] *We are upright men:* Gen. 42:11.
[188] *We are verily guilty:* Gen. 42:21.
[190] *If a man comes:* a talmudic teaching (Yoma 38b).
[191] *I am the man:* Lam. 3:1.

[194] *The radiance of Moses' face:* a talmudic tradition (Baba Batra 75a).

[195] *Arise, cry out:* Lam. 2:19.

[196] *Thine iniquity:* Isa. 6:7.

[198] *The Yehudi:* Yaakov Yitzhak of Pzhysha (see pp. 224-233).

[199] *And everyone that was in distress:* I Sam. 22:2.

[205] *My son, I and you:* Talmud (Shabbat 33b).

[205] *God himself prays:* Talmud (Berakhot 7a).

[205] *And I shall bring them:* Isa. 56:7; the translation follows the talmudic interpretation. The correct translation is: ". . . in My house of prayer."

[209] *My soul failed me:* Cant. 5:6.

[209] *And Moses went down:* Exod. 19:14.

[216] *A king is not saved:* Ps. 33:16.

[218] *The righteous . . .:* Prov. 10:25 (the usual translation is: "The righteous is an everlasting foundation").

[218] *He hangeth the world:* Job 26:7.

[218] *The world rests:* Talmud (Hullin 89a).

[219] *Whoever occupies himself:* Talmud (Hagigah 12b).

[221] *Darkness, cloud:* Deut. 4:11.

[222] *The air of the land of Israel:* a talmudic saying (Baba Batra 158b).

[230] *How long shall I take counsel:* Ps. 13:3.

[230] *And Moses spoke:* Deut. 31:30.

[231] *And he stood over them:* Gen. 18:8.

[235] *Pardon, I pray:* Num. 14:19-20.

[235] *Love thy neighbor:* Lev. 19:18.

[240] *Pharaoh:* Exod. 5:2.

[242] *Bright-colored dress:* they reminded Rabbi Bunam of the white shrouds.

[242] *Thou shalt surely give him:* Deut. 15:10.

[245] *Elijah found Elisha:* I Kings 19:19-20.

[248] *All joys:* see Tales of the Hasidim: The Early Masters, p. 135.

[249] *Taste and see:* Ps. 34:9.

[249] *All my bones:* Ps. 35:10.

[250] *I am earth:* Gen. 18:27.

[252] *Be not like servants:* Sayings of the Fathers, I,3.

[253] *And I am prayer:* Ps. 109:4.

[257] *The Lord has put away:* II Sam. 12:13.

[259] *Curse upon the serpent: see* Gen. 3:14, 16, 17.

[259] *And now, lest he put:* Gen. 3:22.

[260] *Both of them together:* Gen. 22:6.

[260] *And the children of Israel:* Exod. 2:23.

[260] *And I will bring you out:* Exod. 6:6.

[261] *And ye shall be unto me:* Exod. 19:6.

[261] *And he set before them:* Exod. 19:7.

[261] *I am the Lord:* Exod. 20:2.

[261] *We will do:* Exod. 24:7.

[262] *And Korah took:* Num. 16:1.

[262] *Golden calf:* see Exod. 32.

[262] *Sin of the spies:* see Num. 13.

[262] *I saw all Israel:* I Kings 22:17.

[263] *Who healeth the broken:* Ps. 147:3.

[263] *The sacrifices of God:* Ps. 51:19.

[263] *As in water:* Prov. 27:19.

[263] *Open to me:* Ps. 118:19.

[264] *And they two made a covenant:* Gen. 21:27.

[264] *Seek peace:* a talmudic saying (Palestinian Talmud, Peah 15d).

[264] *There is no peace:* Ps. 38:4.

[265] *Return, O backsliding children:* Jer. 3:14; to this quotation the "Voice from Heaven" added: all except Aher. A talmudic story (Hagigah 15a).

[270] *This is my God:* Exod. 15:2.

[271] *It is good for a man:* Lam. 3:27.

[272] *If a disciple is banished:* a talmudic statement (Makkot 10a).

[274] *But a trustworthy man:* Prov. 20:6.

[274] *And in His temple:* Ps. 29:9.

[275] *Thou shalt not steal:* Exod. 20:15.

[275] *Passed by a castle:* Genesis Rabbah XXXIX.1.

[275] *And thou shalt see My back:* Exod. 33:23.

[276] *The ordinances of the Lord:* Ps. 19:10.

[276] *This is the law:* Lev. 6:2.

[277] *The waters of immersion of Israel:* Mishnah Yoma VIII. 9, in interpreting Jer. 17:13.

[278] *We do, we hear:* Exod. 24:7.

[278] *And these words which I command:* Deut. 6:6.

[278] *There shall no strange God:* Ps. 81:10.

[278] *Thou shalt have no other gods:* Exod. 20:3.

[278] *Thou shalt make thee:* Exod. 34:17.

[279] *Take heed unto yourselves:* Deut. 4:23.

[279] *Speak thou with us:* Exod. 20:19.

[281] *And ye shall be holy men:* Exod. 22:30.

[281] *Am I a God:* Jer. 23:23.

[281] *Let the wicked forsake:* Isa. 55:7.

[282] *Ye shall serve the Lord:* Exod. 23:25.

[283] *How the angels formed:* Genesis Rabbah VIII.5.

[283] *Controversy:* Sayings of the Fathers, V,20.

[284] *He that increaseth knowledge:* Eccles. 1:18.

[284] *Only take heed:* Deut. 4:9.

[286] *Thou shalt not steal:* Exod. 20:15.

[287] *And the fear of thy master:* Sayings of the Fathers, IV, 15.

[287] *Wherefore criest thou:* Exod. 14:15.

[287] *Three pillars:* Sayings of the Fathers, I,2.

[287] *Zion shall be redeemed:* Isa. 1:27.

[288] *He setteth an end:* Job 28:3.

[291] *I shall not die:* Ps. 118:17.

[292] *That they take for Me:* Exod. 25:2.

[292] *About Rabbi Zera:* Megillah 28a.

[293] *You shall do all your host:* Talmud (Pesahim 86b).

[293] *He that is banished:* II Sam. 14:14.

[293] *Return, O backsliding children:* Jer. 3:14; see the story "The Test" in the chapter "Simha Bunam of Pzhysha."

[294] *Can any hide himself:* Jer. 23:24.

[296] *Sufficient and too much:* Exod. 36:7.

[296] *Heaven and the heaven of heavens:* I Kings 8:27.

[296] *King Solomon made himself:* Cant. 3:9.

[296] *The inside thereof:* Cant. 3:10.

[297] *This is the blessing:* Deut. 33:1.

[300] *And all the people saw:* Exod. 20:18.

[300] *There is no speech:* Ps. 19:4.

[300] *Simeon of Emmaus:* Pesahim 22b.

[301] *Thou shalt fear the Lord:* Deut. 6:13.

[301] *For God hath heard:* Gen. 21:17.

[301] *And she opened:* Exod. 2:6.

[304] *Man should take the Torah:* Talmud (Abodah Zarah 5b).

[305] *The ox knoweth:* Isa. 1:3.

[306] *Israel joined himself:* Num. 25:3.

[306] *If I am not for myself:* Sayings of the Fathers, I,14.

[307] *Depart from evil:* Ps. 34:15.

[307] *He who has no shame:* Talmud (Nedarim 20a).

[307] *And though God did say:* Gen. 3:1.

[308] *Why is thy countenance:* Gen. 4:6.

[308] *When Esau my brother:* Gen. 32:18.

[308] *Reflect upon three things:* Sayings of the Fathers, III, 1.

[308] *They saw not:* Exod. 10:23.

[308] *And Israel saw the great hand:* Exod. 14:31.

[309] *And this shall be the token:* Exod. 3:12.

[309] *It went on no more:* Deut. 5:19.

[309] *If ye will hearken:* Exod. 19:5.

[311] *Thou shalt love:* Deut. 6:5.

[311] *Even if He takes:* a talmudic teaching (Berakhot 61b).

[313] *The secret counsel of the Lord:* Ps. 25:14.

[314] *The children of Israel sighed:* Exod. 2:23.

[314] *Our sages compare this world:* Talmud (Erubin 54a).

[315] *The children of Israel lifted their eyes:* Exod. 14:10.

[315] *And Moses said:* Exod. 14:13.
[316] *The Lord will fight:* Exod. 14:14.
[316] *He split the sea:* Ps. 78:13.
[316] *Moses bade the sea split:* Exodus Rabbah XXI
[316] *The sea saw it and fled:* Ps. 114:3.
[316] *I come unto thee:* Exod. 19:9.
[316] *The mountain burned:* Deut. 4:11.
[317] *He will do the desire:* Ps. 145:19.
[317] *The heavens are the heavens:* Ps. 115:16.
[318] *Cast me not off:* Ps. 71:9.
[318] *Who reneweth the creation:* Morning Prayer.

GLOSSARY

ABAYYI: talmudic sage of Babylonia, third, fourth centuries. He was born an orphan.

ADDITIONAL PRAYER: Hebrew, *Musaf. Musaf* was originally an additional sacrifice on the Sabbath and holidays; later as its substitute, an additional prayer service recited after the general Morning Prayer.

AHER: *see* ELISHA BEN ABUYA.

AKIBA: leading Palestinian teacher of the second century C.E.

ALL VOWS: *see* KOL NIDRE.

AMORA, *pl.*, AMORAIM: talmudic sage quoted in the Gemara.

BADHAN: master of ceremonies and merry-maker at a wedding.

BAR MITZVAH ("son of commandment"): upon the completion of his thirteenth year a boy accepts the responsibility of fulfilling the religious law. He becomes a *Bar Mitzvah*. This event is festively celebrated.

BENEDICTION OF SANCTIFICATION *(Kiddush)*: benediction pronounced over the wine at the commencement of the Sabbath and holidays.

BENEDICTION OF SEPARATION *(Havdalah)*: "separation" (of the holy and the profane); benediction pronounced over the wine, spices, and the light at the conclusion of the Sabbath and holidays.

BLESSING OF THE NEW MOON: outdoor benediction service on the appearance of the new moon, which marks the beginning of a month according to the Hebrew calendar.

BOOK OF THE ANGEL RAZIEL: a kabbalistic work.

BOOK OF SPLENDOR: the book *Zohar*, the foremost work of Jewish mysticism, composed, in Aramaic, as a commentary on the Pentateuch (thirteenth century).

Breaking Of The Vessels: *see* Sparks.

Breastplate Of Judgment *(Hoshen Mishpat)*: one of the four parts of the Shulhan Arukh, the authoritative code of Jewish law.

Counting Of The Fifty Days: *see* Lev. 23:15.

Curtain: the Talmud (Hagigah 12b) speaks of seven heavens and their names and functions; the curtain is the lowest heaven.

Day Of Atonement *(Yom Kippur)*: the last of the "Ten Days of Turning" (and repentance) which commence with the New Year. It is a day of fasting and uninterrupted prayer for atonement.

Days Of Awe: the New Year's days and the Day of Atonement.

Divine Chariot *(Merkavah)*: a mystical interpretation of Ezekiel's vision (Ezek. 1), the basis of kabbalistic theosophy.

Divine Presence: *see* Shekhinah.

Eighteen Benedictions: one of the oldest parts of liturgy, occurring in the regular prayer service. After silent recitation by the worshippers it is repeated aloud by the reader.

Elijah: after his ascent to heaven, the prophet Elijah, according to legend, continued to help and instruct the world of man in his function as a messenger of God. Especially, he appears at every feast of circumcision and at every Seder celebration. To behold him and to receive instruction from him are considered an initiation into the mysteries of the Torah.

Elisha: the disciple and successor of Elijah the prophet.

Elisha Ben Abuya: talmudic sage, teacher of Rabbi Meir. Under the influence of foreign, probably Gnostic teachings, he deserted pharisaic Judaism, hence is called *Aher* ("the other").

Elohim: name of God, in rabbinical literature interpreted as referring to the divine attribute of rigor. *See* Mercy-Rigor.

Elul: the month preceding the Days of Awe and the days of heavenly judgment. It is devoted to inner preparation and self-examination.

EMDEN, JACOB: rabbi in Germany (Emden and Altona); eighteenth century.

ESCORT OF THE SABBATH QUEEN: the meal taken after the departure of the Sabbath. This meal is understood as bidding farewell to the Sabbath Queen. It "escorts" her away. It is also called "the feast of King David." According to the legend, David was told by God that he would die on a Sabbath; he therefore feasted after every Sabbath in celebration of his continued living.

EVIL URGE: the inclination to evil, which is opposed to "the inclination to good." It is not considered as evil *per se*, but as a power abused by men. It is rather the "passion" in which all human action originates. Man is called upon to serve God "with both inclinations," directing his passion toward the good and the holy.

EXILARCH *(Resh Galuta)*: title of the head of the autonomous Jewish community in the Babylonian diaspora; an especially active office in the period between the seventh and the eleventh centuries.

EXILE FESTIVAL: the three festivals of Passover, Feast of Weeks and Feast of Booths are observed in the countries of the Diaspora one day longer than in Palestine. The additional day of observance is called Exile Festival.

EZRA THE SCRIBE: leader of Palestinian Jewry in the fifth century B.C.E. His institutions and ordinances greatly influenced the development of traditional Judaism.

FEAST OF BOOTHS *(Sukkot)*: tabernacles; an eight-day holiday beginning on the fifth day after the Day of Atonement. It commemorates the wandering in the desert. During this period the houses are abandoned and the people live in booths covered with leaves.

FEAST OF WEEKS *(Shavuot)*: a two-day holiday (in Palestine, one day), seven weeks after Passover. It is the feast of the first fruits and a season dedicated to the memory of the revelation on Mount Sinai. Pious Jews stay awake at night to read and study holy writings.

FIRST GATE *(Baba Kamma)*: a talmudic tractate.

GALUT: the dispersion of Israel; according to Jewish tradition, the Divine Presence takes part in the sufferings of exile and also waits for redemption.

GEMARA ("completion") : part of the Talmud which consists of discussions of the Mishnah.

GLORY AND FAITHFULNESS: ancient mystical hymn recited by many hasidim among the prayers on Sabbath morning.

GREAT ASSEMBLY *(Keneset ha-Gedolah)*: legislative body in Palestine at the time of the Second Temple.

GREAT PRAYER OF SALVATION: chanted on *Hoshana Rabba* ("The Great Salvation") observed on the seventh day of the Feast of Booths.

GREAT SABBATH: the Sabbath which precedes Passover.

HAGGADAH ("narrative") : usually, *Haggadah shel Pesah*, the collection of sayings, scriptural interpretations, and hymns pertaining to the exodus from Egypt, as recited in the home service on Passover night *(see* SEDER*)*.

HALLEL ("praise") : a group of psalms recited in the prayer service at certain festivals.

HANUKKAH ("dedication") : an eight-day holiday beginning on the twenty-fifth day of *Kislev* (November or December) and commemorating the rededication of the Temple by the Maccabees (167 B.C.E.) and their victory over the Syrian Greeks who had desecrated it. In remembrance of the Maccabean Feast of Lights, candles are lighted in Jewish homes on each of the eight evenings, one candle the first evening, two the second, etc.

HIDDEN ZADDIK: *see* THIRTY-SIX HIDDEN ZADDIKIM.

HILLEL AND SHAMMAI: Palestinian teachers and founders of schools in the first century B.C.E.

HOLY BROTHERHOOD *(Hevra Kaddisha,* "holy society") : its members devote themselves to the burial of the dead.

HOSHANOT: prayers for help and salvation during the Feast of Booths.

HOUSE OF LIFE: cemetery.

HOUSE OF STUDY *(Bet ha-Midrash)*: identical, usually, with the House of Prayer. It is a place of learning and worship. Travelers without lodgings are put up in the House of Study.

IMMERSION: the ancient bath which, in the Kabbalah and especially among the hasidim, became an important ceremony with mystical meanings of its own. Immersion in a river or stream is higher in value than the ordinary ritual bath.

JOURNEY (to the zaddik): *see* TRAVEL.

KAVVANAH, *pl.*, KAVVANOT: mystical meaning of scriptural phrases, prayers, or religious acts; also, the concentration on this meaning. Direction of the heart towards God while performing a religious deed. In Jewish mysticism, *kavvanot* denote also the permutations of the divine name that aim at overcoming the separation of the forces in the Upper World.

KOL NIDRE ("All Vows"): the initial words in the solemn formula of absolution from unfulfilled and unfulfillable vows, pronounced on the eve of the Day of Atonement.

LAMENTATIONS AT MIDNIGHT: the pious are accustomed to rise at midnight from their beds, sit down on the floor, without shoes, put ashes on their forehead, and read lamentations on the fall of Zion and prayers for redemption.

LURIA, ISAAC: Safed, Palestine, sixteenth century. The outstanding representative of later Kabbalah.

MEIR: talmudic sage of Palestine, second century; post-talmudic legend describes him as a "miracle-worker."

MERCY-RIGOR: the chief attributes of God.

MESSIAH SON OF JOSEPH: a Messiah who will prepare the way, gathering Israel together and re-establishing the kingdom, and who will then fall in a war against the Romans led by Armilus. Another tradition holds that he reappears "from generation to generation."

METATRON: name of an angel, mentioned in talmudic and kabbalistic literature; among other functions he mediates between God and the material world. He is referred to as "Prince of the Divine Face," or "Prince of the Innermost Chamber."

MIDRASH, *pl.*, MIDRASHIM ("exposition, interpretation"): books of the talmudic and post-talmudic times devoted to the homiletic exegesis of the Scriptures. They are rich in legends, parables, similes, and sayings.

MIRIAM'S WELL: due to the merits of Miriam, sister of Moses and Aaron, a well, according to a talmudic legend, accompanied the children of Israel through the desert (*see* Taanit 9a).

332

MISHNAH ("repetition, teaching") : the earliest and basic part of the Talmud.

MITNAGED, *pl.*, MITNACDIM ("opponent, antagonist") : the avowed opponents of hasidism.

MOSES BEN MAIMON: Maimonides, born 1135, Cordova; died 1204, Cairo. Foremost Jewish thinker of Middle Ages.

NEW MOON: *see* BLESSING OF THE NEW MOON.

NEW YEAR'S DAY *(Rosh ha-Shanah)*: observed on the first and second day of *Tishri* (September or October), the days of judgment.

NEW YEAR OF THE TREES: observed on the fifteenth day of *Shevat* (January or February) ; arbor day.

NINTH DAY OF AV *(Tishah be-Av)*: *Av*: July or August. A day of fasting and mourning in memory of the destruction of the first Temple by Nebuchadnezzar and the second Temple by Titus. The worshippers sit, like mourners of the dead, without shoes, on the floor of the darkened House of Prayer and recite the Book of Lamentations. According to tradition, the Messiah was born on the Ninth Day of Av and will re-appear on that day.

NOTES OF REQUEST (in Yiddish, *kvittel*) : addressed to the zaddik, written on slips of paper containing the name of the supplicant, the name of his mother, and his request.

PASSOVER *(Pesah,* "passing over," i.e., the sparing of the houses of the children of Israel) : eight-day holiday (in Palestine seven days) beginning on the fifteenth day of *Nisan* (March or April) and commemorating the exodus from Egypt.

PATH OF LIFE *(Orah Hayyim)*: one of the four parts of the Shulhan Arukh, the authoritative code of Jewish law.

PENITENTIAL PRAYERS *(Selihot)*: prayers recited especially on the days preceding the New Year's days, in the period between these and the Day of Atonement, and on the latter day itself.

PHYLACTERIES *(tefillin)*: leather cubicles containing scriptural texts inscribed on parchment. Following the commandment in Deut. 11:18, *tefillin* are attached to the left arm and the head during the weekday morning service. They are a sign of the covenant between God and Israel. An error in the written text disqualifies the phylacteries. There is a talmudic conception (Berakhot 6a) of the "phylacteries of God," which are said to contain the verse II Sam. 7:23.

PRAYER OF BENEDICTIONS: central prayer in the synagogue service. *See also* EIGHTEEN BENEDICTIONS.

PRAYER SHAWL *(tallit)*: a rectangular shawl worn at prayers; its four corners have fringes *(tzitzit)* attached.

PRESENCE OF GOD: *see* SHEKHINAH.

PRINCIPLES OF FAITH: a section of the Morning Prayer arranged according to the formulation of the articles of Jewish creed by Moses ben Maimon (Maimonides) in the twelfth century.

QUORUM *(minyan)*: the minimum of ten males (all past thirteen years of age) required for community prayer.

RABBI: *see* RAV.

RAM'S HORN *(shofar)*: sounded in the synagogue, principally on the New Year. A blast on the ram's horn will announce the coming of the Messiah.

RASHI: abbreviation for Rabbi Solomon (ben) Isaac (of Troyes), the classical commentator on the Bible and the Babylonian Talmud (died 1105).

RAV ("master, teacher"): the leader of the religious community. He teaches the law and, as the "head of the law court," supervises its fulfilment; whereas *rabbi*, in most cases, denotes the leader of the local hasidic group. In some instances the rabbi, also called zaddik, was, in addition, the rav of his town.

READER OF PRAYERS *(Hazan, Baal Tefillah)*: the man who, "standing in front of the Ark," or the Reader's desk, leads the congregation in the synagogue worship; cantor.

REJOICING IN THE LAW *(Simhat Torah)*: feast on the day following the Feast of Booths. The Torah scrolls are taken out of the Ark and are carried through the House of Prayer by a festive procession.

RIGOR: *see* MERCY-RIGOR.

RITUAL BATH: *see* IMMERSION.

SABBATAI ZEVI: born in Smyrna, Turkey, in 1626. He proclaimed himself Messiah; central figure of the greatest messianic movement in the history of the Diaspora. The movement broke down and its founder embraced Islam.

SABBATH OF SONG *(Shabbat Shirah)*: the Sabbath on which the song of the Israelites at the Red Sea is sung (Exod. 15).

SABBATH OF TURNING *(Shabbat Shuvah)*: the Sabbath within the Ten Days of Turning between the New Year's Day and the Day of Atonement.

SABBATIANS: followers of Sabbatai Zevi.

SAMMAEL: post-biblical name for Satan, the prince of demons.

SANCTIFICATION OF THE NAME (of God): designates every sacrificial act of man; by it man participates in the establishment of the kingdom of God on earth. The death of a martyr is the highest instance of Sanctification of the Name.

SAYING TORAH: At the communal meal with the hasidim, the zaddik delivers a discourse on a topic of hasidic teachings usually based on a scriptural passage.

SECTION OF SONGS *(Perek Shirah)*: a compilation of scriptural verses which, it is said, are recited by all kinds of living creatures in praise of God, each one speaking a particular verse.

SEDER ("order"): the festival meal and home service on the first and second (in Palestine, only the first) night of Passover. In this celebration, each succeeding generation identifies itself anew with the generation that went out of Egypt (*see* HAGGADAH).

SEFIROT: the mystical and organically related hierarchy of the ten creative powers emanating from God, constituting, according to the kabbalistic system, the foundation of the existence of the worlds.

SEVEN BENEDICTIONS: recited at weddings, and after Grace on the seven days following, if new guests are present.

SEVEN DAYS OF THE FEAST: observed after the wedding day.

SEVEN SHEPHERDS: the three patriarchs, together with Joseph, Moses, Aaron and David, who are greeted by the pious as guests in the holiday booths during the Feast of Booths.

SHAMMAI: *see* HILLEL AND SHAMMAI.

SHEKHINAH ("indwelling"): divine hypostasis indwelling in

the world and sharing the exile of Israel; Divine Presence among men.

SON OF COMMANDMENT: *see* BAR MITZVAH.

SPARKS: according to the Kabbalah, in the primeval creation preceding the creation of our world, the divine light-substance burst and the "sparks" fell into the lower depths, filling the "shells" of the things and creatures of our world.

TANNA, *pl.*, TANNAIM ("repeater, teacher"): the masters of the Mishnah.

TENT OF MEETING *(Ohel Moed; Mishkan)*: the portable sanctuary (Tabernacle) built by Bezalel for the Israelites when they were in the desert. *See* Exod. 26, 27; and 35-38.

THIRD MEAL: the principal meal of the Sabbath, eaten after the Afternoon Prayer, and accompanied by community singing and an address by the zaddik.

THIRTY-SIX HIDDEN ZADDIKIM: the Talmud (Sukkah 45b) speaks of the thirty-six pious men who welcome the presence of God every day; in later legends they are described as humble, unrecognized saints. Disguised as peasants, artisans, or porters, they go around doing good deeds. They constitute the true "foundation of the world."

TORAH: teaching, law, both the written (biblical) and the oral (traditional) law.

TOSEFTA ("addition"): a collection of laws closely related to the Mishnah and supplementing it.

TRAVEL (to the zaddik): to become a follower of a zaddik, to receive his teachings, and to visit him from time to time.

TURNING *(Teshuvah,* usually "repentance"): man's turning from his aberrations to the "way of God." It is interpreted as the fundamental act by which man contributes to his redemption.

UNIFICATION: the overcoming of the separation of forces and principles in the Divine Realm, the accomplishment of which is attempted by man through religious action and sacred ceremonies.

UNLEAVENED BREAD *(matzah)*: eaten during the week of Passover.

WORLD OF CONFUSION *(Olam ha-Tohu)*: the realm in which the souls exist after death before they achieve their redemption.

336

WORLD OF EMANATION: according to the kabbalistic doctrine the World of Emanation and of Divinity is the highest among the four "Worlds" which are placed between the Infinite and our earthly cosmos.

WORLD OF ILLUSION *(Olam ha-Dimyon)*: a realm "in which the souls of all those who died deluded by their vanity stray."

YHVH: the tetragram for the name of God which, according to tradition, was not to be pronounced; usually *Adonai* (the Lord) is substituted. In rabbinical literature YHVH is interpreted as referring to the divine attribute of mercy. *See* MERCY-RIGOR.

ZADDIK: the leader of the hasidic community (*see* RAV).

GENEALOGY OF THE HASIDIC MASTERS*

*The numerals in square brackets refer to the main portions in *Tales of the Hasidim* dealing with the masters in question: I indicates *The Early Masters*; II, *The Later Masters*.

16. Mordecai (Motel) of Tchernobil, d.1837 [I. 55]

17. David Leikes [I. 55, 174]
18. Wolf Kitzes [I. 63-64, 72-73, 77]
19. Meir Margaliot [I. 42-43]
20. Zevi the Scribe [I. 77-78]
21. Leib, son of Sarah [I. 59, 86, 107, 169]

DESCENDANTS OF DOV BAER OF MEZRITCH.
"THE GREAT MAGGID," (NOS. 22-27):

22. Abraham "the Angel," d.1776 [I. 113-117]

HIS SON:

23. Shalom Shakhna of Probishtch, d.1803 [II. 49-51]

SON OF SHALOM:

24. Israel of Rizhyn, d.1850 [II. 52-69]

SONS OF ISRAEL:

25. Abraham Yaakov of Sadagora, d.1883 [II. 70-72]
26. Nahum of Stepinesht [II. 73-74]
27. David Moshe of Tchortkov, d.1903 [II. 74-78]

DISCIPLES OF DOV BAER OF MEZRITCH
(NOS. 28.29.30.37.38.39.43.44.52.57):

28. Menahem Mendel of Vitebsk, d.1788 [I. 175-181]
29. Aaron of Karlin, d.1772 [I. 195-202]
30. Shmelke of Nikolsburg, d.1778 [I. 182-194]

HIS DISCIPLES (NOS. 31.32.36):

31. Abraham Hayyim of Zlotchov
32. Moshe Leib of Sasov, d.1807 [II. 81-95]

SON OF MOSHE LEIB:

33. Shmelke of Sasov

DISCIPLE OF MOSHE LEIB:

34. Menahem Mendel of Kosov, d.1825 [II. 96-98]

SON OF MENAHEM MENDEL:

35. Hayyim of Kosov [II. 98-99]

36. Yitzhak Eisik of Kalev, d.1821 [II. 100-104]

37. Levi Yitzhak of Berditchev, d.1809 [I. 203-234]
38. Meshullam Zusya of Hanipol, d.1800 [I. 235-252]
39. Elimelekh of Lizhensk, Zusya's brother, d.1786 [I. 253-264]

341

ALPHABETICAL INDEX TO THE GENEALOGY

Peretz (82)
Pinhas of Kinsk (71)
Pinhas of Koretz (8)

Rafael of Bershad (9)

Seer of Lublin, Yaakov Yitzhak of Lublin (57)
Shalom of Belz (68)
Shalom Shakhna of Probishtch (23)
Shelomo Hayyim of Kaidanov (50)
Shelomo of Karlin (44)
Shelomo Leib of Lentshno (66)
Shmelke of Nikolsburg (30)
Shmelke of Sasov (33)
Shneur Zalman of Ladi, the Rav (43)
Simha Bunam of Pzhysha (76)

Uri of Strelisk (45)

Wolf Kitzes (18)

Yaakov Joseph of Polnoye (6)

Yaakov Yitzhak of Lublin, the Seer (57)
Yaakov Yitzhak of Pzhysha, the Yehudi (69)
Yaakov Zevi of Parysov (73)
Yehezkel of Shenyava (61)
Yehiel Mikhal of Zlotchov, the Maggid of Zlotchov (10)
Yehudah Zevi of Rozdol (63)
Yehudah Zevi of Stretyn (46)
Yehudi, the; Yaakov Yitzhak of Pzhysha (69)
Yehoshua Asher (72)
Yerahmiel of Pzhysha (70)
Yisakhar of Wolborz (56)
Yisakhar Baer of Radoshitz (67)
Yitzhak of Vorki (78)
Yitzhak Eisik of Kalev (36)
Yitzhak Eisik of Zhydatchov (64)
Yitzhak Meir of Ger (80)

Zev Wolf of Zbarazh (12)
Zevi Hirsh of Rymanov (41)
Zevi Hirsh of Zhydatchov (62)
Zevi the Scribe (20)
Zusya, Meshullam, of Hanipol (38)

Sephardic pronunciation has been followed in the spelling of the proper names in *Tales of the Hasidim*, exception being made for some names which here appear in their equivalents in the English Bible.

The names of geographical locations appear in a transliteration of their popular Jewish versions. Thus we say Alexander for Alexandrowo, Apt for Opatów, Hanipol for Annopol, Koretz for Korzec, Koznitz for Koziniec, Lizhensk for Leżajsk, Mezbizh for Miedzyborz, Mezritch for Miedzyrzecze, Polnoye for Polennoje, Primishlan for Przemyślany, Pzhysha for Przysucha, Rizhyn for Rużyn, Roptchitz for Ropczyce, Tchernobil for Czernobiel, Zlotchov for Zloczów.

INDEX TO THE TALES

The Descendants of the Great Maggid

From the School of Rabbi Shmelke of Nikolsburg

From the School of Rabbi Elimelekh of Lizhensk

From the School of Rabbi Shelomo of Karlin

From the House of the Maggid of Koznitz

From the School of the Rabbi of Lublin

Pzhysha And Its Daughter Schools

ABOUT THE AUTHOR

MARTIN BUBER was born in Vienna in 1878 and raised in Lemberg by his paternal grandparents, Solomon and Adele Buber. He studied philosophy at the University of Berlin.

At the age of twenty-six, Buber commenced his life-long fascination with Hasidism, publishing two volumes of his retelling of classic hasidic tales, *The Tales of Rabbi Nachman* (1906) and *The Legend of the Baal Shem* (1907). Over the years, Buber wrote numerous books on the religious meaning of Hasidism, in addition to his work on Bible and Bible translation, Judaism, and philosophy. His famous work, *I and Thou* (1923), which presents his philosophy of dialogue, comes out of his study of Hasidism.

Buber taught at the University of Frankfort, where he served as professor of religion until 1933, when he was forced to resign his position by the Nazis. In 1938 he left Germany for the land of Israel. He was professor of social philosophy at the Hebrew University, a post created for him, until his retirement in 1951. He lived in Jerusalem until his death in 1965.

This edition of *Tales of the Hasidim*, an expanded edition of his earlier work in German, was published in English in 1947 as one of the first Schocken books published in America.

Printed in the United States
by Baker & Taylor Publisher Services